between *Dreams* and *Realities*

At the end of the game, the king and the pawn go back in the same box
ITALIAN PROVERB

between
Dreams
and
Realities

SOME MILESTONES IN PAKISTAN'S HISTORY

SECOND EDITION

SARTAJ AZIZ

Foreword by
Syed Babar Ali

OXFORD
UNIVERSITY PRESS

OXFORD
UNIVERSITY PRESS

Oxford University Press is a department of the University of Oxford.
It furthers the University's objective of excellence in research, scholarship,
and education by publishing worldwide. Oxford is a registered trade mark of
Oxford University Press in the UK and in certain other countries

Published in Pakistan by
Oxford University Press
No. 38, Sector 15, Korangi Industrial Area,
PO Box 8214, Karachi-74900, Pakistan

ISBN 978-0-19-070258-8

Typeset in Minion Pro
Printed on 80gsm Offset Paper

Printed by Delta Dot Technologies (Pvt.) Ltd., Karachi

To my wife Hameeda, and our three children,
Tahmina, Shahid, and Farhana,
who have given me much respect and affection, quietly and sincerely.

Contents

Foreword

I feel greatly honoured that Sartaj Aziz asked me to write the Foreword for this book. I am proud to have known him for over forty years and hold him in great esteem for his consistency, competence, integrity, and humility. He has had an outstanding career and has played an important part in the development of Pakistan, especially in the area of food and agriculture.

I recall with pleasure my first meeting with Sartaj Aziz when I was asked to talk to Pakistani students at the Harvard University in 1962. After my presentation, one of the students, Sartaj Aziz, talked to me briefly on the economic situation in Pakistan. I was deeply impressed by his wide ranging knowledge of development economics and his vision of Pakistan's future and I always looked to him as a person dedicated to the development of Pakistan.

He has had a remarkable career. In 1969, Lester Pearson, former prime minister of Canada, invited him to serve on the staff of the Pearson Commission on international development sponsored by the World Bank. In 1971, he joined the Food and Agriculture Organization (FAO) of the United Nations in Rome as director of commodities and trade division where he played a leading role in organizing the World Food Conference in Rome in 1974.

In her Foreword to Sartaj Aziz's book, *Hunger, Politics & Markets: Issues in the Food Crisis* (1975), Dame Barbara Ward wrote:

> Without Sartaj Aziz, there would have been no Rome Forum. I admire him for his wisdom, dedication, and hard work with which he organized the World Food Conference. He is a good man, dedicated to improving the human condition and his work for the welfare of the hungry and the poor deserves better recognition. I wish he had continued at FAO for a few years longer—and served a term or two as its Director General.

The International Fund for Agricultural Development (IFAD) was one of the major outcomes of the Rome conference and Sartaj Aziz's pioneering work at FAO. IFAD was given a fund of $1 billion to focus primarily on increasing food production and reducing poverty in the developing world. Sartaj Aziz served IFAD with distinction from 1978 to 1984. He was also one of the founding members of the Third World Forum designed to bring together social scientists and policymakers from developing countries and devise new initiatives for South–South cooperation.

In 1978, he was elected president of the Society for International Development for three years and initiated two major programmes: North–South Round Table, and Research on Alternative Development Strategies.

In 1978, his book, *Rural Development: Learning from China* was a major landmark and an absorbing guide for governments to rethink their rural priorities. According to M S Swaminathan, UNESCO professor of eco-technology and president of the Pugwash conferences on science and world:

> Sartaj Aziz's analysis of the reasons for the phenomenal progress made by China in eradicating hunger has helped many developing countries to re-orient their rural development strategies in order to pay concurrent attention to on-farm and non-farm employment.

It was Pakistan's good fortune that at the height of a very productive and promising international career, Sartaj Aziz was persuaded by his close friend, Jamil Nishtar (for whose blessed memory I have great respect and regard), head of Agricultural Development Bank of Pakistan, to return to Pakistan. He then devoted his energies and skills to the development of the country. My personal friendship and professional interaction with him was further reinforced from this period onwards.

We were happy to see him elected to the Senate of Pakistan and he joined the cabinet of Prime Minister Mohammad Khan Junejo as minister of state for food and agriculture. I had the honour to serve on the National Commission of Agriculture under Sartaj Aziz's chairmanship and the commission submitted its recommendations in March 1988. These recommendations played an important role in formulating government policy, enabling Pakistan to achieve accelerated growth in the agricultural sector between the years 1985 and 2000. Much credit goes to Sartaj Aziz for ensuring the implementation of the commission's recommendations.

In November 1988, when I was serving on the board of World Wildlife Fund International, its then president, the Duke of Edinburgh, remarked to me after his visit to Pakistan that he was very impressed with Sartaj Aziz who was our minister of agriculture. He said that Sartaj Aziz was an outstanding leader in his field with a strong commitment to environment and conservation of natural resources.

In 1990, Sartaj Aziz entered into the political arena with full commitment by being appointed as the minister of finance, in which position he served with credit till 1993. With the fast changing political scene in Pakistan, he maintained his prominence, and in 1998 he took over the important portfolio of foreign affairs in the Government of Pakistan.

The best turning point in Sartaj Aziz's career came in 2004 when he decided to accept the position of vice chancellor of the Beaconhouse National University (BNU) at Lahore. He was always committed to the cause of education in Pakistan. His decision to utilize his rich experience in building a first rate liberal arts university in Lahore is truly praiseworthy.

In 2013, as his party won the elections, Sartaj Aziz resumed his political career as the de facto Foreign Minister and also National Security Advisor at a very critical time in the country's history. According to reports I received from many friends, his performance during this tenure was again above or at par with some of the great diplomats and Foreign Ministers around the world.

I share Sartaj Aziz's dream of a better Pakistan. I sincerely hope that the publication of his book will help awaken the conscience of all concerned to dedicate themselves towards building our young nation-state to the visionary heights dreamed of by our founding fathers, Allama Muhammad Iqbal and Quaid-i-Azam Mohammad Ali Jinnah.

Syed Babar Ali

Preface to the Second Edition

The reviews, following the publishing of the first edition of this book, highlighted many themes and sub-themes which were mentioned briefly in different chapters.

Khaled Ahmad in his review published in *Daily Times* of 12 August 2009 says, 'Sitting in the Planning Commission in 1964, the economist, Sartaj Aziz was made uncomfortably aware of the mismatch between the country's economic resources and its diplomatic and military strategy on the eve of the 1965 War. This policy mismatch between economic reality and policy formulation', continued to be his principal worry throughout his career and can be categorized as the defining theme of this book. Another intellectual thesis of this book, as Khaled Ahmad says, is Sartaj Aziz's statement that 'the Pakistan Army is "tactical" rather than "strategic" in its thinking'.

Shahid Hamid, in his review published in *The Nation* on 23 August 2009, says 'Sartaj Aziz's recounting of the events of the Kargil crisis is simply fascinating, but we need to set up a Kargil Commission of Inquiry to find out who knew what and when and what did he do about it'. He then also asks an important question: 'Has the fact of our being a nuclear power gone to our collective head?'

Shahid Kamal in his review published in *Dawn* of 11 October 2009, says, 'the way Pakistan responded to the dilemma of whether or not to conduct the nuclear tests has become a landmark example of decision making in Pakistan's history. But we need to know much more: when was the decision to conduct the tests taken and during the intervening period, Nawaz Sharif was resolute, indecisive or calm? Also, what was the mood of the Army at that time?'

I have tried to answer these questions in the second edition of my book.

Mani Shankar Aiyar in his review says, 'it is a sad, sad book—the autobiography of a promising Pathan boy who is asking, six decades after the creation of Pakistan, what went wrong? What has dried up the dream? What has stoked the reality? Would it not be true to say that the central dilemma of Pakistan's quest for national identity is that while it is Islam which unites Pakistan but it is Islamization that divides it'.

In addition to these themes, highlighted in different reviews, I was also struck, especially during my tenure in the Foreign Office, by the overwhelming implications of Pakistan's geographic location in the formulation of a coherent foreign policy. We cannot forget that the region in which Pakistan is located, has been a graveyard for many different empires. During the past 100 years:

- The Ottoman Empire disintegrated in the beginning of the twentieth century leading to many prolonged crises in different countries of the Middle East.
- The British Empire withdrew in 1947, leaving behind many unfortunate legacies like inter-communal riots, mass migration and the unresolved problem of Kashmir.
- The USSR collapsed in 1990, following its defeat in Afghanistan, laying the foundation for a prolonged civil war in Afghanistan and many problems for other countries in the region.
- Soon, we will also witness the end of another mini Empire after the withdrawal of US troops from Afghanistan.

The continuing turmoil caused by the collapse of these empires, has resulted in Pakistan becoming a melting pot of many global fault lines. One of the most important challenges, which will determine, in many ways the future of Pakistan, will be to find ways and means of converting Pakistan's strategic geopolitical location from a liability into an asset.

The new Chapter 14 covers the five-year tenure of the PPP government under President Asif Ali Zardari from 2008 to 2013.

In Chapter 15, Nawaz Sharif's third term as Prime Minister from 2014–2017, along with Shahid Khaqan Abbasi's ten months tenure is analysed. The chapter includes a score card to assess factors behind Nawaz Sharif's long and successful political career and also those that led to the premature termination of each of the three tenures.

Chapter 16 describes in some detail the untold story of how the historic landmark objective of mainstreaming the Federally Administered Tribal Areas (FATA) through its merger with Khyber Pakhtunkhwa Province was achieved.

The final Chapter 17, 'Imran Khan as Prime Minister', was not easy to write because one year is too short for a decisive assessment of success or failure. I have tried to present an objective assessment of his government based on one year's record and different policy pronouncements.

The dream, which I saw when the Pakistani flag was raised for the first time on 14 August 1947 in front of me, in Abbottabad, has received many serious blows in the past seven decades. I have held on to this dream all my life. I am confident that the future generations of Pakistanis will bring forth outstanding political leaders who will convert this dream into a permanent reality.

Sartaj Aziz

Preface to the First Edition

As I reflect over different phases of my educational, professional and political career, I am overwhelmed by the intensity of my dreams and the equally strong jolts of reality.

When I came to Lahore in 1944 to join Islamia College, the dream of an independent homeland, which Pakistan's founding fathers had seen in 1940, was about to become a reality. The capacity of a young man to dream about his own future and the emerging prospect of a free homeland was limitless. Islamia College, Lahore, was a dynamic centre of activity for the Pakistan Movement. In March 1946, when Quaid-i-Azam Mohammad Ali Jinnah, urged the students of Islamia College to move on and become Maimar-e-Pakistan (the builders of Pakistan), I felt that he was speaking neither to the nation nor to the college body as a whole, but to me directly and personally. And these words changed the course of my career.

But as I returned to Lahore in September 1947 after the summer break, I was shaken by the reality of Partition—thousands and thousands of refugees streaming through every part of Lahore with nothing but their worn-out clothes. This seesaw effect between my dreams and the devastating reality on the ground has marked every phase of my life in which I have witnessed many turning points and many economic and political milestones.

I am not an historian nor is this book a comprehensive and authoritative history of Pakistan. But having participated in the political life of Pakistan from 1984 onwards, I considered it my duty to record my version of events, decisions and acts of commission and omission that I witnessed, so that historians can draw on this record. At the same time, future leaders may be able to learn from past mistakes and draw inspiration from noble deeds and sincere efforts. While in terms of identifying milestones and turning points, this book covers the entire history of Pakistan, a more detailed account is presented for the period after April 1984, when I returned to Pakistan from Rome and started my political career.

The eternal dream which I will continue to cherish as long as I am alive, will remain the advent of a vibrant and self sustaining democracy in Pakistan. I have explored in this volume, some of the causes of failure of democracy in Pakistan.

Sartaj Aziz

Acknowledgements

I am grateful to many who directly or indirectly participated in my early life and the four different phases of my career over six decades, reflected in this book. I was a civil servant for the first twenty years, from 1950 to 1970, and in international civil service for the next thirteen years, from 1971 to 1984. My political tenure lasted fifteen years, from 1984 to 1999. I am now in the fourth and most satisfying phase of my career in the education sector since 2004.

I have had a wonderful family. My father grew up in a spiritual family and passed on to me, at a very early stage, the importance of faith in one's life. Because of his influence, I kept away from many vices including smoking and drinking throughout my life. My own mother died when I was four, but our stepmother, called Mummy by everyone, was very kind. My sister, Nisar, even though only one year older, became a foster mother to me very soon and protected me and guided my intellectual growth. My two brothers, Javed Aziz and Kamal Aziz and sisters, Jamila and Rukhsana, always treated me like their father.

My immersion in the Pakistan Movement and direct interaction with Quaid-i-Azam, Mohammad Ali Jinnah, at the young age of 16–18 not only matured me early but also strengthened my commitment to serve Pakistan above all else and probably shaped the basic traits of my character like integrity, capacity for hard work and a positive attitude to other people and life in general. That is perhaps one reason why at every stage of my career I had excellent relations with people I worked with or worked for. These included Jari Ahmad Saiyid, S.S. Haider, Qamar-ul-Islam, M.M. Ahmad in Pakistan; Eric Ojala, A.H. Boerma, John Hannah and Al-Sudeary in my international career; and Mohammad Khan Junejo and Nawaz Sharif in my political career.

A very large number of my professional colleagues have contributed to my intellectual growth and my worldview. Some highlights of this interaction are mentioned in the book. I wish to thank them all.

It has taken me three years to write this book. In determining its scope and content at different stages, I received very helpful advice and assistance from many friends, specially Anwar Dil, Dr Hafiz Pasha, and Dr Liaquat Ali. My sincere thanks to them.

I wish to thank my Personal Assistant Rafiq-ud-Din for typing and revising the manuscript many times.

I am also grateful to Arshad Saeed Husain, Managing Director, Raheela Baqai, Marketing Director and Samuel Ray, Editor of Oxford University Press, for the speed and efficiency in publishing the Second edition of this book.

Abbreviations and Acronyms

AFPAK	Afghanistan-Pakistan Cell
ANP	Awami National Party
ANSF	Afghan National Security Forces
APC	All Parties Conference
APDM	All Parties Democratic Movement
APEC	Asia-Pacific Economic Forum
APHC	All Parties Hurriyat Conference
BISP	Benazir Income Support Programme
BJP	Bharatiya Janata Party
BNA	Balochistan National Alliance
BNU	Beaconhouse National University
BRI	Belt and Road Initiative
CCDNS	Cabinet Committee on Defence and National Security
CCI	Council for Common Interest
CENTO	Central Treaty Organisation
CGS	Chief of General Staff
CJCSC	Chairman, Joint Chiefs of Staff Committee
COAS	Chief of Army Staff
COD	Charter of Democracy
COP	Combined Opposition Parties
CPEC	China-Pakistan Economic Corridor
CTBT	Comprehensive Nuclear-Test-Ban Treaty
DCC	Defence Committee of the Cabinet
DGMO	Director General Military Operations
EBDO	Elected Bodies Disqualification Order
ECC	Economic Committee of the Cabinet
ECL	Exit Control List
ECNEC	Executive Committee of the National Economic Council
ECO	Economic Cooperation Organization
FATA	Federally Administered Tribal Areas
FATF	Financial Action Task Force

FCA	Foreign Currency Account
FCNA	Force Command Northern Areas
FCR	Frontier Crimes Regulation
FOB	Forward Operating Base
GCC	Gulf Cooperation Council
HRCP	Human Rights Commission of Pakistan
ICRC	International Committee of the Red Cross
IDP	Internally Displaced Person
IHK	Indian Held Kashmir
IJI	Islami Jamhoori Ittehad
IMF	International Monetary Fund
IOC	Indian Occupied Kashmir
IPG	Independent Parliamentary Group
IPP	Independent Power Producer
IRS	Institute of Regional Studies
ISAF	International Security Assistance Force
ISI	Inter-Services Intelligence
ISIL	Islamic State of Iraq and the Levant
ISPR	Inter-Services Public Relations
ISSI	Institute of Strategic Studies, Islamabad
ISSRA	Institute for Strategic Studies, Research, and Analysis
JIT	Joint Investigation Team
JUI(F)	Jamiat Ulema-i-Islam (Fazlur Rehman Group)
JWP	Jamhoori Watan Party
KP	Khyber Pakhtunkhwa
KRL	Khan Research Laboratories (previously known as Kahuta Research Laboratories)
KSG	Kashmir Study Group
LOC	Line of Control
MFN	Most Favoured Nation
MI	Military Intelligence
MMA	Muttahida Majlis-e-Amal
MQM	Muttahida Qaumi Movement
NAB	National Accountability Bureau
NACTA	National Counter Terrorism Authority
NAM	Non-Aligned Movement
NBFIs	Non-Bank Financial Institutions
NDU	National Defence University

NPT	Non-Proliferation Treaty
NRO	National Reconciliation Ordinance
NSA	National Security Advisor
NSC	National Security Committee
NWFP	North West Frontier Province
OBL	Osama bin Laden
OBOR	One Belt, One Road
OIC	Organization of Islamic Countries
OPG	Official Parliamentary Group
PAEC	Pakistan Atomic Energy Commission
PCO	Provisional Constitutional Order
PEMRA	Pakistan Electronic Media Regulatory Authority
PKMAP	Pashtunkhwa Milli Awami Party
PML	Pakistan Muslim League
PML(N)	Pakistan Muslim League (Nawaz Sharif group)
PML(Q)	Pakistan Muslim League (Quaid-i-Azam group)
PPP	Pakistan Peoples Party
PPPPP	Pakistan Peoples Party Parliamentarians-Patriots
PSDP	Public Sector Development Program
PTI	Pakistan Tehreek-e-Insaaf
QCG	Quadrilateral Cooperation Group
RAW	Research and Analysis Wing (Indian Intelligence agency)
SAFRON	Ministry for States and Frontier Regions
SBP	State Bank of Pakistan
SCO	Shanghai Cooperation Group
SEATO	South East Asia Treaty Organisation
TTP	Tehrik-i-Taliban Pakistan
UNDP	United Nations Development Programme
UNMOGIP	United Nations Military Observer Group in India and Pakistan

CHAPTER 1

Early Life

The compulsion to record and publish my memoirs, it seems, is a part of my inherited legacy. My grandfather, Haji Mohtadullah published his life long search for knowledge in 1914 in the form of a 256-page Urdu book entitled *Ilaj-ul-Qulb* which in essence means 'Rediscovery of One's Soul'. He died in 1930.

My father, Mian Abdul Aziz published a smaller, 110-page English book with the title of *What is Man and What he Ought to Do* in 1946, six years before he died in December 1952. I reproduce below the English translation of some extracts from the foreword of my grandfather's book:

I am very grateful to God Almighty that I am a Muslim and a *momin* (true believer). I consider any other person as a *momin* who is a believer and is pious, no matter what his religion or race. I wrote this book in 1913 in the Frontier, which is a province of India, which in turn is ruled by the British, whose religion is Christianity. Today, Muslims throughout the world are in great distress. Italy is trying to occupy Trablus (Tripoli), the French are making plans to takeover Marakhash (Morocco) and other territories of North Africa. Russia has already digested Bukhara and is now advancing towards Iran and Armenia. Afghanistan is fearful of both its overbearing neighbours. In Central Asia, the interests of rival European powers are colliding and it is quite possible that a part of the Ottoman Empire may collapse in this struggle. These warring European powers could also destroy each other. Many hostile forces are trying hard to convert the Islamic bonds between the Turks and the Arabs into strong hostility. The Muslims of Java are under pressure from the Dutch. The Chinese Muslims are suffering in isolation. The Indian Muslims are also affected by these developments and feel totally directionless. All in all, Muslims are in distress in every part of this planet.

The principal cause of this distress and decline of the Muslims is their lack of knowledge and their decadent moral values...

I have written this book to distil knowledge from the divine books and the sayings and lives of prophets, saints and scholars. Those who read it without religious or racial prejudice will get to know themselves. And those who discover themselves can also reform themselves. This is not a religious book, it is book of ethics. I appeal to the government to include it in the educational syllabi of schools and colleges.

Haji Mohtadullah Kakakhel
4 October 1913

On the eve of the First World War (1914–18), he talks passionately about the enormous pressure which the Western powers were exerting on Turkey and other Muslim countries. His conclusion was that Muslims were backward and decadent mainly because they lacked knowledge and education. 'The main purpose of my life', he says in the foreword, is to collect as much knowledge as possible, in the light of Qur'an and Sunnah, and leave it for the next generation'. His opening statement that 'I am a Muslim and *Momin* (true believer) and consider any other person who is a believer and pious as a Momin, whatever his religion or race' is also a testimony to his grasp of the real meaning of Islam.

My father wrote his memoir to show how he, while totally overwhelmed by the early death of his first wife (my mother), and problems in his civil service career caused by unkind British officers, found peace through the pursuit of spiritual values. He sought guidance from the eight-volume works of the Indian mystic, Swami Rama Teerath, *In Woods of God Realization*. Swami Rama Teerath who was born in Gujranwala in 1873, got a Master's degree in mathematics from Government College, Lahore. Allama Iqbal knew him well and wrote a poem in his memory when he died.

I was born in Mardan on 7 February 1929, in the home of my maternal grandfather, Farman Ali. While hailing from Sialkot, he was posted as deputy collector irrigation in Mardan in 1924. My father was *naib tehsildar*, Mardan, at that time. When he first met Farman Ali to congratulate him on the award of the title of 'Khan Sahib' by the British, he was very impressed by his kindness and piety. He soon heard that Farman Ali had seven daughters and no son. He promptly sent one of his aunts with a marriage proposal for the eldest, who was 15 years old. To his delight, the proposal was accepted and they were married in 1925. Their first child, my sister Nisar, was born in 1927, and was said to have caused another burst of sorrow and anguish that had greeted the birth of eight successive females in that well-to-do household. My birth two years later thus became an especially joyous occasion. The celebration to greet the first male child after so many girls coincided happily with *Shab-e-Barat* (the Night of Blessings). The whole town of Mardan that night was ablaze with lights and festivity.

I have no memory of my mother, because she died when I was only four, but my aunts tell me she was very efficient and caring. She was also very fond of buying good clothes for me. This is clearly borne out by my childhood photograph, taken just before my mother died in 1933. After her death, my sister, Nisar, provided physical and emotional protection to me throughout our lives together.

My father remarried when I was five. Our stepmother, whom we called Mummy, was very kind and affectionate and never behaved like a stepmother. That is perhaps one reason why my relationship with her four children—Jamila, Javed, Rukhsana, and Kamal—was warmer and stronger than is normally seen even among full brothers and sisters. Tragically, Javed died when he was only 26, bringing the family even closer.

My father as a provincial civil servant in NWFP, started as *naib tehsildar* in 1920, moved on to become *tehsildar*, and retired as extra assistant commissioner in 1950. He was frequently posted from one district to another. I passed the primary school from Charsadda, sixth class from Abbottabad, middle school from Haripur, and matriculation from Dera Ismail Khan, in which I secured first position in the district, and second in the province.

My father would have liked to send me to Islamia College, Peshawar, since he was one of the first graduates from that college in 1918, but I had to go to Lahore and join Islamia College, Lahore, as my sister, Nisar, who had passed matriculation with distinction a year earlier, had to join Islamia College for Women in Lahore. Before partition there was no girls' college throughout the NWFP. It would be easier for her to travel back and forth between Lahore and Peshawar, I was told, if I was there to accompany her. The eventual stories of our train and bus journey in those days of underdeveloped communications, with missed connections, train accidents, loss of baggage, provided rich material for many short stories that Nisar wrote and eventually for her autobiography *Gaye Dino ka Suragh* (*The Search for Days Gone By*) published in 2004.

Joining the Muslim Students Federation (MSF)

My arrival in Islamia College, Lahore, in May 1944 was very exciting. The level of political activity was very high. The faculty with Dr Omar Hayat Malik as principal (who later became Pakistan's ambassador to Germany), Dr M. Aslam (Psychology), Dr Zaheeruddin (Chemistry), Professor Abdul Qadir (History), and Maulana Abdul Sattar Niazi (Islamiyat) was very impressive. The Islamia College cricket team at that time was well ahead of the rival cricket team from Government College, Lahore. It included five of the twelve players selected subsequently for the 1954 test tour of England (Abdul Hafeez Kardar, Khan Mohammad, Fazal Mahmood, Imtiaz Ahmad, and Maqsood Ahmad). The Government College provided two players—Shuja and Waqar and two players Hanif Mohammad and Mushtaq, were Karachi based.

Islamia College had a very active branch of the Muslim Students Federation (MSF), founded in 1937 by Hameed Nizami, soon after the 1937 elections in which the Muslim League had won only two seats in Punjab. Quaid-i-Azam Mohammad Ali Jinnah soon recognized the potential role Muslim students could play in the Pakistan Movement. He therefore invited Hameed Nizami, who was a student leader at that time, to setup a Muslim Students Federation as a student wing of the All-India Muslim League. As recorded in history, Quaid-i-Azam visited Islamia College, Lahore eleven times between 1937 and 1947. I had the good fortune of being present during three of these visits.

Other political parties were also keen to enlist the support of students from the largest Muslim educational institution in the Punjab. Maulana Maudoodi, Amir of Jamaat-e-Islami, came to Islamia College every Thursday, led the *maghrib* (evening) prayers in the new hostel mosque and spent an hour with the students explaining different aspects of Islamic teachings. These magnificent lectures left a deep imprint on my mind and ignited my interest in studying as many books as possible especially on Islamic history and the life of Prophet Muhammad (PBUH).

There was also an active Khaksar Tehrik in Islamia College. This Tehrik led by Allama Mashriqi, required its members to wear a green uniform and carry a *belcha* (shovel) in the daily parade. Mahmood Ahmad, the head of Khaksars in the college approached me to join the Tehrik. 'Without discipline and active, military-like training, the Muslim minority in India will not be able to secure a free homeland from the Hindu majority.' This argument was quite persuasive but by a happy coincidence, Quaid-i-Azam came to Lahore at that juncture and addressed a public meeting in the university ground. After listening to his inspiring address, I promptly went to Aftab Qarshi, the president of MSF in Islamia College and offered to work actively for it. I think he must have been impressed by my enthusiasm since within three months, he co-opted me in the executive committee, and gave me the responsibility for finance and accounts. This responsibility became very important a few months later, because Mian Mumtaz Daultana, then the treasurer of the Punjab Muslim League provided the hefty sum of Rs22,000 (in two instalments) for MSF's election campaign. The principal, Dr Omar Hayat Malik, also helped by exempting students who volunteered for election duty, from the detention tests in December 1945, under which the students were required to qualify to take FA or BA exams. This brought a flood of volunteers the next day. With these volunteers and the funds provided by Mumtaz Daultana, the MSF was able to send 1,200 students to over 80 out of 86 Muslim constituencies of Punjab in batches of six to ten students. Each student was given money for a third class train ticket and one rupee per day for meals. Some batches would return Rs10 out of Rs100 given to them because two meals were provided by the candidate. That was the real spirit of the Pakistan Movement. Qasim Rizvi, vice president of the MSF was a very good speaker and was the main organizer of this election campaign.

In the elections for the provincial assemblies held in February 1946, the Muslim League won 73 out of 86 Muslim seats in the Punjab and in India as a whole, 423 out of 493 Muslim seats. This was a decisive show of the overwhelming support of Muslim voters for the Muslim League, negating the repeated claims of the Indian National Congress that it represented not only Hindus but also Muslims of India. The

British could no longer ignore this democratic endorsement of the demand for Pakistan and soon sent a Cabinet Mission led by Sir Pethick Lawrence. The Cabinet Mission first presented, in May 1946, its own plan for a united India but with three semi autonomous components, one consisting of Punjab, NWFP, Sindh and Balochistan, the second comprising Bengal and Assam, and the third the rest of Hindu majority provinces. The Muslim League accepted this plan because it had a provision that after ten years, a group could opt out of the Indian union, if it so wished. The Indian National Congress however rejected the plan precisely because of this provision. As this gulf widened and Hindu–Muslim riots erupted throughout the subcontinent, the British realized that partition of India was the only option. Lord Mountbatten was sent to India in March 1947 as the new viceroy. After prolonged negotiations he announced, on 3 June 1947, the partition plan, which also included the partition of Punjab and Bengal, as demanded by Congress, to transfer the Hindu majority districts of these provinces to India. That is how the dream of Pakistan became a truncated reality on 14 August 1947.

Soon after the results of the 1946 elections were announced, the MSF branch of Islamia College distributed certificates of 'Mujahid-e-Pakistan' (The Warriors of Pakistan) to all the students who had taken part. These were in classes A, B, C based on number of days a student had devoted to the election campaign. Ten students, including the main office bearers and myself, however, received special class certificates.

In recognition of the role played by the students of Islamia College, Quaid-i-Azam came to the college in March 1946 to preside over the annual prize distribution function. I received from the Quaid, the prize for standing first in my class. The prizes were given in the form of books which the student himself selected. For Rs 20, which was the value of my prize, I selected three books: the *Chambers Dictionary*, *Dialogue with Plato* and the correspondence between Iqbal and Jinnah. I still use that dictionary.

In his speech on that occasion, the Quaid said: 'Now that many of you have won the certificates of Mujahid-e-Pakistan, I urge you to become Maimar-e-Pakistan (Builders of Pakistan)'. He also urged those present to pay more attention to commerce and industry 'because these sectors, so far dominated by Hindus, will be very important for the new state of Pakistan.'

The next day I accompanied a delegation of MSF led by Aftab Qarshi to Mamdot Villa to meet our beloved Quaid. During our conversation, I asked somewhat hesitantly 'Sir, what can the students do for commerce and industry. You might ask the landlords with money to invest in these sectors.' In his usual affectionate tone, in which he always addressed students, he said: 'My boy, diversion for students means diversion in studies'.

These words changed the course of my career. Instead of pursuing a career in law, which my father wanted me to do, I decided, along with twelve other fellow students, to join the Hailey College of Commerce. This, as narrated later in this chapter, was quite an adventurous experience, but for me that day, i.e. 24 March 1946, proved a turning point in life. The excitement of receiving a prize from the Quaid, was elevated by Quaid's directive to me personally on what career to pursue.

The next month, of April 1946, was also full of intense political activity. Qasim Rizvi had written to Chaudhry Khaliquzzaman, a key party lieutenant of the Quaid and Liaquat Ali Khan, from the United Provinces (UP) of India and offered the services of a batch of students from Islamia College, Lahore, to assist in his election campaign. On receiving a positive response, Qasim Rizvi quickly selected seven top campaigners, including myself, at the ripe age of seventeen years and two months, and the delegation left for Lucknow by the Calcutta Mail, which plied between Peshawar and Calcutta every day. (Another train, Bombay Express, provided a daily service between Peshawar and Bombay).

At the railway station, Qasim Rizvi after purchasing the rail tickets, gave me Rs800 in my capacity as member finance, for the remaining expenses including the return train journey. There was a longish stop at Tundla Junction during the middle of the night. I was sleeping on an empty seat with my coat under my head as a pillow. As a jolt woke me up, I discovered the coat was missing along with entire sum of Rs800. After some time, in the early morning light, a lineman found the coat near the railway line but the money was gone. We arrived in Lucknow virtually penniless and all the members cursing me for starving them. But I did not lose my nerve and sent a telegram to

Hasan Ahmad Rizvi, a friend in Aligarh University, to come to Lucknow with as much money as he could arrange. He came the next day with Rs250, which was enough for our return tickets and entertained me to a sumptuous lunch, which I desperately needed.

Chaudhry Khaliquzzaman received us very warmly and arranged our stay in the basement of the three-storey house of Begum Aizaz Rasool. We were to go to the nearby house of Raja Mahmoodabad for meals twice a day. But his political briefing took us by surprise. 'The election strategy you followed in Punjab,' Chaudhry Khaliquzzaman said, 'is not relevant for UP. Punjab will be a part of Pakistan and your main slogan—*Pakistan ka matlab kya—La Illaha Illallah* (Meaning of Pakistan: Only One God) had a strong impact. But UP will be a part of India. Muslim voters will ask you, why are you making Pakistan and leaving us at the mercy of the Hindu majority.'

In the evening, we discussed our election strategy in the light of these remarks and decided that instead of holding corner meetings, we would organize small public meetings in the Muslim majority localities of Lucknow. Our focus would be to emphasize that in the absence of Pakistan, the entire 100 million Muslim population of India will be a minority. Now at least two-thirds of them will get their own independent homeland and the remaining one-third will have a strong independent country watching over their interests according to international law and tradition.

We did not realize at that time the vicissitudes of local Shia–Sunni politics. Chaudhry Khaliquzzaman was facing two rivals: Ali Zaheer, a Shia (who later became India's ambassador to Iran), and Badi-uz-Zaman, a Sunni. Ali Zaheer was attacking Chaudhry Khaliquzzaman for starting Madah-e-Sahaba (the praise of Prophet Muhammad's four companions) when he was chairman of Lucknow city council. Badi-uz-Zaman was blaming him for stopping Madah-e-Sahaba in the mosques. When we asked Chaudhry Khaliquzzaman about it, he said, without any embarrassment: 'It all depends on who is in majority in the city council at a given point of time, Shias or Sunnis?' We left Lucknow after a week, fully convinced that Chaudhry Khaliquzzaman would lose the election. But we were pleasantly surprised when we heard that he had won without leaving his house for a single day during the campaign.

We returned to Lahore just in time to join the mass agitation against the Unionist government of Khizar Hayat Khan Tiwana. Following the death of Sir Sikander Hayat Khan in 1942, Khizar Tiwana was elected president of the Unionist Party. In the 1946 elections, all Muslim parties and groups had joined the Muslim League, but Khizar Tiwana's Unionist Party joined the Indian National Congress and won all the three seats he contested in the Punjab by spending at least Rs3 lakhs (a fortune at that time). Muslim League won 73 out of 86 Muslim seats but these were not enough to form a government. Khizar Tiwana became chief minister in April 1946, by joining members of the Congress and the Sikh Akali Dal. The majority of Muslims in Punjab was angry with him and soon found an issue to agitate against him when he banned the Muslim League national guards as a paramilitary organization. The agitation launched by All-India Muslim League brought thousands on to the streets all over the province and jails filled up beyond their capacity. I was also arrested along with about thirty other students but we did not spend more than one night in jail. We made so much noise throughout the night that next morning we were bundled into a police van and left on Multan road, about thirty miles from Lahore. We walked to the nearest railway line, raising slogans. The third train that passed had a Muslim driver. He stopped. We got into the train. He again stopped the train just short of Lahore city railway station, so that we could jump off.

Khizar Tiwana's government could not withstand the widespread agitation and was forced to resign within a few months. Khizar Tiwana retired from politics after that and remained aloof until he died in 1986.

The Shift to Hailey College of Commerce

In May 1946, I along with twelve other fellow students went to Hailey College to seek admission in compliance with the Quaid's wishes (which I took as his command). The Sikh head-clerk looked at us with dismay and said: 'You Muslims (*O' musleo*), it will not be easy for you to get admission in Hailey College because we admit FA/FSc with first division only'. As we learnt later, there was only one Muslim faculty member (Professor M. Hasan for economics) and only three Muslims out of 350 students: M. Masood, the well known chartered accountant of Lahore; Abdul Jabbar, who retired as president of the National Bank of Pakistan; and Maqsood, who later started his own business.

Fortunately, ten out of my thirteen fellow students who had applied got enough marks to get admission. I got a first division in my FA exam even though I had had very little time to prepare. I was in Quetta at the end of June along with two other students (Fazal Hussain and Ayub Khan) to raise funds for the Islamia College trust fund when I received my result and immediately sent a telegram to my father in Parachinar because he was convinced I would not pass the FA exam, even in the third division.

When we joined Hailey College in September 1946, we found it was also a very well managed place with a good faculty. But it was very different from the Islamia College. Most Hindu and Sikh students were from well-to-do business families. They were very well dressed and came to the college in private cars. Majid Nizami had joined Hailey College with me, and for the same reason, but he did not like the 'dull accountancy courses' and transferred to Government College after a few months to prepare for MA in political science. While he was there, we struck up many common friendships. One such close friend was Darshan Singh, who like Majid Nizami belonged to Sangla Hill. They had met in school. Darshan and I became lifelong friends.

In the first few weeks of 1947, the city of Lahore was overtaken by tension and hatred. Hindus could not walk through Muslim areas and vice versa. In all parts of Lahore, political processions and rallies were gaining momentum. Both sides were also preparing for low intensity war, with bamboos, hockey sticks, and fire bottles. The number of stabbing cases was increasing by the day. There were also scary rumours that Sir Radcliffe, who was drawing the boundaries between India and Pakistan, might award Lahore to India.

These disturbances were especially worrisome for students who were preparing for university examinations. My sister, Nisar, had worked hard to prepare for her BA examination, but many exam centres were disrupted by riots and curfews. After the first paper on 1 April, we learnt that the exam centre at F.C. College was relatively safe, so every alternate day I would escort her to F.C. College, but once the examination was over I did not waste a day in putting her on the train to Peshawar.

Just a few days before our classes were to end for the summer break
in May 1947, a Hindu passer-by was stabbed to death in front of our
college gate. That sent waves of shock and anger through the hostel
students. Darshan came to me late in the evening and said it would be
better if I went to Mozang and spent the remaining days in Asghar's
house (one of our day-scholar friends). Bhatia, our hostel
superintendent, he told me, was actually the district organizer of the
Rashtriya Swayamsevak Sangh (RSS) and they had discussed plans to
take revenge. I and three other Muslim boarders climbed down the
huge banyan tree that touched the roof of the hostel and walked to
Mozang two hours later. The next day I too left for Peshawar.

The Dream Becoming a Reality

I will never forget the memorable radio broadcast by Lord
Mountbatten, on 3 June, announcing that Pakistan would emerge as
an independent and sovereign country on 14 August 1947. My family
had arrived in Abbottabad from Peshawar for the summer months, as
we did every year on 1 June. But the electricity connection for the
house we had rented, had not yet been provided. Therefore, Mummy,
Nisar and I took our radio to a neighbouring house and sought
permission to listen to the leaders' speeches. They readily agreed. Lord
Mountbatten was followed by Pandit Jawaharlal Nehru, Quaid-i-Azam
Mohammad Ali Jinnah and Sardar Baldev Singh. Quaid-i-Azam ended
his speech with a forceful 'Pakistan *Zindabad*', starting waves of
applause, wherever it was heard.

But as these speeches were dissected, a serious issue that was yet to
be decided raised its head—the future of NWFP. The Muslim League
had won majority seats in all the Muslim majority provinces of India,
except NWFP where it had won only 45 per cent of the seats. It would
therefore be necessary, the British authorities decided, to hold a
referendum in NWFP (as also in the Sylhet district of Assam plus a
jirga of sardars in Balochistan) to determine if the people would vote
to join Pakistan or India.

The referendum was to be held in July. The next day, I arrived at
the district headquarters of the Muslim League located in Springfield
Hotel, Abbottabad. Baba Jalaluddin (affectionately called Jalal Baba)

was the district president and Ghulam Hussain the general secretary.
I explained the work we had done in Islamia College, Lahore, and
volunteered to do all the office work connected with the referendum.
They were delighted because dozens of letters seeking information,
instructions, or help were pending action in Ghulam Hussain's office.
I cleared them within a few days. Fortunately, the Red Shirt party (later
National Awami Party) boycotted the referendum and more than 90
per cent of the votes cast were in favour of Pakistan.

But the success of the referendum was marred by great disappointment
over the Boundary Commission award under Sir Cyril Radcliffe.
Gurdaspur, which was a Muslim majority district, was given to India.
That provided a land route between India and Kashmir and became
the root cause of the major dispute between India and Pakistan over
Kashmir for the coming decades.

The historic day of 14 August 1947 has left a lasting imprint on my
mind. We spent the whole day distributing green flags and earthen oil
lamps to as many houses as possible. The formal ceremony for hoisting
the Pakistan flag was to be held in Company Bagh, Abbottabad, where
the British deputy commissioner was to take the salute from a
contingent of the Muslim League national guards. I had one of my
white summer suits dyed in green and merrily marched in front of the
contingent. 'This deputy commissioner, who until yesterday was
ordering *lathi* (baton) charge on our rallies, will be saluting our flag!'
How could I miss the excitement of such an experience?

Before the end of August, I received a letter from Professor Hassan,
the only Muslim faculty member of Hailey College, urging me to
return to college. The vice chancellor had assured him, he said, that if
thirty-five new students joined in September, the college would begin
its post-partition existence with fifty students.

We lobbied hard by addressing Friday gatherings in Government
College and F.C. College and conveying Quaid-i-Azam's emphasis on
commerce and industry. By middle of September, we had managed
thirty new admissions but what about faculty? Professor Hasan finally
arranged part-time faculty members. Rahim Jan for accountancy,
Professor Ziauddin for statistics, Professor Ataullah for economic
history, and Professor Nazar Mohammad for commercial law, and one
full-time faculty member, Hashmi, for economics and marketing.
Hashmi also became the hostel superintendent and eventually served

as principal of the college. Since there were only twelve boarders in the large new hostel, we occupied two or three rooms each and Hashmi took over the entire old hostel for about sixty of his relatives from Agra, who had migrated to Pakistan and had nowhere to live.

Our life at Hailey College for the remaining two years was such a stark contrast to the first year. All the hustle and bustle created by 350 Hindu and Sikh students had gone and was replaced by the gloom and agony of millions of refugees who had poured into Lahore. My friend Ehsan and I would go regularly to the Walton refugee camp and help some of them to trace their relatives. But after a few days it became impossible to stomach so much misery and distress.

After the gloom subsided, we began to enjoy the vast funds and facilities left by the college authorities in the sports fund, the union fund, and the welfare fund. We purchased new furniture, crockery, curtains, and carpets for the common room and the hostel kitchen. We bought new sports gear including two boats for the boating club. With only fifty students, every student was either a winner or a runner up in different sporting events at the annual sports. The principal sanctioned liberal scholarships for most new students and as a result in September 1948, we had 110 new students (the full capacity), and a great demand for starting evening short courses in accountancy and banking to fill expanding job opportunities in these sectors following the departure of the Hindus.

I earned a B.Com. degree with very good marks in May 1949, and joined an internship programme, as required, at the Colony Textile Mills in Shahdin Building on Mall Road in Lahore.

I was very keen to take up a career in banking but unfortunately the scheme to directly recruit officers in the bank, started by Zahid Hussain, governor of the Central Bank three years later, did not exist at that time. I therefore decided to prepare for the Central Superior Services examination in 1951, and take up whatever appointment came my way for the interim period. Within a few months, in response to an advertisement, I was selected by the Punjab/NWFP Public Service Commission for the post of deputy director information, government of NWFP.

Information Department, Peshawar

This stopgap employment in Peshawar for the next two years proved an enriching experience. Khan Abdul Qayyum Khan was the chief minister of NWFP and was very keen to publicize the development activities being undertaken in the province—new schools, new roads and extension of electricity to new villages. The director information, A.K. Qureshi was an outstanding journalist and a very fine human being. Unfortunately, he died a few years later in the PIA crash near the Cairo airport. The group of journalists that I escorted on the chief minister's entourage was very lively and friendly and included Mufti and Safdar Qureshi of APP, Faiq Kamran of daily *Shahbaz*, Sanaullah of daily *Khyber Mail* and Hashmi, news editor of Radio Pakistan. The provincial cabinet had only two other ministers, Mian Jaffar Shah (education) and Faridullah Khan (health).

Even as a young entrant in the provincial setup, I developed good personal relations with all the ministers and heads of departments because of frequent trips with the chief minister. Having secured a job, my parents were anxious, as most parents of that era were, to marry me off to my childhood fiancée, Hamida, as early as possible. Since I was posted in Nathiagali, the summer headquarters of the NWFP government, to officiate for the director, A.K. Qureshi, who had gone to USA for a long study tour, a brief marriage ceremony took place in Abbottabad on 2 August 1951. However, the *valima* had to be delayed until 13 August, when all heads of departments would descend in Peshawar for the 14 August celebration. My family was very pleased when they saw that their 'boy's' wedding at the Services Hotel Peshawar was attended by Governor Shahabuddin, Chief Minister Qayyum Khan, the two ministers, Mian Jaffar Shah and Faridullah Khan and all the twelve heads of departments in the provincial government apart from all my journalist friends.

While I learnt a lot and greatly enjoyed this limelight, I also discovered some uncomfortable aspects of a bureaucrat's life. The provincial elections held in October 1951 were heavily managed and the deputy commissioners and police officials who participated in this 'management' were rewarded, while those who wanted to act honestly were sidelined. This experience helped me greatly in choosing my future career.

The Central Superior Services (CSS)

I had appeared in the CSS examination held in February 1951 and had obtained a good position. But I was surprised when I learnt in August that I had been assigned to the police service of Pakistan. I sent a letter of regret to the establishment division and said that unless I was given a service of my choice I would forego this chance and would try again next year.

By some coincidence at that time, most of the top positions governing the country were from the audit and accounts service of undivided India. These included Ghulam Mohammad, (finance minister, later governor-general); Chaudhry Mohammad Ali (secretary general, later prime minister); Zahid Hussain (governor State Bank); Abdul Qadir (finance secretary later finance minister); and many other prominent officials like S.A. Hasnie, Mumtaz Hasan, and Rashid Ibrahim. I often told my colleagues that if you are a deputy commissioner or a commissioner, you only manage a limited area and are open to many pressures. But if you become a *policy professional*, and are able to make a good budget or evolve sound commercial and economic policies, you can make a difference in the lives of the entire nation. In terms of temperament, I always felt more comfortable dealing with challenging ideas rather than handling troublesome people, as a police official is generally required to do.

In the face of these considerations, I readily accepted the offer to join the Pakistan military accounts service, which I received a few weeks later and joined the Military Accounts Service Academy in the office of CMA, Lahore cantonment, which was modest, compared to the impressive Civil Service Academy on the Mall Road in Lahore. Jarri Ahmad Sayyid as controller military accounts was also the principal of the academy. Other colleagues in military accounts, who became life-long friends, included Nurual Hassan Jafri, A.P. Hassumani, S.S. Iqbal Hussain, Tajammal Hussain, Aftab Ahmad, M.A.G.M. Akhtar, Abdul Jalil, and Abdul Malik.

In the first two decades after the creation of Pakistan, the merit system it seems was quite strong in Pakistan. I cannot think of any other explanation for the rapid advancement in the career of someone like me, who came from a rural background of a small province, with no powerful connections to recommend him.

After less than three years' service, I was selected for a course in organization and methods and elementary computer training in the UK. After this three months' training in the summer of 1955, I was posted to the O&M Division in Karachi to assist in improving financial and economic services provided by various organizations (e.g. collector of customs, passport office, and speedy loan processing by the Agricultural Development Bank (then called ADFC).

After General Ayub Khan declared martial law in October 1958, he setup more than twenty-five commissions and committees to reform the system, ranging from land reforms to education reforms. One such committee was the Administrative Reorganization Committee (ARC). It was chaired by G. Ahmad, then chairman of Planning Board and included all the senior secretaries to the government (G. Mueenuddin, Hafiz Abdul Majid, Nasir Ahmad, M. Ayub, Hardy, and Vaqar Ahmad). The committee was to review the justification, performance, and strength of all the ministries and their subordinate organizations, including all the foreign missions abroad. I became the secretary of this committee to assist my joint secretary, S.S. Haider. It was the first major assignment of my career and I gave it all that I possessed in my head and heart.

Instead of submitting one consolidated voluminous report after many years, G. Ahmad decided that the committee would submit separate reports on each ministry or subject in the form of a summary for the cabinet. The committee submitted sixty such reports over the next two years. These included reports on introducing the section officers' scheme in the secretariat to replace the old hierarchical system of assistant, superintendent and assistant secretary, and also the new system of financial management to make the secretary of a ministry the principal accounting officer to control and spend the approved budget, with assistance from a financial adviser. One report also recommended the creation of an economic pool, under which the best officers drawn from the CSP (later district management group) and other accounts and revenue services were to be drawn and trained for senior reserved positions in all the economic ministries and organizations. I was readily selected for this pool in 1960, because most of the members of the selection committee were also members of the ARC. Earlier in October 1959, I had also received *Tamgha-e-Khidmat* from Ayub Khan for my services to ARC.

The following year, as the work of ARC ended, G. Ahmad asked me to join the Planning Commission as deputy secretary plan coordination. Thus, I was promoted as deputy secretary with only nine years' service. The year after that I was selected for a Master's degree course in development economics at Harvard University, starting from September 1962. During Christmas vacations in Washington that winter, I met Munir Hussain, economic counsellor in the embassy. As deputy secretary cabinet, he had processed the list of candidates selected for the economic pool in 1960, and was surprised that instead of opting for one of more 'attractive' posts like collector customs, commissioner income tax or chief controller imports and exports, I had chosen to join the Planning Commission. 'Instead of wielding real powers and in the process making some money for yourself and family, you will be writing long notes and useless papers on different subjects.' Munir Hussain said sarcastically. I replied with a laugh, 'The power of ideas, I believe, is much greater than the power that comes from executive authority or money.' A few years later, in 1969, Munir Hussain's name was near the top of the list of 303 officers sacked by General Yahya Khan for corruption.

The Planning Commission Experience

My ten years' stay in the Planning Commission was extremely fruitful. Under its reorganization, President Ayub Khan had become its chairman. The deputy chairman, Saeed Hasan and later M.M. Ahmad had a minister's status. Apart from formulating five-year plans and sectoral plans, its main function was to promote the preparation and approval of good, viable development projects and also assist in the formulation of sound economic policies. Finance Minister Shoaib had readily agreed to delegate the responsibility for the approval of development projects and for making up the annual development programme for the public sector to the Planning Commission. The economic affairs division was also a part of the Planning Commission for better coordination of rupee allocations and provision of foreign assistance for different projects. The administrative and institutional infrastructure for development activities (NEC, ECNEC, ECC, CDWP, PC-I Proforma) in vogue at present was put in place at that time.

But the real delight of my tenure in the Planning Commission was the dream economic team and the life-long friendships we developed.

When I joined the Planning Commission in October 1961, Dr Mahbub ul Haq, as chief of the perspective planning section was the rising star on the economic horizon. Another remarkable member of the team was Dr Moinuddin Baqai as chief of fiscal and monetary section.

Mahbub's brilliance and passionate articulation was highly infectious. He stimulated, challenged, and co-opted anyone who came in contact with him and had something to add or contribute. He had topped every examination he had taken, right up to his double PhD in Cambridge (1954) and Yale (1957). After a short tenure in the State Bank, he joined the Planning Board at the request of Mueenuddin Qureshi who had joined the Planning Board three years earlier as assistant chief.

The third member of the 'famous Trio', Moinuddin Baqai, with a rare combination of intellectual brilliance and the superb human quality of humility, was a perfect member of the team, which soon added a second layer of young, excellent economists as potential successors. These included Javed Azfar, Khalid Ikram, Javed Hamid and Meekal Ahmad. Moinuddin Baqai had completed his education under difficult circumstances since his father died when he was only twelve. After completing his Masters in economics from Government College, Lahore in the first division, he joined the State Bank's research department in 1953, along with his friends Mahbub ul Haq and Parvez Hasan. He soon got a scholarship for a PhD from Kansas University which he completed in just two years.

Because of its expanding role in policy making, the Planning Commission had also attracted many professional experts from other fields, i.e. Shafi Niaz as chief of agriculture, N.N.A. Qureshi as chief of industries, Dr M.S. Qureshi as chief of water and power (with Masiduddin as his deputy chief), Khalid Shibli as chief of housing, and Dr Siddiqui as chief of education. Qamar-ul-Islam as secretary planning, and Saeed Hasan (and later M.M. Ahmad) as deputy chairman, provided very good leadership to this talented group of experts. There was also a five-member advisory group from Harvard

University, led by Richard Gilbert which provided support to the basic analytical and research work of the Planning Commission.

During the 1960s, most budget speeches originated in the Planning Commission and not in the ministry of finance as did proposals for annual trade policies. The final briefs for President Ayub Khan on all cabinet summaries were prepared in the Planning Commission and provided the basis for the most important economic decisions.

The excitement, the tensions and the accomplishments that we went through in the 1960s, would deserve a full volume. But the most important part of this story was not the usual hassle of meeting difficult deadlines, for five-year plans, the annual plan and the documents for the annual World Bank's aid to Pakistan consortium; it was our collective intellectual growth in understanding the process of economic and social change, and the difficulties of reconciling the conflicting objectives of freedom and equality, growth versus macro economic stability, and the complex issues of poverty and regional inequalities especially in the context of East and West Pakistan.

Mahbub's contribution to development theory and practice has been monumental. Its culmination was the concept of human development and its quantitative indicator, the human development index, which he introduced through UNDP's annual reports on human development in 1990.[1] But unlike many other intellectual stalwarts Mahbub had the intellectual honesty to accept a conflicting viewpoint and accommodate it in his thinking. We used to have long arguments about the thesis presented in his first book *The Strategy of Economic Planning* (Oxford 1963) that developing countries should first concentrate on economic growth and worry about income distribution later because increase in inequality was inevitable in the initial phase of development. I think he was finally convinced about my viewpoint when we together paid our first ten-day visit to China in December 1967 as a part of an eight-member Economic delegation led by M.M. Ahmad. As we returned to Dhaka on 23 December 1967, I could not resist the urge to record the firsthand account of this momentous visit in my diary, despite the fatigue of the journey. Next morning at breakfast, I read out the concluding portion of this entry in my diary. He was overwhelmed. He said, 'Taji, this is the essence of development theory you have captured. Please continue the search and record it fully as your contribution to the theory and practice of development.' I, of course, followed his advice and ten years later, published *Rural Development: Learning from China* in 1978 through Macmillan in London.

In this book I distilled, from the Chinese experience, five main elements of a comprehensive rural development strategy: (i) Equitable distribution of land, (ii) opportunities for collective efforts to develop land and water resources, (iii) Diversification of rural economy to increase social productivity and expand non-farm employment, (iv) active promotion of social development, not only through better education and health services but also by eliminating barriers to social progress often created by the landowner, the middlemen or the local official, and (v) finally to create a positive political and economic framework for rural development, that will protect the terms of trade for agriculture and prevent transfer of resources from the rural sector through taxation or exchange rate policies.

While recognizing the cultural and political uniqueness of China, I spelt out in the book, certain intermediate or partial solutions for those developing countries which cannot overcome the political obstacles for a comprehensive rural development strategy.[2]

Here for the record, I also reproduce the extract from my diary that I read out to Mahbub ul Haq on the morning of 25 December 1967:

As the plane took off (from Canton to Dacca), I realized that I had answers to many of the questions that were on my mind when I reached Beijing:

a. First and most important, Communism as practiced and evolved in China is not merely a political system or even a politico-economic framework; it is almost a 'religion', comprehensive in concept and decisive in its impact.

b. Politically, it mobilizes the support of the masses for benefiting the masses at the cost of the elite (unlike democracy in which the elite rule the country but to get the power they do the minimum necessary to keep the masses happy).

c. Economically, it creates powerful non-material incentives to supplement limited material incentives to make people sacrifice and work hard. Material incentives are essentially relative and are always running behind aspirations. Those who have more, want still more. For countries like ours, which can't afford to beat the incentives race and provide material rewards necessary to get everyone to do his best, we have to find some way of creating non-material incentives for our scientists, engineers and civil servants.

d. The main purpose of the Cultural Revolution was to make the people work hard for another spell without corresponding material rewards. China had now started developing surpluses which could be given to the people to let them relax a little after eighteen years of hard work and that is what people like Liu Shao-chi wanted, but Mao had seen the degeneration of Russia, once the craze for consumer goods started and wanted to avoid it by re-igniting the ideological fervour. Another purpose was to stimulate the younger generation, which had not seen the 1949 revolution and needed to feel its impact.

e. Having decided not to distribute its surplus internally, China will spend an increasing proportion on defence, space and nuclear weapons, and foreign aid.

f. China is prepared for a nuclear war. Having industrialized after the nuclear age had begun, it has decentralized on a massive scale. This plus their policy of self-reliance from a village to a city would ensure that if half of China is destroyed, the remaining half would be functioning.

g. The most impressive part of China's performance was its social and moral transformation. A country which was internationally known for all the sins and crimes one could think of, is now virtually free from thefts, smuggling, prostitution, gambling, or organized crimes. Even if we achieve economic development, but degenerate morally (as many countries have) what is the use? Perhaps the only country in the world where economic development is accompanied by satisfaction and contentment and much-needed social harmony is China. Elsewhere, as in Pakistan, economic development means the enrichment of a small minority, which also degenerates morally, and as human beings.

The crucial question, however, is how long will the system go on like this. Historically, man has tried to control the human instincts only on a limited scale and when he failed, the society adjusted its values. Here the instincts of 700 million people have been harmonized and channelized for a new system or a new religion, as Islam had done 1400 years ago. How long will this last? How far will this spread and by what means?

As I pondered over these reflections, I had a strange uneasy feeling about our own future. Intellectually, communism or some brand of socialism is far superior to anything we have, but psychologically we are not ready for it. Even our present alliance with China looks so artificial. They are so warm and gracious in their attitude to us, and we are so reactionary.

These question marks aside, my visit has been a memorable one: It may change my whole attitude toward things and life. It has been an experience of a new kind.

The East Pakistan Crisis

My last two years in the Planning Commission were very painful and difficult. In 1968, I was still recovering from the shock and grief of the sudden death of my 26-year-old younger brother, Captain Javed Aziz, who was a commando and had drowned in the upper Jhelum canal during an exercise, when the country was overtaken by a massive political agitation against Ayub Khan. He was forced to resign on 25 March 1969 and handed over power to General Yahya Khan who promptly declared another martial law and later promised fresh elections in October 1970. I recorded the following in my diary on 28 March 1969:

> The most serious implication of the current crisis, apart from Ayub's ouster, is the distinct possibility of a break between East and West Pakistan. There were only two binding factors, Islam and the fear of India. Islam, we never developed actively as a major driving force in our political and social life. The fear of India was exploded by the 1965 war, when East Pakistan was completely isolated, and they realized that West Pakistan could not really defend them. Since then the demand for autonomy has been mounting. As soon as the political debate about the future of the country started, the agitation for regional autonomy gathered momentum. In fact, East Pakistan

economists are convinced they would be better off economically if they were separate. They have no large defence burden to carry, they would be responsible for only 10–15 per cent of the total debt, and they could get food under PL-480 from the USA to balance the inter-wing trade. They would still be left with Rs100 crores of foreign exchange for development, unlike West Pakistan which will give up all its foreign exchange in debt, defence, barter, and bonus voucher scheme.

Whatever the outcome, Pakistan will never be the same again. That Pakistan for which we fought and struggled in 1947, has proved to be unviable and 'our dream come true' is now shattering. I have the feeling of a person whose legs are being chopped, but he will die if his legs are not chopped.

We in the Planning Commission did our best to push ahead with the fourth plan, and make it an element of national unity by promising a substantial transfer of resources from West to East Pakistan. We succeeded to some extent but the result of the elections held in December 1970, overtook everything and as recorded in Chapter 3, shattered the dream of a united Pakistan.

NOTES

1. The term human development was first used by Mahbub in a small booklet we published in 1968 on socio-economic objectives of the fourth five-year plan.
2. Chapters 6 and 7 of *Rural Development: Learning from China* are reproduced in *Hunger, Poverty and Development: Life and Work of Sartaj Aziz* edited by Anwar Dil, published by Ferozsons, Lahore in 2000.

A significant phase of Sartaj Aziz's early life, as a student, was his role in the Pakistan Movement, as a
Member of the Executive Committee of the Muslim Students Federation (MSF)
of Islamia College, Lahore (1944–1946). A precious legacy of that role are these photographs
with the Father of the Nation, Quaid-i-Azam Mohammad Ali Jinnah.

Receiving a prize from the Quaid-i-Azam at the Annual Convocation
of Islamia College, Lahore, 21 March 1946
Photo Courtesy: Islamia College, Lahore

Members of the Islamia College MSF with the Quaid-i-Azam
(December 1945). Sartaj Aziz is second from left in the front row.
Photo Courtesy: Islamia College, Lahore

The Quaid-i-Azam with the faculty and proctors of Islamia College, Lahore
(March 1946). Front row from left: Prof. Zahiruddin, Qasim, Dr Omar Hayat Malik, Quaid-i- Azam,
Prof. Abdul Qadir, Sartaj Aziz, Prof. Mohamed Aslam
Photo Courtesy: Islamia College, Lahore

In 1958, Sartaj Aziz served as Secretary of Pakistan's Administrative Reorganization Committee. That assignment earned him the award of Tamgha-e-Khidmat which he received from President Ayub Khan on 27 October 1959
Photo Courtesy: Press Information Department (PID), Islamabad

Receiving Tehrik-e-Pakistan Gold Medal from Chief Minister Nawaz Sharif,
23 March 1990
Photo Courtesy: Author's personal collection

Sartaj Aziz at age 3
Photo Courtesy: Author's personal collection

Sartaj Aziz at age 21
Photo Courtesy: Author's personal collection

My brother, Late Captain Javed Aziz, who died in
June 1968, aged 26 years, during a commando exercise
Photo Courtesy: Author's personal collection

My brother, Brigadier Kamal Aziz
Photo Courtesy: Author's personal collection

My daughter, Tahmina with her husband, Arif Ayub soon after their wedding in May 1982
Photo Courtesy: Author's personal collection

My daughter Farhana
Photo Courtesy: Author's personal collection

(My sister Nisar on left) and my wife Hameeda at my nephew Ahmar's wedding
Photo Courtesy: Author's personal collection

With my sister Jameela and my wife Hameeda at Santa Barbara, California in 2003
Photo Courtesy: Author's personal collection

My sister Nisar with her husband Asghar Butt
Photo Courtesy: Author's personal collection

My sister Nisar's son Ashar with Ayesha
Photo Courtesy: Author's personal collection

Celebrating our 50th wedding anniversary with
friends and relatives in August 2001
Photo Courtesy: Author's personal collection

My sister **Rukhsana** with her husband
Shafqat Kakakhel
Photo Courtesy: Author's personal collection

With my son and grandson Sharez
Photo Courtesy: Author's personal collection

With Jamil Nishtar and Mahbub ul Haq
Photo Courtesy: Author's personal collection

CHAPTER 2

Milestones and Turning Points

Many individuals, events, and interactions shape the history and the future of all nations. Historians record and analyze each of these from different perspectives, assigning credit for outstanding achievements, apportioning responsibility for failures and explaining causes and results over a period of time. Many of these historical accounts create controversies, depending on the political, religious, or ethnic orientation tilt or bias of those involved.

Any attempt to analyze the different facets of Pakistan's history in a meaningful and objective manner is particularly difficult because of the exceptional circumstances in which Pakistan came into existence on 14 August 1947, and the heterogeneous society that Pakistan has become since then. That is why most of the historical studies or essays so far written leave the students of history somewhat confused about the causes and effects of different events and the role of various actors on the stage of history. Even more serious, these confused and often conflicting versions of Pakistan's history give succeeding generations of political leaders and policy makers the excuse to ignore the real lessons of Pakistan's sad and turbulent past. That is why there is today no national consensus on such fundamental issues as the ideology of Pakistan as visualized by the country's founding fathers, the place of Islam in the society, the real causes of the failure of democracy in Pakistan and the role of the military in the country's political system.

In this volume, I have attempted to identify certain milestones of Pakistan's journey through history, in an effort to highlight the significant landmarks and to sift the essential from the trivial, in the expectation that it will provide some guidance to present and future rulers in evolving a wider national consensus on certain basic issues of state and governance without which no nation can survive or prosper.

The Failure of Democracy

A milestone is essentially a significant political development or a major economic event that has a substantial and lasting impact on the political or economic life of the country.

A turning point, by comparison is a much bigger event or catastrophe, which can change the direction of the country's political history, its geography or system of governance. It is either the result of a major external convulsion or an historic opportunity grasped by the leadership of the country.

The creation of Pakistan was obviously a major and positive turning point, just as the break up of Pakistan in 1971, when East Pakistan became Bangladesh and shattered the dream of Pakistan's founding fathers, was a negative turning point.

As my personal progress in my career proceeded parallel with Pakistan's progress as a nation, I witnessed, often from close quarters many more milestones and turning points—both positive and negative, adding to my dreams and their realization and also tragedies and upheavals which shattered some dreams and left a legacy of difficulties and obstacles.

The death of Quaid-i-Azam Mohammad Ali Jinnah in September 1948 followed soon after, by the tragic assassination of Prime Minister Liaquat Ali Khan was the first negative turning point because the departure of these founding founders made it more difficult to erect the constitutional edifice on which a democratic and workable political system could be built for the new state of Pakistan. This prepared the ground for the next paradigm shift in 1958, when General Ayub Khan abrogated the 1956 constitution, postponed the first general elections scheduled for February 1959, and took over as martial law administrator.

General (later Field Marshal) Ayub Khan's tenure was bad for politics but good for the economy. As I joined the National Planning Commission in 1961, my dreams were again lifted to a high point, as I suddenly realized that with sustained growth, Pakistan could join the selected group of middle-income countries within a decade and perhaps this economic upsurge would be followed by healthy political development.

But the 1965 war with India, another negative milestone brought about by a series of ill-conceived and poorly executed strategies, not only shattered that dream but also led to the eventual break-up of the country in 1971.

The tragic turning point of 1971, when East Pakistan became Bangladesh was essentially brought about by the failure of democracy in Pakistan. Even though East Pakistan economy had performed reasonably well in the 1960s, the people of East Pakistan were getting increasingly disillusioned. With limited representation in the armed forces and the civil services, they had no sense of participation in decision making. Under the highly centralized rule of Ayub Khan, the 1962 constitution gave more powers to the nominated governor than the elected chief minister of the province. Only the fear of a hostile neighbour, India, kept the two wings together but even that factor disappeared with the 1965 India–Pakistan war. Sheikh Mujibur Rehman won 160 out of National Assembly's 162 seats in East Pakistan in the 1970 elections, based on his six-point formula of maximum provincial autonomy. That also gave him a majority in the National Assembly of 300 seats. Yet he was denied the opportunity to become prime minister. Negotiations to give autonomy to East Pakistan, under the Awami League also failed. The repression that followed, after the arrest of Mujibur Rehman in March 1971, sent millions of refugees to India, giving it a good excuse to intervene militarily in November 1971 to 'liberate' East Pakistan and create the new state of Bangladesh.

The democratic interlude of the PPP government under Zulfikar Ali Bhutto, from 1972 to 1977, was a positive turning point, as it pulled the nation out of the trauma caused by the 1971 tragedy and as described in Chapter 3, restored the ownership of the country's political system to the people.

However, this interlude was once again overtaken by another negative turning point consisting of three separate milestones: Ziaul Haq's military takeover of July 1977; hanging of Z.A. Bhutto in April 1979; and Pakistan's involvement in the Afghan war in 1980. These were essentially political milestones as they intensified the struggle of the society to choose its identity. Since Islam has not had an overall renaissance so far, every Muslim society is witnessing a serious struggle between its conservative and liberal elements. Ziaul Haq's Islamization programme and the support for the *jihad* in Afghanistan added a new and violet dimension to this struggle in Pakistan.

The next five chapters, describing the tenure of Mohammad Khan Junejo from 1985 to 1988 and two tenures each, of Benazir Bhutto and Nawaz Sharif highlight many positive and negative milestones culminating finally in a new turning point with the military takeover of October 1999, followed two years later, by the tragic events of 9/11.

The 1998 nuclear tests also constitute a major turning point in Pakistan's history. This effectively countered Indian doubts about Pakistan's nuclear capability and by restoring the strategic balance between the two countries improved the prospects of peace and meaningful negotiations, culminating in the historic Lahore visit of Prime Minister Vajpayee in February 1999. This short lived but significant peace process was effectively derailed by the misadventure in Kargil and then by the military takeover of October 1999.

Apart from the creation of Pakistan, under the dynamic leadership of Quaid-i-Azam Mohammad Ali Jinnah in 1947, no other leader in Pakistan has been able to engineer a turning point in Pakistan's history or match the extraordinary qualities of vision and integrity that its founder possessed. Pakistan in fact has not been very lucky in terms of leadership. Unlike India, where Pandit Jawaharlal Nehru provided guidance and inspiration for 17 years after independence, Quaid-i-Azam died on 11 September 1948 and Prime Minister Liaquat Ali Khan was assassinated three years later on 16 October 1951. The reservoir of political leadership that Pakistan inherited was in any case much smaller than that in India where the Indian National Congress had been spearheading the freedom movement for a much longer period than the All-India Muslim League, which provided a rallying point and organized platform to the Muslims of the subcontinent. Yet, under the dynamic leadership of Quaid-i-Azam, within a short period of seven years the vision of Pakistan presented on 23 March 1940 in the historic Pakistan Resolution at Lahore became a reality.

The narrowness of political base of the Pakistan Muslim League (PML), the limited nature of its democratic ethos, weakened further by displacement of its main leaders from their political grassroots after partition, created a serious political vacuum. This space was gradually filled, first by civil bureaucratic elite, followed a few years later by the armed bureaucracy, thus setting in motion a dry rot of power politics.

The frequent military takeovers from 1958 onwards were the main factor responsible for the paucity of good political leadership in Pakistan. This not only weakened the democratic foundation of the political system by assigning a larger role to the military, but stultified the political process which could have developed and projected outstanding political leaders. Almost all the political leaders in Pakistan after 1958, were the product of the managed political system which the army inevitably created to provide a civilian facade to the military rule for as long as possible and then to share power with the army, if elections became unavoidable.

Democratic institutions and traditions take a long time to develop strong roots. Free and fair elections, held regularly, enable political parties to present their programmes to the people. Political leaders who promise but do not deliver are rejected by the people and gradually stronger political parties and better political leaders, with a broader support base among the masses, emerge and consolidate the democratic process. This process has never been given a fair chance in Pakistan.

In 1947, Muslims of India secured a homeland in Pakistan under the dynamic leadership of Quaid-i-Azam, but did not get the opportunity to elect their own government for twenty-three long years. The first general elections in Pakistan, it is often forgotten, were held only in December 1970. The first constituent assembly of Pakistan composed of sixty-eight members, who were elected to central legislature in 1945 from the five provinces that were included in Pakistan, was unable to frame a constitution, because of sharp differences over several fundamental issues such as the degree of provincial autonomy, presidential versus parliamentary form of government, and the role of Islam in the new state. The Assembly was dissolved by Governor-General Ghulam Mohammad in 1953, just when it had almost agreed on many of these contentious issues. The second eighty-member constituent assembly, elected indirectly by the respective provincial assemblies was convened in July 1955, adopted the new constitution in February 1956, after passing the One Unit Act to merge all the provinces of West Pakistan into one province to create an artificial 'parity' with East Pakistan. The new constitution was based on a parliamentary system of government and created high expectations that finally after nine years' delay, the people of Pakistan would be able to participate in general elections to elect their own government.

But before these elections could be held, President Iskandar Mirza, in collusion with General Ayub Khan, then commander-in-chief of the army, abrogated the constitution on 7 October 1958, imposed martial law and derailed the system. Only twenty days later, General Ayub Khan removed Iskandar Mirza and himself took over as president and chief martial law administrator. Ambitious civil servants who had gradually arrogated more and more political power to themselves were rudely reminded of the fact that when the niceties of 'democracy', 'popular will' and 'legitimacy' are done away with and pure and simple pursuit of power is the only game in play, a pen-pushing bureaucrat is no match for gun wielding generals.

It is also a strange coincidence of history that every military takeover in Pakistan has somehow occurred at a time when major international events required Pakistan's active participation as a frontline state. In 1958, when Ayub Khan took over, the cold war between USA and Russia was heating up and USA was evolving a network of security pacts like the Baghdad Pact (later renamed CENTO) and SEATO to encircle the Soviet Union. Pakistan readily joined these pacts and Ayub Khan became one of the most popular leaders in western capitals.

In 1979, two years after General Ziaul Haq dismissed the elected government of Zulfikar Ali Bhutto and assumed power as chief martial law administrator, the Soviet Union invaded Afghanistan and Pakistan again became a frontline state to organize, train and arm thousands of mujahideen (holy warriors) to take on and eventually defeat the Russians, forcing them to retreat in 1989. In return, Ziaul Haq received unflinching support and substantial economic and military assistance from USA and its allies.

In 2001, two years after General Musharraf removed the duly elected government of Nawaz Sharif and took over as chief executive, the tragic events of 11 September 2001 occurred, leading to a major international campaign against terrorism and a ferocious military attack on Afghanistan to change the Taliban regime which had provided a safe haven to the Al-Qaeda network. Pakistan once again became a frontline state and President Musharraf a much sought after leader in the western world.

Thus, ever since Pakistan's creation in 1947, it has been under direct military rule for twenty-four years and indirect military rule for another ten years. But the transition to civilian rule in 1971, in 1985 and in 2002, was always manipulated through dubious constitutional changes, managed elections and carefully selected political figures, partly to protect the military establishment and partly to give a continuing role to the armed forces to supervise the new system and save it from 'corrupt politicians or various vested interests'. The military has thus been casting a long shadow over the political landscape of Pakistan, even during periods of civilian rule. Therefore, it has never really gone back to the barracks throughout Pakistan's history. This is the most fundamental reason for the failure of the democratic process in Pakistan.

The civil bureaucracy has also played a supplementary role in weakening democratic institutions. Pakistan started its independent existence with institutions inherited from the colonial era. The colonial powers had deliberately weakened those structures and institutions which could empower the people and redesigned them to keep their colonies under tight control, by giving maximum powers to the bureaucracy and by tolerating bureaucratic corruption at lower levels. In Pakistan, unlike India where strong political leadership managed to bring the military establishment and the bureaucracy under political control, the early departure of torch bearers of the freedom movement like Quaid-i-Azam in 1948 and Liaquat Ali Khan in 1951, gave an opportunity to senior bureaucrats like Ghulam Mohammad and later Iskandar Mirza to further strengthen pre-independence institutions, which effectively prevented political institutions from taking root. This inevitably paved the ground for repeated military takeovers.

A number of books have been written about the political history of Pakistan, covering the martial law period of Ayub Khan from 1958 to 1969, that of Yahya Khan from 1969 to 1971 which saw the tragic saga of the break-up of the country in 1971, the brief interlude of civil rule under Zulfikar Ali Bhutto and the Ziaul Haq years from 1977 to 1988. Many of these also discuss the wide range of factors that have been responsible for the failure of the democratic process in Pakistan. This volume also explores the theme from the perspective of a ringside observer.

CHAPTER 3

The Shattered Dream (1947–1971)

In less than twenty-five years after Pakistan was created, East Pakistan, the majority province, broke away and became Bangladesh in December 1971, shattering the vision which the founding fathers had seen for Pakistan. This was undoubtedly the most tragic turning point in Pakistan's brief history but the causes underlying this tragedy are still being discussed and the generation of Pakistanis born after 1971 are still asking different questions: Did history play a joke on us by giving us a country that we could not preserve? Has the worst already happened in Dhaka in December 1971 or is there a possibility of similar tragedies in what is left of Pakistan? What is the real basis of Pakistan's unity and vitality which will ensure its survival as a strong and viable nation?

The problems of political and national viability are not new nor confined to Pakistan. In the past three decades, sixty-five small and large countries in Asia, Africa, and Latin America have attained their independence after long periods of colonial rule. Some of these, like Egypt and Iran, were fortunate enough to be born with a basic national viability, grounded in their traditional cultures and a proud heritage of history. In others, the new boundaries were often the result of historical accident, and cut across tribal or traditional communities. The worst example of this was perhaps Nigeria, where Biafrans felt their tribal affinities were more important than Nigerian nationalism and fought a gruesome civil war for several years.

The most outstanding example of the building of a new nation on fresh foundations was probably Indonesia where Soekarno succeeded in creating a great deal of enthusiasm for Indonesian nationalism among the inhabitants of his country who are spread over hundreds of islands. But to achieve this he had to adopt a policy of confrontation with Malaysia, build a strong army, and construct many expensive monuments. The economic cost of this nation building, despite

Indonesia's vast natural resources, proved unbearable, and with rampant inflation for ten years, it became difficult to fill people's stomachs with slogans year after year. As a result, Soekarno had to leave, but he left a strong basis for Indonesia's political viability and since then the economic situation has also been improving.

The movement for the creation of Pakistan started in the late 1930s and rapidly gained widespread support among the Muslims of the Indian subcontinent. Initially, the Indian Muslims were a part of the Indian freedom movement, but their leaders soon realized that being one-fourth of the total population of India, they would not, in a land dominated by Hindus, achieve any real freedom in the absence of adequate safeguards. It proved impossible to agree on the nature and adequacy of these safeguards, and the resultant bitterness and hatred between Hindus and Muslims led to the demand for the partition of the country. The Pakistan Resolution of 23 March 1940 visualized two Muslim states, one consisting of Bengal and Assam, and the provinces now included in West Pakistan. By 1946, however, the common struggle for Pakistan had created, or at least seemed to have created, so much unity of purpose that the leaders of Bengal decided to support the concept of one Pakistan.

In any analysis of the genesis of the Pakistan ideology, or a search for the future ideology of Pakistan, it is important to understand the complex motives for which the Muslims of the Indian subcontinent supported the Pakistan Movement. It is clear that different groups supported the Pakistan Movement for different reasons. The intellectual and political leadership of the movement was of course provided by Quaid-i-Azam and his colleagues, who were inspired by the Islamic reformist movement of the preceding two centuries and wanted to build a truly modern Islamic state. For most of the common Muslims, however, it was the threat of Hindu domination in the economic or the political sense that spurred them to seek their own country. There were also those who saw in Pakistan their only safeguard to preserve their identity, language, culture, and way of life.

A careful analysis of these motives in support of Pakistan will show that they were not consistent or entirely adequate for evolving a positive ideology. If economic discrimination on the basis of religion was the main cause of disunity, then in strict logic it could not be solved through greater religious hatred but, at least theoretically, by creating a secular society. Again, those who saw the preservation of their culture or language in Pakistan were essentially thinking in secular terms, and many 'nationalist' Muslims of India had argued in favour of an 'Indian culture' as an amalgam of Hindu and Muslim cultures. The only group which could have provided a viable basis of the Pakistan ideology consisted of those who genuinely advocated Islam but their efforts were seriously undermined by the other groups, which, while supporting Pakistan to save themselves from the economic and political domination of the Hindus, did not accept the role of Islam in developing a modern progressive state. As a result, the search for a Pakistan ideology alternated in vain between two possibilities, a semi-secular concept of 'Pakistan nationalism' and what many considered would be a 'theocratic Islamic state'. The first concept did not take root because most of the usual elements of secular nationalism, like historical heritage, language, and culture became less relevant as they were not really common between East and West Pakistan. The Islamic basis, whose potential as an ideological force was much greater, also did not develop because the political leadership of the early 1950s, instead of harnessing and translating into political and economic institutions those Islamic forces which led to the creation of Pakistan, got too involved in internal power politics. The task of interpreting and pursuing Islam for the individual and for the society thereafter gradually and inevitably shifted to different groups of ulema and religious leaders, who did not often agree among themselves but almost all went back to various forms of traditionalism.

In this virtual ideological vacuum which was visible very soon after Pakistan was born, the only factor which lent some significance to Pakistan's geographical boundaries was the fear of a hostile neighbour. This fear was sustained by India's reluctance to resolve the Kashmir problem in accordance with the wishes of Kashmiri people, and gradually developed into a kind of negative ideology which lasted effectively till September 1965, when it was eroded by the India–Pakistan war of that year. For the first time, the people of East Pakistan felt isolated and began to realize that their fear of India was unreal since Kashmir which symbolized the conflict between India and Pakistan was really an issue for West Pakistan, and that in any case, West Pakistan would be unable to defend East Pakistan if the need ever arose. Only six months later, Sheikh Mujibur Rehman's six points, which were in effect a concealed plan for gradual separation, came out on the political platform and provided a rallying focus to the movement for Bengali nationalism which quickly superseded whatever segments of the Pakistan ideology were still scattered in East Pakistan. It took only six more years for the Quaid-i-Azam's dream to be fully shattered in the face of persistent failure in West Pakistan to understand the painful fact that Pakistan as a Muslim state or as an Islamic ideological state, was gradually losing its significance for growing segments of the people in East Pakistan. Many still recognized the importance of common economic interests, but the political leaders interested in separation, gradually and successfully destroyed the economic basis of the country's unity by overplaying the so-called 'injustices' and 'economic exploitation' of East Pakistan by West Pakistan. The fear of India, already weakened by the 1965 war, also disappeared in the next few years in the wake of sustained Indian publicity, and tacit Indian support to a separatist movement to an extent that those very followers of A.K. Fazlul Haq and H.S. Suhrawardy who had suffered much more at the hands of the Hindus in the past, and had as a result spearheaded the Pakistan Movement, soon joined the same Hindus in killing their Muslim countrymen. It will take us a long time to recover from the shock, humiliation, and impact of this tragic experience.

The 1965 War

The year 1965 was a remarkable year in the political life of Ayub Khan. He rose to the pinnacle of his success in the first half of 1965 and within three months, the 1965 war for which he must take a considerable share of the responsibility proved to be the beginning of his end.

The second Five-Year Plan (1960–65) has been widely accepted as the most successful period of economic progress in Pakistan. From virtual stagnation in the 1950s the rate of economic growth had jumped, from 3.5 to 6.7 per cent per annum (in West Pakistan), industrial production had increased by 12 per cent per annum and investment rate by 14 per cent a year. The rate of inflation was only 2 per cent.

On the political front, Ayub Khan's international profile was rising, especially after Prime Minister Nehru's death in October 1964. Ayub Khan's foreign minister, the young and articulate Zulfikar Ali Bhutto was equally active on the diplomatic front. He advocated a pro-China policy and a hard-line policy against India, both very popular on the domestic scene. Bhutto played an active role in the abortive summit of non-aligned nations in Algeria in June 1965, by meeting many leaders including the foreign ministers of Vietnam, China, and Indonesia. From there he went to England for the Commonwealth Summit and before the arrival of Ayub Khan, effectively thwarted Malaysia's efforts to condemn Indonesia. Encouraged by this obvious shift in the foreign policy of Pakistan, which was still an active member of CENTO and SEATO, President Nasser of Egypt invited Ayub Khan to stopover in Cairo on his way back to Pakistan. When Ayub Khan reached Cairo, he was received by three world leaders then regarded as the arch enemies of America: President Nasser, Prime Minister Zhou Enlai of China, and President Soekarno of Indonesia. The very next week, the US State Department submitted a confidential assessment to President Johnson saying Ayub Khan was growing too big for his boots and needed to be cut down to size. As a first step, it recommended that the World Bank Consortium meeting scheduled for 27 July 1965 to pledge foreign assistance of $550 million for the first year of the Third Five-Year Plan (1965–70) should be postponed.

I was present in the cabinet meeting held in the third week of June, when Ayub Khan presented a glowing account of his meetings in London and Cairo, and displayed the glow of a global statesman (an Asian de Gaulle as *Newsweek* called him at that time). He was followed by Saeed Hasan, the deputy chairman of the Planning Commission, who presented a report on the successful pre-consortium meeting in Washington D.C., when Pakistan's economic performance under the Second Plan (1960–65) was applauded and its requirements of $2.7 billion for the Third Five-Year Plan (1965–70) were fully endorsed. Mahbub ul Haq and I had accompanied Saeed Hasan for this presentation at the cabinet.

As Mahbub ul Haq, Moinuddin Baqai, and I sat for lunch after the cabinet meeting, we could not reconcile these two presentations. In the face of such a drastic shift in our foreign policy stance, how could we count on such substantial flows of economic and military assistance (by then almost 6.8 per cent of Pakistan's GDP). We were of course not aware at that time of the communication which the US government had sent to the World Bank, asking them to postpone the consortium meeting scheduled for 27 July 1965.

I received an urgent call on 4 July from Saeed Hasan to join him in his meeting with President Ayub Khan in Murree. Ayub was furious, 'You had reported to the cabinet that everything had been agreed upon in the pre-consortium meeting, then why this postponement?' he asked. Saeed Hasan hesitated a little and then said 'Sir, I hope you realize that our foreign policy and our economic requirements are not fully consistent, in fact they are rapidly falling out of line.' Ayub Khan sobered up and asked him to meet the American ambassador and explain to him that having a few meetings with leaders who are not in the western camp, does not mean a basic change in Pakistan's foreign policy. In fact such contacts can be useful in building bridges', he said.

But before Saeed Hasan had a chance to convey these clarifications to the US ambassador, Zulfikar Ali Bhutto appeared three days later in a National Assembly session in Karachi, and made a thundering speech. 'Mr Speaker, US would like us to change our independent foreign policy and if we do not, they will not give us aid of $200 millions (US share in the $550 million pledged for the first year). Is the nation willing to sell its foreign policy for $200 million?' There was uproar and shouts of No! No! No! The same evening a big procession came out of nowhere and burnt the US information centre on Bunder Road. The tension between US and Pakistan, which the US had expected Pakistan to handle in a subtle manner, was now a full-blown crisis. We were told, there should be no contacts with US officials in view of the strong public reaction to this news.

The irony of this bizarre situation was further magnified in the first week of August, when Bhutto, totally ignoring this new turn of events, gave the green signal for Operation Gibraltar under which several thousand Kashmiris, supported by some army personnel would enter Indian occupied Kashmir and engineer an uprising. Ayub Khan had been persuaded a few weeks earlier to approve this plan as a last desperate bid to liberate Kashmir from Indian occupation. The operation however fizzled out within a fortnight. Some of the Kashmiri freedom fighters who had entered Kashmir were either killed or captured, and the rest fled back into Azad Kashmir.

If Ayub Khan had recognized the inappropriate timing of this misadventure and called it off, Operation Gibraltar would have hardly got a footnote in history books. But advised by his brilliant generals, he went even further and authorized an open tank attack on Akhnoor on 1 September 1965 to cut the only access road from India into Kashmir. That gave India a very good opportunity to attack Pakistan at a time when 'USA was looking the other way.'

Two days before India's full-scale attack on Lahore, on 6 September, Bhutto had made a categorical statement in the cabinet, that Pakistan's incursion into Indian occupied Kashmir, at Akhnoor, on 1 September, would not provide India with the justification for attacking Pakistan across the international boundary because Kashmir was a disputed territory.

According to some Canadian experts, who participated in a case study of the 1965 India–Pakistan war, the city of Lahore was indefensible against a full-scale tank attack. A more viable strategy, they concluded, would have been to abandon the defence of Lahore and dig in along the western banks of the river Ravi, which is the first major natural defence between India and Pakistan on that front. That assessment may have some value in terms of classical theories of military strategy but not for those inspired soldiers for whom the defence of every inch of Pakistan was a sacred duty, which had to be carried out to the last drop of their blood. They therefore defied the proverbial logic of military strategy and successfully defended the city of Lahore with valour and dignity. A single company of three hundred soldiers led by Major Aziz Bhatti, for example, withstood the onslaught of an entire Indian brigade for that fateful day of 6 September, until new reinforcements arrived and repulsed the Indian attack. The Indian general, who had boasted that on the evening of 6 September, he would have his 'chota peg' (small drink of whiskey) in the Lahore gymkhana, was humiliated.

The seventeen-day war in 1965 was at best a draw, despite the vast superiority of Indian forces and equipment, but it revived the spirit of the Pakistan Movement among the people in every part of Pakistan. There were stirring songs on the radio and many programmes on the valour of Pakistani soldiers. Within the army, however, there were rumours of discontent among the officers about the genesis and conduct of the war.

The longer-term economic and political consequences of the 1965 war were extremely damaging. In many ways, this war represented the beginning of the end of the Ayub era. The United States had already suspended its economic assistance in July 1965, two months before hostilities broke out between India and Pakistan, but with the outbreak of war, an arms embargo was imposed. In addition, the war also effectively blocked credits from other western donors, as the postponed consortium meeting was never held. The assistance was resumed on a limited scale in April 1966 after the Tashkent agreement, because the wheat crop of that year had declined in West Pakistan from 4.5 million tons in 1964–65 to 3.8 million tons in 1965–66, leading to shortages, price escalation, and food riots.

During a visit of Finance Minister Mohammad Shoaib to Washington in April 1966, USA offered $50 million as commodity assistance, one million tons of wheat under PL-480, and a resumption of negotiations to finance a steel mill of half a million tons (These negotiations were never successfully concluded, forcing Pakistan to seek Russian credits for building a million ton plant at Karachi). Despite this limited resumption, the overall flow of foreign assistance declined from 6 to 3 per cent of GDP. At the same time in the wake of the war, defence expenditure went up from 2.2 per cent of GDP in 1964–65 to 4.0 per cent in 1969–70. As a result, the overall share of East Pakistan in the pool of resources, promised under the Third Five-Year Plan, could not be protected.

The political consequences of the 1965 war were however far more damaging and eventually led to the crisis that led to the break-up of the country. In the 1964 presidential elections, voters in East Pakistan (40,000 councillors) had cast more votes in favour of Miss Fatima Jinnah who had been put up as a candidate of the Combined Opposition Parties (COP) to contest the presidential elections against Ayub Khan. Now in the wake of the 1965 war, there was a widespread perception that West Pakistan could not really defend East Pakistan against an attack from India. The Kashmir centred conflict between India and Pakistan was in any case distant for the average citizen in East Pakistan. It was a very good opportunity for the charismatic Awami League leader, Sheikh Mujibur Rehman to announce, in March

1966 in Lahore his six-point programme, which was in effect a political demand for greater provincial autonomy for East Pakistan to replace the highly centralized form of government provided for in the 1962 constitution.

Bhutto, as a shrewd politician, readily saw that the fall of Ayub Khan was imminent. He therefore resigned as foreign minister in June 1966, after criticizing the Tashkent Declaration as a 'surrender'. The Tashkent Declaration was brokered by Prime Minister Kosygin of USSR between President Ayub Khan and Prime Minister Lal Bahadur Shastri of India to convert the temporary ceasefire between the two countries into a permanent ceasefire and facilitate the exchange of POWs.

It took Bhutto almost eighteen months to launch a new political party rather than join one of the existing anti-Ayub's parties (the Council Muslim League or Abdul Wali Khan's National Awami Party for example). He was persuaded by several leaders with leftist leanings like J.A. Rahim, Mubashir Hasan, Mumtaz Bhutto, Mairaj Mohammad Khan, Mustafa Khar, and Mohammad Hayat Sherpao. At a convention held in Lahore on 30 November and 1 December 1967, ten foundation documents were adopted along with a manifesto of the Pakistan Peoples Party (PPP). For Bhutto's colleagues who wrote these documents, socialism was the answer to all the problems facing Pakistan. But Bhutto was more pragmatic. He knew that a socialist ideology would not appeal to the conservative masses of Pakistan. He therefore called his framework 'Islamic socialism'. He wanted to oppose Ayub Khan's rule based on issues with mass appeal, strong stand on Jammu and Kashmir, reducing US influence in Pakistan, exploitation of the poor by the rich and a combined struggle for the restoration of democracy. He wanted to oppose Ayub Khan by winning the support of the masses on these issues but without emphasizing a particular ideology.

Ayub Khan retaliated by launching a campaign to damage Bhutto's image and reputation but Bhutto continued on his mass mobilization campaign undeterred by these allegations, raising the catchy slogan of *Roti, Kapra, aur Makan* (Food, Clothing and Shelter). This campaign coupled with consistent agitation in East Pakistan became too much for Ayub Khan. He had a serious heart attack in early 1968 and had to fly to USA for open-heart surgery. He returned after three months with much weaker physical and emotional capacity to handle the deteriorating political situation. Bhutto's attempts to convert the '22 families' slogan into a major issue of inequality were overshadowed by the demand for provincial autonomy according to Mujibur Rehman's six points. These political issues combined with economic difficulties created by the suspension of aid, provided greater momentum to a civil disobedience movement in East Pakistan. Many leaders including Bhutto and Mujibur Rehman were arrested but the situation did not improve. Finally, in a desperate bid, Ayub Khan convened on 10 March 1969, a Round Table Conference (RTC) in Lahore to reconcile various conflicting demands. Mujibur Rehman and Bhutto were released unconditionally to enable them to attend the conference. Mujib did but Bhutto refused. Even though Ayub Khan announced in advance that he would not be a candidate in the next elections, that the presidential system would be replaced by a parliamentary system, and the parity formula would be given up in favour of one man–one vote, giving the majority vote in East Pakistan its due weight, the RTC was a failure because the demands from various leaders and parties kept growing. Ayub Khan saw no option but to hand over power to the army commander-in-chief, General Yahya Khan on 25 March 1969. Yahya abrogated the 1962 constitution and assumed charge as chief martial law administrator. *The Economist* (London) reported this news under the title 'Tweedle Khan Takes Over.'

The Tragic Tenure of Yahya Khan

Soon after taking over, General Yahya Khan began to introduce many changes in the political setup based on the concessions President Ayub had already announced:

- A One Unit Dissolution Committee was setup to reorganize West Pakistan into four provinces (Punjab, Sindh, NWFP, and Balochistan) to share, along with the fifth province—East Pakistan, power with the federal government under the 'New Constitutional Framework'.
- This new constitutional framework for parliamentary system was announced through a Legal Framework Order (LFO) on 28 March 1970, which provided for a 300-member directly elected assembly,

with 162 seats for East Pakistan and 138 for the four provinces of West Pakistan. Another 13 seats were reserved for women, to be elected indirectly by elected members of each province. This formula effectively abandoned the principle of parity on which the 1956 constitution was based.

- The elections were scheduled for 5 October 1970 and the newly elected assembly was given four months to agree on a new constitution. If it did not meet this deadline, it would be dissolved to make way for fresh elections. Due to a major cyclone in October in East Pakistan, the elections were postponed to 7 December 1970.
- The LFO also laid down five fundamental principles for the new constitution. It said: 'The provinces shall have provincial autonomy but at the same time provinces shall be so united in a Federation that the independence, territorial integrity and national solidarity of Pakistan are ensured and that the unity of the Federation is not in any manner surpassed'.

There were several contradictions in the LFO announced by President Yahya Khan in March 1970. The decision to replace the presidential system, introduced by President Ayub Khan under the 1962 constitution, by a parliamentary system was fully justified. But it did not accommodate certain essential features of a parliamentary system in a federation. To balance the representation of large and small provinces in the lower house, all federal constitutions provide for an upper house or a senate, in which all provinces have equal representation. The 1956 constitution had attempted to solve the imbalance problem by merging the three West Pakistan provinces plus the federally administered territory of Balochistan into one unit—the province of West Pakistan—and opting for the principle of parity by giving equal seats to East and West Pakistan. This formula was resented in East Pakistan because it had denied them seats in proportion to their population. It was also unpopular in the smaller provinces of West Pakistan because their people were now required to travel to Lahore to redress their complaints. A more viable option of creating an upper house was ignored in 1956 and again by Yahya Khan in 1970 with disastrous consequences.

Another serious shortcoming in Yahya Khan's political reform was the total lack of consultation with the political leadership of the country. Unlike Ayub Khan, he was entirely dependent on the advice of three or four colleagues in the army. If he had allowed political leaders from the two wings to come up with agreed proposals before the LFO was finalized, the course of Pakistan's history might have been different. Bhutto, for example, had criticized the LFO in a speech on 15 May 1970 and had proposed a bicameral legislature. 'No other way can create unity between the two wings', he had said.

My friend Jamil Nishtar who was also very disturbed by the LFO, said that only West Pakistan leaders like Z.A. Bhutto and Khan Abdul Wali Khan could work out an arrangement with Mujib and his colleagues that could keep the country together. He also felt that this was a good opportunity to break-up the one unit of West Pakistan into fifteen smaller provinces corresponding to fifteen divisions and not four provinces. He in fact prepared a paper on the subject which was presented to Yahya Khan by General Sher Ali Khan Pataudi, his information minister but Yahya Khan did not accept the proposal.

Yahya Khan tried to counter Mujib's six points by presenting a formula for provincial autonomy in the LFO but allowed the Awami League to run their entire election campaign on the basis of the six-point programme. Nor did he declare that the six points were in conflict with the LFO. Mujibur Rehman was a charismatic leader and the Awami League had become a well-organized party. The cyclones of October and November 1970 further intensified the anti-West Pakistan feeling, and Awami League won 160 out of 162 seats, allocated to East Pakistan, in a landslide victory.

In West Pakistan, most parties were not as well organized as the Awami League in East Pakistan, but Bhutto's personal popularity had skyrocketed. Even though his platform of Islamic socialism was criticized by both the right and the left, his call for widespread reform in every sphere of life, his slogan of *Roti, Kapra aur Makan*, and his call for an independent policy and his anti-India stance were enough to secure a decisive victory for the PPP. It won 81 out of 138 seats allocated to the four provinces of West Pakistan, including 61 in Punjab, 18 in Sindh and 1 in NWFP.

These election results were a big disappointment for the regime of Yahya Khan. The Awami League had not only won a decisive victory on the basis of the six-point programme of maximum autonomy but also commanded absolute majority in the assembly with 160 out of 300 seats. In West Pakistan, Bhutto's PPP, with a socialist agenda, had won 81 or about 60 per cent of 138 seats allocated to West Pakistan. For all practical purposes, Yahya Khan, who expected a hung parliament, saw that his regime had lost political control. His negotiations with Mujibur Rehman over the next three months were fruitless as deadlock over the six points persisted. Finally, when the confrontation reached a boiling point in the first week of March, he conceded the six points. But it was too late. Having tasted the peoples' war, Mujib was now demanding virtual independence, under the title of a confederation. Yahya having been driven to the wall, could not be pushed further, and resorted to military crackdown on 26 March 1971 'to save the country'.

The Shattered Dream

I was serving in the Planning Commission at that time as joint secretary (plan coordination) and was involved in the painful process through which East Pakistan gradually drifted away and became Bangladesh. The extracts from my diary recording that eventful period recall the trauma and the pain of that process. They are reproduced in the appendix to another volume.[1] This firsthand account of the tragic events from December 1970 to December 1971 shows clearly that had Pakistan evolved a genuine democratic political system, East Pakistan would not have become Bangladesh.

NOTE

1. See Anwar Dil (ed.), *Hunger, Poverty, and Development: Life and Work of Sartaj Aziz*, Intercultural Forum, San Diego, California. Lahore: Ferozsons, 2000, pp. 484–525.

Chapter 4

The Democratic Interlude under Zulfikar Ali Bhutto (1971–1977)

Bhutto's emergence on the national scene was a major milestone in the country's history. He joined General Ayub Khan's first martial law cabinet in October 1958 as a young and bright lawyer, but as mentioned in the previous chapter, formed a new political party, the PPP, in 1966, which within a short period of five years, won 82 seats out of a total of 138 National Assembly seats in West Pakistan in the 1970 elections and thus became a major political force for the future.

Ironically, Bhutto assumed power on 20 December 1971 as president and chief martial law administrator despite being an elected leader of West Pakistan. Yahya Khan had to hand over power after a bitter civil war and humiliating surrender by the Pakistan army to General Jagjit Singh Aurora. But there was no constitutional arrangement in place under which Bhutto could takeover as prime minister. He therefore opted for the dubious distinction of being the head of a martial law regime led by a civilian political leader.

As Rafi Raza recalls in his book,[1] Yahya Khan had proposed to Bhutto that he should remain president with Bhutto as prime minister. When Bhutto refused, Yahya Khan suggested he should be allowed to continue as chief martial law administrator (CMLA) and commander-in-chief of the army while Bhutto became president. But Bhutto wanted full and effective control as president and CMLA. When it was suggested that martial law should be scrapped immediately, Bhutto said, he could not withdraw martial law till it was replaced by a constitutional arrangement approved by the assembly.

One of the first acts of Bhutto was to appoint Nurul Amin, the only leader from East Pakistan who was elected to the National Assembly from West Pakistan, as the vice president of Pakistan. He had no significant functions but it was a symbolic gesture to give representation to East Pakistan. Bhutto himself had four offices: president, CMLA, president of the constituent assembly, and chairman of PPP.

The 1973 Constitution

The most significant achievement of Bhutto's tenure was the adoption of the 1973 constitution by consensus among the four provinces. The history of constitution making in Pakistan has been very sad. As already mentioned, it took nine years after the creation of Pakistan for the first constitution to emerge from the constituent assembly in 1956. But before elections could be held under this constitution, General Ayub Khan took over in October 1958 and abrogated the 1956 constitution. Ayub Khan then promulgated his 1962 constitution with a presidential system and a strong centre, the president being elected indirectly by 80,000 basic democrats elected to local councils. On 25 March 1969, Ayub Khan handed over power to General Yahya Khan who assumed power as CMLA and abrogated the 1962 constitution. On 28 March 1970, Yahya Khan promulgated a LFO to formalize some important constitutional changes he had announced on 28 November 1969: dissolution of one unit, ending the principle of parity between the two wings, and conceding the system of one man–one vote for the next elections.

Bhutto thus assumed power in a virtual constitutional and legal vacuum. As a brilliant lawyer, he knew that a new constitution was required as early as possible, and it had to emerge as a compact among the four provinces. He therefore lifted the ban on Wali Khan's NAP soon after he took over and also opened discussions with Jamiat-i-Ulema-i-Islam (JUI) led by Mufti Mahmud. By April 1972, he had achieved a consensus on an interim constitution under which the legitimacy of government was confirmed through a vote of confidence and a committee of the house was setup to draft a permanent constitution. Martial law was consequently withdrawn on 21 April 1972.

When the committee setup by the National Assembly failed to reach agreement on several substantive issues (like presidential versus parliamentary form of government, the role of Islam and the degree of provincial autonomy), Bhutto called a series of meetings with leaders of all the parliamentary parties in the first week of April 1973 and by 12 April, achieved a consensus on the constitution which was signed by the representatives of all the political parties represented in the assembly. The 1973 constitution entered into force on 14 August 1973, twenty-six years after Pakistan came into existence.

The 1973 constitution was parliamentary in nature, drew on the 1935 Act and 1956 constitution for the division of subjects between the federation and the provinces. Two significant new features, however, were the creation of an upper house to provide equal representation to all provinces in the Senate (Article 59) and the creation of a Council of Common Interest (Article 153) to formulate policies relating to inter-provincial matters which before 1971 were provincial subjects but after the break-up of one unit, could not be handled by the provinces (like railways, natural gas, water and power and industries sponsored by the federal government). The council was to function under the parliament in joint sitting.

To safeguard against military intervention in politics, the 1973 constitution introduced Article 6, under which any attempt to abrogate or subvert the constitution by force, would be punishable as high treason. This provision could not, however, prevent military takeovers in 1977 and again in 1999.

Bhutto had to give up his preference for a presidential system, as a part of the compromise reached with other parties, but in the process he made sure that the 1973 constitution would allocate maximum powers to the prime minister, making the office of the president a purely ceremonial one. Under Article 48, the advice of the prime minister was binding on the president and all the orders issued by the president had to be countersigned by the prime minister. That is why the amendments made by President Ziaul Haq in March 1985, shifted the balance of power entirely in favour of the president; the Eighth Amendment of October 1985 tried to restore the imbalance to some extent but the division of powers between the president and the prime minister continues to be a burning controversial issue.

The Nationalization Policy of Zulfikar Ali Bhutto

Another major step by Bhutto, soon after taking over was to fulfil the PPP manifesto's socialist agenda, by nationalizing ten basic industries on 1 January 1972: iron and steel, heavy engineering, automobiles, tractors and trucks, petrochemicals, heavy chemical, cement, oil refineries and public utilities like gas and electricity. Under the Economic Reforms Order of 1972, only the management of thirty-two units in these industries was taken over by the government, without assuming ownership. In this way, they avoided the fiscal burden of paying compensation to the owners. Subsequently some owners were given long-term (15–20 years) bonds as compensation but these in effect had only nominal value.

In September 1973, the government nationalized another twenty-six units producing vegetable ghee, followed by shipping companies, petroleum companies, life insurance companies, and the export trade in cotton and rice. But a major extension in the scope of public service activities came with the nationalization of banks in January 1974 to enable the government 'to use capital concentrated in the hands of a few rich bankers for rapid economic development of the country and the more urgent social welfare projects to distribute bank credit equitably to different classes, sectors and regions and to coordinate banking policy without eliminating healthy competition among banks.'

The extension of the public sector was not confined to the so-called 'strategic sectors' of the economy. In August 1976, it extended to 3,000 flour milling, rice husking, and cotton ginning industries. These small-scale operations, based on local technology, were run mostly by middle-class industrialists in rural areas. As uproar intensified, the government yielded some ground and denationalized most of the rice mills and cotton ginning units but retained the larger rice mills. Of the major sub-sectors of the economy, this drive for public-sector control left only textiles and sugar untouched. Many prominent industrialists and businessmen left the country during this turbulent period.

While in retrospect, this major reversal of the country's policies and large scale policy of nationalization had disastrous economic consequences, the measures enjoyed great popularity at the time, reflecting widespread concern about the concentration of economic power in a few hands and the inadequate distribution of benefits to the 'bottom 40 per cent' of the population. The prevailing view held that a market-based system would not achieve vital social goals until the economic system became fully subservient to socio-political objectives.

Bhutto assumed power in difficult economic circumstances: with the separation of East Pakistan, the foreign exchange earnings of the country were halved, but the inter-wing trade which was equal to 40 per cent of total exports from West Pakistan also came to a sudden halt, disrupting the sub-sectors dependent on such trade. In 1972, Bhutto took the bold decision of devaluing the rupee by 120 per cent (from Rs4.76 to 10.20 for a dollar). This step along with the diversion of inter-wing trade to the export markets led to a sharp 150 per cent increase in exports in 1972–73. But the sudden increase in oil prices in 1973 consumed a substantial portion of the additional foreign exchange earnings.

Despite the paucity of resources, Bhutto managed to implement many of the promises made in the PPP manifesto of 1970 like the shift to basic industry. Apart from substantial public sector investment in fertilizer and cement, the construction of Pakistan Steel Mills was taken up during this period with Russian assistance. Much of the expansion in public spending was met through deficit financing, which naturally led to double digit inflation. The overall growth rate in this period (1972–77) was just over 4 per cent with agriculture growing at only 2.1 per cent.

Bhutto could not really fulfil his election slogan of 'Roti, Kapra, aur Makan' for everyone but he did succeed in securing a sufficient increase in the real wages of industrial workers along with many other benefits. In effect the Bhutto era brought about a qualitative change in the power of the trade union and the relations between employees and employers, a legacy that keeps his name alive today.

Land Reforms

The 1970 manifesto of PPP had assured land reforms in these words 'To destroy the power of feudal landowners is a national necessity that will have to be carried through by practical measures of which a ceiling is only a part.' The ceiling on individual holdings was reduced from 500 acres of irrigated land to 150 acres (and from 1000 to 300 in case of rain-fed holdings). About 3.2 million acres were resumed by government, without any compensation and over 130,000 tenants received proprietary rights. To improve the incomes and working conditions of tenants, land revenue and water rates were made the responsibility of the landlord who was also required to bear 50 per cent of the cost of seed, fertilizer and pesticides. The actual implementation of these land reforms was far below Bhutto's expectation because many of his colleagues were feudal landlords who created loopholes to minimize the impact of the reforms.

In January 1976, Bhutto announced further land reform to lower the ceiling for irrigated areas from 150 to 100 acres and for un-irrigated holdings from 300 to 200 acres. These surprise reforms annoyed the feudal segments on the country's political right but did not fully satisfy his leftist supporters who were expecting a ceiling of only 25 acres.

The Fall of Zulfikar Ali Bhutto

Bhutto's tenure of five-and-a-half years was a remarkable democratic interlude sandwiched between twenty-two years of military rule in the period 1958 to 1985 and was marked by the kind of dynamic leadership Pakistan had not experienced before. Relations with India were re-established on the basis of equality and dignity, Pakistan's stature in the outside world soared to new heights. Bhutto's popularity within the country, particularly among the working classes and the peasants, was unprecedented, many important mega projects were undertaken as a part of economic restructuring. But the most significant change was perhaps bringing the Pakistan army under civilian control. The military was no longer the ruling class of the country, but just another institution of state.

But one basic flaw in Bhutto's personality—his lack of tolerance for other political leaders and the opposition parties—led not only to his political downfall but also to the premature end of his promising life. Bhutto, despite his political intellect, had not gone through the rough and tumble of politics at the grassroots level and did not in the process learn to reconcile differences amicably and with tolerance. Of course, his feudal background and the autocratic streak that goes with it did not help either.

By the end of 1976, Bhutto had totally sidelined the opposition and achieved, in his own calculation, the pinnacle of political power which would guarantee his continuity in office for an indefinite period. This dream could have been realized, if he were to achieve a decisive majority of more than two thirds in the next elections.

On 7 January 1977, Bhutto announced that general elections would be held for the National Assembly on 7 March and for provincial assemblies on 10 March. This announcement was a rallying call for the opposition and within four days, nine political parties including Jamaat-e-Islami and National Awami Party formed the Pakistan National Alliance (PNA) for contesting the elections. It announced, within a month, a very good manifesto and organized many successful public meetings and rallies. It was therefore expecting to expand its tally in the National Assembly even if it did not win a majority. But when the results came in, PNA had won only 18 per cent or 36 seats out of a total of 192 seats while Bhutto's PPP had won 146 or over 75 per cent of the seats, including 108 in Punjab. With nine unopposed victories, the tally of PPP went up to 155 seats.

The PNA rejected the election results and started a major agitation which gathered momentum with each passing day. As police were unable to control the deteriorating law and order situation, the army was called in to assist, but many soldiers refused to fire on their own citizens who were now calling for 'Nizam-e-Mustafa' (a system ordained by Prophet Muhammad [PBUH]). Under pressure, Bhutto started negotiations with political parties but just as he was reaching a settlement, the army intervened and General Ziaul Haq took over on 5 July 1977, declaring martial law and announcing fresh elections within ninety days. These were of course postponed and held eight years later in March 1985 as non-party elections so that PPP could be kept out as long as possible.

Bhutto had declared on 28 April that there was an international conspiracy to remove him, but according to Rafi Raza, the creation and unity of PNA was mainly the consequence of his own actions over the preceding four years.[2]

After the passage of the 1973 constitution, Bhutto had used the first amendment of the constitution (May 1974) to ban the NAP and arrest Wali Khan and many other party stalwarts. The fourth and fifth amendments curtailed the independence of the judiciary and damaged the reputation of Bhutto as someone determined to convert Pakistan into one party authoritarian state. Many allegations regarding rigging the March 1977 elections were largely true, although how much of these excesses were committed by overzealous local leaders, being more loyal than the king, is difficult to assess.

Bhutto's intolerance for the opposition was particularly harsh when it came from those whom he regarded as his supporters. Ahmad Raza Kasuri, MNA, was one such staunch supporter turned opponent. On 10 November 1974, there was an unprovoked attack on Ahmad Raza Kasuri's car in Lahore, in which his father was killed. Ahmad Raza Kasuri named Bhutto as a co-accused in the FIR. Once Bhutto was removed from power, that FIR was invoked to start proceedings against him. On 2 March 1978, the Lahore High Court unanimously sentenced Bhutto to death for ordering members of the Federal Security Force to 'finish off' Ahmad Raza Kasuri. The Supreme Court which heard the appeal decided on 6 February 1979 to uphold, by a 4–3 decision, the sentence awarded by the Lahore High Court. Appeals by many leaders, including heads of state and government to pardon Bhutto were rejected by General Ziaul Haq, and he was hanged in Rawalpindi on 4 April 1979.

It is one of the many ironies of our history that one of the most outstanding political leaders, who secured a unanimous constitution for the country, was hanged while all the military generals who created circumstances that eventually led to the break-up of the country, lived on without much accountability.

NOTES

1. Rafi Raza, *Zulfikar Ali Bhutto and Pakistan 1967–77*, Karachi: Oxford University Press, 1997, p. 142.
2. Op. cit., p. 357.

CHAPTER 5

Ziaul Haq and His Legacy (1977–1985)

When Prime Minister Bhutto appointed General Ziaul Haq as chief of army staff in 1976 over the heads of five senior generals, to replace General Tikka Khan, he could not have anticipated that within a year, this non-political and self-effacing general would oust such a strong and popular political leader.

Before the general elections scheduled for March 1977, all political observers were convinced of a major victory for Bhutto, because the nine-party combined opposition, under the banner of PNA did not pose any real challenge. But some of Bhutto's enthusiastic supporters were not content with a simple majority in parliament. They wanted their leader to gain a two-thirds majority so that he could amend the constitution and stay in power indefinitely. These expectations were realized and Bhutto's PPP won 155 out of 192 seats and PNA only 36. The opposition led by Air Marshal Asghar Khan alleged massive ballot rigging and launched an unprecedented agitation to challenge the results. PNA gave a religious colour to the agitation by calling for Nizam-e-Mustafa, an Islamic system ordained by Prophet Muhammad (PBUH). This movement, in effect, provided a strong basis for the Islamization programme of General Zia and also for the *jihad* against the infidel Russians in Afghanistan in 1979.

Bhutto called in the army to quell the agitation but soon there were reports of reluctance on the part of many army personnel to fire on their own people. The ground was thus ripe for another army intervention after a brief democratic interlude of five and a half years. Bhutto along with some leaders of PNA was taken into protective custody on 5 July 1977 and Zia announced that fresh elections would be held within ninety days on 17 November 1977. But within sixty days, the elections were postponed and Zia effectively ruled the country for eleven years, till his mysterious plane crash on 17 August 1988. The Russian attack on Afghanistan in December 1979 had provided a big boost to Ziaul Haq at a time when his international image had plummeted by his stubborn rejection of all the domestic and international appeals to spare the life of Bhutto.

In many ways, Ziaul Haq followed in Ayub Khan's footsteps by gaining some degree of legitimacy for his rule. In 1979, like Ayub Khan's system of basic democracies, he introduced a new local bodies system of union councils and district councils and held elections to these councils in 1979 and then in 1983. The system also brought into forefront a new line of political leaders, who supported Ziaul Haq and many of whom eventually became candidates for the provincial and national assemblies in the 1985 elections.

The Process of Islamization

But Zia went a step further and initiated a series of changes 'to create an Islamic state'. He no doubt genuinely believed that an Islamic system was better for Pakistan than the western parliamentary system, but this strategy also provided him additional political space by winning the support of some of the Islamic parties. Gradually, he also saw a continuing role for himself under an Islamic system, as the undisputed *Amir*, ruling according to the injunctions of the Quran and Sunnah, with advice from a Majlis-e-Shoora, partly elected, partly nominated.

Building on the work of a number of committees and working groups, Zia introduced over a period of six years, a number of changes to put in place different elements of an Islamic system.

- Hudood Laws were promulgated in 1979, prescribing Islamic punishments such as amputation of hands for theft, stoning to death for adultery and lashes for consumption of alcohol. It also tightened provisions for testimony requirements in different cases. Although these harsh punishments have not been actually carried out, these new laws have provided the grounds for continuing agitation by various women's organizations against these laws.
- In 1981, Zia announced many changes in the economic system to introduce an interest free banking system. While there was no outright ban on the use of interest, the banking system was required to offer Islamic alternatives like mark-up, *musharka* and *modaraba*.

- In 1983, he introduced a new system of Zakat to deduct 2.5 per cent from all deposits in banks. The Shia community protested violently and was exempted from this levy.
- From 1980 to 1982, he brought about major changes in the country's legal system, by instituting a Federal Shariat Court to examine and decide if any law was repugnant to the injunctions of Islam, as laid down in the Holy Quran and Sunnah of the Holy Prophet. This permitted anyone to appeal to the judicial system under two different laws, the pre-independence law as incorporated in various statutes and validated for Pakistan after independence and the Shariat laws. The writ jurisdiction of courts was also withdrawn under these amendments.
- Pakistan's education system also underwent a fundamental change during Ziaul Haq's eleven-year rule. The madrassahs, which had been providing classical Islamic religious teaching long before Pakistan was created, gained prominence by training volunteers for the Afghan war against the Russian occupation. There is now a gulf in the perception and outlook of students coming out of about 10,000 madrassahs, and those who are studying in English medium or some of the Urdu medium schools. This conflicting world view of students coming out of different school systems does not auger well for the creation of a homogenous society or for national integration. In 1982, Zia issued orders to equate, for the purpose of employment, the degree awarded by various religious madrassahs or colleges, with the degrees awarded by accredited colleges and universities, without realizing that twenty years later this decision will lead to far reaching consequences in the 2002 elections in which only degree holders could participate.

Zia's Political Strategy

Apart from taking measures to Islamize the legal and economic system of Pakistan, Zia also began to build a political coalition that could support him whenever a civilian system was restored and in this process keep out the main opposition, consisting of the PPP and some other groups.

The new local bodies system of the union councils and district councils was introduced in August 1979. In the same year, Zia issued a presidential ordinance to amend the Political Parties Act of 1962, requiring all political parties to register with the Election Commission, to publish their manifestos and submit their annual accounts. One of the aims of this amendment was to deny registration to a party whose manifesto, according to his interpretation, did not adhere to Islamic principles.

In March 1981, Zia promulgated a Provisional Constitutional Order (PCO) to create a Federal Council or Majlis-e-Shoora of 200 nominated members 'to perform such functions as may be specified in an order made by the President.' The PCO allowed limited political activities but only to those political parties that had been registered by the Election Commission. The PPP had refused to register itself under those conditions.

In July 1983, Zia setup a sixteen-member commission under Zafar Ahmad Ansari 'to undertake an in-depth examination of the form of the government that should be setup, keeping in view the conditions of the country and the interest of the *Millat* [nation].'

The Ansari Commission submitted its Report on 4 August 1983. It recommended:

a. A presidential system, in which the head of the state called *Amir-e-Mumlikat*, would also be the head of government and would be elected by the central Majlis-e-Shoora and the provincial Majlis-e-Shoora.
b. Elections to the Majlis-e-Shoora would be held on a non-party basis and the candidates would be sponsored by at least 2000 voters of a constituency. All political parties would be dissolved.
c. In addition to specific qualifications for candidates (like good character and knowledge of Islam), some additional qualifications were proposed for women candidates that they should not be less than fifty years of age, and they should produce written permission of the husband if he was alive, to take part in the elections.

Ziaul Haq was very keen to establish an Islamic system on the lines recommended by the Ansari Commission, but almost all his colleagues in the cabinet, particularly Finance Minister Ghulam Ishaq Khan and Interior Minister Mahmud Haroon, and his external advisors were equally emphatic that any effort to change the basic parliamentary character of the 1973 constitution would open a Pandora's box. Reports of widespread agitation under the banner of 'Sindhu-desh movement' from different parts of Sindh also played some role in convincing Ziaul Haq to moderate his ambitions and refrain from changing the basic character of the 1973 constitution. The first half of August 1983 was thus marked by these hectic and intense discussions between Ziaul Haq and his team of advisors.

Finally, Ziaul Haq addressed a special session of the Majlis-e-Shoora on 12 August 1983 and announced that elections to the national and provincial assemblies would be held in March 1985, after which martial law would be withdrawn and the 1973 constitution restored with some amendments to correct the balance of powers between the president and the prime minister. Initially, Ziaul Haq planned to announce his elections plan on 14 August. But the Movement for Restoration of Democracy (MRD) suddenly announced an agitational campaign from 14 August 1983. He advanced his speech by two days to take the wind out of MRD's sails.

Zia did not say anything about the role of political parties, nor about the procedure for electing the president. But two days later, in his address to the nation on 14 August he announced that the president would be elected by the two houses of parliament, in accordance with the 1973 constitution. He also said there would be no referendum on the constitutional amendments since the Supreme Court had given him the power to amend the constitution as necessary.

I was on home leave from Rome and was present, along with my friend the late Jamil Nishtar and my sister Nisar Aziz, in the assembly chamber on 12 August, when Zia announced his political road map for the elections. We all had mixed feelings about the proposed package. Jamil was strongly in favour of a presidential system to ensure political stability as long as the president was directly elected by the people. In his view, it was not possible to select a competent cabinet from the National Assembly. Under a presidential system, most of the cabinet members could be selected from outside on the basis of merit. He also felt this half way house, in which a parliamentary system is revived with a strong presidency, would not be sustainable because of the continuing tussle between the two centres of power, with the third real centre of power—namely the army—looking for opportunities to play one against the other.

My sister, Nisar, was even more pessimistic about the future of democracy. She said, as I recorded in my diary that evening:

- Ayub Khan had built a very nice pyramid, from where he ruled with the help of the bureaucracy and the support of the business community. He used the army initially but then sent them to the barracks.
- Bhutto tried to inverse the pyramid and for the first time broke the barrier between the intellectuals and the people. But he soon realized that the right was better organized than the left, and slowed down his reforms. Yet, when the right got their chance, they eliminated him, since they knew he would move towards the left whenever he saw the opportunity.
- The big dilemma for the Third World is the ever-present fear in USA about the spread of socialism. To keep socialism in check, they want a legitimized military to continue to rule. That makes the task of the left to get organized even more difficult. Many of the leftist elements have personal stakes (jobs, a house or some privileges) which they would not like to lose. Those who have tried have faced prisons, lashes or other difficulties.
- The generals are prolonging their rule only to protect their necks and the wealth they have accumulated. But their necks are not more important than the country's future. In the final analysis only a revolutionary movement, like that in Iran, could bring about a fundamental change but we do not seem to have the ingredients of such a movement at present.

As we returned home, after listening to this historic address by Ziaul Haq, Jamil Nishtar abruptly asked me, 'Now that the revival of the political process is round the corner, shouldn't you start thinking seriously about returning to the country and playing a role in the political and economic life here?' That question set into motion a mental process that culminated, seven months later in the premature end of my international career and the advent of the third phase of my career in the political arena.

My long life search for more meaningful alternatives for economic and social development had culminated in a book titled *Rural Development: Learning from China*, published in 1978. In several seminars held in Rome, Oxford, and New York over the next three years, to discuss the rural development model presented in this book, I was asked repeatedly if the model could work in Pakistan. I replied that the book had presented a conceptual framework for rural development, with intermediate options and partial solutions for countries, which did not meet the political and the institutional pre-requisites for the comprehensive approach. There was need for thorough socio-economic research in Pakistan to determine the model under which the rural population could be organized to help themselves.

From then onwards, I became more actively involved in intense discussions with several colleagues on different approaches to rural development in Pakistan. My closest friend, Jamil Nishtar was insistent that to pursue this task in a serious manner, I would have to return to Pakistan.

An opportunity presented itself within three months of President Ziaul Haq's address on the revival of the political system on 12 August 1983. In November 1983, Fakhar Imam, minister for rural development had resigned because he had lost his elections as chairman, district council, Multan. Jamil Nishtar rang me up the next morning and said, 'President Ziaul Haq has been urging you to return and join his cabinet, but now the slot of rural development you wanted, has become available. Should I speak to him?' After some discussions, I agreed. President Ziaul Haq, when I met him in February 1984, was enthusiastic about my return but wanted me to join as minister of state for agriculture, rather than the minister for rural development. Eventually, I agreed and took my first oath of a political office on 17 April 1984 (out of a total of seven oaths that I was to take, over the next thirteen years), to replace Mir Zafarullah Khan Jamali, who took his oath as minister for rural development at the same ceremony. The stages by which I pursued the cause of promoting rural development in Pakistan are described briefly in this and subsequent chapters of the book.

After joining the cabinet of President Ziaul Haq in April 1984, eleven months before the restoration of 'civilian rule', I had a very rare opportunity to observe at first hand, the implementation of Ziaul Haq's political strategy to create a civilian facade for his continuing hold on real power.

Zia's Game Plan

By May 1984, political activity was heating up and newspapers were publishing detailed accounts of meetings between different leaders and their plans for election alliances. In a meeting called to review the political situation on 7 May, President Ziaul Haq asked if such a rapid increase in the political temperature would not reach a boiling point by election time in March 1985. Almost everyone present said such activities were a part of the political process that had to begin in preparation for the elections. Mahmud Haroon, the minister for interior, was particularly vocal in presenting this viewpoint. The opposition was organizing itself, he said, because they want a real sharing of power. They will obviously build on the widespread discontent among the masses and will raise issues like unemployment and corruption. The only way to restore democracy in an orderly fashion is to initiate a dialogue with those moderate elements, which have public roots. If we do not manage to secure the support of some of the political forces in the country, we will have to be prepared for the worst, Mahmud Haroon said.

Ziaul Haq was not yet ready for laying his political game plan on the table. He did not answer these points and virtually ignored the views of his cabinet colleagues and announced his decision to impose some restrictions on the press to curtail coverage of political activities. Addressing the information secretary, General Mujib-ur-Rehman (rather than the information minister, Raja Zafarul Haq), he said: 'we are not imposing censorship—only 'press advice'—so that the political temperature in the coming months does not become too hot.'

Next month, on 7 June 1984, there was another strategy meeting to discuss political activities and matters relating to the elections. Many ministers raised the issue of the president's election and said there may be problems if the president's election was deferred till after the general elections. Some formula should be found to confirm Ziaul Haq as president in advance. Others made suggestions for strengthening the 'president's party' and complained that the provincial governors were lukewarm about cabinet ministers and were not supporting the sitting members of Majlis-e-Shoora who were 'the president's men'. Ziaul Haq did not comment on the first topic but on the second he said, we certainly need a majority of those in the National Assembly who would support my policies, but to achieve this we will give only legitimate support to 'our candidates'. There will be no rigging and no naked use of the administration. He welcomed the suggestion to setup an 'election cell' to select suitable candidates for different constituencies and to meet politicians in preparation for the elections in March 1985.

In July 1984, there was another interesting meeting chaired by President Ziaul Haq. In his review of the political situation, the Interior Minister Mahmud Haroon said that the gap between the reality on the ground and our perception of that reality was growing. 'As the political process is unfolding, many external forces are emerging to accentuate the causes of tensions. The challenge before us is to manage the transition without jeopardizing our stability or security. For this, we have to build on our strengths and anticipate potential problems.'

Some participants again emphasized the importance of closer interaction with political forces in the country. As usual, Ziaul Haq patiently listened to all the statements and did not reveal any reaction to views with which he did not agree. He only expressed in general terms his lack of trust in most politicians and reaffirmed his earlier decision that only limited political activity be allowed and the press be handled firmly.

On 10 September 1984, political discussions were postponed because the issue of Kalabagh dam took much longer than expected. Before the end of the meeting, I felt, he was about to give a green signal to WAPDA to start work on the Kalabagh dam project, while the issues raised were being sorted out gradually (the threat of flooding Nowshera in years of high floods, increased silting of river Kabul, the minimum flow of water below Kotri Barrage to prevent inflow of saline water from the sea and to preserve the mangroves). But the final intervention of General Fazal-e-Haq, governor of NWFP was so forceful and hostile that President Ziaul Haq took shelter behind some of the issues raised by Ghulam Ishaq Khan (final height of the dam and preliminary discussions with donors on financing the dam) and postponed the final decision without realizing that this postponement would continue for decades.

In October 1984, tensions with India suddenly grew while the Russian offensive in Afghanistan was threatening our western borders. Many ministers including myself, argued for a change of course in

Afghanistan because the Russians could work through India by raising the ultimate cost of our Afghan policy. The president while agreeing with the logic of these arguments said something very unusual: 'I know it will not be easy to defeat a superpower and I am also aware of all the problems and obstacles but I also believe in miracles.' The first 'miracle' happened on 31 October 1984, when Indira Gandhi was assassinated, leading to a sudden reduction of tensions between India and Pakistan. In the next three years, the Russian forces in Afghanistan suffered heavy casualties, and began to look for some face saving ways to retreat from Afghanistan. The proximity talks in Geneva gained momentum and by March 1988 the Geneva Accords were signed. In a meeting held to 'celebrate' the Geneva Accord, Zia was full of pride and satisfaction and reminded some of the cabinet members of that statement in 1984: 'You see my belief in miracles. The Russians are now leaving Afghanistan.'

There was a very eventful meeting on 15 November 1984. The chief election commissioner, Justice S.A. Nusrat gave a report on election arrangements and the president said the basic issue was whether the elections should be party-based or held on non-party basis. Most of those who spoke said, under the constitution, everyone has a right to form associations or unions, therefore, non-party elections would be contrary to the spirit of the constitution. Ziaul Haq virtually ignored these views and said the elections would be held on a non-party basis. The Ansari Commission, he emphasized, had already pointed out the evils of a party-based system. Islamic principles demand that elections on party-based system should be disallowed in Pakistan because they lead to polarization and feuds. He had therefore decided to hold the next elections on non-party basis on 25 February 1985. In his assessment the opposition, grouped under MRD would boycott non-party elections to make them less credible. And that is exactly what happened when PPP and other opposition parties of the MRD met in Abbottabad two days later and decided to boycott the elections, thus leaving substantial political space for the political coalition Ziaul Haq was trying to build.

At this meeting on 15 November, after Zia announced the decision to hold non-party elections, there was an interesting discussion on how to organize 'our party' and Zia asked: 'How do we choose good candidates who are committed to Islam and Pakistan and can win at least 60–70 seats in the 200-member house?' Most of those present said, 'If you want to win, forget about good people and commitment to Islam'. People vote for *biradari* (their own clan) and to win, a candidate has to spend at least one or two million rupees. How does he recover that amount, if he is really honest? Some members like General Fazal-e-Haq, governor of NWFP, reminded Ziaul Haq not to underestimate the opposition. 'Despite the boycott, they will support anti-establishment candidates. We have to disqualify some of these candidates otherwise the agitation will become unbearable,' he said.

Ziaul Haq was visibly shaken by these comments. He concluded the discussion by saying, 'Let us elect as many good candidates as possible, giving them legitimate support but do not go to the extent of rigging the elections, to retain the credibility of the electoral process.' He asked the governors to coordinate the selection of candidates in their respective provinces. But deep down, he was smiling because he had started preparing his political game plan much earlier. In 1979, he had held local bodies' elections in all four provinces. Many of those elected in 1979, gradually moved upwards and had become strong candidates for the provincial and national assemblies. Similarly, the nominated Majlis-e-Shoora setup in 1981 as a kind of advisory body of two hundred members had started working as a 'shadow' National Assembly. About half those members of Majlis-e-Shoora contested the 1985 non-party elections and forty-four of them actually succeeded in winning their seats.

The next important issue came up for discussions on the following day—16 November 1984. Mahmud Haroon, the interior minister opened the discussion by saying, 'No matter how well we choose our candidates, the team won't be able to play cricket without a captain. The option of delaying the election of the president until after the assemblies are elected will impose a major question mark on the whole electoral exercise. It is in any case uncertain if the assemblies once elected, will also elect Ziaul Haq as president. The only viable option is to elect the president in advance through a referendum'. Most members supported the idea. The same question arose as a major political issue faced by another general, in 2002 and surprisingly the same solution was found.

Two weeks later, on 1 December 1984, a surprise meeting was called to announce that the president had decided to go for a referendum on

19 December 1984. I recorded in my diary that day: 'According to official results, 67 per cent of the registered voters voted in the referendum, with 97 per cent yes vote. There is no doubt that all the officials worked diligently not only to allow everyone to vote but added votes wherever the turnout was low. No one will ever find out the extent of these additional votes cast by officials and not by voters. But having legitimized himself, the president need not interfere actively in the electoral process because most of those elected will have to cooperate with the sitting president.' In 2002, a subsequent referendum to legitimize a subsequent military ruler had once again a similar participation rate and 'yes' percentage.

Constitutional Amendments

On 12 February, a fortnight before the elections, Ziaul Haq presented the list of constitutional amendments he intended to carry out 'to restore the balance of powers between the president and the prime minister' and to give legal cover to all the martial law orders, ordinances and regulations issued between 1977 and 1985. Under these amendments, he would retain the power to appoint provincial governors, chiefs of armed forces and chief justices of the Supreme Court and High Courts. He would acquire the power to dissolve the National Assembly by adding Article 58(2-b) to the constitution. There would also be a new Article 152(A) to create a National Security Council chaired by the president. Thus, except for chairing the periodical meetings of the cabinet, the president wanted to retain most of the powers through these constitutional amendments.

Although many of us felt that the amendments proposed were against the spirit and purpose of the constitution and its basic parliamentary character, no one said this openly. Everyone in fact was conscious of the fact that Ziaul Haq had no intention of transferring real power to a civilian setup. He wanted to share power only to create a civilian façade for his continuing rule. The logic of a genuine democratic process would require that there was a strong and effective prime minister, answerable to the parliament, with the president performing a residual and ceremonial role. But President Zia could not afford such a setup because he knew that even an assembly elected on a non-party basis would feel its independence and may create a hostile political atmosphere in which he could be removed, impeached or even tried under Article 6, for subverting the constitution in 1977. In the face of this dilemma, Zia declared in the 12 February meeting that the proposed amendments would not be unveiled in advance, but incorporated in a presidential order to be issued after the elections along with the order to restore the 1973 constitution. He also said martial law would remain in force at least until the new National Assembly had ratified the proposed constitutional amendments.

Zia announced these sweeping constitutional amendments on 2 March 1985 through the Restoration of Constitution Order 1985, to concentrate political powers in the hands of the president. In all, there were fifty-six amendments but the following were particularly important:

- The Objective Resolution initially included as a preamble, was made a substantive part of the constitution of 1949, by including it as Article 2A. The original Article 2 merely said: 'Islam shall be the state Religion of Pakistan'. The new Article 2A, it was emphasized, would now ensure that Islam would henceforth provide the legal and moral basis for the exercise of political power.
- Twenty-three articles were amended to give discretionary powers to the president. These included powers to call a referendum [Article 48(6)], appoint the prime minister [Article 91(2)], fix the date of election of the National Assembly after dissolution [Article 48(5)(a)], appoint a caretaker cabinet [Article 48(5)(b)], appoint governors [Article 10(1)], dismiss governors [Article 101(3)], provide for functions of governors in areas not provided for in the constitution [Article 101(5)], modify terms of appointment of a Federal Shariat Court judge and assign him other functions [Article 203-C(4B) a,b&c)], appoint chief election commissioner [Article 213(1)], appoint chairman, Federal Public Service Commission [Article 242(A)], appoint chairman, joint chiefs of staff, and appoint three services chiefs [Article 243(2)(c)]. In the original 1973 constitution, most of these powers could be exercised by the president, only on the advice of the prime minister.

- Sub-Article 2(b) was added to Article 58, to give the president the power to dissolve the National Assembly at his discretion, 'if an appeal to the electorate was necessary'.
- Article 91 was amended by adding sub-Article (5): 'The prime minister shall hold office during the pleasure of the president but the president shall not exercise this power under this clause unless he is satisfied that the prime minister does not command the confidence of the majority of the members of the National Assembly'.
- Article 152(A) was added to create a National Security Council, chaired by the president.

Many of these enhanced powers of the president and the institutional role of the army through the National Security Council were intensely debated six months later, when the draft of the Eighth Amendment Bill was introduced in the National Assembly.

The Non-Party Elections of 1985

The polling to elect a new National Assembly was scheduled for 25 February 1985, eight years after the fateful elections of March 1977. The opposition having boycotted the elections had prepared an elaborate plan to disrupt the polls. There were large-scale arrests on the eve of the elections, generating considerable tensions in all the four provinces but particularly in Sindh. The BBC in its lead story that morning said: 'Pakistan is going to polls today with 1500 opposition leaders in prison'.

Elections were held on 25 February 1985 for 207 National Assembly seats and on 27 February for 483 seats in the four provincial assemblies. On the average, there were five candidates for each National Assembly seat and eight candidates for each provincial assembly seat. The voter's turnout was quite impressive. Out of 33 million registered voters, 17.3 million or 53 per cent cast votes for National Assembly candidates and 18.5 million or 57 per cent for provincial assembly candidates. This turnout in retrospect was better than all the four-party based elections held subsequently (43, 45, 40 and 35 per cent respectively for National Assembly seats). The main surprise of the elections, however, was the disappointing results of candidates belonging to Islamic parties. Despite Zia's open policy to introduce an Islamic system, the Jamaat-e-Islami, which fielded sixty candidates for the non-party elections, succeeded in winning only eight seats.

Soon after the elections, speculation about the next prime minister and the four chief ministers became the main topic of discussions. By the first week of March, the rumours narrowed down to three names, Mohammad Khan Junejo and Ilahi Bakhsh Soomro from Sindh and Zafarullah Khan Jamali from Balochistan. Pir Sahib Pagara, it seems finally prevailed upon President Zia to nominate Mohammad Khan Junejo. Nawaz Sharif became the chief minister of Punjab, General Fazal-e-Haq in NWFP, Akhtar Ali G. Kazi in Sindh and Mir Zafarullah Khan Jamali in Balochistan.

The National Assembly was convened on 21 March 1985 to elect a speaker and meet again the following day to elect the leader of the house, i.e. the prime minister. President Zia experienced the first setback to his political game plan even before the National Assembly met on 21 March. He wanted Khawaja Mohammad Safdar, who was the speaker of his nominated Majlis-e-Shoora and had been elected from Sialkot, to continue as speaker of the new assembly and he was certain that the neatly tailored assembly would carry out his wishes by electing him unopposed. But to his surprise, some members filed the nomination papers of Syed Fakhar Imam. To General Zia's dismay and surprise and despite his best efforts, the new National Assembly elected Syed Fakhar Imam as the speaker by 155 votes.

But Ziaul Haq did succeed in having Ghulam Ishaq Khan, the finance minister in his cabinet from 1978 to 1985, as chairman of the Senate. He called all the newly elected senators to a meeting in the President's House and pleaded with them to elect Ghulam Ishaq Khan as chairman. Ishaq Khan was initially not happy with this 'elevation'. Having managed the economy for eight years with an impressive growth rate of over 6 per cent, he would have preferred to stay on as finance minister, but eventually this appointment prepared the ground for his rise to the highest office of the president of the country, three-and-a-half years later.

CHAPTER 6

Controlled Democracy under Junejo (1985–1988)

Mohammad Khan Junejo, a decent, upright man and a respected and shrewd politician from Sindh, assumed the office of the prime minister on 23 March 1985, amidst great expectations. The 1973 constitution was being revived after a lapse of eight years. The two houses of parliament with a National Assembly of 210 members and a Senate of 87 members and the four provincial assemblies had many prominent politicians and technocrats, anxious to play a role in strengthening the democratic process. Despite the opposition's boycott, 53 per cent of the total registered voters had taken part in the National Assembly elections and 57 per cent in the elections for provincial assemblies. That gave the new setup a certain degree of legitimacy.

The first order of business was to form a new cabinet. Junejo took eighteen days to select his new ministers after prolonged consultations with Ziaul Haq. That was the first glimpse of his political acumen, as over the next three years he reshuffled his cabinet at regular intervals to accommodate as many members from different provinces and districts as possible, while retaining a core group for important ministries.

The first elected cabinet, after the 1985 election was introduced on 10 April 1985 and included the following thirteen ministers and seven ministers of state:

Ministers	Ministers of State
Sahabzada Yaqub-Khan	Mir Haji Tareen
Dr Mahbub ul Haq	Zain Noorani
Salim Saifullah Khan	Rai Mansab Ali Khan
Prince Mohiuddin Baloch	Begum Attiya Inayatullah
Syed Zafar Ali Shah	Islamuddin Sheikh
Yousaf Raza Gillani	Maqbool Ahmad
Hamid Nasir Chatta	Syed Qasim Shah
Iqbal Ahmed Khan	
Haji Hanif Tayyab	
Ghulam Mohammad Ahmed Khan Manika	
Mohammad Khaqan Abbasi	
Nawabzada Abdul Ghafoor Khan Hoti	
Zafarullah Khan Jamali	

Junejo added another six ministers on 22 May 1985: Lt.-Gen. (retd) Jamal Said Mian, Mian Mohammad Yasin Khan Wattoo, Qazi Abdul Majid Abid, Malik Noor Hayat Khan Noon, Mohammad Aslam Khattak, and Syed Qasim Shah.

After the initial nineteen-member cabinet inducted in April/May, he had the first reshuffle within ten months, in January 1986, when he inducted a new cabinet of twenty-two ministers and thirteen ministers of state. He retained ten members from the previous cabinet and added twelve new members. A significant change in this 1986 reshuffle was the appointment of Yasin Wattoo as finance minister in place of Dr Mahbub ul Haq, who was asked to continue only as planning minister. Initially, Mahbub ul Haq refused this 'down-grading' but Jamil Nishtar and I persuaded him to accept and stay on in the cabinet as planning minister. Fourteen months later, in the March 1987 reshuffle, Mahbub ul Haq was also allocated the commerce portfolio, but that cabinet did not last very long since Ziaul Haq dissolved the National Assembly and the cabinet on 29 May 1988.

I was not included in the first cabinet of March 1985 but was appointed as special assistant to the prime minister in October 1985 and as minister of state for food and agriculture in the January 1986 reshuffle. My induction in the cabinet was the result of a gradual process of involvement in different assignments. In April 1985, I was appointed chairman of a special committee to formulate the rules of procedures and conduct of business in the Senate and over the next few weeks, I devoted all my time to this task by studying the rules of procedures of as many parliaments as possible. In July 1985, Prime Minister Junejo asked Dr Mahbub ul Haq to start work on preparing a manifesto which he would like to announce whenever the martial law was lifted. Mahbub was too busy as finance minister and passed on the task to me. I discussed the subject with him and Jamil Nishtar and suggested that manifestoes were issued by political parties. The first step for Muhammad Khan Junejo would be to revive the Muslim League and also to create a Muslim League Parliamentary Group within the parliament. They readily agreed and in the next two weeks, I prepared a paper entitled 'Evolving a Stable Political Structure in Parliament'. This paper Mahbub ul Haq gave to Muhammad Khan Junejo in the first week of August 1985, just as he was boarding the plane on a visit to Tokyo and South Korea.

On 3 September 1985, I met Junejo at a dinner hosted jointly by the chairman Senate, Ghulam Ishaq Khan and speaker of the National Assembly, Fakhar Imam for all the members of parliament. I told him that the committee setup to formulate the rules of procedures for the Senate had finished its work but there were some recommendations regarding the role of the Senate on which I would like to have his views before submitting the report. He invited me three days later to meet him. I told him that under the constitution, the budget was presented to and approved by the National Assembly, but the committee felt it would be useful if the budget were also presented to the Senate for discussion, not approval.[1] The National Assembly could then take into account the views of the Senate, while approving the budget. Senate members could also be included in a joint public accounts committee. Junejo said the committee was at liberty to submit these recommendations to the Senate. Follow up action could then be considered in consultation with members of the National Assembly, because it would require amendments to the constitution. This discussion slowly drifted into a review of the overall political situation and the prospect of organizing a Muslim League party in parliament. Having prepared a detailed paper on the subject, which Dr Mahbub ul Haq had already given to the prime minister, I was well prepared for this discussion. As I began to spell out various steps, Junejo found them in line with his own thinking. He asked me to stay on for dinner and we finished well past 11 p.m. He complimented me on my strong commitment to the Muslim League and its role in the country's political life. He said, he was sorry he had not met me before. He indicated that I would be included in the next cabinet whenever it was reshuffled but meanwhile I should start working as his special assistant, with the status of minister of state.

Prime Minister Junejo's Five-Point Programme

When I joined the prime minister's secretariat as a special assistant in October 1985, Junejo had already started thinking about his programme and the statement he would present to the nation on 31 December 1985, when martial law would finally end: 'Sartaj Sahib, please suggest a comprehensive agenda but with an attractive slogan like Zulfikar Ali Bhutto's *Roti, Kapra aur Makan*. I immediately responded by saying, 'It was important to determine your priorities first and what you wanted to achieve during your tenure, then we can find the words or the slogans to package the priorities.' He thought for a while and said, 'I belong to a very poor region and I feel very disturbed when I recall the poverty stricken eyes of my people. I want to bring about a fundamental change in the lives of those people.

I felt very excited when I heard these words and said, 'That means a comprehensive programme of rural development. That is the objective, to pursue which I came back to Pakistan after leaving a very comfortable and well-paid career in Rome. I will give you some concrete ideas and proposals within a few days.'

For the next four weeks, I worked intensively on what came to be known as Prime Minister Junejo's five-point programme, which he announced on national television on 31 December 1985, the day on which martial law was lifted. This programme brought about a massive increase in the financial allocations for rural programmes, from Rs10 billion ($800 million at the exchange rate in 1986) to Rs23 billion ($1.8 billion) a year for rural education, health care, drinking water, rural roads and rural electrification. Since 50 per cent of the allocations were earmarked for education, the total expenditure on education went up sharply between 1985 and 1988, from Rs10.2 billion to Rs17.5 billion, or from 1.6 to 2.3 per cent of GDP. Even though after the dismissal of the Junejo government on 29 May 1988, the five-point programme was discontinued as a separate programme, the higher expenditure on rural infrastructure made possible by the programme, became a benchmark and therefore continued with periodical but modest increments.

Another assignment, which Prime Minister Junejo entrusted to me at that stage, was the chairmanship of the National Commission on Agriculture. In his address to the nation on 31 December 1985, he said: 'Agricultural development is the basic pillar of rural progress. If agricultural development is accelerated, it not only increases incomes and job opportunities but also generates avenues of development in agro-industrial units and allied fields. But the pace of agricultural development at present is unsatisfactory and yields of many crops are still too low, I have therefore decided to setup a high powered agricultural commission to propose practical solution to these problems.'

The composition and terms of reference of the National Commission on Agriculture were announced on 20 April 1986 with an outstanding list of thirteen members: Malik Khuda Bakhsh Bucha, Shafi Niaz, Dr Amir Mohammad, Syed Babar Ali, Dr Zafar Altaf, Syed Qamar Zaman Shah, Agha Atta Mohammad, Nisar Hassanally Effendi, Dr Imtizaj Hussain, Fateh Mohammad Khan, Faqir Mohammad Khan, Abdur Rehman Jamali, and Sardar Ali Asghar. The commission took about two years and submitted its 640-page report to the prime minister on 15 March 1988, based on the work of twenty different committees consisting of over 200 well-known experts for each major crop or sub-sector. The commission recommended a comprehensive strategy for accelerating the rate of agricultural growth from 3.7 per cent in the period 1965–87 to 5.0 per cent per annum in 1988–2000, diversifying the sector towards high value sub-sectors like horticulture and livestock and conservation and development of the country's land, water and forest resources.

While the preparation of this report itself was a major undertaking, even more challenging was the task of implementing its recommendations. It so happened that two years after the report was submitted in March 1988, I was elevated to the position of minister of finance from 1990 to 1993. This gave me a valuable opportunity to reorient the overall macro-economic framework in favour of agriculture largely by ensuring a positive relationship between the prices which farmers pay for inputs and those they receive for their output. As a result of these policies and the improvement of rural infrastructure, the actual growth of the agricultural sector in 1987–99 was very close to the 5 per cent target set by the commission, i.e. 4.6 per cent per annum, which was ahead of average industrial growth of 4.4 per cent during this period. My only regret is that one of the most important recommendations for the creation of a Watersheds and Arid Land Development Authority (WALDA) has not so far been implemented. Just as WAPDA has responsibility for 23 million hectares of irrigated areas, there is need for a similar authority to look after the 60 million hectares of non-irrigated areas—starting from the northern glaciers to Balochistan's range lands and the arid areas of Cholistan and lower Sindh.

Revival of Pakistan Muslim League (PML)

After my eventful meeting with Junejo on 6 September about the revival of the Muslim League, I could see my most cherished dream of establishing a stable democratic system in the country, moving closer to reality. I not only included the objective of strengthening democratic institution and traditions as a top priority item in the prime minister's landmark 31 December address but also reinforced his plans to convert the 'Official Parliamentary Group' in parliament to a Muslim League Parliamentary Group, as early as possible. An 'Official Parliamentary Group' with more than two-thirds of the assembly members had been formed in mid-1985, with an 'Independent Parliamentary Group' of about twenty members functioning as opposition. The Political Parties Act had been passed by the National Assembly on 9 December 1985, which partly amended the ordinance issued by General Ziaul Haq on this subject on 30 August 1979 and also included an anti-defection clause. The ground was therefore ready for Junejo to announce the revival of Pakistan Muslim League. Simultaneously, he setup a committee to propose a new constitution and a manifesto for the party. The committee was chaired by Iqbal Ahmed Khan, secretary general of the party. At its first meeting on 13 January 1986, I was given the task to prepare the drafts of these two documents. I took several months to finish this task and finally in July 1986, the Muslim League council met to formally approve these basic documents and to elect Junejo as president of the party.

As subsequent events have shown, this revival of the Pakistan Muslim League as a political party, with a strong presence in the National Assembly, was a major landmark in the political history of the country. The party, which won freedom for the Muslims of India, had fallen into disarray after the death of Quaid-i-Azam Mohammad Ali Jinnah in 1948 and Prime Minister Liaquat Ali Khan in 1951. In 1958, the party was dissolved along with other political parties when Ayub Khan imposed martial law. In 1962, President Ayub Khan, feeling the need for a political platform to get himself elected through basic democracies under the 1962 constitution, revived the Muslim League. But some diehard Muslim Leaguers refused to join the new Muslim League because the decision to elect Ayub Khan as party president was taken during a convention of the party. The dissidents called a meeting of the PML council to elect Pir Pagara as president. It was, therefore, called the Council Muslim League. The two Leagues contested against each other in the 1964 presidential elections, when the Council Muslim League selected Miss Fatima Jinnah, the sister of Quaid-i-Azam to contest against President Ayub Khan. Two years later, Bhutto, who was Ayub Khan's campaign manager in the 1964 presidential elections, resigned from the cabinet and formed his own party, the PPP, which within four years became very popular and in the elections of 1970, won 81 seats out of 138 seats in the National Assembly reserved for West Pakistan. The two Muslim Leagues together won only 18 seats.

After its revival in 1986, Muslim League gradually improved its political standing and laid the basis for a two party political system. The strength of the party increased further after Nawaz Sharif was elected as its president in April 1993. In each of the four elections, held in 1988, 1990, 1993, and 1997, the two main political parties, namely PML and PPP, won 75 to 80 per cent of all seats as shown in the following table:

Seats won by PML and PPP in the National Assembly (200 Seats)

	1988		1990		1993		1997	
	Seats	Votes (Million)	Seats	Votes (Million)	Seats	Votes (Million)	Seats	Votes (Million)
PML	54	5.90	106	7.90	73	8.12	137	8.84
PPP	93	7.55	45	7.80	89	7.82	18	4.21
Total	147	13.45	151	15.70	162	15.94	155	13.05
% of seats	73.5		75.5		81		77	

Note: The total seats in the National Assembly for the elections were 200. Pakistan Muslim League contested the 1988 and 1990 elections as part of an alliance called IJI (Islamic Jamhoori Ittehad). The seats and votes shown above were won by the alliance but if the result of other parties in the alliance in two subsequent elections are taken into account, 90 to 95 per cent of seats were won for the alliance by Pakistan Muslim League. Similarly, the PPP contested the 1990 elections as a part of an alliance called PDA (Pakistan Democratic Alliance) but 90–95 of the seats won in that elections (44) were due to the vote bank of the PPP.

The disruption of this two party system after the military takeover in October 1999, and during the manipulated elections of October 2002, has been a major setback because a two-party system, with roots in all the provinces, is necessary for the strength and unity of the federation.

The Eighth Amendment

Prime Minister Junejo's first year in office was dominated by the debate on the constitutional amendments made by President Ziaul Haq in March 1985, when he revived the constitution. Under a well-thought out political strategy, Ziaul Haq largely succeeded in engineering a smooth transition to civilian rule while maintaining a firm grip on political power. But he also faced many pitfalls he had not fully anticipated. The Movement for Restoration of Democracy (MRD) was a strong political force although its agitational campaign launched in Sindh on 14 August 1983, did not spread to Punjab and was effectively crushed by killing at least sixty demonstrators and arresting 5,000 supporters of MRD. Ziaul Haq was acutely conscious of the strong resentment against him that had become more acute after the hanging of Zulfikar Ali Bhutto. This factor also influenced his decision to select a Sindhi as prime minister. But Prime Minister Junejo soon started showing signs of independence.

His first defiant act was to announce at a public meeting in Lahore on 14 August 1985 that martial law and democracy cannot co-exist and therefore martial law must be lifted before the end of 1985. Ziaul Haq told him that this could only be done once the parliament had passed an Indemnity Bill giving constitutional protection to all the laws passed during martial law, including the constitutional amendments announced in March 1985 through P.O. 14 of 1985.

The draft Eighth Amendment Bill was submitted to parliament on 10 September 1985 to facilitate the lifting of martial law, by giving legal cover to all martial law orders, ordinances, and regulations issued between July 1977 and March 1985, including the constitutional amendments promulgated through P.O. 14 of 1985.

The legal formula under which the constitutional amendments made by President Ziaul Haq were ratified was quite ingenious. First Article 270-A was replaced by a new Article-270A, which made a specific reference to the Referendum Order 1984 and the Revival of Constitution Order 1985 (P.O. 14 of 1985) and thus validated all the constitutional amendments made by Ziaul Haq as part of the constitution. But then it proceeded to amend sixteen articles of the constitution to alter some of the amendments made earlier by Ziaul Haq himself. These included amendments in Articles 48, 51, 56, 58, 59, 60, 75, 90, 91, 101, 105, 106, 112, 116, 130, and 155 of the constitution.

President Ziaul Haq had accepted the requirement that his constitutional amendments should be ratified by parliament, because the Official Parliamentary Group (OPG) enjoyed the support of 180 out of 200 members in the National Assembly and more than 70 members in the 87 member Senate. But he was both surprised and upset when the small Independent Parliamentary Group (IPG) under the leadership of Haji Saifullah from Rahimyar Khan, started moving a series of amendments to curtail the powers which Ziaul Haq had assumed under P.O. 14 of 1985. Prime Minister Junejo did not openly confront Ziaul Haq on these amendments moved by the opposition, but by encouraging a candid debate in the National Assembly on the issues involved, he created an atmosphere in which a blanket approval of P.O. 14 of 1985, which Ziaul Haq had expected, could not be secured. This started a long and acrimonious process of behind the scene negotiations in which Ziaul Haq was forced to compromise on a number of points. Finally, the Eighth Amendment was passed by the National Assembly on 17 October 1985 and by the Senate in November 1985. It received the assent of the president on 9 November 1985.

According to some independent experts like the late Justice M. Yaqub Ali Khan:

> The Eighth Amendment was not a free and voluntary action of the members of the Parliament. It was the result of a bargain struck between the usurper who held the coercive apparatus of the state and the members of the Parliament who did not have the backing of political parties. The latter had no option but to bow before the will of the dictator.[2]

Some other experts like S.M. Zafar, however, highlighted some positive aspects of the Eighth Amendment:

> Out of the various aspects of the Eighth Amendment, I find the matter relating to the powers of the Senate, the jurisdiction of the Senate and the addition to its membership in the interest of the nation. It is for the first time that the Senate has been given the power to initiate any legislation other than money bills. This satisfied the part relating to provincial autonomy. The extension of the electorate for the election of president to include the members of the provincial assemblies is also in the interest of the federation. As for the balance of powers between the president and the prime minister, neither the type of balance that is available in the original 1973 constitution is a good example of such relationship nor the one created by the Eighth Amendment can be called a good example. If this provision has to be amended, it will require a new substitution and not a mere repeal of the provision brought about by the Eighth Amendment.[3]

Other expert comments at that time brought out some other positive features of the Eighth Amendment in modifying the amendments made by Ziaul Haq: Article 58(2b) amended in March 1985, for example, gave the president the power to dissolve the National Assembly at his discretion 'if an appeal to the electorate is necessary'. The Eighth Amendment added the words, 'if a situation has arisen in which the government of the federation cannot be carried on in accordance with the provisions of the constitution' and an appeal to the electorate is necessary. This addition made it possible for the Supreme Court to intervene and adjucate if the use of power under this article was justified. This power was used four times—in 1988, 1990, 1993, and 1996. Twice, in 1988 and 1993, the exercise of this power was declared to be unconstitutional and on the other two occasions (1990 and 1996) the decision was upheld.[4]

Another important amendment was made in Article 91(5) which was promulgated in March 1985 read 'The prime minister shall hold office during the pleasure of the president but the president shall not exercise this power under this clause unless he is satisfied that the prime minister does not command the confidence of the majority of the members of the National Assembly'. The Eighth Amendment added the words 'in which case he shall summon the National Assembly and require the prime minister to obtain a vote of confidence'. This amendment effectively nullified Ziaul Haq's game plan to change the prime minister every year.

The Eighth Amendment also eliminated Article 152(A) to setup the National Security Council (NSC). In retrospect, it would have been better to retain the NSC, but under the prime minister as chairman rather than the president and use the forum to deal with real national security issues, rather than supervise the political system. Since in 1985 and again in 1997 and 2002, the NSC was created primarily to provide an opportunity to the army establishment to supervise the political system, it became controversial and the real function of evolving an effective national security policy has gone by default.

After the passage of the Eighth Amendment, martial law was lifted on 30 December 1985. The martial law courts were closed and fundamental rights were fully restored. Many cabinet colleagues of Prime Minister Junejo including two chief ministers were opposed to the restoration of fundamental rights but Junejo overruled them and insisted that only by restoring those fundamental rights, after twelve years, would people experience real democracy. However, President Ziaul Haq refused to take off his uniform and announced that he would stay on as chief of army staff and thus keep the armed forces involved in supervising the new system. Junejo thus started his eventful tenure as prime minister under the shadow of a strong military ruler. He was an honest person with a firm belief in democratic institutions and traditions. He was also an astute politician and had therefore evolved his strategy after careful thought and consultations. He did not believe in dramatic initiatives or impulsive slogans to play to the gallery. He therefore started asserting himself in areas in which he would not come in conflict with the military—such as bureaucratic inefficiency and corruption. In an effort to promote austerity, he ordered that senior civil servants entitled to official cars would use only 800 CC Suzuki cars and ministers no more than 1300 CC cars. He sacked at least two ministers in the first two years when he heard complaints of corruption or allegations of serious violation of rules. While the first cabinet was largely chosen by Ziaul Haq, within ten months he reshuffled the cabinet to imprint his own stamp and to secure greater political support within the parliament. Junejo also grew with the job and gained considerable confidence as he went along. But despite his cautious and gradual approach to strengthen the role of the prime minister and the parliament, there were certain unexpected political developments, which did not allow him to complete his five-year tenure.

The first major challenge to the new political system emerged on 10 April 1986 when Benazir Bhutto returned from abroad and landed at Lahore to an historic welcome by her supporters. Having already refused to register itself as a political party under the new Political Parties Act, passed by the National Assembly on 9 December 1985, the PPP began a campaign against the Eighth Amendment to further reduce the powers assumed by the president. In August, the MRD insisted on having a public meeting in Lahore so as to celebrate Independence Day, despite restrictions on such meetings. That gave the authorities the opportunity to arrest Benazir Bhutto and many other MRD leaders. There was no large-scale reaction in the streets, as MRD leaders had expected and the government quietly released Benazir Bhutto in September 1986. Next month Ghulam Mustafa Jatoi returned from abroad and announced the formation of a separate political party, the National Peoples Party. Within a few days, Air

Marshal Asghar Khan announced his party's withdrawal from the MRD. These developments eroded MRD's image and cooled down its agitational campaign and the resultant threat to the stability of the government.

By the end of 1986, just as the overall political situation was becoming more stable, certain other events overshadowed the political landscape. On 14 December, following a clean up operation in Sohrab Goth near Karachi, certain Pathan groups attacked the Orangi township and killed more than a hundred innocent civilians including women and children. Most of the residents in Orangi were immigrants (Mohajir) from India who had recently organized themselves in a political party called the Mohajir Qaumi Movement (MQM) under the leadership of Altaf Hussain. The MQM workers launched a counter attack on Sohrab Goth and killed more than fifty Pathans. The local authorities moved quickly, arrested Altaf Hussain and brought the situation under control, but the psychological aftermath and the deep sense of anxiety that these incident generated lingered amid concerns about a tie-up between old Sindhis and new Sindhis (Mohajirs) in a sustained campaign 'to get rid of' Punjabis and Pathans settled in Sindh.

That atmosphere of uncertainty was also reinforced by a large number of incidents of bomb blasts in NWFP, which were linked to the intense fighting in Afghanistan between the Russian troops and the Mujahideen supported by Pakistan. Hundreds of violations of Pakistan air space by Russia and Afghanistan were reported in 1986 and 1987.

In the beginning of 1987, I told Prime Minister Junejo in one of my meetings that the weight of negative factors in the overall balance sheet of his two years in office was now larger than the positive factors. The euphoria arising from the removal of martial law and restoration of fundamental rights was now over. The initiatives like the five-point programme and the recommendations of the National Commission on Agriculture were useful but needed time to have an impact on the lives of the people. However, negative factors like the growing tensions between Sindhi and non-Sindhis, the influx of millions of refugees into NWFP and Balochistan from Afghanistan along with the large-scale inflow of weapons and drugs were becoming more ominous. The unrest in most urban areas of the country, constantly exploited by members of parliament from urban areas, who even though smaller in numbers, were vocal and defiant, was also a major cause of concern. The MRD was therefore waiting for an opportunity to re-launch its agitation, if any burning issue emerged and was preparing itself for the next elections on the platform of *Amariat versus Jamhooriat* (Autocracy versus Democracy).

Prime Minister Junejo generally agreed with my analysis but said without much hesitation, 'You know, Sartaj Sahib, all the policies whose negative consequences you mentioned are not in my control. The Afghan policy is handled by the president and the ISI. Everyone knows, why and how the MQM was created; PML can easily win the next elections, if it succeeds in curtailing the role of the president and the armed forces in the political life of the country and in the process strengthen the role of the parliament. But such a course might jeopardize the democratic process itself. President Ziaul Haq has already been criticizing the weaknesses of the democratic process and highlighting the virtues of an Islamic *shoora-i-nizam* in which an *Amir*, elected for life, can run the country smoothly with advice and guidance from a nominated *shoora* (Consultative Council).'

Subsequent events proved how prophetic these words of Junejo were and how serious the political divide was between Junejo's democratic instincts and Ziaul Haq's ambitions to stay on in the power as the virtual ruler. Basically Ziaul Haq was convinced that unbridled politics was not good for the country and that he had a moral duty—a kind of divine mandate—to discipline the political forces in the country and maintain order and stability. That is why he was prepared to share some powers but not transfer real power. He therefore organized non-party elections in March 1985 and amended the constitution to retain the main levers of power, including the power to change the prime minister, as frequently as necessary.

Prime Minister Junejo upset these plans by creating the Muslim League Parliamentary Party and keeping it together in his support and amending Article 91(5) through the Eighth Amendment to shift the power of changing the prime minister from the president to the

National Assembly. By the end of 1987, Junejo had consolidated his power and Ziaul Haq had somehow reconciled to a lesser role. But the Afghan peace talks in early 1988, pushed him beyond the limits of his patience.

In January 1988, I participated in two four-hour meetings which President Ziaul Haq had convened to prepare for his successive meetings with Michael Armacost, the US under secretary of state and Yuli Vorontsov, the Russian deputy foreign minister. These meeting were attended by only four civilians (Sahabzada Yaqub-Khan, Ghulam Ishaq Khan, Dr Mahbub ul Haq and myself), and four senior army officers (General K.M. Arif, General Akhtar Abdul Rehman [DG, ISI]; General Imranullah [Commander 10 Corp] and General Rafaqat [PSO to General Zia]). Zia was unusually agitated and angry that under the Geneva Accord, the Russians were ready to leave but two important issues had remained unsolved: First, who will rule Afghanistan after the Russians leave and second, will there be a ban on the supply of weapons to various factions in Afghanistan? Sahabzada Yaqub-Khan explained that the four instruments negotiated in Geneva had taken three years. It would be impossible to reopen these negotiations by introducing any new issues. The issue of power sharing would have to be discussed with the main commanders in Afghanistan after the Russians left, and it would not be practicable to monitor the flow of arms to Afghanistan, even if the principle of 'negative symmetry' was to be accepted in advance. Ziaul Haq summed up the discussion with the prophetic words: 'You will have a bloody civil war in Afghanistan.'

For Zia, the opportunity was ripe for a military solution of Afghanistan, as the commanders who would capture Kabul would automatically assume power and these would largely be groups supported by Pakistan. Junejo was in favour of a negotiated settlement and a faithful implementation of the accord negotiated in Geneva. To strengthen his hands, he convened an all parties conference in March 1988, including Benazir Bhutto and other opposition leaders. The conference endorsed Junejo's policy on the Afghan issue. Zia, who had handled the Afghan policy for ten years, was not invited. His unhappiness with the unfolding Afghan policy was further compounded by the removal of Sahabzada Yaqub-Khan as foreign minister in March 1988, leaving Zain Noorani, the minister of state as incharge of the foreign ministry at such a critical time. Many minor irritations like Junejo's reluctance to allow many ministers to accompany Ziaul Haq at the OIC Summit in Kuwait or on his impending US trip scheduled for the second week of June 1988 were pushing Ziaul Haq's patience beyond the limits of his tolerance.

Then came the Ojhri camp disaster on 10 April 1988, when an ammunition depot, located in a thickly populated area between Rawalpindi and Islamabad, was rocked by massive explosions, sending thousands of projectiles all over Rawalpindi and Islamabad, killing at least one hundred people and injuring twice as many. Junejo responded to the strong public resentment by appointing a six-member parliamentary committee to enquire into the causes of the Ojhri disaster. The committee chaired by Aslam Khattak submitted its report in the third week of May amid rumours that the committee had pointed the finger at ISI and its head General Akhtar Abdul Rehman, who was regarded as the hero of the Afghan war, in which the Mujahideen had defeated a super power with only small arms. This report was due to surface in the National Assembly session scheduled for 8 June 1988. Ziaul Haq decided to act before the report on the Ojhri camp disaster could surface in the National Assembly. On 29 May 1988, he dissolved the parliament and dismissed the government of Prime Minister Junejo under Article 58(2-b), which he had inserted in the constitution under P.O. 14 of 1985.

Junejo had just returned from a very successful visit to China, Japan, and the Philippines. I was present at the crowded press conference he addressed at the airport at 5 p.m. A journalist standing next to me was telling another journalist, 'President Zia has also called a press conference at 6 p.m. Are you going there?' The other journalist said: 'I don't think so. Zia is going to China the next day, so it must be a routine pre-visit briefing. I can use the official press note.' The few journalists who did attend Zia's press conference were stunned when they heard the proclamation to dismiss the cabinet and dissolve the national and provincial assemblies. The charge sheet was relatively brief: 'Rampant corruption, nepotism, and maladministration, finally leading to a complete breakdown of morality and law and order in the country.'[5] In its verdict in October 1988 (after Zia's death), the Supreme Court held Zia's action as unconstitutional in terms of Article 58(2-b), which says, 'If a situation has arisen in which the government of the federation cannot be carried on in accordance with the constitution.' The charges based by Ziaul Haq did not amount to a constitutional deadlock.

While the immediate trigger for Zia's drastic action was provided by the Afghan policy and the Ojhri camp disaster, he was deep down unhappy with the civilian setup throughout the three-year period since he revived the parliamentary political system. He therefore decided, after dismissing the assemblies, to resume total power once again. He announced on 16 July 1988 that general elections would be held on 16 November 1988, but he was working on plans to ensure that political activity including the elections was conducted according to his ground rules. And if the political parties were not prepared to play the game according to his rules, he would again suspend the constitution and re-impose martial law or at least emergency, to retain absolute power, preferably with a civilian facade. But if the facade became too heavy, then he would prefer to rule with the support of those who backed his programme to Islamize the society.

I heard first hand, the explanation for this line of thinking when I met President Zia on 4 August. He said, the geo-political circumstances surrounding Pakistan were very grave and complicated and beyond the comprehension of most political leaders. Thirteen days later in the fateful air crash on 17 August 1988, he died along with General Akhtar Abdul Rehman, and many other senior army officers and the American ambassador, Arnold Raphel.

On 19 August, as Zia's coffin arrived at the airport from Bahawalpur, I could not help thinking about the cruel timing of his death. Supposing he had died three months earlier, when the National Assembly was intact and the parliamentary system was functioning, his successor would have been chosen without any difficulty by the parliament and the provincial assemblies and in the absence of his strong desire to stay in power, the political process would have become even stronger. Now that the power under Article 58(2-b) to dismiss the National Assembly had been used once, it could be used again on one pretext or another, making it difficult for the democratic process to take root.

The Split in the PML

Ziaul Haq had already announced on 16 July, a month before his fatal air crash, that elections to the national and provincial assemblies would be held on 16 November 1988. But his sudden death on 17 August created a turbulent political situation in which the main players had launched their game plans even before Ziaul Haq was buried on 20 August.

In the very first emergency meeting of the cabinet, held within three hours of the air crash, Ghulam Ishaq Khan, who as chairman Senate, had assumed the charge of acting president, clearly indicated that he would strictly follow the constitutional route and would not do anything extraordinary to ensure the return of the ruling establishment to power. He refused to suspend fundamental rights or hold non-party elections. But he did assure the military establishment, as we learnt later, that their vital interests would be fully protected. These included protection of the budget allocations for defence, continuing support to the Afghan mujahideen, and a strong stand on the Kashmir policy. In an astute move to persuade the army to follow a constitutional path rather than think of other options, Ghulam Ishaq Khan went straight to the GHQ to extend these assurances and then came to the cabinet along with the three services chiefs. This was, in fact, the start of the uneasy 'Troika System', under which the president, the prime minister and the army chief would somehow run the 'managed democratic system' for the next eleven years.

General Fazal-e-Haq, the governor of NWFP convened a meeting the following day at the Frontier House to which he invited the other three chief ministers and ten ministers: Chaudhry Shujaat Hussain, Wasim Sajjad, Dr Mahbub ul Haq, and Chaudhry Nisar Ali Khan from Punjab; Mahmood Haroon and Mir Hazar Khan Bijrani from Sindh; Aslam Khattak, Mir Afzal Khan and myself from NWFP; and Fateh Mohammad Hasnie from Balochistan. Fazal-e-Haq started the meeting by saying that by refusing to suspend fundamental rights, Ghulam Ishaq Khan was preparing the ground for the acceptance of Benazir Bhutto's petition in the Supreme Court, that taking part in the elections was the constitutional right of political parties even if they were not registered. That effectively meant handing over the elections on a platter to the PPP. Everyone attending the meeting agreed with this conclusion but no one could suggest any workable alternative. The only counter point that emerged from the discussion was the importance of unifying the Pakistan Muslim League, which had split into two factions over the issue of leadership a fortnight before Zia's air crash. Nawaz Sharif as president of the Punjab Muslim League felt strongly that Mohammad Khan Junejo would not be able to take on the PPP in the next elections against the charismatic leadership of Benazir Bhutto. Since Junejo and his supporters did not agree to give up, the faction led by Nawaz Sharif elected Fida Mohammad Khan as the president of PML at a meeting of PML council on 12 August and the next day, a bigger meeting of PML council presided over by Junejo ended in scuffles without transacting any business. Thus, the anti-PPP political forces were in total disarray in preparing for the elections. Their internal squabbles continued right until election time. This, in a way, facilitated the emergence of PPP as the largest party in the 1988 elections, although without an absolute majority.

On 20 August, Majid Niazmi and I met Nawaz Sharif and Shahbaz Sharif at Ziaul Haq's funeral. We agreed to meet at my house soon after the funeral to discuss the prospects for unifying the Muslim League.

I first met Nawaz Sharif in the speaker's gallery of the National Assembly on 22 March 1985, when members of the newly elected assembly were to take their oath. I had been elected to the Senate from NWFP and was sitting in the same gallery, duly elated by the exuberant atmosphere surrounding the restoration of civilian rule. I knew Nawaz Sharif had won seats in both the National Assembly and the Punjab Assembly, so I was surprised that being a member elect, he was sitting in the gallery and not on the main floor. I spontaneously asked him, 'Are you getting ready to takeover as chief minister of Punjab?' He gave me a strange glance, full of meaning and mystery, but did not answer the question. In later years, this glance became characteristic of him, appearing whenever he could not answer a question straight, yet could not fully conceal his inner reactions or conflicts. On this occasion, he was hoping to become chief minister of Punjab but had not received a nod from the real masters of the political game plan, so he was sitting in the National Assembly as a visitor.

He did become chief minister of Punjab and I saw him regularly at cabinet meetings and other inter-provincial meetings, after I joined the government as special assistant to the prime minister in October 1985 and as a minister of state for food and agriculture in January 1986. He always struck me as a strong and shrewd personality. He would seldom follow any discussion with keenness or diligence but would suddenly intervene very forcefully, coming up with the most unexpected and often original contribution, for which he had obviously come prepared.

But our meeting on 20 August 1988 after Ziaul Haq's funeral was particularly significant because it proved to be the beginning of a long association for revitalizing the Muslim League, as one of the two main political parties in the country. Ziaul Haq's burial in the compound of Faisal Mosque was an overwhelming experience, with half a million people spilling from the burial ground on all sides of the Faisal Avenue right up to Zero Point. I had not fully recovered from this experience and was still working out in my mind how to begin the discussions, when Nawaz Sharif shook me into an intense conversation by asking straightaway, 'Sartaj Sahib, what do we do now?' He was referring to the strange meeting a week earlier in which the two factions of PML nearly came to blows. Recalling our discussions at Frontier House two days earlier, I said, 'We have to keep the party together, otherwise PPP will win the elections.' 'But under whose leadership?' he asked with unusual force. 'We are entering a new and active phase of politics. The 1985 elections were held under the army's supervision on a non-party basis. The forthcoming elctions in November 1988 are the first elections on a party basis after a gap of eleven years. Benazir Bhutto will be riding the populist wave created by her father eighteen years earlier. I do not think Muslim League under Junejo can take her on. I am the only leader within the party who can counter her populist platform and present an even stronger political alternative.' I was stunned by his frankness, his determination, and his vision for the future, but to keep the conversation going I said, 'But at present, you are a provincial leader. It will take some time for you to make the transition to national leadership and elections are only three months away.' 'I know that,' he replied. 'But if the party will give me a free hand in Punjab, to select strong candidates and launch an effective campaign, PML can win enough seats to form the next government. In the other three provinces, the party does not have a viable organizational structure. Junejo Sahib has revived the party only in the parliament and not at the grass roots level. Only in Punjab, due largely to the efforts of Ghulam Haider Wyne (secretary general of the Punjab Muslim League) and myself, the party has developed roots. So please talk to Junejo Sahib and work out some arrangement under which we can participate in the next elections as a unified party. I am ready to accept Junejo Sahib as president of PML, if he will accept me as president of Punjab PML.'

As I pondered over this meeting during my several visits to the airport that evening to see off different VIPs, I could clearly see Nawaz Sharif's burning ambition of reaching the top and ruling with full authority, as his inevitable destiny. His uncontrollable desire for absolute power, which propelled this ambition, unfortunately also contained the germs of his destruction.

In the next few days, the party instead of coming together formally, split into two. On 26 August, the anti-Junejo faction convened its council members and elected Fida Mohammad Khan as president and Nawaz Sharif as secretary general. Three days later, on 29 August, the pro-Junejo faction convened its council and elected Junejo as president and Iqbal Ahmad Khan as secretary general. At the same meeting, the council decided to amend the PML constitution to lay down that a party office cannot be combined with a ministerial office. It also expelled all the caretaker ministers from the party except three—Shujaat Hussain, Wasim Sajjad, and myself, because we had responded positively to a letter of 17 August from Iqbal Ahmed Khan. The three of us called on Junejo on 2 September at his house to thank him. That gave me the opportunity to explore the unification proposal which Nawaz Sharif had asked me to pursue. After emphasizing the importance of a unified party for the next elections, I said, 'If the chief ministers were to accept you as president of the unified PML, would you accept them as provincial chiefs? If so, Fida Mohammad Khan can be made co-president and a joint parliamentary board setup to select candidates.' Junejo in his typical mild and dignified manner, showed a lot of interest in the package and said, 'Why don't you consult all concerned and then come back to me.'

I met Nawaz Sharif and Fida Mohammad Khan at my house on 4 September, after the inauguration of the new PML office at Margalla Road. Fida Mohammad Khan readily agreed to step down in the interest of unity. But what about the other three chief ministers? Nawaz Sharif suggested that the subject could be discussed in greater depth on 6 September in Lahore, when everyone would be present for the Defence Day public meeting at Mochi Gate.

When the meeting began after lunch at the chief minister's office on 6 Club Road, Lahore, I made a long and frank presentation on the dismal election prospects facing the party: 'Muslim League has damaged its reputation and its election chances by splitting into two factions. Neither faction can do well on its own, but if they unite many other parties, inimical to PPP, will join PML in an election alliance. But we should not underestimate the obstacles to unity. The faction led by Fida Mohammad Khan is considered as the legacy of Ziaul Haq and is counting on the establishment's support but the faction led by Junejo is considered as anti-Zia and that is its main election platform. That is why the army may not be enthusiastic about unifying the PML under Junejo. Within the party, there are strong personality clashes since all those who were outside the caretaker setup are against those who were inside. In Sindh, Pir Sahib of Pagara is not in favour of unification since that will reduce the importance of his faction. Despite these obstacles, the compulsions for unity are much stronger. We should therefore overcome the obstacles.'

The discussion was fairly disgusting because most participants were more interested in their own narrow political space, rather than the larger interest of the party. Finally, they all agreed on the minimum necessary conditions for unity. If the two factions of PML had separate candidates for each seat, most would lose. But if there was a joint parliamentary board, then the chances would improve at least for those candidates who have a strong vote bank of their own, because in their case the additional party votes would not split. And in that context, Prime Minister Junejo should be allowed to continue as president, provided he accepted all the four chief ministers as provincial presidents of the party.

I conveyed this package to Junejo on 9 September, when he returned to Islamabad from Karachi. His position had become less flexible. He said he would accept them as provincial party chiefs but they have to resign as chief ministers because under the new party constitution (adopted on 29 August 1988), a party office could not be combined with a government office.

Junejo's reluctance was in fact strengthened by certain judicial developments. The Supreme Court had already decided that political parties do not have to be formally registered with the Election Commission to participate in the elections. That prepared the ground for the PPP to launch its election campaign in a very charged atmosphere, created by Zia's unexpected departure. But suddenly, in September 1988, the Lahore High Court declared on a petition submitted much earlier by Haji Saifullah that the dissolution of the assemblies by Ziaul Haq on 29 May was illegal, arbitrary and malafide. But the court did not provide relief by restoring the assemblies, since preparations for new elections were already underway. As the appeal went to the Supreme Court to seek the relief of reviving the assemblies, Junejo became more hopeful.

On 4 October, Majid Nizami arranged a midnight meeting between Junejo and Nawaz Sharif at a local hotel. At this meeting, Junejo agreed to the 'package' because he wanted Nawaz Sharif to persuade Ghulam Ishaq Khan to agree to the revival of the National Assembly for at least one year. Nawaz Sharif tried but did not succeed. 'The shooting of the horse was wrong and illegal but the dead horse cannot come to life again,' was the answer he received.

The next day, on 5 October, the Supreme Court upheld the decision of the Lahore High Court, dashing Junejo's hopes for the revival of the assembly. He therefore stuck to his position once again. On 6 October, Manzoor Wattoo, Chaudhry Shujaat Hussain, and I spent several hours with Junejo to follow up on his meeting with Nawaz Sharif two days earlier, but without much success.

That evening, the PML faction led by Fida Mohammad Khan joined an election alliance with eight other parties under the label of Islami Jamhoori Ittehad (IJI) or Islamic Democratic Alliance. The Jamaat-e-Islami joined this alliance three days later. The alliance was cobbled together by the 'establishment'. That is why Nawaz Sharif was so desperate to reach an agreement with Junejo that day, but Junejo was so upset by the Supreme Court decision announced a day earlier that he could not forestall the emergence of IJI. If he had accepted the proposed package on that day, PML could have contested the November 1988 elections on its own symbol, with seat adjustment arrangements with eight other parties that were included in the IJI.

Despite the formation of IJI, Manzoor Wattoo and Hamid Nasir Chatta, the two other mediators did not give up their efforts to unify the PML, 'because that will effectively prevent the PML faction led by Prime Minister Junejo to put up candidates against the PML candidate belonging to the faction led by Fida Mohammad Khan, technically the IJI candidates'. Manzoor Wattoo told me this on 10 October. Three days later, he called me and said somewhat excitedly that they had found a formula that might be acceptable to Junejo and Nawaz Sharif. He asked me if I could reach Lahore immediately because the formula had to be given concrete shape and then the unification had to be announced at a press conference at the PML Secretariat at 6 p.m. the next day—14 October. The formula was, I was somewhat amused to learn, that the chief ministers would resign their party posts, as demanded by Junejo but Junejo would keep these resignations pending until after the elections. In other words, the principle of separating government offices from party offices would be accepted but would be implemented after the elections. 'Political expediency must have some limits,' I said to myself as I heard the formula.

The next day, it took several hours to work out the 'formula', as Manzoor Wattoo and I shuttled continuously between the Governor House, where Nawaz Sharif and three other chief ministers had assembled, and the Avari Hotel where Junejo and his colleagues were holding a marathon party meeting. The main issue that took time to resolve arose from the suggestion that since Junejo would be the president of the unified Muslim League, someone from the Fida faction should be the secretary general, i.e. Nawaz Sharif. Junejo, however, remained adamant that Iqbal Ahmed Khan would remain the secretary general and that he had made enough concession by allowing Nawaz Sharif and other chief ministers to remain provincial presidents until after the elections.

Everyone finally appeared at the press conference at 11 p.m. instead of 6 p.m. to announce the 'unification' of the PML and at midnight at the chief minister's residence for the celebration dinner.

But the so-called unification was not only too late but also very half hearted. Only three days were left for filing nomination papers and the reconstituted parliamentary board faced enormous difficulties in reaching agreement on candidates. Many potential candidates revolted and filed the papers as independent candidates when they failed to get the party ticket, thus splitting the party vote. But more importantly, the mistrust among leaders continued and affected the results of the 1988 elections, which Benazir Bhutto's PPP won by a wide margin—93 out of 204 National Assembly seats against 54 by PML and other parties of the IJI. But she could not win enough seats in the provincial assemblies of Punjab and Balochistan to form a government or join a coalition and that proved to be a major handicap as she assumed power in November 1988.

NOTES

1. The recommendation to place the budget before the Senate for discussion and comments was not approved at that time, but was adopted seventeen years later, in 2002.
2. *The Nation*, 28 March 1989.
3. *The Nation*, 8 February 1989.
4. Sartaj Aziz, '8th Amendment: The Real Issues', *The Nation*, 25 February 1989.
5. *Dawn*, Karachi, 31 May 1988.

Members of the National Commission on Agriculture (1986–88)
Front Row: Zafar Altaf, Dr Amir Mohammad, Shafi Niaz, Sartaj Aziz (Chairman),
Malik Khuda Bakhsh Bucha, Qamar Zaman Shah, Taj Jamali, Javed Burki.
Second Row: Syed Babar Ali, Imtiaz Hussain, Faqir Mohammad and members of the Secretariat
Photo courtesy: Press Information Department (PID), Islamabad

Presenting Report of the National Commission on Agriculture to Prime Minister
Mohammad Khan Junejo, Rawalpindi, 3 April 1988
Photo courtesy: Press Information Department (PID), Islamabad

In 1985, Sartaj Aziz was elected a member of the Pakistan Senate from NWFP. He was re-elected for a six-year term from Islamabad Capital Territory in 1988. In 1994, he was re-elected from NWFP for another six years.

The newly elected Senators with the Senate Chairman, Wasim Sajjad, and Prime Minister Nawaz Sharif, March 1991

Photo courtesy: Press Information Department (PID), Islamabad

Leader of the Opposition, Nawaz Sharif on a Train March during
Tehrik-e-Nijjat (Deliverance Movement), September 1994
Photo courtesy: Ali Balti from author's personal collection

With Hakim Mohammad Said during a visit to Hamdard University, Karachi, March 1993
Photo courtesy: Author's personal collection

Being sworn in as Director Commodities and Trade Division of
UN Food and Agriculture Organization at Rome, August 1971
Photo courtesy: Author's personal collection

A meeting with Henry Kissinger, US Secretary of State in August 1974; with Sayed A. Marei,
Secretary General of the World Food Conference. Sartaj Aziz was
Deputy Secretary General of the Conference
Photo courtesy: Author's personal collection

A memorable dinner on the eve of the World Food Conference, November 1974.
From left: Mrs Marei; Mr A.H. Boerma, Director General of FAO; H. M. A. Onitiri of Nigeria; Escott Reid of Canada; Barbara Ward (Lady Jackson); Syed A. Marei; Mrs Boerma

Photo courtesy: Author's personal collection

As President of the Society for International Development (1976–79), Sartaj Aziz organized the first meeting of the North South Round Table in May 1978, which was chaired by Barbara Ward.

From left: Dr Mahbub ul Haq, Amb. Richard Gardner of USA, Amb. Donald Mills of Jamaica, Barbara Ward, Sartaj Aziz, Dame Judith Hart of UK, and Paul Marc Henry of France

Photo courtesy: Author's personal collection

Addressing the second meeting of the North South Round Table, May 1979
From left: James P. Grant, (later Head of UNICEF); Mr Hernan Santa Cruz
(Chile); Julio Andreotti, Prime Minister of Italy; Sartaj Aziz; Inga Thorsson
(Sweden); and Aurelio Peccie (Italy)
Photo courtesy: Author's personal collection

IFAD was the first international agency to provide financial support
to the Grameen Bank of Bangladesh when it was set up in 1982. Sartaj Aziz,
as Assistant President of IFAD, personally went to Bangladesh to finalize the loan.
Here he is distributing loans to some of the recipients in Tangle, near Dhaka.
Photo courtesy: Author's personal collection

CHAPTER 7

Benazir Bhutto as Prime Minister
(1988–1990)

The circumstances, in which the November 1988 elections were held, were extremely difficult in the wake of many far-reaching events: the Ojhri camp disaster of April 1988, the dissolution of the National Assembly in May 1988, and the sudden death of Ziaul Haq in August 1988. The fact that the fragile structure was able to withstand these shocks and get back on the constitutional path within six months, created a measure of optimism on the eve of the elections, relegating for the time being, the more chronic weaknesses of the system.

As expected, the PPP emerged as the largest single party in the 1988 elections but did not get an absolute majority. It won 93 out of 196 contested seats in the National Assembly as shown in the following table.

1988 Elections for the National Assembly						
Party	Punjab	Sindh	NWFP	Balochistan	ICT	Total
PPP	53	31	7	1	1	93
IJI	44	–	8	2	–	54
Other Parties	4	15	7	6	–	32
Independents	12	–	3	2	–	17
Total	113	46	25	11	1	196
Source: Election Commission of Pakistan						

The IJI, consisting of PML and eight other parties, won only 54 seats in the National Assembly but captured 108 out of 240 seats in the

Punjab Assembly, enough to form the provincial government under Nawaz Sharif with the support of most of the independent members. In Balochistan also, the Jamhoori Watan Party (JWP) and JUI(F) captured enough seats to form a government that was opposed to PPP. This created a difficult situation for the PPP, the party in power at the centre, which consequently had to cope with hostile governments in two provinces. The resultant tug of war ultimately lead to the demise of the PPP government in less than two years.

The main surprise of the 1988 elections was the emergence of the MQM, which captured 15 out of 17 National Assembly seats allocated to urban centres of Karachi and Hyderabad.

In many ways, 1988 was a watershed year in the political life of the country. The Zia era, which prevailed in the country for eleven long years, had finally ended, leading to elections and the advent of democracy, but it also brought out the inevitable pitfalls of the transition from a military regime.

The army was not comfortable with PPP's victory in the elections and as a result, President Ghulam Ishaq Khan took two weeks to hold consultations with different political parties before calling upon Benazir Bhutto to form the government. But in the process, he extracted assurances from her that she would not interfere in senior appointments in the armed forces or try to change the course of foreign policy in Afghanistan. As she said subsequently in the course of several interviews, she formed a government in 1988 with her hands tied and that she was overthrown in 1990 because she chose to dictate her own security agenda.

Despite the assurances Benazir Bhutto gave to the armed forces, through Ghulam Ishaq Khan, she could have asserted herself, like her predecessor, in strengthening the role of parliament and other democratic institutions, but she concentrated primarily on consolidating and expanding the political space of the party. To start with, the 1988 elections had produced a split mandate. PPP did not get an absolute majority in the centre and in three of the four provinces. Only in Sindh, it secured a sweeping mandate—67 out of 100 seats (Zulfikar Ali Bhutto in the period 1971–77 did not have a majority in NWFP and Balochistan, but in the largest province of Punjab, he had a comfortable majority).

The first task taken up by the new PPP government was to try to capture the Punjab government by winning over at least twenty-five members of the IJI government led by Nawaz Sharif. This failed attempt was the first serious blunder which had a lasting effect on our politics and the democratic system in the coming years. If Benazir Bhutto had accepted the voters' mandate in Punjab and told Nawaz Sharif that he should rule peacefully in the Punjab as required under the constitution, while cooperating with her at the centre, she would have relegated him to the position of a provincial chief and also strengthened democracy. But by confronting him, she elevated him to national politics and also gave him the opportunity to use the Punjab card and stir up Punjabi nationalism. The second major mistake she made was to keep the chief ministers of Punjab and Balochistan out of the decision-making fora at the centre. Only chief ministers of Sindh and NWFP were invited to attend cabinet meetings. Similarly, the provincial governments of Punjab and Balochistan and the district councils in these provinces were bypassed in implementing the Peoples Works Programme through a new parallel machinery, mostly under the district heads of the PPP. Attempts were also made to weaken the role of the Senate because PPP did not have a majority in the Senate.

The IJI, under Nawaz Sharif, retaliated against these discriminatory policies. As chief minister of Punjab, he did not accept many posting orders of senior officers to or from Punjab. He started the Bank of Punjab because the nationalized commercial banks had been directed by the central government to stop financing facilities for the Ittefaq Group and businesses owned by other PML leaders. The Punjab government also objected to the new structure created for implementing the Peoples Works Programme, in place of the district and union councils elected in 1983.

Once when Nawaz Sharif was attending a meeting in early 1989 to prepare himself for a meeting of the National Economic Council, I asked him if the strategy of non-cooperation with the federal government and the use of the 'Punjab card' were really in the longer term national interest. He replied without much hesitation: 'Did the

PPP not run its 1988 election campaign on the Sindhi platform? That is why IJI did not win a single seat in the National Assembly in Sindh and only one seat in the provincial assembly. PML has to develop strong roots in Sindh to become a truly national party in the next elections.'

There were other divisive undercurrents as a result of the 1988 elections. In NWFP, IJI won 27 provincial seats against PPP's 20, but because of its majority at the centre, PPP was able to form the government in NWFP with the support of thirteen MPAs from Awami National Party (ANP) and some independent members.

In Balochistan, the mandate was totally divided between five parties. JUI(F) emerged as the largest party with 11 seats, followed by IJI with 8 seats and Balochistan National Alliance (BNA) with 6 seats, PPP won only 3 seats, Pakistan National Party (PNP) 2 seats, and Pakhtoonkhwa Milli Awami Party 2 seats. There were seven independent members. Mir Zafarullah Jamali could not get the support of JUI(F) because they wanted the chief ministry, so he put together a fragile government with a majority of only one (which was the Speaker's casting vote) with the help of three PPP members, the smaller parties and some independents. But within twelve days, on 14 December 1988, one minister shifted to the opposition and the government was faced with a serious post-election crisis. Eventually, Nawab Akbar Bugti was able to form a BNA government in Balochistan with the help of JUI(F). He soon joined Nawaz Sharif to confront the federal government.

In Sindh, even though PPP had a two-thirds majority in a house of 100, it entered into an agreement with the MQM and invited them to join the government, but within a year, the agreement broke down amid wild accusations from both sides, leading to serious ethnic violence between the 'old' and the 'new' Sindhis, causing the death of 1,200 persons with 2,500 injured.

The election manifesto of PPP was full of promises to improve the life of the common man by accelerating the pace of investment and growth. But ethnic violence in Sindh seriously affected the industrial sector in the province. Many non-Sindhi industrialists moved back to Punjab and the rate of industrial growth slowed down from an average of 8–9 per cent in the preceding five years to less than 4 per cent in

1988–89—recovering only to 5.7 per cent in 1989–90. As a result, the overall GDP growth was less than 5 per cent during the PPP government. This also affected the employment situation in the country.

Benazir Bhutto's election as the first woman prime minister in a Muslim country was warmly welcomed in the West. This also led to increased flow of foreign assistance. Total commitments went up by 28 per cent from $2.6 billion in 1985–96 to $3.4 billion a year in 1988–90. But before these commitments could be translated into actual disbursements, the government of Benazir Bhutto had been dismissed on 6 August 1990.

Many of the problems during Benazir Bhutto's tenure arose from the concentration of economic and financial powers with the prime minister. During her first tenure, as in the second tenure from 1993–96, she did not appoint a finance minister. She retained the finance portfolio and herself frequently chaired meetings of the economic committee of the cabinet, which is primarily responsible for the day-to-day management of the economy. She appointed, on President Ghulam Ishaq Khan's recommendation, V.A. Jaffery as economic advisor to handle the enormous file work of the finance ministry, and Ehsan-ul-Haq Paracha as minister of state for finance to handle all the work in parliament and present the national budget in the National Assembly. She also created a new Board of Investment, chaired by her to issue permissions for setting up new industrial units, and appointed a cell in the prime minister secretariat to monitor and supervise all loans advanced by the nationalized commercial banks. In addition, a 'placement bureau' was created in the prime minister secretariat to recommend candidates for all vacancies in different ministries and divisions. During its twenty-month rule, the PPP government 'placed' about 200,000 personnel in different grades, recommended by PPP members of parliament and the party leaders. When Ghulam Ishaq Khan dismissed the PPP government on 6 August 1990, he listed all these examples to show that national wealth and official patronage was used to promote the interest of the party to such an extent that 'the word 'corruption' became the trade mark of politics in Pakistan'.

But the premature end of Benazir Bhutto's government was finally triggered by her effort to establish her control over the army. She tried to reduce the involvement of ISI in politics, by replacing General Hamid Gul with a retired general, Shamsur Rehman Kalu. She also tried to change the CJCS, Admiral Sirohey, but President Ghulam Ishaq Khan refused to sign the order thus bringing out into the open the interpretation of the new division of powers between the president and the prime minister after the Eighth Amendment. While the issue itself was not resolved, despite prolonged discussion in parliament, the establishment realized that Benazir Bhutto was trying to go back on the understanding she had reached with Ghulam Ishaq Khan in November 1988.

Meanwhile, the political situation became extremely volatile when in September 1989, MQM with its fourteen members in the National Assembly, withdrew their support from the government, alleging that most of the promises made to them in November 1988 had not been fulfilled. The PPP government retaliated by starting a crackdown against MQM activists and disarming them forcibly. When Ghulam Ishaq Khan dismissed the Benazir government in August 1990, he cited this as one of the grounds of his action in the following words: 'According to statistics supplied by the governments' own agencies, during the period of only seven months, from 1 January to 31 July 1990, after the elected government has been in office for one full year, 1187 persons were killed and 2491 injured in various incidents in Sindh. Of these 635 were killed and 1433 injured in ethnic troubles.'[1] In a single incident of ethnic violence in Hyderabad, Sindh, about 200 Urdu speaking people were gunned down in September 1989.

As tensions mounted and the local police efforts seemed unable to disarm the MQM activists, the federal government called upon the army to do the job. The army leadership indicated in response that there were militant elements on both sides and they would like to follow an even-handed approach to the issue. For that, they required full powers under Article 245 of the constitution. Under clause 3 of this article, a High Court cannot exercise any jurisdiction under Article 199 (governing unlawful detentions) in relation to any area in which the armed forces of Pakistan are acting in aid of civil power in pursuance of Article 245. The government was reluctant to give them these powers. This further increased tensions between the government and the army, which at that time was under growing pressures from large-scale movement of Indian forces along the border between Rajasthan and Sindh.

The erosion of the government's strength in parliament, after the withdrawal of MQM support, provided an opportunity to the Combined Opposition Parties (COP) to launch a motion of no-confidence against the PPP government. The motion was moved by Ghulam Mustafa Jatoi, the leader of COP in November 1989, and led to a series of high tension dramas in all parts of the country. PPP at that time had a majority of 44 in a house of 217. If in addition to MQM's fourteen seats, eight independent members from tribal areas, which invariably support the government in power, had also shifted sides, the government would have lost its majority. The opposition therefore needed to win only three or four members from the government's side to carry the motion of no confidence. The scramble for these three to four members led to an unprecedented level of political bribery from both sides. The ruling party was so apprehensive about this onslaught that it moved all its members to Swat for 'safe custody' and brought them back only on the day of voting. In a dramatic move, PPP showed on television three members of the opposition sitting with the prime minister a day before the voting. The no-confidence motion did not succeed but left the ruling party much weaker, after only one year in the saddle.

In the next few months, confrontation between the federal government and the two provinces intensified. The tension in Sindh continued to escalate and the clouds of uncertainty became darker. Rumours began to circulate in the early months of 1990 about a possible military takeover.

I had a meeting with Ghulam Ishaq Khan on 14 June 1990 and he shared his concerns with me. Referring to rumours about an army takeover he said, 'In our system, the army intervenes when, in their and in the public perception, there is an imminent breakdown of the civilian system. At present, the situation in Sindh is very bad. The army is generally uneasy that it is being diverted from the borders and asked to tackle the crisis in Sindh. The public is also greatly concerned about the growing incidence of corruption. We have a constitutional safeguard under Article 58(2-b) when by calling for fresh elections, the democratic process can be saved but I am reluctant to use these powers at present because it is a drastic alternative. However, I have to ensure that the army's perception about the complete breakdown of the civilian system does not reach a point, when even fresh elections are considered an inadequate solution.'

He probably reached this judgement in the first week of August 1990. I had just returned from a three-week trip to the United States on 5 August, when I received a message that the president would like to meet me immediately. When I met him three hours later, he told me that he had decided to dissolve the National Assembly under Article 58-2(b) and would like me to join the caretaker government as finance minister. He also told me not to share this information with anyone else. I guarded this secret to such an extent that even my wife was surprised to see me at the swearing in ceremony on television the next evening.

Ghulam Ishaq Khan had done careful homework before he issued the orders to dissolve the National Assembly and dismiss the government of Benazir Bhutto. He and his team had carefully studied the Supreme Court judgement of 5 October 1988, in which similar action by Ziaul Haq under Article 58(2-b) to dismiss the government of Mohammad Khan Junejo was held to be unconstitutional and unlawful. The Article, as amended by the Eighth Amendment, says: 'If a situation has arisen in which the government of the Federation cannot be carried on in accordance with the provisions of constitution and a reference to the electorate is necessary.' Allegations like corruption, inefficiency, and inability to Islamize the system, which Ziaul Haq had framed in 1988, did not amount to a constitutional impasse. Ghulam Ishaq Khan, on the other hand found sufficient grounds in support of his decision to dismiss the PPP government, i.e. the confrontation between the centre and two provinces, inability to form and activate constitutional bodies like the National Finance Commission and the Council of Common Interest and the continuing ethnic strife. The decision was challenged in the High Courts of

Peshawar, Karachi, and Lahore but both the latter courts ruled that the decision was in order in terms of Article 58(2-b).

In August 1988, after Ziaul Haq's death, Ghulam Ishaq Khan, on becoming acting president, carried on with the caretaker cabinet which Ziaul Haq had setup in May 1988 but did not appoint a caretaker prime minister. This was primarily because he was somewhat reluctant to elevate someone from within the cabinet. He felt it would be safer to retain the role of chief executive with himself. Aslam Khattak, who as minister of provincial coordination, considered himself the senior-most minister, convened several meetings of ministers to pressurize Ghulam Ishaq Khan to appoint a caretaker prime minister. But Ghulam Ishaq Khan did not oblige. As I learnt later, he would have preferred someone like Sahabzada Yaqub-Khan as caretaker prime minister if he had to, but anticipating opposition from ministers like Aslam Khattak, he decided not to appoint one.

In August 1990, however, when he dismissed the government of Benazir Bhutto, he appointed Ghulam Mustafa Jatoi as caretaker prime minister. He was one of the founding members of PPP but was now the head of a breakaway faction of the PPP called NPP. He could therefore play a useful role in supporting the anti-PPP coalition to victory and in the process, vindicating Ghulam Ishaq Khan's decision to dismiss the government of Benazir Bhutto. I was surprised to see Ghulam Mustafa Khar in the caretaker cabinet but was happy at the inclusion of Rafi Raza and Kamal Azfar. As I told some colleagues, I would have been prepared to see a neutral caretaker cabinet but in politics, it is difficult to be a total puritan.

The COP which had launched the no-confidence motion in November 1989 included almost all the parties that were opposed to the PPP government at that time: Pakistan Muslim League, Jamaat-e-Islami, JUI, BNP, MQM and a number of smaller parties. It was not therefore difficult to organize a strong anti-PPP coalition under the umbrella of IJI to contest the 1990 elections, with some of the COP parties.

The COP had also setup in 1989, a number of committees to work on various economic, social, political and legal issues to convey the image of a credible 'government in waiting' with a popular and acceptable programme. This process had helped to narrow differences even on important divisive issues like provincial autonomy.

In one of the meetings of COP high command, Nawab Akbar Bugti, then chief minister of Balochistan said that the participation of his party in COP was based on the assurances given to him that the subject of maximum provincial autonomy would be an important component of the COP's policy platform. He distributed copies of a three-year-old document entitled 'Declaration of Autonomy of Federating Units', signed on 2 August 1986 by leaders of component parties of MRD at Lahore, including Begum Nusrat Bhutto on behalf of PPP. All the leaders had committed that if MRD or any of its component parties came into power, it would be bound to have these autonomy provisions incorporated in the 1973 constitution. The declaration said the federal government would have only four subjects—defence, foreign affairs, communications, and currency. All other subjects, including foreign trade, would be handled by the federating units. Akbar Bugti said that PPP, which was one of the components of MRD in 1986, had been in power for one year but had taken no steps to implement the declaration. He would now like the COP to endorse the declaration and faithfully implement it if it won the next elections.

This demand took many of the COP leaders by surprise. Nawaz Sharif said that Pakistan Muslim League had already setup a committee on provincial coordination. He would ask it to examine the subject of provincial autonomy. The PML working committee would be able to take a policy decision on the issue in the light of this committee's report, which would then be shared with other leaders of COP.

Next week, a sub-committee of the PML committee on provincial coordination was setup under my convenorship. Other members were Raja Zafarul Haq, Ghous Ali Shah, and Nawabzada Jehangir Shah Jogezai. After several meetings, I submitted a comprehensive report on 7 February 1990. The report presented a comparative analysis of the nature and quantum of provincial autonomy as endorsed in 1956, 1962 and 1973 constitutions and concluded that:

A constitution on the MRD formula, which allocates only four subjects to the centre, would not guarantee a viable federation of Pakistan. Without minimum powers for economic coordination and financial resources to manage its functions and also promote the development of less developed regions in all the provinces, it will not be able to fulfil the concept of a unified Pakistan.

It recommended a number of measures to strengthen national unity, including a drastic reduction in the concurrent list, and a review of Schedule IV to the 1973 constitution to increase the degree of provincial autonomy, larger financial allocations to provinces and adequate representation to all provinces in military and civil services.

This report not only provided certain basic guidelines which were included in the election manifestoes that the Pakistan Muslim League announced in 1993 and 1996, but also reassured leaders like Akbar Bugti that the Pakistan Muslim League had at least seriously considered the issue of provincial autonomy.

There were other divisive issues and personality conflicts in the new election alliance. Nawaz Sharif was the head of IJI but Junejo was the head of the Pakistan Muslim League, by far the largest component of IJI. But the compulsion to win the next elections kept the coalition together, including the MQM in Sindh, the ANP in NWFP and Nawab Akbar Bugti in Balochistan.

The PPP also tried to strengthen its position for the elections by forming an electoral alliance called PDA (Pakistan Democratic Alliance) with the Tehrik-e-Istiqlal of Air Marshal Asghar Khan, the Shia Tehrik-e-Jafferia and a splinter group of Pakistan Muslim League with Hamid Nasir Chatta, as its leader.

IJI's victory in the 1990 elections was bigger than we had expected. In the pre-election meetings of the alliance, the most optimistic estimate was between 95 to 100 seats, but it won 106 out of 199 contested seats, almost twice the number of seats it had won in 1988. PPP's tally of 45 seats was less than half its bag of 93 seats in 1988. Thus the prediction of another split mandate which had led to so much uncertainty in the preceding two years was rejected by the voters as shown in the following table.

1990 Elections for the National Assembly

Party	Punjab	Sindh	NWFP	Balochistan	ICT/ FATA	Total
IJI	92	3	8	2	1	106
PDA	14	24	5	2	–	45
MQM	–	15	–	–	–	15
ANP	–	–	6	–	–	6
JUI (F)	–	–	4	2	–	6
Independents	6	4	3	–	8	21
Total	112	46	26	6	9	199

Source: Election Commission of Pakistan

As the head of the caretaker government, which supervised the 1990 elections, Ghulam Mustafa Jatoi was naturally very keen to continue as prime minister. During many meetings of the caretaker cabinet, whenever he would comment on various policies and initiatives, he would invariably say, 'Inshallah, after the election, we would pursue it more vigorously or implement it with peoples' mandate.' But the result of the elections threw cold water on these aspirations as Nawaz Sharif suddenly emerged as the new star on the political horizon.

Within two years of that meaningful conversation on 20 August 1988, soon after Ziaul Haq's burial, Nawaz Sharif had in fact made a swift transition from the provincial arena to national leadership, partly by confronting the federal government of Benazir Bhutto. After becoming the head of IJI, he managed to form a broader anti-PPP alliance, called the COP, which included many important provincial, regional, and ethnic parties, like MQM, ANP and JWP, apart from JI and JUI, which were already a part of IJI. This not only facilitated victory in the elections but also paved the way for bringing these parties in the mainstream of national politics after elections. Nawaz Sharif also campaigned very aggressively on the IJI election symbol of bicycle, particularly in the Punjab, where his three-year tenure as chief minister was perceived very positively by the public, and where his defiant attitude to protect the rights of Punjab had won him many supporters. Eventually, IJI won 92 seats of National Assembly from

Punjab out of 112 contested seats. It also won 8 seats in NWFP but only 3 in Sindh and 2 in Balochistan. With such an impressive tally in the elections, his election as prime minister by the National Assembly should have been a smooth formality, but it was not.

Ghulam Ishaq Khan took almost ten days before convening the session to elect a Speaker and then a prime minister. Rumours about Ghulam Mustafa Jatoi as the first choice of the establishment began to circulate. One morning, a week after the elections, I received a phone call from Nawaz Sharif, saying he was about to leave Murree for Lahore, but would like to stop over at my house in Islamabad. He arrived two hours later and wanted to know why Ghulam Ishaq Khan had not convened the National Assembly session so far. 'I have heard rumours about Jatoi,' he said without much hesitation. 'Maybe the establishment wants a more pliable prime minister. But how would he get the required vote of confidence from the National Assembly? I am the leader of IJI and IJI has won 106 out of 199 seats that were contested, 92 of them in Punjab. Will the establishment coerce or browbeat every member to vote according to their directives? We have to gradually reduce the role of these invisible forces in the political life of the country. Let the assembly choose its leader according to democratic principles and the constitution.'

When I met Ghulam Ishaq Khan the next day and conveyed these concerns in more discrete language, he just smiled and said, 'Nawaz Sharif's concerns are misplaced. No one is trying to deny him the prime ministership. Before the elections, Mr Jatoi was one of the contenders, but even during the elections, while Nawaz Sharif's standing as a potential leader was going up, Mr Jatoi, with a weak stamina literally collapsed in the middle of the elections, and could not even complete the schedule of election rallies planned for him.'

Nawaz Sharif was sworn in two days later on 6 November 1990, as the fourteenth prime minister of Pakistan. It was the first Punjabi prime minister in almost three decades with a much broader base of political support than almost anyone of his predecessors.

NOTE

1. *Dawn*, Karachi, 7 August 1990.

CHAPTER 8

Nawaz Sharif and His Economic Reforms
(1990–1993)

As a human being, Nawaz Sharif is a complex personality. Even after observing him closely in different facets of his remarkable career for more than twenty years, I cannot claim that I understand him fully. He has no doubt some outstanding qualities as a political leader, which elevated him to the highest political office in the country in less than six years after he entered politics. Again, his courageous defiance, as leader of the opposition from 1993 to 1996, boosted his popularity to such an extent that in the February 1997 elections, he won more than two-thirds of the seats in the National Assembly, a distinction no other leader in South Asia had ever achieved. But like all populist leaders he has his weaknesses and shortcomings. He is very impulsive by nature and therefore thrives on dramatic moves rather than well-considered decisions. He has a strong belief, based perhaps on his popularity among the party workers and the people at large, in the importance of his personal power. He therefore ran the government on his terms through a system of personalized decision making, without adequate consultations or participation of his cabinet colleagues, parliament or other relevant bodies—a pattern subsequently seen in UK under Tony Blair. This desire to strengthen his personal power base rather than strengthen the institutions that are the main pillars of a viable democratic process, eventually led to his dramatic downfall.

Nawaz Sharif's first tenure as prime minister, from November 1990 to July 1993, was certainly one of the most successful periods in the country's history. He initiated certain basic reforms that transformed the nature of the Pakistan economy from a closed and over regulated system to a more open and de-regulated economy and brought about a fundamental change in the environment for investment and business in Pakistan. In this sense, Pakistan preceded India in the process of liberalization and this fact caught the attention of the Indian media. Sankarshan Thakur, for example, wrote in *The Telegraph* of Calcutta on 7 May 1992:

> Genial, businesslike and oppressively articulate on economic issues, Sartaj Aziz as the nuts and bolts man of the new economic structure Pakistan is trying to build on the debris of the old one and tasks and challenges he faces make an ideal soul mate for Dr Manmohan Singh, who too, very often, must look for one. With staggering speed in the last nine months, Sartaj Aziz has altered the foundations of the Pakistani economy, bulldozing regulations out of the way, privatizing both the public sector and the banking system and opening up the arena till the doors creaked at the hinges. Big business has suddenly boomed in Pakistan. It finds its manifestations as much in the buoyancy of the Karachi Stock Exchange which has quadrupled its capital, raising Rs (Pakistani) 17.3 billion in just the last year as in the rush for grabbing hitherto unsought spaces in commercial buildings down Islamabad's desolate Shahrah-e-Quaid-i-Azam. Non-resident Pakistanis have overnight been seduced to invest Rs4 billion and the finance ministry assures $1 billion worth of foreign investment is already in the pipeline. The South Koreans, for instance, have taken up a 500-acre plot near Karachi to setup an industrial estate of their own.

Nawaz Sharif was not only the first leader from Punjab to become prime minister in three decades, but was also the first political leader from urban areas to occupy that position. This factor plus his record as a development and result oriented chief minister of Punjab raised high expectations within the business community and created a euphoric atmosphere on the stock market, when he took over in November 1990.

I vividly remember the swearing in ceremony of the first Nawaz Sharif cabinet on 7 November 1990. As I recall the same ceremony for his second stint on 25 February 1997, the contrast could not have been more glaring. In November 1990, he climbed into the top political office with the help of President Ghulam Ishaq Khan, who had created the opportunity by dismissing the government of Benazir Bhutto after only twenty months in office and then by imposing a charge sheet of corruption and bad governance, which was upheld by the Supreme Court. Ghulam Ishaq Khan also played a role in convincing the establishment that Mustafa Jatoi may have been their first choice but according to democratic norms, Nawaz Sharif's claim was stronger since as head of IJI he had managed to win for the alliance 92 seats in Punjab out of 106 seats captured by it.

The composition of the first Cabinet was therefore largely decided by Ghulam Ishaq Khan. But within a few months, Nawaz Sharif started asserting his authority. While Ghulam Ishaq Khan was always conscious of the political space and opportunities he had created for Nawaz Sharif in 1990, Nawaz Sharif for his part, wanted to forget this reality and grow out of the shadow of Ghulam Ishaq Khan. This gap in perceptions, as described in the latter part of this chapter was one of the principal reasons for growing differences between the two and the fateful decision by Ghulam Ishaq Khan to dismiss the government of this 'thankless' prime minister on 18 April 1993.

I had joined the caretaker cabinet setup by Ghulam Ishaq Khan in August 1990, as finance minister under Ghulam Mustafa Jatoi. I had met Nawaz Sharif many times when I was minister of state for agriculture in Junejo's cabinet from 1985 to 1988, but did not know him intimately. However, after my active role in 1988 to unify two factions of the Muslim League and as a member of the opposition in the Senate, we had developed a strong working relationship. I was in no doubt therefore that I would continue as finance minister in the new cabinet. I had already been re-elected to the Senate in 1988, from Islamabad for a six-year term, which ran until March 1994. Under the constitution up to one-fourth of the federal ministers can be selected from the Senate.

The first meeting of the new cabinet in November 1990 was like a benign earthquake. Nawaz Sharif had come prepared with his agenda. The first priority, he said, would be accorded to economic reforms so that the system is liberated from the tyranny of bureaucratic controls and the economy can begin to move. He wanted six committees to be setup to prepare far-reaching reforms and policy initiatives on: (1) privatization and deregulation, (2) industrial policy, (3) export policy, (4) exchange and payments system, (5) tax policy and resource mobilization, and (6) self reliance.

He wanted recommendations on the composition and terms of reference of these committees the very next day. With difficulty, I persuaded him to give me forty-eight hours. I was used to a rapid pace of work and regarded myself as an expert in meeting deadlines and coordinating difficult assignments. But the impossible deadlines I had to contend with in the next three years became really challenging.

Instead of following the normal practice of appointing the senior-most secretary or the deputy chairman Planning Commission as the head of such committees, I decided to look towards some of my colleagues in the Senate, I asked Saeed Qadir, who was the minister of production in the Ziaul Haq cabinet, to chair the committee on privatization and deregulation, Mazhar Ali the committee on tax policy and resource mobilization and Professor Khurshid Ahmed the committee on self reliance. Yusaf Shirazi from the private sector was requested to chair the committee on industrial policy. Qazi Aleemullah the finance secretary chaired the committee on exchange and payments system.

That evening when I was driving home from office late at night, I fondly remembered my late friend, Jamil Nishtar, at whose initiative, I had returned to Pakistan in April 1984 after resigning from a UN assignment at the level of assistant secretary general which was to run for four more years. He was then the head of the Agricultural Development Bank and was very excited about the prospects of an agricultural breakthrough in the next ten to fifteen years. But he needed to supplement his plans on credit and technology with strong policy support from government. 'If you could join the ministry of agriculture and promote sound macro economic policies in favour of agriculture' he wrote to me, 'the agricultural growth rate could accelerate from less than 3 per cent in the 1970s to over 5 per cent in the next decade.' We actually achieved an agricultural growth rate of 4.6 per cent in the fifteen-year period, 1984–1999, but alas Jamil, having died suddenly on 9 June 1986, only two years after I came back, was not there to celebrate that achievement.

When our common friend, Dr Mahbub ul Haq became finance minister in the first Junejo government in March 1985, Jamil made an impressive speech at the dinner he had hosted to mark his appointment:

Mahbub, now you will enjoy real power in the economic field; these powers are bigger than those exercised by the prime minister. But remember, the real task of the finance minister is to make sound policy decisions and not to exercise power. And these decisions will have an impact not just on your ministry but the entire economy. History will judge you on the merit, integrity, and quality of these decisions.

These words of Jamil Nishtar echoed in my ears once more, as I went to bed that night and remained with me throughout my two terms as finance minister for more than five years.

The first hundred days of the first tenure of Nawaz Sharif would go down as a turning point in the country's economic history, when the most far-reaching reforms were introduced in the country.

When I presented the composition and terms of reference of the six committees to the prime minister forty-eight hours later, he wanted to give them only one month's time to submit their recommendations. I however persuaded him to extend the time limit to two months but he wanted to have at least one meeting with each committee for preliminary discussions within a month.

Privatization

When the prime minister met the committee on privatization and deregulation, Senator Saeed Qadir presented very useful proposals for setting up a proper machinery for the privatization process, i.e. a privatization commission with clear guidelines on the selection of enterprises to be privatized, the criteria for fixing the minimum reserve price below which it would not be sold and a transparent procedure for advertising, opening of bids and finalizing the recommendations for consideration by a cabinet committee on privatization chaired by the finance minister. This infrastructure, once created was followed by all the successive governments in implementing the privatization programme.

When the prime minister issued instructions for the immediate setting up of the privatization commission he also said that at least one bank should be privatized as early as possible. The choice fell on the Muslim Commercial Bank (MCB) because its valuation and other preparatory work had already been completed by the consultants, M/s Rothschild and M/s Ferguson in 1989.

The public announcement for the privatization of MCB was issued on 15 December 1990, with a reserve price of Rs35 per share, bids were received within two weeks and evaluated by a committee chaired by the governor of the State Bank of Pakistan. A letter of acceptance was issued to a group of twelve sponsors at the highest bid price of Rs56 per share on 9 January 1991, after approval by the cabinet committee on privatization.

This dazzling pace of privatization was maintained for the next two years. Sixty-six industrial units and two commercial banks were privatized between January 1991 and June 1993 and considerable preparatory work was undertaken to privatize Pakistan Telecommunication Corporation Limited (PTCL), after restructuring, as well as several units in the powers, oil and gas sectors. It was repeatedly emphasized to all stakeholders that the primary objective of privatization was to eliminate or reduce state intervention in many sub-sectors of the economy.

In at least four important sub-sectors—cement, vegetable oils, fertilizers and automobiles—Public Sector Enterprises (PSEs) had a dominant share of the market. Politically determined pricing policies discouraged investment in these sub-sectors and weakened incentives for modernization and more efficient management. The nationalization of banks in 1974 had not fulfilled initial expectations of more equitable distribution of credit to the agricultural sector and to small borrowers. On the contrary, the nationalized commercial banks had been used extensively as instruments of political patronage. They were heavily overstaffed, and the quality of their service to the public had deteriorated sharply. Privatization of banks, along with a policy of allowing new financial institutions in the private sector, thus represented a major step forward in improving the investment climate in the country and in liberalizing the financial sector.

Certain social objectives such as providing facilities to less-developed areas or disadvantaged people probably had furnished a greater justification for a large public-sector role in providing essential services and infrastructure facilities like telecommunications and power than for setting up or managing industries. Inadequate investment and poor management, however, can cripple even these sectors to the detriment of the economy as a whole. In the case of telecommunication services, for example, the T&T Department in Pakistan could not cope with rising demand because of chronic budgetary constraints. In the forty-year period from 1950 to 1990, the telephone system had a total capacity of 900,000 lines, while the number of people on the waiting list had swelled to 800,000. Despite a 40 per cent return on investment, funds provided from the budget were adequate to add annually only about 30,000 and, in later years, 50,000 lines to the system. Since demand was growing much faster, the waiting list could only grow longer. Similarly, in the power sector, electricity demand increased at about 8 to 10 per cent a year and public sector resources could not finance the capacity expansion required to meet it. The familiar problems of overstaffing and avoidable losses of revenues persisted, the latter a result partly of thefts and partly due to inadequate investment in modernizing the system of transmission and distribution.

Up to a point, solutions to these problems could lie in giving greater autonomy to these organizations and freeing them from budgetary constraints, with authority to borrow in the domestic and international markets in order to finance their expansion programmes. Nevertheless, unless such organizations could determine their prices on commercial principles, they could not earn enough profits to service their loans. Profits also depend on optimum levels of staffing in relation to given levels of output, and on technological and managerial efficiency. As experience has shown in many countries, a carefully planned privatization programme, accompanied by the required regulatory mechanisms, can achieve these objectives largely under public-sector management. The privatization policy in Pakistan therefore included plans to privatize infrastructure, but at a pace slower than that adopted for the industrial sector, mainly in order to evolve an adequate regulatory framework before privatization.

Unlike many other developing countries, Pakistan did not take up privatization, nor in fact the broader policy of deregulation, in response to a financial crisis or under pressure from the IMF or other multilateral agencies. It clearly recognized that public-sector enterprises or banks were not as efficient as comparable enterprises in the private sector and that the national budget could not really afford the growing subsidies, some concealed, some open, to state enterprises and public monopolies such as railways or power companies. The annual review reports of the IMF and the World Bank, and the structural adjustment programme agreed with the IMF in December 1988, therefore contained recommendations to reduce subsidies or to introduce commercial criteria for determining interest rates or power tariffs; but no immediate compulsion for reforms arose from a budgetary or foreign exchange crisis similar to those witnessed in Latin America in the 1980s.

The process of privatization was undertaken by taking workers into confidence. They were not only provided a liberal golden handshake if they opted for voluntary retirement but many of them participated in the employee buy-out plans. At least six such units were sold to employee groups, apart from Allied Bank, which was also purchased by its 7,500 employees. No employee of public sector enterprise lost his or her employment because the new management of these industries undertook expansion plans. Preliminary results show that most of the privatized units have improved their efficiency and profitability with positive results for the economy as a whole.

Exchange and Payments System

The next important committee which completed its work in less than two months was the committee on exchange and payments system chaired by Qazi Alimullah, special secretary, ministry of finance. 'Why do we need all these restrictions on foreign exchange for the citizens and the business community?' Nawaz Sharif told the committee at the very outset: 'If you are travelling abroad, you have to fill a dozen forms to get permission from the State Bank of Pakistan to take along a few hundred dollars; if your son is studying abroad, you need specific permission to remit his fees and living expenses; if you return from abroad with one hundred or two hundred dollars you have to surrender the amount after declaring it on arrival.'

Nawaz Sharif was delighted when the committee submitted its report because the degree of deregulation recommended was beyond even his expectation. Under the reforms announced in February 1991, virtually all restrictions on the movement of foreign exchange were lifted. Anyone could bring in or take out foreign currencies without any questions or restrictions. Pakistanis living abroad could open foreign currency accounts in Pakistan and those living in Pakistan could keep foreign currency in any bank abroad, and to use these accounts as collateral to obtain rupee loans. Business houses could raise foreign currency loans, as long as they did not require a government guarantee. Dealers were allowed to buy and sell foreign currency at the prevailing rate, as in any other country with a free market economy.

The foreign currency deposits built up as a result of these reforms, were very helpful in the short run in financing at least one-fourth of the external payments deficits in the next few years (1992–97), but the absence of deeper reforms in the financial sector delayed the other complementary reforms in the balance of payments. These financial sector reforms were carried out in our second tenure, which started in February 1997.

Tax Reforms and Resource Mobilisation

The committee under Senator Mazhar Ali made radical proposals for reform of the tax system, especially of the income tax. The approach suggested by Hafiz Pasha, secretary of the committee was to extend the tax net through the regime of withholding and presumptive taxes involving deductions at source. The objective was to not only check tax evasion but also to simplify the tax system, reduce corruption and harassment of taxpayers. The prime minister greatly appreciated these proposals and withholding taxes on interest income, dividend income and export income, were introduced.

The reforms led to a phenomenal jump in income tax revenues of over 46 per cent in 1991–92 and 32 per cent in 1992–93. The share of direct taxes in total tax revenue increased and the tax-to-GDP ratio rose significantly. To this day, withholding taxes account for over 60 per cent of income tax collection.

Industrial Policy

A new industrial policy, based on the recommendations of the committee on Industrial Policy, was announced in March 1991 to achieve several important objectives: (1) To diversify the country's industrial base from simple industries like spinning and sugar manufacturing towards more sophisticated and value-added industries like engineering, electronics, and chemical industries. Even in textiles and leather, the scope for producing value-added goods mainly for exports was emphasized. (2) To finance future investment in industries largely by attracting foreign private capital rather than through foreign loans contracted by government, to reduce the country's dependence on foreign aid, and to bring a higher level of technology and managerial skills to Pakistan.

The objective of attracting foreign private investment to supplement and gradually replace official loans was the main pillar of the new economic policy. It would not only move the country towards greater self-reliance, but also improve Pakistan's competitive advantage in the world for value-added industries. Such a policy could thus help to expand and diversify the country's export of manufactured goods.

In its efforts to attract foreign investment, the government announced many new incentives and concessions in 1991. The government allowed foreign investors to hold up to 100 per cent equity in companies operating in Pakistan and gave them permission to repatriate profits and capital without any restrictions. All sectors of economy were opened for foreign investments except some areas like arms or alcoholic beverages. Incentives allowed to Pakistani nationals were also made available to foreign investors without any discrimination.

To take Pakistan to a higher level of industrialization, industry specific incentives were also provided. Plant and machinery not manufactured locally and imported for establishment of key industries, biotechnology, electronics, fertilizers, fibre-optics, and solar energy were exempted from customs duty and sales tax. Additionally, a four-year tax holiday was provided throughout Pakistan to these industries. Machinery and equipment required for certain industries like engineering, cement, dairy, mining and electronics, but not manufactured locally were exempted from customs duty and sales tax.

For export processing units, additional incentives were provided to move gradually towards an export-led growth. Not only were procedures simplified but considerable financial incentives were provided for boosting the country's exports. It was decided that concessions once granted would not be withdrawn. Tariff commission was made effective and the setting up of industries based on imported raw material for re-exports was made easier. Special incentives were provided for value-added exports and non-traditional exports.

The country's non-traditional exports showed a marked rise as a result of these policies despite the continuing global recession. Special Industrial Zones (SIZs) were planned to ensure provision of all infrastructure facilities to industrialists and foreign investors at one place. Credit provision to industries on merit from public sector banks and development finance institutions was facilitated by setting deadlines within which these financial institutions had to either approve or reject financing for a project, with reasons for the decision stated.

The industrial policy adopted, along with measures to bolster private sector, led to an investment boom in the large-scale manufacturing sector, which jumped up in real terms by over 40 per cent in 1991–92 and attained the peak level for the 1990s. The number of new companies listed on the stock market between January 1991 and April 1993 exceeded 200. Some of the capacity created in this period became available for the supply response to expansionary policies in recent years.

Infrastructure

The second important prerequisite for industrialization and foreign investment, apart from a positive and dynamic policy framework, is adequate infrastructure. Recognizing the adverse impact of past neglect in these sub-sectors of the economy, the government initiated several infrastructure projects by according high priority to the development of telecommunications, roads, air services, electricity, ports, and shipping.

A key element in the success of this policy was the policy of privatization. By opening up many sectors previously reserved for the public sector, such as telecommunications, power generation, air services, ports and shipping, the government was able to implement a much bigger programme in these sectors that would have been possible only with budgetary funds. Simultaneously, the government reviewed and improved the policy framework for investment in gas, petroleum, ports and shipping.

Telecommunications

Nobody believed the announcement that all the pending applications for telephones would be cleared within twenty months. With the expansion of the telephone network at an unprecedented pace, the government was able to more than double the number of telephone connections within a period of two years from 800,000 in 1991 to 1.7 million in 1993 (and to 4 million in 1999). In fact, during the period from December 1990 to June 1993, Pakistan Telecommunication Corporation was able to install more telephones than all the telephones installed in the previous forty-three years of Pakistan's history.

The telegraph and telephone department was converted into an autonomous corporation, Pakistan Telecommunication Corporation Ltd. (PTCL). Its efficiency increased manifold and it was made independent of the government budget, making further expansion easier by entering into contractual arrangements with international companies to install new telephone systems in different regions. As a result, the number of telephones per 100 persons quadrupled—from 1 to 4. This ratio was again doubled to 8 phones per 100 persons by 1999, which is the Asian average.

The telecommunication sector was also deregulated. Services like paging, pay phones, telephone directory, and radio equipment were opened to the private sector. Optical fibre link was initiated and digital telex facilities introduced. The most exciting feature of the developments in the telecom sector was the introduction of the state of art technology notably the cell phone technology, which was to play such a dominant role in the years to come.

Electricity

Inadequate investment in the power sector had not only retarded the pace of investment and production in the country but also caused hardship to the people through persistent load shedding. In the very first years after coming to power, the government almost doubled the total financial allocation to Water and Power Development Authority (WAPDA) from Rs12 billion in 1990–91 to Rs23 billion in 1991–92 to enable it to accelerate its programmes for power generation and transmission. As a result the total power generation capacity in the country increased by 36 per cent from 7,770 MW in June 1990 to 10,600 MW in June 1993. About 1.5 million new electricity connections were provided during this period and 6,500 new villages and rural settlements were electrified.

Roads

Far-reaching changes were undertaken in the system of building roads in Pakistan. To overcome delays in approval of road related projects and to make the system of implementation more effective, the National Highway Council was setup under the chairmanship of the prime minister. Similarly, a National Highway Authority (NHA) was established to undertake the implementation of road related projects. NHA prioritized the country's major road development projects and undertook implementation within the national resources at a very fast pace. Pakistan Motorway (M2) from Lahore to Islamabad was a key project of that period and was implemented in record time.

Apart from dualizing the national highway (N-5) joining Karachi-Hyderabad-Multan-Lahore-Rawalpindi-Peshawar and Torkham, the pace of construction on the Indus Highway project was also accelerated. It envisaged a second highway linking Karachi with Peshawar. This much-delayed project when completed would shorten the distance between Karachi and Central Asia via Peshawar by 400 km.

Social Sectors

The most important item of the social agenda was the launching of the Social Action Programme (SAP) in 1992. It responded to the urgent need to improve basic health and education services, expand the provision of safe drinking water and promote population welfare. The programme was aimed at rectifying the past neglect of the social sectors both in terms of financial allocations and implementation capacity. In addition to the increased funding of both development and current expenditures, SAP tried to tackle a number of bottlenecks in implementation. These included such constraints as finding adequate numbers of female staff in rural areas, access of girls to schools, and private sector participation.

The SAP was aimed at taking the fruits of development to those who lived at the lower strata of society, especially in the rural areas, by addressing the imbalances between: (i) primary and secondary education, (ii) rural and urban facilities, (iii) male and female education, and (iv) between current and development expenditure.

The SAP prepared in close cooperation with the four provincial governments, doubled the total government expenditure in these sectors. The government financed this additional expenditure on SAP by providing 50 per cent of additional expenditure itself, 25 per cent from the provincial budgets, and 25 per cent from international donors.

Plans were under way to setup a high level 'SAP Authority' in each province for the implementation of SAP because the education and health infrastructure, with traditional departments under a grade 20 officer who was in practice transferred almost every year, could not handle such a large programme. But with the dismissal of the government in April 1993, these plans could not be implemented and despite larger allocations, the physical and qualitative results were disappointing. Primary school enrolment did in fact double in the 1990s from 10 to 20 million and more than doubled for girl students from 3.7 million to 8.7 million, contributing to a rise in the rate of literacy from 30 to 45 per cent, yet the programme was terminated a year after the military took over in October 1999 because of administrative and institutional weaknesses in the implementation of the programme.

A new education policy was announced by the government on 20 December 1992 by the education minister, Fakhar Imam for the next decade. The policy aimed at universal primary education, fulfilling the basic learning needs, within ten years. Secondary education was to be diversified into general and vocational streams along with expansion of graduate and post-graduate level courses, shifting education from supply to demand orientation and reforming the examination system. Other key elements of the policy were to open up avenues for participation of the private sector in higher education.

Self-Employment Programme

Under the self-employment programme about 35,000 loans involving a total amount of Rs4,500 million were sanctioned in 1992–93 to enable educated youth to setup small scale industrial and other enterprises. These loans ranging from Rs50,000 to Rs300,000 provided permanent employment to about 90,000 persons, apart from providing goods and services for the economy.

A public transport scheme was started in February 1992 to provide loans to unemployed persons to buy yellow taxicabs, coaches, and buses. In the first eighteen months loans totalling Rs23,100 million for 95,000 vehicles were approved. It is estimated that each taxi provided employment to at least three persons, and a larger vehicle employed directly or indirectly five to ten persons. The transport scheme thus provided additional employment opportunities to about 400,000 persons, besides meeting the growing transport needs of the country. But in the second year of its implementation the yellow cab scheme attracted considerable criticism. In some banks, like United Bank Limited, the employees union had influenced the managers to sanction many loans to fake applicants. Under pressure from car importers, built-up cars, including luxury cars were included in the scheme for duty free imports. That not only adversely affected the local industry but also damaged the image of the scheme. Despite these shortcomings, the overall benefits of the scheme on employment and on providing improved public transport were considerable.

Bait-ul-Mal

A Bait-ul-Mal scheme was launched with Rs2,000 million in 1991 to provide financial assistance to widows and very low income families. Food stamps scheme for people earning less than Rs1,000 per month was also launched to enable them to buy their food at reasonable prices.

Distribution of Lands to Haris

As a part of its policy to give a due share in the distribution of assets to low income people, a scheme was initiated to distribute government owned lands to *haris* in Sindh. This difficult task was undertaken despite the resistance of big landlords. *Haris* were also provided with loans to start cultivating their lands and elaborate plans were chalked out to make this exercise as beneficial as possible for people who had been disenfranchised for generations. A total of 300,000 acres of government land was distributed to 50,000 landless *haris* between 1991 and 1993.

Macro-Economic Management

The Pakistan economy withstood very unfavourable external circumstances like difficulties emanating from the Gulf crisis of 1991, a prolonged global recession, and unprecedented floods in September 1992, and performed reasonably well:

- The annual growth rate for the three-year period from July 1990 to June 1993 was 5.6 per cent, 7.7 per cent, and 2.3 per cent respectively, yielding an average of 5.2 per cent.
- Gross investment in the economy jumped by 70 per cent from Rs162 billion in 1990 to Rs277 billion or 20.3 per cent of GDP in 1992–93. The corresponding increase in gross domestic savings was from 10.5 per cent in 1988–89 to 12.2 per cent in 1992–93.
- The general index of share prices went up sharply by 116 per cent over these three years. The corresponding increase in aggregate market capitalization during the period was 256 per cent.
- The average growth in exports during the three-year period was 14 per cent per annum.

The net impact of the far-reaching economic reforms to liberalize the economy was however neutralized to some extent, by macro-economic problems. Although the average growth in the period 1990–1993 was over 5 per cent and total investment at 20 per cent of GDP was the highest for that period, the government's inability to control the fiscal deficit meant a higher rate of inflation and balance of payment pressures. With larger expenditure on infrastructure and the social sectors, the budget deficit remained at 8 per cent of GDP, creating inflationary pressures and raised the current account deficit to over 7 per cent of GDP in 1992–93.

It is somewhat ironic to recall that the much-delayed economic liberalization programme of 1991–93 coincided with the Pressler sanctions imposed by the United States in October 1990 due to Pakistan's nuclear policy. Any economic liberalization programme has to be accompanied by larger investment in infrastructure so that the additional demand for electricity, telephones, and transport generated by the higher level of investment can be met. Pakistan undertook these investments in the expectation that multilateral and bilateral donor agencies, which had been urging a programme of economic liberalization for so long, would support the required investments. But the stoppage of American assistance under the Pressler Amendment reduced the net flow of foreign assistance in terms of new commitments from $3.4 billion in 1990 to $1.9 billion in 1993.

The stoppage of American military assistance also had a strong impact on the defence budget which had already reached 6.9 per cent of GDP in the final year of the Zia era (1988–99). The effort to finance military equipment and spare parts, previously available from USA on soft terms, as well as from other commercial sources, created a serious strain on the federal budget.

Another consequence of the reforms programme was its effect on the rate of industrial growth. As tariffs were reduced to shift investment from inefficient and over-protected industries to more efficient value-added industries, many industrial units closed down and the rate of industrial growth started slowing down from an average of 8 per cent in the 1980s to around 4 per cent in the 1990s. That brought down the overall GDP growth rate from 6.5 per cent in the 1980s to 4.6 per cent in the 1990s. The expectation that the potential loss of production from inefficient industrial units would be compensated by higher production from new investment was thwarted by many unexpected developments—the Asian economic crisis of the 1997–98, the sanctions imposed on Pakistan after the nuclear test of May 1998, and the image of recurring political instability due to premature dismissal of elected governments in 1988, 1990, 1993 and 1996.

Inter-Provincial Accords

As a part of the reform process, Nawaz Sharif identified two other issues of vital importance. One was the 70-year old dispute among the provinces, notably Sindh and Punjab, over the sharing of Indus water. The second was the sharing of revenues between the federal and provincial governments. 'We cannot strengthen the foundations of our federal structure and create inter-provincial harmony unless we resolve these fundamental issues,' he said while opening the first meeting of the newly appointed Council of Common Interests on 12 January 1991 and urged the chief ministers to reach an agreement on the water issue within three months. The inter-provincial Water Accord was signed on 16 March 1991 and the unanimous report of the National Finance

Commission was signed on 9 April 1991, establishing two important milestones in the country's economic history.

A number of committees and commissions had been setup in the past—the Fazl-e-Akbar Commission in 1970 and Justice Abdul Haleem Committee in 1983—to 'find a permanent solution of the water issue on a fair and equitable basis, after taking into consideration the legitimate interests of the provinces on one hand and the overall national interest on the other.' But they could not reach a consensus even though the differences were of the order of only 1.5 or 2.0 MAF (million acre feet), out of a total of 126 MAF of usable water. The CCI at its meeting on 12 January setup an inter-provincial committee[1] to examine all previous reports and formulate recommendations on the apportionment of water and submit its recommendations within thirty days. The committee identified the main issues and proposed options which were considered by the four chief ministers at Lahore on 3 March 1991 and again at Karachi on 16 March 1991, when a final consensus agreement was reached and signed. A key element of the agreement was the formula for the distribution of additional supplies from future storages and floods, under which Punjab and Sindh were given an equal share of 37 per cent, with NWFP 14 per cent and Balochistan 12 per cent. This was a considerable improvement for the smaller Provinces over the distribution of existing water supplies in which Punjab had a share of almost 50 per cent, and Sindh 42 per cent, NWFP and Balochistan receiving only 5 and 3 per cent respectively. Nawaz Sharif had discreetly persuaded Ghulam Hyder Wyne, the chief minister of Punjab, to accommodate the concerns of the smaller provinces in order to reach a consensus.

The 1990 National Finance Commission was originally setup on 23 July 1990, but before it could hold its first meeting, the PPP government was dismissed on 6 August 1990. The commission was therefore reconstituted on 30 December 1990, with the new federal and provincial finance ministers and new non-official members.

Two earlier commissions, setup in 1979 and 1985, had failed to reach a consensus. The 1979 commission worked for two years but could not submit a formal report because the 1981 census had changed the assumptions on which its recommendations were based. The ad hoc arrangements already in force were therefore continued with some modifications through an order issued in 1983. Similarly, the 1985 commission held nine meetings over three years but before it could finish its work and evolve a consensus, the elected government was dismissed in May 1988. The next government that assumed power in 1988 did not hold any meeting of this commission until the life of the commission expired in 1990.

One important lesson that emerged from this experience was the futility of exchanging technical arguments among bureaucrats over long periods of time. If there is broad consensus among the top political leaders of the country on the main issues involved, then it is easier for the civil servants concerned to evolve necessary formulae to implement the consensus. After the 1991 commission held its first meeting on 16 January 1991, I informed the prime minister that the two key issues were, (1) the payment of development surcharge on gas, and (2) the net hydel power profits to the provinces. Despite a clear provision in Article 161 of the 1973 constitution, these obligations had not been met in the preceding seventeen years. The prime minister readily agreed that instead of picking up large revenue gaps in the budgets of NWFP and Balochistan through special grants and subventions, it would be more prudent to assign permanent sources of revenues to the provinces, in accordance with the constitution. This decision made it possible for the National Finance Commission to evolve its historic consensus within only three months, to enable the provinces to increase their non-development expenditure at the rate of 14 per cent every year.

For NWFP, the projected transfer of Rs6 billion on account of electricity profits virtually doubled the total federal transfer to Rs12.4 billion in 1991–92 leaving the province with a surplus of Rs1.2 billion.

The government of Balochistan, according to the estimates presented by the commission, was to have an even bigger surplus of Rs2,444 million in 1991–92, after the transfer of Rs4,993 million on account of gas development surcharge.

The Curse of Political Instability

Nawaz Sharif started his first tenure as prime minister in November 1990, with a comfortable political base. The IJI coalition of which he was the head had secured in the October 1990 elections, 106 seats out of 200 against 45 secured by the Opposition Alliance, Pakistan Democratic Alliance (PDA) of which PPP was the main party. IJI had also won a very large majority in the Punjab (208 out of 250 seats) and the largest proportion of seats in NWFP (32 out of 80 seats). By joining the MQM in Sindh and certain small parties in Balochistan, the IJI managed to form the provincial governments in all the four provinces. This was a considerable advantage for Nawaz Sharif, when compared to the tenure of Benazir Bhutto who had to face confrontation with governments of two provinces—Punjab under Nawaz Sharif and Balochistan under Nawab Akbar Bugti. This confrontation eventually led to her downfall in August 1990. Nawaz Sharif also had smooth working relationship with the president, the army and the bureaucracy. The Afghan war was nearing its end with the departure of the Soviet troops.

Despite these positive factors, Nawaz Sharif was unable to complete his term and was dismissed by President Ghulam Ishaq Khan on 18 April 1993. The principal reason for this unfortunate end of Nawaz Sharif's first tenure was a serious misunderstanding with the president. Mistrust between the two actually started soon after Nawaz Sharif took over. The main reasons can be summarized as follows:

- Nawaz Sharif was a great believer in the dynamism of the private sector and wanted to deregulate and liberalize the economy as fast as possible, whereas Ghulam Ishaq Khan had an inherent mistrust of private business. He would have preferred a much slower and measured pace of reforms.
- Nawaz Sharif hated rules and regulations and wanted to throw out all the age-old restrictions and lengthy procedures for the approval of projects and their implementation. Ghulam Ishaq Khan having drafted many of the rules over the years was a stickler for rules and was very upset when rules were not followed strictly or short cuts were adopted.
- Nawaz Sharif loved mega projects and dramatic announcements of new initiatives because of their political impact. But Ghulam Ishaq Khan was by nature very cautious and did not want major commitment of funds at the cost of fiscal stability.

• Ghulam Ishaq Khan kept sending notes or comments to the prime minister whenever he felt any rule or procedure was being violated or a decision was made without following the rules of business. Nawaz Sharif was invariably annoyed over these notes. 'I have received a mandate from the electorate; the President has only contingency powers under the constitution, with no responsibility for day-to-day policy making; so why should he interfere?' was his common refrain.

Ghulam Ishaq Khan was also guided by the vivid memory of the role he had played in the dismissal of the first Benazir government, thus paving the way for Nawaz Sharif to step into power. He also felt that he had decades of rich experience in administration and in managing the economy and Nawaz Sharif should look up to him for guidance and advice. But this model did not fit into either Nawaz Sharif's impulsive personality or his political ambitions.

These strong differences in views, style, and substance somehow remained under the surface for the first two years of Nawaz Sharif's government, but suddenly exploded into the open by the end of 1992, when Ghulam Ishaq Khan discovered that Nawaz Sharif did not want him to be re-elected as president in November 1993, when his five years term expired. There was a cabinet meeting in December 1992, at which Nawaz Sharif advised his cabinet colleagues not to make any statements about the president's election, which was still eleven months away. Surprisingly this advice was prominently published in most of the newspapers next morning. When I met Ghulam Ishaq Khan about ten days later along with a director of the International Monetary Fund (IMF), he asked me to stay on after the meeting. He was quite angry. 'There were only two statements from Ilahi Bux Soomro and Ijazul Haq in support of my re-election in November 1993. In stopping such statements, Nawaz Sharif has revealed his real '*niyat*' (intention)'. Ishaq Khan had already spoken to me on this subject complaining about some decision or the other, just as Nawaz Sharif had also complained about the difficulties of dealing with a president who acted like a headmaster. But this time Ghulam Ishaq Khan's attitude and tone was much harsher. This relationship, I said to myself after the meeting, has now crossed the limits of tolerance and acceptability.

A brief account of the events leading to the dismissal of the first Nawaz Sharif government on 18 April 1993, its restoration by the Supreme Court on 26 May, and the renewed crisis in the month of June, leading to the resignations of both Nawaz Sharif and Ghulam Ishaq Khan was recorded in my diary at that time. These entries are reproduced below:

24 April 1993

The crisis leading to the dismissal of Nawaz Sharif government and the dissolution of the National Assembly had started simmering in January 1993. No one could foresee at the time that it would become so serious in such a short time or lead to such uncontrollable consequences.'

As one correspondent wrote in the *Nation* on 16 April, the roots of the discord actually started in early 1991, when Ijlal Zaidi was sacked. Other Ishaq loyalists were also elbowed out or sidetracked (Sahabzada Yaqub-Khan, Roedad Khan, and Aziz Munshi). Nawaz Sharif's failure to play to Ishaq's ego was the key problem. But it was not a benign omission. I think Nawaz Sharif wanted to follow the logic of the constitution and relegate Ishaq to a constitutional head (a mistake Junejo had committed in relation to Zia).

I think initially it was the potential threat of army chief, Aslam Beg's ambitions that kept the two together throughout 1991–92. By comparison, General Asif Nawaz's ambitions and his initiative to crush MQM through the Sindh operation in June 1992 created more problems for Nawaz Sharif. Soon after this, PPP also decided to shift its guns from Ishaq to Nawaz Sharif, culminating in the Long March of November 1992, which fizzled out. This gave confidence to Nawaz Sharif to strengthen his position for the remainder of his term, by announcing on the Senate floor on 28 February 1993, his intention to repeal Art. 58(2b) of the constitution to curtail president's power to dissolve the National Assembly. In fact it was due to this power that most of the opposition leaders and the armed forces looked towards the president rather than the prime minister. He was sure PPP would support his move to repeal this provision validated by the Eighth Amendment.

The situation was complicated by two unexpected deaths of General Asif Nawaz on 9 January 1993 and Mohammad Khan Junejo on

18 March 1993. The first brought into open the rift between the prime minister and president on the appointment of a new chief of army staff and the second gave an opportunity to the anti-Nawaz group in the Muslim League to start a chain of resignations from 27 March onwards, with open encouragement from the president, as was clear from the inclusion of Anwar Saifullah (his son-in-law) in the first group of resignations along with Hamid Nasir Chatta and Haji Gulsher Khan.

Because of my own delicate position, I did not make any major mediation efforts in January–February, but on 16 March, Chaudhry Nisar told me to find out if there was any way out. I met Roedad Khan the same evening. He agreed that there was need for re-establishing communications and for diffusing the tension. The next morning, soon after a meeting in the Central Board of Revenue, I rode with Nawaz Sharif to the airport (he was going to Sukkur) and told him that preparations for dissolving the assemblies were going on and lists of caretakers were being drawn up. He said that he was in politics and therefore always ready for elections. I asked, 'But why have them two years earlier?' If he could complete his tenure, he would have a good chance to win again on the basis of his record. Now everyone would turn against him. There would be an open charge sheet from the President. Those at the margin would desert him. The Muslim League party will also be better organized in two years. 'So why now? Just because Ishaq is annoyed? That's not much of a reason'.

He agreed to meet the president soon to clarify matters. The next day, on 18 March, Mohammad Khan Junejo died and at the funeral, Hamid Nasir Chatta kept them apart, spreading even more rumours about the widening gulf. They finally met on 21 March exactly eight weeks after their meeting in mid-January regarding chief of army staff's appointment, but it was already too late.

From 26 March to 2 April, I was in the UK and then Germany with the prime minister. I again emphasized that his real political fight was with PPP and not with Ishaq Khan. He has to keep him happy, as long as he has the Eighth Amendment power to dissolve the National Assembly. His mind accepted these arguments but his heart (and instincts) was not in line.

On 3 April, when Nawaz Sharif returned from Germany, his father literally ordered him to go and reconcile with Ishaq Khan. He did, and yielded on both the key points, but it was too late. Ishaq Khan had made up his mind to remove him. He was not prepared to give him another chance. His next meeting on 14 April was the last chance. He briefed the cabinet that afternoon and said there would be a joint press release, and a draft had been sent to the presidency. Instead of accepting that draft, a terse eight-line release came out of the President's House saying the president had told the prime minister what to do to resolve national and international issues and he should report to the president on the actions taken. This, if accepted, would have meant political suicide for Nawaz Sharif. So, on the 15 April, the decision was made to go for confrontation. That led to the prime minister's famous speech of 17 April and the dissolution order of the president on 18 April.

Six days earlier, i.e. on 12 April, I was in Karachi to inaugurate the Bear Stern's new branch office in Pakistan and to address the customs staff on 13 April. I suddenly realized the gravity of the situation and called the president's military secretary to seek an appointment. The appointment was fixed for 17 April at 10 a.m. but had to be shifted to 3 p.m. because Nawaz Sharif asked me to preside over the foundation stone laying ceremony of the new Honda car plant near Lahore that morning on his behalf.

My meeting with the president was very tense. I told him that political uncertainty was not good for the economy, foreign investments, or aid prospects. With great difficulty, I had lined up additional support from the IMF and World Bank in preparation for a donor's consortium meeting in Paris on 22 April. Nothing should be done to deprive the country of these resources.

He said the ball was in the prime minister's court. 'I have already told him what is to be done. So many ministers had resigned. The real issue is not his re-election but the viability of the system'.

I told him, his assessment of the government's performance, particularly in the economic field and regarding privatization was not objective or even fair. In fact, the period 1990–93 will be remembered for its far-reaching reforms which were overdue for two decades. He said I didn't know all the facts. I replied, 'You are surrounded by disgruntled elements and defeated politicians, who are giving you wrong advice.' He said that he was not so naïve as to be misled.

Finally, I asked what was the object of all this? 'Whom do you want to bring in place of Nawaz Sharif? If the strategy is to bring back PPP, then it is working very well. Otherwise, I don't see the purpose.'

He said, 'What is wrong with that?' (bringing back PPP) and I literally sank in my chair, as I could not imagine he would forget 'Go Baba go' so soon. Before I could say anything, he raised his voice and said, 'You are taking undue advantage of our friendship to ask such questions.' I said I was saying these things because I was his well-wisher and what he was doing would not be good for him or the country. As I got up to leave, I could not restrain myself from saying, 'You have had such an illustrious and spotless career but now you are spoiling your 'aqibat' (life hereafter) by diving so deep in politics and dismissing another elected government in less than three years.'

After the meeting, I rushed to the PM House to telephone Nawaz Sharif on the hotline. But he was locked up working on his speech. In his place, Shahbaz Sharif came over the telephone. I told him this was not the right time for the prime minister to make a speech. He should first call the National Assembly, get a vote of confidence, and then make a defiant speech. 'It is too late,' Shahbaz said, 'He is bent upon addressing the nation today.' Three hours later, Nawaz Sharif made his historic speech which according to some observers proved a turning point in his political career: 'I would not accept dictation from the presidency. I would uphold the principles of democracy and the constitution,' he thundered.

The next day all the cabinet colleagues had assembled in the PM House, expecting the retaliatory blow from the president. It came at 9 p.m. Ishaq Khan spoke under great strain, reading out the charge sheet for dismissing the prime minister and dissolving the National Assembly. The greatest surprise, of course, was the inclusion of Asif Ali Zardari in the caretaker government the next day.

On 19 April, the day after the dismissal of the government, the PML council met in Islamabad and elected Nawaz Sharif as president in place of Junejo. That decision marked an important milestone in the life of the party since only four years later Muslim League emerged as the largest political party in the country winning more than two-thirds of the seats in the National Assembly in February 1997.

There was great excitement in the council meeting which had convened at only four days' notice. Almost all members had arrived in

Islamabad the previous evening, just before Ishaq Khan made his dismissal speech. If the meeting had been a day later, the Punjab government would have ruthlessly blocked the entry of at least half the council members.

The next day Nawaz Sharif left for Lahore by Awami Express and was greeted by cheering crowds at every railway station.

In the past six days, since the dismissal of Nawaz Sharif's government, I have been trying to reach an objective assessment of these events. Where did the prime minister go wrong? What were his serious mistakes?

That he was a strong and decisive leader was his best quality. Without this quality, we would not have been able to implement these important economic reforms with such speed. He also had the instincts of a populist leader and that dictated his priorities: motorways, self-employment scheme, yellow taxi scheme, flood relief, visit to victims, and land distribution in Sindh. But whatever he did, he pursued the task with excessive zeal thus making the timetable unrealistic and the costs unnecessarily high.

His greatest defect from my point of view was his lack of financial discipline. It was not easy for me and the rest of the economic team to restrain him all the time. But I think we managed to keep the slippages within reasonable limits and did not allow the fiscal deficit to get out of control. Basically, he had the mandate and like Z.A. Bhutto, he was gambling with a little inflation in return for tangible infrastructure. But the economic situation as a whole did not provide the fiscal space for too many mega projects.

In the end he overplayed his hand. He didn't realize he couldn't trust PPP in reducing the presidential powers. His announcement on the Senate floor (on 28 February 1993) that he had started the process to delete clause 58.2(b) of the constitution (power of the president to dissolve the National Assembly) was a very ill-advised move. His tendency to condone the irregularities of some of his own colleagues probably also played a part in Ishaq's decision.

Despite these problems, there was no justification, legal or moral for Ishaq's action. As I have pointed out in the notes prepared by me in the past three days for Khalid Anwar to challenge the dismissal in the Supreme Court, there was no constitutional crisis or any economic justification for such drastic action.

A major area of research and study to which Sartaj Aziz devoted his time and effort was the development experience of the People's Republic of China. He visited China 14 times starting in 1967 during the Cultural Revolution. These photographs record some of his visits to China

On a visit to China in December 1967, as part of Pakistan's economic delegation.
Sartaj Aziz is standing behind Prime Minister Zhou Enlai
Photo courtesy: Author's personal collection

With the Finance Minister, People's Republic of China, November 1991
Photo courtesy: Author's personal collection

Arriving to sign an agreement with the Finance Minister, People's Republic of China,
November 1991
Photo courtesy: Author's personal collection

Signing an agreement with the Finance Minister, People's Republic
of China, November 1991
Photo courtesy: Author's personal collection

After signing an agreement with the Finance Minister,
People's Republic of China, November 1991
Photo courtesy: Author's personal collection

With Zhu Liang, Chairman, Foreign Affairs Committee of the National People's
Congress, November 1995
Photo courtesy: Author's personal collection

With Madam Li-Shuzheng, Head of Headquarters of Communist Party of China
November 1995
Photo courtesy: Author's personal collection

Prime Minister Nawaz Sharif 's visit to China, March 1991
Photo courtesy: Author's personal collection

But going from an analysis of the past to prospects for the future, it is difficult to make any firm predictions. Each one of the scenarios leads to possibilities that may leave the country in a more difficult bind than the assumed crisis of mid-April that led to the dissolution.

The first question is whether PDA will stick to the caretaker setup if provincial assemblies are not dissolved. They are gambling on winning the next elections and will not like to lose electoral support which their actions have already eroded.

The next big question is whether the Supreme Court will uphold the dissolution. It will start hearing Nawaz Sharif's appeal from 26 April and there is a strong possibility it may declare it unconstitutional. That will throw the whole system in a terrible spin.

Restoration of Assembly

The Supreme Court proceedings challenging the dismissal of the assembly by President Ishaq Khan on 18 April 1993 were truly historical in nature. The level of presentation was very high and all those involved realized the momentous nature of the case and came out with their best. But the star was our chief lawyer, Khalid Anwar. I spent long hours with him and his team (Akram Shaikh, Ashtar Ausaf and occasionally assisted by Khalid Ishaq)) to prepare material on the charges levelled by Ghulam Ishaq Khan. I also prepared a long written brief on these subjects. Khalid Anwar was really impressive in his grasp of the main issues.

I attended almost all the sessions and took long notes of the main arguments because it was a highly educative exercise. The atmosphere was very tense and charged. Finally, when the ten to one judgment of the Supreme Court was announced on 26 May by Chief Justice Nasim Hassan Shah to restore the assembly, it was one of the most exciting and popular political news. There was widespread jubilation throughout the country. About 10,000 people thronged the residence of Chaudhry Shujaat, where six of us, surrounding Nawaz Sharif, heard the decision just after 3 p.m. At 4 p.m. everyone went to Faisal Mosque for thanksgiving prayers because the crowd could not be accommodated on Street 72. At eight o'clock, we had a cabinet meeting to regain control of the government machinery. I would never forget the overwhelming feeling of relief, joy, and excitement, which I had that night when I finally retired at midnight.

The month of June was dominated by budget preparation and approval through the National Assembly. The whole process was squeezed into twenty days instead of the usual six weeks and therefore quite arduous.

Even before the budget session ended, the second phase of the confrontation between Ishaq Khan and Nawaz Sharif had started. The Supreme Court verdict had revived the National Assembly, but the provincial governments under Manzoor Wattoo in Punjab and Mir Afzal Khan in NWFP, were hostile to Nawaz Sharif. Ishaq Khan therefore started mulling over the possibility of intensifying confrontation between the federal government and these two provincial governments to provide renewed justification for dissolving the assembly. He had not forgotten or forgiven the humiliation he had suffered with the verdict of the Supreme Court to set aside his order.

Instead of countering this game plan with tact and patience, Nawaz Sharif followed his aggressive instincts and decided to impose governor's rule in the Punjab. Amid high tension, he got a resolution passed by a joint session of parliament on 30 June to this effect, dissolving the provincial assembly and appointing Mian Azhar as the new governor. Ignoring legal advice, he did not send this resolution to the president for assent, as required under the constitution, before sending it to the provincial government for implementation. The provincial government refused and the army, under the president's advice, declined to intervene.

This naturally led to a constitutional deadlock. A series of meetings were held between the president, the prime minister and the chief of army staff, Gen. Abdul Waheed Kakar. Eventually it was decided that both would quit their respective offices—Nawaz Sharif by advising the president, under Article 58.2(a) to dissolve the National Assembly, and Ghulam Ishaq Khan by resigning under Article 43.

The arrangements under these decisions to be implemented were not easy to work out. The most difficult part was to reach agreement on the caretaker prime minister. General (retd) Majid Malik and I were assisting Nawaz Sharif in these negotiations and had many meetings with General Javed Ashraf Qazi (DG, ISI), who was to consult the PPP leadership in an effort to reach a consensus. Contrary to popular perception, I had not suggested the name of Moeenuddin Qureshi. It was put forward by Nawaz Sharif himself following a suggestion from a close friend in Washington. At the penultimate meeting in the presidency, when the agreed transitional arrangements were almost final, Ishaq Khan asked, 'We have finalized this road map but do we have a caretaker prime minister?' At this General Qazi said, 'There seems to be an agreement on Moeenuddin Qureshi but we don't know how to find him.' For me this news was a surprise but I said, I can find him, because he talked to me from Karachi last week, before proceeding to China.

When I contacted Beijing I was told he had left for Bangkok two days earlier. The embassy in Bangkok reported that he had just left for Singapore. Finally, I caught up with him at Singapore. He was surprised. 'Sartaj, you know, I am suffering from cancer and have to enter hospital in ten days for the next round of chemotherapy. How can I accept in such a state of health?' When he did not agree despite my persuasion, I informed both Nawaz Sharif and General Qazi that he had declined on health grounds.

Early next morning, on 18 July, I was woken up by a call from Singapore. Moeen Qureshi was on the line: 'I have been persuaded to accept. Can you now make arrangements for me to get to Islamabad by 6 p.m. the time fixed for swearing in?' Apparently the friend who had suggested his name in the first place had called him and said, 'Don't worry about chemotherapy. Once you are prime minister all arrangements will take shape automatically.'

I immediately telephoned General Qazi to tell him that Moeen Qureshi had accepted. He said, 'But my man has just left to inform Justice Haleem, the next choice, that he will be sworn in at 6 p.m.' I telephoned Nawaz Sharif who said, 'Please insist on Moeen Qureshi.' I don't know whether General Qazi's message had reached Justice Haleem before he withdrew it but I got his confirmation in about ten minutes.

That day, 18 July was a Sunday, so it was not possible to charter a plane. The Pakistan High Commissioner in Singapore told me, 'But there is a flight via Bangkok which would reach Karachi at 6 p.m.' From there a special plane could take him to Islamabad in two hours. The time of the swearing in ceremony was accordingly rescheduled from 6 to 10 p.m.

Moeen eventually arrived at the Islamabad airport just after 9 p.m. and the ceremony took place just before midnight. Another thirty minutes' delay would have required changes in all the documents because they were prepared for 18 July.

The final document entitled 'Agreed Arrangements on the Transition dated 18 July 1993' reads as follows:

It is hereby agreed between the signatories of this document and its annexes/appendices that:

a. PM shall in his discretion advise dissolution of National Assembly on 18 July 1993. The President shall dissolve the Assembly the same day and the PM and his Cabinet shall cease to hold office.
b. The present PM shall not be eligible for any caretaker appointment.
c. The President shall give oath of office to the caretaker PM and depart from the scene.
d. President shall resign and avail four months leave after the effective date of laying down his office, i.e. w.e.f. 19 July 1993 (FN).
e. Chairman Senate shall takeover as Acting President.
f. All care-taker appointees in the Federal and Provincial Governments shall be non-political persons and shall not take part in the forthcoming general elections. (2) Caretaker PM, Chief Ministers, Governors and Acting Governors shall be as per Annex-1 attached and they shall not take part in the forthcoming general elections.
g. General elections for National Assembly shall be held on 6 Oct and for Provincial Assemblies on 9 Oct 1993 with the assistance of the Armed Forces.
h. All 'modalities' given out at Annex-2 and its appendices attached shall be deemed to be part of the agreed arrangements.
i. These arrangements shall be unalterable till the installation of new elected governments at the Centre and in all the Provinces as a result of general elections.

It was signed by President Ghulam Ishaq Khan; Prime Minister Nawaz Sharif; Chairman Senate Wasim Sajjad; and Caretaker Prime Minister Moeenuddin Qureshi.

Decisions about the choice of caretaker governors and chief ministers were not so difficult. We reached a consensus within about two hours on Lt.-Gen. (retd) Mohammad Iqbal, Hakim Muhammad Said, Lt.-Gen. (retd) Khurshid Ali Khan and Brig. (retd) Rahim

Durrani as governors of Punjab, Sindh, NWFP and Balochistan respectively and on Sheikh Manzoor Ilahi, Justice (retd) Ali Madad Shah, Mufti Abbas and Naseerullah Mengal as chief ministers. These were listed in annexure-I to the transition document.

The next day I spent several hours with Moeen Qureshi to help him finalize the list of his cabinet members. Syed Babar Ali joined the caretaker government as finance minister but Moeen Qureshi also invited Shahid Javed Burki to join his team as economic adviser. He soon launched many initiatives and policy changes. These were basically sound moves in the right direction but led to some criticism in the press that the main task of a caretaker government is to hold elections and not to make basic changes in policy.

On 19 August 1993, Moeen Qureshi addressed the nation on the media, recounted the economic problems facing the country and said, 'These problems cannot be ascribed to any one government, they are the cumulative results of the acts of omission and commission in the past two decades.' He then announced a series of measures to reduce the budget deficit by raising utility charges and cutting subsidies.

When Moeen Qureshi appeared in the Senate a fortnight later—he was criticized by Professor Khurshid Ahmad and some other members for going beyond the mandate of a caretaker government and imposing additional burden on the masses. He reacted by recalling how difficult the economic situation was. Many mega projects like the motorway and the yellow cab scheme, he said, had created serious strains on the economy and the balance of payments.

I was on a visit to Nepal when Moeen Qureshi spoke in the Senate, but I saw a tape of his speech when I returned. In his earlier address of 19 August, he had not blamed any particular government, but in his address to the Senate he strongly criticized the economic policies of Nawaz Sharif. I therefore wrote a longish letter to counter his criticism. I said:

Our government had introduced between 1991–1993 fundamental economic reforms which were overdue for almost two decades. The growth rate of the economy in 1990–91 and 1992–92 was 5.6 per cent and 7.7 per cent respectively. The lower 1992–93 growth of 2.6 per cent was due to unprecedented floods of September 1992, but other indicators were still positive. Stock market had quadrupled in value and investment level in these three years had climbed to over 20 per cent of GDP for the fist time in our history. Many expatriate Pakistanis were returning to the country to take advantage of the opportunities that had been created. Our government had also signed the historic Water Accord and finalized the unanimous NFC Award after a delay of 17 years. You totally ignored these achievements in presenting your assessment.

In organizing these elections, a caretaker government had to provide a level playing field to all political parties. This Senate speech of yours marked a tilt in favour of the opposition parties which is neither fair nor justified.

He invited me for lunch next day and tried his best to convince me that the few negative factors he had mentioned in his speech would not detract from the long list of achievements of the government in the preceding three years, but I kept insisting that he had in fact caused irreparable damage to our electoral prospects.

The 1993 Elections

Nawaz Sharif was elected as president of the Pakistan Muslim League on 19 April 1993, a month after Mohammad Khan Junejo died on 18 March and only a day after President Ghulam Ishaq Khan had dismissed his government. He could not, however, pay much attention to party matters in the next three months, with the Supreme Court hearing of his appeal against his dismissal throughout May, the short lived revival of his government on 26 May, the continuing tensions with the president, culminating in another dissolution of the assembly, this time on the advice of the prime minister, together with the resignation of the president on 18 July 1993.

On 19 July, a day after Moeen Qureshi was sworn in as caretaker prime minister, Nawaz Sharif came to my house with Lt.-Gen. (retd) Majid Malik to initiate preparations for the elections scheduled for 6 October. We agreed that we must convene within a week, i.e. on 26–27 July 1993 a two-day meeting of the central working committee of the party and rent premises to establish the secretariat of the party. Fortunately, after frantic efforts, I found a spacious house at 72 Margalla Road within a few days, but it was not ready in time for the meeting of the central working committee on 26 July. The meeting was therefore arranged in my house at 25 Park Road in F-8/1.

After intense discussion, the committee decided unanimously that the party would contest the October 1993 election as PML(N) and not as a part of the IJI as was done in 1990. The committee also decided to appoint me secretary general of PML(N).

My first task as secretary general was to setup the secretariat and secure the appointment of other office bearers. An important mechanism created at the very outset was an informal core group, consisting of the prominent members of the central working committee of the party, which met almost every week for the next four years to take all important decisions, continuously evolve party strategy, initially for the elections and then for its role as the opposition party.

The core group, chaired by Nawaz Sharif, consisted of Raja Zafarul Haq, General Majid Malik, Chaudhry Shujaat Hussain, Chaudhry Nisar Ali Khan, Sheikh Rashid Ahmad, Mahtab Abbasi, Mushahid Hussain, Syed Ghous Ali Shah, and myself.

A manifesto committee was setup under my chairmanship to prepare the party manifesto. It included Mushahid Hussain, Ahsan Iqbal, and Ahmad Raza Kasuri. The draft manifesto was submitted to the central working committee in the last week of August and was published a month before the election.

Mushahid Hussain was appointed secretary information and he quickly organized a strong media centre in the PML secretariat consisting of Siddiq-ul-Farooq, Khalil Malik, and Irfan Ghazi.

But the task of selecting candidates for the award of party tickets proved exceptionally difficult. The old PML secretariat, setup in 1986, when PML was revived by Junejo, had now been taken over by the dissident group led by Hamid Nasir Chatta. It was called PML(J) with Hamid Nasir Chatta as president and Iqbal Ahmad Khan as secretary general. They inherited all the records of the party. Even the provincial PML office in Punjab, which had built a very strong party organization at district and lower level, had been taken over by PML(J) when Manzoor Ahmad Wattoo was the chief minister.

There was a reasonably good response from potential applicants for PML tickets but in the absence of proper homework, tickets were awarded in a very ad hoc fashion. Negotiations with certain parties, previously a part of the IJI alliance on seat adjustment were also quite cumbersome and lengthy.

In 1990, PML, as part of IJI, had fought and won the election with the bicycle as its symbol. I was directed by the core group to make sure, for the sake of continuity, that the symbol of bicycle was again allotted to PML(N). When I appeared in the Election Commission, I found that Iqbal Ahmad Khan, secretary general of PML(J) had made the same request. The chief election commissioner decided that the issue would be decided by a draw. When the draw was held, Iqbal Ahmad Khan picked up the slip with the bicycle and I drew a blank. I was almost panicky because most of the other election symbols had already been allotted. I asked for a fifteen minutes break to verify what symbols were still available. I could not believe that the symbol of tiger was still available and quickly grabbed it. That turned out to be a blessing in disguise because our candidates used this symbol to full advantage in their posters, stage decorations, and election songs. Sheikh Rashid Ahmad even brought a live tiger to the Liaquat Bagh for the final election rally addressed by Nawaz Sharif.

The elections held on 6 October 1993, produced a result similar to that of the 1988 elections. PPP emerged as the largest party but without a clear majority: 92 seats in 1988 and 86 in 1993, in a house of 200. By comparison, PML(N) won comfortable majorities in 1990 and 1997, i.e. 105 and 138 respectively, in the two elections which brought in Nawaz Sharif as prime minister.

Results of October 1993 Elections for the National Assembly

Name of Party	Punjab	Sindh	Frontier	Balochistan	Others	Total
PPP	47	33	5	1	–	86
PML (N)	52	11	9	–	1	73
PML (J)	6	–	–	–	–	6
IJM	–	–	2	1	–	3
ANP	–	–	3	–	–	3
PIF	–	1	2	–	–	3
Others	3	1	2	7	–	13
Independent	4	–	2	2	7	15
Vacant seats*	3	–	1	–	1	5
Total	**115**	**46**	**26**	**11**	**9**	**207**

Source: Election Commission of Pakistan, 1994

* Elections on five seats had to be postponed due to the death of one of the candidates. Three of these five vacant seats went to PPP, taking its total strength to eighty-nine, one seat to IJM and the fifth went to an independent member from FATA. The election turnout was 41 per cent (i.e. 22.5 million votes).

Benazir Bhutto with 86 seats however gained the support of the PML(J) with 6 seats and 14 independent and other members to secure a majority and was sworn in as prime minister on 17 October 1993.

In the provincial elections held three days later on 9 October 1993, PPP won an absolute majority only in the Sindh province. In Punjab, the PML(N) won more seats than PPP as shown in the following table, but PPP managed to form a coalition government with the help of PML(J).

Results of October 1993 Elections for the Provincial Assemblies					
Name of Party	**Punjab**	**Sindh**	**Frontier**	**Balochistan**	**Total**
PPP	94	57	22	3	176
PML (N)	106	8	15	6	135
PML (J)	18	–	4	–	22
MQM	–	26	–	–	26
ANP	–	–	21	–	21
PIF	2	–	4	–	6
BNM (H)	–	–	–	5	5
Others	3	3	2	17	25
Independent	17	6	12	9	44
Total	**240**	**100**	**80**	**40**	**460**

Source: Election Commission of Pakistan, 1994

NOTE

1. This Committee was chaired by me as finance minister and included Shah Mahmood Qureshi and Chaudhry Mazhar Ali from Punjab, Syed Muzaffar Hussain Shah and Mohammad Alim Baloch from Sindh, Nawabzada Mohsin Ali Khan and Khalid Aziz from NWFP, Zulfiqar Ali Magsi and Muhammad Amin from Balochistan.

CHAPTER 9

The Second Benazir Government (1993–1996)

When Benazir Bhutto started her second tenure as prime minister on 17 October 1993, she had already decided that she would co-exist with the army and would not challenge its authority in certain vital sectors. The trauma of her dismissal by Ghulam Ishaq Khan on 6 August 1990, only twenty months after she was sworn in, was probably still fresh in her mind. As she admitted in several interviews after 1996, she had chosen the path of realism over idealism.

Another factor that must have persuaded her to follow the path of compromise was the tenuous nature of her election victory. The PPP had won only 86 out of 207 seats in the National Assembly, compared to 73 for PML(N), and therefore had to depend on certain defectors and independent members to form a coalition government. Her entire focus throughout her second tenure was to eliminate potential threats to her continuity in office, for the next five years.

The first and key step in gaining security for her tenure was to have 'her own trusted man' as president. By a happy coincidence Ishaq Khan's five-year tenure was to end in November 1993, only a month after Benazir Bhutto started her second tenure. Almost everyone assumed that in dismissing the government of Nawaz Sharif in April 1993, the inclusion of Asif Zardari in the caretaker setup, and the campaign of vilification against Nawaz Sharif by the interim government were based on a tacit understanding between Benazir Bhutto and Ishaq Khan that he would continue as President. And a day before the date fixed for filing the nomination papers, Ishaq Khan did arrive in Islamabad, only to face a shocking surprise: the PPP had decided to put up Farooq Ahmed Khan Leghari as its candidate for the office of president.

Farooq Leghari of course had impeccable credentials: a loyal member of the party for seventeen years, had suffered imprisonment many times while protesting against General Zia and then against the dismissal of the first Benazir's government in which he was the minister of water and power. Above all he was one of the few ex-colleagues of Zulfikar Ali Bhutto (the 'uncles') who were ready to serve the party under the leadership of Benazir Bhutto.

I have never seen Benazir Bhutto happier on the TV screen than the day when Farooq Leghari was elected as president. 'Now I am absolutely safe from dismissal for the next five years', she must have thought, without anticipating the cruel irony of history when three years later, her handpicked president would dismiss her government on 5 November 1996.

The third major threat, having forestalled the first two, from the army and the presidency, was of course, Nawaz Sharif. He led a formidable opposition with 73 members in the National Assembly, and a virtual majority in the Senate. In Punjab, Nawaz Sharif's PML(N) had won more seats than the PPP (106 and 94 respectively out of a total of 240). But Benazir Bhutto managed to capture the provincial government in Punjab, the power base of Nawaz Sharif, with the help of a breakaway faction of PML, under Hamid Nasir Chatta, with eighteen seats in the Punjab Assembly. In return, Manzoor Wattoo of PML (Chatta) was appointed as chief minister.

Economic Management

Having secured her own party stalwart as president and the government of the largest province, Punjab, apart from Sindh and NWFP, she began implementing her economic agenda. In this context, it is significant that despite its inherited image of a 'left of centre party', the PPP government after assuming office in November 1993, continued the reform process for a liberal market-oriented economy initiated in 1991. The privatization programme was continued along with the liberal investment framework. The investment boom that had started in the early 1990s continued to yield results in the textile sector with installed capacity expanding dramatically from 5.50 million spindles in 1991 to 8.50 million by 1996–97. But a key element in stimulating foreign investment was the new power policy announced in March 1994. Although in essence, this policy was based on the medium term energy plan approved by the cabinet committee on energy, chaired by Prime Minister Nawaz Sharif on 10 February 1993, calling for the induction of the private sector in the generation of electricity, the new energy policy of March 1994 greatly improved the incentives package. Under this package a two tier price system was introduced—a fixed capacity price of 6.5 cent per KWH at which government through WAPDA was to purchase at least 60 per cent of electricity produced by private investors and a variable price based on the cost of furnace oil and its transport cost. This package attracted a large number of foreign investors, raising the annual inflow of foreign investment to over $1.3 billion a year in 1994-95 and 1995-96. But there was also strong criticism of this policy due to the high capital cost of new plants, its dependence on imported furnace oil and the higher cost of electricity provided by these plants.[1] But in retrospect, even expensive energy is better than no energy.

The decline in GDP growth rate from well over 6 per cent in 1980s to less than 5 per cent in the 1990s continued during the second tenure of Benazir Bhutto's government, averaging about 4.3 per cent per annum in the period 1993-97. The principal cause of this slow down was the decline in investment GDP ratio from over 20 per cent of GDP in 1991-92 to less than 18 per cent in 1993-96. This was at least partly due to a decrease in total public expenditures from 26 per cent of GDP to 22 per cent, following the imposition of Pressler sanctions by USA in October 1990.

Political Confrontation

The first few months of the second Benazir government were fairly smooth. Nawaz Sharif, in his first speech as leader of the opposition in the National Assembly assured the government of Benazir Bhutto that the opposition would respect the mandate of the people and would fully cooperate with the government in the affairs of the state. This sent a wave of relief through political circles who felt reassured that despite the split mandate given by the electorate, the country might see a period of stability. In our informal contracts with the treasury benches, some areas were identified for joint legislative initiatives. These included the restoration of reserved seats for women, where the twenty-year provision in the 1973 constitution had expired in 1993, and the repeal of Article 58-2(b) of the constitution giving power to the president to dissolve the National Assembly. Both parties were also keen to find some formula to prevent floor crossing in the assemblies.

But this optimism about political accommodation and goodwill proved short lived. Having captured the Punjab government, with the support of PML(J), the political heavyweights of the PPP hatched a plan to oust the PML(N)/ANP government in NWFP led by Pir Sabir Shah. PPP had won 24 out of 80 seats in the Provincial Assembly, but PML(N) and ANP together had 36 seats. With the help of several independent members, a coalition government was sworn in with Pir Sabir Shah as chief minister.[2]

Within four months of the election, the PPP leadership in NWFP, led by Aftab Sherpao, had collected enough funds to lure away eleven independent members who had initially supported the Sabir Shah government. On 5 February 1994, a vote of no-confidence against Pir Sabir Shah's government was moved and carried. This step proved to be the beginning of a confrontation between PPP and PML(N) that dominated the country's politics throughout the next few years. The opposition resorted to frequent walkouts from the assembly and hardly permitted any legislation in the first half of 1994. Amid threats of resignations from the assemblies, both sides started blaming each other for corruption and misconduct. In retaliation the government arrested prominent PML leaders like Chaudhry Shujaat Hussain and Sheikh Rashid Ahmad.

In July 1994, we started receiving reports and rumours that the government was making plans to arrest Nawaz Sharif on some pretext or the other. A core group of the top leadership of the party met in the PML secretariat almost every week to review the prevailing situation and also review the implementation of decisions made, or initiatives launched previously. At one such meeting, one of the participants reported a conversation which Asif Ali Zardari had had with Majid Nizami in Jeddah: 'Nawaz Sharif has lot of experience in selling iron, but he has not yet worn iron himself (meaning handcuffs). That time is now approaching.'

I could almost feel the rage I saw in Nawaz Sharif's eyes. Within a month he announced his counter strategy to forestall such an eventuality: 'Tehrik-e-Nijjat', i.e. 'a deliverance movement to get rid of a corrupt and incompetent government.' He called a meeting of the central working committee in Lahore and made a passionate speech to mobilize the party to launch the 'Tehrik'. Many members were bewildered: 'The PPP government has not even completed a year, isn't it rather early to launch such a movement?' Another said, 'In Pakistan you need the support of 3 'A's to get into power: Army, America and Allah. How many A's do you have?' Nawaz Sharif laughed and said, 'So far only one: Allah.'

The Tehrik-e-Nijjat launched in September 1994, was a thumping success. Party workers from Karachi and Peshawar took out rallies and processions and organized public meetings. The climax was a train march led by Nawaz Sharif himself, from Karachi to Peshawar. He was accompanied in the train by all the prominent party leaders and was greeted by thousands of enthusiastic workers at every railway station. The provincial governments retaliated by arresting thousands of workers including about fifty members of the National and Provincial assemblies. The lawyers' wing of the party was activated in all district headquarters to file appeals for bail and release. A special committee was setup to visit detainees in different jails and assist their families, where necessary. The publicity surrounding their arrest and legal proceedings served the underlying purpose. The PPP government realized that the arrest of Nawaz Sharif, if attempted, could lead to mass agitation in the country. Nawaz Sharif was never arrested but the seeds of mistrust and confrontation between the two main parties of the country became even more intense, all because of an indiscreet remark of Asif Ali Zardari.

We had hardly recovered from the heat and turmoil of Tehrik-e-Nijjat when another mini crisis exploded: On 13 November, a day before President Farooq Leghari was to address the joint session of parliament, Nawaz Sharif's father, Mian Mohammad Sharif was arrested. At about 11 a.m. Nawaz Sharif telephoned me and said: 'Abbaji has just been arrested from his office and taken to Islamabad. Can you send some people to the airport to find out the location where they might take him?' I sent three teams, but Mian Mohammad Sharif was whisked away without being brought to the terminal. So when

Nawaz Sharif arrived two hours later, we did not know where his father was. By the evening, however, one of our teams, taking a round of all the 'safe houses' detected unusual activity at one of the houses in F-8/3. We finally persuaded the official in charge to deliver a small bag containing his clothes and medicines.

Next day, Mian Sharif had a mild heart attack and was shifted to the cardiac ward of PIMS (Pakistan Institute of Medical Sciences). The public reaction to the arrest, without any reason, of a 75-year old man, with a heart ailment was very adverse and very widespread. The government realized its folly the very next day. The Interior Minister Naseerullah Babar telephoned me at 10:30 p.m. to say that Mian Mohammad Sharif was no longer under detention, could we make alternative arrangements to look after him in the hospital.

The purpose of this senseless arrest, as we were to learn later, was a strange plan by some of Benazir's colleagues to generate maximum anger in the opposition ranks so that they would protest as violently as possible to disrupt the formal address of President Farooq Leghari to the joint session of parliament on 14 November. This 'plan', it seems was the beginning of the mistrust between Benazir Bhutto and Farooq Leghari which was to lead to her dismissal two years later.

Another factor which widened the gulf between Benazir Bhutto and Farooq Leghari was Benazir's ongoing tussle with the judiciary. To safeguard her position against adverse judgments from the courts, she wanted to appoint lawyers sympathetic to her party to the High Courts and the Supreme Court. She withdrew all the names proposed by the caretaker government of Moeen Qureshi to fill the vacant posts of judges in different courts. One of her remarks in 1993, that judges were influenced by *chamak* (money), created a strong reaction in the legal fraternity. This eventually led to a petition in the Supreme Court seeking its intervention in laying down proper criteria for the appointment of judges. The landmark judgment of 20 March 1996, on this case, required that all cases of appointments of judges, in which the consent of the chief justice had not been obtained, should be reviewed. Benazir Bhutto refused to comply, forcing the Supreme Court to seek the intervention and support of the president.

The president moved a reference to the Supreme Court, asking for an opinion on whether he had powers to appoint judges in his discretion or was bound to act on the advice of the prime minister. He also wrote letters to chairman Senate and speaker National Assembly containing proposals for setting up an accountability process. Nawaz Sharif responded to this suggestion by submitting a draft law on accountability to the National Assembly on 8 September 1996, as a private members' bill.

Meanwhile the law and order situation was rapidly deteriorating. The MQM which had boycotted the elections for the National Assembly but had won 27 out of 100 seats in the Sindh Assembly, had become a formidable opposition to the PPP government in Sindh, along with PML(N) which had won 15 seats. As terrorist activities increased in Karachi, the government launched a crackdown against MQM. There were complaints of large-scale extra judicial killings of MQM activists. The climate of insecurity reached such a point, after the murder of two American consulate officers in broad daylight on 8 March 1995, that most diplomats shifted their families from Karachi to Islamabad.

The PPP government's relations with PML(J) with whom it had formed a coalition government in Punjab, under Manzoor Wattoo, also came under strain. As a result, in September 1995, Manzoor Wattoo was sacked under Article 234 of the constitution and Sardar Arif Nakai was sworn in as chief minister. Mian Manzoor Wattoo filed an appeal in the Lahore High Court. After one year, on 3 November, the Lahore High Court reinstated the government of Manzoor Wattoo and declared the presidential proclamation, the governor's advice and the election of Sardar Arif Nakai as without lawful authority. This caused considerable embarrassment to the federal government.

The final straw in this saga was the tragic murder of Benazir Bhutto's brother Murtaza Bhutto, in Karachi on 20 September 1996. Amid allegations that he was assassinated by police officials, there were rumours from influential quarters that some agencies might be involved in the plot to assassinate Murtaza Bhutto.

The month of October was full of many unexpected developments. At a secret meeting between Shahid Hamid and Nawaz Sharif at the residence of Begum Abida Hussain, I learnt that Farooq Leghari was fed up with so many acts of commissions and omissions, reflected in poor governance, rampart corruption and misuse of authority. The excessive use of force in Karachi had created a strong reaction and the tussle with the judiciary had created a virtual constitutional crisis.

Early on the morning of 5 November I was woken up by a telephone call from Shahbaz Sharif at 4 a.m. 'The party is over,' he said. Then Nawaz Sharif came on the line and said he would reach Islamabad from Murree at about 9:30 a.m. and I should assemble as many leaders of the party as I could. To my surprise, despite the short notice, about hundred members of the parliament and provincial assemblies had reached the PML secretariat by 9:30 a.m. to start the ball rolling for the next general elections—fifth in a period of twelve years since March 1985.

The 1997 Elections

Unlike 1993, when PML(N) was confronted with fresh elections at very short notice, in 1996, the party was now fully prepared for the elections.

In November 1993, soon after the October elections, the core group of the party leadership had intensively analyzed the election results by district and by constituencies, and evolved a coherent strategy to re-organize the party by appointing new office bearers at district and lower levels, and started the process of reconstituting the PML councils at the central and provincial levels, through fresh elections as required under the PML constitution.

Simultaneously I began to organize the party secretariat by enlisting the support of as many leaders and experts as were prepared to spare time for work in the secretariat on a voluntary basis. In 1962, when I was studying at Harvard, I had purchased a book by Theodore White entitled *The Making of a President*. This book was about Kennedy's campaign for the presidential election of 1960 and explained at some length how Kennedy's campaign managers had attempted a systematic analysis of the real power structure in each of the fifty states, i.e. the relative strength of different trade unions, the farm lobbies, different religious groups, the big business, as also the key players and power brokers in each state. Based on this analysis, Kennedy's campaign had identified specific election issues and platforms for each state and evolved a strategy to win voter support on these issues. The result was a landslide victory for Kennedy in November 1960.

I pulled out this book from my library and evolved a similar strategy with the help of a small team, which included Lt.-Gen. (retd) Saeed Qadir, Sadiq Saeed Khan, a retired federal secretary, Dr Liaquat Ali, and Bilal Hasan, a professional researcher. This strategy was implemented through many stages over the next two years.

- About hundred or half the total constituencies were chosen for in-depth political analysis. The results of the remaining half were easily predictable as 'safe seats' of either PML(N), the PPP, or some other party.

- The political analysis started with a brief profile of the district, its economy, natural resources, extent of irrigation, main crops, and industries, and any specific economic or social issues.

- Within each district, the constituency wise analysis focused on voter composition (Shia, Sunni, ethnic, occupational or tribal classification), the main political families and personalities and their political affiliations. Newspaper reports on earlier elections giving such information were also accessed.

- The results of the preceding four elections (1985, 1988, 1990 and 1993) were computerized and compiled in comparative charts for each constituency, clearly showing in different columns, the ascending or descending position of PML, PPP and some other parties.

- Based on this analysis, a brief (10 to 20 pages) report was prepared for each district/constituency, leading to certain recommendations for alignments between different factions or groups. In constituencies, where PML(N) did not have its own strong candidate, attempts were made to identify independent candidates who had secured substantial votes in earlier elections.

- These draft reports were circulated for comments to members of parliament belonging to PML(N), candidates who had contested but had not won, and party office bearers at district level. During sessions of parliament, I convened several district or division-wise meetings of members to discuss these reports. The reactions were mixed. Some said, they were already aware of these facts about their constituencies, others said they had never looked at their constituency in such a perspective. Many were intrigued by the proposal to join a rival faction, until it was explained to them, that the two groups together would command enough votes to win both the National and Provincial Assembly seats.

• Throughout the preceding three years, the media centre of the PML secretariat under Syed Mushahid Hussain had published a series of fact sheets to criticize the record of the PPP government on such issues as human rights, judiciary, corruption and economic management. As elections approached, Dr Liaquat Ali prepared briefs for election speeches based on these fact sheets, which were circulated to PML candidates.

Within a few days after the dissolution of the National Assembly, a concerted campaign of 'accountability before elections' began to surface. In a statement on 1 December only two days after the JI and PML(N) had already agreed on seat adjustments in the elections, Qazi Hussain Ahmad proposed that the elections should be postponed till the accountability process had screened out corrupt politicians. President Leghari and caretaker Prime Minister Malik Meraj Khalid initially supported this proposal. Justice (retd) Mujjadad Mirza had been appointed chief ehtesab commissioner on 20 November. On 5 December, an ordinance was issued to amend the Representation of People Act 1976 so that those who were loan defaulters or had their loans written off, would not be allowed to take part in the elections. On 29 December the State Bank of Pakistan also published a list of 15,000 loan defaulters including 450 politicians.

There were strong rumours that the president might postpone the elections to allow the caretaker setup continue for a year or two, but the country's foreign exchange reserves were low and the efforts of the caretaker government to borrow funds from abroad were not very successful. President Farooq Leghari therefore decided to go ahead with the elections within 90 days but in January 1997, setup a national council on defence and security, chaired by the president to reassure the establishment that even if Nawaz Sharif came to power as a result of the elections, he would be under the supervision of this council. Nawaz Sharif instructed his party stalwarts to offer no reaction to the establishment of this body, possibly to convey his acceptance of the idea.

Finally the election schedule was announced on 16 December 1996 fixing 21 December as the last date for filing nomination papers.

Even before the election schedule was formally announced, the PML secretariat was flooded with applications for party tickets. Meetings of the central parliamentary board were scheduled for Lahore, Karachi, Quetta, and Abbottabad (for NWFP), with detailed charts for each constituency showing the lists of all applicants, results of preceding four elections and brief recommendations on the election strategy for that constituency based on the political analysis undertaken in the preceding two years.

The parliamentary board invited all the candidates to appear before it and gave them an opportunity to present their case. Any comments received from voters about a particular candidate in response to consolidated advertisements in all major newspapers listing all the candidates, were also made available. After this elaborate exercise a list of 178 candidates was finalized for as many seats in the National Assembly. The remaining 21 seats out of a total of 199 were either given to other parties under the seat adjustment formula or not contested.

The election campaign was very intense. The helicopter which the party had leased from a Russian company for the 1993 elections and had been grounded by the PPP government on one pretext or another, was reactivated under Supreme Court's order, in November 1996. This enabled Nawaz Sharif to cover almost all the constituencies and address four to five election rallies each day, ending with seven on the last day.

The outstanding success achieved by PML(N) exceeded our own expectations. We were all confident about winning an absolute majority, but the most optimistic estimate went to 120 out of 200 seats. In the end PML(N) won 137 or 67 per cent of the total, compared to 73 in 1993. PPP went down from 89 to 18 seats, all in the province of Sindh only. It did not win a single seat in the other three provinces.

The results of the Provincial Assembly elections held on the same day, were even more impressive. In Punjab, PML(N) won 212 or

88 per cent of all seats and in NWFP 33 seats or 40 per cent of all seats (or 62 seats if the seats won by the allied party, the ANP, are taken into account). Even in Sindh, PML(N) won 15 out of 100 seats and in Balochistan 4 out of 40 seats.

By 3 a.m. PML leaders and supporters had started to arrive in the secretariat with large baskets of sweets, because even before the complete results were available, the overwhelming nature of the victory won by PML(N) was clearly visible. The jubilation went on in Islamabad, Lahore, Karachi, Peshawar, and Quetta throughout the next three days.

Results of the National Assembly Elections held in February 1997						
Name of Party	**Punjab**	**Sindh**	**Frontier**	**Balochistan**	**Others**	**Total**
PML (N)	107	12	14	3	1	137
PPP	–	18	–	–	–	18
MQM	–	12	–	–	–	12
ANP	–	–	8	2	–	10
BNP	–	–	–	3	–	3
Other	–	2	2	2	–	6
Independent	8	2	2	1	7	21
Total	**115**	**46**	**26**	**11**	**9**	**207**

Source: The Election Commission of Pakistan, 1997

Results of the Provincial Assembly Elections of February 1997					
Name of Party	**Punjab**	**Sindh**	**Frontier**	**Balochistan**	**Total**
PML (N)	212	15	33	4	264
PPP	3	34	4	1	42
ANP	–	–	29	–	29
MQM	–	30	–	–	30
BNP	–	–	–	9	9
Other	4	6	3	18	31
Independent	22	14	11	8	55
Total	**240**	**100**	**80**	**40**	**460**

Source: The Election Commission of Pakistan, 1997

NOTES

1. See for example, the author's article entitled 'The Perils of High Cost Imported Energy', *The Nation*, Lahore, 28–29 November 1994. Also published as Chapter 36 of *Hunger, Poverty and Development*, Ferozsons, 2000.

2. Since ANP was the larger of the two parties, I had expected that it would ask for the post of chief minister. I was surprised, however, when in a meeting between Nawaz Sharif and Begum Nasim Wali Khan in the PML secretariat, she suggested that PML(N) should nominate a chief minister. She also proposed that Pir Sabir Shah would be an acceptable candidate. Nawaz Sharif had to ask for a break in the meeting to move to another room and explain to Mahtab Abbasi, who was his first choice as chief minister that he had to defer to ANP's advice because they had more seats in the Provincial Assembly.

CHAPTER 10

The Perils of a Heavy Mandate (1997–1999)

Nawaz Sharif looked larger than life, when he was sworn in as the prime minister, for the second time on 17 February 1997, after he received the support of 177 members in the vote of confidence. This unprecedented victory in general elections or 'the heavy mandate', as the media repeatedly emphasized, had probably changed his political mindset forever.

After his defiant speech of 17 April 1993, which transformed Nawaz Sharif from a shrewd politician to a popular leader, he was catapulted once again into a higher orbit of populism. But as Francis Pym, a Conservative Party stalwart in UK had observed after the third consecutive landslide victory of Margaret Thatcher, in 1987, 'Heavy mandates are not good for the Party.' Mrs Thatcher was removed from office after a bitter division in the Conservative Party. The heavy mandate of 1997 cast a similar dark shadow on Nawaz Sharif's political future.

Even in a stable democracy a heavy mandate leads to intemperate decisions, such as introduction of the 'poll tax' by Margaret Thatcher in 1988, Iraq war plus illiberal legislation of Tony Blair in 2001–2004 in the United Kingdom. It is even more dangerous in new democracies with weak institutions.

Nawaz Sharif became prime minister with a vote of confidence from 177 members of the lower house. This crushing weight of mandate and exhilaration of popular support created an overwhelming instability which led to a series of actions and reactions culminating in the calamity of October 1999, the effects of which will be with us for a long time.

Born out of this feeling of massive responsibility to provide quick justice were the steps leading to the judicial crisis. Armed with all the instruments for constitutional amendments, the temptation to repeal Article 58-2(b) of the constitution became unbearable.

Alarmed and frightened by these events, other individuals and state institutions such as the Supreme Court, the president, and the army chief attempted counter measures to protect their respective interests but were swept away.

Nawaz Sharif also gradually isolated himself from his cabinet colleagues and did not have many consultations on important issues like the election of a new president or the Shariat Bill. Consultations in democratic states are like electricity stored in water dams. Excess power is used to replenish the dam so that excess power can be generated in times of extraordinary need.

On 25 February, a small cabinet of only seven members was sworn in: Ishaq Dar (commerce), Chaudhry Shujaat Hussain (interior), Chaudhry Nisar Ali (petroleum), Gohar Ayub Khan (foreign affairs), Abida Hussain (population), Asghar Ali Shah (MOS housing) and myself as finance minister. Mushahid Hussain and Khalid Anwar were appointed as advisors on information and law respectively and Khawaja Asif as chairman privatization commission. Azam Hoti joined the cabinet as communications minister on 2 March. Illahi Bakhsh Soomro had already been elected as speaker of National Assembly. As I discovered later, Nawaz Sharif's hesitation to fill all the cabinet positions was partly due to the difficulty he was facing in choosing a few out of so many contenders. It took him almost five months to add thirteen new members to the cabinet, on 10 July 1997. They consisted of nine ministers (Raja Zafarul Haq, General Abdul Majid Malik, Yasin Wattoo, Javed Hashmi, Ghous Ali Shah, Sheikh Rashid Ahmad, Abdul Sattar Lalika, Khalid Maqbool Siddiqui, Sardar Yaqub Nasir) and four ministers of state (Tehmina Daultana, Siddiq Khan Kanju, Haleem Siddiqui, and Ahmad Mahmud).

Meanwhile, PML was able to form governments in all the four provinces. In Punjab, where it had won 212 or almost 90 per cent out of 240 seats, Shahbaz Sharif was sworn in as chief minister on 21 February 1997 and Shahid Hamid as governor on 11 March 1997. In NWFP, where PML had won 33 out of 80 seats, Sardar Mahtab Abbasi became chief minister with the support of ANP, with 29 seats. In Sindh, MQM had won 30 out of 100 seats (against PPP's 33 seats) but Liaquat Jatoi of PML(N) which itself had won 15 seats, was sworn in on 22 February 1997, after prolonged negotiations with MQM. But it took almost twenty days for the sixteen-member cabinet, equally divided between PML and MQM, to take office on 13 March. Initially Kamal Azfar took the oath of office as governor but within four days he resigned and Lt.-Gen. (retd) Mueenuddin Haider was appointed governor.

In Balochistan, PML(N) with only 4 out of 40 seats in the Provincial Assembly formed a coalition government with BNP (9 seats), JUI(F) (7 seats) and JWP (6 seats). Akhtar Mengal of BNP became chief minister on 22 February and Abdul Jabbar of JWP was elected speaker and Maulana Allah Dad of JUI(F) as deputy speaker. Lt.-Gen. (retd) Imranullah Khan was appointed governor.

On 12 March 1997, elections to half the seats falling vacant in the Senate were held. With the decisive shift in favour of PML(N) and its allied parties in all the four provincial assemblies, they were able to secure a clear majority of 56 in the upper house of 87. Wasim Sajjad was re-elected chairman senate and Humayun Marri as deputy chairman.

Revival of the Economy

Having established a stable setup at the centre and the four provinces and with more than two-thirds majority in both houses, Nawaz Sharif turned his attention to his economic agenda. He addressed the nation on 23 February 1997 and announced the following policies and measures:

The federal and provincial cabinets will be small.

My government will not allot plots to any one at concessional rates. Only the disabled and sons and wards of martyrs will be given plots at concessional rates.

Official guards will be withdrawn from the residences of all Ministers, advisors and senior officials. Though the Government is responsible for the law and order and security, this responsibility is equal for every citizen, the rich and the poor alike. Everyone is equal before the eyes of the government and has equal right to receive protection.

All signboards publicizing names of individuals at public sector schemes will be removed immediately. Nobody has the right to get his name displayed at schemes funded by the state exchequer through hard-earned money of the people. Whosoever wants to display his name should volunteer and sponsor schemes of public interest from his own pocket and then put his name on them.

The green channel has been reopened. Pakistanis returning home will be accorded the same regard and respect as used to be given to them till 1993.

The right to vote will be accorded to overseas Pakistanis and those who have obtained passports abroad will be exempted from visa restrictions like the Pakistanis in Britain.

An independent authority will be setup to issue driving licences. The driving standards for highways and motorways will be brought at par with the international standards. This authority will also be responsible for the standard of driving as well. If its licence holder is found unsatisfactory in driving, the issuing authority will also be penalized.

Insha Allah, I will try to get the remaining work of the motorway completed this year to open it for traffic. You might have noted that the blueprint prepared by us for revival of the economy and wiping off the national debt puts no restriction on defence expenditures. As long as the Kashmir dispute is there and there is no guarantee of peace in the sub-continent on a just and equitable basis, we cannot do so. Defence is our foremost priority and we will always strive to strengthen it even if we have to go without food.

There will be a complete ban on smoking in all government offices, trains and domestic flights. Local and national sports will be encouraged and patronized in order to provide healthy entertainment to the youth. I am directing the Provincial Governments to promote and evolve a uniform national culture. Sports be patronized in every province and then national level competitions held.

Nobody will be allowed to import a duty-free car in Pakistan including the President, Prime Minister, Governors, Chief Ministers and the Chiefs of the Armed Forces.

No political personalities or government servants will be allowed to proceed abroad for medical treatment from the national exchequer.

Probe will be conducted into the affairs of all those government officials who have organized lavish marriage ceremonies since 1990 to date and if the expenditure is found to be in excess of their income the same will be recovered from them and they will be held accountable.

All government servants will have to declare their assets within the next fifteen days. All assets which will be found in excess of the declaration would be confiscated and those filing wrong declarations will be penalized. The government servants will give the declaration of their assets to their respective heads of the departments.

In future all government appointments and promotions in the federal and provincial governments will be made on merit.

I would now focus more attention on the rural population than done in the past. Small farmers and agriculturists will be provided yellow tractors and tubewells on easy instalments. They will also be given fertilizers and pesticides of international standards and it would be necessary to follow the standards.

The prices of fertilizers and pesticides will also be reduced. Government lands will be distributed among landless *haris* and agricultural labourers in all the four provinces.

The current price hike has troubled all and sundry from Karachi to Khyber. The poor and middle classes are the worst hit. It is my earnest desire to raise their pays and pensions to the maximum. The empty exchequer restrains me from realizing this desire. Yet, I announce an increase of Rs300/- per month in the salaries of all government employees from grade 1 to 16 from 1 March 1997. The pensioners in these grades will also get a raise of 10 per cent per month. The private sector will also implement an increase proportionate to this. I hope it will mitigate the sufferings of the poor to some extent.

Three days later and only a day after the new cabinet was sworn in on 25 February, he convened a convention of business leaders to discuss the prevailing economic situation and solicit new ideas for the future course of action. A detailed brief on the economy was presented at the convention, clearly bringing out the difficult economic situation the new government had inherited:

- The overall GDP growth had slowed down from an average of 5.2 per cent in 1990–93 to 4.2 per cent in 1993–97 and only 1.8 per cent in 1996–97.
- A crisis in the manufacturing sector was the principal cause of this slow down. After recording low growth of 1.7 per cent and 1 per cent in 1994–95 and 1995–96, large scale manufacturing had actually suffered a decline of 2.1 per cent in 1996–97 for the first time in Pakistan's history.
- The agricultural sector had also experienced a bad year with near zero growth in 1996–97, resulting in record wheat imports of four million tons in 1997–98.
- The cumulative current account deficit in these three years was almost $11 billion, virtually eroding the country's exchange reserves.

Exports had declined by 3 per cent in 1996–97, the current account deficit was close to $4 billion and foreign exchange reserves had declined to the precarious level of $500 million by the end of 1996. The value of the rupee had correspondingly declined by 33 per cent from Rs30 to Rs39 per dollar.

- The rate of inflation had jumped to double digits in the entire three year period at 13.0, 10.8 and 11.8 per cent per annum respectively.
- The most serious dimension of the economic situation was however the institutional decay. PIA's profits had dropped from Rs700 million in 1992–93 to only Rs65 million. Liabilities outstanding against Water and Power Development Authority (WAPDA) and Karachi Electricity Supply Corporation (KESC) had reached Rs42 billion. Bad debts of banks and financial institutions had increased from Rs83 billion in October 1993 to Rs130 billion by the end of 1996. This had increased the sense of despondency and frustration not just among the business community but also the public at large. That was a major reason for the dramatic decline in the total votes cast for PPP, from 7.82 million in 1993 to 4.21 million, in 1997.

I could see the spark of determination in Nawaz Sharif's eyes as he setup eleven different committees to present concrete proposals on tax reforms, exports, industrial revival including revival of sick units, agricultural incentives, recovery of defaulted loans, capital market reforms, human development and poverty reduction. Each committee was given one or two experts in the field and only one month to submit their recommendations. I met each committee as it started its deliberation to provide a sense of direction and also had frequent meetings with the officials providing expertise and secretariat services to these committees to ensure complementarity and consistency in their approach.

The first committee to finish its work in less than four weeks was the Committee on Tax and Tariff Reforms chaired by the late Ejaz Shafi, MNA. This was followed by the Committee on Industrial Revival and Export Promotion. On 28 March, I presented a programme of economic revival in the National Assembly, based on the recommendations of these committees. The main objective of tax reforms was to shift the country's dependence on trade related taxes like customs duty to domestic income and sales taxes, by introducing far reaching changes in the structure and rates of duties. Maximum tariffs were reduced from 65 to 45 per cent for most imports and the number of duty slabs was reduced from 13 to 5, to stimulate industrial production and investment. The standard general sales tax (GST) rate was also reduced from 18 to 12.5 per cent. GST was also extended to retail trade in the form of a turnover tax at the rate of 3 per cent. Similarly, maximum rate of personal income tax was reduced from 35 to 25 per cent and on corporate income, from 45 to 35 per cent.

Five days after the announcement of these fundamental tariff and tax reforms, a new agricultural incentives package was announced by the prime minister at a largely attended farmers' convention in Islamabad on 3 April 1997. The agricultural minister, late Abdul Sattar Lalika, and I had extensive meetings with the committee members, representing various farmers' associations for evolving a comprehensive package.

From my long international experience in FAO and IFAD, between 1971 and 1984, I had discovered the most important secret for stimulating agricultural growth, namely improving its terms of trade by ensuring that the prices paid by farmers for various inputs were in line with the prices they received for their output. Recognizing that these terms of trade had deteriorated in the preceding three years (the price of urea alone had gone up by 60 per cent), support prices of all major crops were increased and prices of many of the inputs were reduced by adjusting duties on tractors and harvesters and expanding agricultural credit.

As the prime minister announced an unprecedented increase of 40 per cent in the support price of wheat, from Rs173 to Rs240 per 40 kg, the entire convention centre echoed with wild applause. The year 1998 was declared a, wheat year, to ensure that the great 'Indus Food Machine' which was once the granary of the subcontinent should again become a wheat exporter. That vision was achieved within two years, as the 1999-2000 wheat crops reached a record 22 million tons, yielding an exportable surplus of 3 million tons.

Just before the convention ended, a farmer came to the podium and said, 'Prime Minister, in the Indian Punjab, government provides free electricity to tuebwells and that is why Indian Punjab is doing so much better than our Punjab in agriculture. Please announce today 'free electricity for tube-wells' and then see what the farmers of our Punjab can do.'

My breath literally stopped in my throat. While we were working on the agricultural package, chairman WAPDA had sent me a note to point out that the policy of flat rates of electricity for tube-wells announced in 1992 (Rs60 per HP) had led to large scale leakage of revenue because almost all electricity consumption in rural areas including air-conditioners were now connected to tube-well meters. He had suggested discontinuing the system of flat rates and going back to metered rates for tube-wells. 'WAPDA will go bankrupt if this suggestion of providing free electricity for tube-wells was accepted' went through my mind like a flash.

Thankfully, before making an announcement, the prime minister looked towards me. I quickly scribbled the following on a piece of paper: 'Providing free electricity will not be a sound policy, but if the flat rates were to be replaced by installing meters, we can reduce the electricity tariffs for tube-wells to half the industrial tariffs.' The prime minister was probably relieved that he managed to extract some concession from me. He made this announcement amidst an enthusiastic applause. Most of those clapping had not, of course, realized that even at half the industrial tariffs, WAPDA would realize more revenues from tube-wells than under the misused flat rate system.

The month of April was spent on fine-tuning capital market reforms, which were announced on 6 May 1997. The key feature of these reforms was the creation of the Securities and Exchange Commission of Pakistan to replace the outdated Corporate Law Authority, with new powers to regulate the capital markets, oversee the management of stock exchanges and modernize their operations and to promote the mutual funds industry and broaden the investor base in the country. These reforms were supplemented by certain fiscal incentives. The period of capital gain tax exemption was extended by three years and turnover tax on shares was removed.

Next on the list were reforms in the banking and financial sector. The first Nawaz Sharif government had already initiated many reforms in this sector by denationalizing two of the five nationalized commercial banks, namely Muslim Commercial Bank and Allied Bank Limited, and allowing ten new commercial banks and twenty investment banks to be setup in the private sector. To further accelerate the process of financial liberalization and expand reliance on market based instruments of monetary control, a number of legal and administrative measures were taken:

a. To strengthen the autonomy of the State Bank of Pakistan to formulate and implement monetary and credit policies;
b. To give greater autonomy to board of directors of banks to manage their banks and evolve their lending policies, under the supervision of the State Bank of Pakistan;
c. To improve the process of loan recovery through a unified system of banking courts and giving foreclosure rights to banking companies to sell mortgaged properties;
d. To reduce infected portfolios of stuck up loans;
e. To reduce markup rates for the private sector by curtailing the administrative expenses of nationalized commercial banks.

To achieve these objectives, five major laws were amended through the parliament in 1997, the Pakistan Banking Council was abolished and twenty-four new banking courts were established. The Federal Bank for Cooperatives was merged with the Agricultural Development Bank, Equity Participation Fund with Industrial Development Bank, the Regional Development Finance Corporation with the National Development Finance Corporation and the Youth Investment Promotion Society with the Small Business Finance Corporation.

The government had already appointed three prominent bankers from the private sector, Shaukat Tarin, Mohammad Mian Soomro, and Zubair Soomro, as heads of three nationalized commercial banks (Habib Bank Limited, National Bank of Pakistan, and United Bank Limited, respectively). On 3 June 1997, at a meeting with heads of all development finance institutions (DFIs) and commercial banks at the State Bank in Karachi, the prime minister announced the composition of new boards of directors for these three banks, consisting entirely of prominent persons from the private sector. When an official of the finance ministry hesitantly suggested that at least one director should be from the ministry, considering that these banks are owned by the government, Nawaz Sharif said without hesitation that these nominated directors can serve the interests of the government better than an official of the finance ministry, because they will manage the banks more efficiently. This prediction was vindicated by subsequent events as in the next twelve months, the three government banks succeeded in reducing the portfolio of stuck up loans by Rs28 billion and increasing their profits. By June 1997, the country's foreign exchange reserves had also increased from $1.7 billion in February to $2.0 billion by 30 June 1997, largely due to an inflow of $350 million under the national Debt Retirement Programme (*Qarz utaro mulk sanwaro*). Incidentally, as the 2002 annual report of the State Bank confirmed, deposits under this scheme were not frozen in May 1998 and were returned to contributors with markup on the expiry of the stipulated term of 2–5 years.

The mood of optimism and hope generated throughout the country by these far reaching reforms was clearly reflected in my upbeat budget speech when I presented the 1997–98 budget to the National Assembly on 13 June. I was also conscious of the recurrent criticism of political parties that they present lofty manifestoes before every election but forget all the promises made, after the elections. I therefore made it a point to incorporate the key elements of the PML's election manifesto in my budget speech by converting them into the main medium term objectives of government's economic and social policy:

a. To double the country's income within a decade and thus increase per capita income by at least two thirds. For this we will have to modernize our industry and to increase production and productivity in agriculture. We intend to induct new technologies and to simultaneously ensure that the fruits of progress are not concentrated in a few hands or a few regions.
b. To ensure fiscal and financial stability by increasing revenues and controlling government expenditures.
c. To reduce dependence on external loans and improve the balance of payments by accelerating exports and home remittances, and to take such steps as would attract foreign direct investment and the rapid transfer of technology.
d. To speed up the recovery of stuck up loans and to take stern action against defaulters.
e. To accelerate the pace of progress in the social sectors; in particular, in basic education, health, population welfare and rural water

supply and sanitation. To increase employment opportunities, to stabilize prices and to reduce the level of poverty by formulating special programmes for less-developed areas and disadvantaged groups.

f. To ensure better law and order and to provide protection to the life and property of all citizens, to provide quick and cheap justice, to uphold the rule of law, to eradicate corruption, and to accelerate the process of accountability.

g. To reform the administrative structure, to down size the public sector to increase its efficiency and to encourage the private sector in all fields.

h. To strengthen the defence of the country and to ensure an effective role for Pakistan in regional and world affairs.

i. To propagate Islamic values and to effectively introduce the Islamic economic system in the country.

Before I concluded my budget speech, I also said: 'I hope by now, you, Mr Speaker, this august house and the entire nation of Pakistan would have realized that this budget has not imposed any new taxes on the people of Pakistan and I have the honour to present the first tax free budget in the history of Pakistan.'

The treasury benches broke into wild applause and several members shouted *mukarar*, i.e. encore. As I repeated these words, the surprise and bewilderment on the face of Benazir Bhutto and other stalwarts of the opposition benches was clearly visible. She raised her hands in disgust as if to ask her colleagues, 'How is this possible?'

At that exciting moment, no one could have forecast that these economic reforms and the far reaching programme would soon be overtaken, before they had yielded tangible results, by several earth-shaking, global events and by an unexpected series of crises at home.

In July 1997, the sudden collapse of the Thai currency set into motion the Asian economic crisis which soon engulfed Malaysia, Indonesia and South Korea, with ripple effects on all the developing countries including Pakistan. In February 1999, when I met Dr Mahathir Mohamad, prime minister of Malaysia at a summit meeting of eight Islamic countries (D-8) in Dhaka, he gave me a very succinct account of the causes of this crisis and Malaysia's efforts to deal with it. Next year, recalling our conversation, he sent me, through the Malaysian embassy in Islamabad, copies of three articles he had written on the subject in August 2000, although I was no longer in the government at that time. These articles explained how by imposing controls on capital transfers, in defiance of IMF's advice, Malaysia was able to meet the crisis.

While the Asian economic crisis damaged the investment prospects and stock markets of all emerging markets, Pakistan did not suffer the currency contagion of this crisis because in 1991, when Pakistan had liberalized the buying and selling of foreign currency on current account, it had not liberalized the movement of currency on capital account. Its limited exchange reserves did not therefore suffer the onslaught of foreign currency traders. Pakistan's exports however were adversely affected by the crisis and virtually stagnated at about $8 billion.

But more damaging for the economy were a series of other crises: the judicial crisis of October–December 1997, the imposition of wide ranging sanctions following the nuclear tests of May 1998, the Kargil conflict with India in May–June 1999, and the military takeover of October 1999.

The Judicial Crisis

Nawaz Sharif had two-thirds majority in both the houses, but he was still apprehensive of other threats to the stability of his government. One of these was the power of the president to dissolve the National Assembly under article 58-2(b) of the constitution, which had been assumed by General Ziaul Haq when he restored the 1973 constitution in March 1985. This power, ratified by the Eighth Amendment in October 1985, had already been used four times, in May 1988 by General Ziaul Haq, in August 1990 and April 1993 by Ghulam Ishaq Khan, and November 1996 by Farooq Leghari. Soon after Farooq Leghari's address to the joint session of parliament on 26 March, there were ripples in the PML(N) circles that he had delivered his own speech and had discarded the text sent to him by the government. Nawaz Sharif decided that this was the right moment to eliminate the power of the president under 58-2(b) to dissolve the assembly. After a meeting with army chief General Jehangir Karamat, he flew to Choti, in Dera Ghazi Khan, where Farooq Leghari had gone for a three-day visit and sought his endorsement to this proposal. Late at night the same day, he addressed the nation and said President Leghari had accepted his proposal to delete this undemocratic provision of the constitution. The federal cabinet met at midnight to approve the draft of the Thirteenth Amendment to the constitution which was moved the next day and passed unanimously by 190 members of the National Assembly to delete Articles 58-2(b) and 112-2(b) from the constitution.

Benazir Bhutto warmly supported this amendment because she had been removed from office twice under these powers. Many leaders of other parties also supported the move to end this 'black law'.

The Thirteenth Amendment Bill was also passed unanimously by the Senate the next day. A week earlier, Nawaz Sharif had invited Nawab Akbar Bugti and Ataullah Mengal to Islamabad as his guests and had secured their support for the Thirteenth and the Fourteenth Amendments. Without the votes of these two parties, Nawaz Sharif could not have managed a two-thirds majority in the Senate.

The passage of the Thirteenth Amendment was widely hailed in the Western media. President Clinton also issued a statement praising this move towards real parliamentary democracy.

Three months after the passage of the Thirteenth Amendment Bill, Nawaz Sharif's government moved the Fourteenth Amendment Bill to add a new article 63-A to the constitution to prevent floor crossing in parliament by requesting members to vote according to the instructions of the leaders of the parliamentary party on all important matters. Those who violate party discipline become liable to lose their seats. This amendment, meant to forestall internal threats to the stability of the government, was passed by the Senate on 30 June 1997. The next day it was passed by the National Assembly with 181 votes. JUI(F) members opposed the amendment and walked out in protest.

Having forestalled these two perceived threats to the stability of the government by strengthening the role of the parliament, Nawaz Sharif turned his attention to the third pillar of state, namely the judiciary. On 16 July he initiated a proposal to establish a parallel system of special courts to provide 'speedy justice' at a meeting of the cabinet. Several members expressed strong reservations on this initiative. Even loyal members like Syed Ghous Ali Shah warned that this proposal could lead to confrontation with the judiciary. The proposal was therefore deferred. But in less than a month a draft law on special courts and anti-terrorism was presented and passed by both houses of parliament on 13 August, setting into motion a serious crisis with the judiciary. Chief Justice Sajjad Ali Shah had repeatedly suggested that the existing judicial system could provide speedy justice if given adequate resources and a parallel judicial system was not required. He also met the prime minister in Lahore at the airport to dissuade him, but Nawaz Sharif was extremely worried about the growing violence, especially in Sindh, reflected in the high profile killing of more than 240 persons between March and July including Shahid Hamid, managing director, KESC, on 5 July. After some time another prominent business executive, Shaukat Mirza was assassinated.

The anti-terrorism legislation was challenged in the Lahore and Rawalpindi High Courts on 15 August. On 21 August the federal government decided to reduce the number of judges from 17 to 12 which was also challenged in the Supreme Court on 5 September and the Chief Justice Sajjad Ali, while admitting the petition issued a stay order. As the hearing of this petition began on 15 September, Shahbaz Sharif persuaded Nawaz Sharif to withdraw the presidential order reducing the number of judges, but the approval of five judges recommended by the chief justice was withheld, amid rumours that the government had reservations about two of the five judges and therefore government might pass a law reducing the number of judges from 17 to 15.

In this crisis with the judiciary, Justice Sajjad Ali started meeting President Farooq Leghari more frequently. Contrary to accepted traditions, he also made several press statements saying the judiciary had a role in ensuring good governance in the country and that parliament had a right to legislate but the judiciary had to decide whether or not the legislation was within the framework of the constitution.

The PPP suddenly realized it had an opportunity to take advantage of this crisis and filed a number of petitions in the Supreme Court on 18 October and 21 October seeking disqualification of Nawaz Sharif.

Meanwhile, there was a strong reaction within the judiciary to the 'political activism' of Chief Justice Sajjad Ali Shah. On 10 October 1997, after the Chief Justice went to Saudi Arabia on a five-day visit, the Acting Chief Justice, Ajmal Mian, while talking to the media, at his swearing in ceremony said that the chief justice had not consulted other judges on the names of the proposed new judges or on the issue of the strength of the Supreme Court. He also said according to the best judicial tradition, judges speak only through their judgements but Justice Sajjad Ali Shah had been making anti-government statements for the past several months. Justice Ajmal Mian also convened a full Supreme Court session on 13 October to discuss the issue of appointment of judges. Justice Sajjad Ali Shah, when he heard about the full court session cut short his visit, arrived on the morning of 13 October and cancelled the full court session. Later on the same day, a reference against Justice Ajmal Mian was submitted before the chief justice alleging that by calling the full court session, he had violated the constitution and the matter should be referred to the Supreme Judicial Council.

Between 15 and 22 October, the Supreme Court admitted several petitions from PPP leaders and lawyers against the prime minister, Senator Saifur Rehman and some other PML leaders.

On 20 October, six Supreme Court judges posted in Lahore and Karachi met in Lahore and submitted a requisition for convening a full court session. This was followed on 21 October by a letter addressed to the president, saying the chief justice's own appointment was not based on the principle of seniority. This letter was signed by 9 out of 12 Supreme Court judges.

This confrontation between the judiciary and the executive branches of government took a new turn, when on 24 October, the Supreme Court admitted a petition challenging the Fourteenth Amendment, passed to prevent floor crossing in legislative bodies. Disallowing the attorney general's pleas for adjourning the case to a later date, a three-member bench of the Supreme Court decided, on 29 October, to suspend the operation of the Fourteenth Amendment. The law minister, Khalid Anwar, said that this decision to suspend a constitutional provision was unprecedented in the judicial history of the Commonwealth. In the National Assembly, many members of parliament openly criticized the chief justice for suspending the Fourteenth Amendment with the help of two other judges who were appointed on an ad hoc basis and were confirmed in disregard of 20 March 1996 judgement on the appointment of judges.

The very next day on 30 October, a petition was filed in the Supreme Court that three speeches in the National Assembly against the suspension of the Fourteenth Amendment amounted to contempt of court. On 31 October, another petition was filed by advocate Iqbal Haider, seeking the annulment of the Thirteenth Amendment and restoration of the president's power to dissolve the National Assembly and dismiss the elected government under a restored Article 58-2(b).

The game plan of the opposition and other anti-government elements in the system was now clear. Having created a judicial crisis on the issue of appointment of judges, having secured the suspension of the Fourteenth Amendment from the Supreme Court and by forestalling effective opposition to such decisions, through filing of contempt proceedings against those who criticized them, the stage was now ready for the final assault: namely the suspension of the Thirteenth Amendment to restore the power of the president to dissolve the National Assembly.

Nawaz Sharif and his political and legal colleagues reacted to this dangerous game plan in three different ways. First, they relented on the issues of appointment of judges by passing a law on 31 October to increase the number of judges from 12 to 17, from both houses of parliament. This was welcomed by the president and by the chief justice. Second, as a three-member bench of the Supreme Court, on 3 November, had issued a contempt notice to the prime minister and several of his colleagues, Nawaz Sharif agreed to appear in the Supreme Court on 17 November and file a written statement to express full respect for the Supreme Court and its decisions. The same night the National Assembly passed an amendment in the Contempt of Court Act, giving the affected person the right to file an inter-court appeal, which would be heard by those judges of the Supreme Court, who were not on the bench which admitted or heard the contempt petition. The Senate also passed the bill the next day but the Supreme Court issued an order two days later, on 20 November, to restrain the president from signing this Act. This Act was also challenged in the High Courts of Lahore and Karachi. Addressing a meeting of the parliamentary party held on 17 November, Nawaz Sharif said that even after the chief justice's proposal to appoint five new judges had been accepted, there had been no change in his attitude at the behest of the president.

At the same time, i.e. on 18 November, advocate Raja Afsar Khan, submitted an application in the Quetta Circuit Bench of the Supreme Court at Quetta, to propose that the appointment of Sajjad Ali Shah as chief justice was contrary to the 20 March 1996 judgement. He should therefore resign. Similar petitions were filed a week later, on 25 November, by advocate Qazi Mohammad Anwar, in the Peshawar High Court and the Peshawar Circuit Bench of Supreme Court.

On 26 November, the Quetta Bench of the Supreme Court, consisting of Justice Irshad Hasan Khan and Justice Khalilur Rahman, admitted the constitutional petition against the appointment of Sajjad Ali Shah and suspended the notification under which he had been appointed. The chief justice immediately declared this decision as illegal but the federal government sent a summary to the president the same day, recommending the appointment of Ajmal Mian as acting chief justice. Next day, a five-member Bench of the Supreme Court decided by 4 to 1, (with Justice Mamun Qazi dissenting) to suspend the decision of the Quetta Bench amid noisy reaction from pro-government lawyers and PML workers raising slogans against the chief justice.

This crisis deepened when the two-member Peshawar Bench of the Supreme Court consisting of Justice Saeed-uz-Zaman Siddiqui and Justice Fazal Ilahi Khan, held on 27 November that being a party, the chief justice could not suspend the decision of the Quetta Bench. It directed the registrar to submit all important cases to the next senior judge, Ajmal Mian and not to Justice Sajjad Ali Shah. The next day Justice Saeed-uz-Zaman Siddiqui, convened a 15-member full Bench to hear all the petitions against the appointment of the Chief Justice Sajjad Ali Shah. In retaliation Justice Sajjad Ali Shah sent references to the president against Justices Saeed-uz-Zaman, Fazal Ilahi Khan, Irshad Hasan Khan, Nasir Aslam Zahid and Khalilur Rahman.

This was the charged atmosphere on 28 November in which Prime Minister Nawaz Sharif appeared before the Supreme Court in the contempt case, along with hundreds of his supporters and workers. There were strong rumours that in the face of the growing 'revolt' by the majority of the Supreme Court judges against Justice Sajjad Ali Shah, he would convict the prime minister of contempt of court to force him to resign. That a prime minister, elected by an overwhelming majority of voters was to be dragged into this artificial 'judicial crisis' to weaken his position to this extent, within a short period of nine months, was totally unacceptable to PML workers. Some of them were apprehensive that if the Supreme Court was allowed to conduct its business, the prime minister would be convicted. As a result he would also lose the political battle. They therefore resorted to violence to disrupt the court proceedings. The chief justice and other members of the Bench left the court and went to their chamber to mark one of the most disgraceful episodes in the judicial history of Pakistan.

The next day, while the registrar issued a cause list on behalf of Justice Sajjad Ali Shah to hear the contempt petition against the prime minister, the deputy registrar issued another cause list convening the 15-member full court under Justice Saeed-uz-Zaman Siddiqui to hear the petitions against the appointment of Sajjad Ali Shah, who meanwhile had written letters to the president and the army chief for army protection. While the army chief, General Jehangir Karamat sent the letter addressed to him to the defence secretary, the president sent the letter received by him to the prime minister, requesting to make adequate security arrangements for the Supreme Court and the chief justice. He also recommended that the reference against Justice Saeed-uz-Zaman Siddiqui should be sent to the Supreme Judicial Council. The prime minister replied saying he had already condemned the 28 November attack on the Supreme Court and taken action against those involved. There was no need for calling the army to protect the Supreme Court as adequate security had been provided. The prime minister also blamed the president for becoming a party in the confrontation between the government and the chief justice.

The prime minister addressed the nation on 30 November and said that he had been elected by the people to solve their problems, but he was being dragged by the opposition in collusion with the president and the chief justice, into an endless web of hostile court cases and the President's House had become a centre for intrigues.

This bizarre drama reached its climax on 2 December 1997, when Chief Justice Sajjad Ali Shah, chairing a three-member Bench, decided after hearing arguments for only ten minutes to suspend the Thirteenth Amendment and restore the power of the president to dissolve the assembly under Article 58-2(b) of the constitution.

By midday on that fateful day, the entire cabinet and about hundred members of parliament had already reached the PM House, awaiting news from the Supreme Court. As I drove past the presidency, towards the PM House, I saw more than hundred media representatives crowding the main entrance gate of the presidency. One of the members of parliament was the first to receive a call on his cell phone, which he readily relayed to all those present. 'The chief justice has suspended the Thirteenth Amendment. Two former members of President Leghari's caretaker setup (Irshad Haqqani and Najam Sethi) have personally taken this judgement to the presidency, along with, according to rumours floating around, the draft of an order dissolving the assembly and a list of the caretaker cabinet that will takeover after the dissolution.' Everyone was stunned but no one knew if there was anything the government in power could do, except to wait for the next move.

Apparently in a flash of prudence, President Farooq Leghari decided to consult the army chief, before taking such drastic action, within only ten months of a general election. As I learnt later directly from General Jehangir Karamat himself, Farooq Leghari narrated at some length the confrontation between the prime minister and the chief justice and some other charges of one-sided accountability and said that the country's administration could no longer be run according to the constitution. 'I believe in democratic principles and traditions and would not do anything that is against the law and the constitution,' Farooq Leghari said. 'But when the situation becomes so bad, these drastic remedies become unavoidable. I hope you will support my decisions.' According to General Jehangir Karamat, he did not respond to him directly but just looked the other way and the game plan was over.

By 2 p.m. we learnt that the army chief had left the presidency but no dissolution order had been issued. One could hear a visible sigh of relief followed by loud applause. Several members suggested that every member of the National Assembly, who was present, should sign a motion of impeachment of the president under Article 47 of the constitution, so that it could be tabled in the house the very next day. Within two hours a draft motion had been prepared and signed by more than hundred members. This news of a move to impeach the president had travelled quickly to the presidency because by 5 p.m., the president had sent his resignation to the speaker of the National Assembly.

While these dramatic developments were taking place in the presidency and the PM House, the final phase of the drama was also being played out in the Supreme Court. While Justice Sajjad Ali Shah had convened his 3-member bench in Court Room No. 1 to hear the appeal against the Thirteenth Amendment, Justice Saeed-uz-Zaman Siddiqui had convened a 10-member full court in Court Room No. 2 to hear four identical petitions challenging the appointment of Justice Sajjad Ali Shah as chief justice. The full court upheld the earlier decision of the Quetta Bench, suspended the notification appointing him as chief justice and asked the senior most judge, Justice Ajmal Mian, to takeover as acting chief justice. When informed of the decision of the Bench convened by Justice Sajjad Ali Shah to suspend the Thirteenth Amendment, the full court also suspended that decision.

A summary signed by the prime minister was sent to the president the same afternoon, recommending the removal of Justice Sajjad Ali Shah and the appointment of Justice Ajmal Mian as acting chief justice. President Farooq Leghari convened a press conference and said since he was unable to sign this recommendation, he was resigning. He could have dissolved the assembly, but did not because he believed in democracy.

Wasim Sajjad, chairman Senate, who assumed the charge of acting president, promptly signed this summary bringing to a close one of the most unfortunate judicial crises in the political history of Pakistan. Justice Ajmal Mian took oath as chief justice of Pakistan on 23 December, after a 10-member full court decided unanimously, after further hearings from 11 to 19 December, that the initial appointment of Justice Sajjad Ali Shah was illegal and unconstitutional.

As dust settled over this crisis, I had lengthy discussions with many of my colleagues, especially Khalid Anwar and Chaudhry Nisar, about the real reasons behind the crisis and the lessons we could learn from it. We all agreed that the crisis started with the decision of Nawaz Sharif to setup a separate judicial system for trying cases involving terrorism. But when prominent opposition elements saw a confrontation in the making, they started conspiring to accentuate the confrontation and bring down the government by restoring the president's power to dissolve the assembly. Justice Sajjad Ali Shah's insistence on having five additional judges to increase the strength of the Supreme Court to seventeen was obviously intended to enable him to constitute a full bench of his choice to hear constitutional petitions. President Farooq Leghari was also unhappy when the prime minister suddenly had the Thirteenth Amendment passed from both houses to curtail his power to dissolve the National Assembly. Having dismissed the government of Benazir Bhutto and making way for Nawaz Sharif in the February 1997 elections, he naturally expected better cooperation from the prime minister. But there was no real crisis, economic or constitutional, to justify dismissal of an elected government so soon after an election in which the ruling party had won more than two-thirds majority. On 4 December, Nawaz Sharif wrote a letter to Farooq Leghari saying we should bury the past and work together for the future. Farooq Leghari replied that they had differences in the past but no bitterness. He conveyed his goodwill and best wishes for the future.

Election of the New President

On 3 June 1997, i.e. six months before President Leghari actually resigned, in the meeting of the parliamentary party of PML(N), one member, rising on a point of order, proposed that Sartaj Aziz should be adopted as the PML candidate in the next presidential election, whenever it took place. I was taken aback by this proposal as were many other members because no presidential election was on the horizon at that time, but the proposal was greeted by spontaneous applause and there was no further discussion. Next day some newspapers carried a small news item that the PML(N)'s parliamentary party had decided that Sartaj Aziz would be its candidate for the next presidential election. This was obviously a crude attempt to send a message to Farooq Leghari.

Soon after Farooq Leghari's resignation on 2 December, speculation about who would be the candidate for the office of president caught the front pages of all the newspapers. Many PML leaders like Chaudhry Nisar Ali Khan and Ilahi Bakhsh Soomro, supported my candidature indirectly by suggesting that since both the prime minister and chairman Senate were from Punjab and the speaker National Assembly was from Sindh, the president should be from one of the smaller provinces. But many newspapers columns openly advocated my election, in fact selection, because the formal election process was in effect dependent on the decision of one man—Prime Minister Nawaz Sharif. A typical comment by Ikram Sehgal that appeared in *The News* of 8 December 1997, under the title 'Who is who in the Presidential Race':

> Sartaj Aziz has been a bureaucrat, a technocrat, a legislator, a government minister and now a politician. Through all this he has maintained a clean reputation for honesty and resolve, as finance minister he was easily the most clean and had the most integrity. Even in the partisan role as the PML secretary general, Sartaj Aziz remained above the dirt of day-to-day politics, keeping the game clean, at least at his level. At this time, Senator Sartaj Aziz is definitely a reluctant dark horse. Self-effacing and humble by nature, he has not shown any inclination that he would like to be president what to talk about lobbying on his own behalf as the others are doing. He is a tested man, coming through the vicissitudes of political life in Pakistan and emerging as a man for all seasons. Among a number of extremely good candidates for the president of Pakistan, Sartaj Aziz comes across a patriot who is always there to serve his country selflessly. Qualifications alone put him head and shoulders over the rest of the field, one only hopes that the major political groups would mutually agree on making this outstanding Pakistani the President of this country.

As I learnt later, the prime minister had also asked the army chief, General Jehangir Karamat, to prepare an assessment of the relative merits of different presidential candidates. In a list of fifteen candidates, I was rated as the top candidate in an assessment presented to the prime minister on 10 December.

Meanwhile the prime minister was holding consultations with other political parties, MQM agreed to support the PML(N) candidate when many of their demands, like the release of 1,250 detained persons, payment of Rs50 million to affectees and withdrawal of Rangers, were accepted. After some hesitation, ANP also agreed to support the PML(N) candidate unconditionally. But in these consultations Nawaz Sharif did not reveal the name of the PML(N)'s candidate.

As many analysts pointed out later, the prime minister wanted a low profile and totally loyal president, who would never question any decision or proposal made by the prime minister. In the cabinet meeting held on 12 December, the power to nominate the PML(N) candidate was given to the prime minister who revealed his mind partially, when he enthusiastically agreed with one or two ministers who said, 'This time you should not take any risk whatsoever. That is more important than the province to which the president belongs.'

In another cabinet meeting on 15 December called for 9 p.m., the prime minister announced to the surprise of most of his cabinet colleagues, the name of Justice (retd) Rafiq Tarrar. He had invited three of the potential candidates, Ghous Ali Shah, Gohar Ayub Khan, and myself to meet him individually, just before the cabinet meeting. When he told me about his decision, I only said: 'We are all bound to respect your decision but I will always harbour one regret that I could not win your trust after everything I have done for the party so sincerely in the past twelve years.' He responded after a long silence and said, 'finance ministry is the nerve centre of my reform programme and you are the best finance minister. I will not be able to find another finance minister like you if you were elevated as president.'

Incidentally, Rafiq Tarrar's name was not on the list of fifteen candidates given by the prime minister to the army chief for their assessment. On 18 December, Rafiq Tarrar's nomination papers were rejected by the acting chief election commissioner because of some newspaper comments he had been casting aspirations on the judiciary and the chief justice. But a three-member bench of the Lahore High Court under Justice Malik Mohammad Qayyum overruled the decision of the acting chief election commissioner (CEC) and allowed Rafiq Tarrar to take part in the elections.

The election was held on 31 December and Justice (retd) Rafiq Tarrar was elected president by 374 votes against 58 received by the opposition PPP candidate Aftab Shaban Mirani. Maulana Sheerani of JUI(F) received 22 votes.

Ironically, the controversy surrounding Nawaz Sharif's decision to nominate Justice (retd) Rafiq Tarrar resurfaced in the media, after the military takeover in October 1999. Someone with a higher status and wider acceptability, it was emphasized, would have raised the tone of political discourse in the country and served as a bridge between the political establishment led by the prime minister and the military establishment. Instead of quietly signing the dismissal orders of General Pervez Musharraf, he might have forestalled the military takeover, by persuading the prime minister to wait for his return from

Sri Lanka and then inviting them both for a meeting to sort out the differences.

Population Census of 1998

In the first tenure of Nawaz Sharif from November 1990 to 18 July 1993, one of the most important unfinished agenda items for me, as finance minister, was the population census due in 1991, after the prescribed ten-yearly interval. In March 1991, I had presented a proposal to the cabinet to hold the census in November 1991, preceded by a housing census in October. This proposal was approved but the results of the housing census created a strong reaction, especially in the Punjab. The late Ghulam Haider Wyne, chief minister of Punjab, pointed out unprecedented irregularities in the housing census and demanded a postponement of the November census, until fool proof arrangements could be made for an accurate count. 'Punjab does not wish to lose its majority in the country's population, along with its representation in the assemblies and its due share in national resources, due to a faulty census,' he said with some emotion.

I had lengthy consultations in all the provinces and went back to the cabinet twice in 1992, to seek approval for undertaking the census, first in March 1992 and then in November 1992, but the prime minister overruled me, despite my outburst on the second occasion that 'We are becoming like Lebanon which because of the Muslim– Christian imbalance had not had a census in the past fifty years. A country which cannot conduct a proper census does not have any credible basis for planning its development programmes and priorities.'

For reasons, I have never understood, the PPP government, from October 1993 to August 1996, never took up this issue of conducting a population census in the country. But for me, this was a top priority item and within a month, I went back to the cabinet and got approval for conducting a census in October 1997, in consultation with the provinces. The proposal was approved without much debate because I had assured the chief minister of Punjab, Shahbaz Sharif, in advance that Punjab's concerns would be fully met.

From the intensive consultations I had with officials in 1991–92, I knew that the large number of enumerators that would actually undertake the exercise, i.e. the primary school teachers and lower grade officials in districts, were not really under the effective control of provincial governments. If they were convinced by local politicians that a higher count would give their province more seats in the National Assembly or larger resources through the National Finance Commission (NFC), they would exaggerate the results. One way to ensure a fair and accurate census, I thought, would be to announce that these vital matters would be based on the 1981 census and would not be affected by the 1997 census. But I was not confident that this would be accepted by the provinces if different results came out. The only other course, I decided, was to request the army to attach one army enumerator with each civilian enumerator.

I met the army chief, General Jehangir Karamat, in April 1997, and conveyed this proposal to him. First he was baffled. 'You are asking me to spare 160,000 soldiers to conduct this census. Can we bear the financial cost and handle the logistics?' he asked. I replied, 'I will provide whatever financial resources you need, if you can handle the logistics.' He asked for a week's time to give his response. He called back in less than a week and said, 'Yes, we can support the census. I am sending Major General Zahid Ehsan and his team to discuss the details and prepare for the operation.' When General Zahid Ehsan called on me, we constituted joint teams from representatives of the census organization and army to make detailed operational plans for carrying out the census through joint teams in October 1997. The proposal was presented and approved by the cabinet on 16 July, to hold the population census from 16 October 1997.

In the first week of October 1997, however, I received an urgent call from General Zahid Ehsan that they would like to postpone the census to early 1998, because the census could provide a valuable opportunity to build a national database and for that purpose a larger questionnaire had to be prepared and printed in the next few months. I readily agreed to this useful proposal, which was then presented to the prime minister and approved in a special briefing session.

The task of designing a revised questionnaire and printing and distributing 50 million copies in all parts of the country proved quite challenging but it was completed in record time. On 7 January 1998, the cabinet decided formally that the population census would be conducted from 2 to 18 March 1998. In choosing these dates we had considered the fact that in that week, India would also be holding its general elections and the deployment of a large segment of the Pakistan army on civilian duty would not therefore ignite any adventurous ideas across the border.

The joint census was an outstanding success. It was largely conducted peacefully except in some parts of Balochistan, where there were protests and incidents of violence. The date for the completion of census was therefore extended in Balochistan to 18 April. The provisional results of the fifth population census announced on 8 July 1998, were a pleasant surprise. The total population of the country in March 1998 was 132.35 million and not 140 million as projected by the Planning Commission for 1998 by applying the assumed population growth rate to the 1981 population figure of 84 million. It meant that apart from correcting the exaggerated 1981 base, this was clear evidence that the population growth rate had also slowed down from 3.1 per cent in the 1970s to 2.6 per cent in the 1980s and 2.3 per cent in the 1990s. This was welcome news because without this continuing decline in the rate of population, it would be difficult for the country to manage the growing demand for food, education, housing and transport in the coming decades.

The provincial breakdown of the new census figures (Punjab: 73.6 million, Sindh: 30.4 million, NWFP: 17.7 million, Balochistan: 6.5 million, FATA: 3.1 million, and Islamabad 0.8 million) was also broadly in line with the percentage shares of the 1981 census. There would thus be no consequential changes in the number of seats in the Assembly or the provincial shares in the NFC Awards.

Even before the census results were announced, I had submitted a proposal to the prime minister in April 1998 to create a new organization, called National Database and Registration Authority (NADRA), to takeover and process all the data forms collected during the census. In the process, I was able to persuade the interior minister, Chaudhry Shujaat Hussain to transfer the function of issuing national ID cards from the ministry of interior to this new registration authority for issuing computerized ID cards. There was an understanding that NADRA would absorb some staff from the old Registration Organization, but this promise was not really fulfilled. I was somewhat amused a few years later, when General Musharraf started claiming credit for creating NADRA, an organization that had been created eighteen months before Musharraf took over.

Nuclear Tests of May 1998

Another major event with far reaching regional, international and domestic consequences for the future was the nuclear tests of 28 May in response to India's tests of 11 May 1998.

Pakistan's nuclear programme had actually started in the 1960s, when it established the Pakistan Atomic Energy Commission (PAEC) to promote nuclear technology for peaceful purposes. In 1962, PAEC acquired a small research reactor for setting up the Pakistan Institute of Nuclear Science and Technology (PINSTEC) near Islamabad. In the late 1960s, Canada also agreed to build, under IAEA safeguards, a 120 megawatt nuclear power plant near Karachi.

At that time, Pakistan was aware that India's nuclear programme was secretly aimed at developing nuclear weapons, but it avoided the temptation to follow the same route in the expectation that the Non-Proliferation Treaty (NPT) being actively negotiated would prevent India from going nuclear. But it did not and in May 1974 India carried out a nuclear explosion codenamed 'Buddha Smiles'.

Zulfikar Ali Bhutto, who was Pakistan's prime minister at the time and had never concealed his resolve to develop nuclear weapons if India did so, responded to the Indian tests by launching plans to implement this resolve. In 1975, he invited Munir Ahmad Khan, then working in the International Atomic Energy Commission in Vienna to come back as chairman of the Pakistan Atomic Energy Commission. A year later, in 1976, he persuaded another outstanding metallurgist Dr Abdul Qadeer Khan to return to Pakistan to build a uranium enrichment plant at Kahuta, near Islamabad. Having failed to secure a plant to reprocess spent uranium fuel into plutonium from France, under agreement signed in 1973, Pakistan with the help of these two scientists and their teams, started on the alternative technological route of building centrifuges to enrich uranium for building an explosive device. It took the A. Q. Khan Research Laboratories six years to achieve that objective. Meanwhile PAEC completed its tasks of developing a guidance system and other related requirements by 1982. Despite insurmountable technical and logistical obstacles, Pakistan had the first atomic explosive device by 1983 but sensitive to global concerns it kept it under wraps.

Pakistan was surprised that the international reaction to India's nuclear test of May 1974 was so muted. It therefore launched, from then onwards, a two-track strategy. Under track one, it took a diplomatic initiative by moving a resolution in the UN General Assembly in September 1974 to establish a nuclear free zone in South Asia. This resolution was carried by the large majority of General Assembly members. The same resolution was moved and passed year after year. Pakistan also isolated India on the issue, by offering to sign the Comprehensive Test Ban Treaty (CTBT) and the Non-Proliferation Treaty (NPT) if India would do the same.

Under the second track, Pakistan, as already mentioned, was developing its own capacity to respond in kind. USA had detected these efforts but in view of the valuable support Pakistan was offering to counter the Russian invasion of Afghanistan, it did not take any action, although under the 1977–78 Symington and Glenn amendments, it could stop economic assistance to Pakistan. In 1987, however, USA enacted the so-called Pressler Law under which the US president had to certify each year that Pakistan was not developing a nuclear device, to qualify for economic and military assistance. The certificate was issued for three years, but in 1990 as soon as the Russian forces left Afghanistan in the wake of the Geneva accords of 1988, the president did not sign the certificate invoking sanctions under the Pressler Law.

On 1 October 1990, when I was finance minister in the caretaker cabinet of Ghulam Mustafa Jatoi, I received an urgent message that the US ambassador would like to call on me that afternoon. He came and delivered a letter saying Pakistan had violated the Pressler Law and due to sanctions imposed under this law, it would no longer receive any economic assistance or military supplies from USA. When I enquired if the supply of sixty F-16 planes which were not a part of military assistance but were being purchased on a commercial basis through Pakistan's own resources would be affected, the reply was yes. I conveyed to the ambassador, Pakistan's strong reaction and said, on the nuclear issue, India was the independent variable which USA should have focused on. Pakistan was only a dependent variable in the sense that if India went ahead with the nuclear option, Pakistan had no option but to follow suit in order to safeguard its security. This is a remark that I also repeated to US deputy secretary of state, Strobe Talbott, in July 1998, when he was persuading both India and Pakistan to sign the CTBT and has been quoted in his book *Engaging India* (p. 104).

The timing of imposing Pressler sanctions on Pakistan was both ironic and significant. These came only two months before Pakistan embarked on a major programme to liberalize and deregulate its economy, a policy long advocated by USA and other bilateral and multilateral donors. But USA was unable to support this policy throughout the 1990s, because of these sanctions.

Throughout the preceding four decades Pakistan had been dependent on USA for its defence capability, under various defence cooperation agreements. This cooperation was at its peak in the 1980s after the Russian invasion of Afghanistan, taking Pakistan's defence budget from Rs9 billion in 1977–78 to Rs90 billion 1989–90 or 6.9 per cent of GDP. This unexpected termination of not only military assistance but also commercial purchases of spare parts imposed a very heavy burden on Pakistan's finances, because Pakistan had to buy these spare parts at much higher prices. It forced Pakistan to borrow from abroad on harder terms to pay its debt service obligations. The net result of these developments on the national budget is shown in the following table:

The Changing Composition of the National Budget (% of GDP)					
Head	1980–81	1984–85	1989–90	1994–95	1999–2000
Current Expenditure	13.8	17.7	19.3	18.5	18.2
Interest Payments	2.2	3.5	5.4	5.2	6.8
Defence	5.6	6.7	6.9	5.6	4.3
Other Federal Expenditure	2.9	3.5	3.0	3.1	2.9
Provincial Expenditures	3.1	4.0	4.0	4.6	4.2
Development Expenditure	9.4	7.0	6.6	4.4	2.8
Total Budget Expenditure	23.2	24.7	25.9	22.9	21.0
Source: Pakistan Economic Survey—different years					

As can be seen, development expenditure which in 1980–81 was the largest budget item at 9.4 per cent of GDP had declined to 2.8 per cent of GDP by 1999–2000 and had become the smallest item. In 1989–90, defence expenditure at 6.9 per cent of GDP had become the largest item, but as interest payments rocketed to 6.8 per cent of GDP by 1999–2000 (compared to 2.2 per cent in 1980–81 and 5.4 per cent in 1989–90) it became the largest item, followed by defence and then development.

After the nuclear tests in May 1998, other donor countries and multilateral agencies also imposed sanctions. Total new annual commitments in 1998–2000 were therefore 30 per cent lower than the average of the preceding three years, despite the fact that Pakistan had fulfilled all the conditions of an IMF agreement signed in 1997. In fact an IMF mission which visited Pakistan in May 1998 had recommended the release of the third tranche of its loan only a week before the nuclear tests. The agreement was suspended despite this positive recommendation because of nuclear related sanctions, and not due to slippages in conditionalities, as repeatedly publicized by the Musharraf regime.

The Decision to Test

After the victory of Bharatiya Janata Party (BJP) in March 1998 elections, speculation that India would conduct another nuclear test and openly claim the status of a nuclear weapons state had started gathering momentum. Even then, India stunned the world on 11 May 1998, when the Indian Prime Minister Vajpayee announced at a hurriedly convened press conference that India had conducted three nuclear tests at Pokhran in Rajasthan. Two days later, it conducted two additional tests.

These tests undoubtedly constituted a grave threat to the security of Pakistan because the strategic 1:3 balance which it had maintained with India over the years had now become less relevant. The provocative tests also presented Pakistan with a serious dilemma. However, the way Pakistan responded to this dilemma has become a landmark example of decision making in Pakistan's history.

Prime Minister Nawaz Sharif was in Kazakhstan on an official visit when the Indian tests were conducted on 11 May. He cut short his visit and returned the next day. Before he landed, we received information that the Defence Committee of the Cabinet (DCC) would meet at 10 a.m. on 13 May.

The DCC, chaired by the prime minister, was attended by three ministers, Gohar Ayub Khan (foreign minister), Chaudhry Shujaat Hussain (interior minister), and myself as finance minister and the three service chiefs, General Jehangir Karamat (chief of army staff), Air Chief Marshal Parvaiz Mehdi Qureshi (chief of air staff), and Admiral Fasih Bokhari (chief of naval staff). In addition, Dr Abdul Qadeer Khan (director of Khan Research Laboratories (KRL)) and Dr Samar Mubarakmand (member technical, PAEC). The chairman PAEC, Dr Ishfaq Ahmad was abroad at that time.

The DCC meeting reviewed in some depth, the diplomatic, the economic, the strategic and the security dimensions of Pakistan's response to India's nuclear tests. In the process, the Indian objectives in carrying out these tests were clearly highlighted:

- India's basic objective is to become a de facto member of the nuclear club without signing the NPT.
- The tests will improve India's status as a regional power and strengthen, in the medium term, its claim for the permanent membership of the UN Security Council.
- The nuclear status will give a strategic edge to India in its relations with Pakistan, and enable it to adopt a more aggressive policy on Kashmir.
- Forcing Pakistan to follow suit in conducting its nuclear tests at a time when its economy is much more vulnerable than India's. Since India already has a strong edge in conventional and nuclear capacity, the deepening economic imbalance will bring about a decisive shift in the balance of power between India and Pakistan.
- As I learnt later, Prime Minister Nawaz Sharif had already reached a firm decision, even before he returned from Kazakistan, that Pakistan had no option but to respond to the Indian tests. He, therefore asked Dr A. Q. Khan and Dr Ashfaq Ahmed about the minimum time that would be required to carry out these nuclear tests. They all agreed that a minimum period of two weeks would

be required. The DCC then authorized all the preparatory work that had to be undertaken.

- Meanwhile, India launched its own diplomatic offensive to justify its nuclear tests. Indian Prime Minister Vajpayee sent letters to the heads of state and government of all the UN members, justifying the test. The letters to the US and other western leaders highlighted the potential threat from China to the largest democracy in the world.

- In the next few days, the Prime Minister had several meetings with the Army Chief and the country's top scientists including Dr A. Q. Khan, Dr Ashfaq Ahmed and Dr Samar Mubarakmand to review arrangements for the tests.

Since the media and the public were not aware that a minimum period of two weeks would be required to carry out these tests, there was speculation that the Prime Minister was hesitant or uncertain about the issue.

There was also some concern that the US and the western reactions to the Indian tests had not been as forceful as expected. Sanctions under the 1994 law had been imposed but these would affect new bilateral loans only. Two-thirds of total foreign loans received by India, $3.2 billion a year, were however from multilateral sources.

As expected, the main focus of US and western diplomacy shifted, soon after the Indian tests, to the objective of preventing Pakistan from testing. President Clinton telephoned Nawaz Sharif and offered a package of economic and military assistance including the F-16 planes whose delivery had been suspended under the Pressler sanction since October 1990.

Nobody could be more aware than me, of the historic opportunity that was knocking at our door, not only to jump start the economy but also to rebuild the country's eroded defence capability. But I was equally aware of the growing threat to our security and the strong public sentiment that Pakistan had to give a befitting response to India's tests. In my comments, therefore, I emphasized that even a substantial package of economic and conventional military assistance would not address our longer term security concerns. If Pakistan did not test, or at least delayed its option to test, India would conduct further tests to force Pakistan to respond; it could take aggressive military initiatives in Kashmir; it could intensify subversive activity in various cities of Pakistan. We should therefore ask for a security umbrella in addition to an economic package. But if India's nuclear test was only an opening shot in BJP's strategy of using its nuclear blackmail for forcing Pakistan to give up its claim on Kashmir, then even a security umbrella would prove to be only a short term and ineffective palliative.

A cabinet meeting was held the next day, 14 May 1998, and to my surprise the discussion and the reaction was very sober and constructive. Only three members took a hawkish line and advocated that unless we retained strategic parity with India, our very existence would be threatened. The US would offer a package but then prolong the negotiations till Pakistan's bargaining power, having postponed the testing option, was virtually over, making it impossible for Pakistan to test in the future.

In comparison at least six members took a more dovish line, by emphasizing that everyone including India knew that we had the weapons. We could always test at a time of our choosing, but meanwhile why not take advantage of this opportunity: (i) to isolate India diplomatically, while elevating Pakistan's stature in the world, (ii) secure the repeal of the Pressler amendment to resume the flow of conventional military hardware including F-16 planes, (iii) receive substantial economic assistance and debt relief. The test of true leadership, some said, was to take the public along in support of sensible policy options that are in the longer term national interest.

Another six members used hawkish rhetoric but advocated restraint to gain more time for decision making. These members were neither hawks nor doves but could perhaps be categorized as 'Hoves'.

As expected, the cabinet left the vital decision to the prime minister but authorized the preparation of a contingency plan to counter the effect of sanctions, in case Pakistan decided to go for the option to test. It also decided to contact friendly countries through special envoys or letters to gain their support and expose India's continuing threats to Pakistan's security.

In the Cabinet meeting, the Prime Minister listened to all his colleagues but didn't express his opinion. He, however, seemed very composed and confident, as if looking forward to his tryst with history.

On 14 May and again on 17 May, leaders of eleven political parties demanded immediate testing. In the Senate, the main opposition party, the Pakistan Peoples Party (PPP) moved a resolution calling for an effective response to India's test. The resolution was carried unanimously. The leader of the opposition, Benazir Bhutto, made a statement on 17 May that India was issuing threats to Pakistan. 'We must respond to them by conducting nuclear test, which is our right.' The people of Pakistan were ready for all sacrifices.

These domestic pressures were greatly accentuated by several statements that Indian leaders made during this period to force Pakistan to test. The Indian Home Minister, L. K. Advani warned that the Indian tests had changed the strategic balance in the subcontinent, Pakistan should, therefore stop all cross border activities in Kashmir or be prepared for consequences. The Indian spokesman Krishan Lal Sharma said, India was now in a position to take control of Azad Kashmir. These statements were followed by intense Indian firing along the Line of Control in Kashmir.

Strobe Talbott, the US deputy secretary of state visited Pakistan along with General Anthony Zinni, commander of the US central command, to dissuade Pakistan from testing. As he records in some detail in his book *Engaging India*, he got a 'bombastic no' from the foreign ministry and a 'polite no' from the 'cool customer' in Rawalpindi, i.e. General Jehangir Karamat (p. 63).

In fact, General Karamat while quietly supportive of the decision to test, did not display any enthusiasm or anxiety in the DCC meeting on 13 May or in subsequent meetings.

Having decided to go for the tests immediately after India's nuclear tests, Nawaz Sharif was much more restrained in his statements during that fateful interval of seventeen days. But he was closely monitoring all the preparations for the tests. An L-shaped one kilometre long tunnel had been built fifteen years ago at Ras Koh Hills in the Chagai district of Balochistan. By 19 May, two teams of PAEC and KRL scientists with all support personnel and equipment had reached the site. It took them five days to prepare the nuclear devices and establish the command and observation post. The test tunnel was sealed on 25 May. On 26 May the prime minister was informed that everything was ready for carrying out a series of nuclear tests.

On 27 May, having been alerted by his own intelligence agencies that a test was imminent, President Clinton made the last of his five phone calls to Nawaz Sharif. This time Nawaz Sharif was frank and forthcoming. 'I am sorry to disappoint you, but I have no choice but to go ahead with the test,' he told Clinton.

On 28 May, at 3:40 p.m., Pakistan conducted five nuclear tests with a cumulative weight of 50 kilotons, producing an explosion of 4.5 on the Richter scale. As the radiation inside the tunnel hit the surface, the accumulated earth on the hills was dislodged, turning the mountains white. On the 30 May, Pakistan conducted one more test.

On the evening of 28 May, Nawaz Sharif addressed the nation and said Pakistan has already become the seventh nuclear nation of the world and restored the strategic balance with India. We are ready for dialogue with India on all issues but we are also ready for every sacrifice to defend our security and vital national interests. The nation has to prepare for a comprehensive austerity programme, in the wake of sanctions that are now inevitable.

The successful nuclear tests by Pakistan led to spontaneous jubilation, not just in Pakistan but throughout the Muslim world. There were jovial processions in every city, national flags went up on every house and shop and tons of sweets were distributed. Nawaz Sharif received a tumultuous welcome when he landed in Lahore on 30 May.

The very next day on 31 May, President Clinton signed the declaration imposing sanctions on Pakistan. Similar action was taken by Japan, Canada, Sweden and Australia. But UK, Germany and France refused to follow the US and Japan. France said that sanctions seldom realize their objectives. Germany said that non-proliferation can be pursued only through dialogue. The same day, the US moved a resolution in the Security Council seeking imposition of sanctions, but it was opposed by Germany and France and vetoed by China. The resolution was therefore amended only to express concern over the tests and appeal to India and Pakistan to avoid an arms race. Resolution 1172 passed by the Security Council on 6 June demanded that the two nations refrain from further testing, sign CTBT and resume dialogue to find mutually acceptable solutions that addressed the root cause of these tensions including Kashmir.

On 12 June, however, the foreign ministers of G-8 countries (Canada, France, Germany, Italy, Japan, Russia, UK, and the US) issued a communiqué that they would oppose grant of loans by World Bank and other international financial institutions to India and Pakistan, except those for basic human needs. This meant virtually cessation of new loans for Pakistan.

As described in Chapter 11, these sanctions were partly relaxed within seven months, i.e. by January 1999, when the donor countries agreed not to oppose resumption of multilateral loans to Pakistan. The IMF provided an ESAF loan of $1.2 billion to Pakistan and the Paris Club agreed to reschedule some of the outstanding loans for one year. But the real and substantial relief came from Saudi Arabia. A friend in need is a friend indeed.

What would have happened if Pakistan had chosen the alternative path of restraint? This question has been constantly on my mind. But four years later, in 2002, the paramount significance of the decision to test became obvious, when India mobilized half a million troops to the Pakistan border after the attack on the Indian parliament on 13 December 2001. The forces remained on the border, ready for offensive action for ten long months, but were finally withdrawn due to the danger of a nuclear retaliation by Pakistan.

Economic Contingency Plan

In the cabinet meeting of 14 May 1998, it was decided that the ministry of finance should formulate, in consultation with the ministries concerned and the State Bank of Pakistan, an economic contingency plan, in case Pakistan decided to go ahead with the nuclear test option and had to face economic sanctions. A small team consisting of Dr M. Yaqub (governor, State Bank of Pakistan), Dr Hafiz Pasha (deputy chairman, Planning Commission), Mueen Afzal (finance secretary), and Ghafoor Mirza (special secretary ministry of finance) worked round the clock for the next four days. Based largely on proposals submitted to the team by Dr Yaqub, the team finalized and submitted to me a detailed note on 18 May, which I reviewed and finalized in a meeting with the team on 19 May. In view of the sensitive nature of the proposals, all the papers and notes were handwritten. A copy of the note, which I presented to the prime minister personally on 19 May, is reproduced in Appendix I.

Since the prime minister was very busy at the time, he invited me to join him on a flying visit to Karachi on 20 May, along with Hafiz Pasha. During the journey, he read the handwritten note containing the economic contingency plan. He was satisfied with most of the recommendations except those concerning the foreign currency accounts (FCA). The contingency plan had recommended that the FCAs of resident Pakistanis (about $7 billion) be converted into rupees at the official exchange rate (Rs46=US$1), but FCAs of non-resident individuals and financial institutions ($4 billion) be only temporarily brought under State Bank restrictions and some withdrawals allowed on a case to case basis. Simultaneously, holding of FCAs by residents be discontinued and the business of money changers suspended for the time being.

The prime minister felt that compulsory conversion of FCAs of resident Pakistanis at the official rate would be too drastic. Why not treat them at par with non-residents, i.e. just suspend withdrawals without State Bank permission. I said, 'We will discuss this option and present final proposals for approval in the next few days.' But that opportunity never arose. A week later, on 28 May, I learnt only two hours before the actual test that Pakistan was about to go for the nuclear option. After some last minute consultations, the team concluded that since the prime minister had not approved the two separate options for resident and non-resident FCAs, we had to follow the single uniform option tentatively proposed by the prime minister, i.e. to place restrictions on withdrawals from all FCAs. I rushed to see the law minister, Khalid Anwar, who was working on the Proclamation of Emergency under Article 232 of the constitution, to draft another Foreign Exchange (Temporary Restrictions) Ordinance along with the proclamation. Both were issued the same evening.

In the weeks that followed, the decision to freeze the FCAs became highly controversial. I explain below the circumstances leading to this decision.

The foreign currency accounts (FCA) scheme was introduced in February 1991 as part of the exchange and payments reforms to liberalize the capital account of the balance of payments. The expectation was that these deposits would help raise the low level of savings and investment in the economy.

Incentives offered to FCAs included (i) no questions asked about the source of foreign exchange, (ii) attractive rates of markup, (iii) no income tax on the profits earned, (iv) exemption from wealth tax for six years if any assets were purchased from these funds, (v) facility of obtaining local currency loans against the security of these deposits at concessional rates of markup.

As a result of these liberal incentives the total amount in FCAs increased rapidly from $2.1 billion in February 1991 to almost $11.1 billion by April 1998, with the bulk of the increase coming from residents and NBFIs, who accounted for almost 80 per cent of these deposits.

If these FCAs had remained a part of the foreign exchange reserves, then they could have played a useful role despite their high real cost. But instead they were largely spent to finance current account deficits by successive governments from 1992 to 1998, especially after 1993. Consequently, reserves were down to only $1.3 billion at the time of the nuclear explosions in May 2008.

An extremely important point to keep in mind in assessing the decision to freeze FCAs was that residents accounted for almost two-thirds of the deposits. These did not represent actual remittance of foreign currency from abroad but conversion of rupees into dollars by purchase from local moneychangers. The objective in most cases was to benefit from the extremely liberal tax treatment of these accounts, as described above.

The average exchange rate at which these deposits were built up over the period 1992 to 1998 was Rs30 to the dollar. Therefore, the conversion at Rs46 per dollar after the freeze did not mean any actual loss to depositors as they had availed of various tax benefits and also got a significant return due to exchange rate depreciation.

During the period that the FCAs were in operation, the scheme was criticized in various quarters, including international financial institutions, on the ground that the FCAs had created a debt overhang problem, which would constrain growth prospects in the future. It was also argued that the FCA scheme required banks to sell all the foreign exchange deposited with them to the State Bank of Pakistan which in turn provided foreign exchange cover to the commercial banks. The SBP provided the forward cover at subsidized rates. Given the cumulative exchange rate depreciation of 77 per cent from 1991 to

1998, this implied large annual losses to the central bank. Therefore, SBP was determined to get out of the existing FCA scheme whenever possible.

Following the difficult decision to freeze the FCAs, the government announced a number of facilities to the account holders including, first, a number of tax benefits following conversion and, second, the option of converting their deposits into dollar bonds of varying maturities with attractive returns and tax and other benefits.

Overall, the FCA scheme had failed to achieve its objectives. There was little impact on investment and savings. Instead, it contributed to profligacy in imports and rather than lead to greater stability through buildup of foreign exchange reserves it made the economy more vulnerable to external shocks, of the type imposed on Pakistan after the nuclear blasts. It might, of course, be argued that the transition from the FCAs could have been more orderly in nature. Unfortunately, the prospect of imminent sanctions after the nuclear tests brought with it the apprehension of a run on these deposits leading to a depletion of the already low foreign exchange reserves. That was the principal justification for the decision to freeze these accounts in the immediate aftermath of the blasts.

Soon after the nuclear tests, there were misleading rumours in the media that the news about freezing FCA had leaked out and certain influential persons had withdrawn millions of dollars from the bank just before the nuclear test. These rumours were also played up by the opposition in parliament. In contradicting these reports I presented to the Senate, details of daily withdrawals from FCA during the month of May 1998, to show that the total withdrawals of $155 million in the twenty-day period, between 11 and 28 May were only slightly more than the normal withdrawals of $67 million in the first ten days of May.

The decision to freeze the FCAs has understandably come under severe public criticism mainly because the government had gone back on its commitment to protect all economic reforms under the Economic Reforms Act of 1992. As indicated above, this option could not be presented to the cabinet for consideration because of grave implications of a possible leakage, which could have led to a run on the banks. The prime minister was so preoccupied with working off international pressures, that he could not spare enough time to carefully discuss various options on this crucial issue and give clear-cut directions. I came to know about the decision to test only two hours before the actual event. I felt that I had no option but to fall back on the tentative decision which the prime minister had indicated. in retrospect, the initial proposal that I had presented to the prime minister, namely compulsory conversion of the FCAs of resident Pakistanis and protecting the FCAs of non-resident Pakistanis, would have been a better option

The Resignation of Jehangir Karamat

The fourth military takeover in October 1999 and the resultant end of the democratic process with the dismissal of Nawaz Sharif's government was a major negative turning point in Pakistan's history. Historians will debate for a long time the real reasons for this setback. Some will trace the crisis to intricacies of civil military relations and especially the Kargil misadventure. Others will blame Nawaz Sharif for many mistakes he made. But in my view, the most serious of these mistakes was Nawaz Sharif's decision to remove General Jehangir Karamat as chief of army staff in October 1998.

On 5 October, Jehangir Karamat, while addressing naval officers at the Naval Staff College in Lahore, proposed the setting up of a National Security Council which would help to strengthen political institutions. He also called for greater attention to the situation in Sindh, the sense of deprivation in smaller provinces and improvement of relations with neighbours.

If these suggestions had remained as confidential remarks at a military establishment, no one would have taken any notice, but surprisingly, the director general, ISPR issued a press note highlighting the suggestions.

The national press naturally took notice of these 'important proposals', and Nawaz Sharif was naturally furious. I met him two days later at Murree where he was hosting a lunch for Prince Mohammad, defence minister of UAE. General Jehangir Karamat was also there, besides Shahbaz Sharif, Shahid Hamid, the governor of Punjab and some other officials.

When I asked General Jehangir Karamat about this statement, he said there was no doubt need for such a forum, but he was surprised that the statement had been released to the press. I told him about the proposal I was developing to convert the Defence Committee of the Cabinet (DCC) into a Cabinet Committee on Defence and National Security (CCDNS) chaired by the prime minister (see Chapter 11). He said that would also serve the purpose he had in mind. After lunch he invited me to join him for his return journey to Rawalpindi by helicopter. During the journey I suggested to him that while clarifying his position, he could refer to the proposed CCDNS.

I was taken aback the next day, when I heard that General Jehangir Karamat had offered to resign during his meeting with the prime minister. The news of this resignation spread like wildfire, sending conflicting signals in different directions: about Nawaz Sharif's unchallenged powers to the political quarters and alarm bells to some other quarters.

Within hours, speculation about the next army chief gripped the country. I was almost certain the position would go to General Ali Kuli Khan, the chief of general staff and a very competent officer, next in seniority to General Jehangir Karamat. But Nawaz Sharif decided, in consultation with Shahbaz Sharif and Chaudhry Nisar Ali Khan, to appoint General Pervez Musharraf as the next army chief.[1]

The day after General Pervez Musharraf was appointed as army chief. I suggested to Nawaz Sharif that he might appoint General Ali Kuli Khan as CJCSC to redress the injustice done to him. He seemed quite receptive and said, he would think about it.

Next evening, I received a phone call from Shahbaz Sharif saying he was on his way to Lahore, and the time before his departure was not enough for him to stop by at my house. Could I meet him at the airport? When half an hour later we met in the VIP Lounge, he said: 'Mian Sahib (PM) had asked me to speak to you in the context of your suggestion to appoint General Ali Kuli Khan as CJCSC. He was seriously considering this proposal but by some coincidence, just when you were discussing the proposal with the PM in Islamabad, I and Chaudhry Nisar Ali were calling on General Jehangir Karamat in Rawalpindi. During our conversation, General Karamat said that he was under great pressure from colleagues like General Ali Kuli Khan to takeover rather than resign but he had decided to respect the constitution. After we reported this to Mian Sahib, he changed his mind about General Ali Kuli Khan and has especially asked me to convey this reason to you.'

I could hardly say anything to Shahbaz Sharif at that time, but later on when I asked Ali Kuli Khan, he denied the allegation. In 2006, after Musharraf wrote some derogatory remarks about Ali Kuli Khan, he issued a detailed rejoinder in which he said:

> General Karamt told me that Sharif was furious and the situation was worse than he had told me. In the presence of ISI Chief Lt. Gen. Nasim Rana, the question of General Karamat's resignation also came up for discussion. I told him don't even think of resigning because the verdict that you would receive would be so damning that you would not be able to live with it. This is what I said and I own it even now. But at no stage, whether it was the corps commanders' conference or that of the principal staff officers, I asked him to stage a coup. In fact, it was Musharraf who subsequently removed the elected prime minister.

Many years later, when during several informal conversations, I asked General Jehangir Karamat if the statement he had made at the Naval Staff College was the only reason for his resignation, he said there were also some other reasons caused by certain statements wrongly attributed to him but these need not be discussed in public.

As I reflected on this unfortunate chain of events after the military takeover in October 1999, I came to the conclusion that in removing General Jehangir Karamat, Nawaz Sharif had committed a blunder. He also failed to recognize that despite his heavy mandate, it was not advisable for him to dismiss two army chiefs in less than a year. In doing so he had overplayed his hands and effectively derailed the democratic process for nine long years.

NOTE

1. In an article in the *Defence Journal* (September 2007, page 93) Ikram Sehgal recalled 'Once he became Lt.-Gen. and Corps Commander, Mangla, Musharraf very deliberately gave the ruling PML the impression of being least powerful among the contenders for COAS, quite different from his actual personality. Being a Mohajir and therefore taken wrongly to be someone without a 'constituency' in the Army added to his profile as the most suitable COAS in Nawaz Sharif's eyes. In Lahore every other weekend having a good time, Musharraf seemed least likely to buck the PM's authority.'

CHAPTER 11

The Foreign Office: A Melting Pot of Global Fault Lines

My transition from the ministry of finance to the ministry of foreign affairs in August 1998 generated an interesting debate in the media but was not a surprise for me. In January 1998, I had accompanied Nawaz Sharif to the annual World Economic Forum meetings in Davos. One of his bilateral meetings was with William Richardson, then US permanent representative to the UN in New York. During the discussions, Richardson asked about the situation in Afghanistan. Nawaz Sharif asked me to answer the question. As we were driving for lunch after the meeting, Nawaz Sharif praised my succinct summation of the Afghan situation and said: 'I think you should become the foreign minister in the next cabinet reshuffle.' I said, 'As a member of your team, I will fulfil whatever role you assign to me, but only two months ago, you did not elevate me as president of Pakistan because, as you said, you could not find anyone else to replace me at the finance ministry'. He was visibly embarrassed but spontaneously said, 'That is also true.' He must have been relieved that by then we had reached the venue of the lunch. He raised the issue again in May 1998, during a flight from Lahore to Islamabad when he asked me as to who would be the best person to replace me in the finance ministry, after the budget session. I replied, 'Ishaq Dar'. He said, 'For the time being he is all right in the ministry of commerce but what about Hafiz Pasha? Can he manage the finance ministry?' I said, 'Of course. He is very competent and an excellent economist but since he is not a member of parliament, he can only be appointed as advisor. That can create some complications in his role as the principal coordinator of economic policies because ministers are reluctant to participate in the economic or other committees of the cabinet when it is chaired by an advisor.' My prediction proved right, because Hafiz Pasha could last as advisor finance only for two months and was promptly replaced by Ishaq Dar in October 1998.

Pakistan's Foreign Policy in Retrospect

As I was driving towards the foreign office on the morning of 6 August 1998 to take charge of the ministry, I was overwhelmed by the formidable array of political security and social problems of Pakistan and by the realization that Pakistan had become a melting pot of many global fault lines. The growth of extremism and so called Islamic fundamentalism in Afghanistan and its spillover into Pakistan was a direct legacy of the proxy war between the United States and the USSR, which started in 1979, with the Russian invasion of Afghanistan. Another global faultline whose long shadows continue to fall on Pakistan was the unending and tragic saga of the Middle East. Many mujahideen and their networks that had been fighting the Russians in Afghanistan traced their desperation to the continuing occupation of Palestine and other Arab lands. Pakistan could not therefore find solutions to these problems by acting alone.

I was also struck by another paradox. I was the foreign minister of a country that had just become the first Islamic country to possess nuclear weapons. But the price it had paid for achieving that status was rising by the day. In 1990, USA had suspended economic assistance and military supplies by imposing sanctions under the Pressler Amendment. Now in 1998 after the nuclear tests, all the G-7 countries had imposed comprehensive sanctions which also included loans from multilateral agencies like the World Bank, IMF and the Asian Development Bank. Our foreign exchange reserves were only $1 billion, enough to cover one month's imports. The net flow of foreign assistance had already become negative. Tensions with India were growing after the nuclear tests. My foremost priority would be to end this isolation and enable the country to concentrate on strengthening its economy. The Soviet Union had collapsed in 1990 and split into fifteen countries despite its vast nuclear arsenal because of its economic decline.

In the next few days I literally dived into my mental and physical archives to prepare myself for these two tasks. Having participated in the Pakistan Movement as a student, I was fully aware of the circumstances in which the Muslims of pre-partition India had successfully struggled for a homeland and achieved it in 1947. I was also deeply conscious of the enormous difficulties under which the new nation, in the face of growing hostility with India over Kashmir, had started its independent existence. Pakistan's foreign policy was therefore always dominated by its relations with India which in 1947 was four times larger in terms of population and seven times larger after 1971 when East Pakistan became Bangladesh. Throughout this period, Pakistan's relations with other regions and countries were largely influenced by this overriding compulsion to safeguard its security against actual and potential threats from a larger neighbour which had refused to resolve its differences and especially the Kashmir dispute on the basis of UN resolutions and through negotiations in accordance with the principles of international law.

This was the perilous context, in which Pakistan had joined the western alliances which USA was building in the 1950s to counter the growing Soviet influences in the developing world. In 1954, Pakistan signed the first Mutual Defence Assistance Agreement with USA. A few months later, it joined the South East Asia Treaty Organization (SEATO) and in 1955, the Baghdad Pact, renamed the Central Treaty Organization (CENTO) in 1958. In 1959, Pakistan signed another bilateral Pakistan–US Cooperation Agreement. As a result of these alliances and despite strong protests from India, military and economic assistance to Pakistan expanded rapidly in the next few years.

But these alliances also involved heavy costs. Pakistan's policy of throwing its lot with USA was unpopular at home. This became vividly clear in the Suez crisis of 1956, but reached a high pitch in 1962–63, when in the wake of the border skirmish between India and China in October 1962, USA offered military assistance to India. In response, Pakistan moved closer to China. PIA started flying to Shanghai and Premier Zhou Enlai was given a rousing reception when he visited Pakistan in February 1964. In March 1965, President Ayub Khan made his 'historic' visit to China followed by the first ever visit by a Pakistani head of state to USSR. In retaliation, USA cancelled Ayub Khan's planned visit to USA.

Meanwhile, after carrying out six rounds of inconclusive negotiations on Kashmir in 1962 and 1963, India had initiated from October 1963 several measures to change the special status of Jammu and Kashmir. The president of Kashmir was re-designated as governor and the prime minister as chief minister to bring Kashmir at par with other states (provinces) of India. This was followed by further moves in December 1964, to extend certain provisions of the Indian constitution to Kashmir to further erode its special status. A visit to Pakistan by the Kashmiri leader Sheikh Abdullah in May 1964, with a message from Prime Minister Nehru that he wanted a settlement, and wanted Ayub Khan to visit New Delhi, did not go very far because a day after Sheikh Abdullah returned to India on 26 May, Nehru died.

Having been repeatedly frustrated by lack of progress on reaching a negotiated settlement of Kashmir, and boosted by its success in a limited military operation in the Rann of Kutch in April 1965, Pakistan decided to explore another alternative—to send Kashmiri volunteers into Kashmir to convert the Kashmiri agitation that was already under way for several months, into an uprising that would takeover Kashmir by force. The plan called Operation Gibraltar was launched on 5 August 1965 but did not lead to any uprising by Kashmiris. Initially, the 'volunteers' inflicted heavy losses on the Indian troops but were soon overwhelmed by reinforcements. India attacked the territory of Azad Kashmir in the Kargil and Poonch Sectors. Pakistan tried to cut the link between India and Kashmir, at Akhnoor. In retaliation, India attacked the international boundary near Lahore on 6 September 1965, aimed at capturing the city of Lahore. The bravery of Pakistani soldiers and boldness of Pakistan Air Force not only saved Lahore but secured a 'draw' in the seventeen-day war, till the UN Security Council agreed on a ceasefire resolution on 23 September 1965.

In retrospect, as I recalled, Operation Gibraltar and the subsequent war in 1965 were the first major foreign policy disasters brought about by a military government in Pakistan. USA, the main supplier of military and economic assistance, had already withdrawn from its special relationship with Pakistan. Indian defence budget had increased by 150 per cent between 1960 and 1965 in the wake of the India–China border conflict of 1962, from Rs3500 million to Rs8500 million, while Pakistan's defence budget had gone up marginally from Rs1080 million to Rs1350 million in the same period. It is unthinkable that any group of competent military strategists would launch such an unrealistic operation in the face of these realities and on the assumption that India would not attack the international boundary. In fact at that time there was a fundamental flaw in Pakistan's foreign policy because it was not in line with Pakistan's security requirements and its economic realities.

I wondered, as I recalled this unfortunate phase of our history if we were facing a similar disconnect in our security needs, foreign policy and economic realities once again in the late 1990s.

This sobering assessment of Pakistan's foreign policy in its historical context, led to a clearer identification of priorities I set for myself as I started my tenure in the foreign office: (a) How to promote durable peace with India? (b) How to build a more stable and mutually supportive relationship with USA? (c) How to deal with the disastrous civil war in Afghanistan?

But on that fateful day of 6 August, when I joined the foreign ministry, I was not aware that I was literally jumping into the fire. The very next day, on 7 August, the US embassies in Nairobi and Darussalam were attacked by terrorists killing more than 250 people. The attack was immediately blamed on Osama Bin Laden and his network in Afghanistan. That raised the Afghan situation to the top of my agenda.

The Turmoil in Afghanistan

On 8 August, a day after the Nairobi bombing, the Taliban recaptured Mazar-e-Sharif, the capital of Northern Alliance, killing many senior Iranian military and intelligence personnel who were assisting the Northern Alliance under the Uzbek leader, General Rashid Dostum in their fight against the Taliban.

Early on 9th morning, I received an urgent phone call from Kamal Kharazi, the foreign minister of Iran saying eleven of their senior diplomats posted in Mazar-e-Sharif were missing. Could I help in tracing them? I rushed to the Ministry and after a hurried briefing with senior officials on the ground situation; I telephoned Mullah Omar, the undisputed *Amir* of the Taliban in Afghanistan, and spoke to him in Pashto, the only language he could speak. He professed ignorance and asked, 'Why did Iran need eleven senior diplomats in a small place like Mazar-e-Sharif?' A few days later I discovered from independent sources that they had all been killed on the day of the attack. I telephoned Mullah Omar again and said, even if they had been killed, it was his Islamic duty to return the bodies to their families. I also added that the Taliban forces had captured thirty Iranian trucks carrying arms and ammunition for the Northern Alliance. Could they release these trucks and their drivers? It took almost a month, and prolonged negotiations and joint investigations by the UN and ICRC before nine bodies of Iranian officials mostly from Iranian Revolutionary Guards were found and returned to Tehran. Meanwhile throughout this period, there was strong resentment in the Iranian media and official statements against the Taliban and their supporters (Pakistan).

Throughout that month we had a series of in-depth briefing and policy sessions within the ministry and with other agencies to identify ways to defuse the situation and avert an Iranian attack on Afghanistan. I soon realized the irony of the whole situation. The Taliban (students of religious seminaries or madrassahs) had emerged on the Afghan scene in 1994 in the city of Kandahar and within four years they had captured almost 90 per cent of the country's territory without much fighting. They had brought relative peace to the areas under their control by disarming gangs and petty warlords; they had succeeded in eradicating poppy cultivation, and restored reasonably good governance in different parts of the country. People who were sick of the Russian occupation and the brutal civil war among different warlords after the Soviets left in 1990 had welcomed them.

But the negative side of the Taliban was now bulging rapidly. As long as they controlled the largely Pashtun areas of south and south-east Afghanistan, they were on safer ground, but as they spread to the northern areas capturing areas populated by Hazara (Shia), Uzbek and Tajik communities, the resistance and hostility had increased. Iran naturally wanted a broad based government in Kabul with a fair share for Hazaras and Tajiks. That is why they were helping the exiled government of the Northern Alliance, after the fall of Kabul in 1996, with arms and ammunition. Another fatal flaw in the Taliban's strategy was their dependence on foreign supporters. During the jihad against the Russian invasion from 1979 onwards, many foreign mujahideen had joined the seven warlords who were fighting the Russians, supported by arms, training and money from USA. These foreign supporters included prominent persons like Osama Bin Laden, who had shifted to Sudan when the Russians left in 1990. But in early 1996 he returned to Jalalabad in Afghanistan which was in the middle of a new civil war. At that time Jalalabad was ruled by Haji Qadeer. Taking advantage of the power vacuum in a ravaged country he setup his network near Kandahar and supported the Taliban with money and foreign volunteers. Six days after the terrorist's attack on Nairobi and Darussalam, the UN Security Council passed resolution 1189 on 13 August 1998, condemning these attacks and calling upon all states to take steps to prevent such attacks. The USA directly blamed Osama Bin Laden for these attacks and a week later, on 20 August, fired 100 low flying cruise missiles from ships in the Persian Gulf to target the reported hideouts of Osama Bin Laden near Khost. These missiles violated Pakistan's air space but no permission was sought from the government of Pakistan. The commander of the central command, General Zinni, however, landed at the Chaklala air base half an hour before the missile attack for a hurriedly arranged dinner meeting with General Jehangir Karamat, the chief of army staff at the air base and informed him that they were launching these missiles to punish Osama Bin Laden and that he was telling them in advance so that Pakistan was aware that these were US and not Indian missiles!

Next day, there were noisy scenes in Parliament at this violation of Pakistan's sovereignty. I explained at length that we had strongly protested to the US government and were also lodging a formal complaint with the President of the UN Security Council.

Even at that early stage, I could see that another global faultline was now threatening Pakistan, primarily because the USA and its allies after setting up with Pakistan's support hundred of madrassahs in Afghanistan and Pakistan to train thousands of volunteers to fight and eventually defeat a super power, had walked away from Afghanistan, pushing it into a prolonged civil war.

The Geneva Accords of 1988 were signed on 14 April 1988 by the foreign ministers of Pakistan, Afghanistan, USSR and USA. The Soviet Union, having suffered huge casualties (estimated 13,000 dead and 35,000 injured) was anxious to withdraw from territories that in 1979, it desperately wanted to integrate into the Union. As the BBC pointed out in its Century series on revolutionary wars, both the super powers were defeated in the twentieth century: USA in Vietnam and the Soviet

Union in Afghanistan. But these defeats were not inflicted by superior arms but essentially by ideology—the communist ideology in Vietnam and the Islamic ideology in Afghanistan. Those who organized and armed the Afghan mujahideen in the 1980s to expel the 'infidels' from Islamic Afghanistan were not aware of the potential dangers of creating such a force, until it mushroomed into the tragic disaster of 11 September 2001.

As described in Chapter 6, in January 1988, I had participated in two four-hour meetings which President Ziaul Haq had convened to prepare for his successive meetings with Michael Armacost, the US under secretary of state and Yuli Vorontsov, the first deputy foreign minister of Soviet Union. Ziaul Haq had predicted at the concluding session that since the issue of power-sharing after the Russians left, had not been resolved, the Afghans would be pushed into a prolonged civil war, which would also threaten the security of Pakistan.

The civil war, predicted by Ziaul Haq broke out with full force in 1990. During the struggle to oust the Soviets, Afghanistan had lost a million people and another five million had left the country as refugees, for Pakistan (3.5 million) and Iran (1.5 million). The people of Afghanistan therefore wanted peace and reconstruction of their ravaged country. What they got instead was an unending civil war despite two power-sharing accords, in Peshawar on 24 April 1992 and in Islamabad on 7 March 1993.

The Taliban emerged as a new force in Afghanistan in August 1994, when Mullah Omar led a small revolt against a local commander in Kandahar. Once the Taliban, who were students of his madrassahs, captured Kandahar, he was welcomed by the Taliban in other provinces which he captured without any fight because people were sick of the continuing civil war among different warlords. The advancing Taliban had however stiff battles in Herat in September 1995, with the pro-Iran Tajik warlord Ismail Khan. When the Taliban captured Herat, the Burhanuddin Rabbani and Ahmad Shah Mahsud government in Kabul blamed Pakistan. As a consequence, the Pakistan embassy in Kabul was burned, and the ambassador Humayun Qazi narrowly escaped but received serious injuries. Thirty other employees of the embassy were also injured. One employee was killed. A year later, in September 1996, the Taliban captured Kabul. Rabbani and Hekmatyar fled to Iran. By the middle of 1997, the Taliban had also captured several other provinces and were controlling 75 per cent of the territory of Afghanistan.

In May 1997 General Rashid Dostum's deputy, General Malik revolted against Dostum and with support from the forces of Gulbuddin Hekmatyar and Jumbish-e-Milli whose commander Haqqani was killed in Mazar-e-Sharif by Dostum loyalists, captured Mazar Sharif along with the Taliban forces. General Malik had signed a written agreement with the Taliban that he would be in-charge of the Northern provinces. But when the Taliban appointed Mullah Abdul Razzaq as the leader of the north, General Malik, who was only offered the post of deputy foreign minister in Kabul, revolted once again, this time against the Taliban. He said the Taliban had disarmed other areas captured by them because they were Pashtun areas. Uzbeks in the north would not surrender their weapons to the Taliban. Malik's forces were joined by Hizb-e-Wahdat's Shia faction and thousands of Taliban were brutally killed in the last week of May, as General Malik regained control of Mazar-e-Sharif and the provinces of Faryab, Jowjan, Sar-e-Pul, Balkh and Samangam.

Without anticipating that the Taliban would lose control of Mazar-e-Sharif within a week, the Pakistan government went ahead and recognized the Taliban government as the legitimate government of Afghanistan only a day after they 'captured' Mazar-e-Sharif. Apparently the instructions to recognize the Taliban government were received by the foreign office from the DG ISI, General Rana,[1] and Foreign Minister Gohar Ayub Khan promptly announced the decision at a press conference the next day—Sunday, 25 May 1997. In the next two days, Saudi Arabia and United Arab Emirates also followed suit and recognized the Taliban regime. But the rest of the world, very concerned about their appalling record on human rights and treatment of women, did not recognize the Taliban till they were ousted from power by US forces in October 2001. The Northern Alliance government, led by Burhanuddin Rabbani, which controlled only 10 per cent of the country continued to represent Afghanistan at the United Nations throughout this period.

After the ouster of the Taliban from Mazar-e-Sharif on 31 May 1997, Pakistan had launched hectic diplomatic efforts in pursuit of its policy of promoting a broad based government through an intra Afghanistan peace process. Ahmad Shah Masood who had now re-emerged as the de-facto leader of the Northern alliance, wanted to share power with the Taliban in Kabul, as long as he retained control of his Panjsher Valley. Iran was keen to gain a share of the broad based government for the Hazara Shias and the Northern Alliance and were involved in a UN supported Pak–Iran initiative to find a political solution to the problem.

The Taliban were listening to the foreign office officials from Pakistan about various proposals, but were quietly pursuing their own strategy of recapturing Mazar-e-Sharif. Taking advantage of the infighting among various factions constituting the Northern Alliance, especially after the return of Dostum to Mazar-e-Sharif in June 1997, the Taliban gradually advanced to capture Shibbergan, the stronghold of Dostum on 2 August 1998. That persuaded several commanders in Balkh and Samangan to switch over to the Taliban once again. The Taliban blocked all the supply routes to Mazar-e-Sharif and eventually entered Mazar-e-Sharif on 8 August 1998 without much resistance. As mentioned already, on that day, they also violated the Iranian consulate, killing 9 out of 11 'diplomats' (actually senior Iranian military and intelligence officers). The other two escaped and reached Iran after a few days.

This incident led to a serious stand off between Iran and Afghanistan, in which Pakistan was also criticized by the Iranian leaders. Before the end of August 1998, the Iranians had moved more than 100,000 troops to the Afghan border and a military invasion of Afghanistan seemed imminent. I flew to Tehran in the middle of September and persuaded the Iranian leadership to pursue the path of negotiation under the UN formula of working through the groups of six plus two, i.e. Afghanistan and its five neighbours and USA and Russia.

USA, already unhappy with the Taliban for their narrow and extremist view of Islam became openly hostile after the attacks on US embassies in Nairobi and Darussalam on 7 August 1998.

As Pakistan was coming under increasing pressure for supporting the Taliban, we decided, soon after my return from the General Assembly session in New York in September 1998, that Pakistan should forcefully ask the Taliban to persuade Osama bin Laden to leave Afghanistan voluntarily. I had a series of meetings with the Afghan ambassador Mullah Haqqani and their foreign minister Wakil Ahmad

Mutawakil. I told them that Osama bin Laden may have played a very important role in the Afghan jihad but now he was becoming a liability for Afghanistan. If he was really a well wisher of the Taliban regime, he should leave Afghanistan voluntarily and take refuge in another country. Pakistan would be prepared to provide transport and other facilities for his safe exit from Afghanistan. The response was always vague and non-committal. They said they would convey these proposals to Mullah Omar. Sometimes they would say, he was a guest and it was against their traditions to expel a guest. I also raised the issue with the Afghan prime minister, Mullah Rabbani, during one of his visits to Islamabad. I could feel from the body language of Afghan officials that they saw the force of my arguments, but were helpless. As I learnt later, it was Osama, and not Mullah Omar who made key policy decisions in Kandahar at that time. That is why Mullah Omar kept his headquarters in Kandahar while the formal government functioned from Kabul.

In December 1998, I was asked to join a meeting between Prime Minister Nawaz Sharif and Prince Turki, Saudi Arabia's intelligence chief. As the meeting started, I was surprised to hear from Prince Turki that Mullah Omar had promised him in September 1998, that Osama bin Laden, who was a Saudi citizen, would be handed over to Saudi Arabia within three months. Now that three months had passed, he wanted to visit Kandahar and ask Mullah Omar to fulfil his promise. We agreed that DG ISI, General Ziauddin, and the additional secretary for Afghanistan and Central Asia, Iftikhar Murshed would accompany him to Kandahar next morning to meet Mullah Omar.

Prince Turki returned from Kandahar the same day and had another meeting with the prime minister the next day. He was very angry. He said, 'Mullah Omar denied point blank that he had made any promise to hand over Bin Laden within three months. The translator had probably conveyed something he had never actually said, he told me. He then accused me of siding with Iran, which had massed their troops along the Afghan border to attack Afghanistan. He then insulted me by calling me a hypocrite and said, 'You are even unable to defend yourself against Iraq and have allowed the Americans to enter the holy land to defend you." After such a rude response, Prince Turki said, 'I am going to recommend to my government to withdraw our envoy from Kabul and stop any further support to the Taliban regime.' This actually happened within a few days.

After Prince Turki had left, the prime minister asked us to stay on. Addressing the DG ISI, General Ziauddin, the prime minister said, 'Is this the behaviour you expected from the Taliban's supreme leader after all the support we had given them? And the proposal we are making about Bin Laden is in their own best interest.' Then without waiting for an answer from DG ISI, he turned towards me and said: 'Sartaj Sahib, we must review our entire relationship with the Taliban regime. The international community has criticized our decision to recognize the Taliban in May 1997. Ever since Naseerullah Babar, PPP government's interior minister called the Taliban 'our boys' in 1995, they are perceived to be a force created and supported by Pakistan. The kind of fifteenth century Islam they preach and follow has brought a bad name to Islam which is a religion of peace and moderation. We still give shelter to more than three million Afghan refugees and yet, we have zero influence on their policies and actions. Please prepare, in consultation with DG ISI, a comprehensive position paper on our future relationship with the Taliban regime and bring it to a special meeting of the DCC within two weeks.'

As we left the PM House, I told the DG ISI that he should initiate work on the position paper the prime minister had asked for, and we in the foreign office would also prepare a brief. We could meet after a few days to evolve a joint summary for the DCC.

The very next morning, Major General Parvez Masud, in-charge of the Afghan desk in ISI, appeared in my office without any appointment. When I saw him after I finished another meeting, he said, 'Please persuade the prime minister to defer his decision to review Pakistan's relationship with the Taliban regime for some time. After a long time, we see the prospect of having a peaceful and friendly neighbour in Afghanistan, because the Taliban are expanding their influence. All other alternatives will be worse.'

I heard him with great anguish. I knew that the Taliban were ideologically motivated and considered Osama bin Laden a true mujahid. They were also convinced that they were following the right course. But they did not realize the enormous dangers they were facing by protecting Bin Laden. Pakistan was caught in the middle of this historical tragedy. It genuinely wanted peace and stability in

Afghanistan and had been working actively to create a broad-based government in Afghanistan so that after twenty years of war, Afghans could live in peace. But there was enormous mistrust among the Pashtuns of Southern Afghanistan and Uzbek-Tajik-Hazara leaders of the North. 'We are in a real bind, by following a policy that is not sustainable' I said to myself.

In the next few days I conveyed the message from ISI to the prime minister and said, 'I will pursue the subject and revert to him after some time.' Meanwhile we were actively engaged with the UN special representative for Afghanistan, Lakhdar Brahimi, to find a political solution between the Taliban and the Northern Alliance under the 'Six plus Two Group'. In preparation for these efforts I also invited the foreign ministers of Tajikistan, Turkmenistan and Uzbekistan to visit Pakistan for in-depth discussion in the months of January and February 1999.

True to their style, the Taliban while participating in each stage of these negotiations were also preparing to capture the remaining 10 per cent of Afghanistan and continue their suicidal course. But Ahmad Shah Masood was also a dogged fighter. He held on to his territory for the next two years, but on 9 September 2001, two days before the tragedy of 9/11, he was blown up by two suicide bombers who posed as journalists and had concealed their explosives inside the camera they were carrying.

Before the Taliban could take advantage of the sudden disappearance of Ahmad Shah Masood, the terrorist attack on the World Trade Centre in New York on 11 September 2001, marked the beginning of the end of the Taliban regime in Afghanistan. When they failed to respond to the UN resolution to expel Osama bin Laden, the coalition forces led by USA attacked Afghanistan with massive airpower. The anti-Taliban forces of the Northern Alliance quickly re-grouped and marched into Kabul, ahead of the Allied troops in October 2001. The Taliban, unable to fight such a formidable force, decided to melt away with their weapons, in different parts of Afghanistan and in the tribal belt between Afghanistan and Pakistan, to challenge the occupying forces through guerrilla action at a time of their choosing. Seven years after their occupation of Afghanistan, the coalition forces have not been able to capture either Bin Laden or Mullah Omar and attacks by the Taliban have been rising gradually, creating problems not just for the coalition forces but also for Pakistan.

Many prominent Taliban and Al-Qaeda leaders have apparently found safer hideouts in North and South Waziristan and enlisted the support of many local volunteers to give them shelter, and active support against the paramilitary forces which Pakistan started deploying in the tribal areas, to flush out these areas and to prevent cross border incursions into Afghanistan. Between 2004 and 2007, the radical movement expanded rapidly, especially in South Waziristan, creating serious concerns within the NATO forces in Afghanistan and in western capitals. The pressure on Pakistan 'to do more' has been growing incessantly and finally the US Congress passed a new law in July 2007, under which, henceforth, the US must certify every year that 'Pakistan is making demonstrated, significant and sustained progress towards eliminating support or safe haven for terrorists and showing a commitment to eliminate from its territory any organization such as Taliban, Al-Qaeda or any successor, engaged in military, insurgent or terrorist activities in Afghanistan.' Thus another Pressler Law has re-appeared as a sword of Damocles over Pakistan.

Simultaneously top level threats that US and NATO forces themselves can launch attacks inside the territory of Pakistan, if Pakistan itself is unable to do this job, have been growing louder and louder, undermining the sovereignty of, not an adversary, but a close non-NATO Ally of the US. This particular global faultline had actually become red hot and the final act of this Greek tragedy is yet to be played.

The Search for Durable Peace with India

As already mentioned, the foreign policy of Pakistan has throughout been dominated by its relations with India and by the constant threat to its security from a much larger and hostile neighbour.

In the first phase, from 1948 to 1965, Pakistan's diplomatic efforts were focused on securing the implementation of UN resolution of 21 April 1949, calling for measures 'to bring about cessation of fighting and to create proper conditions for a free and impartial plebiscite to decide whether the state of Jammu and Kashmir is to accede to India or Pakistan.' Since India rejected subsequent proposals by two special UN representatives, Judge Owen Dixon of Australia in 1950 and Frank P. Graham in 1952 on the issue of demilitarization of Kashmir, this and five subsequent UN resolutions could not be implemented. After 1957, India had persuaded the Soviet Union, which was in any case unhappy with Pakistan over its defence agreement with USA, to block further action at the UN Security Council on the Kashmir issue.

The disappointment arising from Pakistan's inability to secure a just settlement of the Kashmir dispute pushed it to the alternative of Operation Gibraltar which led to the war of September 1965.

India's audacious resolve to continue its illegal occupation of Kashmir on the principle of 'might is right' became clearer in January 1966 when in the post-war Tashkent Declaration, concluded by President Ayub Khan and Prime Minister Lal Bahadur Shastri, under the auspices of the Soviet Prime Minister Kosygin, India refused to include any reference to 'the settlement of the Kashmir dispute' and only agreed to an ambiguous formulation saying 'the two sides will continue meetings, both at the highest level and at other levels, on matters of direct concern to both countries.' This effectively shifted Pakistan's diplomatic efforts from the international arena to the bilateral mode.

This transition to bilateralism was further reinforced by the Simla Agreement signed on 2 July 1972, after the 1971 war between India and Pakistan. 'In order to achieve this objective (durable peace) the governments of India and Pakistan have agreed', the Simla Agreement stipulated in para (ii) 'that the two countries are resolved to settle their differences by peaceful means through bilateral negotiations or by any other peaceful means mutually agreed upon between them.'

Although Pakistan has never accepted the Indian interpretation of this paragraph that Pakistan could no longer seek 'third party intervention nor raise Pakistan–India disputes at the United Nations, in practice, the Kashmir issue, despite being on the formal list of subjects for the General Assembly, virtually disappeared from the active agenda of the United Nations after 1971. According to Abdul Sattar, 'Pakistan paid a high price for securing vacation of its territory. Under normal circumstances, it would not, and could not accept the provision regarding bilateral settlement of disputes.'[2]

Having agreed to resolve differences and disputes through peaceful negotiations under the Simla Agreement, India did not show any willingness for meaningful dialogue, throughout the next two decades either on Kashmir or many other disputes like Sir Creek, involving the demarcation of an agreed line in the Rann of Kutch, or those arising from India's bid to build new dams at Salal, Wuller and Baglihar. The Indus Water Treaty of 1960, allows India to construct 'run of the river power plants' but not storage dams that will divert more water to India than prescribed under the Treaty. In each of these, India went ahead, without providing the required information to Pakistan.

In 1984, India added a new dispute to this list by occupying 30,000 square km in Siachen Glacier where the Line of Control was not demarcated and compelled both countries to deploy their forces and engage in intermittent combat in a war zone that is located at a high altitude of over 20,000 feet.

The same year there was renewed tension between the two countries when there were reports about an imminent air attack on Pakistan's nuclear facilities at Kahuta. This led to an agreement in December 1985 between President Ziaul Haq and Prime Minister Rajiv Gandhi, under which both countries agreed not to attack each other's nuclear facilities.

This gloomy phase in the India–Pakistan relations, marked by periodical rise in temperature, finally entered a new paradigm in 1990, when the resentment of the people of Kashmir against Indian occupation, turned into a popular uprising. This was triggered partly by growing Indian repression and partly by widespread corruption by the government of Indian held Kashmir (IHK). The elections in March 1987 were heavily rigged, forcing the United Muslim Front to launch a movement to secure their right of self determination. Starting with strikes and protest rallies, the movement became more violent.

From the early 1990s, Kashmiri militants from Azad Kashmir and some other Pakistan based organizations, including mujahideen who had participated in the jihad in Afghanistan, began to join this liberation struggle. As the tempo of the liberation struggle gained momentum, the Kashmir issue re-surfaced as a live problem and attracted considerable international attention. The Indian government was forced to increase the strength of its forces to 700,000 by mid

1990s and in the process, at least 60,000 freedom fighters had lost their lives. Kashmiri sources claim this figure to be 100,000.

In February 1993, thirty political parties of IHK joined hands to form the All Parties Hurriyat Conference (APHC) with the aim of 'ending Indian occupation and rescuing the Kashmiri people from repression.' It boycotted the state elections held in September 1996 and its leaders suffered even greater repression and harassment at the hands of the Indian security forces.

The Lahore Process

The seeds of the Lahore process were sown in August 1996. Frank Wisner, then US ambassador to India, was visiting Pakistan and also called on the leader of the opposition, Nawaz Sharif in Islamabad. General Majid Malik, Chaudhry Shujaat Hussain, Gohar Ayub and I arrived a few minutes earlier to prepare for this meeting. In his typical style Nawaz Sharif abruptly asked me in Punjabi: 'Sartaj Sahib, is there no way out. Are we going to confront each for another fifty years and neglect the development so badly needed by people on both sides of the border.' I said, 'In fact, no negotiation can ever succeed if both sides are stuck on their maximum position. To make progress both sides have to show flexibility'.

Nawaz Sharif asked Frank Wisner the same question, when he came a few minutes later: 'Mr Ambassador, will India ever negotiate seriously on Kashmir?' Surprisingly, Wisner gave the same answer which I had given. 'Only if both sides show flexibility. All of you are so stuck or your maximalist positions that no negotiation can actually succeed if that is the national consensus on both sides.'

After Wisner left, Nawaz Sharif said, 'If we get back to power, we can show flexibility in negotiations because no-one can doubt my *niyyat* (good intention and patriotism) even if I negotiate on something less than Pakistan's stated position.'

Three months later, the PPP government of Benazir Bhutto was dismissed and elections announced for February 1997. During the election campaign Nawaz Sharif made at least two statements, in which he said that 'One of my priorities will be to hold intensive and serious negotiations with India on Kashmir and try to improve relations with

India.' He made these statements deliberately because when he came to Islamabad later, he told me in Punjabi: 'Sartaj Sahib, *mai oh gal kar detiye* (I said that thing) so that tomorrow people cannot object to negotiations with India. This is now a part of my election platform.'

When Nawaz Sharif was elected prime minister, after winning an unprecedented two-thirds majority in the National Assembly—137 out of 200 seats, he received a congratulatory message from prime minister, H.D. Deve Gowda. Nawaz Sharif showed me this letter and the formal draft reply submitted by the Foreign Office. I said, 'What about starting serious negotiations?' I was then finance minister and not foreign minister. Why don't we add a sentence? The sentence added was, 'I share your desire for improved relations but that requires serious negotiations and I suggest that we begin these negotiations at the Foreign Secretary's level, if possible, before the end of March 1997.'

A positive reply came promptly and the first meeting was held between the two foreign secretaries. Shamshad Ahmad and Salman Haider met in New Delhi from 28 to 31 March to carry out, 'as directed by their respective two prime ministers, wide ranging and comprehensive dialogue on all outstanding issues between the two countries' and decided to meet again in June 1997 in Islamabad.

In May 1997, Nawaz Sharif met Prime Minister I.K. Gujral in Male, Maldives, during the Summit of the South Asian Association for Regional Cooperation (SAARC). After his return, Nawaz Sharif sounded very positive. He told me, 'I said to Gujral, we may not find a solution quickly, but let us at least start serious negotiations.'

The next meeting at the foreign secretaries' level, held in Islamabad from 19 to 23 June 1997, was something of a breakthrough. The joint statement issued after the meeting said:

With the objective of promoting a friendly and harmonious relationship between Pakistan and India, the Foreign Secretaries have agreed as follows:

- to address all outstanding issues of concern to both sides including, inter alia: (a) Peace and security, including CBMs, (b) Jammu and Kashmir, (c) Siachen, (d) Wullar Barrage Project/Tulbul Navigation Project, (e) Sir Creek, (f) Terrorism and drug-trafficking, (g) Economic and Commercial Cooperation, (h) Promotion of friendly exchanges in various fields.

- to setup a mechanism, including working groups at appropriate levels, to address all these issues in an integrated manner. The issues at (a) and (b) above will be dealt with at the level of Foreign Secretaries who will also coordinate and monitor the progress of work of all the working groups.

The two foreign secretaries also had a preliminary exchange of views on the composition of the working groups and their methodology. It was decided to continue the consideration of this matter through diplomatic channels.

Thus not only had India accepted Jammu and Kashmir as an outstanding issue but had also agreed to setup a working group at foreign secretaries' level to discuss the issue.

Diplomatic exchanges were in progress to convene the next round of meetings when in November 1997, the Gujral government fell. But the 'mechanism for integrated dialogue' agreed between the two countries in June 1997, was revived in 1998, after the nuclear tests.

The nuclear tests conducted by India on 11 May and by Pakistan on 28 May 1998, sent shock waves throughout the world and highlighted the importance of resolving underlying disputes to avoid a nuclear stand off between the two countries. The Security Council Resolution 1172 of 6 June 1998 urged India and Pakistan to remove tensions by finding 'solutions that address the root causes of those tensions, including Kashmir'. This was followed by a similar resolution by G-8 countries in London on 12 June 1998.

In the face of these international pressures, I met the Indian Prime Minister Atal Behari Vajpayee in Durban, South Africa in the last week of August 1998 during the Summit of the Non-Aligned Movement (NAM). Nawaz Sharif had to cancel his participation at the last minute and asked me to lead the Pakistan delegation. I had taken over as foreign minister only three weeks earlier. It was agreed during this meeting that the formula for composite dialogue evolved by the foreign secretaries in June 1997 would be revived but a formal announcement would be made after the scheduled meeting of the two prime ministers in September in New York on the sidelines of the General Assembly.

The September meeting between the two prime ministers went a step further than the June 1997 formula. The joint statement issued in New York on 23 September 1998, said:

They reaffirmed their common belief that an environment of durable peace and security was in the supreme interest of both India and Pakistan, and of the region as a whole. They expressed their determination to renew and reinvigorate efforts to secure such an environment. They agreed that the peaceful settlement of all outstanding issues, including Jammu and Kashmir, was essential for this purpose.

The two leaders reiterated their commitment to create conditions which would enable both countries to fully devote their resources, both human and material, to improving the lives of their people, particularly the poorest among them.

The two prime ministers noted with satisfaction the agreement reached between the Foreign Secretaries on operationalizing the mechanism to address all items in the agreed agenda of 23rd June 1997 in a purposeful and composite manner. They directed the foreign secretaries, accordingly, to resume the dialogue on the agreed dates.

In pursuance of these decisions, the two foreign secretaries met in Islamabad on 15–18 October 1998 to discuss peace, security, and Jammu and Kashmir, while other officials met in New Delhi in November 1998 to discuss the other six issues.

One of the decisions emerging out of meeting of the two prime ministers was to start a direct bus service between New Delhi and Lahore to facilitate the movement of people.

In January 1999 as the date for the inaugural bus service came closer, Nawaz Sharif told an Indian correspondent that he would like to welcome Vajpayee to lead the inaugural bus himself. To our surprise, within a few days, a positive response came that Vajpayee would travel to Lahore on the inaugural bus on 20 February 1999.

While excited about the prospect of such a visit, the actual date created a logistic problem. Several weeks earlier, Pakistan had accepted a proposal from China that the Chinese defence minister pay an official visit to Pakistan on 20 February, the same day as indicated by Prime Minister Vajpayee for his visit. The foreign office suggested that Vajpayee's visit be postponed for a day, but with the Indian parliament commencing its budget session from 22 February, the visit could not be rescheduled. At a meeting convened by Prime Minister Nawaz Sharif and attended by the army chief, General Pervez Musharraf, it was decided that I would not accompany the prime minister to the Wagah border in Lahore to receive the Indian prime minister, but instead receive the Chinese defence minister at mid-day at Islamabad. Since there was no separate defence minister in the cabinet, I was to receive him, hold formal talks in the afternoon and host a formal banquet for the Chinese guest in the evening. I would however go to Lahore next morning to join the formal talks with the Indian prime minister.

Similarly the three services chiefs, it was decided, would join me at the Islamabad airport to receive the Chinese defence minister, and then fly to Lahore to join the formal reception line for the Indian prime minister at the Governor House and return to Islamabad in the evening to attend the formal banquet for the Chinese defence minister.

In the light of this background the speculation in the media and the statement of Qazi Hussain Ahmad on 21 February that General Musharraf and other senior chiefs had refused to go to Wagah to receive the Indian prime minister is not factually correct. They duly carried out the decision which the prime minister had made in my presence.

Vajpayee's 28-hour visit to Lahore was full of drama. He was accompanied by a large entourage of dignitaries, editors and film stars. There was great excitement among all sections of the society, but Jamaat-e-Islami declared 20 February as a black day and organized large-scale demonstrations in Lahore. Even the cars of diplomats which were going to Lahore Fort for the formal banquet were attacked. There were reports that Jamaat-e-Islami was encouraged by certain 'agencies' which were against the peace process with India, to organize these protests.

At the formal banquet Vajpayee in his response to Nawaz Sharif's speech said, 'We welcome the opportunity for meaningful negotiation on all pending issues including Kashmir. In the interest of future generations, we have to bury our differences and restore trust between the two countries.'

Next day, Vajpayee visited Minar-e-Pakistan (previously Minto Park, where the Pakistan Resolution was passed by the Convention of All India Muslim League on 23 March 1940) and said, 'My friends advised me not to visit Minar-e-Pakistan because that would put my approval seal on the creation of Pakistan but, a strong and prosperous Pakistan is in our own interest.' These words he also recorded in the guest book.

The same afternoon, at a citizens' reception on the lawns of the Governor House in Lahore, Vajpayee said, 'We have suffered enmity for so long. Now is the time for friendship. I know how to win this friendship: difficult decisions would have to be made, a solution of the Kashmir problem would have to be found, but we are ready.'

This statement was a major change in the traditional Indian position that Kashmir was a part of India and there was nothing more to discuss. Nawaz Sharif also said in his speech that to solve Kashmir, both sides would have to move beyond their stated position.

The Lahore Declaration, signed by the two prime ministers on 21 February 1999, reflected these positive vibrations of Vajpayee's visit (Appendix II).

The declaration, sharing 'the vision of peace and stability' of the two prime ministers records their commitments to inter alia:

- Intensify their efforts to resolve all issues, including the issue of Jammu and Kashmir;
- Intensify their composite and integrated dialogue process for an early and positive outcome of the agreed bilateral agenda;
- Take immediate steps for reducing the risk of accidental or unauthorized use of nuclear weapons.

Along with the Lahore Declaration, a Memorandum of Understanding was also signed between the two foreign secretaries on nuclear and security issues. (Appendix II)

As the formal meeting between the two prime ministers started, Nawaz Sharif, departing from his formal opening statement, startled everybody present by thanking Vajpayee 'for providing us an opportunity to become a nuclear power. The Indian ambition to become a nuclear power by bringing the weapons out of the closet, also forced Pakistan to respond in kind and become a declared nuclear power.' Vajpayee, caught unaware, only smiled and did not say anything.

A little later, Nawaz Sharif also proposed that since both countries were under pressure to sign the CTBT, they could benefit by evolving a joint position through regular exchange of information. This point was reflected in the subtle formulation of paragraph 8 of the Memorandum of Understanding.

The joint statement issued on the occasion also recorded the decision that the two foreign ministers would meet periodically to discuss all issues of mutual concern including nuclear related issues.

The Chenab Formula

The main outcome of Vajpayee's Lahore visit, in terms of the implementation of the Lahore Declaration, was the decision to accelerate the back channel discussions on Kashmir. During their luncheon meeting in September in New York, Nawaz Sharif startled Vajpayee when he said, 'We have asked the two foreign secretaries to meet, but you know and I know that such sensitive and important issues cannot be resolved by civil servants. We as political leaders have to come to grips and take initiatives that will lead to solutions. You come up with any reasonable proposals on Kashmir and I promise to move forward responding to your proposals. Are you ready?' Vajpayee, with his typical caution, looked right and left and said, 'let us meet alone after lunch.'

At that one-to-one meeting, they agreed to setup a back channel to undertake serious discussions on Kashmir. They also agreed to nominate one representative who would report directly to the prime minister.

After our return, I proposed Shaharyar Mohammed Khan. But the Foreign Secretary Shamshad Ahmad persuaded Nawaz Sharif to nominate Niaz A. Naik. Vajpayee nominated R.K. Mishra. These two representatives met several times between October 1998 and May 1999. The focus of their discussion was what came to be known as the 'Chenab Formula.'

The origin of the Chenab Formula can be traced to the proposal put forward by UN mediator, Judge Owen Dixon of Australia in 1950. He had said: 'Since India's agreement would never be obtained to de-militarization in any such form as would permit the plebiscite to be conducted in conditions sufficiently guarded against intimidation and other forms of influence and abuse.'[3] He then suggested an alternate approach of 'regional plebiscites' and 'allocation of each section or area according to the results of the votes therein.' As an alternative he also suggested that actual voting would take place only in the valley of

Kashmir, the other three regions with Muslim, Hindu and Buddhist majorities would be assigned to Pakistan and India respectively without an actual vote, because their voting pattern can be predicted with certainty.

According to Owen Dixon, Prime Minister Jawaharlal Nehru was willing to consider the alternative of holding a plebiscite in the valley only in the expectation that Sheikh Abdullah, the then prime minister of occupied Kashmir could swing the vote to India's favour. But Prime Minister Liaquat Ali Khan rejected the proposal because under the Security Council resolution 'the destiny of the state of Jammu and Kashmir as a whole should be decided by a single plebiscite taken over the entire state.'

By the time, the next serious negotiations took place between India and Pakistan on Kashmir in 1962 during six rounds of talks between the two foreign ministers, Zulfikar Ali Bhutto and Swaran Singh, India initially responded positively to proposals of 'a partition based on the presumed wishes of the people,' but then it backtracked and reverted to their idea of making the line of control a permanent 'Line of Peace'.

The proposals evolved by the Kashmir Study Group (KSG)[4] in 1998 were also based on the Owen Dixon approach: called the Livingston Proposal 'Kashmir, A Way Forward', the KSG proposal recommended that portions of the former state of Jammu and Kashmir be re-constituted as a sovereign entity or entities (but without an international personality) enjoying free access to one another and from both India and Pakistan on the following lines:

1. Three entities, Kashmir, Jammu and Ladakh, would be established in the portion of the pre-1947 state now administered by India. These three self-governing entities would each take part in a body that would coordinate issues of interest to all of them, such as internal trade and transportation.
2. Two entities, Azad Kashmir and the Northern Areas, would be established on the side now administered by Pakistan. Like the entities on the Indian side, they would each be represented in a coordinating body that would consider issues in which they both had an interest.

3. An All-Kashmir body would be setup to coordinate areas of broader interest such as regional trade, tourism, environment, and water resources. This body would include representatives from each of the five entities as well as from India and Pakistan.

4. Each of the new entities would have its own democratic constitution, as well as its own citizenship, flag, and legislature which would legislate on all matters other than defence and foreign affairs. India and Pakistan would be responsible for the defence of the entities, and the entities would maintain police forces to maintain internal law and order. India and Pakistan would be expected to work out financial arrangements for the entities.

5. Citizenship of the entities would also entitle individuals to acquire Indian or Pakistani passports (depending on which side of the Line of Control they live on). Alternatively, they could use entity passports subject to endorsements by India or Pakistan as appropriate.

6. The borders of the entities with India and Pakistan would remain open for the free transit of people, goods, and services in accordance with arrangements to be worked out between India, Pakistan and the entities.

7. While the present Line of Control would remain in place until such time as both India and Pakistan decided to alter it in their mutual interest, both India and Pakistan would demilitarize the area included in the entities. Neither India nor Pakistan could place troops on the other side of the Line of Control without the permission of the other state.

8. All displaced persons who left any portion of the entities would have the right to return to their home localities.

The 1998 KSG proposal was revised successively in the light of comments received. The final version was published in 2005 (www. kashmirstudygroup.net).

Since Niaz A. Naik was a member of the Kashmir Study Group, his discussions with R.K. Mishra started on the basis of these proposals and evolved gradually into what came to be known as the Chenab Formula.

According to the 'Chenab Formula', 'Pakistan may consider 'Doaba', a narrow strip of land between Chenab and Ravi rivers in the suburbs of Shakargarh (district Sialkot) stretching up to Chamb, Dhodha and Rajwari districts as international border. The town of Kargil might go to India under this 'give and take' but from Kargil upward, India will have to agree to give territory to Pakistan.' Most of the districts in Jammu and on the left bank of the Chenab are Hindu majority in the state of Jammu and Kashmir while in most of the districts on the western side of the Chenab, the Muslims are predominant. 'Pakistan may also agree to forego its claim over Buddhist majority Ladakh region as well, but there will be no compromise on the Valley. The Muslim majority valley will be partially autonomous and there will be major changes on the borderline to adjust tehsils and town surrounding the valley between India and Pakistan. In short, the River Chenab will form the separation line between the Pakistan and Indian held areas.'

Since India was no longer willing to go back to the concept of Hindu versus Muslim majority, the Chenab formula basically converted a communal formula into a geographic formula since most of the Hindu majority is east of Chenab and Muslim majority districts are west of Chenab.

The Lahore Declaration had called upon the two foreign ministers to meet periodically to discuss all issues of mutual concern. An opportunity for such a meeting emerged within a month when I and Jaswant Singh, the Indian foreign minister were together at the SAARC foreign ministers' meeting in Nuwara Eliya, Sri Lanka from 17 to 19 March 1999. We met on a bench perched in the middle of a lotus filled lake, away from all glares and cameras.

I started the discussion by saying that for the first time, the two prime ministers had accepted, first in New York and then in Lahore, that the peaceful settlement of all outstanding issues including Jammu and Kashmir was essential to create an environment of durable peace and security in the region. Both the leaders had also showed flexibility by not insisting on their traditional viewpoints. Vajpayee did not say Kashmir was an integral part of India and there is nothing to discuss. Nawaz Sharif also conceded that to resolve Kashmir, both sides will have to move beyond their stated positions. Now it is for you and me to move further. You cannot expect me to move 90 per cent, without further movement from your side. We have to find that mid point somewhere. Future generations will not forgive us if we do not clinch this window of opportunity within the next 12 to 18 months.

Jaswant Singh listened carefully and then said, 'So, how should we proceed?'

I said, 'Let us list all the options identified so far on the Kashmir issue, eliminate those that are totally unacceptable to either side and narrow the discussion to options in which there is some common ground.'

He said, 'Let us start.'

I said, let me clarify that we are not negotiating at this stage. So if I list any option, it does not mean that our latest negotiating position has changed. We are exploring, off the record, the overall direction or approach on the basis of which serious negotiations can begin. He said, 'I agree.'

After listing various options, I said, I found some common ground in the formula for district wise or region wise voting or ascertainment. Under such a formula, the Hindu majority areas, east of Chenab will go to India, and Northern Areas and Azad Kashmir to Pakistan, narrowing the problem to the Kashmir valley, for which the maximum autonomy formula put forward by the KSG might be the best option.

He said, it would be difficult to accept the principle of voting for some areas or to go back to Hindu majority versus Muslim majority but these are matters of detail. Give me four to six weeks and I will get back to you for a meeting at some mutually convenient location and date. Please nominate someone who can facilitate such a meeting.

I told him, 'You can call our high commissioner, Jehangir Ashraf Qazi and tell him when and where you will be going and he will get back to you within 24 hours with my response.' I of course briefed Jehangir Ashraf Qazi on the subject the same day, as he was a part of the delegation to the SAARC meeting.

On my return I briefed Nawaz Sharif and my colleagues in the foreign office. We all felt that for the first time in decades, we could see some light at the end of the tunnel. But this optimism did not last long. The four to six weeks Jaswant asked for never finished because the Vajpayee government fell in less than four weeks, on 17 April 1999. In May the Kargil crisis, and in October the military takeover totally derailed the peace process with India, and Pakistan lost an historic opportunity to find a durable solution to the problem of Kashmir.

As recorded in the next chapter, when I met Vajpayee in New Delhi on 12 June 1999, he said with a voice chocked with emotions: 'I had travelled to Pakistan with such sincerity and with high hope for durable peace between India and Pakistan. The real casualty of the Kargil crisis is trust between the two countries.' On hearing these words, I controlled my own emotions with great difficulty.

I had the opportunity to revisit this subject in March 2005 and May 2006, when I met Dr Manmohan Singh, the prime minister of India. On both occasions, when I was in India for different conferences, he was kind enough to invite me for a private one-to-one lunch and a frank, though informal, exchange of views. On both occasions, he emphasized his deep commitment to the composite dialogue process to promote durable peace with Pakistan. 'If I succeed in fulfilling this high priority agenda during my tenure, I might get a footnote in history', he said.

US–Pakistan Relations

The central challenge of Pakistan's foreign policy over the years has been its relations with USA. This relationship has seen many negative and positive milestones, created largely by external events and pressures.

In the late 1950s, as tensions with India over Kashmir continued, Pakistan began to look for ways to defend its security. It therefore readily accepted the option to join the alliances and the defence pacts which USA was building in the 1950s, to counter the Russian influence in the region. While in the process, Pakistan acquired modern weapons, but lost the opportunity to evolve an independent foreign policy and gradually slided into the position of a satellite of a super power. That faultline in Pakistan's foreign and security policy has never been fully repaired.

This new partnership with USA suffered its first setback in 1962 when after the outbreak of border hostilities between India and China, USA offered military assistance to India. This opened the opportunity for Pakistan to adopt a more independent foreign policy by moving closer to China and some other non-aligned countries like Indonesia and Libya. USA however felt that Pakistan, while still dependent on its military and economic assistance, was drifting too far from its sphere of influence. It therefore engineered a crisis in the US–Pakistan relations by cancelling the Consortium meeting convened by the World Bank in July 1965 to pledge assistance for the first year of the Third Five-Year Plan.

This slide in the relationship with USA continued for the next few years and hit a very low point in December 1971, when in the wake of military aggression by India in East Pakistan, Pakistan's request for military assistance against Indian aggression under the 1959 Cooperation Agreement, was turned down. The USSR, in contrast, was faithfully implementing its treaty with India by providing arms and vetoing every Security Council resolution calling for a ceasefire and withdrawal of troops.

In November 1972, after East Pakistan became Bangladesh, Pakistan withdrew from SEATO but retained its membership of CENTO. USA responded by resuming military assistance to Pakistan during Zulfikar Ali Bhutto's visit to USA in September 1973.

Basically there were many contradictions in the structure of Pakistan's relations with USA. Its desperate need for arms to gain a certain strategic balance with India was understandable but in the process it was not always easy for it to accommodate all the priorities of a major world power. As a new Muslim nation, the people of Pakistan wanted stronger links with other Islamic countries but USA was averse to many such countries. Again the people of Pakistan felt very warmly towards China, which had extended strong moral, economic and military support to Pakistan in every hour of its need. But one of the top priorities of the US foreign policy from the outset was to counter China's rise by building up India. That is why Pakistan was very disappointed at the lukewarm political support it received from USA on the issue of Kashmir throughout this period.

These contradictions in the US–Pakistan relations crossed another threshold in the mid-1970s, as India, in its search for the status of a regional superpower, tested a nuclear device on 18 May 1974 and called it 'Buddha Smiles'. Prime Minister Zulfikar Ali Bhutto had already embarked on a programme to build nuclear weapons soon after taking over in December 1971. But the Indian tests gave a strong fillip to these efforts. Simultaneously, Pakistan launched a parallel diplomatic track, by moving a resolution in the UN General Assembly in October 1974 to declare South Asia a nuclear free zone. It also offered to sign NPT and CTBT if India would do the same. This resolution was adopted by the General Assembly every year for the next twelve years, but had no effect on India's policy of going ahead with its nuclear options.

USA, while tacitly accepting India's nuclear capability, increased the pressure on Pakistan by offering to sell 120 military planes if it would cancel its agreement with France to buy a reprocessing plant to produce plutonium. When Pakistan refused, USA forced France to cancel the contract. Pakistan then quietly opted for the alternative technology of uranium enrichment in the Kahuta plant under the supervision of Dr A.Q. Khan. In a short period of seven years since his appointment in 1976, the first atomic device had been manufactured and cold tested.

In 1977–78, the US Congress passed the Symington and Glenn amendments to the Foreign Assistance Act to impose sanctions on a country that imported equipment, material or technology for the production of plutonium or for enriching uranium.

USA was aware of the nuclear capability Pakistan was developing but two years after the Symington and Glenn amendments were adopted, the Soviet Union invaded Afghanistan in December 1979. As Pakistan joined USA in arming Afghan mujahideen and their foreign supporters, it became a key ally once again. That made it difficult for USA to impose sanctions on Pakistan and the US president issued an annual certificate required under the Pakistan specific Pressler Law passed in 1985. But in October 1990, as the Soviet forces began to withdraw, Pressler sanctions were imposed on Pakistan, terminating the annual flow of $700 million in foreign assistance and the delivery of sixty F-16 planes for which Pakistan had already paid half the amount in cash foreign exchange.

Thus the stark contradiction in the basic policy framework of US–Pakistan relations re-emerged with full force. From the start, Pakistan had no option, in the face of growing Indian nuclear capability, but to develop its own nuclear capability. For USA, however, its nuclear non proliferation agenda was more important than Pakistan's security. It walked away, once again, from a warm and genuine relationship with Pakistan as soon as its strategic objective of defeating the Soviet Union in Afghanistan had been achieved. This naturally revived memories of similar betrayals in the past among the people of Pakistan.

In October 1990, US sanctions under the Pressler Law were limited to its own bilateral assistance, but after the May 1998 nuclear tests, all bilateral and multilateral assistance to Pakistan had been stopped.

Is it possible, I asked myself as I reviewed these bitter lessons of history in August 1998 to build a more stable relationship with USA based not just on the temporary need to tackle 'common enemies' but on shared values, respect for international law and a fuller understanding of each other priorities and constraints?

Nuclear Diplomacy

After the nuclear tests by India and Pakistan, USA intensified its efforts to persuade both countries to sign the CTBT and desist from further nuclear tests. As Strobe Talbott, the US deputy secretary of state records in his book *Engaging India*,[5] 'But the Indian government was, from the very outset, disinclined to compromise. Its short-term goal was to resist precisely the sort of abnegation the United States proposed. Its strategy was to play for the day when the United States would get over its huffing and puffing and with a sigh of exhaustion or a shrug of resignation, accept a nuclear armed India as a fully responsible and fully entitled member of the international community.' This prediction proved right ten years later when India was accepted as a de facto nuclear power, with the signing of an Indo–US nuclear agreement in October 2008.

For Pakistan, India's reluctance to sign the CTBT provided a way out, since it could sign the treaty but link its ratification to India's ratification. But the public opinion in Pakistan was strongly opposed to any unilateral signing by Pakistan. I therefore decided to take the issue to parliament. A joint meeting of the foreign affairs committees of the National Assembly and the Senate was convened to debate the issue. The meeting was opened to all other members and at least hundred members attended. I explained in my opening statement that Pakistan could secure many benefits if it offered to sign the CTBT. In practice I emphasized the signing would be only of symbolic significance because without ratification it would not prevent Pakistan from carrying out further tests if necessary. Many opposition members wanted to know the details of benefits Pakistan would get. I responded by saying that unless we indicated that in principle, we were ready to sign, we could not ascertain or negotiate the likely benefits we would get. After many lengthy speeches over two days and protest by Islamic parties, the parliamentary committees endorsed the line proposed by the foreign office on the issue without adopting a formal resolution: that the prime minister in his statement in the UN General Assembly could offer to sign the CTBT within a reasonable time but Pakistan would not ratify unless and until India had ratified the Treaty.

This symbolic concession provided a very positive atmosphere for Nawaz Sharif's first meeting with President Clinton. It was agreed at this meeting that the prime minister would be invited for an official visit to USA in December 1998. In the meanwhile the possibility of a partial relaxation of sanctions would be explored by resuming blocked loans from IMF. Discussions would also be intensified to return the whole or a substantial part of the remaining amount Pakistan had paid for F-16 planes.

Nawaz Sharif's official visit to USA in the first week of December 1998 coincided with the impeachment proceedings against President Clinton in Congress. I was anticipating a very nervous and tense host but I was amazed at Clinton's confidence and composure throughout the four hours we spent at the White House on 2 December, only three days before the final vote in the Senate. He was well briefed and totally focused. During the official lunch, he asked about the impact of the Asian economic crisis on Pakistan and pros and cons of the phenomenon of globalization for developing countries.

As expected, the outcome of the visit was positive. IMF received the green signal to resume lending and initiate, through the Paris Club, the rescheduling of Pakistan's loans. On the F-16 issue, President Clinton was very apologetic and said it was not good business practice nor very fair that his side should refuse to deliver the planes for which we had paid and also hesitate to return the money. 'But fortunately or unfortunately, Washington is ruled by lawyers. USA has a settlement fund, from which it can pay its obligations arising from legal disputes. Our lawyers have determined that if Pakistan were to go to court on this issue, it had 70 per cent chance of winning. So we can pay Pakistan 70 per cent of the remaining amount, i.e. $325 million. You may get more if you go to court but it may take several years and will also involve heavy legal costs. Also I promise to retrieve the remaining

30 per cent ($100 million) for Pakistan, through the aid programme in the next year or two.'

Nawaz Sharif looked towards me. I told him in quick Punjabi that we should accept in principle but their delegation should meet us the next day to discuss details and explore certain options on the remaining 30 per cent. Clinton was delighted. He got up and shook Nawaz Sharif's hands and said, 'I am greatly relieved.'

The next day, Karl Inderfurth, US assistant secretary for South Asia, came to my hotel with a team of six lawyers, each representing a different department, and a six-page draft agreement to the effect that Pakistan was accepting 70 per cent payment in full and final settlement of its claim.

I started the discussion by reminding the team that this money was paid 8 to 10 years ago and Pakistan could legitimately claim interest on the amount paid. In normal times we would have gone to the court and recovered the full amount with interest. But in view of the difficult situation created by the nuclear related sanctions, we will accept the offer made by President Clinton on three conditions. First, the 70 per cent will be paid within a month, i.e. before the end of December 1998. Second, the remaining 30 per cent should also be included in the proposed arrangement, if USA will agree to give it in the form of wheat on a grant basis. (That year Pakistan had imported one and half million tons of wheat at a cost of $300 million in foreign exchange). Third, instead of a long legal agreement, the agreed understanding will be formalized through an exchange of letters between Pakistan's ambassador in USA and Karl Inderfurth.

After three hours of discussions these arrangements were finalized and Pakistan received $325 million[6] before the end of December 1998. With a bumper wheat crop in 1999, a part of 30 per cent allocation for wheat was however switched to edible oils. But eventually Pakistan received the entire amount it had paid for the F-16 planes, $555 million in cash and about $100 million in the form of commodities.

By January 1999, the other important component of the understanding reached with President Clinton in September 1998 was also implemented, as IMF signed an ESAF Loan of $1.2 million and the Paris Club rescheduled some of the outstanding loans for one year. This helped to increase the country's foreign exchange reserves from

$1 billion in December 1998, to $1.7 billion in the first week of October 1999.

Pakistan had thus achieved a measure of diplomatic success in securing, within a short period of seven months, some relaxation in the sanctions imposed in May 1998, after the nuclear tests, but its overall relationship with USA was still very problematic. Pakistan's continuing support for the Taliban regime in Afghanistan, which was providing safe haven to Osama Bin Laden and his Al-Qaeda network was constantly played up in Washington by the Indian lobby in USA and some members of the Congress. India was also urging the US to accept India as a nuclear power but deny such a status to Pakistan. As Strobe Talbott records, 'Jaswant had come to Washington with a subliminal message in support of an overarching goal to persuade the American government that, unlike Pakistan, a democratic, socially cohesive, politically confident India could be trusted with the bomb. A nuclear armed India was a natural ally of the United States in the struggle against Islamic fundamentalism, while a nuclear armed Pakistan was a threat to both countries. Therefore the United States should back off its insistence on India's acceptance of the non-proliferation benchmarks which he called the 'four legs of the elephant' and stop pestering his prime minister for a timetable that required a public commitment to signing the CTBT within a year.'[7]

We in the foreign office were fully aware of this Indian onslaught to bracket Pakistan with Islamic fundamentalists in an effort to build a strategic partnership with USA and also seek a de facto nuclear status for India. We had therefore decided, in principle, to adopt a more positive attitude on the non-proliferation benchmark, without compromising our vital objectives. Under this policy, Nawaz Sharif's statement at the UN General Assembly on 23 September 1998, that 'Pakistan will, within a year, adhere to the CTBT in conditions free from coercion or pressure', was more positive than the 'convoluted' statement made by Prime Minister Vajpayee the next day. That in turn led to greater relaxation of sanctions in the case of Pakistan, when compared to India, in December 1998.

However, our efforts to continue this policy could not be sustained during 1999. In the spring of 1999, the foreign office had prepared a brief suggesting that if Pakistan were to sign the CTBT by September 1999, as promised, but linked its ratification to Indian ratification, the signing would have no legal significance, nor would it prevent Pakistan from testing if India carried out another test. Initially the prime minister was inclined to approve this brief, in preparation for his visit to the UN General Assembly in September 1999. But after the Kargil crisis in June/July 1999, he anticipated stronger domestic opposition to even the 'symbolic' signing of the CTBT and decided to cancel his programme to attend the General Assembly. This decision, as I gathered during my own visit to New York in September 1999, also contributed to Nawaz Sharif's ouster from the government a month later.

The military takeover of 12 October 1999 further increased Pakistan's isolation and attracted democracy related sanctions, which further increased the country's economic difficulties. This isolation continued for the next two years, when the tragic events of 11 September 2001, suddenly catapulted Pakistan into centre stage of a major international campaign against terrorism, ending its isolation of the preceding eleven years. But at the same time, this dramatic change in the geo-political landscape of the world had also heightened tensions between the West and the Islamic World, especially after the military action in Afghanistan in October 2001 and in Iraq in April 2003, setting into motion once again, an undercurrent of contradiction in the US–Pakistan relations.

As already mentioned in Chapter 2, it is a strange coincidence of Pakistan's chequered history that each time Pakistan is required to participate in a great global game, there is military rule in Pakistan. General Ayub Khan took over in 1958 as the Cold War was heating up and USA was building military alliances to encircle the USSR. Two years after General Ziaul Haq imposed martial law in Pakistan, the Soviet Union invaded Afghanistan and USA enlisted Pakistan's support to defeat the Russians with the help of thousands of mujahideen.

Now once again, when USA and its allies launched a major international campaign against terrorism after 9/11, General Musharraf was in the saddle to make Pakistan an active participant in this campaign.

I hope some security and foreign policy experts will find it possible to go deeper into the records of US think tanks and policy cells to determine if this coincidence is really accidental.

It will be equally revealing to explore if Pakistan would have adopted a different course or played a more balanced role, if there had been a democratically elected government with a strong parliament in Pakistan in the 1960s, 1980s and the 2000s and if Pakistan had also evolved, like many other countries, an effective national security system to debate and select the most appropriate foreign policy options.

Failure to Evolve an Effective National Security System

All major countries of the world have evolved their respective national security system in the light of their own political and administrative structures. The most successful of these, in my assessment, is the national security process in the United States. As Henry Kissinger, the most influential national security advisor USA has ever had, documents in his writings, the roots of most important strategies and initiatives in US foreign policy can be traced to the intensive research done by the staff of the National Security Council (NSC). For example, the Domino Theory is spelled out in NSC document No. 64 of February 1950 and American official statement on the cold war strategy is presented in NSC document No. 68 of April 1950.

Unfortunately, after 60 years of independent existence, Pakistan has yet to evolve an effective national security system. The reasons for this failure, in my assessment, are complex and mutually reinforcing. For 27 years, from 1958 and 1985 (except a brief interval of civilian rule from 1972 to 1977), the country was under military rule. In a military regime, security issues are discussed and decided only by the military and its inter-services structure. The need for bringing in civilian leaders and functionaries into these discussions was not therefore considered necessary.

In 1985, on the eve of the general elections in March 1985, when President Ziaul Haq revived the 1973 constitution, he introduced under the powers given to him by the Supreme Court (PLD 1977 SC 657), several constitutional amendments. These included insertion of Article 152-A to create a NSC 'to make recommendations relating to the issue of a Proclamation of Emergency under Article 232, security of Pakistan and any other matter of national importance that may be

referred to it by the president in consultation with the prime minister.'
The NSC was to consist of the president, the prime minister, the
chairman of Senate, the CJCSC, the three services' chiefs and the chief
ministers of the provinces. From the composition of the NSC and its
terms of reference, it was clear that it had been created to give the
president and heads of the armed forces a constitutional role in
supervising the functioning of the government rather than evolving a
coherent national security policy.

The National Assembly elected in March 1985, debated at great
length all the amendments made by General Ziaul Haq and finally
passed the Eighth Amendment in October 1985, which apart from
providing constitutional cover to all the martial law orders, ordinances
and the constitutional amendments made between 1977 and 1985,
amended Articles 48, 58 and 91, 101, 105 and 112 and also deleted
Article 152-A to create a NSC. Thus that NSC died without holding a
single meeting.

Another half-hearted attempt to create a NSC was made in January
1997 by President Farooq Ahmad Leghari during the caretaker
government of November 1996–February 1997. Since the National
Assembly had been dissolved and a constitutional amendment could
not be made through an ordinance, the 1997 Council on Defence and
National Security (CDNS) was created by amending the Rules of
Business. The CDNS was given wider functions and was to be chaired
by the president. The CDNS also never met and died without serving
any useful purpose.

Finally, in 2004, a NSC was created, through an ordinary law, rather
than the Seventeenth Amendment. Its functions are,

> to serve as a forum for consultation on strategic matters pertaining to the
> sovereignty, integrity and security of the State; and the matters relating to
> democracy, governance and inter-provincial harmony. The President shall
> be the Chairman of the National Security Council and its other members
> shall be the Prime Minister, the Chairman of the Senate, the Speaker of
> the National Assembly, the Leader of the Opposition in the National
> Assembly, the Chief Ministers of the Provinces, the Chairman Joint Chiefs
> of Staff Committee, and the Chiefs of Staff of the Pakistan Army, Pakistan
> Navy and Pakistan Air Force.

This council which has met several times between 2004 and 2008 is modelled on the council created by General Ziaul Haq in 1985 with the same objective—to give an institutional role to the armed forces to supervise the political system. As General Musharraf says in his book, *In the Line of Fire*,

> With the National Security Council composed thus and meeting at least once a quarter, I am convinced that we have instituted a check on the three power brokers. The prime minister has to perform, or he will come under pressure from the NSC, or at least from the leader of the opposition and the uniformed members. The president had better not be impulsive when no member of NSC is with him. The army chief can never takeover, because he has an institution available to voice his concerns (and the concerns of a worried public) to the prime minister and can then allow the constitution and the political process to take their course.

The NSC created in 2004, has effectively changed the nature of the constitutional setup from a Parliamentary system to a semi-presidential system. The main characteristic of a parliamentary system is that both in matters of legislation and executive authority, the parliament and its representatives enjoy supremacy. There can be many variations within the parliamentary system but the system loses its parliamentary character, if the supremacy of parliament is compromised or if the powers of the chief executive do not vest in the prime minister who is responsible to the parliament. To institute a system in which the army chief is expected to convey 'the concerns of a worried public' to the prime minister, rather than the elected representatives in parliament, will be a serious violation of the basic principle of democracy and the distribution of powers under the constitution between the executive, the judiciary and the parliament.

Inadequacy of the Present System

When I joined the foreign office in August 1998, I was struck by the absence of a viable institutional framework that could help military planners to coordinate more effectively with makers of foreign policy like the NSC in USA. I therefore began intensive discussions with my colleagues in the foreign office and in various military establishments.

My findings and recommendations which I incorporated in a formal proposal for the cabinet by February 1999, included the following:

- The armed forces have well-structured intelligence organizations and joint services arrangements to review security issues from time to time, but there is limited input in these reviews from policy makers or experts in the field of foreign policy and economic management.
- There is very limited coordination between the civilian intelligence agencies and the intelligence agencies of the armed forces.
- The defence committee of the cabinet has had a very limited role, primarily because it does not have its own secretariat and has not traditionally been used for discussing major national security issues. That is why, at present, in the absence of a NSC with its own secretariat and supporting mechanisms, there is no high level forum which can take an integrated view of all the elements affecting national security and formulate policy options and strategies for dealing with internal and external threats to national security. Periodical assessments of various issues and developments affecting national security are presented to the prime minister and some of his cabinet colleagues but these are more in the nature of a briefing rather than a part of the decision making process.
- As an inevitable consequence of the absence of an effective national security system, there is a wide gap between the military establishment and the elected civilian setup on different aspects of national security policies. This gap is also partly responsible for recurrent political instability and for periodical tensions between the two.
- In the absence of a system, which could facilitate regular interaction between the military establishment and the civilian establishment, the foreign policy of the country, for all practical purposes, has been formulated by the military establishment, particularly in critical areas like the policy on Kashmir, relations with India and Afghanistan. Various civilian governments, which assumed office from time to time after 1985, did not have a major impact on the conduct of foreign policy, partly because there was no forum where major changes in foreign policy could be discussed with the military establishment. That is why some initiatives taken by the political

governments, such as the bus diplomacy of early 1999 and the signing of the Lahore Declaration widened the gulf between the military and civilian establishments.

Overall, it would be fair to say that Pakistan's foreign policy has been taking shape largely in isolation not only from the mainstream political thinking but also without the benefit of advice from foreign policy experts in the foreign office and various think tanks. This would at least partly explain why in 1965, overlooking the widening gap between Pakistan and India's defence budgets (from a ratio of 1:3 in 1965 to 1:7 in 1965, after the India–China border conflict of 1962), Pakistan launched Operation Gibraltar that led to the 1965 war. Again in 1971, we allowed the internal political crisis in East Pakistan to blow up, in size and intensity, to a point where India found enough excuses to intervene militarily and break Pakistan into Pakistan and Bangladesh. The Afghan policy Pakistan pursued between 1980 and 2000 has not been, it now seems in retrospect, a great success. In fact, its negative fall out far exceeds any positive economic gains Pakistan may have achieved in the 1980s. The Kargil crisis is another example where a major initiative was launched without taking into account all the international and diplomatic implications.

It should be absolutely clear from this chronicle of catastrophic decisions, that the task of bringing together all the elements of a national security policy, i.e. military, economic and foreign policy, is so important that other considerations, such as giving a constitutional role to the armed forces in the governance of the country through 'checks and balances', should not be allowed to influence the composition and the terms of reference of the Council or its substantive functions.

The Proposed Model

The main objective of an effective national security system, I emphasized in the formal proposal for the cabinet, should be to translate the national strategy into policy options or more specifically to orchestrate various elements of national power, allocate priorities and objectives and select foreign policy options within a strategic framework. These comprise political, diplomatic, economic and commercial, moral and psychological, geographic, demographic, cultural and technological elements. It is unthinkable that any viable national security policy can be evolved without a proper institutional setup with the best minds and expertise available to the nation to analyze and evaluate different internal and external threats to national security, to assess and orchestrate various elements of national power and to explore concrete options for policy changes, redirection of efforts or concrete initiatives to avert or meet the potential threats.

My recommended model for the proposed body for decision making on national security issues, as outlined in the formal proposal, was as follows:

a. The Defence Committee of the Cabinet (DCC) should be reconstituted as the Cabinet Committee on Defence and National Security (CCDNS).
b. The CCDNS would be chaired by the prime minister and should include the ministers of foreign affairs, defence, interior and finance, the CJCSC and chiefs of staff of the Pakistan army, navy and air force. (At present service chiefs are not members of DCC but are invariably invited to attend its meetings).
c. The CCDNS would have its own secretariat located in the PM secretariat. It would be under a national security advisor, who, depending on the status and seniority of the person chosen, can be a minister or minister of state.
d. The CCDNS would be assisted by a planning committee on national security which will be chaired by the national security advisor and would include secretary foreign affairs, secretary interior, secretary finance and heads of all the civil and military intelligence agencies. The planning committee will prepare policy briefs, position papers and policy guidelines on different aspects of national security for consideration and approval by the NSC. Once approved, appropriate policy papers can also be presented to parliament or published for general discussions by the public and the media.
e. The CCDNS would also have the advice of an advisory committee on national security, consisting of heads of all the public and private think tanks dealing with strategic and foreign policy studies.

f. The terms of reference of the CCDNS would be broad yet specific and would cover all dimensions of national strategy. The committee would meet at least once every quarter and more frequently when the situation demanded and would adopt a business-like approach involving intense and frank discussions to evolve a consensus on major foreign policy issues.

One of the main objectives of the proposed CCDNS, I pointed out, would be to narrow the gap between the perceptions of the army establishment and the civilian leadership on security issues. This would not be easy because a military perception is inherently based on a threat perception which can be countered only by covert or overt military operations and hence the need to constantly upgrade the military strength of the country. A civilian perspective, on the other hand, is broader and much more cognizant of the economic constraints and diplomatic or international implications of different initiatives or responses. As a result, wherever possible, civilian political leadership will give preference to the diplomatic option because in the final analysis, war is always the inevitable consequence of the failure of diplomacy. But constant interaction between the civilian leadership and the top brass of the armed forces in a body like the CCDNS can help to narrow this gap in perceptions, gradually leading to a national consensus on different aspects of the national security.

It was not easy to convince the prime minister to submit these proposals to the cabinet for approval. Anything resembling a security council that will give an institutional role to the armed forces in the political setup had become highly controversial since 1985. But I kept emphasizing that we were not creating a security council but reconstituting the DCC, and a cabinet committee is always chaired by the prime minister or a member of the cabinet. Finally in April 1999, he authorized me to consult all concerned about these proposals and also submit a parallel proposal for a national command authority to coordinate and supervise the work of all the civilian and military organizations dealing with nuclear and strategic activities. After intense consultations with Dr A.Q. Khan, Dr Ishfaq Ahmad (chairman PAEC), and General Bajwa (head of strategic plans division), a paper to create a national command authority was also ready by the beginning of May 1999.

In the second week of May, I convened a meeting in the Foreign Office to discuss these two proposals—the creation of a new CCDNS and a National Command Authority (NCA). The meeting was attended by General Pervez Musharraf; General Tauqir Zia (DGMO), and General Bajwa. After the meeting General Musharraf asked if he could meet me in my office. When we sat down, he said, 'Sir, you have proposed a national security advisor with the status of a minister to serve as secretary of the CCDNS. If appointed, such an advisor would effectively become the defence minister. Could I instead propose a Grade-22 officer for this position rather than a minister?' I said that I had made this proposal on the assumption that Anwar Zahid, then special assistant to the prime minister, could possibly assume this position. But he, unfortunately, had died recently. Since I cannot readily think of another substitute, I could accept your proposal and recommend a Grade-22 (federal secretary level) official for this position. I then amended the proposal accordingly.

It took me another three months to obtain the required clearances from all concerned to these two proposals. Finally on 4 October, the prime minister authorized the inclusion of these two proposals in the agenda of the next cabinet meeting scheduled for the middle of October 1999. But that meeting and these proposals were washed away by the military takeover of 12 October, leaving Pakistan without an effective national security system for one more decade. As mentioned above, a NSC was created in 2004, but without the right composition or focus. The NCA created in February 2000 was based largely on the proposal initiated by me in 1999. General Musharraf's contention in his book (p. 286) that he had 'submitted a written plan calling for a National Command Authority but it remained unapproved during Nawaz Sharif's term in office', is not therefore correct. The proposal, as prepared by the foreign office, in consultation with Dr A.Q. Khan and Dr Ishfaq Ahmad, would have been approved by the next cabinet meeting in mid-October, if he had not taken over a few days earlier.

Future Outlook

A nation has security when it does not have to sacrifice its legitimate interests to avoid war and is able to protect them through war if challenged.

After 11 September 2001, a new global political order is gradually emerging, based on the right of pre-emptive unilateral action against sovereign nations in cases of threats of terrorism, which the nation state itself is unable to counter. This evolving doctrine launched with attacks on Afghanistan and Iraq in 2001 and 2003, if carried to its logical conclusion, will strike at the root of the global system based on the UN charter and could have serious consequences for the global economic order.

Partly as a reaction to these events, terrorists have been increasing in different parts of the world. The relations between the western world and the Islamic world have reached their lowest point. Initially all Islamic countries condemned the attacks but generally that sympathy has been replaced by hostility. A campaign against terrorism is being perceived as a campaign against Islam. A part of western media has played a major role in demonizing Islam and projecting fundamental Islam as the main enemy. This has seriously vitiated the investment climate in Pakistan and other Muslim countries.

Due to its geographical location, Pakistan has also become the melting pot of many global fault lines: like the Russian invasion of Afghanistan and the unresolved problem of Palestine. After the Russians left, Afghanistan became a safe haven for many extremist groups like Al-Qaeda, because the West literally abandoned Afghanistan in 1991. America's growing strategic relationship with India is also a cause for concern in Pakistan. Although, the apparent motivation is India's potential as a large market for trade and investment but a serious imbalance in the military capacity of India and Pakistan cannot be overlooked.

Support to USA after 9/11 has polarized the internal political situation in Pakistan, increasing internal threats to Pakistan's security. As in many other developing countries, the chief threat to national security in Pakistan now comes from internal dissent.

Pakistan is one of the few countries created in the name of Islam. It is an active member of the 57-nation Organization of Islamic Conference and has taken active part in all the international issues involving the rights of Islamic countries or entities like Algeria, Palestine, Bosnia, Kashmir, Al Quds and the Russian invasion of Afghanistan. Pakistan, while being a member of South Asia, has strong cultural and political ties with most countries in West Asia, especially with Iran, Turkey, and Saudi Arabia.

Pakistan has an equally strong set of relationships with the non-Muslim West. It joined the security pacts with USA in the 1950s. It has been an active member of the British Commonwealth and has very strong economic and trade links with Europe. Its political system is based on the Westminster model of parliamentary democracy and its official language is English.

With its strategic location as a bridge between South Asia, Central Asia, and West Asia and the network of positive relations with the West and the Islamic world, Pakistan is thus well placed to become a positive and important stabilizing force in the region.

But after 1980, as USA recruited, trained and funded, in close cooperation with Pakistan, thousands of Islamic volunteers or 'mujahideen' to fight and eventually defeat the Russians, there was unprecedented growth in extremism and what is called Islamic fundamentalism. This movement had its roots in Pakistan through the madrassahs setup to train such volunteers. But after 2001, as USA and allies invaded Afghanistan, thousands of Taliban and their supporters took refuge in the tribal areas between Pakistan and Afghanistan, with a destabilizing effect on both countries.

To realize Pakistan's potential as a stabilizing force in the region, it is equally important to understand its history. It has already fought three wars with a much bigger and hostile neighbour, India, losing in the process, half the country. It has suffered the burden of three million refugees from Afghanistan and the influx of weapons, drugs and militants. Its economy has suffered from unjustified sanctions because of its nuclear policy forced upon it by India's insistence to develop nuclear weapons. These have further compounded its internal difficulties associated with ethnic violence in Sindh and Balochistan. Forces of extremism have naturally benefited from these conditions of political instability and internal strife and have tried to deepen their roots in different parts of the country.

These difficulties have remained within manageable limits, thanks to the resilience of the nation. This resilience can play an important moderating role, if stability is restored in Afghanistan, if the peace process with India is strengthened further and full-fledged democracy is restored in Pakistan. But Pakistan needs continuing understanding and support of the international community in dealing with all these global fault lines and in building a strong economy and internally cohesive political structure.

NOTES

1. Iftikhar Murshed, *The Taliban Years*, Bennet & Bloom, London, 2006, p. 82.
2. Abdul Sattar, *Pakistan's Foreign Policy: 1947–2005*, Karachi: Oxford University Press, 2007, p. 141. Abdul Sattar was a member of the Pakistan delegation at the Simla Conference in 1972 and was later Foreign Minister of Pakistan from October 1999 to September 2002.
3. Quoted by Abdul Sattar, ibid., p. 28.
4. The Kashmir Study Group convened by Farooq Kotwari, a US citizen of Kashmiri origin, consisted of Admiral Nair and S.K. Singh from India and General K.M. Arif and Niaz Naik from Pakistan. In December 1998, the group developed the Livingston Proposal 'Kashmir, A Way Forward'.
5. Strobe Talbott, *Engaging India*, Brooking Institution Press, Washington DC, 2004, p. 5.
6. Pakistan had purchased sixty F-16 planes for $1.2 billion and had paid about $650 million, when the Pressler sanctions were imposed in October 1990 blocking the delivery of these planes. By 1992, twenty-eight planes had been manufactured. In 1995, under the Brown amendment, USA returned $230 million which had not yet been spent by the company for the manufacture of the remaining planes. The remaining amount of $425 million represented the cost of twenty-eight planes already manufactured.
7. Op. cit., p. 121.

With Nelson Mandela, President of South Africa, 1991
Photo Courtesy: Press Information Department (PID), Islamabad

With Prime Minister Li Peng of China, March 1991
Photo Courtesy: Author's personal collection

With Princess Diana of the United
Kingdom, 1992
*Photo Courtesy: Press Information
Department (PID), Islamabad*

With Prime Minister Mahathir
Mohamad of Malaysia, 1993
*Photo Courtesy: Press Information
Department (PID), Islamabad*

With Chandrika B. Kumaratuna,
President of Sri Lanka, 1997
*Photo Courtesy: Press Information
Department (PID), Islamabad*

With former President George Bush of the United States, September 1997
Photo Courtesy: Author's personal collection

With Jiang Zemin, President of China, 1998
Photo Courtesy: Author's personal collection

With HRH Shaikh Zayed Bin Sultan Al-Nahyan of the United Arab Emirates, June 1998
Photo Courtesy: Author's personal collection

With King Fahad Bin Abdulaziz of Saudi Arabia, June 1998
Photo Courtesy: Author's personal collection

Addressing the UN General Assembly, September 1998
Photo Courtesy: Author's personal collection

With Kofi Annan, Secretary General of the United Nations, September 1998
Photo Courtesy: Author's personal collection

Meeting with President Bill Clinton, December 1998. From left: Shahbaz Sharif, Mushahid Hussain, Ishaq Dar, Sartaj Aziz, and Prime Minister Nawaz Sharif
Photo Courtesy: Author's personal collection

With President Bill Clinton, July 1999
Photo Courtesy: Author's personal collection

With King Abdullah of Jordan, 1999
Photo Courtesy: Author's personal collection

With Boris Yeltsin, President of the Russian Federation, April 1999
Photo Courtesy: Author's personal collection

With Prime Minister of India, Dr Manmohan Singh, May 2005
Photo Courtesy: Author's personal collection

Showing Indian ingress after 1972 and Indian-alleged Pakistani incursion

Source: Cartographics by ISSI

CHAPTER 12

The Kargil Crisis 1999

The Kargil operation of 1999 has become an extraordinary event in the country's history because it not only prepared the ground for a prolonged military takeover in Pakistan in October 1999 but also derailed the peace process between India and Pakistan, which had started with such high hopes following Prime Minister Vajpayee's historic visit to Lahore on 20–21 February 1999. It also caused irreparable damage to Pakistan's principled and legitimate stand on Kashmir in the international arena.

Because of these disastrous consequences of the Kargil operation, no one is prepared to take responsibility for this misadventure. Success, as they say, has a thousand fathers but failure has none. The controversy surrounding this crisis has degenerated, over the years, into a verbal duel between Nawaz Sharif and Pervez Musharraf about whether or not the prime minister was fully briefed on the operation in advance.

Historical Background

In understanding the objectives of the Kargil operation, it is important to recall certain historical facts concerning the 'line of control' in Kashmir. Kashmir is one of the oldest disputes on the agenda of the United Nations. In 1846, the British defeated the Sikhs in Punjab and sold Kashmir to Gulab Singh under the Treaty of Amritsar. Kashmir was one of 500 princely states, which were under British suzerainty but were not directly ruled by the British. Under the partition plan, most of these states joined either India or Pakistan on the basis of their geographical proximity and religious correspondence to either of the two countries. There were, however, three states over which there were serious problems. The Muslim ruler of Junagadh with a Hindu majority announced his decision to join Pakistan, but India forcibly annexed it

249

through 'police action'. Hyderabad, with a Muslim Nizam but Hindu majority, wanted independence. India refused and occupied the state through military force and deposed the Nizam. In the Jammu and Kashmir state, the situation was the opposite. The ruler of the State, Maharaja Hari Singh was a Hindu, but the population was 80 per cent Muslim and wanted to join Pakistan. But Hari Singh deliberately delayed his decision to accede to Pakistan and fled to the Hindu majority province of Jammu. Pakistan should have followed the Indian example of annexing Junagadh and Hyderabad, and occupied Jammu and Kashmir by force. But its troops were still in transit from various parts of India. It therefore resorted to the alternative of sending a tribal *lashkar* to capture Srinagar. That it did in a matter of days but ignored the strategic safeguard of blocking the Srinagar airport. The very next day, Indian forces landed in Srinagar and expelled the tribes from Srinagar. Based on a dubious Instrument of Accession,[1] Kashmir was provisionally 'accepted' into the Indian union pending a free and impartial plebiscite. In 'accepting' the accession on 27 October 1947, Lord Mountbatten made it clear that the state would only be incorporated into the Indian union after a plebiscite to ascertain the wishes of the people of Kashmir.

Meanwhile some Pakistani troops were dispatched to Kashmir to join the fighting. On 1 January 1948, India took the Kashmir dispute to the United Nations. After twelve months, on 1 January 1949, the UN Security Council adopted a ceasefire resolution between the two countries, and deployed the United Nations Military Observer Group (UNMOGIP) to monitor the ceasefire line. This was followed by several resolutions calling for the holding of a 'free and fair plebiscite under UN supervision' to ascertain the 'wishes of the Kashmiri people.' But India prevented the implementation of these resolutions on one pretext or another.

The ceasefire of 1949 left three-fourths of the population of Kashmir in Indian occupied Kashmir, and one-fourth on the Pakistan side, subsequently called Azad Jammu and Kashmir. The two countries have been building fortifications and bunkers along this ceasefire line.

In the 1971 war between Pakistan and India the hostilities were largely concentrated in East Pakistan, but taking advantage of the state of war, India also succeeded in improving its position along the ceasefire line in Kashmir, by occupying 3,000 sq km at Kargil, Tithwal, and Chachro.

Under the Simla Agreement of 2 July 1972, India agreed to withdraw from certain territories in West Pakistan (Shakargarh, Sehjra, Islamgarh, and Chachro) but not those occupied in Kashmir. Under Para 4(ii) of the Simla Agreement, both sides agreed to 'respect the *Line of Control* emerging from the ceasefire of 17 December 1971 without prejudice to the recognized position of either side.' The Ceasefire Line of 1949 was thus effectively replaced by the Line of Control (LOC) of 1972.

India did not however adhere to para 4(ii) of the Simla Agreement which also stated: 'Neither side shall seek to alter it unilaterally, irrespective of the mutual differences and legal interpretations. Both sides further undertake to refrain from threat or use of force in violation of the Line.' Since then India has committed at least four major violations of the Simla Agreement:

- In 1972, immediately after the Simla Agreement, Indian forces crossed the LOC in Chorbat La sector and occupied about 10 sq km on the Pakistan side to gain further tactical advantage.

- In 1984, the Simla Agreement was further eroded when Indian troops captured about 3000 sq km in the Siachen glacier, along with passes at Saltoro range. The LOC was not determined beyond NJ-980420. According to one Indian army officer, Lt.-Col. Tewari 'No one in his right mind could possibly want that terrifying wasteland at heights of 18,000–22,000 feet, between that point and the Great Wall of China.'[2] But India did advance beyond the position it occupied in December 1971, forcing Pakistan to mobilize its troops. For the next two and half decades, despite a series of discussions, the Siachen issue has not been resolved and both sides have lost precious resources in men and materials.

- In 1988, India intruded into the Qamar sector, across the LOC and occupied 33 sq km of area to establish several posts.

- In the 1990s India also violated the Dras sector and established posts at Bhinbet and Maspola.

Apart from these specific violations, the LOC has never been peaceful because of regular shelling and mortar fire from both sides. In 1994, however, India started incessant firing in the Neelum valley in Azad Kashmir. According to Dr Shirin Mazari:

> The interdiction was on such a scale that the Neelum valley road had to be closed. The extent of civilian suffering was so extensive that UNMOGIP reportedly took up the matter with UN headquarters in 1997–98 seeking the running of humanitarian convoys to provide relief to the besieged population of the area. With the construction of an alternate route, through the Kaghan valley, around 1996, Pakistan was able to respond more effectively to the continuing Indian interdictions. In retaliation, Pakistan targeted the Dras–Kargil road, which negatively impacted Indian supplies to Siachen. It was then that India offered, through their DGMO, to refrain from targeting each other's line of communication. However, the Indian side did not live up to this commitment and the firing exchanges along the LOC continued with Indians targeting civilians on the Azad Jammu and Kashmir (AJK) side of the LOC.[3]

This in essence was the context in which the Kargil operation was planned as a kind of retaliation for the Indian action in the Neelum valley in 1994–96. According to Dr Shirin Mazari's analysis of the Kargil conflict based on official sources, 'It was a limited tactical defensive operation which incrementally escalated as a result of India raising the military, political and diplomatic ante.'[4]

Apparently this 'tactical defensive operation' got out of hand for several unexpected reasons. The planners of this operation had obviously assumed that if India could get away with several violations of the LOC in the past, without much international reaction, it was time that Pakistan should attempt to gain some tactical advantage, with the help of the Kashmiri freedom fighters who had waged a relentless struggle for their right of self determination since 1990.

On 17 April 1999, less than two months after his Lahore visit, the Vajpayee government in India faced a no confidence motion and had to resign preparing the ground for fresh elections in October 1999. The Kargil issue burst into the open only a month later on 7 May 1999 and immediately became a hot election issue. As a direct result of the election fever, India mobilized enormous troops, heavy Bofor guns and the Indian air force 'to defend every inch of Indian territory', sending alarm signals that the Kargil conflict may spread to other areas of Kashmir and eventually to the international boundary.

The international reaction to the Kargil conflict was very strong because unlike the 1980s, both the countries had become nuclear powers in 1998 and any danger of a nuclear stand off was totally out of line with the global non-proliferation agenda.

In March 1999, as the mujahideen, with assistance from the Northern Light Infantry occupied several heights in the Kargil–Dras sector, General Musharraf and his team decided to 'brief' the prime minister about the operation. Two sessions were held on 12–13 March, in which the first item was a presentation on the report of the Kashmir Study Group, in the context of ongoing negotiations on Kashmir with India after Prime Minister Vajpayee's visit to Lahore twenty days earlier. In the second session, the usual review of the situation inside occupied Kashmir was presented without indicating that any new initiative or operation was being launched. The briefing however highlighted that the mujahideen's activity inside Kashmir was intensifying particularly in the Kargil–Dras sector and that should have a positive impact on the ongoing negotiations on Kashmir because India would recognize the urgency of solving the Kashmir problem. There was no mention during this briefing of the involvement of the Pakistan army or paramilitary personnel or of any plans to cross the LOC to occupy positions previously occupied by India. They only highlighted intensification of mujahideen activity in the Kargil sector and a plan to provide them stinger missiles.

I attended this meeting in my capacity as foreign minister, along with Lt.-Gen. (retd) Abdul Majid Malik, the minister for Kashmir affairs. General Majid Malik was quite emphatic in his comments. He said, 'The proposal to provide stinger missiles to the Mujahideen will be treated by India as an act of war. It will also debunk our basic stand that Kashmiris inside occupied Kashmir were waging their own struggle for self determination, and Pakistan was only providing moral and diplomatic support.'

In my comments, I referred to the visit of Prime Minister Vajpayee to Lahore only three weeks ago and said that after signing the Lahore

Declaration and showing their willingness to start serious negotiations on Kashmir, they were expecting some reduction in the level of cross border activity in Kashmir, to improve the atmosphere for negotiations. Intensified mujahideen activity would in all probability derail the Lahore process.

The response to these comments from the army chief, General Pervez Musharraf, was rather strong: 'We know the Indians. They will negotiate seriously only under maximum pressure. Besides we cannot take responsibility for restraining mujahideen activity inside occupied Kashmir. We can however postpone the proposal to give stinger missiles to mujahideen if that would create any complications.'

The next day, when I met the prime minister, I pointed out that the briefing we had heard a day earlier implied a course of action that was contrary to that advocated by the foreign office and approved by the DCC two months earlier. He agreed with me and said, 'You can raise this issue in the next meeting of the DCC.' I had hardly realized at that time that the actual departure from the approved policy guidelines was much more serious and fraught with grave dangers. I think at that stage even the planners of the Kargil operation had not anticipated the strong Indian reaction or the dangers of a wider conflict and that in all probability was the reason for which only partial information was conveyed to the prime minister and his team without revealing the actual plan of operation.

The Kargil operation burst into the open in the first week of May 1999. According to the account presented by General Musharraf in his book:

The first confrontation between the two armies took place on 2 May, when Indian troops bumped into our position in the Shyok sector. The second encounter was with freedom fighters in the Battalik sector on 7 May. The Indians suffered heavy casualties. Alarm bells started ringing at the Indian high command when another skirmish took place with the freedom fighters in the Dras sector on 10 May. India over-reacted by bringing its air force into action. Helicopter sorties were flown to ascertain the ingresses made by the freedom fighters. However, the actions of the Indian Air Force were not confined to the freedom fighters' locations; the Indians also started crossing over and bombarding positions of the Pakistan Army. This resulted in the shooting down of one of the Indian helicopters.[5]

The Indian version of these events is presented by Lt.-Gen. V.P. Malik: 'I was informed by my DGMO on 12 May that about 100–150 jihadi militants appeared to have infiltrated into Kargil, mostly in the Batalik sector.' On 15 May, Lt.-Gen. V.P. Malik, then on a visit to Poland, was informed that the number of infiltrators was 250–300. At that stage the Indian assessment was that 70 per cent of the intruders were jihadi militants and 30 per cent Pakistani regulars. By the end of May, the Indian NSC secretariat reported that nearly 70 per cent of the intruders appeared to be Pakistani regulars and only 30 per cent were jihadi militants.[6]

The Kargil Review Committee setup by the government of India records the strategic and tactical intelligence failure of India in the following words:

> The Review Committee had before it overwhelming evidence that the Pakistan armed intrusion in the Kargil sector came as a complete and total surprise to the Indian government, army and intelligence agencies as well as to Jammu and Kashmir state government and its agencies. The committee did not come across any agency or individual who was able to clearly assess before the event, the possibility of a large-scale Pakistani military intrusion across the Kargil heights. What was conceived of was the limited possibility of infiltrations and enhanced artillery exchanges in this sector.

The 17 May Meeting

As the news of clashes between India and Pakistan began to mount in the domestic and the international media, after the initial clash on the Batalik sector on 7 May, General Musharraf and his team could not delay a full disclosure of their plans to the political leadership. A briefing session was therefore called at the ISI station in Rawalpindi, at short notice, on 17 May 1999. This briefing was attended by General Musharraf (COAS), Lt.-Gen. Aziz Khan (CGS), Lt.-Gen. Mahmud Ahmad (commander 10 Corps), Lt.-Gen. Ziauddin (DG ISI), General Iftikhar Ali Khan (secretary defence), General Tauqir Zia (DGMO), and Maj.-Gen. Javed Hasan (commandant FCNA). The prime minister was accompanied by three ministers namely Maj.-Gen. Abdul Majid

Malik (minister for Kashmir affairs), Raja Zafarul Haq (minister for religious affairs), myself, Shamshad Ahmad (foreign secretary), and Tariq Fatemi (additional secretary in the PM secretariat).

Responding to reports of intensified Indian movements in the Shaqma sector, the meeting was informed, the Frontier Corps Northern Areas (FCNA), a paramilitary force, had been directed by HQ 10 Corps, to take 'defensive measures' to forestall the Indian designs. Accordingly, some battalion of FCNA had occupied in March 1999, the watershed on the Indian side of the LOC. The areas occupied were pointed out on the map of the area. This would not only frustrate any Indian design to improve its position on the LOC but also make it easier for Pakistan to interdict the movement of supplies from Srinagar to Siachen because the Kargil–Dras road was now visible from many heights occupied by units of FCNA.

I do not know what went through the mind of my other cabinet colleagues, but I was immediately struck by the enormity of the news, revealed to us in such a matter of fact and low key briefing: 'that the Pakistan army had crossed the LOC and occupied several Indian posts, contrary to the commitments made under the Simla Agreement, which had again been reiterated in the fifth preambular paragraph of the Lahore Declaration signed three months earlier ('Reiterating the determination of both countries to implementing the Simla Agreement in letter and spirit') could become a major diplomatic debacle for Pakistan', was the sum total of my initial reaction.

I was shaken out of this introspection, by the remarks made by the prime minister, 'How have you succeeded in moving so many personnel and supplies without being detected?'

'Sir, it has been a brilliant tactical operation and the credit goes to our men and officers for carrying out their tasks under such difficult conditions,' General Aziz said.

'But India will naturally react strongly and try to re-occupy these posts. Can we hold on to them?'

'Absolutely!' was the reply. 'Even 8 or 10 persons occupying a position on such a commanding height can not be dislodged by an entire company, without suffering an unacceptable level of casualties.'

'Finally, Pakistan has succeeded in capturing some areas along the 'unmarked LOC', in retaliation of the increasing incursions India has undertaken on this sector over the years,' someone said. That defused the underlying tension and the prime minister asked, 'Will this road eventually lead to Srinagar?' 'Inshallah,' many participants said simultaneously.

General Majid Malik was not however impressed by this euphoria. He said he had been a DGMO and had first hand knowledge of that sector. He could not understand the logic of this operation. From a purely military perspective, we should be absolutely clear that the Indian side in this sector is connected with metalled roads. They will mobilize their troops and equipment in a matter of days. We, on the other hand, would have an impossible task of supplying our forces occupying these heights across several mountain ranges. Once they launch a full scale counter offensive to dislodge our troops from these heights, supported by heavy artillery and air force fire, our forces will have a limited chance of holding out. Our air force or artillery would not be able to help them because we are treating it only as a mujahideen operation and not a full-scale war. How long will their ammunition or other supplies last?'

'Looking beyond these ill conceived military dimensions, one thing is clear,' General Majid Malik said, 'The Indians will either have to dislodge us from these positions on the Indian side of the LOC or if they fail, as our military commanders are predicting, then they will have no option but to broaden the theatre of war to other sectors of their choice, in Kashmir or even across the international frontier between the two countries. Are we prepared for an open war between the two countries?' he asked in a very excited voice.

General Musharraf himself responded to this tirade from one of his own senior army colleagues. He said, 'India was mobilizing so many troops for Kashmir that they would be left with only limited offensive capacity for an open war between the two countries across the international boundary. And in Kashmir, we can take them on if they broaden the theatre of war.'

At this point, I made my comments on the situation. I said: 'The basic advice given to every commander is to first define his objectives, then develop a strategy and then the tactics to implement that strategy. In this case, I see that the tactics are brilliant but the strategy does not seem viable. And the objectives of the operation are even less clear. It cannot be just interruption of supplies to Siachen because we have been doing that from our side of the LOC for the past two years. If the objective is to increase pressure for meaningful negotiations on Kashmir, then the timing is unfortunate because the Lahore process was, in any case, on hold for the present, following the defeat of the Vajpayee's government in the Indian parliament on 17 April and the resultant preparations for fresh elections in October 1999.' The meeting ended with joint prayers for the success of the operation.

General Majid Malik and I travelled together from Rawalpindi to Islamabad after the meeting. He agreed with my remarks that the operation may have been brilliant from the tactical point of view but could become a strategic disaster. How long could we conceal the fact that the persons who crossed the LOC were not mujahideen but paramilitary forces, was our major concern.

General Majid Malik asked me, 'Do you think the prime minister knew about this operation already?' I said I am not sure but I think he was not aware of the entire plan. As far as I know, in the earlier briefing on 12–13 March, there was no mention of the involvement of FCNA or of crossing the LOC. I am not aware of any other briefing. But looking at it from a political point of view, I can understand why the prime minister accorded, what amounted to ex-post facto approval, even if he was not informed earlier. Regaining a slice of Indian occupied Kashmir is something no prime minister of Pakistan can object to in public.

Then after a pause, I added: 'But one thing is certain. As Pakistan's foreign minister, I was not aware of this operation till this morning, nor was I consulted about the possible diplomatic fall out of this dangerous operation. This is a very sad reflection on Pakistan's governing structure, the civil–military relationship and the total absence of an effective infrastructure for decision-making on national security issues. In the absence of such infrastructure and in the face of prolonged periods of military rule, such major decisions are still being taken by the army leadership without adequate consultations with the political leadership and the civilian bureaucracy.'

In an interview with Sohail Warriach, in 2006, Nawaz Sharif had said: 'As prime minister I was not taken into confidence about Kargil. Four months after the operation, when some details were revealed they also reaffirmed that this attack would not lead to any complications, no major loss of life is expected and the mujahideen rather than the Pakistan army would be mostly involved in the operation. But when the operation was concluded, the Northern Light Infantry (a regiment of FCNA) had suffered heavy losses with 2,700 casualties, which is higher than that suffered in 1965 and 1971 wars. After these losses occurred, I asked General Musharraf, 'You had said our forces would not suffer losses?' He replied, 'Indian forces had resorted to carpet bombing.' I asked, 'Did you not anticipate such retaliation?' He said, 'Not really.' In fact, contrary to General Musharraf's assurances, by the time the Washington accord was reached on 4 July, the Indians had re-occupied half the posts on their side of the LOC and were advancing further. I thus saved the army from a larger debacle.'

Surprisingly, General Musharraf in his book *In the Line of Fire* and in an earlier TV interview on 12 July 2006, made the unbelievable assertion that Nawaz Sharif was briefed on the Kargil operation on 5 February 1999, when he visited the Kel sector in Neelum valley. I was present in this briefing. It was specifically related to the Indian interdiction in the Neelum valley road and the successful completion of an alternative road through the Kaghan valley.[7] There was no mention of the Kargil sector.

The Kargil War

After occupying posts in the Shaqma sector in March 1999, the 323 Brigade of FCNA occupied some dominating features overlooking Turtok and Gora Lungpa in the third week of April 1999. At the same time the 62 Brigade occupied vacant heights/features covering Indian approaches or routes through Gragrabar and Gragrio Nullahs. In the Gultari sector, features overlooking Batakulain Nullah were occupied. These positions were reinforced in June with extra troops, after the Indians counter-attacked. According to Brian Cloughley, Pakistan had established about 130 pickuets and not posts, which have better physical facilities.

The Pakistan army, in planning this 'tactical operation', had made certain assumptions that in view of the difficulties and expense of moving and inducting additional forces, India would employ a maximum of 4–5 brigades against the FCNA while the two strategic reserve divisions would be committed to redress the vulnerabilities opposite 12 Division and 23 Division areas. This would reduce the possibility of India responding militarily at the strategic level in other areas. These assumptions proved to be totally unrealistic. As General V.P. Malik describes in some detail, India mobilized, as predicted by General (retd) Abdul Majid Malik, massive additional forces and launched them with strong artillery and air force support in a very short time.

A strong attack was launched by India in the third week of May, centring on the Tololing sector and Tiger Hill. Four squadrons of the Indian air force were launched from four different bases. Two IAF fighters were shot down by Pakistan on 27 May, when they intruded into the Pakistan side of the LOC. This raised the morale of the public in Pakistan but also the international concerns about the possibilities of a wider war.

By mid-June, with the Indian deployment of additional troops, artillery, and mirage 2,000 aircraft, the ground situation began to change. The Indian media started highlighting acts of extreme bravery leading to recapture of several important positions in different sectors. Simultaneously, India also launched a diplomatic offensive by sending messages and envoys to all the major countries saying Pakistan had deliberately violated the LOC and disturbed the status quo. While India would do everything to expel the intruders, it was exercising maximum restraint to prevent a wider, possibly nuclear conflict in South Asia. The national security advisor, Brajesh Mishra, was sent to Paris to meet his US counterpart, Sandy Berger to deliver a letter to President Clinton to raise the issue at a G-8 summit on 18–20 June 1999 at Cologne and record India's warning that 'India might attack Pakistan if Pakistan did not pull out troops who had seized Indian outposts in the disputed territory of Kashmir'. The G-8 summit, without naming Pakistan, said:

Any military action to change the status quo (along the LOC) was irresponsible. We therefore call for the immediate end of these actions, restoration of the Line of Control and for the parties to work for an immediate cessation of the fighting, full respect in the future for the Line of Control and the resumption of dialogue between India and Pakistan in the spirit of the Lahore Declaration.

Eight days after the 17 May meeting, another meeting was called in the PM House on 25 May which was attended by the top army leadership. Since General Musharraf had gone on a visit to China, he was represented by the acting COAS, Lt.-Gen. Saeed-uz-Zaman Zafar (GOC 11 Corps, Peshawar). Lt.-Gen. Zafar said, 'Several Indian shells had fallen on the Pakistan side of the Line of Control. We should play up this fact in the media and emphasize that Pakistan had no option but to mobilize troops to retaliate if necessary'. Then a taped conversation between the two DGMOs that very morning was played in the meeting. The Indian DGMO said, 'These infiltrators could not have been there without Pakistan's support because they had artillery and sophisticated weapons, but we will flush them out.' The Pakistan DGMO, Maj.-Gen. Tauqir Zia asked for details about how many and where, 'so that we can investigate'. He also warned his Indian counterpart about the military build up, including large number of aircrafts. 'Any misadventure on Pakistan's side of the LOC will be suitably dealt with.' 'There was no reason for alarm or panic,' the meeting was told.

On 26 May, Lt.-Gen. Aziz Khan gave a detailed report on this high level meeting held on 25 May to General Musharraf through a telephone call to Beijing. This conversation and a subsequent conversation on 29 May were apparently intercepted by the Indian intelligence agency, RAW. The transcripts of both these conversations were released by the Indian foreign minister on 11 June 1999 and were published in every major Indian newspaper on the morning of 12 June 1999, the day I arrived in India. These transcripts made my task in answering hostile questions from 300 angry Indian journalists extremely difficult. These transcripts (reproduced in Appendix III) virtually knocked off the bottom of the entire case Pakistan had been trying to build to justify the Kargil operation, that it was only a mujahideen operation.

The transcript however also contains one very revealing sentence: 'We told him (the prime minister) there is no reason of alarm and panic. Then he said, since I came to know seven days back, when were the corps commanders told? The entire reason of the success of this operation was this total secrecy. Our experience was that our earlier efforts failed because of lack of secrecy. So the top priority is to accord confidentiality to ensure our success. We should respect this and the advantage we have from this would give us a handle.'

This is the clearest proof, if any was needed, that the prime minister was told only a week before this 25 May meeting that is at the 17 May briefing. That is why General Musharraf asked after Lt.-Gen. Aziz finished his emphasis on the importance of secrecy: 'Is Mian Sahib okay?'

Notwithstanding the value of such taped conversations for revealing the truth on Kargil, it is really unbelievable that the two senior most officers of the Pakistan Army would conduct such prolonged conversations on such an important and sensitive subject on an open and insecure international telephone line. Lt.-Gen. V.P. Malik in his book, while admitting the failure of Indian intelligence in detecting the initial movement across the LOC by Pakistani troops, claimed considerable credit for RAW in their success in intercepting these two conversations.[8]

After the briefing on 25 May, we at the foreign office had very detailed strategy sessions on how to deal with the mounting international pressure. The domestic public opinion was in an upbeat mood, following the shooting down of two Indian planes on 27 May. For them the distinction between army personnel and mujahideen was in any case immaterial because of Pakistan's strong political, moral and legal case on the Kashmir issue. In fact, even moderate Pakistanis would have welcomed the prospect of Pakistan's military victory over India to regain Kashmir.

But for Pakistan, the diplomatic battle was becoming highly problematic as the international opinion was rapidly turning against Pakistan. Our initial contention that Kashmir freedom fighters had occupied certain vacant positions on the Indian side of the LOC was exposed within days, when the Indian forces found and displayed evidence of the involvement of Pakistan's paramilitary forces. But throughout the Kargil crisis, we could not own this involvement because under the Simla Agreement, we had undertaken 'to respect the line of control, without prejudice to the recognized position of either side.' The DG ISPR, Maj.-Gen. Rashid Qureshi, in his daily press briefings, did not even admit what General Musharraf has now revealed in his book:

> On 15 May, I ordered FCNA to improve our defensive position in coordination with the freedom fighters to deny access to the watershed by India.' By now the freedom fighters occupied over 500 square miles of Indian occupied territory, and that 'our field commanders were fully engaged in supporting them, in the face of the growing momentum of the Indian operation we wanted to dominate the areas held by the freedom fighters. We established outposts to act as eyes and ears and made raids and ambushes.[9]

In the foreign office, as we received queries from our missions abroad, we had to stick to the official line which no one believed. After pushing the foreign office and the political leadership into such a tight corner and then blaming them 'for displaying total lack of statesmanship and for not making any serious effort to rally the country' is an unbelievable travesty of justice.

The expert assessment of the foreign office was leading to some inescapable conclusions: If India was unable to dislodge the 'intruders' from positions on the Indian side of the LOC, as repeatedly anticipated by the army leadership in Pakistan, they would have no option but to broaden the theatre of war to other parts of Kashmir, or even the international boundary. But if they somehow succeeded through massive mobilization of their ground and air force, it would be a military debacle for Pakistan. Hence the need for exploring options to defuse the situation. ·

On 28 May, after the Indian planes were shot down, Prime Minister Vajpayee telephoned Nawaz Sharif and complained bitterly about the reported escalation, contrary to the spirit of the Lahore Declaration. Nawaz Sharif told him that instead of reacting so strongly with massive mobilization and the use of the air force they should have waited for a diplomatic solution. He then made an offer that the foreign minister could visit New Delhi to explore the possibility of defusing tensions. Vajpayee agreed in principle.

The prime minister briefed me and my colleagues in the foreign office and said that I should hold a meeting with the army leadership to explore the basis on which the situation could be defused. This meeting was held the next day, 29 May in the committee room of the ministry of foreign affairs and was attended by Lt.-Gen. Saeed-uz-Zafar (who was officiating as COAS in the absence of General Musharraf), Lt.-Gen. Aziz Khan (CGS), Lt.-Gen. Mahmud (GOC 10 Corps) and Lt.-Gen. Ziauddin (DG, ISI). At this meeting, General Zafar suggested that during my visit I should insist that the LOC in the Kargil sector is un-demarcated and we have been along our watershed of the LOC for years. I could say that we were ready for dialogue but I should not give any assurance on the military or the ground situation. I should not even accept a ceasefire because then their vehicles could start moving on the Dras–Kargil road. 'We have caught the leopard by the tail and we should not let it go.'

In the follow up review meeting within the foreign office, I said there was no point in my going to New Delhi with the kind of brief indicated in the morning meeting. We should therefore delay the visit for a few days. The foreign secretary, Shamshad Ahmad, while agreeing with the postponement, kept insisting that under no circumstances should we withdraw from positions we have occupied. Some of my colleagues then pointed out the stark prospects of a wider war, but the Foreign Secretary discounted that prospect because of our nuclear capacity.

Two days later on 1 June, the Indian prime minister addressed a press conference and said: 'A warlike situation had evolved. This is a kind of aggression, an attempt to alter the frontier and grab the land.' Simultaneously the Indian forces launched a major offensive in several areas.

On 5 June, there was a cabinet meeting, where a detailed briefing on the Kargil situation was given by the defence secretary and the DGMO. The discussion was remarkably frank and constructive. Some of my colleagues started with the 'how and why' of the situation. Was the government consulted? Who authorized the detailed plan? What are the objectives? Did we look at all the implications? Some even suggested that this operation may have been designed to derail the Lahore process and dissipate the prospects of serious dialogue with India.

Several members of the cabinet shared their assessment of the emerging crisis along the following lines:

- That India would not accept this situation, particularly in the face of the forthcoming general elections. They will even go to war if they cannot retrieve the captured areas because Vajpayee needs a 'victory' to win the election.

- A war with India will not however suit us at this juncture because most western nations are convinced that we have precipitated this crisis. We will not get much sympathy or support from them in case of wider hostilities.

- Our economy is much more vulnerable than India's. We can come under further squeeze if sanctions partially relaxed in January 1999 were re-imposed.

In contrast to these statements, two or three members led by Raja Zafarul Haq took a hawkish line and said, 'We should stand firm, neither panic nor apologize. We are a nuclear power. It will not therefore be easy for India to take the risk of a full-scale war. The morale of the Kashmiri mujahideen is high and we should try to derive maximum advantage from this crisis. Any talk of premature withdrawal could have serious political implications.'

The final conclusions that emerged from the discussion can be summarized as follows:

- If we can keep the crisis at the tactical level, i.e. confined to the Kargil sector or at the most at the operational level, i.e. beyond Kargil but within Jammu and Kashmir, we can derive some advantage at the negotiating table, but under no circumstances should we allow the crisis to escalate to the strategic level, i.e. to the international boundary.

- That the prime minister should telephone Vajpayee and suggest a visit by the foreign minister as early as possible.

On 8 June, Prime Minister Nawaz Sharif proposed to Prime Minister Vajpayee that Pakistan's foreign minister could visit New Delhi on 12 June. Vajpayee accepted but said that the talks must have a definite, specific purpose. At present the subject is one and one alone: the intrusion and how Pakistan proposed to undo it.

I was extremely uneasy about my visit to New Delhi in the absence of any clear-cut strategy to defuse the situation. Just as I was preparing to leave office that afternoon, I received a phone call from Tariq Fatemi to say that the prime minister had asked General Musharraf to call on me at my house that evening. The purpose of the visit, he said, was three fold:

- To make an accurate assessment of the ground situation because the official briefing given to the prime minister a day earlier did not tally with independent media reports;

- To determine if Pakistan had the capacity and the stamina to hold on till winter sets in;

- To discuss different options of defusing the situation in case the ground situation turns against Pakistan in the coming weeks.

General Musharraf arrived at 7 p.m. and was accompanied by Lt.-Gen. Aziz Khan (CGS) and Brigadier Nadeem Ahmad (DMO). In anticipation of the first agenda item, Brigadier Nadeem had brought with him maps of the Kargil sector clearly showing areas occupied by NLI forces and the mujahideen on the Indian side of the LOC. It also showed in a different colour, the areas occupied by India, after the Simla Agreement, i.e. Chorbatla in 1972, Siachen in 1984 and Qamar in 1988.

They insisted that the ground situation was fully in Pakistan's control and despite the Indian onslaught, they were holding out. General Musharraf's major concern was of course my forthcoming visit to New Delhi and the approach I would adopt in defusing the situation. He repeated the points that were emphasized in the high level meeting held in the foreign office on 29 May. 'At this stage we should not agree to a ceasefire, nor make a promise for any change in the ground situation, we should continue to insist that we don't know who these intruders are but meanwhile India should not raise tensions on the LOC.'

I asked if we should explore the possibilities of a reciprocal withdrawal, i.e. we could assist in getting these new areas vacated if they will withdraw from areas they had illegally occupied after the Simla Agreement. The response was not enthusiastic, almost implying that the areas now controlled directly or indirectly by Pakistan, were of greater strategic significance than those occupied by India in 1972, 1984, and 1988.

The hour-long meeting ended without improving the brief I was supposed to carry to New Delhi. I did however ask in very specific terms if we could firmly hold on to the commanding positions we have occupied under all circumstances and the answer was an emphatic 'of course'. In that case, I said to myself, the inflexible brief being given to me has some justification.

The next day (9 June) my colleagues in the foreign office suggested that I should pay a quick visit to China before going to India. The Chinese government readily agreed to receive me on 11 June. On 10 June, I convened a meeting of about ten former foreign ministers and diplomats including Sahabzada Yaqub-Khan who was foreign minister from 1978 to 1988. At the outset, Sahabzada Yaqub-Khan said, 'You deserve our special compliments. Policy makers do occasionally consult retired experts in evolving longer term policies or strategies. It is rare for such experts to be consulted on a topical hot issue of such strategic importance.' Then he went on to give his frank assessment: 'With my military background, I can say that this adventurous operation will not bring any credit to the Pakistan army or to Pakistan as a responsible state. You must therefore find a speedy solution for an honourable exit. The longer you stay across the LOC, the greater will be the national loss and a growing diplomatic setback.' Other participants also agreed that it would be extremely difficult for Pakistan to hold on to the positions it had occupied. And if it does, India would have to retaliate elsewhere. The meeting, in effect, endorsed the position which the foreign office had evolved for a diplomatic solution: that we should offer to persuade the mujahideen to withdraw if India would agree to a reasonable deadline for resolving the Kashmir dispute.

I left for Beijing on the evening of 10 June and arrived there early on the 11th morning. After a briefing session at the embassy, I arrived for my meeting with the Chinese Foreign Minister Tang Jiaxuan at 11 a.m. The meeting was very cordial and was followed by lunch. During the course of discussions, after I had given a brief introduction to the crisis in Kargil, my Chinese colleague repeated in very polite language, the message which the Chinese president, Jiang Zemin, had conveyed to Pakistan in the joint session of parliament in August 1996.

He then concluded by saying that China had always supported Pakistan's principled stand on the issue of Kashmir, but at this time, it is of utmost importance to defuse tensions and find a way out of the prevailing situation.

After lunch I called on Li Peng, chairman of National Peoples Congress and caught the 5 p.m. flight for my return journey to Islamabad. At the Islamabad airport I addressed a press conference and circulated the press note issued after my meetings in Beijing:

> China assured Pakistan of its deep and abiding interest and support for the sovereignty, territorial integrity, independence and security of Pakistan. Chinese leaders also emphasized that the preservation of peace and security in the region is of great importance.
>
> Both Pakistan and China agreed on the need to de-escalate the dangerous situation that has developed at the Line of Control in Jammu and Kashmir. They also agreed on the need for a peaceful, negotiated and just settlement of the Jammu and Kashmir dispute.[10]

Visit to India

My day long visit to New Delhi on 12 June was very tense. I arrived by special plane, with the additional secretary foreign affairs, Tariq Altaf and five journalists. Jaswant Singh, the Indian foreign minister had come to the airport to receive me, but apart from shaking hands and the confirmation that he would expect me at the venue of the meeting by 11 a.m., there was no other exchange. The Indian authorities had blocked all traffic on the entire route from the airport to the Pakistan High Commission. My convoy was accompanied by dozens of vehicles including army units, ambulances and fire brigades. I felt as if I was travelling through a war zone.

On arrival at the high commission, the high commissioner, Jehangir Ashraf Qazi showed me a stack of newspapers, each carrying the taped conversations between General Musharraf, then on a visit to China and Lt.-Gen. Aziz Khan on 26 and 29 May 1999 (Appendix III). I read through the transcript as rapidly as I could, and my heart literally began to sink. Our entire plank that certain Kargil heights were occupied by the Kashmiri mujahideen during winter months and that the LOC in that sector was not fully demarcated, so we needed to take steps to demarcate them and that in the meanwhile India should not raise the tempo of hostilities, stood fully exposed. One Indian newspaper had a separate box story about my visit, headlined 'Pakistani Foreign Minister arrives in New Delhi with his hands tied behind his back.' It referred to the conversation between General Musharraf and Lt.-Gen. Aziz Khan and their joint recommendation that 'the Foreign Minister should make no commitment in the first meeting on the military situation.'

During the hour long meeting with Jaswant Singh, I presented a three-point formula: (a) immediate ceasefire, (b) a joint working group to review the LOC and its demarcation on the ground, and (c) a return visit by the Indian minister of external affairs, if possible, within a week. Jaswant Singh however kept insisting on one point that Pakistan must vacate the areas it had occupied across the LOC in violation of the Simla Agreement. He was a bit surprised when I said India had also occupied certain areas across the LOC after the Simla Agreement. The press reports on the following day succinctly summarized, on the basis of our two separate press conferences, the gist of the discussions:

Pakistan Foreign Minister Sartaj Aziz arrived here this morning in pursuance of Prime Minister Nawaz Sharif's proposal to the Indian Prime Minister Atal Bihari Vajpayee to defuse the tense situation developed along the LOC. After holding discussions with his Indian counterpart Jaswant Singh at the Hyderabad House here, Sartaj Aziz called on Prime Minister Vajpayee in the afternoon. The two ministers, who also had a working lunch, were assisted by their respective high commissioners and senior officials. Both the foreign ministers later addressed separate press conferences.

At the crowded media conference at the Pakistan High Commission, Sartaj Aziz said his 70 minutes talk with India would have to continue, to cool escalating military hostilities along the LOC in Jammu and Kashmir. Stressing the need for further talks over the issue, Sartaj told reporters that he had no illusion of resolving the current difficulties in a day's visit to New Delhi.

His Indian counterpart, however, told media that both countries could not afford the luxury of talks without any conclusions. 'We don't want talks for the sake of talks. We will move only if other side shows some flexibility and responsibility in its stand and understanding of the situation,' said the eloquent Indian Foreign Minister. The ball is in Pakistan's court, they should reply as to when they are going to pull out their troops and Mujahideen from the Kargil sector, added Singh. He also called upon Islamabad to uphold the 'sanctity of the LOC'.

Jaswant Singh reiterated the sanctity and inviolability of the LOC, which was vital for the maintenance of peace and security. He pointed out that the LOC as well-defined and well-delineated on authentic maps by the military authorities of the two countries. Its location had been known for 27 years.

Sartaj Aziz categorically denied that Pakistan has ever violated the LOC. It is India that has violated it thrice in 1972 and in 1984 and 1988, while moving its troops to Chorbatla, Siachen heights and Qamar. 'We have never questioned the validity and sanctity of the LOC,' said Sartaj. 'Last year in October too, India tried to cross over the LOC and occupy Pakistani territory.' 'Kargil situation is just tip of an ice-berg,' said Pakistan Foreign Minister, adding it is part of a larger problem of Jammu and Kashmir. 'It will go on happening. If it is now Kargil, it will be Srinagar tomorrow. We need to address the issue in totality and the cause of escalation'.[11]

Another report dramatized the tense atmosphere surrounding the talks: Official sources said the talks, which took place amid tight security, were held in a 'serious and business-like atmosphere'. The atmosphere of the dialogue was unusually cool and sombre. The two ministers did not even exchange niceties like handshakes or customary hugs. A bitter atmosphere hung over the talks, as the tension prevailed all over the Indian capital. As many as four demonstrations were held near the Hyderabad House with the activists of the National Akali Dal,

Youth Congress, Shiv Sena and Hindu Mahasabha staging demonstrations against Pakistan.

The contrast was remarkable between the two foreign ministers' briefings, which were twice postponed in apparent manoeuvring to see who would get the last word. Sartaj Aziz was affable and polite to a hostile press pack, consisting mostly of the local press but with a leavening of foreign correspondents. His statement was couched in the standard language of diplomacy. Jaswant Singh, on the other hand, was abrasive, curt and spoke of demands and what was acceptable and unacceptable. While Sartaj held out hopes of future talks, Singh bluntly said there was no dialogue going on: 'Sartaj Aziz's visit took place at the request of the Government of Pakistan, and we have conveyed our views to him to convey to his government.'

The difference of perception was clear even before Sartaj Aziz landed in New Delhi by special aircraft on Saturday morning for an 11-hour stay in the Indian capital. India insisted that it would talk on only two points: Its demand that Pakistan withdraw the Kargil infiltrators, and that it punish the perpetrators of the mutilation of its six soldiers. Pakistan wished to engage in a dialogue defining what was the nature of the supposed violations and what Pakistan was supposed to have done.

In that respect, Sartaj Aziz did not expect to come away with anything more than, as he put it, the hope that there would not be any further escalation, and that a process of engagement would start. That he claims to have got. However, Jaswant's reaction to this conclusion was a dry, 'I am heartened by the comment of His Excellency the Foreign Minister.'

India was having none of it. In his briefing, Sartaj Aziz described a process of considering measures to de-escalate, saying that India received certain proposals from Pakistan, but refusing to discuss them until the Indians had a chance to give them some consideration, and to make a response.

The response was there within minutes, before Sartaj Aziz's plane left Delhi, and given not to him directly, but to the international press. Jaswant Singh first disclosed them as being a call to cease cross-LOC artillery fire, and to stop aerial bombardments. He then proceeded to dismiss them as calls for partial de-escalation, as opposed to India's call for total de-escalation by Pakistan withdrawing the so-called infiltrators.

There was also an element of grim comedy in the two ministers' schedules. Sartaj Aziz was originally supposed to brief the press as soon as he had made his call on Prime Minister Vajpayee. Jaswant Singh then scheduled his own briefing to merge with the daily defence briefing on the Kargil situation.

However, Sartaj Aziz moved his briefing up to 6 p.m. Jaswant Singh then moved his to 6 p.m. too. Sartaj moved his to 7 p.m. Pressmen who turned up at Shastri Bhavan for Jaswant's briefing were told at about 6:15 p.m. that the briefing was postponed to 7:30 p.m. At this point, Sartaj stuck to his guns, and went ahead and held his Press conference. Jaswant did not arrive at his until 8 p.m., at which point he had probably been given a rushed update on Sartaj's statement. Apart from debating points, the substance of the matter is that Pakistan has taken a diplomatic step in the right direction, and it is now up to India to decide how it wishes to resolve the ground situation in Kargil. Pakistan wanted de-escalation, in the sense of an assurance that the situation would not be allowed to move beyond Kargil. India on the other hand wanted Kargil resolved first.

Indian armed forces have not been able to contain the Kargil situation, and has to face the prospect of heavy losses if it is to reoccupy the positions held by the freedom fighters. The BJP can neither take the disgrace of being unable to handle a few hundred Pakistani soldiers, nor of having thousands of soldiers' coffins going to towns and villages all over India, just before a general election.

However, Sartaj Aziz has conveyed to India that Pakistan is neither going to bail out the Indian army, nor is it going to act as the BJP's campaign manager. That is the apparent bottom line on this visit.[12]

I met Prime Minister Vajpayee soon after my lunch with Jaswant Singh. He was extremely emotional. He said almost with a choked voice in chaste Urdu: 'I had travelled to Lahore with such sincerity and high hopes for durable peace between India and Pakistan. The real casualty of this crisis is the trust between the two countries and without trust, relations can't improve.'

When I arrived back in Islamabad by 10 p.m., two messages were waiting for me at the airport: That the COAS, General Musharraf, along with his colleagues was waiting for me at the joint services headquarters and second, the prime minister had called a meeting at Lahore the next morning at 9:30 a.m. for which a special plane would take me to Lahore at 8 a.m.

During the short journey from the airport to the joint services headquarters, I wondered if I should ask General Musharraf about his indiscreet telephonic conversations with Lt.-Gen. Aziz Khan on 26 and 29 May. I decided that it would be inadvisable to embarrass him by raising the subject in front of all his colleagues, but to show him the transcript as published in the Indian press, at a subsequent occasion.

The meeting at joint services headquarters was also attended by the chief of air staff and deputy chief of naval staff (the naval chief was travelling back from London that very evening) along with the respective heads of their military operations. After I had given a brief summary of my discussions in New Delhi, the heads of military operations of the three services gave me a briefing on the large-scale movement of Indian forces into Kashmir and along the international frontier and then recounted the preparations they had undertaken to meet any possible threats from India in Kashmir or elsewhere. General Musharraf had repeatedly emphasized one point: 'Now that the Indians have moved several divisions to the Kargil sector, there is virtual parity in the size of confronting troops across the international boundary.'

As I travelled to Islamabad past midnight after this briefing, I could almost hear the inaudible drums of war in the distance.

The meeting in Lahore next morning was quite eventful. I asked Tariq Altaf (additional secretary) to present a detailed account of the discussions I had held in New Delhi. After the presentation, I added only a few sentences: 'India is not prepared to accept our version of the Kargil crisis. They have adequate proof that personnel of the Pakistan army had crossed the LOC and occupied many positions several kilometres inside the Indian side of the LOC. They want us to vacate this 'aggression' or be prepared for a wider conflict.'

At this General Musharraf asked the heads of military operation of the army, air force and navy to describe the preparations they had undertaken to counter the eventuality of a wider conflict and repeated his assessment of 'strategic parity' across the international frontier. As the presentations concluded, the naval chief, Admiral Fasihuddin Bokhari, who had been in England for the preceding two weeks due to the illness of his wife, stunned everyone when he asked: 'Since I have been away, may I ask what are the objectives of this large scale mobilization? We want to go to war over a few desolate heights that we may have to vacate anyway during the forthcoming winter?'

Before anyone could attempt to answer this question, the prime minister cut short the discussion by saying, 'We will discuss this separately and then turned towards me and said: 'So what else did Vajpayee say?'

After the meeting, Nawaz Sharif asked me to travel with him in his car to the airport, where I was to catch a PIA flight to Islamabad at 2 p.m. 'Musharraf has landed us in a terrible mess, but we have to find a way to get out of this impossible situation.' He said in Urdu and then suggested that I should immediately contact Niaz Naik and ask him to invite R.K. Mishra to visit Islamabad as soon as possible. As already mentioned they were both involved in back channel diplomacy to explore an acceptable solution of the Kashmir problem.

R.K. Mishra arrived two days later, on 15 June. Nawaz Sharif met him and told him, we can find a way out of the crisis if India would agree to a time schedule for a solution of the Kashmir issue. Since at that time, the ground situation was still difficult for India and reports of mounting Indian casualties were adversely affecting BJP's election campaign, Mishra showed interest in the proposal and asked for a 'non-paper' spelling out the precise terms of this 'way out'. Tariq Fatemi (additional secretary in the PM secretariat) and Niaz Naik put together three paragraphs saying that both sides agreed on the importance of reducing tensions and restoring peace in Jammu and Kashmir, and undertook to intensify discussion under the Lahore Declaration in order to resolve the Kashmir issue possibly by October 2000. On its part Pakistan undertook to persuade the mujahideen to withdraw from any positions occupied on the Indian side of the LOC.

Mishra came back three days later, with some minor amendments. It was agreed that after his forthcoming visit to China from 27 to 29 June, Nawaz Sharif would stop over in New Delhi and sign the agreed document with Prime Minister Vajpayee. But from the second half of June, the ground situation and the diplomatic see saw had started turning decisively in favour of India.

On 13 June, the Indian forces launched a massive attack on Tololing peak in the Dras sector and captured the peak on 17 June, after five days of fierce fighting. It then went on to capture Point 5140 on 20 June. In the Batalik sector, point 5203 was captured on 21 June, three Pimples in the Dras sector was captured on 29 June, the Jubar Complex in Batalik on 2 July, Tiger Hill on 4 July and Point 4875 in Mashkoh sector on 7 July. Prime Minister Vajpayee himself flew to Kargil on

14 June to celebrate the imminent capture of Tololing peak and motivate the troops to intensify their attacks.

On the diplomatic front, External Affairs Minister Jaswant Singh visited China from 13 to 15 June to seek their support. On 15 June, the US President Bill Clinton telephoned Prime Minster Nawaz Sharif and urged him to pull back from Kargil. On 17 June, Brajesh Mishra, national security advisor of Prime Minister Vajpayee, visited Geneva to meet his US counterpart and presented a letter from Prime Minister Vajpayee to President Clinton in which he had threatened that 'India might have to attack Pakistan if Pakistan did not pull troops who had seized Indian outposts in the disputed territory of Kashmir.' As a result of this intervention G-8 passed a resolution calling for 'the restoration of the line of control.' Following this resolution Prime Minister Vajpayee made a statement saying, 'India had the world community's understanding for its military offensive but it would not accept mediation to end its attack on "Pakistan backed Mujahideen".'

Encouraged by these developments on the ground and in the diplomatic arena, Vajpayee and his colleagues started having second thoughts about the formula worked out by R.K. Mishra and Niaz Naik. Niaz Naik discovered this when he arrived in New Delhi on 28 June, in preparation for Nawaz Sharif's arrival on 30 June to sign the agreed document. When he met Vajpayee he was told that 'dialogue with Pakistan will be possible only after intrusion has been vacated.' Nawaz Sharif's projected visit to New Delhi which was never announced in the first place was quietly cancelled.

This change in the ground situation in favour of India was however an important factor in keeping the war confined to the Kargil sector. According to General V.P. Malik the Indian chief of army staff during the Kargil war:

> The middle of June was the most anxious period of the war and possibly the closest when we came to enlarging the conflict area. Bitter fighting was going on in all sectors but we had yet to win any battle. On 16 June, Brajesh Mishra informed the US national security advisor, Sandy Berger, that India would not be able to continue with its policy of 'restraint' for long and that our military forces could not be kept on leash any longer. He added that the Government of India might have to let them cross the border any day.

According to Brajesh Mishra, the US Administration took this message quite seriously.

Our military build-up along the western border was going on smoothly. Along with the concerned Army commanders, I visited every Corps Headquarters to discuss and 'lock in' their operational plans. Gradually, military operations staff and operational logistics staff in the Army Headquarters redeployed the strike and reserve formations and issued instructions for stocking forward logistics bases in accordance with approved operational plans. Also, 108 Infantry Brigade from the Andaman and Nicobar Islands was positioned on the west coast for 'training in amphibious operations'. The juggernaut was moving steadily.

The escalation was avoided when our forces recaptured Tololing and Point 5140 in the Dras sector. Thereafter, we began achieving steady success in our operations.[13]

The Blair House Summit

Nawaz Sharif returned from China on 30 June, amid an avalanche of bad news regarding the ground situation. Reports from GHQ did not tally with the media reports from India, fully backed by TV coverage that India had recaptured several important peaks and positions. His efforts to reach a bilateral agreement with India to redress the situation along the LOC in return for a deadline for resolving the Kashmir dispute had fizzled out because of the unexpected reversals faced by Pakistan on several fronts. As he said subsequently in an interview, he had to 'find some honourable exit strategy to save the honour of the armed forces of Pakistan.'

On 25 June, just before Nawaz Sharif's visit to China, General Anthony Zinni, commander of the US central command, had visited Islamabad. He gave a stern message from the White House. 'If you do not pull back you are going to bring war and nuclear annihilation down on your country.' Giving an account of his visit, General Zinni writes in his memoirs:

Nobody actually quarrelled with this rationale. The problem with the Pakistani leadership was the apparent national loss of face. Backing down and pulling back to the Line of Control looked like political suicide. We needed to come up with a face-saving way of (sic) this mess. What we (the USA) were able to offer was, a meeting with President Clinton, which would end the isolation that had long been the state of affairs between our two countries, but would announce the meeting only after a withdrawal of forces. That got Musharraf's attention and he encouraged Prime Minister Sharif to hear me out.[14]

Virtually picking up the threads from the offer made by General Zinni and General Musharraf's pleas for an early meeting with President Clinton, Prime Minister Nawaz Sharif telephoned President Clinton on 2 July 1999, and asked for an early meeting. Seeing the prospect for resolving the situation, President Clinton readily agreed to receive him on 4 July, which was not only a Sunday but also a closed holiday as it was the US Independence Day.

I had returned to Islamabad from Upper Volta, via Paris on the morning of 3 July, after attending a meeting of OIC foreign ministers. I had hardly finished my briefing sessions with my colleagues to get updated on developments during my absence, when I got a phone call from the prime minister that I was to accompany him to Washington later that evening for a meeting with President Clinton. I was also informed that there would be a meeting at the airport two hours prior to our departure, with the service chiefs.

General Musharraf, who was spending that weekend at the Bhurban Golf Club, had to cut short his holiday to join this meeting. He was much quieter than he was in earlier meetings and did not contest or contradict the negative reports presented at this meeting about the ground situation, including the news of the imminent ejection of Pakistani personnel from the most important theatre of the Kargil war—the Tiger Hill. He generally agreed with the basic brief prepared for the visit, that we should agree to a restoration of the line of control, if President Clinton would take personal interest in resolving the Kashmir issue.

We arrived in Washington D.C. at about 11 a.m. by the PIA commercial flight which was scheduled from Islamabad to New York, but made a special stopover in Washington for our delegation.

The meeting with President Clinton took place an hour later at Blair House. He was accompanied by Sandy Berger (national security advisor); Strobe Talbott (deputy secretary of state); Bruce Riedel (director for Near East and South Asia in the NSC); and Rick Inderfurth (assistant secretary for South Asia). Nawaz Sharif was assisted by me and Foreign Secretary Shamshad Ahmad.

President Clinton started the conversation by pulling out an editorial cartoon published in that day's *Chicago Tribune*. It showed two soldiers each on two large nuclear bombs, throwing mortar shells at each other. 'Our foreign policy and our conduct in the post-war era had been circumscribed by one overwhelming realization, that we are a nuclear power. Apart from the Cuban missile crisis of 1962, we have fully discharged this responsibility of being a nuclear power throughout the past five decades. But you, the two South Asian neighbours, have come to blows within a year of becoming de-facto nuclear powers.' Bill Clinton said. Somewhat baffled by such a strong opening statement, Nawaz Sharif had no option but to stick to his brief. He said he did not expect India to overreact so strongly to incidents along the LOC, which have been of common and frequent occurrence. But Pakistan had been urging restraint and doing its best to defuse the situation. 'Ever since I assumed power two years ago with a heavy mandate, I have been trying to resolve differences between India and Pakistan over Kashmir. Unless and until this issue is resolved, crises like Kargil will continue to occur. President Clinton, you should show leadership and persuade India to be more flexible.'

Clinton referred to the Lahore visit of Vajpayee as an important breakthrough and said: 'If you want me to intervene with the Indians, you have to withdraw across the line of control. But India would never agree to negotiate on Kashmir because of the pressures generated by the Kargil crisis. Once Pakistan's forces have returned to their side of the line, then after some time, USA might be able to help the Lahore process move further.'

At this point, Nawaz Sharif suggested that he would like to have a one-to-one meeting with President Clinton. I and Shamshad moved out along with Sandy Berger and Strobe Talbott, but Bruce Riedel stayed back.[15]

Nawaz Sharif came out from the meeting with a draft statement, which was to be issued as the outcome of the meeting.

The draft statement was discussed while we all ate a hurried sandwich lunch. Several amendments were made in the draft to sharpen the language on Kashmir, including a commitment by President Clinton to visit South Asia before the end of the year for this purpose.

The revised draft communiqué emerging from this review was readily accepted and issued to the press within an hour. The text is reproduced below:

- President Clinton and Prime Minister Nawaz Sharif share the view that the current fighting in the Kargil region of Kashmir is dangerous and contains the seeds of a wider conflict.

- They also agree that it was vital for peace in South Asia that the Line of Control in Kashmir be respected by both parties, in accordance with their 1972 Simla Agreement.

- It was agreed between the President and the Prime Minister that concrete steps would be taken for the restoration of the Line of Control in accordance with the Simla Agreement.

- The President urged immediate cessation of the hostilities once these steps are taken. The Prime Minister and the President agreed that the bilateral dialogue begun in Lahore in February 1999 provides the best forum for resolving all issues dividing India and Pakistan, including Kashmir.

- The President said he would take personal interest in encouraging expeditious resumption and intensification of those bilateral efforts once the sanctity of the Line of Control has been fully restored.

- The President reaffirmed his intent to pay an early visit to South Asia.

After the draft communiqué was finalized, and Clinton was about to say good bye and leave, Sandy Berger said in a loud voice:

'Mr President, I hope you have advised our Pakistani guests that once the communiqué is issued, there would be no supplementary or explanatory statements, because that could lead to speculations or misunderstanding.' President Clinton looked towards us enquiringly. Before Nawaz Sharif could answer, I said, 'Yes, of course, on the understanding that this applied to both sides.' Looking towards his delegation Clinton said, 'Yes, of course.'

Despite this commitment at the highest level, I was surprised to see in next morning's *Washington Post* a statement by Rick Inderfurth, explaining the implications of different sentences in the press communiqué. I knew that at 8:30 that morning, Nawaz Sharif would be taking his wife and children to the White House to meet President Clinton and his wife. I telephoned him about the press statement of Rick Inderfurth and suggested that he should protest to the president. He did and the president was quite apologetic.

Soon after the meeting in Blair House, we were literally invaded by the media to find out what had happened. After a quick check in at the hotel, because there was no time to do so before the meeting, the delegation travelled to the Pakistan embassy for a review session. From there we had to go with the prime minister for a dinner hosted by his friend, Saeed Sheikh. By midnight, as I went to bed, I recalled that after four nights in a plane seat, I would finally get a full night's sleep in a bed, but that was not to be because at 5:30 a.m. Mushahid Hussain, our information minister telephoned from Islamabad, saying he needed my recorded interview with the Radio and TV before the evening bulletins. I knew at that unearthly hour that the next two nights were also destined to be spent in flights from New York to London and then from London to Islamabad.

We flew from Washington to New York in the afternoon for a meeting with the UN secretary general before taking a flight to London. In New York I received a call from Tim Sebastian of the BBC for a 'Hard Talk' interview. The interview took place at my hotel soon after I had checked in. During this interview, referring to the joint statement of President Clinton and Nawaz Sharif, Tim Sebastian bluntly asked me: 'How will you now go to Pakistan? The army will not be happy with Nawaz Sharif's agreement to pull back the troops from the Kargil heights. They might just takeover.'

In December that year, Tim Sebastian received the 'TV Interviewer Award of the Year' for accurately predicting the military takeover in Pakistan, three months in advance!

That afternoon we went to 10 Downing Street for a meeting with Prime Minister Tony Blair. He received us in the open terrace overlooking the back lawn of the house over a cup of typical British afternoon tea. After a brief discussion on the facts and the controversy surrounding Kargil, Prime Minister Blair expressed considerable satisfaction at the outcome of the meetings in Washington and offered to assist in any way he could, in the follow up discussions with India.

We arrived in Islamabad amid a very tense atmosphere marked by a mixture of relief, anxiety and uncertainty. A series of meetings to order a ceasefire and disengagement of troops took place over the next three days, but what was happening outside the formal meetings was more worrisome. The whole nation wanted to know the truth. Why did we undertake this operation if we could not sustain it?

In Chapter 11 of his book *In the Line of Fire* General Pervez Musharraf has presented his version of the Kargil conflict, 'to lay bare what has been shrouded in mystery'. 'The time has come for me,' he says 'to deal with some of the myths and faulty perceptions and present the truth, as I know it.' He then proceeds to list what he calls the five myths:

a. That the operation was launched without the army's taking the political leadership into confidence.

b. That the military situation on the ground was precarious and the prime minister dashed to Washington to get the army out of it.

c. That the military hierarchy was not informed and that even the senior army leaders were unaware of our manoeuvres.

d. That we came to the brink of a nuclear war.

e. That Pakistan army suffered a large number of casualties.

President Musharraf, after presenting his afterthoughts on the whole crisis and on the outcome of the Washington visit of the Prime Minister, made several statements which are self-contradictory. He says:

> The briefing given by me personally to the Defence Committee of the Cabinet on 2 July 1999, actually laid out the entire military picture. I covered all possible hypotheses of enemy actions in the air, at sea, and on land. The conclusions that I derived were:
>
> • That the Indians were in no position to launch an all-out offensive on land, at sea, or in the air.
>
> • That Pakistan was in a strategically advantageous position in case of an all-out war, in view of the massive Indian troop inductions inside Kashmir, resulting in a strategic imbalance in India's system of forces.
>
> • That the Indian forces, despite their massive strength, would never be able to dislodge the freedom fighters and the NLI from the ingresses and positions held by them.

At that briefing the prime minister asked me several times whether we should accept a cease-fire and withdraw. My answer every time was restricted to the optimistic military situation; I left the political decisions to him. I would like to state emphatically that whatever movement has taken place so far in the direction of finding a solution to Kashmir is due considerably to the Kargil conflict.[16]

This hypothesis of General Musharraf has many holes:

• There is no evidence of an 'optimistic military situation', while there is concrete and overwhelming evidence to the contrary not just from India but independent sources that India has recaptured many important positions despite heavy losses in men and material. In other localities, it was becoming increasingly difficult for the Pakistan army to keep the lines of supply open and as a result most of their occupants were running short of ammunition and food.

From mid-June, the military situation was becoming more and more difficult for Pakistan.

- The second plank of General Musharraf's thesis, that Indians were in no position to launch an all out offensive on land, sea and air, and that Pakistan was in a strategically advantageous position in case of an all out war is even less tenable. Almost all independent observers ranging from President Clinton to military experts like Brian Cloughley have repeatedly expressed apprehensions about the danger of an all out war between two nuclear armed neighbours. This quote from General Talat Masood in *Dawn* of 17 July 1999 sums up the alarming situation created by the Kargil adventure. 'The Kargil crisis has once again exposed the bankruptcy of Pakistan's national policy. Events in and around Kargil brought India and Pakistan dangerously close to an all-out war, dealt a shattering blow to the peace process, have done immense damage to the already faltering economy, isolated Pakistan internationally and proved highly divisive internally...', (Quoted in Cloughley, p. 322)

- General Musharraf's statement that he left the political decision to the prime minister and that his agreement in Washington to an unconditional withdrawal amounted 'to political mishandling' is a total distortion of facts and of history. A military commander, without consulting the political leadership or the foreign office, initiates a major military operation that violates the Simla Agreement and effectively derails the Lahore peace process, achieved after such sustained efforts and then expects the political leadership to handle all the adverse consequences. An army commander can and should handle smaller operations at the local level but cannot and should not initiate operations that have such widespread diplomatic and international implications without the explicit approval of the political leadership. Limited ex-post facto briefings (like those on 17 May and then 2 July, for example) are not an adequate substitute for proper consultation with the political leadership, before a major initiative is actually launched.

- From the point of view of military strategy and tactics, the operation was ill conceived and did not achieve any purpose whatsoever. Even if General Musharraf's contention that the army could hold on to the positions is accepted, then the danger of all out war would have correspondingly increased at a time, when no country would have supported Pakistan even for such basic needs as fuel and ammunition because the blame for starting the crisis was placed squarely on Pakistan's shoulder.

- The most hilarious and controversial line in the whole book, as future historians would record after Musharraf's departure from the scene would probably be: 'I would like to state emphatically that whatever movement has taken place so far in the direction of finding a solution in Kashmir is due considerably to the Kargil conflict.'

The real issues raised by the Kargil crisis are however much deeper and more complex. The nation has a right to know if those responsible for the operation had clearly defined its ultimate objectives, and whether or not they had adequately anticipated the obstacles on the ground and the full diplomatic implications of the operation. A subsidiary set of questions then follow about the timing and adequacy of consultation with the political leadership and other important components of the government, especially the ministry of foreign affairs. Briefing the prime minister on some aspects of the operation after the operation was already under way, could hardly be a substitute for proper and timely decision making in consultation with all the stakeholders and formal approval by the political leadership at the highest level for such a major initiative with long term strategic implications.

In 2005, I was sitting in a seminar next to a retired army general who had served during the tenure of General Ziaul Haq. One of the speakers said, the Kargil operation had been launched deliberately to sabotage the Lahore process. I asked for the general's comments on a piece of paper. Without any hesitation he scribbled: 'Kargil was a very badly planned and poorly executed operation for which General Musharraf should have been court martialed.'

It is really sad to recall that almost all the major milestones of Pakistan's history and especially military history, are not only shrouded in mystery but have been presented in very distorted versions: No one knows the real story of the assassination of Prime Minister Liaquat Ali Khan in Rawalpindi on 16 October 1951. The lessons from the 1965 war, especially the responsibility for the September's ill-planned attack near Jammu have never been fully recalled.

The story of the 1971 war, in which we lost half the country, was documented by the Hamood-ur-Rahman Commission, but its report was suppressed for thirty years. In 2003, it somehow surfaced in the Indian press. By then it was too late to digest the main findings and take the required action against those involved.

President Ziaul Haq's air crash of 17 August 1988 remains a well-guarded secret amid all kinds of speculative stories, and finally the Kargil fiasco has produced more questions than answers. The Indian government setup a Kargil Review Committee in the year 2000 which submitted a full report within a few weeks admitting weaknesses drawing lessons and making concrete recommendations on all aspects of national security. We can never learn from our mistakes and safeguard our national security if we continue to conceal facts to protect those in power.

In 1965, the Operation Gibraltar launched on 5 August had fizzled out by 20 August. If Pakistan had not attacked the Chamb sector in Kashmir on 1 September 'to interrupt the Indian line of communication to Kashmir', the 1965 war could have been avoided and Operation Gibraltar would have only deserved a footnote in history.

Pakistan was confronted with a similar situation in 1999. The leader who saved Pakistan from a disastrous all-out war with India, was deposed and then exiled from the country and the army general who overstepped his authority and caused irreparable damage to the Kashmir cause, became the undisputed ruler of the country for nine long years. It is difficult to imagine a more ironic and unjust episode in history.

NOTES

1. Alastair Lamb in his book *The Legacy of Kashmir*, 1992, has concluded that this 'fake' instrument of accession was signed after the Indian invasion of Kashmir.
2. Brian Cloughley, *A History of the Pakistan Army*, Karachi: Oxford University Press, 1999, p. 226.
3. Dr Shirin M. Mazari, *The Kargil Conflict, 1999*, Ferozsons, Islamabad, p. 25.
4. Op. cit., p. 15.
5. Pervez Musharraf, *In the Line of Fire: A Memoir*, Simon & Schuster, 2006, p. 90.
6. General V.P. Malik, *Kargil: From Surprise to Victory*, Harper Collins, India, 2006, pp. 106 and 111.
7. This is also confirmed in Shirin Mazari's account op. cit., p. 57.
8. General V.P. Malik, op. cit., p. 99.
9. Op. cit., p. 91.
10. *The Nation*, Lahore, 12 June 1999.
11. *The Nation*, Lahore, 13 June 1999.
12. *The Nation*, Lahore, 13 June 1999.
13. Ibid., pp. 146–148.
14. Tom Clancy and Anthony Zinni, *Battle Ready*, New York: Berkley Books, 2004, p. 346.
15. Strobe Talbott in his book *Engaging India* (Brookings, 2004) admits that he and Rick Inderfurth advised President Clinton to insist on a one-to-one meeting to keep Sartaj Aziz and Shamshad Ahmad out because 'they would prevent Sharif from making concessions or would pull him back from the ones he had already made'. (p. 113). He also highlights the fact that President Clinton's team had 'to conduct its dealings with the Pakistanis in a way that protected and even advanced Indian interests.' In my view, the US reasons for seeking a one-to-one meeting were different. Clinton wanted to ask Sharif whether or not he knew his military was taking steps towards deployment of nuclear weaponry and also he wanted to repeat the US plea for help to bring Osama Bin Laden to justice. Eventually, as Strobe Talbott records, it was Nawaz Sharif who asked for the one-to-one meeting and Bill Clinton, having agreed, asked Bruce Riedel to stay on for a two-to-one meeting.
16. Pervez Musharraf, op. cit., pp. 96–98.

CHAPTER 13

The Fourth Military Takeover, October 1999

The 'counter coup', launched by General Pervez Musharraf on 12 October 1999 was the fourth army takeover in Pakistan's chequered history, after Ayub Khan's martial law of October 1958, Yahya Khan's transitional martial law from March 1969 to December 1971, and Ziaul Haq's coup in July 1977. The real story of this fourth military takeover is still hidden beneath layers of fabricated theories and a deliberate campaign of disinformation.

As I recall the angry words uttered by Nawaz Sharif on 13 June during the car journey in Lahore, after the de-briefing session on Kargil following my visit to New Delhi ('Musharraf has landed us in a terrible mess'), I have no doubt in my mind that he had made up his mind at that fateful juncture to remove Musharraf as chief of army staff at the earliest opportunity. Musharraf had exceeded his lawful authority, by launching an ill-planned operation in Kargil, with such serious diplomatic and political consequences, without any consultation with the foreign ministry or the approval of the prime minister.

If Nawaz Sharif had dismissed Musharraf two or three weeks after the end of the Kargil stand off, there would have been no reaction at all, even in the armed forces, because the corps commanders and the other two service chiefs had never been taken into confidence about the Kargil plan. But that would have also confirmed India's position on the Kargil episode and brought a bad name to the army as a whole.

This delay in implementing his decision to remove General Musharraf proved fatal. During the month of August, Musharraf visited all the formations and corps headquarters. Apprehending his imminent dismissal, he sought the support of his army colleagues for a 'counter coup' if any action was taken against him. As he admits in his book, *In the Line of Fire*, he 'told them to stop brooding over the forced resignation of General Karamat and get on with our jobs. We would not allow another humiliation to befall on us in case the prime minister tried something like this again, but we would only react, never act unilaterally.'

In September 1999, I heard from certain reliable friends that Brigadier Salahuddin Satti, the commander of the 111 Brigade of the Rawalpindi Corps had carried out a secret exercise to identify target locations which had to be occupied in case of a military takeover and assigned them to officers of his brigade.

Before I left for New York on 19 September to attend the UN General Assembly, I learnt from a close friend that Musharraf's team was collecting names of potential ministers and other senior officials who could be asked to join the new government 'whenever the need arose'.

In New York and Washington DC, I met many persons with close links to the White House and the national security staff and my apprehensions about the future of Nawaz Sharif's government became more ominous.

I also learnt that USA had not fully digested Nawaz Sharif's defiance in carrying out six nuclear tests in May 1998, despite five telephone calls from President Clinton and many more from other Western leaders. His lukewarm willingness shown in his address to the General Assembly in September 1998, to sign the CTBT (but not ratify) was a partial consolation but even that was not being implemented.

Another issue worrying the US authorities, I was told, was the impending passage of a Shariat Bill. This bill, passed by the National Assembly in October 1998 as the Fifteenth Amendment, was now pending before the Senate. At that time the Nawaz Sharif government did not have the required two-thirds majority in the Senate but after the next elections to renew half the Senate members, due in March 2000, the government would have secured the required majority to pass the Shariat Bill giving the prime minister 'absolute dictatorial powers to enforce Shariat Law in Pakistan'. This had to be stopped.

During my stay in USA there were spates of media reports that Nawaz Sharif had sent his brother Shahbaz Sharif to USA from 14 to 20 September to seek the support of US administration in the face of mounting pressures on the government from the army. As a result the official spokesman of the state department, James Rubin, issued a statement saying 'We are confident that the Pakistan army will respect the constitution and democracy and we will oppose any extra constitutional actions.' BBC's comment on this statement was very cryptic. It said, despite apparent support for the government of Pakistan, this American statement does not rule out a change of government through the army. *The Far Eastern Economic Review* also echoed the same line in its comments that week.

When I returned to Pakistan on 2 October, I was very anxious to convey these apprehensions to Nawaz Sharif but he had already left for Lahore to spend the weekend with the family. I therefore met him on Monday 4 October for about two hours and briefed him about my concerns. He told me that five days earlier, General Pervez Musharraf had been appointed CJCSC, in addition to his own duties as army chief, for a further period of 18 months (up to 16 October 2001). That should end any speculations about a change. On the issue of the Shariat Bill he accepted my suggestion that we should move some much needed amendments in the bill in the Senate. As a result the draft bill passed by the National Assembly would become ineffective for the time being, since the amended bill will have to go back to the National Assembly.

The same evening while attending a session of the Senate, I learnt that a day after the notification extending General Musharraf's tenure as CJCSC was notified, he made a press statement that he 'had not made any deal with the government for this extension. I am also not aware if this decision will give greater stability to the government.'

This statement obviously exuded defiance and over confidence Nawaz Sharif must have realized that his initiative to give this extension to General Musharraf would not curb any game plan he may have developed to intervene.

On 7 October General Pervez Musharraf called for an explanation from Lt.-Gen. Tariq Parvez (corps commander Quetta) for meeting the prime minister and transferred him to GHQ. General Tariq Parvez who was the brother of Federal Minister Raja Nadir Parvez, resigned in protest. Three days later, when Pervez Musharraf had already left for Sri Lanka, General Tariq Parvez said in an interview with a newspaper that he had not met the prime minister, nor had he resigned. He had in fact been forcibly retired.

This incident must have further strengthened Nawaz Sharif's resolve to remove General Pervez Musharraf from his position. But unfortunately he did not follow a prudent course to implement this resolve. He should have anticipated that the decision to appoint General Ziauddin, then DG ISI, would not be well received in the armed forces. But to remove Musharraf when he was out of the country and the decision to prevent his plane from landing in Karachi ostensibly to facilitate General Ziauddin's induction as the new army chief before General Musharraf's landing, were not only unwise but also rash.

It is also surprising that Nawaz Sharif was not fully aware of the 'action plan', the army leadership had developed to launch a 'counter coup' if General Musharraf was removed. Some media representatives had reported that this plan called the 'Solidarity Operation' was hatched during two successive meetings in Rawalpindi on 17 and 24 September.

The actual events of 12 October have been recorded in great detail during the trial of Nawaz Sharif on charges of 'hijacking' in the first quarter of the year 2000. But it must be the first time in aviation history that the person convicted for hijacking a plane was not on board but was sitting 1000 km away! It could at best be an indirect obstruction in the permission for the plane to land.

It is also a great irony of human nature that Musharraf should have felt so sore about his dismissal for which there was plenty of justification flowing from the Kargil fiasco, but he did not have the same feelings when he dismissed an elected prime minister, with a two-thirds majority in parliament, and subsequently a president and then a chief justice!

On that fateful day, I returned home shortly before 6 p.m. A few minutes later, I received a phone call from a relative asking me to switch on the TV because the army chief had been changed. To my surprise the news was announced at 6:14 p.m., just before the end of the news bulletin. Within minutes, my driver came running and said: some army soldiers had arrived and said: 'The minister is under arrest'. I locked the bedroom door. As the major in-charge of about ten soldiers, knocked at the door, I told him to wait for a few minutes so that I can make some phone calls. I called the PM House on the green line and talked to the ADC I said, some soldiers have arrived to arrest me. What should I do? He said, 'They have also arrived at PM House' and put the phone down. I then called Chaudhry Shujaat Hussain and asked in Punjabi 'Have they arrived?' He said yes. I replied that in that case we might meet, if they took us to the same place, recalling my frequent visits to him when he was in Adiala Jail in 1995. After that I opened the door and walked with the major to the lounge downstairs. He told me, I was only under house arrest and then telephoned his boss to report that 'the subject' was in his custody.

In a short while my wife, who had gone to Peshawar to offer condolences on the death of a relative, returned with her friend Mrs Jamil Nishtar. As they saw so many soldiers near the gate, Mrs Nishtar said, 'It seems Musharraf is again visiting Sartaj Bhai!' She was aware of his two earlier visits to the house in the month of June. On seeing the ladies, the major asked the three soldiers who were guarding the front and back doors of the house while standing inside, to go out. He was very apologetic that he had to carry out this unpleasant duty because he had the highest respect for me. At about 10:30 p.m., after eating a pizza dinner in his presence, I asked his permission to go up to sleep. He readily agreed. BBC and Voice of America called just after 11 p.m. to talk to me. When my wife told them I had already gone to sleep, they said, 'Thank God, that means he is okay.'

For the next three days, I only read newspapers and watched television. On Friday the 15th, I asked the major, if I could go to the mosque to offer Friday prayers. He checked with his boss and said, 'Yes, but I will have to accompany you'. Most of the *namazis* who used to greet me before or after the prayers stayed away this time when they saw a major in uniform with me.

That very night at about 10 p.m., the major informed me that they had been ordered to leave so I was free. This ended my painless house arrest after three days. As I learnt later, all the ministers had been released from detention except three: Ishaq Dar, Chaudhry Nisar Ali Khan, and Mushahid Hussain. Ishaq Dar was shifted to NAB headquarters in Lahore and the other two remained under house arrest for almost two years.

Six other leaders and officials—Shahbaz Sharif, Ghous Ali Shah, Shahid Khaqan Abbasi, Saifur Rahman and Saeed Mehdi had been arrested on 12 October, along with Nawaz Sharif, to be tried on charges of abetting the hijacking.

Gradually, as I recovered from the initial shock of the military takeover, I was struck by so many paradoxes. On 13 October, Benazir Bhutto, in an interview with BBC had welcomed the military takeover and said, General Musharraf was a 'neutral person'. She also said that Musharraf should hold elections within ninety days and that he 'should also talk to me because I can play an important role in defusing this crisis'. Apparently she tried to contact the military leadership but did not succeed.

On 14 October, Qazi Hussain Ahmad said, the military takeover was inevitable but the army should not extend its rule but appoint a neutral caretaker government. Other leaders who welcomed the military takeover included Maulana Fazlur Rehman of JUI(F), Altaf Hussain (MQM), Tahir-ul-Qadri (Pakistan Awami Tehrik) and Ijaz-ul-Haq (PML).

The US state department in a statement on 13 October said, the US had tried to restrain Nawaz Sharif but he could not control the situation. The administration was not therefore surprised by the military takeover. However, it hoped the army would respect the constitution and restore democracy. UK and Germany made similar statements.

As I read these reactions, I recalled the jubilation of opposition politicians under PNA, including Air Marshal (retd) Asghar Khan, Mufti Mahmud, and Shah Ahmad Noorani, when Ziaul Haq had declared martial law on 5 July 1977 and removed the government of Zulfikar Ali Bhutto. They expected the general to hold elections within ninety days and transfer power to the newly elected leaders. But Ziaul Haq promptly postponed the elections and stayed on in power for eleven long years. Our politicians, I said to a colleague, never seem to learn any lessons from history.

I also felt sad and depressed throughout the next few weeks that the government of Nawaz Sharif having achieved a record-breaking electoral victory in February 1997, could complete only half its five-year tenure. Even in his earlier tenure, his government was dismissed after two years and nine months. This meant he had also learnt no lessons from history. What are these lessons, I asked myself repeatedly as I discussed the subject with many of my colleagues who were also involved in similar introspection and self criticism.

We all agreed that the fundamental reason for the recurring political instability in Pakistan has its roots in the continuing tussle between the army and the civilian political leadership for a larger slice of the pie. As a result of the prolonged periods of military rule, the military bureaucracy along with its intelligence agencies, i.e. the ISI and Military Intelligence (MI), called the 'Establishment', had fully entrenched itself in the power structure of Pakistan. Civil bureaucracy had also provided a supporting role. In contrast, each relatively brief period of civilian rule had been the result of a managed process through which the army establishment shared power with the 'elected representatives', through a leader or a political party chosen by it. As the civilian leaders settled down and tried to expand their political space in the power structure, they faced resistance and whenever they went too far, they were sent home, hanged or exiled.

In March 1985, Ziaul Haq had transferred only 30 per cent power to Prime Minister Junejo by drastically amending the constitution to retain the powers to change the prime minister, dissolve the National Assembly and make all major appointments like the service chiefs, governors of provinces and in the higher judiciary. But in October 1985, through the Eighth Amendment, Junejo managed to extend his political space from 30 to 60 per cent. Zia tolerated that but when in early 1988 Junejo took over the Afghan policy, he had crossed the tolerable limits and was dismissed in May 1988.

Benazir Bhutto and Nawaz Sharif both tried to deal with this perennial tussle with the 'Establishment' by appointing their own choice as head of ISI and not the one recommended by the army chief. This only increased misunderstanding and tensions with the army leadership. Benazir's nervous attempts to clip the wings of the establishment lasted only twenty months in her first tenure (November 1988 to August 1990) and thirty-six months in the second tenure (December 1993 to November 1996).

Nawaz Sharif during his second tenure felt that after such a heavy electoral mandate, he would be able to bring about a decisive change in the country's power structure by establishing the supremacy of the civilian government over the armed forces. But he went too far, by dismissing two army chiefs in less than a year and not only saw the demise of his government but also the derailment of the democratic process.

In this miscalculation, his first major blunder was the passage of the Thirteenth Amendment to do away with the power of the president to dissolve the National Assembly. While in principle this power is highly undemocratic but in practice it has acted as a safety valve against the imposition of martial law. At least four times, in 1988, 1990, 1993 and 1996, when a change of government became unavoidable, this power was used but there were elections within ninety days and the democratic process remained on track, I am certain that even in 1999, the army would have persuaded the very 'loyal' President, Justice (retd) Rafiq Tarrar to dissolve the assembly and call for fresh elections within ninety days, thus avoiding the prolonged military rule after 1999.

Nawaz Sharif's political struggle for restoring full democracy was fully justified but he failed to recognize the essential requirements of a system based on the rule of law and democratic principles. The success of such a system can only be assured on the basis of strong institutions, especially an independent judiciary, a sovereign parliament, a strong election commission and free media. Nawaz Sharif somehow assumed that if an elected leader is more powerful, he can deliver democracy, without realizing that the real strength of an elected leader comes from these institutions. His tussle with the judiciary in October/November 1997 was actually the beginning of the end of his tenure.

In addition as mentioned in Chapter 10, a heavy mandate even in stable democracies can lead to intemperate decisions. There were plenty of those between February 1997 and October 1999. But despite those miscalculations or shortcomings of Nawaz Sharif in handling the perennial civil–military see saw, there was no real justification for a military takeover.

Appeal to the Supreme Court

In December 1999, a constitutional petition, No. 63/99, was filed by five leaders, Syed Zafar Ali Shah, Wasim Sajjad, Illahi Bux Soomro, Raja Zafarul Haq and Chaudhry Pervez Elahi, on behalf of PML(N) to challenge the validity and legal effect of the army takeover of the country on 12 October 1999. It prayed inter alia that the said takeover be declared illegal and violative of the 1973 constitution. The petitioners had also prayed that the Provisional Constitution Order No. 1 dated 14 October 1999, the proclamation of emergency of the same date and all orders, enactments and instruments issued hereunder may be also declared as illegal, ultra vires of the constitution and of no legal effect.

The Supreme Court, after hearing this petition for four months, issued a short order on 12 May 2000 and a detailed judgment on 29 May 2000, rejecting the pleas made by the petitioners and observed as follows:

a. That the military action of the 12-10-1999 was validly taken, being justified on grounds of state necessity.
b. That the Constitution of Pakistan 1973 still remains the supreme law of the land subject to the condition that certain parts thereof have been held in abeyance on account of state necessity.
c. That the Superior Courts continue to function under the constitution and that the new oath taken under the 'Oath of Office (Judges) Order No. 1 of 2000' does not in any manner derogate from this position.
d. That the chief executive is entitled to perform all such acts and promulgate all legislative measures as enumerated in the judgement and has also powers to amend the constitution, subject to certain conditions stipulated therein.
e. That the Superior Courts continue to have the power of Judicial Review to judge the validity of any act or action of the armed forces in the light of principles underlying the law of state necessity.
f. That the chief executive be allowed a period of three years from 12 October 1999 to achieve his declared objectives and that not later than ninety days before the expiry of the afore-mentioned period, he shall appoint a date for holding of general elections to the National Assembly, the Provincial Assemblies and the Senate of Pakistan.

A review petition was submitted under Article 188 against this Supreme Court judgment of 29 May 2000. This petition acquired renewed significance after the Presidential reference filed seven years later against Justice Iftikhar Muhammad Chaudhry on 9 March 2007. Some extracts from this review petition are reproduced in Appendix

IV to show that had this movement for the independence of the judiciary taken place before 1999, the military takeover of October 1999 would not have been declared valid by the Supreme Court on grounds of state necessity.

The review petition was not accepted and General Musharraf utilized the power given to him to consolidate his position. To avoid the stigma of martial law, he decided to call himself chief executive and assumed the full powers of the head of state. Justice (retd) Rafiq Tarrar was allowed to continue as president, without any power, till June 2001, when in preparation for the Agra summit with India, Musharraf issued the Proclamation of Emergency Order 2001 on 21 June 2001. Under this order he amended the earlier Proclamation of Emergency Order of 14 October 1999 and dismissed President Rafiq Tarrar whose term of office was to end on 1 January 2003. The next day he himself assumed the office of president.

The 2002 Referendum

As the three-year period given to Musharraf by the Supreme Court was nearing its end, he realized that it would be risky for him to hand over his fate to the new assembly created after the October 2002 elections. He therefore organized a dubious referendum on 5 April 2002 to get himself 'elected' as president. Musharraf himself admits in his memoirs:

> There were some irregularities, though, I found that in some places overenthusiastic administrative officials and bureaucrats had allowed people to vote more than once, and had even filled out ballot papers themselves. I also later found that this absolutely unwarranted 'support' was helped along by the opposition in certain areas where they have a hold and where they stuffed ballot boxes in my favour so as to provide supposed evidence for claims of foul play. The whole exercise ended in a near catastrophe.

Musharraf did not of course admit a more fundamental flaw in his decision to get 'elected' as president through a dubious referendum, before the next general elections. Under Article 48(6) of the constitution, 'if at any time, the president considers that it is desirable that any matter of national importance should be referred to a referendum, the president may cause the matter to be referred to in a referendum in the form of a question, that is capable of being answered either 'Yes' or 'No.' Even the most liberal and flexible interpretation of this provision would not allow its use, in fact misuse, to elect a president, in total disregard of the procedure laid down in Article 41 of the constitution for the election of the president. But Musharraf decided to follow the footsteps of his predecessors, Field Marshal Ayub Khan and General Ziaul Haq along this dubious course, because he could not face the democratic alternative of presenting his candidature to the new parliament, after the 2002 elections.

Almost the entire international and local media condemned this farce in the strongest possible terms and considered it a serious violation of the Supreme Court decision of May 2000, under which General Musharraf was to hold elections within three years and transfer power to elected representatives. These commentators were not in fact aware at that time that many more violations and distortions of the constitution and the rule of law lay in store for this unfortunate nation over the next five years.

General Elections 2002

Almost all independent observers agree that the 2002 elections broke all previous records of rigging, malpractices and manipulation.

All military governments, to gain a certain degree of legitimacy, have tried to create a civilian façade by co-opting certain political parties and leaders. In such a scheme the military establishment retains real power but gives a marginal and largely ceremonial share to those political parties and leaders who are ready to be content with this marginal share. Some of them are coerced while others are bribed.

Musharraf's game plan to build such a civilian façade started taking shape soon after he took over. Immediately after Nawaz Sharif was 'convicted' in the hijacking case on 10 April 2000, efforts to capture the Pakistan Muslim League (PML) as a pro-Musharraf political party were launched. Initially the main focus of these efforts was to find a PML leader, around whom 'PML dissidents' would gather and either takeover the party from Nawaz Sharif or if that was not possible, to create a new and larger faction of the PML. For this purpose, Mian Azhar, a former governor of Punjab and a well-respected member of PML, was selected. After that the ISI functionaries in each district started contacting the 140 PML members of the 1997–99 National Assembly to persuade or coerce them to part company with Nawaz Sharif. Some were shown NAB files to threaten them with dire consequences, others were promised favour or a 'party ticket' for the next elections. In his first meeting with Musharraf, Mian Azhar had only five PML members with him, but in July when the 'dissidents' assembled at the residence of Syed Fakhar Imam in Islamabad, they were thirty. In November, at an *iftar* party organized by Mian Azhar, the number had risen to 62. On 25 November, the establishment, supported by some PML supporters of Mian Azhar, stormed the PML(N) secretariat on Margalla Road, to take it over for the dissident group later called PML(Q). As secretary general of PML, from 1993 to 1999, I had acquired and furnished this headquarters in 1997 with the support of many party members. I was greatly disturbed when I learnt that those who captured the building had destroyed all the records, including many valuable books and reference material I had placed in the party library. They had also pulled down and burnt the curtains, as if they were entering enemy property. That building, whose title is still in my name as secretary general PML, is easily the best office of a political party in the country.

After Nawaz Sharif's dramatic exile to Saudi Arabia a fortnight later, on 10 December 2000, the dissidents' pool began to swell at a faster pace. Finally when the 'Establishment' organized a meeting of the PML council in Islamabad in March 2001, 108 out of 140 PML former MNAs elected in 1997, attended to formalize the birth of a 'King's Party' with Mian Azhar as the president. But before the 2002 elections in August 2002, Mian Azhar was replaced by Chaudhry Shujaat Hussain as president of PML(Q).

Those PML members and leaders who resisted these moves to defect from PML(N) came under great pressure before, during and after the elections but most of them remained firm in their loyalty to Nawaz Sharif. As is often said, the true test of a politician's commitment to political principles comes in times of adversity.

Since each election held in Pakistan after 1985, has been micro-managed by the army establishment, it had acquired by 2002, considerable experience in managing and manipulating the electoral process. This is no longer confined to what is commonly called 'ballot rigging' on the election day. The process is very comprehensive and starts long before the election day. It can be distinguished in four stages: (i) system rigging, (ii) pre-poll rigging, (iii) polling day rigging, (iv) post-poll rigging.

The system rigging in this case started with the military takeover, under which the constitution was suspended and amended and all major institutions including the judiciary and the election commission were brought under the control of the martial law administrator or the chief executive as he was called. Pervez Musharraf's 'election' as president through a dubious referendum, in violation of the procedure laid down in the constitution, was another dimension of 'system rigging'. Thus extra constitutional forces were placed over and above the parliament. The judiciary was weakened and brought in line, through the PCO, because six independent judges of the Supreme Court, who refused to take oath under the PCO, in violation of the constitution, had to resign. In 2001, to the surprise of all legal experts, Justice Irshad Hasan Khan was appointed as chief election commissioner, as soon as he retired as the chief justice of Pakistan. Normally according to tradition, chief justices do not accept any other office after their retirement. In this case Justice Irshad Hasan Khan had also become controversial because he made several judicial appointments only six days before his retirement allegedly on the recommendations of the government. As a result, for the first time in judicial history, his colleagues had refused to give him a full court reference.

The phase of pre-poll rigging started several months before the elections. A new cell was established in the National Reconstruction Bureau (NRB) to undertake re-alignment of all the constituencies according to the wishes of the King's Party [PML(Q)] and some other allied parties like the National Alliance and MQM. The election commission, which is responsible for the demarcation of constituencies on the basis of certain well established criteria, was kept out of this exercise.

Another and more gruesome part of the pre-poll circus was the systematic disqualification of opposition candidates through discriminatory accountability. Some like Makhdoom Javed Hashmi were arrested on fake charges (although he still won his seat from the prison cell), others were pressurized to withdraw or face the wrath of the administration. The nomination papers of Shahbaz Sharif and Begum Kulsum Nawaz were rejected on the flimsy ground that in their absence, the returning officer could not verify their signatures on the nomination papers.

Large-scale postings and transfers of district officials were made on the recommendations of 'official' candidates, although under election laws these are not allowed for a period of six months before the election date. When the media raised a storm over these postings, the chief election commissioner issued a belated order on 23 July to stop any further transfers.

The governors openly campaigned for the King's Party and announced allocation of millions of rupees for development projects in constituencies of officially supported candidates. Musharraf himself campaigned extensively while wearing his uniform. Public funds were used for projecting a positive image of the government and a negative image of the opposition parties through the electronic and print media.

Just a day before the polling date, Musharraf announced certain changes in his Legal Framework Order (LFO), under which those winning elections as independent candidates would be free to join any political party within three days. The retirement age of judges of the High Courts and the Supreme Court was also extended by two years.

On the polling day of 10 October 2002, rigging was undertaken on a horrendous scale. Polling agents and workers of the opposition were harassed or evicted from polling stations and fake votes were cast with the connivance of election staff. These were widely reported in the media but the election commission took no notice.

The post-poll rigging under which many declared results were changed overnight was also undertaken on a substantial scale partly by stuffing ballot boxes with bogus votes and partly by manipulation in counting votes. The European Union Observer Group and the Commonwealth team declared serious flaws in the electoral process. Many local organizations like the Human Rights Commission and the Liberal Forum also criticized the elections as faulty and fraudulent. The western media was also critical of the 'democratization' process. But the western governments generally took a charitable view because of Musharraf's whole-hearted support for the war on terrorism after 9/11.

Despite these massive efforts to manage and rig the 2002 Elections, the 'Establishment' could not secure a simple majority for the pro-Musharraf coalition, as shown in the following table:

2002 Election Results of National Assembly							
	Punjab	Sindh	NWFP	Balochistan	FATA	Islamabad	Total
Total General Seats	148	61	35	14	12	2	272
PML(Q)	68	4	4	2			78
MMA	3	6	29	6		1	45
PPPP	35	27				1	63
PML(N)	14			1			15
MQM		13					13
NA	7	5		1			13
PML(F)		4					4
PML(J)	2						2
PPP(S)		2					2
BNP				1			1
PTI	1						1
PML(Z)	1						1
MQM(H)		1					1
JWP				1			1
PPP(SB)	1						1
PAT	1						1
PKMAP				1			1
Independents	15	1		1	12		29
Source: Election Commission of Pakistan							

The election planners of the 'Establishment' had expected PML(Q) to secure over 100 out of 272 contested seats but it won only 78 seats. By comparison the Muttahida Majlis-e-Amal (MMA) which they expected to win only 25–30 seats won 45 seats mainly from NWFP and Balochistan. This was largely because both the mainstream political parties, namely PML(N) and PPP, which between the two had won 75 to 80 per cent of all National Assembly seats in the preceding four elections (1988, 1990, 1993 and 1997) were vilified, divided and weakened. This created larger political space for the MMA, an alliance of six religious political parties, which had been engineered by the 'Establishment' a year earlier under the name of Afghan defence council. This was the first time when these six parties participated in an election on a single platform and symbol. Thus while the mainstream parties were deliberately discredited and divided, this alliance was encouraged as a counterweight. That much for Musharraf's liberal credentials and policy of 'enlightened moderation'!

In terms of total votes, the PPP emerged as the largest party with 24.56 per cent of polled votes. Even PML(N) which won only 15 seats, polled more popular votes (10.96 per cent) than MMA's 10.61 per cent, with 45 seats:

Total Votes secured by different Political Parties						
Parties	Contesting candidates	Returned candidates	Contesting candidates (%)	Votes Secured	Polled votes (%)	Regis- tered votes (%)
PPP-P	232	63	27.15	7,361,423	24.56	10.24
PML(Q)	197	78	39.6	6,898,587	23.01	9.59
PML(N)	171	15	8.77	3,292,659	10.96	4.6
MMA	183	45	24.6	3,181,483	10.61	4.42
NA	75	13	17.33	1,269,268	4.26	1.76
MQM	60	13	21.66	920,381	3.00	1.30
Source: Election Commission of Pakistan						

Under the Seventeenth Amendment, in addition to the 272 directly elected members, 60 additional seats were reserved for women candidates to be elected indirectly by the elected members, in proportion to the seats secured by each political party from the province. Another ten non-Muslim candidates were to be elected in a similar manner. The final party position, in a house of 342 seats, after the election of these 70 indirectly elected members and considerable horse trading, was as follows:

Party	General	Women	Minorities	Total
PML(Q)	92	22	4	118
PPP(P)	63	15	2	80
MMA	47	12	2	61
PML(N)	15	3	1	19
MQM	13	3	1	17
NA	13	3	0	16
PML(F)	4	1	0	5
PML(J)	2	1	0	3
PPP(S)	2	0	0	2
FATA	12	0	0	12
Independents	1	0	0	1
Others*	8	0	0	8
Total	272	60	10	342

*Others include one seat each of BNP, JWP, PAT, PML(Z), PTI, MQM(H), PKMAP, and PPP(SB).
Source: Election Commission of Pakistan

To form a pro-Musharraf government at the centre, the 'Establishment' needed at least 172 seats. With PML(Q)'s initial tally of 104 seats (after adding 22 women and 4 minorities seats), MQM's 17 seats, National Alliance's 16 seats and 12 independents from FATA, they had only 149 seats. In a bizarre saga of horse trading and pressure tactics, the strength of PML(Q) was increased to 118. Even then the required majority could not be managed. Finally, 10 members of the PPP-Parliamentarians were won over to form a breakaway faction called PPPP-Patriots, to elect Zafarullah Jamali as prime minister with 172 votes or a margin of only one vote. In return, ten members of the breakaway faction (PPPPP) were allocated six cabinet posts of their choice. This was not a very happy start for the experiment of democracy.

But within about eighteen months, even Jamali could not retain Musharraf's trust. As Musharraf records in his book (pp. 178–179) that apart from differences with Chaudhry Shujaat:

I felt that Jamali could not cope with the demands of the office. I had also come to the conclusion that Shaukat Aziz, our successful Finance Minister, would make the best Prime Minister. But the difficulty was that Shaukat Aziz was in the Senate, and the Prime Minister had to be a member of the

National Assembly. It was therefore decided that Jamali would resign as Prime Minister, that party president Chaudhry Shujaat Hussain would become Prime Minister for a couple of months and Shaukat Aziz would run two by-elections for seats voluntarily surrendered for him in the National Assembly.

Can there be more glaring proof that the National Assembly elected in October 2002, was in effect a rubber stamp parliament which was not given even the authority to discharge its constitutional responsibility of electing one of its own members as prime minister? That was perhaps the most overbearing face of 'khaki democracy' imposed on Pakistan in October 2002.

The Seventeenth Amendment

Out of seventeen amendments moved in the 1973 constitution, thirteen were passed and four became infructuous. Half of those passed became highly controversial but the Seventeenth Amendment took the cake, in terms of constitutional manipulation for certain pre-conceived purposes.

The first seven amendments were passed by the PPP government of Zulfikar Ali Bhutto, in May 1974, September 1974, February 1975, November 1975, September 1976, December 1976 and May 1977, partly to gain powers to ban certain political parties and partly to curtail the powers of the judiciary. The second amendment had pronounced Qadianis as non-Muslims.

The Eighth Amendment passed in October 1985, while curtailing some of the powers assumed by the president, Ziaul Haq, when he revived the 1973 constitution in March 1985, also validated the presidential order of July 1977 and all other martial law orders and regulations including the referendum order of 1984.

The Ninth Amendment Bill (as also the Fifteenth Amendment Bill) concerning the enforcement of Shariat remained bills and were never enacted to become a part of the constitution.

Under the Tenth Amendment, the number of days for which the National Assembly was required to meet was reduced from 160 to 130.

The Eleventh Amendment Bill, introduced in the Senate on 31 December 1989, sought to restore twenty women's seats in the

National Assembly because the provision for these seats under Article 51 of the Constitution had expired with the third general election. The bill was however withdrawn by its movers on 23 August 1992.

Under the Twelfth Amendment, passed on 28 July 1991, the first Nawaz Sharif government established special courts for the trial of heinous offences and raised the salaries and pensions of judges.

The Thirteenth Amendment, passed unanimously by both houses in April 1997, repealed the infamous article 58-2(b) under which the president had dismissed national and provincial assemblies four times in 1988, 1990, 1993 and 1996.

Under the Fourteenth Amendment, a new clause was inserted in Article 63, under which any member of a parliamentary party committing a breach of party discipline or voting contrary to party direction, could be disqualified.

The Fifteenth Amendment Bill, as already mentioned, was introduced for the enforcement of Shariat in the country. It was passed by the National Assembly in October 1998 and was pending in the Senate for approval but became infructuous with the dissolution of the Senate in October 1999.

The Sixteenth Amendment Bill was a comprehensive bill on the subject of provincial autonomy, introduced by members of many political parties as a private members bill, but it was never enacted.

The groundwork for the Seventeenth Amendment was laid down in the LFO No. 24 of 2002, issued by the chief executive, General Musharraf on 21 August 2002 in preparation for the 2002 elections. Under this Order many important amendments and changes were made:

- The 1973 constitution was revived but with several amendments in the constitution.
- The results of the dubious referendum held on 1 May 2002 were sanctified by giving a 'democratic mandate' to General Musharraf to serve as president for five years (Article 41).
- Article 58-2(b) was restored to revive the powers of the president to dissolve the National Assembly.
- The number of seats in the National Assembly was increased from 210 to 342 and in the Senate from 87 to 100. Correspondingly the provincial assembly seats also increased from 250, 100, 80 and 40

to 371, 168, 124 and 65 for Punjab, Sindh, NWFP, and Balochistan respectively (Article 106).

- The provision for a NSC, abolished under the Eighth Amendment, was revived (Article 152-A) with the president as chairperson.
- Under the original Article 224(i), a general election to the national or provincial assembly was to be held within a period of sixty days immediately preceding the day on which the term of the assembly was due to expire. Through the LFO 2002, the word 'preceding' was substituted by the word 'following', thus opening a constitutional pandora's box in 2007.
- The president was given powers to appoint, in his discretion, service chiefs and members of the superior judiciary.

Having managed the 2002 elections to form a coalition government under Jamali, Musharraf's next major priority was to get a constitutional cover for retaining the office of the army chief while serving as president. Article 43 says very clearly that 'the president shall not hold any office of profit in the service of Pakistan or occupy any other position carrying the right of remuneration for the rendering of services.'

Since the pro-Musharraf coalition did not have the required two-thirds majority in parliament, a major political marathon began with the MMA that lasted fourteen months, until the Seventeenth Amendment was adopted in December 2003.

Under the Seventeenth Amendment all the constitutional amendments promulgated by General Musharraf under the LFO No. 24 of 2002, were validated, allowing him inter alia to keep his uniform, along with the Presidency, but with the following proviso added to Article 41-7(b): 'Provided that paragraph (d) of Clause (1) of Article 63 shall become operative on and from the 31st day of December 2004.' This paragraph (d) says that 'a person shall be disqualified from being a member of parliament, if he holds an office of profit in the service of Pakistan other than an office declared by law not to disqualify him.'

The MMA leaders were jubilant that they had managed to persuade General Musharraf to take off his uniform by December 2004. General Musharraf himself appeared on the television and made a promise to the whole nation that he would relinquish the post of army chief by the end of 2004. This promise he never fulfilled. The Seventeenth

Amendment thus caused irreparable damage to the democratic process.

The MMA in return, for legalizing Musharraf and his two offices under the Seventeenth Amendment, received three major concessions: (1), a promise that their governments in NWFP and Balochistan would not be de-stabilized; (2), the cases in the Supreme Court challenging the equivalence of a madrassah degree with a normal degree, would remain in abeyance. If these degrees had been declared insufficient, the majority of MMA parliamentarian would have been disqualified; (3) the ban on a prime minister not to hold office for the third term, also provided them a fig leaf that in the absence of Nawaz Sharif and Benazir Bhutto, the two mainstream political parties would not do as well, leaving more space for the MMA.

The most bizarre constitutional amendment through LFO No. 24 of 2002, which the MMA failed to detect and prevent under the Seventeenth Amendment, was in Article 224. Musharraf and his supporters had already hatched a plot to get Musharraf re-elected as president for another five years from the same assembly, by changing the word 'preceding' (the day on which the term of the assembly is due to expire) into 'following'. This anomaly created a serious political and constitutional anomaly by requiring an assembly which is about to end its tenure, to elect a president for the next five years in total violation of the spirit of the constitution or accepted democratic principles and, as described in a subsequent section in this chapter, created a major political crisis in the last quarter of 2007.

The Tussle with the Judiciary

It will not be easy to draw up a comprehensive list of legal deviations and constitutional distortions that have been unleashed on the hapless Pakistani nation in the nine-year rule of General Musharraf, but the climax certainly occurred on 9 March 2007, when he tried to unceremoniously dismiss the chief justice of Pakistan, Iftikhar Muhammad Chaudhry by declaring him 'non-functional' simply because he wanted a more pliable judiciary that would remove all legal hurdles in the way of his re-election as president and also find a way for him to keep his uniform. But the move backfired. The chief justice refused to resign and the entire legal fraternity and civil society rallied behind his defiance. The mishandling of the chief justice by police officials on 12 March 2007, when they insisted on taking him to the Supreme Court by car, rather than allow him to walk in procession with his lawyers and supporters, provided the turning point. All the bar associations throughout the country passed resolutions in support of the chief justice and many invited him to address their members. The chief justice's road journey from Islamabad to Lahore on 5 May 2007 that took twenty-six hours was shown live by all television networks with thousand of lawyers, political party workers and ordinary citizens welcoming him at every stop. This show of massive public support not only further deepened the civil–military divide but also generated considerable optimism that this movement for the supremacy of the rule of law was now unstoppable.

But there was tragic anti-climax a week later, when the chief justice landed in Karachi on 12 May 2007 at the invitation of the Karachi Bar Association. The chief justice was not allowed by the local authorities to leave the airport 'to prevent a breakdown in the law and order situation' and all the roads leading to the airport were blocked by large containers and other barricades. As lawyers and other supporters of the chief justice tried to cross these barricades to move towards the airport, they were killed in cold blood by gunmen in civilian clothes. AAJ TV station which showed these gory scenes in great detail was also attacked. In all, more than fifty innocent people were massacred on that day sending waves of outrage throughout the country. The chief justice had no option but to return to Islamabad in the evening after waiting at the airport for several hours.

To pour salt on the wounds of a traumatized nation, a vulgar show of festivity was organized for Musharraf the same evening in Islamabad to which thousands of civil servants and ordinary workers were brought and fed at state expense. The purpose was to demonstrate peoples' support as a counter weight to the support the Chief Justice was receiving, totally ignoring the sadness generated by the gory bloodletting in Karachi. All in all, the 12 May incident further deepened the ethnic divide that has been haunting the country's politics since the early 1980s.

The chief justice's visits to other cities like Hyderabad, Peshawar, and Faisalabad however went off peacefully and attracted not only large crowds but also serving judges of various courts, generating widespread enthusiasm.

Meanwhile the hearing of the reference against the full Supreme Court continued with wide coverage in the media, especially of the brilliant presentation by Aitzaz Ahsan and Munir Malik. Finally on 20 July 2007 the unanimous and historic judgement came. The full court set aside the reference against the chief justice, declared the appointment of acting chief justice illegal and restored the chief justice to his office. This judgement will go down as a landmark in the country's judicial and political history, reviving the prospect of a new and independent judiciary with far reaching consequences in the years to come.

While the legal fraternity was still celebrating this landmark judgement and the imminent birth of a new and independent judiciary, the declaration of emergency on 3 November 2007 landed as a thunderbolt. The main target of this fifth martial law was the independence of the judiciary.

Nawaz Sharif's Return

Nawaz Sharif went into his exile in Saudi Arabia on 10 December 2000, after spending one year and two months in confinement at different prisons in Islamabad, Karachi, and Attock. For the first five years, he did not take any active part in politics, apart from occasional statements, released by those who met him in Jeddah or Madina. But in January 2006, he got permission to travel to London for the treatment of his ailing son, Hasan Nawaz. He arrived in London on 29 January 2006 to a rousing welcome. I also arrived in London from Zurich after attending the World Economic Forum in Davos, just in time to receive him. He addressed the PML workers who had come to receive him at a community centre in Southall soon after landing. He ignited the crowd when he said:

I first want to ask you and the 160 million people of Pakistan why the Muslim League government was dismissed by General Musharraf?
- Was I the enemy of Pakistan?
- Did I make a deal not to go for a nuclear explosion?
- Did I conspire against the integrity of Pakistan?

- Did I accept any commission or kickback in the purchase of tanks, sub-marines or military aircraft?
- Have they proved any case against me?

Each of these questions was answered by the crowd with an emphatic 'No'. Then he asked: 'Is the situation better today than it was on 12 October 1999? Look, what is happening. The army is bombing and killing its own people in the tribal and adjoining areas. Under the seven-point agenda, Musharraf promised to strengthen the federation. But look what is happening in Balochistan, NWFP and parts of Sindh. There has been record inflation adding to the misery of the people. Unemployment is growing and the unemployed are committing suicide at a rate never seen in Pakistan before.'

Then Nawaz Sharif presented the theme, on which he was to build his and his party's political strategy for the future:

Today the people of Pakistan have to make a fundamental decision. Will Pakistan be governed in future by the elected representatives of the people or by a few generals who capture power through force? The unity of the federation is threatened today and conditions similar to those in 1971 in East Pakistan are developing, the law and order has broken down, the sovereignty of the nation has been compromised and there is widespread despondency and frustration in the country. These problems can be tackled only through a genuine democratic process. That is why I am here today. This is not a struggle to gain political power but to safeguard the future of Pakistan by re-establishing the rule of law and democracy.

Nawaz Sharif addressed two public meetings in Birmingham and Manchester and convened a meeting of the central working committee of PML(N) on 25–26 March 2006 in which certain important organizational changes were made to activate the party.

Two months later, on 14 May 2006, Nawaz Sharif and Benazir Bhutto signed the historic Charter of Democracy. Other component parties of the Alliance for Restoration of Democracy (ARD) signed this charter on 2 July 2006, beginning a new era in the country's democratic history. The two mainstream political parties which between them had won 75–80 per cent of all seats in the National Assembly in the general elections held in 1988, 1990, 1993 and 1997, had realized their shortcomings and had decided to come together to draw up rules for establishing genuine democracy in Pakistan and prevent military takeover in the future. The full text of the Charter of Democracy is in Appendix V.

This charter is neither an election manifesto nor a document for an electoral alliance. It is an agenda to strengthen the democratic process and democratic institutions, with the following objectives, specific measures and reforms:

- Restoration of the 1973 constitution and repeal of the Seventeenth Amendment including the power to dissolve the National Assembly under Article 58-2(b) while protecting some non-controversial provisions, like lowering the age of voters, increase in total seats, and more seats for women and minorities.
- Evolution of a transparent merit-based procedure for constitutional appointments like judges of higher judiciary and the election commission.
- A code of ethics for political parties, not to seek military intervention for political gain, nor to join a military sponsored government, and setting up a national democracy commission to eliminate horse trading and corruption in elections to reserved seats.
- Strengthening the federation through maximum provincial autonomy and a new national finance commission award, in consultation with provinces.
- Integration of FATA in the province of NWFP after consultation with the people of FATA.
- Providing improved governance to the people with a focus on providing quality education and health facilities to ordinary citizens, on reducing poverty and unemployment, and on promoting simplicity and austerity at all levels.
- Ensuring free and fair elections by appointing a neutral caretaker setup and an independent and effective election commission.
- Evolving a new framework for civil–military relations by abolishing, inter alia, the political wings of military intelligence agencies.

The Musharraf government was naturally unnerved by this understanding between the two main opposition parties. It therefore launched a secret mission to strike a deal with Benazir Bhutto. Different emissaries both civilian and military met her and some other

PPP leaders in Pakistan, Dubai and London. In these negotiations all the major demands put forward by Benazir Bhutto were initially accepted in principle, namely: allowing her safe passage to return to Pakistan after the withdrawal of cases against her and other leaders and civil servants, removal of constitutional ban on the third term of a prime minister, deletion of Article 58-2(b) of the constitution, and holding free and fair elections in the country. In return she promised to support, directly or indirectly, the re-election of Musharraf as president, but without his uniform and joining a coalition government with PML(Q) and other so-called liberal parties after the elections.

These secret negotiations were in full swing, when Nawaz Sharif convened an All Parties Conference (APC) in London on 7–8 July 2007. It was attended by 38 heads of opposition parties. It was also attended by a seven-member delegation from the PPP led by Makhdoom Amin Fahim, but Benazir Bhutto, while in London, stayed away. PPP also did not sign the final APC Declaration (Appendix VI) because of para 3 of the declaration ('To strongly resist the election by the incumbent assemblies of General Musharraf for the office of the president of Pakistan through all means including resignations from parliament and the provincial assemblies.')

The representatives attending the APC met again two days later, on 10 July 2007, to consider a mechanism for follow-up and agreed to setup an All Parties Democratic Movement (APDM) with an action committee to implement the APC Declaration in a coordinated manner. PPP did not join the APDM on the plea that it could not sit with the MMA on a joint platform. Musharraf had thus succeeded in dividing the opposition, by offering a 'deal' to the PPP.

But at the same time, Musharraf could not afford to let PPP 'steal the show' and become a dominant player after the elections. A month before the presidential elections, there was an orchestrated campaign by PML(Q) leaders to criticize the 'deal' and strongly oppose the removal of restrictions on the third term of a prime minister or the repeal of Article 58-2(b). According to newspaper reports, the main foreign supporters of this deal (USA and UK) were also used to persuade Benazir Bhutto to lower her demands on the understanding that the remaining conditions would be fulfilled at a later stage. Apparently a 'non paper' was signed in London on these lines between the representatives of Benazir Bhutto and Musharraf and the foreign interlocutors. This also meant that even after signing a Charter of Democracy with Nawaz Sharif, Benazir Bhutto was ready to part ways with PML(N) and other opposition parties ostensibly 'to ensure a smooth transition to democracy'.

The second major threat to Musharraf's re-election as president was Nawaz Sharif. In a judgement on 23 August 2007, the Supreme Court declared that as a citizen of Pakistan, Nawaz Sharif and his family members had every right to return to Pakistan. The court also ruled that 'the return and entry of Sharif brothers into the country shall not be restrained, hampered or obstructed by the federal or provincial government agencies in any manner.'

A week after this judgement, Nawaz Sharif announced, after hectic consultations with the party's top leadership that he would return to Pakistan on 10 September, landing in Islamabad and then driving in a procession to Lahore. This announcement, while creating strong ripples in the political landscape, also created panic in the ruling circles. The expected shift of PML(Q) members towards PML(N) would have eroded Musharraf's vote bank in parliament needed for his re-election. A plan was therefore hatched to send Nawaz Shairf back to Saudi Arabia soon after his arrival. All the diplomatic levers were pulled to persuade Nawaz Sharif, through Saad Hariri, son of former Lebanese premier Rafiq Hariri, who had played a role in Nawaz Sharif's exile in 2000, and Saudi intelligence chief, Muqrin bin Abdul Aziz, to persuade Nawaz Sharif to defer his return till after Musharraf's re-election. When he refused, they appeared on television in Islamabad and said: 'Nawaz Sharif must honour the deal that sent him into exile seven years ago and stay out of the country until 2010'.

Just before his departure Nawaz Sharif realized that notwithstanding the clear Supreme Court decision, he would be sent back to Jeddah. He therefore asked Shahbaz Sharif to stay back in London. His arrival and forced exile was reported by the media (*Nation*, 11 September 2007) in the following words:

Under unprecedented security measures at Islamabad International Airport, PIA flight PK-786 landed with former premier Mian Nawaz Sharif on board but in a most dramatic fashion he was once again bundled out to Saudi Arabia on a special plane after a stay of about four hours. As the whole city was sealed off, the PML(N) delegations coming from various parts of the country to welcome their leader were stopped by the authorities. However, in small bunches they engaged in scuffles with security officials at various places in the city but could not make it to the airport due to heavy deployment of police force and barricades erected at all the entry and exit points of the airport.

· Mian Nawaz Sharif was travelling in the club class but as the plane reached the apron, on the suggestion of his companions, he moved to the economy class where he stayed with his entourage for about one and half hours. During this period some security officials asked him to provide them with his passport so that they could complete the necessary immigration requirements, but Mian Nawaz Sharif refused to hand them his passport and insisted to complete the process himself. After negotiations, Mian Nawaz Sharif along with his companions and media team was moved to the Rawal Lounge where he himself got the immigration clearance.

The officials present at the airport said that during this period, some officials kept on negotiating with him probably trying to bring him round to follow their plan. But when Mian Nawaz Sharif insisted to remain here and face the cases against him, a National Accountability Bureau official, Lt.-Col. (retd) Azhar Mahmood Qazi came and served on him the arrest warrant issued by NAB Chairman Naveed Ahsan. Mian Nawaz Sharif received the warrants and later was told that they would now take him to Karachi jail. They forced him to the rear gates of the Rawal Lounge, pushing back his team members who insisted on accompanying him but the security officials in plain clothes pushed them back and in the process also roughed up Mian Nawaz Sharif. Mian Nawaz Sharif was put on a PIA Airbus 310, standing on the Western side of the apron, which immediately took off around 1 p.m. Later it was disclosed by the authorities that Mian Nawaz Sharif had been dispatched to Jeddah where he was likely to complete the rest of his exile term.

On 30 October 2007, as the Supreme Court heard Khawaja Asif's contempt petition, it asked the attorney general to identify a person or persons who had violated the Supreme Court order of 23 August. Apparently, the court remarked, the contemnor was the prime minister since he was reported to have ordered the foreign ministry to arrange a special plane to take Nawaz Sharif to Jeddah. An answer to this question was due at the next hearing of the case on 8 November, but with the declaration of emergency on 3 November, that answer never came.

As the election time came closer and Benazir Bhutto announced on 8 October that she would be returning to Pakistan on 18 October, the pressure on Nawaz Sharif from party leaders and workers became intense.

Finally, Nawaz Sharif landed in Pakistan on 25 November 2007, along with his brother Shahbaz Sharif and wife Kulsum Nawaz and received a historic welcome. Four days earlier Musharraf had specially flown to Saudi Arabia to request King Abdullah to prevent Nawaz Sharif from returning to Pakistan till after the elections due on 8 January 2008. The Saudi king, already concerned about the adverse public reaction among the Pakistani public, over the forcible re-exile of Nawaz Sharif on 10 September 2007, politely told Musharraf that after Benazir Bhutto's return in October 2007 'it would be extremely difficult to hold back another former prime minister'.

The arrival of Nawaz Sharif was reported by the daily *Nation* (26 November 2007) in the following words:

Former Prime Minister and PML(N) Quaid Nawaz Sharif along with his entire family arrived in Lahore on Sunday evening after seven years of forced exile. His return, welcomed by all the opposition leaders including Benazir Bhutto, heralds a new phase of politics in the country. Nawaz Sharif, former Chief Minister Punjab Shahbaz Sharif, Begum Kulsum Nawaz along with their 40 family members arrived here after seven-year exile.

While on 10 September (last), he was sent back to Saudi Arabia hours after he landed in Islamabad, this time he landed quite freely and his party men were given a free hand to organise a befitting welcome to their Quaid, giving the impression among the public that he is coming with a prior understanding with the government which the Sharifs denied strongly.

As a Saudi Royal plane carrying Nawaz Sharif, and other family members touched down at Lahore Airport around 6:30 p.m., thousands of jubilant party workers braving the security reached the airport, greeted the Sharifs on their return after a long drawn-out absence from the country and its politics. Though, it was mainly the show organised by PML(N), leaders from APDM including Liaquat Baloch, Farid Piracha and Sajid Mir were also present at the airport to welcome Nawaz Sharif. In his brief address at the airport, Nawaz said that he had not come to Pakistan for any deal or temptation of office. 'If I had to strike a deal, I would have done this when my father died and so I could bury him with my own hands', Nawaz asserted. Nawaz, facing a very charged crowd, said that together with party workers and people of Pakistan, he would make every effort to restore democracy in the country and end dictatorship.

On this occasion, he demanded of the government to restore judges deposed under PCO as well as the Constitution to its original position. He said that final decision on whether to boycott elections would be taken once the deadline set by APDM expired. He thanked the people who came to welcome him despite all odds. 'Landing in the city and my return to the country is one of the greatest moments in my life' Nawaz, sweating profusely, said. 'I have not returned to get any position but to save the nation and the country', Nawaz said.

Thousands of PML(N) supporters accorded a rousing welcome to their leaders. The PML(N) central leadership included Javed Hashmi, Raja Zafarul Haq, Iqbal Zafar Jhagra, Siddiqul Farooq, Rafiq Tarar, Tehmina Daultana, Saad Rafiq, Ahsan Iqbal, Sartaj Aziz, Sardar Ayaz Saddiq, Sardar Mehtab Abbasi and Nisar Ali Khan.

Although Nawaz Sharif returned to Pakistan only one day before the final date for filing nomination papers for the 2008 elections, his return virtually changed the political landscape of the country. As described later in this chapter, PML(N) emerged as the second largest party, after the PPP, in the National Assembly and as the largest party in the Punjab Assembly.

Musharraf's Re-election

In the last quarter of 2007, Musharraf's re-election as president for the next five years had become the most contentious issue in the political history of Pakistan. Musharraf himself was fully convinced that he had to stay in power to see a smooth transition to civilian rule under his watchful supervision and to tackle extremism and terrorism in the coming years. On the plus side of his game plan, he had the full backing of the 'Establishment' and support of PML(Q) and other components of ruling coalition, which was in any case totally dependent on him for political survival. But the negative side was growing stronger.

The mainstream political parties in the APDM like PML(N), Jamaat-e-Islami and Tehreek-e-Insaf were fully committed to the 'Go Musharraf Go' agenda. But having deported Nawaz Sharif and having made a 'deal' with the PPP, and half a deal with Maulana Fazlur Rehman of JUI(F), Musharraf had ensured that the political opposition would not be able to block his re-election, even if most of them resigned from the assemblies. But more worrisome was the lawyers' movement, supported by a broad segment of the civil society. After winning the case for restoring the chief justice and gaining the support of the public through unprecedented exposure on the media for their struggle to establish the supremacy of the rule of law, the lawyers had become fully involved in the presidential election. Since the main opposition parties were boycotting the president's election through resignations, in order to destroy its credibility, the lawyers nominated a very respectable member of their fraternity, Justice (retd) Wajihuddin Ahmad as their candidate for the presidential election. They knew that they did not have any chance of winning, but at least they would be able to mount a legal battle, in his name, to challenge the candidature of General Musharraf.

The real drama started on 29 September, the day for filing nomination papers in the presidential election. A day earlier, the Supreme Court had decided, in a 6 to 3 verdict to dismiss, on technical grounds, the maintainability of petitions challenging the eligibility of a serving army officer to be a candidate for the presidency of Pakistan. As political leaders and lawyers marched towards the election commission to protest against Musharraf's nomination, the local administration and police unleashed a brutal attack. Even the media representatives who were covering these events were beaten up in the glare of TV cameras. The Supreme Court took suo moto notice of these excesses and suspended the chief commissioner, inspector general police, the deputy commissioner and several other officials, convicting them subsequently, on 1 November, to varying prison terms ranging from one day to one month.

As the election commission accepted Musharraf's nomination papers, a number of cases were filed in the Supreme Court challenging his eligibility on different legal grounds. After many tense sessions, the Supreme Court decided that the elections could go ahead on 6 October, but its result would not be declared until the Supreme Court had ruled on Musharraf's eligibility.

But another act of this drama was being played behind the scene between London, Dubai and Islamabad. Musharraf having decided to take any 'U' turn that may be necessary to secure his re-election was ready to implement the deal with Benazir Bhutto. A statement was placed on record in the Supreme Court that if elected, he would take off his uniform before taking oath as president. One day before the polling date, a National Reconciliation Ordinance (NRO) was issued on 5 October to withdraw all corruption and other cases against Benazir Bhutto and other politicians and bureaucrats under the code of criminal procedure or the National Accountability Ordinance. The relief was applied only to cases filed between 1 January 1996 and 12 October 1999 in order to exclude cases filed against Nawaz Sharif after 12 October 1999. Amidst strong media criticism of this strange piece of legislation, the NRO was immediately challenged in the Supreme Court. There were rumours that having achieved its objective of dividing the opposition, PML(Q) leaders would not mind if the Supreme Court would strike down the NRO.

Another disgusting facet of this drama was unfolding in NWFP. The APDM parties had decided at the meeting in Islamabad on 29 September to implement the APC decision to resign from the assemblies before the presidential elections. They had also decided that the chief minister NWFP would advise the governor to dissolve the provincial assembly so that the electoral college of the presidential election is eroded with the absence of one of the four provincial assemblies. But the chief minister, under the watchful eye of Maulana Fazlur Rehman, delayed the dissolution advice for three days. Meanwhile, the pro-Musharraf opposition in NWFP managed to muster a few votes to file a no-confidence motion against the chief minister. Under the constitution, a chief minister against whom a no-confidence motion has been filed cannot ask for the dissolution of the assembly. As a result of this implicit 'deal', the NWFP Assembly remained intact, and opposition members were able to vote for Musharraf, giving him 18 additional votes. In the absence of these votes, Musharraf's total tally would have been 53 per cent, rather than 57 per cent of total eligible votes. Maulana Fazlur Rehman, to cover this tacit support to Musharraf, went on the offensive against other members of MMA and APDM, saying the resignation of their members from the assemblies before the presidential elections, had left their chief minister exposed in the vote of no-confidence.

On 6 October, Pervez Musharraf bagged 235 votes out of a total of 412 votes that constitute the electoral college in parliament and the four provincial assemblies. Justice (retd) Wajihuddin got two votes. As agreed, PPP did not resign from the assemblies, nor voted for

Musharraf. But by staying in the assemblies and even putting up its own candidate (Makhdoom Amin Fahim) it lent a degree of credibility to the election process. The results of the election were announced with considerable fanfare and jubilation but were not officially notified. Ten days later, the Supreme Court started hearing, on day-to-day basis, the petitions challenging Musharraf's eligibility for contesting the presidential election, mainly on the ground that he did not fulfil the condition laid down in Article 63-1(k) that 'a person shall be disqualified from being elected as a member of parliament if he has been in the service of Pakistan unless a period of two years has elapsed since he ceased to be in such service.' Under Article 41(2) a person shall not be qualified for election as president unless he is qualified to be elected as member of the National Assembly.

Another Mini Martial Law Called Emergency

The *Economist* had predicted a state of emergency in Pakistan in its issue of 13 October, under the title 'Farce in Pakistan':

The re-election of General Pervez Musharraf as Pakistan's president on October 6th was 'fair and transparent'. That was the considered judgment of his chief sidekick, the prime minister. 'Unrepresentative, rigged and at gunpoint' would have been nearer the mark. General Musharraf is inching towards a destination that, in the abstract, appears acceptable: a power-sharing arrangement with Benazir Bhutto, a former prime minister who leads Pakistan's most popular political party from exile. But, to get there, the General is taking so un-democratic a route that he has already almost ensured that such a settlement will be illegitimate and unstable.

The election was legally dubious. The electoral college is made up of the federal and provincial parliaments. A general election is due by mid-January, so logic would suggest that the new bodies should elect the president. General elections, however, might produce less supportive legislatures. As it was, opposition parties resigned from the parliaments rather than endorse this travesty. Even Miss Bhutto's party, although its members stayed out, abstained from the vote.

Also, Pakistan's Supreme Court has been mulling whether General Musharraf can be elected president while still army chief. Bizarrely, it allowed the election to proceed but with no winner to be declared until it has decided on the General's eligibility. General Musharraf has said he will quit his army post before being sworn in as president next month. But he has not done so yet, and his henchmen are hinting that the consequence of an adverse judgment will be a state of emergency. So the court faces a choice between legitimizing military rule by 'election' or provoking military rule by other means.

Unfortunately, Musharraf did not wait for an 'adverse judgment' from the Supreme Court while imposing emergency on 3 November 2007. As Chaudhry Shujaat Hussain confirmed in a story published in the *Guardian* of 5 November 2007, 'The decision to impose emergency was triggered by fears that the Supreme Court would rule against General Musharraf's recent re-election in a legal appeal. A friendly judge passed the information to the government last Wednesday (31 October). So we had no option.'

Under Article 232 of the constitution, the president can declare a state of emergency 'if he is satisfied that grave emergency exists in which the security of Pakistan is threatened by war or external aggression or by national disturbance beyond the power of a provincial government to control'. But under this power, Musharraf could not have achieved the real objective of this action—namely to get rid of the defiant judiciary. So he imposed a state of emergency in his capacity as the army chief, suspended the constitution and issued a new Provisional Constitution Order (PCO) on 3 November 2007 requiring all members of the superior judiciary, namely the Supreme Court and all the High Courts, to take a fresh oath under PCO. The majority refused and they were treated as dismissed from service.

Another subtle obstacle in Musharraf's game plan was the media, especially the electronic media. Musharraf's earlier attempt on 9 March 2007 to have a pliant judiciary, by dismissing Chief Justice Iftikhar Muhammad Chaudhry, had backfired, when the private TV channels like GEO, ARY and AAJ, gave extensive coverage to the sustained protest movement launched by the lawyers and supported by the civil society and opposition political parties, to seek reinstatement of the chief justice. So this time the president promulgated on 3 November 2007 the Pakistan Electronic Media Regulatory Authority (Third Amendment) Ordinance 2007, under which blanket powers were given to PEMRA to seize broadcast or distribution equipment or seal the premises of the licensee in the garb of 'public interest'. Violations of this law could involve three-year imprisonment and a fine up to Rs10 million. Under this draconian law, the government directed all cable operators to block all TV news channels including foreign news channels, like BBC, CNN and Al-Jezirah, as soon as the emergency was declared. In fact, they were not even given the opportunity to 'violate' the new law or even become aware of the amendments before action was taken. The majority of people in Pakistan became aware of some kind of an emergency situation on 3 November, when all TV screens, showing news, suddenly went blank. The actual news was announced by the official PTV two hours later. Instead of calling a spade a spade, Musharraf called this mini martial law an 'Emergency'.

Virtually the entire country revolted against this unwarranted assault on the two main pillars of state namely the judiciary and the media and simultaneously the government agencies resorted to brute force to suppress any agitation or dissent.

On 4 November, all the sixty-five members of the Human Rights Commission of Pakistan, were arrested in Lahore, when they were holding an indoor meeting in the Commission Secretariat, to discuss the human rights implications of the PCO. They were kept in detention for three days and then released on bail. They included many prominent citizens like Salima Hashmi, Shahid Kardar, and Parvez Hassan.

The lawyers who came out in large numbers in Lahore, Karachi, Peshawar, Quetta and Islamabad were beaten up, tear-gassed and their leaders sent to distant prisons, without telling their family members about their locations. The newly elected president of the Supreme Court Bar Association, Chaudhry Aitzaz Ahsan, along with his senior colleagues, Munir Ahmad, Tariq Mahmood, and Ali Ahmad Kurd, were arrested on the evening of 3 November 2007, the day the Emergency was declared.

But the greatest atrocity was inflicted on the superior judiciary. With one stroke, 14 out of 17 judges of the Supreme Court and 45 judges of various High Courts, who refused to take oath under the PCO, which would have violated their basic oath and responsibility to defend the constitution of Pakistan, were virtually dismissed from service. They were the cream of Pakistan's judicial system and at the peak of their respective careers. Along with their dismissal, many of these custodians of the rule of law were also put under house arrest, although they had violated no law. Their telephones were disconnected, their family

322   BETWEEN DREAMS AND REALITIES

members were not allowed to go out or meet anyone and attempts were made to deport them forcibly to their native places. Desperate attempts were made to find new judges or lawyers willing to serve as judges so that at least some of the vacant positions could be filled but without much success. The Supreme Court Bar Association announced an indefinite boycott of the superior courts to prevent its members from appearing before judges who had taken oath under the PCO. In its sixty-year history, Pakistan had never seen such a major crisis virtually paralyzing the country's judicial system.

The game plan under the PCO of 3 November 2007 was not confined to the re-election of Musharraf as president for the next five years but was also meant to facilitate 'positive results at the next general elections, at that time scheduled for 8 January 2008. Under clause 3(2) of the PCO, 'No judgement, decree or writ, order or process whatever shall be made or issued by any court or tribunal against the president, or the prime minister or any authority designated by the president.' This provision effectively eroded the authority of the Supreme Court to provide justice or relief to any person adversely affected by state repression, as widely practiced by arresting judges and lawyers, closing down TV channels, banning certain media anchors from appearing in their popular shows. Having thus ensured unfettered powers for himself to function without any legal or constitutional challenge, the game plan for 'winning' the 2008 elections was elaborately fine tuned.

CHAPTER 14

Revival of Democracy under Zardari (2008–2013)

The prospects of reviving democracy after eight years of Musharraf's rule were further overshadowed by his game plan to retain power as an elected president. Following his re-election as president, by a divided National Assembly on 6 October 2007 and subsequently the passing of an Provisional Constitutional Order (PCO) of 3 November 2007, Musharraf opposed both Benazir Bhutto and Nawaz Sharif's return to Pakistan. Having delivered her part of the deal under the National Reconciliation Order (NRO), Benazir Bhutto announced on 8 October 2007 that she would be returning to Pakistan on 18 October 2007 and would land in Karachi after eight years in exile.

Elaborate preparations were made to transport thousands of PPP supporters to Karachi to welcome her. Unlike the hostile treatment extended to Nawaz Sharif six weeks earlier, the administrative machinery, federal, provincial and local, did everything to facilitate an historic welcome for Benazir Bhutto. From 3 p.m. to midnight her slow moving caravan had covered only half the journey to Quaid-i-Azam's mausoleum through a festive crowd. As it reached Karsaz, there were two loud explosions, killing 150 people and injuring 500, but narrowly missing Benazir and the entire top leadership of PPP travelling with her on the bullet proof truck. The entire nation was shocked at this ghastly tragedy. The authorities quickly blamed the extremists linked to Al-Qaeda but Benazir and some of her colleagues pointed the finger at official agencies. Everyone was worried about the future of politics in the country when workers of a major political party could not even receive their leader without suffering such a major loss of innocent lives. Musharraf's answer to these accusations came a fortnight later when he, in his capacity as chief of army staff, declared a state of emergency in the country on 3 November 2007.

The Tragic Death of Benazir Bhutto

These worries reached their climax with the assassination of Benazir Bhutto in Rawalpindi on 27 December 2007, sending shock waves not only in Pakistan but throughout the world. Every major political leader in the US and Europe sent condolence messages and the UN Security Council passed a resolution condemning her death. All major newspapers and TV channels ran cover stories, highlighting her courageous and turbulent political career.

Within Pakistan, the reaction was violent. Within a few hours, as the news of her death spread, angry mobs attacked life and property in every major city and town, especially in Sindh, burning and destroying shops, banks, industrial units, vehicles, railways and private property. In the next three days, 25 trains, several railway stations, 200 bank branches, many election offices, scores of petrol pumps, and hundreds of vehicles had been burnt by screaming mobs. About 50 innocent people were also killed. The security forces did not intervene ostensibly because they did not want to kill more people and the police simply abandoned their police stations because they could not face the mobs. The economy suffered a serious jolt, the stock market went down by 7 per cent in three days, the rupee lost its value, public transport came to a standstill creating shortages of petrol and other essential items. According to one estimate, the violence and disruption following Benazir Bhutto's death reduced the GDP growth by 1.5 to 2.0 per cent in 2007–8.

The outpouring of grief and sympathy for the bereaved family and the PPP was unprecedented. Leaders belonging to all political parties, the media and the civil society converged on Larkana to offer their condolences. Nawaz Sharif reached the hospital in Rawalpindi as soon as he heard the news and cried spontaneously when he heard the news of her death. 'Benazir Bhutto was also my sister and I will be with you to take revenge for her death. Don't feel alone. I am with you', he said addressing the grief-stricken PPP workers in the hospital. Two days later he, along with sixty leaders from PML(N) and some other political parties visited Naudero to offer condolences. These gestures were very well received in Sindh and according to some observers moderated the violent attacks on non-Sindhi shops and factories at that delicate juncture.

The PPP showed great maturity in handling the crisis created by the sudden departure of their charismatic leader. On 29 December 2007, soon after the *soyem* ceremony in Naudero, the central working committee of the party met. Asif Ali Zardari produced a handwritten Will, which Benazir Bhutto, he said, had sent to her friends in Washington before returning to Pakistan. In compliance with this Will, the central working committee elected Benazir's nineteen-year-old son, Bilawal as the chairman of the party and her husband Asif Ali Zardari as co-chairman. It was announced that Bilawal's name had been changed from Bilawal Zardari to Bilawal Bhutto Zardari. He was to go back to Oxford to complete his studies over the next three years and in his absence the co-chairman, Asif Ali Zardari was to handle the affairs of the party. It was also indicated in less specific terms that since Asif Ali Zardari was not participating in the forthcoming elections, 'someone like' Makhdoom Amin Fahim would be PPP's candidate for the office of the prime minister.

But the government was not equally forthcoming in dealing with the cause of Benazir's death or in identifying those who may have committed this unforgivable crime. While waiting for results of the investigation, a representative of the ministry of interior announced that Benazir had died by hitting her head on the lever of the car's sunroof as she was trying to duck after the blast. But two days later, a film telecast by Britain's Channel 4 showed clearly that she was shot in the head, just before a suicide bomber exploded a device, killing himself and twenty-three other innocent citizens, including her security guard. This bizarre contradiction started a serious controversy which would take a long time to resolve as suspicions spread about the government's involvement in the tragedy. Asif Ali Zardari in an article published in *News Media* in the US, a week after Benazir's death said:

> Her murder does not end her vision and must not be allowed to empower her assassins. Those responsible—within and outside of the Pakistan government—must be held accountable. I call on the United Nations to commence a thorough investigation of the circumstances, facts and cover-up of my wife's murder, modelled on the investigation into the assassination of former Lebanese Prime Minister, Rafiq al-Hariri. I also call on the friends of democracy in the West, in particular the United States and Britain, to endorse the call for an international, independent investigation. An investigation conducted by the government of Pakistan will have no

credibility in my country or anywhere else. One does not put the fox in charge of the henhouse.

In panic, the government invited Britain's Scotland Yard to assist with the investigation. But its report released after several weeks of well publicized activities did not produce any conclusive indication of those involved nor closed the basic controversy, till the new parliament, after the 18 February elections, passed a resolution calling upon the government to approach the United Nations for a full international investigation into this gruesome tragedy.

The UN Commission of Inquiry, chaired by the Chilean Ambassador to UN, Heraldo Munoz submitted its report in 2010. It concluded that the task of assigning criminal responsibility can only be undertaken by competent authorities of Pakistan. The report did however emphasize the following:

- The security arrangements by Pakistan's federal government and local authorities to protect Benazir Bhutto were 'fatally insufficient and ineffective'.
- Subsequent investigations into her death were prejudiced and involved a whitewash, literally of the crime scene also.
- Police actions and omissions, including the hosing down of the crime scene and failure to collect and preserve evidence, inflicted irreparable damage to the investigation.
- Governments' assertions that Mehsud and Al-Qaeda were responsible, was made well before any proper investigation had started, pre-empting, prejudicing and hindering the subsequent investigation.
- Ms. Bhutto faced serious threats from a number of sources, including Al-Qaeda, the Taliban and local *jihadi* groups and potentially from elements in the Pakistani establishment. But the investigation focused on down level operatives linked to Baitullah Mehsud.

The Commission recommended the establishment of a fully independent Truth and Reconciliation Commission to investigate political killings, disappearances and terrorism in Pakistan.

It is really tragic that on 27 December 2007, not only Pakistan lost an outstanding political leader but as a nation, we have not been able to trace the conspiracy that led to her assassination or bring to justice those who committed this most unforgivable crime of this century.

The 2008 Elections

Even judging by the history of flawed electioneering in Pakistan, the prospects of free and fair elections looked very remote. That is why in November 2007, soon after Nawaz Sharif's return to Pakistan, the All Parties Democratic Movement (APDM) met in Lahore and decided to boycott the elections. On 3 December 2007, Nawaz Sharif and some other leaders of APDM met Benazir Bhutto to persuade her party to join the boycott. They agreed at this meeting to formulate a charter of demands and to boycott the elections if their demands were not met. The demands included an independent election commission, a genuinely neutral caretaker setup, and the release of all political and judicial prisoners, rolling back of all politically motivated transfers of officials, suspending the district *nazims*, complete media freedom and no engineering of election results.

But the euphoria over this show of unity by the entire opposition was short-lived, as Pakistan Peoples Party (PPP) continued its preparations for the elections and Maulana Fazlur Rehman also announced they would take part in the elections. A similar announcement soon came from Asfandyar Wali Khan, the head of Awami National Party (ANP). Nawaz Sharif quickly consulted his colleagues and announced that the boycott would provide a useful strategy only if all the opposition parties participate in it. Since that was no longer possible, the PML(N) would also participate in the elections, but under protest against the pre-poll rigging that was in full swing.

Nawaz Sharif pushed for the boycott option once again soon after the tragic assassination of Benazir Bhutto on 27 December 2007, but withdrew this call after his condolence call at Naudero, at the request of Asif Ali Zardari.

A week later, the Election Commission, citing large-scale damage to election offices in Sindh in the rioting following Benazir Bhutto's assassination, postponed the elections from 8 January to 18 February.

The six-week period in the run up to the election was marked by very high tensions throughout the country. The extent of political polarization, which had been high throughout Musharraf's eight-year rule, reached new heights. The internal security situation, tragically dramatized by Benazir Bhutto's death on 27 December, sent out new shock waves, giving the government a new handle to restrict election rallies and public meetings by the opposition leaders. On top of these chronic problems, the apprehensions about massive rigging in the elections, the post-election manipulation of results created widespread concerns. These apprehensions were strengthened by several factors:

- With the illegal removal of the upper layers of the superior judiciary, no one expected any justice or relief from those now responsible for supervising the elections.
- The rejection of the nomination papers of Nawaz Sharif and Shahbaz Sharif on flimsy grounds clearly showed the pro-government bias of election officials.
- The aggressive manner in which the provincial governments in Punjab and Sindh promoted the King's Party and continued their unprecedented advertising and election campaign led to widespread allegations about the misuse of state resources.
- Massive inaccuracies in the electoral rolls strengthened rumours that the ruling party would try to cast bogus votes by those registered more than once, through ghost polling stations or postal ballots.
- Musharraf threw his neutrality to the winds when on the eve of the election, he told Jemima Khan during an interview for a British magazine, only three days before the election that PML(Q) which supported him would certainly have the majority after the 18 February elections.

While these apprehensions were reaching new heights, and threats of a civil war were voiced by Asif Ali Zardari and many other leaders, certain important developments were taking place behind the scenes.

In less than a month after Musharraf doffed his uniform, the new army chief, General Ashfaq Parvez Kayani gave clear signals that he would like to end the army's interference in politics. He issued instructions to withdraw hundreds of army officers from civilian posts and prohibited contacts with political leaders. On the eve of the elections, according to a report in the daily *News* of 24 February, clear instructions were issued to the ISI, MI, district officials and district *nazims* not to interfere with the polls. This was a key factor in defeating the election game plan prepared earlier to ensure a victory for the King's Party. The polling on election day was reasonably fair and complaints about irregularities were promptly investigated. The credit for relatively fair elections thus goes to General Ashfaq Parvez Kayani.

The whole nation heaved a sigh of relief when the election results were declared and the pro-Musharraf parties were defeated. The anti-Musharraf parties gained a clear mandate from the people for launching a transition from military to democratic rule. The final election results including women and minority seats were as given in the following table:

Results of 2008 Elections for the National Assembly

Party	Punjab	Sindh	NWFP	Balochistan	Islamabad	FATA	Women* Minorities	Total
Allocated Seats	183	75	43	17	2	12	10	242
PPP	62	39	13	6	–		4	124
PML(N)	81	–	5	–	2		3	91
PML(Q)	35	6	6	5	–		2	54
ANP	–	–	13	–	–		–	13
MMA	–	–	4	3	–		–	7
MQM	–	24	–	–	–		1	25
PML(F)	1	4	–	–	–		–	5
BNP(A)	–	–	–	1	–		–	1
PPP(S)	–	–	1	–	–		–	1
NPP	–	1	–	–	–		–	1
Ind	3	1	1	2	–	10	–	17
Total	**182**	**75**	**43**	**17**	**2**	**10**	**10**	**339****

* There are 35 reserved women seats in Punjab, 14 in Sindh, 8 in N 1- " and 3 in Balochistan.
The parties are given women seats in proportion to the general seats won in each province. The 10 reserved minorities seats are distributed among the parties in proportion to overall seats secured by them.
** Election in NA-41 suspended, NA-42 postponed and NA-123 withheld.

Source: Election Commission of Pakistan

Results of Elections 2008 for the Provincial Assemblies

Party	Punjab	Sindh	NWFP	Balochistan
Allocated Seats	371	168	124	65
PPP	107	93	30	12
PML(N)	170	–	9	–
PML(Q)	84	9	6	19
ANP	–	2	48	4
MMA	2	–	14	10
MQM	–	51	–	–
PML(F)	3	8	–	–
BNP(A)	–	–	–	7
PPP(S)	–	–	6	–
NPP	–	3	–	–
Others	4	–	11	13
Total	370	166	124	65

Elections in PS-82 and PS-87 withheld

Source: Election Commission of Pakistan

These historic election results virtually heralded the dawn of a new era in Pakistan by frustrating whatever conspiracies were being hatched to maintain the status quo and to keep the PPP and PML(N) out of power. In a remarkable display of maturity and unity, the voters, egged on by the civil society, had voted in favour of democracy and the rule of law and threw out elements which were supporting continuing military rule with a civilian facade.

Despite pre-poll rigging in some areas and the visible partiality of the caretaker setup, the PML(Q) won only 42 out of 268 contested seats in the National Assembly. That was less than 13 per cent, compared to 26 and 20 per cent by PPP and PML(N) respectively. But for the rigging in some constituencies and boycott by some APDM parties, the PML(Q) tally would have been even lower. At least twenty-three ministers, who served in the cabinet of Prime Minister Shaukat Aziz, lost the elections including such stalwarts as Chaudhry Shujaat Hussain, Sheikh Rashid Ahmad, Humayun Akhtar, Wasi Zafar, and Sher Afgan Niazi.

One of the most positive outcomes of the election was ANP's resounding success by capturing 33 seats out of 91 contested seats in the NWFP Assembly, relegating MMA to fourth place with only 10 seats against 54 in the 2002 elections. The voters, contrary to Musharraf's favourite theme that the extremists will take over if he ever left the scene, brought in progressive and moderate forces which believed in democracy, religious tolerance and fundamental rights of the people.

A day after the election, the Human Rights Commission of Pakistan issued the following statement:

> The Human Rights Commission of Pakistan applauds the people of Pakistan who overcame several obstacles and despite pre-poll rigging gave a clear verdict in favour of democratic governance. Regrettably, this opportunity was not available to the electorate in Balochistan. Boycott of worthy political leadership from contesting the elections and their call for staying away from the polls; have not reflected a genuine will of the people of Balochistan in the 2008 polls. This will pose a challenge to the federal parliament as well as the future provincial government of the Province.
>
> The people of Pakistan have placed a monumental responsibility on the winning political parties to ensure that the democratic transition takes place. In addition, there are expectations from the new Parliament to restore the deposed judiciary, improve law and order and to solve the economic crisis. The new government will also be expected to find imaginative ways of combating terrorism, without putting the lives of non-combatants in danger. This will require policies and actions built through consensus. Unilateral and rash decisions of the past have not curbed the rise of 'Talibanization' but added to the miseries of the people. A large number of people have been displaced, lost their lives and been regularly exposed to violence.
>
> Pakistan's civil society, too, must continue to play their role and maintain closer interaction with political parties.

The business community also welcomed the results of the elections, as the Karachi stock market went up by 627 points from 14,354 to 14,981 points within four days after the elections.

The leaders of three main winning political parties, the PPP, PML(N) and ANP announced on 21 February that they had agreed to form coalition governments at the centre and in the provinces. This breakthrough was announced at a joint press conference by Asif Ali Zardari, co-chairman of PPP, Nawaz Sharif, Quaid of PML(N), and Asfandyar Wali Khan, president of ANP. They also indicated broad agreement on various issues including the difficult issue of reinstatement of deposed judges, a key priority for PML(N). With a comfortable 55 seats majority at the centre between the three parties, 57 per cent in the Punjab Assembly, 54 per cent in Sindh Assembly and 53 per cent in NWFP Assembly, the prospects for the advent of genuine democracy could not be brighter. In keeping with democratic principles, it was agreed that the government at the centre and in Sindh would be led by PPP, in Punjab by PML(N) and in NWFP by ANP.

As Yousaf Raza Gillani took his oath as prime minister on 31 March, along with a 23-member cabinet, including eight from PML(N), (Ishaq Dar, Nisar Ali Khan, Khawaja Asif, Ahsan Iqbal, Mahtab Abbasi, Shahid Khaqan Abbasi, Rana Tanwir, and Saad Rafiq), no one could have predicted that this coalition would last only six weeks. But one thing was crystal clear: that these elections had heralded the beginning of the end of the Musharraf's era.

Musharraf's Departure

The month of August 2008 began, for most Pakistanis, with intense anxiety, caused by a formidable array of problems, each compounding the other.

The situation in the Federally Administered Tribal Areas (FATA) and the adjoining areas of the North West Frontier Province (NWFP) had been deteriorating rapidly and the economy was sinking, with independent observers predicting an economic meltdown within a few weeks.

In the middle of these grave threats to the political and economic stability of Pakistan, the gulf between the two main coalition partners in the post-election setup, namely the PPP and PML(N) over the Judges issue, was widening. In July 2008, both Nawaz Sharif and Asif Ali Zardari had gone abroad to London and Dubai respectively, leaving the future of the coalition hanging in mid-air.

Under tremendous public pressure, Asif Zardari and Nawaz Sharif returned to Pakistan in the last week of July and speculation about the judges' issue and the future of the coalition began to mount. Nawaz Sharif convened a meeting of the central working committee of PML(N), a day before his meeting with Asif Ali Zardari on 5 August, preceded by a smaller meeting of twenty-five key leaders and advisors of the party. I met him separately just before the smaller meeting to present some ideas to save the coalition. But when the meeting started, there was virtually no support for a flexible approach on the judges' issue or enthusiasm for saving the coalition.

The news of a breakthrough in the Zardari-Nawaz Sharif talks hit the headlines on 7 August. A written agreement had been reached between the two leaders which was read out by Asif Ali Zardari. The text of this agreement, released subsequently, is reproduced below:

1. Both parties, PPP and PML(N), re-affirm their commitment to restore all the judges, who were removed by General Musharraf unconstitutionally on 3 November 2007 and to bring judiciary back to the position and form in which it existed on 2 November 2007 as agreed between the parties in the Murree Declaration, signed on 9 March 2008.

2. In pursuance of Murree Declaration, both parties agree to proceed in the following manner in order to implement the agreement:

   a) Finalizing the draft of the resolution to be tabled in National Assembly for restoration of judges: Timeline is 11 August 2008.

   b) Tabling and passing of resolution by National Assembly for restoration of judges: Timeline is within one day of vote on impeachment motion or resignation of President.

   c) Issuance of executive order by competent authority to restore the judiciary to 2 November 2007 position in Supreme Court and High Courts: Timeline is instantly upon passing of resolution by National Assembly.

   d) Transfer of official protocol to restored Chief Justice of Supreme Court, Chief Justices of High Courts and the Judges: Timeline is instantly with issuance of executive order:

3. The eight judges of Sindh High Court whose appointment has been held in abeyance shall be restored along with all other judges together. In case there is any legally binding direction received for issuance of notification and administrating oath to the said eight judges, such direction shall not be acted upon until the restoration of all judges removed on 3 November 2007 unconstitutionally by General Musharraf is made as per the Murree Declaration.

4. It is agreed that after the success of the impeachment resolution against the present incumbent or his resignation, a consensus

will be evolved amongst the coalition partners on the name of his replacement along the following lines:

a) In case the office of the President still retains the powers acquired under 17th Amendment, a nationally respected, non-partisan, and pro-democracy figure acceptable to coalition partners will be put forward as the consensus candidate for the office of the President.
b) In case the 17th Amendment is repealed and the powers of the President are restricted to the original powers as envisaged in 1973 Constitution then the PPP will have the right to put forward its own candidate.

As revealed later, an earlier handwritten agreement had been signed on 5 August to begin the process to impeach President Musharraf. This set into motion the chain of dramatic events that culminated in the resignation of Musharraf on 18 August 2008.

The initial reaction from Musharraf and his supporters was one of defiance. 'The ruling coalition has a constitutional right to move the motion for impeachment but he has an equal right to defend himself' his spokesman said. Leaders of PML(Q) also made similar statements about their resolve to defeat the impeachment move.

The second act of this political drama was titled the 'numbers game' under Article 47 of the Constitution; a motion to impeach the president 'for violating the constitution for gross misconduct' can be moved by 50 per cent of the total membership in either house of parliament. After debate it needs the support of two-third members of both the houses, sitting together. Under this formula the coalition needed a total of 295 votes in the joint session of 442 members of parliament—342 in the National Assembly and 100 in the Senate.

On first count, the coalition had a total of 277 votes—237 in the National Assembly and 40 in the Senate. But there were 20 independent members from FATA, who normally voted with the government in power. As the drama began to unfold, the size of the 'forward blocks', namely those members of PML(Q) who were ready to change sides began to swell. 'They want to be on the right side of history at this juncture' one minister said. 'The Q-Leaguers will always be blamed for providing a civilian facade to the military rule. Here was a chance for some of them to whiten their sins, some other observers added to justify their predictions.

This swing in the numbers game in favour of the coalition was confirmed on 11 August when the Punjab Assembly passed a resolution saying, 'General (retd) Pervez Musharraf is unfit to hold the office of the president by virtue of being guilty of violating the constitution and/or gross misconduct on grounds, among others, that General (retd) Musharraf has subverted the constitution twice by holding it in abeyance'. The resolution then called upon General (retd) Pervez Musharraf, 'to take a vote of confidence from his electoral college or resign in terms of Article 44(3) of the Constitution. If he fails to do so, the parliament should give a notice of impeachment in accordance with Article 47 of the Constitution.'

Surprisingly, this resolution was passed by 321 members voting for it, with only 25 against in a house of 370. This showed that the size of the forward block, the breakaway group of PML(Q) which voted with PML(N) and PPP, had swelled from 34 to 56.

Similar resolutions were adopted by the NWFP Assembly on 12 August, by the Sindh Assembly on 13 August, and by the Balochistan Assembly on 15 August. Out of 728 members in the four provincial assemblies, only 29 had voted for Musharraf. The numbers game was over for Musharraf. Foreign friends from the US, UK and Saudi Arabia, who were negotiating with Musharraf to persuade him to resign rather than face the unpleasant impeachment process, were now convinced that the coalition partners had the numbers to impeach him.

The coalition partners also prolonged their discussions on the impeachment charge sheet against Musharraf to give him time to resign, amid speculations that, given his stubborn temperament, he might use the last trump card he still had—Article 58(2-b) to dissolve the National Assembly. The media, however reported discrete leaks that the corps commanders meeting held in the second week of August had decided not to support such a move, in view of the strong public sentiments against Musharraf. Persistent criticisms of Musharraf's policies and illegal actions from a group of retired generals and ex-servicemen perhaps also played a role in this decision.

The curtain finally fell on 18 August 2008. Early that morning there were announcements on the TV that Musharraf would address the nation at 1 p.m., amid rumours that he was going to announce his resignation.

I was in Islamabad that day for a seminar on rural development and decentralization presided over by Prime Minister Yousaf Raza Gillani. As the prime minister left after the inaugural session just before 1 p.m., many of us including rural development minister, Haji Ghulam Ahmad Bilour, rushed to the nearest TV set to listen to the speech.

Midway in his speech, as he was recounting his 'achievements' so forcefully, some of those present in the room started whispering '58(2b) is coming'. But soon his tone changed and with tears floating in his eyes, he said: 'I did nothing wrong and charges against me cannot be proven but I am resigning in the larger interest of the nation. I want to save Pakistan from de-stabilization'.

As I reflect on the rise and fall of Musharraf, I detect the dramatics of a Greek tragedy in which every actor plays the role he or she is destined to play but the end is tragic.

Musharraf's principal folly was his own assessment of his indispensable role in saving Pakistan. He had decided as early as the year 2002 when he first assumed the office of the president, following a dubious referendum, that he must retain effective power not just for five years but at least ten years. The first step in this game plan was the Seventeenth Amendment. The word 'preceding' was replaced, as already mentioned, by the word 'following' in Article 224 through the Seventeenth Amendment so that the outgoing assembly could re-elect him in 2007. The other plank of the same strategy was the attempt on 9 March 2007 to remove Chief Justice Iftikhar Muhammad Chaudhry since Musharraf wanted a more pliant judiciary to endorse his re-election in uniform. When Justice Iftikhar Muhammad Chaudhry refused to resign, he resorted to the unconstitutional act of issuing another Provisional Constitutional Order (PCO) on 3 November 2007 to suspend the Constitution and virtually sack sixty judges of the Supreme Court and High Courts and retain or induct those who were ready to take an oath under the new PCO. This edged the country towards a constitutional crisis caused by these unconstitutional acts that will haunt the nation for a long time.

This stubborn resolve of Musharraf to remain in power was not dampened even by the results of the 18 February elections, when the parties supporting him lost badly. He once again went back on his commitment to quit if 'his party' lost the election. He also forgot the assurance he had given to the Supreme Court in November 2007, that while re-elected by the outgoing assemblies he would also seek a vote of confidence from the new assemblies. Deep down, he was hopeful that the coalition between the PPP and PML(N) would not last long, because of the differences over the judges issue. As soon as PML(N) quits the coalition, he calculated, PPP would have to fall back on the support of PML(Q) and MQM and that would give him a chance not only to stay in office but regain greater leverage in the system. In making these calculations he ignored an important lesson of power politics: that as long as the remnants of the old power structure kept a sizeable slice of the political space, the new legitimate claimants thrown up by the February elections would have to stick together to capture that political space, before splitting over the division of the recaptured political space.

The western media gave very extensive coverage to the dramatic departure of Musharraf from the corridors of power and his legacy. The following editorial that appeared in the *Washington Post* of 21 August 2008 under the title 'Perils of Pakistan' that reflected the general trend of these comments:

> Pervez Musharraf stepped down as Pakistan's president on Monday, brought down by a combination of his own overreaching and the resistance of the parliamentary coalition that won elections six months ago. Having given up command of the Army in November, Musharraf was already a far weaker figure than the brash general who seized power in a 1999 coup. A very real threat of impeachment prompted him to leave four years earlier than planned. Given Musharraf's repressive record in domestic politics and his inconsistent support for US anti-terrorism efforts, his departure is for the best. Now, Pakistan's democratic politicians have what they wanted: full responsibility for governing this nation of 167 million, mostly poor, people.

So far, however, the politicians have spent most of their energy on disputes left over from the Musharraf period. First among these is the question of what to do with Musharraf. One coalition partner, the Pakistan Peoples Party seems to favour allowing him a comfortable exile; the PML(N) apparently wants him to be put on trial. This issue, in turn, is entwined with another struggle over how and when to reinstate the Supreme Court Justices whom Musharraf purged, especially Chief Justice Iftikhar Muhammad Chaudhry. Zardari dislikes the jurist because once refused Zardari's bail when he was jailed on corruption charges; Zardari fears that those charges might be revived.

All transitions from authoritarianism to democracy raise questions of retrospective accountability and justice. The fact that the Pakistani politicians wrestling with these questions are themselves hardly innocent of mistakes and abuses does not make the issues any less legitimate. Obviously, it will be up to the Pakistanis themselves to resolve Musharraf's fate and the future makeup of the Supreme Court. Pakistan's friends, including the United States, will have to show patience.

But Nawaz and Zardari must simultaneously tackle the problems of Pakistan's present and future. Those include not only rising food and fuel prices but also the continuing cross-border insurgency linked to Afghanistan's Taliban. As a deadly Tuesday strike against French troops in Afghanistan and a foiled suicide bombing against US troops the same day show, the West has a strong interest in defeating these guerrillas, and it cannot do so without Pakistan's help, which Pakistan has promised. But the new Pakistani authorities have not yet demonstrated a convincing strategy for keeping that promise, Pakistan's new leaders swept to power on a claim that democracy is better at fighting terrorism than dictatorship. The sooner they start proving it, the better.

It is amazing how soon Musharraf's shadow disappeared from the political scene in Pakistan. For only two or three days there was a brief discussion in the media about whether or not his resignation was based on an understanding that he would not be tried under Article 6 for subverting the constitution. Then like an earthen lamp that drowns in water with a flip, he simply vanished.

My overall assessment of Musharraf's rule is that it was a mixture of good, bad and the disastrous. There were some positive indicators, like higher growth, larger investment and attempts at greater decentralization but the list of negative and adverse consequences of this rule far exceed the positive indicators. In fact, the price the country will pay in the longer run, for supporting the US war on terrorism, in return for short term economic gains, will be very high. The growth of active militancy not only in the Tribal Areas, but in many other parts of Pakistan, directly targeting the security of Pakistan through bomb blasts and suicide bombing is perhaps the most gruesome legacy which Musharraf passed on to his successors.

But the greatest damage during this period was institutional. In an effort to gain legitimacy and build a civilian facade around his rule, he manipulated the electoral process in the 2002 general elections to create a rubber stamp parliament. The same strategy was repeated for the 2005 local bodies election. Then, to perpetuate his rule for another five years, he played havoc with the superior judiciary, virtually destroying it as a major institution of state.

But even greater harm was inflicted on the army as an institution. Unlike the military regimes of Ayub Khan and Ziaul Haq, the army's involvement in civilian affairs during the Musharraf era was unprecedented. It will take considerable efforts on the part of the new military leadership to rebuild the morale, image and capability of the army as a formidable fighting force.

No matter, how efficient and effective a military regime may look on the surface, the real tasks of strengthening the foundations of the federation, creating inter-provincial harmony, and providing participatory governance for the benefit of the common people can be accomplished only by a legitimate government with strong democratic institutions.

Zardari's Election as President

The election of Asif Ali Zardari as the twelfth President of Pakistan on 6 September 2008 with 481 electoral votes out of a total of 702 votes marked the advent of the post-Musharraf dispensation and a welcome transition from military to democratic rule.

As mentioned earlier in this chapter, ever since Benazir Bhutto's tragic death on 27 December 2007, Asif Ali Zardari had demonstrated his political skills to capture, expand and consolidate his political power. Having assumed effective control of the PPP as co-chairman, he ran a successful election campaign and PPP emerged as the largest party in the National Assembly with 124 out of 342 seats and therefore, a mandate to form the federal government. Zardari chose as Prime

Minister, Yousaf Raza Gillani, a decent politician he could trust and also another popular leader, Dr Fehmida Mirza as the first woman Speaker of the National Assembly in Asia. The PPP also emerged as the largest party in Sindh and the second largest party in both NWFP and Balochistan.

Soon after the elections, Zardari and his team launched a well thought out plan to seek the support of other political parties. Although the PPP had an absolute majority of 93 in the provincial assembly of 168, it invited the MQM to join the provincial government (without asking them to join the federal government) in the expectation that MQM would vote for PPPs presidential candidate whenever the opportunity emerged. Similarly, it joined a coalition with Awami National Party (ANP) in NWFP under Ameer Haider Hoti of ANP as chief minister. ANP had 48 seats in a house of 124 and PPP 30. In Balochistan, the PPP formed a coalition with Musharraf's King Party, the PML(Q). PPP had only 12 seats in a house of 65 in the Balochistan Assembly, against 19 for PML(Q), but it secured the post of chief minister for Nawab Akbar Raeesani, the provincial president of PPP, by co-opting most of the 12 independent members.

But Zardari's real success in implementing his political game plan was the six-point Murree Accord signed with Nawaz Sharif on 9 March 2008.

Through this agreement, both the parties took a quantum leap towards democracy, to form a coalition government at the centre which was to include ANP and JUl(F). Based on the promise to restore the deposed judges on the position of 2 November 2007, the PML(N) agreed to be a part of the federal cabinet while PPP was to join the Punjab government.

As the 30-day deadline of the Murree Accord (30 April) approached, prolonged negotiations were held in Dubai, London, and Islamabad and the deadline was extended to 12 May 2008 to find an acceptable formula for restoring the deposed judges. When that deadline was not met, PML(N) ministers withdrew from the cabinet, sending the stock market and the exchange rate into a spin. But Nawaz Sharif also announced that in keeping with the spirit of the Charter of Democracy, PML(N) would continue to support the PPP government.

The month of June was consumed by the budget session of the National Assembly and in July, both Nawaz Sharif and Zardari went abroad. Soon after their return, as mentioned earlier, they met on 5 August 2008 and agreed to go for the impeachment of the president, as the first order of business. They signed two agreements, on 5 August and 7 August 2008 respectively to impeach President Musharraf and then restore the judges in accordance with the Murree Declaration 'within one day of the vote on impeachment motion or resignation of the president.

When the judges were not restored even one week after the resignation of President Musharraf on 18 August, PML(N) decided on 25 August to formally quit the coalition. It had left the cabinet on 13 May 2008 but was still supporting the PPP government in parliament; now it was to sit in the opposition. Nawaz Sharif also announced amid enthusiastic applause, in the meeting of the Central Working Committee, that Justice Saeed-uz-Zaman Siddiqui would be its candidate for the office of the president. Two days later, PML(Q) nominated the secretary general of the party, Syed Mushahid Hussain as its presidential candidate.

Thus, while Zardari could not fulfil his secret ambition to be elected unopposed as the president of Pakistan, just as Yousaf Raza Gillani was elected as prime minister on 31 March, he had through his political game plan ensured the support of at least three parties—MQM, ANP, JUI(F) in his bid for the highest office of the country, vacated by Musharraf on 18 August 2008.

Thirty-seven years after Zulfikar Ali Bhutto assumed the office of the President, his son-in-law, Asif Ali Zardari won the same office on 6 September 2008, with more than two-third of the total votes.

	NA/Senate	Punjab*	Sindh*	NWFP*	Balochistan	Total
Total Votes	442	371	168	124	65	702
Asif Zardari	281	22	63	56	59	481
Saeed uz Zaman	111	35	00	5	2	153
Mushahid Hussain	34	6	00	2	2	44
* Pro-rated to 65 votes						
Source: Election Commission Pakistan						

This election led to some interesting and significant features with many implications for the country's political future:

- Zardari won 64 per cent of the total votes cast in the parliament, 100 per cent in Sindh, 93 per cent in Balochistan and 86 per cent in NWFP. But in the largest province of Punjab, he won only 33 per cent of 63 electoral votes polled.
- The PML(N) candidate on the other hand secured 54 per cent of the votes in the Punjab, thus clearly demonstrating that the party had further consolidated its grip on the provincial government in the Punjab.
- The real loser in the presidential race was the PML(Q) candidate, who received only 44 electoral votes, i.e. only one-third of its 92 members in parliament (52 in the National Assembly and 40 in the Senate) and 66 members in the Punjab Assembly. Only 2 of its 19 members in the Balochistan Assembly voted for Mushahid Hussain.
- The PML(Q) defectors, the so-called 'forward bloc' who did not vote for Mushahid Hussain, shifted their support partly to PPP and partly to PML(N) candidates. Both these candidates therefore received more votes than initially expected in this election, which clearly signalled the virtual end of PML(Q) as a major political party in the future.
- All political parties, created by military dictators as a civilian façade to their rule, invariably disintegrated after the departure of the dictator. In this case, PML(Q) had some residual strength especially in the Senate, as a by-product of the 2002 managed elections, which it could have used to forge a new and unified Muslim League, but it literally squandered that opportunity at the altar of short term publicity for its candidate.

Zardari's electoral victory was celebrated throughout the country amid many questions about his past and about his ability to face the multidimensional challenges that had emerged, as *Daily News* put it in its editorial of 7 September 2007:

Zardari will be walking into the Presidency with a huge burden of history on his shoulders. For a starter, he needs a quick and complete makeover of his image, from a wily politician, winding up his way, not mindful of whether he was breaking his promises or losing his credibility, to an international statesman who carries weight and is taken seriously. To that end he must quickly fulfil all the promises he broke in the past, now that he has come out of the wall of political and physical insecurity that may have bothered him in the past. He must do away with the 17th Amendment, ending the tussle for power between President and Parliament and a power which repeatedly rocked the system and plunged it from one catastrophe to the next. The President will also be moving into the Presidency at a time when multiple crises face us on other fronts too. From across the western frontier, US forces threaten to continue their assaults. The sovereignty of the country is at risk. Within its territory the economic situation seems to be worsening by the day.

As expected, the PPP which captured power in the centre and three provinces soon came under strong pressure from its party stalwarts in Punjab, led by Governor Salman Taseer, to regain the upper hand in the largest province. While Asif Zardari and Yousaf Raza Gillani gave conciliatory statements that they would respect the mandate of PML(N) to form and retain the provincial government, every effort was being made by some provincial PPP leaders to form a PPP government, even if it meant making up with the pro-Musharraf PML(Q). PML(N) with 170 seats in the 371 member Punjab Assembly, was only 16 short of the required majority of 186. In the presidential election, the PML(N) candidate had already received 201 votes with the support of about 30 members of the breakaway 'forward bloc' of PML(Q). The game plan was to woo them back through threats of disqualification combined with offers of ministries or other carrots. Under this game plan, PML(N) had no option but to reconsider its resolve not to destabilize the federal government. The friendly 'separation' between the two parties thus degenerated into a 'bitter divorce':

With these developments, the euphoria created by the 18 February elections that a genuine democratic and stable political order would now take charge from a military ruler, was overshadowed by doubts and apprehensions about the ability of the new setup to tackle the enormous problems facing the nation or the capacity of the PPP leadership to demonstrate that a democratic setup could provide better governance.

As the second anniversary of 9 March 2007 approached, the lawyers announced a long march towards the federal capital from 12 March 2009 followed by a prolonged sit-in, right in front of the Parliament on 16 March till the deposed judges were restored. In the last week of February, four political parties, PML(N), Jamaat-e-Islami, Pakistan Tehreek-e-Insaf, and Pakhtoonkhwa Milli Awami Party announced full support for the long march. Baffled by this onslaught, President Zardari, on 25 February, opted for a pre-emptive but ill-advised move to impose governor's rule and oust the Punjab government, in the wake of a controversial judicial decision to disqualify the top leadership of PML(N). Stung and betrayed once again, Nawaz Sharif and Shahbaz Sharif openly confronted and criticized Zardari in a series of massive public meetings organized in Narowal, Sheikhupura, Multan, Faisalabad, Bahawalpur, Gujranwala and Abbottabad, pushing the political temperature to boiling point.

The government, in retaliation threatened them with charges of sedition, and warned that anyone found guilty would be punished under the law.

Apart from the Chief Minister Balochistan, Nawab Aslam Raisani, Asfandyar Wali Khan and Maulana Fazlur Rehman, also launched mediation efforts in an attempt to avert a major confrontation. I was present in their meeting with Nawaz Sharif on 6 March at Raiwind. Maulana Fazlur Rehman said that President Zardari had agreed in principle to withdraw governor's rule as soon as possible and also to file on behalf of the federal government, a review petition for the revision of the 25 February decision declaring them disqualified, if they would withdraw their support for the lawyers' long march.

Nawaz Sharif immediately clarified that PML(N) was not supporting the long march only to get PML(N)'s government restored in the Punjab. PML(N)'s first priority was the restoration of deposed judiciary; without which it will be difficult to meet the most important pre-requisite of a sustainable democratic system namely an independent judiciary to ensure the supremacy of the rule of law.

Over the next few days, Nawaz Sharif and Shahbaz Sharif intensified their efforts in support of the lawyers' march by meeting not only their party stalwarts but a wider cross section of the society. In response the government launched a major crackdown to prevent the long march. Hundreds of lawyers and political workers were arrested; containers and barricades were placed on all major roads and all entry points into Islamabad. Television stations like Geo and Aaj which showed these draconian measures were curbed through cable operators. In protest, the Information Minister, Sherry Rahman resigned, soon after Raza Rabbani who had resigned a few days earlier. Many other PPP leaders like Safdar Abbasi, Naheed Khan, Enwar Baig and Nafees

Siddiqui also made strong dissenting statements. These cracks within the PPP did not, however, deter Zardari who kept pouring cold water on many compromise proposals that emerged in that fateful week. The reconciliation efforts, openly supported by many foreign envoys, especially from the US and UK, suffered a serious set back on 12 March, when the government offered to restore the judges through a Judicial Commission as proposed in Para 3 of the Charter of Democracy (COD). The long march sponsors promptly rejected this offer, as they wanted reinstatement of judges only through an executive order, without a new oath as that would sanctify their unconstitutional dismissal of 3 November 2007. The Judicial Commission visualized in the COD was in any case for new appointments and offered no solution on the issue of deposed judges.

The sixteenth day of March 2009 will go down in history as a mini revolution when the threat of a massive public uprising forced a besieged Presidency to cave in to their legitimate demand. That morning, Prime Minister Yousuf Raza Gillani addressed the nation and announced on television that 'as per my and the President of Pakistan's promise, I announce the restoration of all the deposed judges including Iftikhar Muhammad Chaudhry, who will take charge as Chief Justice on 21 March on the retirement of Justice Abdul Hameed Dogar'. He also said that the federal government will file a review petition against the decision of the Supreme Court disqualifying Mian Nawaz Sharif and Mian Shahbaz Sharif and called upon them to move forward in the spirit of reconciliation in order to implement the Charter of Democracy.

This was the dramatic climax brought about by peoples' power. A day earlier, on 15 March, the entire nation was gripped with grave apprehensions about the impending violence in the wake of the government crackdown and tear gas shells to crush the lawyers' movement and their supporters and prevent the long march from reaching Islamabad. Tensions reached a new pitch when Nawaz Sharif, defying the ban, came out of his Model Town residence just after mid-day with his enthusiastic workers. As this long march made its way, thousands joined the flood of humanity in vehicles and on foot. The barricades just melted away and many police officials refused to obstruct the long march. It was by now crystal clear that thousands and thousands of ordinary citizens and not just party workers would be unstoppable by the containers and other barricades in Islamabad.

By mid-night, TV channels reported amidst their non-stop coverage of the long march that the Prime Minister, Yousuf Raza Gillani will address the nation at 2 a.m. The Chief of Army Staff, General Ashfaq Parvez Kayani, who had been frequently meeting President Zardari and Prime Minister Yousuf Raza Gillani, had another lengthy meeting that night. News of a breakthrough started spreading by midnight, but the Prime Minister's address was postponed once again. Finally, at six in the morning, Yousuf Raza Gillani made the dramatic announcement.

Nawaz Sharif who was taking a few hours break along with Chaudhry Aitzaz Ahsan, at Gujranwala, welcomed the announcement, thanked the Prime Minister and the President, and called off the long march. The whole nation heaved a sigh of relief. A new wave of optimism and hope for fundamental change in the political life of the country spread like wild fire in every nook and corner. People distributed sweets and congratulated each other and the 'men in black coats' on the re-birth of Pakistan.

As I finally retired at the end of that eventful and exciting day, I could readily predict that Pakistan was entering a new phase of judicial activism under an independent judiciary.

Judicial Activism

In Chapter 10, a very detailed account of 'judicial activism' in the second half of 1997 has been presented. As mentioned a crisis with the Judiciary started when Prime Minister Nawaz Sharif decided to set up, through an Act of Parliament, special courts to provide speedy justice in cases involving terrorism. Chief Justice Sajjad Ali Shah reacted negatively to the legislation and insisted that instead the strength of the Supreme Court should be increased from 12 to 17 Judges. When the opposition saw a confrontation developing between the Government and the Judiciary, they filed a number of cases against the Prime Minister and some Ministers in the Supreme Court. The then President, Farooq Ahmed Leghari was also unhappy because in April 1997, the Parliament had passed the Thirteenth Constitutional Amendment to eliminate the powers of the President under Article

58-2(b) to dissolve the National Assembly. The game plan that emerged from this convergence was to submit a petition in the Supreme Court to declare the Thirteenth and the Fourteenth Amendments illegal; thus restoring the President's powers to dissolve the National Assembly. This 'Plan' did not materialize because at the last minute, the Army Chief, General Jehangir Karamat did not support it. Faced with the prospects of impeachment, President Farooq Leghari resigned with immediate effect. A few days later, Justice Sajjad Ali Sah also resigned when 10 of the 17 Judges of the Supreme Court called a full court and cancelled the notification appointing Justice Sajjad Ali Shah as Chief Justice.

This new phase of judicial activism which started after the restoration of Chief Justice Iftikhar Muhammad Chaudhry on 21 March 2009, was not as dramatic as that in 1997, but created a lot of noise and dust. The newly gained independence of the Judiciary was exclusively used to expand judicial authority and space which largely focussed on the activities of political leaders and politicians.

The first major issue was the change of procedure for appointing superior judges under the Eighteenth Amendment, passed in April 2010. Several rulings by the Supreme Court forced the government to pass the Nineteenth Amendment of the Constitution in 2011 to address these concerns.

Another major issue which greatly increased tensions between the Supreme Court and the Zardari Government was the National Reconciliation Order (NRO) which Pervez Musharraf had issued in October 2007. This NRO provided indemnity to about 8000 corruption and other cases registered between 1 January 1986 and 12 October 1999. This not only closed several cases against Asif Ali Zardari, but had also allowed Benazir Bhutto to return to Pakistan in October 2007.

The Supreme Court in this new phase of judicial activism took up this matter in July 2009 and directed that the NRO plus 36 other orders issued by Musharraf should be submitted to Parliament for approval with a deadline of 28 November for this action. PPP's thin majority in Parliament was further eroded by the reluctance of MQM, its coalition partner, to support the move. As the deadline passed without parliamentary approval, the Supreme Court annulled the NRO on 16 December 2009 and called upon the Government to revive corruption cases against the President, pending in Swiss Courts.

As weeks and months passed and no action was taken on these orders of the Supreme Court, Chief Justice Iftikhar Muhammad Chaudhry summoned Prime Minister Yousuf Raza Gillani and asked him if contempt of court proceedings should be instituted against him. His plea that the Prime Minister has amnesty under Act 248 (2) of the Constitution was not accepted and the Supreme Court issued the following order on 18 January 2012:

- 'Yousuf Raza Gillani had effectively not been PM since April 26, 2011 when he had been found guilty of contempt of court for refusing to comply with a Supreme Court order to re-open dormant fraud investigation against President Zardari. He is sentenced to imprisonment till the rising of the court'.
- This so called 'imprisonment' lasted less than a minute, but was enough to terminate his appointment as Prime Minister.

Next day, Chief Justice Iftikhar Muhammad Chaudhry issued the following clarification:

As a convict, Gillani had been disqualified as a member of Parliament. He has also ceased to be Prime Minister of Pakistan and the Office of the Prime Minister should be deemed to be vacant accordingly, President Zardari should take steps to appoint a new P.M.

This climax of the confrontation between the Supreme Court and the Government was termed by *Dawn* newspaper 'judicial dictationship' as in its comments on 20 January 2012. 'The Constitution was very clear about how the disqualification process is supposed to work. The Supreme Court has quite extraordinarily brushed all of that aside and is making up new rules of the game as it goes along'.

As I read this news story, I recalled Nawaz Sharif's apprehension of 1997, recorded in Chapter 10 of this book: 'Having passed the Thirteenth and Fourteenth Amendments to take away the President's power to dissolve the Assembly and to prevent floor crossing in the Assembly, the next potential threat to political stability will be from the judiciary whenever it became more active in non-judicial matters'.

After hectic consultations, the PPP leadership decided to nominate Shahabuddin as the next Prime Minister. But by a strange coincidence, the same day, NAB filed a reference against Shahabuddin for illegal sale of Ephedrine, a substance used in pharmaceuticals and also for narcotics. This knocked out his candidature and after further consultations, Raja Parvez Ashraf was nominated and elected as the new Prime Minister on 22 June 2012.

In retrospect, some other decisions by the Supreme Court under Chief Justice Iftikhar Chaudhry, under the *suo moto* procedures proved very harmful. One was the cancellation of the government's decision to privatize Pakistan Steel Mills and thus plug the massive losses incurred by it year after year.

The second even more harmful decision was when a three member Bench under the Chief Justice declared that the Chaghi Hill Joint Venture Agreement and all its successor pacts were *void-ab-initio* and the Tethyan Copper Company (TCC) had no legal rights to explore and mine in Reko Diq. As a result of this decision, the World Bank's International Centre for Settlements of Investment Disputes imposed, in July 2019, a massive penalty of $ 5.976 billion (Rs 944 billion) on Pakistan, in compensation of the actual and potential losses incurred by TCC as a result of the cancellation of the contract.

During two years of Chief Justice Saqib Nisar (Dec. 2016–Jan. 2019), judicial activities became even more intrusive and populist. Some commentators described the Judiciary in Pakistan as a Supreme Executive Authority because of its continuing intervention in the executive domain.

The Economy under President Zardari

The economy which President Zardari inherited in February 2008 following 8 years of Musharraf's rule was already in decline. After Musharraf joined the international campaign against terrorism post 9/11, there was a substantial increase in foreign assistance. But unlike many other countries, which used these additional resources for investment in infrastructure and export industries, the Musharraf Government, followed the path of consumption led growth. The boom generated by liberal loans for cars and other consumer durables pushed the average growth to over 6 per cent in the first 5 years of Musharraf rule. But this growth was not sustainable. Many longer term structural weakness, such as low investment GDP ratio, low tax to GDP ratio and over-dependence of the export sector on textiles' were not addressed.

As a result, the growth rate slowed to less than 4 per cent in the last two years of Musharraf's rule. The flow of foreign investment was also affected by the worsening security situation.

In March 2008, the coalition government which the PPP formed with PML(N) gave the Finance and other economic portfolios to PML(N) nominees i.e. Ishaq Dar, Ahsan Iqbal and Khawaja Asif. After the coalition collapsed within six weeks, the PPP began to worry about the economy just as many unfavourable international factors were unfolding. The international banking and financial crisis of 2007–8, caused by massive sub-prime lending by US real estate institutions, created an upheaval in the global markets and the petroleum crude prices rose rapidly to a record high of US$140 a barrel. Pakistan's foreign exchange reserves declined to US$ 3 billion by the end of 2008 equal to one-month imports and inflation levels went well above 17 per cent.

In June 2008, after Ishaq Dar's resigned as Finance Minister, the PPP government appointed Shaukat Tareen as Advisor on Finance after 4 months, on 7 October 2008. After his election as a Senator on 27 July 2009 he became the Finance Minister. Shaukat Tareen was a prominent banker. Nawaz Sharif had appointed him as head of the Habib Bank in 1997. After his retirement from HBL, he was managing a small private bank. After taking over as Advisor, he promptly decided to approach the IMF. The package was negotiated quickly and as a result, the current account deficit declined from 8 per cent of GDP in 2008–9 to 3 per cent in 2009–10 and inflation from 17 to 10.1 per cent.

Another important contribution of Shaukat Tareen was the unanimous inter-provincial agreement in the 7th NFC Award, transferring substantial additional resources to the Provincial Governments.

But this positive news was soon drowned by the unprecedented floods of July 2010. The floods and the devastation they caused also led to heated debates about many chronic issues. Pakistan's water storage capacity was only 14 MAF or 10 per cent of the total annual canal diversions of 140 MAF. If Pakistan had built additional dams, some of this excess water would have been stored, reducing the flood damage. The second major issue that surfaced was the poor maintenance of irrigation infrastructure. Despite large investments in flood protection schemes, the embankments were weak and broke down easily. There were also reports that influential landlords, with the help of irrigation officials breached many embankments to divert water away from their lands. This created artificial ponds and lakes with no natural discharge, causing serious hardship for the people for many months. The floods caused serious damage to the cotton crop.

In December 2010, the PPP government decided to replace Shaukat Tareen with Dr Hafeez Sheikh as the new Finance Minister. He had served in the World Bank from 1992 to 2000 and as Finance Minister in the Sindh Government from 2000 to 2003. After his election as a Senator, he was appointed Federal Minister for Privatization and Investment in 2003. In 2007, he went back to the private sector. In 2010, he was recalled to Pakistan to take over as Finance Minister in the Cabinet of Yousaf Raza Gillani. After becoming Finance Minister, he paid special attention to anti-inflation policies and to the newly set up social safety net programme, called the Benazir Income Support Programme (BISP). In 2012–13, he increased the allocation for the programme to Rs 40 billion.

The overall economic record of the PPP Government from 2008 to 2013 was, however not very enviable, as can be gleaned from the following table:

Economic Indicators (2008–13)

Sectors	2008–09	2009–10	2010–11	2011–12	2012–13	Average 2009–13
GDP Growth (%)	0.4	2.6	3.6	3.8	3.7	2.8
Agriculture (%)	3.5	0.2	2.0	3.6	2.7	2.4
Manufacturing (%)	-4.2	1.4	2.5	2.1	4.9	1.3
Services (%)	1.3	3.2	3.9	4.4	5.1	3.6
Inflation (%)	17.0	10.1	13.7	11.0	7.4	11.84
Current A/C balance (US$ million)	-926.10	-3946.0	214.0	-4658.0	-2496.0	-4029.4
Current A/C Balance (% GDP)	-5.5	-2.2	-0.1	-2.1	-1.1	-2.16
Total Revenue (Rs Million)	1,850,910	2,078,165	2,252,855	2,566,514	2,982,436	2,346,174
Tax Revenues (Rs Million)	1,204,670	1,472,821	1,699,334	2,052,886	2,199,232	1,725,788
Non-Tax Revenue (Rs Million)	646,231	605,344	553,521	513,628	783,204	620,385
Total Revenue (% of GDP)	14.0	14.0	12.3	12.8	13.3	13.28
Tax to GDP Ratio (% of GDP)	9.1	9.9	9.3	10.2	9.8	9.66

There were several exogenous factors that adversely affected the economy during the five year tenure (2008–13) of the PPP government, such as the global financial crisis of 2007–8, the sharp increase in petroleum and food prices and the devastating floods of 2010 and 2011. But there were many internal factors flowing from the government's policies and actions also contributed to this dismal economic record and which had long term consequences.

Zardari's reluctance to honour the commitment made in the Murree Accord of 9 March, to restore the deposed judges by the extended deadline of 12 May 2008 created serious strains in the relation between the government and the judiciary. The resultant political uncertainty was further compounded, when PML(N) ministers decided to resign from the coalition within 6 weeks.

A few months later, in February 2009, the Federal Government decided to dismiss the PML(N) Government in Punjab. This action was set aside by the Court and in terms of negative political fallout, proved to be a disaster.

The civil-military relations during this period were also affected by several factors including efforts to include certain clauses in the Kerry Lugar Bill to link the release of funds to actions against certain terrorist groups and the Memogate Scandal.

Another negative factor for the economy was the worsening energy crisis. With very limited increase in the generation capacity for more than a decade and growing line and recovery losses, the gap between the demand and supply of electricity went on increasing. Load shedding of 8 to 12 hours a day became a serious crisis not only for ordinary citizens but also for industrial and commercial consumers, affecting production and exports. The government's efforts to remedy the situation by setting up, inter alia rental power plants at very high prices also led to many controversies and scandals and further compounded the problem of circular debt.

Terrorism and the Security Crisis

Ever since its creation, Pakistan has experienced violence from different groups claiming ethnic or sectarian rights. But after 9/11 and the US invasion of Afghanistan, a more dangerous phase of violent insurgency began to develop. The mujahideen, whom Pakistan had trained, funded and armed with active US support to fight the Russians, escaped to different parts of Afghanistan and Pakistan after 9/11. Initially, they came to the tribal areas of Pakistan for safety but soon they organized themselves to control parts of North and South Waziristan and then move northwards towards Orakzai, Khyber and Swat. Many international groups, like Al-Qaida, foreign fighters of Arab and Uzbek origin and local Jihadi organizations joined different groups of Taliban, exponentially raising the level of insurgency.

President Musharraf had responded to these threats partly by launching a military operation in the tribal areas in 2004 and partly by signing agreements with certain groups like the Shakai Agreement of 2004 and the 2005 Sara Rogah Agreement with Baitullah Mehsud. But these agreements did not succeed in curbing the level of insurgency which gradually spread from the Tribal Belt to different parts of Pakistan, including the capital city of Islamabad where the Lal Masjid (Red Mosque) Complex had become a major centre for jihadi groups and had hidden a large store of weapons and explosives in the Complex; Students from the Red Mosque, both boys and girls, regularly raided video shops, beauty parlours and radio stores. They even kidnapped some policemen and Chinese workers in July 2007.

Musharraf first tried to negotiate with Maulana Abdul Rashid Ghazi and Maulana Abdul Aziz, the two brothers managing the Complex, but they declared on the media their terms for surrender in a defiant tone. On 7 July a joint police and military operation was ordered by Musharraf which led to fierce battles for several days. More than 150 students and teachers of Lal Masjid including Maulana Abdul Rashid Ghazi were killed in the operation. Maulana Abdul Aziz was arrested while trying to escape in a woman's burqa.

The public reaction to the Lal Masjid Operation was mixed. Musharraf's tussle with the judiciary since March 2007 had already weakened his position. The international reaction to the Lal Masjid Operation was also negative as most observers criticized the prolonged indifference to the emergence of militant groups in the capital city, so close to the seat of power.

One direct and very serious consequence of the Lal Masjid Operation was the creation of Tehrik-e-Taliban Pakistan (TTP)under Baitullah Mehsud. This brought together at least 40 militant groups under one umbrella, including the influential Tehrik-e-Nifaz-e-Shariat-e-Muhammadi (TNSM) with a strong presence in Swat. TTP's creation was primarily responsible for the big upsurge in violent extremism in the next few years throughout Pakistan.

Meanwhile, the Tehrik-e-Taliban Pakistan (TTP) extended its control to other areas and by the end of 2008 had acquired major influence in the Malakand Division and the Valley of Swat, with strong support from TNSM. Maulana Fazalullah, the son in law of Maulana Sufi Mohammad became a fire brand leader of Swat Taliban with several F.M. radio stations calling for the enforcement of *Sharia* day and night. Hundreds of girls schools were either closed or destroyed and the main square in the bazaar of Mingora became a popular place for punishing violators of *Sharia* law in public.

On 21 May 2008, the North West Frontier Province (NWFP) Government led by ANP under Amir Haider Hoti, signed a peace agreement with Maulana Fazalullah, but it did not lead to peace. In August 2008, the frequency of suicide bombings increased further, with major attacks on a police station in Charbagh. In the next few weeks Maulana Fazlullah in an effort to show his influence and writ, began to publically execute 'offenders of shariat' in the public square in Mingora. In some cases, dead bodies were hung in a public square to send a strange and disturbing message to the population.

Baffled by this bizarre situation, the NWFP government decided to concede to the demand of Maulana Sufi Mohammad to introduce an Islamic System of Justice called *Nizam-e-Adl* in Malakand. The justification cited for this move was that it will end illegal executions and punishments in Mingora Square. The new law for establishing *Nizam-e-Adl* in Malakand Division was passed by Parliament in February 2009.

However, the Swat Taliban had different ideas. They regarded this agreement as a first step in their march to gain full control of this region as a whole, under Islamic Law. They openly violated different provisions of the agreement and extended their writ to other areas like Dir and Buner. Newspapers, both national and international started saying 'Taliban are now only 70 kilometres from Islamabad'. In May 2009, Maulana Sufi Mohammad addressed a large gathering of over 100,000 and announced amidst enthusiastic slogans that they no longer accepted the Pakistan Constitution, its Parliament or its Judiciary.

This statement sent shock-waves throughout the country. Prime Minister Yusuf Raza Gillani convened an urgent meeting of all the political parties in May 2009. I was attending a seminar in Murree when I received a phone call from Nawaz Sharif. He said he would be coming to Islamabad next morning for the meeting convened by the Prime Minister. I was asked to prepare a draft statement which should be faxed to him in Lahore the same evening.

The key message conveyed to the All Parties Summit by Nawaz Sharif was that the sanctity of the writ of the State of Pakistan, its Constitution and Parliament. No group can be allowed to use violence in the name of Islam, to undermine this sanctity. This clear and forceful statement effectively neutralized any possible support from Islamic parties for the TTP or TNSM. The meeting then unanimously decided to authorize a mega operation against the militants in Swat.

The military operation in Swat, code named Rah-e-Rast (The True Path) was launched by the Pakistan Army in May 2009 in the Malakand Division, and was a watershed in Pakistan's quest to defeat militancy and extremism.

The Military leadership had made all the preparations for Operation Rah-e-Rast and was waiting for a positive signal from the political leadership. The operation began with about 25,000 troops, circling the valley of Swat from all sides and gradually closing in. About 4000 militants were killed and an equal number captured over the next 10 weeks.

This operation also led to large scale displacement of the population. About 1.3 million people were moved out. They shifted to the adjoining districts of Mardan and Peshawar, some to makeshift camps, others to their relatives' homes. The repatriation and rehabilitation of these displaced people in 2010 was successfully carried out with the support of local communities in a great show of human sympathy combined with efficient administration.

This successful Swat Operation was followed by another operation in South Waziristan in October, 2009, code named Rah-e-Nijat (The Path of Deliverance). In August 2009, Baitullah Mesud was killed by a US drone attack and the TTP was in disarray with two important groups led by Maulvi Nazir Ahmad and Hafiz Gul Bahadar sending positive signals to the Government authorities. The group led by Baitullah Mesud decided not to put up much resistance and the army took control of all major towns and villages.

The TTP now led by Hakimullah Mesud, decided at this stage to respond to the military operations in Swat and South Waziristan by launching suicide attacks throughout the country specially targeting security forces. Their game plan, conceived in 2007, to gain effective control of entire tribal belt to establish an 'Islamic Caliphate', had been halted by the Swat Operation and then reversed by the South Waziristan Operation. After these military operations, extremist elements spread to other cities of Pakistan, notably Karachi, Multan, Bahawalpur, Jhang and Peshawar and began their efforts to join forces with anti-State or hostile elements by supporting them covertly, targeting security forces, exploding bombs to kill civilians and damage state property, where ever possible.

In Balochistan, the militant elements joined with nationalist groups seeking independence or autonomy to create perpetual chaos in Quetta and some other cities. Some elements like the banned Lashkar-e-Jhangvi used this coalition to launch a series of attacks on the Shia population. Some foreign elements, especially from India, had been supplying arms to the militant forces through Afghanistan. Despite many initiatives for political reconciliation and major initiative to transfer resources for development and provide employment and educational opportunities, the security situation in Balochistan became more precarious and fragile.

In Karachi, infiltration of terrorist elements further inflamed the old politico-ethnic rivalries, leading to large scale politically motivated target killings and persistent gang wars among militant wings of different political parties. Since most of recruitment in police in previous years was politically motivated rather than merit based and a large proportion of appointments were made in return for bribes, many criminal elements crept into the Karachi police making law enforcement extremely difficult.

In Khyber Pakhtunkhawa (KPK) formerly North Western Frontier Province (NWFP), proximity to Federally Administered Tribal Areas (FATA), where TTP elements were active, bomb blasts and suicide attacks became more frequent, targeting security personnel and important political figures, who had claimed to provide leadership in tribal areas.

Criminal elements in different parts of the country also penetrated the ranks of security forces or built their own nefarious networks to launch terrorist attacks and undertake unlawful activities like kidnapping for ransom or drug smuggling. Some illegal immigrants and Afghan refugees also joined these elements by providing smuggled arms and safe havens. Cyber security also emerged as a new challenge in this volatile environment. The spread of modern communication technologies and spread of social media further complicated the task of controlling extremism. The extremist elements found it easier to promote radical ideas, encourage violence in the name of Islam and enlist new volunteers for their activities.

According to official figures, between 2002 and 2012 more than 37,000 civilians including 6,530 soldiers and 3,600 personnel of police and paramilitary forces had lost their lives in the fight against terrorism. In 2011–12, with 2,160 deaths, Pakistan was ranked third in the Global Terrorism Risk Index prepared by Maplecroft of the US after Iraq (3,456 deaths) and Afghanistan (3,423 deaths).

As described in the next chapter, a determined effort to counter this growing menace of insurgency was started in 2013 with the Karachi Operation, continued through Operation Zarb-e-Azb in 2014 and Operation Raddul Fasad in 2017.

External Relations

In March 2008, the PPP government under President Asif Ali Zardari started its 5-year tenure, with a commitment to improve the country's external relations. The passage of the Kerry Lugar Bill in 2008 to authorize US$1.5 billion to Pakistan every year, for the next 5 years, was hailed by President Zardari as 'the greatest foreign policy success of his government'. But within a year, a serious controversy developed when efforts were made to introduce conditions that would increase civilian control over the Military. After a meeting of Corps Commanders in October 2009, the media openly criticized the proposed conditions as an infringement of Pakistan's' sovereignty. The conditions were deleted but this controversy created unusual strains between the Pentagon and the Pakistan Army.

These strains in US-Pakistan relations were further compounded by three other incidents in 2011. The first such incident happened on 27 January when Raymond Davis, a CIA contractor killed two Pakistanis on a busy Lahore road. According to reports the victims were armed and were attempting to rob Raymond Davis. Raymond Davis was arrested by police before he could escape. Meanwhile, a vehicle of the US consulate sent to rescue Raymond Davis, driving fast on the wrong side of the road on a one-way street, also killed a pedestrian. The publication of vivid photographs of these incidents created a public uproar which further intensified when the cameras found in Raymond Davis's car had many sensitive photographs of the Frontier Corps Headquarters in Peshawar and of army posts on the India-Pakistan border. The Foreign Minister, Shah Mehmood Qureshi in a press conference announced that Raymond Davis did not have any diplomatic status. Rumours also surfaced in the media that Raymond Davis was part of a much bigger US operation under which a very large number of illegally armed intelligence agents of Blackwater had been sent to Pakistan.

There were intense diplomatic negotiations behind the scenes between the US and Pakistan to find an amicable solution. On 15 March 2011, 46 days after his arrest, Raymond Davis was released and allowed to fly out of Pakistan before the news of his release appeared in the media. Stories appeared that according to *Sharia* Law, the families of the three victims had pardoned Raymond Davis after receiving *Diyat* (blood money).

Within a few weeks of this incident, Shah Mehmood Qureshi resigned as Foreign Minister. President Zardari offered him another portfolio in a cabinet reshuffle. Apparently the US was not happy with his conduct during the Raymond Davis fiasco. Hina Rabbani Khar then replaced Shah Mehmood Qureshi as Foreign Minister in June 2011.

An even bigger storm descended in US-Pakistan relations on 2 May 2011, when US launched a helicopter operation from Afghanistan to capture Osama Bin Laden from a house in Abbottabad. After the US invasion of Afghanistan, Osama Bin Laden, who had been living in the city of Kandahar, rather than the capital city of Kabul, since his relocation from Sudan in 1996, escaped to Torabora mountains, after the US and its Allies invaded Afghanistan in October 2001.

The dramatic US action to kill Osama Bin Laden (OBL) in a midnight raid by the US Marines created a major upheaval in Pakistan. That he was hiding for 5 years within a short distance from the Pakistan Military Academy in Kakul, without being detected, placed the intelligence services of the country in a very difficult situation. There were some stories that certain intelligence operators did in fact have the knowledge of his presence but they did not share it with the political leadership. That started the debate about 'complicity' versus 'incompetence'.

This unilateral US action was taken up by the Parliament and after a heated and stormy debate; it passed a resolution on 14 May 2011. This resolution strongly asserted that:

'these unilateral actions, such as those conducted by the US forces in Abbottabad, as well as the continued drone attacks on the territory of Pakistan, are not only unacceptable but also constitute violation of the UN Charter, international law and humanitarian norms. It called upon the government to re-visit and review its terms of engagement with the United States with a view to ensuring that Pakistan's national interests are fully respected and accommodated in pursuit of policies for countering terrorism and achieving peace and reconciliation in Afghanistan. The resolution also called upon the Government to appoint an independent Commission on the Abbottabad operation to fix responsibility and recommend necessary measures to ensure that such an incident does not recur.

An independent Inquiry Commission was set up on 21 June 2011, under Justice (R) Javed Iqbal as president of the Commission. Other members of the Commission were Ashraf Jehangir Qazi, Lt. Gen. Nadeem Ahmad, and Abbas Khan.

After 18 months' of intense deliberations, the Commission presented its report to the Prime Minister on 4 January 2013. Subsequently the Cabinet decided not to make the report public. However, Al-Jazeera TV on its web page, published extracts from what it called a leaked document and also telecast the findings. According to the Pakistan media, this Al-Jazeera, version was not based on the final report of the Commission but an earlier draft.

I was also invited to meet the Commission on 21 December 2011 or if that was not possible, submit written views on its 5 specific terms of reference. Some extracts from written comments that I submitted to the Commission on 19 December 2011, are reproduced below for record: -

The most important lapse was the inability of our military and civilian intelligence agencies to detect this operation. Two helicopters penetrated deep into Pakistan territory, landed in the vicinity of Pakistan Military Academy, carried out a violent operation for almost two hours and then escaped safely, despite the crash of one of the helicopters, with the body of OBL. This was no doubt a 'victory' made possible by superior technology, but it is a matter of some concern that Pakistani agencies could not detect the intelligence leads that ultimately led to OBL and all the preparatory activities for this operation that must have spread over several months. If Pakistan, itself, had vigorously followed the leads it initially provided to CIA and had traced OBL in Abbottabad, it could have gained enormous diplomatic and political advantage rather than face the damaging charge of 'complicity or incompetence.

The circumstances under which OBL, was able to reside with his family in Abbottabad for so many years, were created by our 'open door' policy for Afghan refugees that was adopted after the Russian invasion of Afghanistan in December 1979. Iran, for example, registered each and every Afghan refugee and kept them in isolated location till most of them were repatriated. Pakistan on the other hand, not only kept the Afghan refugees in camps close to major cities but could not prevent a large percentage of these refugees from acquiring Pakistan ID Cards. This open door policy facilitated the creation of networks through whom a high profile icon like OBL was able to enter Pakistan and live safely with his family members in Abbottabad for many years.

If the government had acted promptly on the recommendations of the Parliamentary Resolution of 14 May 2011 "to revisit and review its terms of engagement with the United States, with a view to ensuring that Pakistan's national interests are fully respected", the 26 November attack on Pakistan posts in Mohmand Agency could probably have been avoided. In other words, "another incident like May 2", has already occurred, further damaging US Pakistan relations and vitiating the atmosphere for the exercise now being undertaken to review the terms of re-engagement with USA.

The third unfortunate incident that seriously damaged US-Pakistan relation was the NATO attack on two border posts at Salala in Mohmand Agency on 26 November 2011. The NATO helicopters and two F-15 E Jet fighters entered 2 kilometres inside Pakistan territory at 02:00 AM and opened indiscriminate fire on these posts, killing 28 Pakistan soldiers and wounding 12 others. The public in Pakistan reacted with protests in all parts of the country. Both houses of Parliament after a prolonged debate condemned 'deliberate attack and called for strong retaliatory measures'. These included the closure of NATO supply lines through Torkham and Chaman borders for US forces and international forces fighting in Afghanistan and the closure of the Shamsi Airfield which was used by NATO forces for aerial operations. Pakistan also called for an official apology from the United States.

Ever since the Salala attack, independent observers have been debating the real facts and the reasons that brought about this major upheaval in US-Pakistan relations. I think some answers are provided by Vali Nasr in his book *The Dispensable Nation* (Doubleday: 2013, p. 85):

In July 2011 (i.e. two months after the Osama Bin Laden episode), National Security Adviser Tom Donilon asked Senator Kerry to talk to General Kayani and see if he would put US-Pakistan relations back on track. The senator and the army chief agreed to a secret meeting in Abu Dhabi, and the two men met for nineteen hours over two days. It was the most substantive and thoroughgoing conversation America had with Pakistan in some time. Kayani and Kerry worked together to put Kayani's thoughts into a white paper for Obama, which Kerry brought back with him to Washington.

Kayani thought the two-day exercise would get the White House engaged in a meaningful strategic discussion that could clear the air, repair the relationship, and chart a course forward. It was an effort on both sides to dial back the relationship to its more productive phase in 2009–2011. Kerry was carrying on where Holbrooke had left off.

The nineteen-hour meeting and the white paper did not elicit an immediate response from Washington. But three months later, in October, Tom Donilon, Marc Grossman, and the White House's AfPak point man, General Lute, went back to Abu Dhabi to meet Kayani. Relations had not improved, and Donilon wanted to smooth things over with Pakistan. Kayani in turn was hoping to hear a response to his paper and more on America's vision for the region – what was the strategy?

The follow-up meeting was much shorter, and soon it became clear Donilon had one agenda: reading Pakistan the riot act for its support of Haqqani network. Donilon made no reference to Kayani's paper or the road map he and Kerry had explored. Instead he presented Kayani with a laundry list of Pakistani misdeeds, backed with intelligence evidence. Pakistan was advised to close up shop in Afghanistan, abandon its strategic goals, and liquidate the Taliban or else. All we cared about was mop-up operations in Afghanistan, and we expected Pakistan to cooperate.

The Salala attack was thus a well-considered decision by the US to 'punish' Pakistan. But as Vali Nasr points out later in the same chapter

it was a very faulty strategy because the total extra cost of diverting NATO supplies through Central Asia was US$100 million a month. The closure would also force US, if Pakistani route remained off limit, to rethink its exit strategy from Afghanistan. The next escalation in this conflict would put the United States and not Pakistan in the pincer.

He then describes the end game (p. 89).

Secretary Clinton all along thought we should say 'Sorry and move on'. Now, as months had passed, Clinton told the White House that enough was enough; she was taking charge. She gave a simple direction to her top deputy at the State Department, Tom Nides: 'I want you to fix this'. Nides flew to Islamabad to negotiate with General Kayani—a tepid U.S. apology in exchange for Pakistan opening the border— and hence preventing the relationship from going over the cliff.

The White House acquiesced to Clinton salvaging the relationship. Not only had their Pakistan policy failed, but Obama also realized that Putin was the main beneficiary of Pakistan's spat with Washington. The alternative supply routes were Central Asian and Russian land and air routes, which gave Putin leverage. Obama decided he preferred apologizing to Pakistan than depending on Putin. It was a critical realization for White House that the real menace to America comes not from states like Pakistan but powers like Russia.

Finally, after difficult behind the scene negotiations, US Secretary of State, Hillary Clinton officially apologised on 3 July 2012, 'for the losses by the Pakistan's military'. Subsequently a new agreement was also concluded to reopen the supply routes. Pakistan's demand to increase the transit fee from US$250 for each truck to US$500 was not accepted but the US agreed to restore the reimbursement of about US$1.2 billion from Coalition Support Funds for the cost incurred by 150,000 Pakistani troops carrying out counter insurgency operations along the border with Afghanistan.

The Shamsi airbase, which was vacated by the US, within a few days, was taken over by the Pakistan military. Since the airbase was used primarily for launching drone attacks, these attacks dropped by 60 per cent in 2012, after the Salala incident.

The Eighteenth Amendment

When the Eighteenth Constitutional Amendment was passed by Parliament on 8 April 2010, it was regarded as a major milestone in the constitutional history of Pakistan because it addressed the critical issue of provincial autonomy and transferred substantial powers and functions from the Federal to the Provincial Governments. It also strengthened the Federal Parliamentary system by securing greater participation of all the federating units.

However, as serious problems slowed down the implementation of reforms visualized under the Eighteenth Amendment in the following years, some political parties and observers began to criticize the reform package as 'over-ambitious'. One view went even further and argued that the Eighteenth Amendment in the long run, may prove to be worse than Sheikh Mujibur Rahman's six points, which eventually led to the breakup of Pakistan in December 1971.

An objective analysis of the Eighteenth Amendment would have to start with the recognition, that any federal system based on power sharing between the federating units is always problematic and will be successful only if the unifying factors like identity, language, ethnicity and culture are carefully recognized and nurtured.

The Eighteenth Amendment was promised in the Charter of Democracy signed in London on 14 May 2006, by Benazir Bhutto and Nawaz Sharif. It called for restoring the 1973 Constitution as on 12 October 1999 i.e. before the military coup, with provisions for joint electorate, minorities and women reserved seats on closed party lists, lowering the voting age and increase in seats in Parliament. It also called for the repeal of Legal Framework Order (LFO) 2000 and the Seventeenth Amendment.

In pursuance of this commitment, a Parliamentary Committee on Constitutional Reforms was set up with Senator Raza Rabbani as chairman and Senator Ishaq Dar as co-chair. After intense deliberations, the Committee submitted a comprehensive report, which was debated at length in both houses of Parliament and 8 April 2010, the Eighteenth Amendment was passed.

The main features of the Eighteenth Amendment, which incorporated a total of 102 Amendments in the Constitution are summarized below:

- The concurrent list of 47 subjects on which both the Federal Parliament and Provincial Assemblies could legislate was abolished, transferring these subjects to Provincial jurisdiction. However, some items were added to Part-II of the Federal legislature list (Schedule-IV) by increasing the number of items from 8 to 18. Under Article 154, policies in relation to subjects in Part-II of Schedule-IV are formulated and regulated by the inter-provincial Council of Common Interests (CCI).

- The powers and functions of the Council of Common Interests were enhanced. In the original 1973 Constitution, a Council of Common Interests was created because after the separation of East Pakistan and the breakup of One Unit in West Pakistan into four Provinces, certain provincial subjects like Railways, Water and Power, Natural Gas and Public Sector Industries had to be federalized. To handle these subjects on behalf of the Provinces, the special mechanism of CCI was created under the direct supervision of both houses of Parliament. Now after the Eighteenth Amendment, the CCI has also become an important forum for inter-provincial coordination for a broader range of subjects.

- Article 58-2(b) was abolished once again. This article was initially inserted by Gen. Ziaul Haq in March 1985, when he restored the Constitution. It was amended by the Eighth Amendment of October 1985 to reduce the discretion of the President. It was used four times in the next 12 years by Ziaul Haq in 1988 (PM Junejo), by Ghulam Ishaq Khan in 1990 and 1993 (PM Benazir Bhutto and PM Nawaz Sharif respectively) and by Farooq Leghari in 1996 (PM Benazir Bhutto). When Nawaz Sharif won the 1997 Election by two third majority the Thirteenth Amendment was passed in March 1997 to abolish Article 58-2(b). However General Musharraf re-inserted this Article through the Seventeenth Amendment. The Eighteenth Amendment by repealing this Article once again restored parliamentary sovereignty.

- A new procedure was prescribed for the appointment of Chief Election Commissioner and other members of the Election Commission and the Judicial Commission to ensure free and fair elections.

- The provisions of Political Parties Act were extended to Federally Administered Tribal Areas (FATA), so that members of National Assembly can be elected directly by the voters and not through selected Maliks.

- Many clauses concerning Fundamental Rights and Principles' of Policy were amended to strengthen the rights of women and minorities.

- Similarly, the autonomy of institutions like Auditor General and the Federal Public Services Commission (FPSC) was enhanced to ensure transparency and accountability.
- The name of North West Frontier Province (NWFP) was changed to Khyber Pakhtunkhwa (KP)

The renaming NWFP as Khyber Pakhtunkhwa was a long standing demand of Awami National Party (ANP). This demand was also discussed in 1990, when PML(N) and ANP formed a coalition government in NWFP. I was present in the final meeting between Nawaz Sharif and Begum Nasim Wali Khan. Nawaz Sharif did not make any commitment but promised to consider the proposal in consultation with his party and other stakeholders.

Now on the eve of the Eighteenth Amendment, the PPP, in order to secure the support of ANP parliamentarians, readily accepted this demand. Nawaz Sharif was aware that at least 40 per cent of the population of NWFP in Hazara Division and in parts of D.I. Khan Division were non-Pakhtuns. They would therefore object to the proposed name. After consultation with PML(N) representatives from Hazara, Nawaz Sharif suggested that the new name should be Khyber Pakhtunkhwa rather than only Pakhtunkhwa. This compromise was accepted and incorporated in the Eighteenth Amendment.

An important step for the timely implementation of the Eighteenth Amendment was the Seventh National Finance Commission (NFC) Award which was unanimously adopted on 20 December 2009, 14 weeks before the Eighteenth Amendment was passed. Under this Award, the share of the Provinces in the divisible Pool was increased from 41.5 to 46.5 per cent for 2010–11, gradually increasing to 57.5 per cent by 2012–13.

While this increase in the Provincial share in the divisible Pool was welcomed by the Provincial Governments, it created serious problems for the Federal Government. With a continuing increase in debt servicing and the defence budget, the remaining fiscal space in the Federal Budget was not enough to cover the minimum necessary administrative expenditures or public sector development programme. This, I believe is one of the main factors for which the Eighteenth Amendment has been criticized.

There have been some other problems in the implementation of the Eighteenth Amendment. In December 2010, five Ministries (Local

Government, Population Welfare, Youth, Zakat and Special initiatives) were wound up and five more (Education, Culture, Livestock, Social Welfare and Tourism) were devolved to provinces. In July 2011, another seven Ministries (Food and Agriculture, Health, Environment, Labour, Sports, Minorities and Women Development) were abolished.

Thus overall, 17 Ministries, 174 functions, and 116 organizations were either closed or transferred to Provinces. It was not easy for the Inter-Provincial Implementation Committee to manage redistribution of assets and resources on such a large scale. Relocating federal employees to different Provinces was also a daunting challenge.

One way to solve these problems was to recreate some of the Ministries under a different name for limited coordination or international functions. Overall the Eighteenth Amendment had a positive impact on relations between the Federation and the Provinces.

Elections 2013

After the non-party elections of 1985, all the other General Elections were essentially between two parties, the Pakistan Muslim League and the Pakistan Peoples Party. As discussed in Chapter 6 (page78) these two parties won 75 to 80 per cent of all seats in the National Assembly in each of the four elections held in 1988, 1990, 1993 and 1997. In 2013, a third political party, the Pakistan Tehreek-e-Insaf (PTI) had entered the arena with a bang.

Imran Khan's first major public meeting in Lahore in October 2011, was very impressive. The crowd was much larger than expected and the participation of well-dressed educated youth, both boys and girls, was a pleasant surprise for everyone. After that PTI launched a successful membership drive. In Punjab, many workers who were dissatisfied with the PPP government joined the PTI in large numbers. In Khyber Pakhtunkhawa (KP), the membership drive was even more successful because unlike Punjab, where the voters were divided between two parties (PML and PPP) in KP, there were at least four other parties with large membership—ANP, JUI(F), JI and PPP (Sherpao) —later renamed JWP.

In Punjab, the vote bank of PML(N) however, remained intact and in Sindh, PPP also retained its vote bank.

The election campaign normally starts 6 to 9 months before the scheduled date of the elections, but electioneering for the May 2013 election started 18 months earlier. PML(N) announced its Manifesto Committee in January 2012 and other parties a few months later.

The Twentieth Amendment to the Constitution passed on 28 February 2012, laid down the process for installing a caretaker set up to hold free and fair elections. It visualized an eight-member committee at the centre and in each province to select the caretaker Prime Minister and caretaker Chief Ministers from a list of 3 names recommended by the Prime Minister and the Leader of the Opposition. If no consensus was reached within 3 days, the matter would be referred to ECP for nominating the PM and the CMs.

In February 2013, the Parliamentary Committee was unable to reach a consensus and the Election Commission nominated Hazar Khan Khoso of Balochistan as caretaker PM.

The results of the 2013 elections held in May 2013, as given below, were a pleasant surprise for PML(N) and a disappointment for other major parties:

Results of 2013 General Election					
Parties	National Assembly	Punjab Assembly	Sindh Assembly	KPK Assembly	Balochistan Assembly
PML(N)	129	214	4	12	9
PPP	34	5	65	2	-
PTI	25	19	3	35	-
MQM(P)	19	-	37	-	-
JUI(F)	8	-	-	13	6
PML(F)	4	-	6	-	-
JI	3	1	-	7	-
PKMAP	3	-	-	-	10
NPP	2	-	3	-	-
PML(Q)	2	7	1	-	5
ANP	2	-	-	4	1
PML(Zia)	1	2	-	-	-
BNP	1	-	-	-	2
NP	1	-	-	-	7
QWP	1	-	-	7	-
AML	1	-	-	-	-
APML	1	-	-	1	-
Total:	237	248	119	81	40

Note: These results cover only contested seats and do not include Women and Minority seats.
Source: Election Commission of Pakistan.

In concluding this brief review of the Zardari led PPP government from 2008 to 2013, it must be acknowledged that despite so many negative external and internal factors, President Zardari left a more settled Pakistan than the turbulent landscape he inherited in 2008. He presided over a smooth democratic transition, in which one elected government completed its 5 year tenure and handed over power to another elected government. Thanks to the Charter of Democracy, signed in 2006, the opposition led by PML(N) also recognized that even a 'bad democracy is better than no democracy'.

President Zardari's commitment to policies of reconciliation was genuine but it did not help to improve his relations with the judiciary and the military establishment. His efforts to control the ISI, through the Ministry of Interior also, created considerable mistrust. Pakistan's relations with US were also adversely affected by the Raymond Davis incident, the Salala episode and the debacle at Abbottabad to arrest Osama Bin Laden.

The rapid expansion of electronic media during this period was an important element in reinforcing the negative image of the PPP government. Stories and scandals exposing stories of mega corruption and governance failures were reported regularly by well-known TV Channels. This was a significant factor in the dismal performance of the PPP in the 2013 elections.

Throughout PPP's tenure (2008–13) there was aggressive reporting and exaggerations and at times outright vilification of PPP leaders in the media. Parallel with that the superior judiciary's activism kept the government under siege. The campaign at the time was largely understood as a natural outcome of a vibrant and free press and an independent judiciary. The same process was repeated with greater vigour and much less sophistication in 2014–6, until the desired results were achieved. PML(N) leadership must share some responsibility for not understanding the game plan and not seeing the bigger picture until it was too late.

CHAPTER 15

Nawaz Sharif's Third Term
as Prime Minister (2013–2017)

Nawaz Sharif's third term as Prime Minister started in a very positive political atmosphere. A democratically elected government had transferred power to another elected government in a peaceful manner to demonstrate that the roots of democracy were growing stronger in Pakistan. Pakistan Muslim League-Nawaz (PML(N) was jubilant at their outstanding electoral success as it had secured about 60 per cent of the seats in the National Assembly and 80 per cent in Punjab.

PML(N) did not need the support of any other political party to form the Federal Government in Islamabad, yet Nawaz Sharif invited Maulana Fazalur Rehman of Jamiat Ulema-e-Islam (JUI(F) and Mehmood Khan Achakzai's Pashtunkhwa Milli Awami Party (PKMAP) to join the government.

Nawaz Sharif also announced that the mandate of the people must be respected and although PML(N) with support of JUI(F) and some independents could form the Provincial Government in Khyber Pakhtunkhawa, Pakistan Tehreek-e-Insaf (PTI), as the largest party, must be given the first option to form the government. Similarly, in Balochistan, the Balochistan National Party (BNP), with support from JUI(F) and PKMAP and PML(N) was able to form the Provincial government. In Punjab and Sindh, the respective mandates of PML(N) and PPP were clear. Nawaz Sharif also discouraged the PML(N) members of AJK Assembly from any attempts to dislodge the AJK government led by PPP at that time.

The 2013 Cabinet

The third Cabinet of Nawaz Sharif was formed on 7 June 2013 and included twenty ministers and eight Ministers of State. The twenty

ministers were: Ishaq Dar (Finance), Chaudhary Nisar Ali Khan
(Interior), Shahid Khaqan Abbasi (Petroleum & Natural Resources),
Khawaja Muhammad Asif (Water & Power), Ahsan Iqbal (Planning,
Development & Reform), Khawaja Saad Rafiq (Railways), Khurram
Dastgir (Commerce), Abdul Qadir Baloch (States and Frontier
Regions), Rana Tanwir Hussain (Defence Production), Sikandar Hayat
Bosan (National Food Security), Ghulam Murtaza Jatoi (Indusries &
Production), Pervez Rashid (Information & National Heritage),
Kamran Michael (Human Rights), Sardar Yusaf (Religious Affairs), Pir
Sadruddin Shah (Overseas Pakistanis), Barjees Tahir (Kashmir Affairs
& Gilgit-Baltistan), Zahid Hamid (Law & Justice), Sheikh Aftab
Ahmed (Parliamentary Affairs), Riaz Hussain Pirzada (Inter-Provincial
Coordination), Akram Durrani (Housing & Works).

There were 8 Minister of State: Muhammad Baligh Ur Rehman
(Federal Education and Professional Training), Saira Afzal Tarar
(National Health), Jam Kamal Khan (Petroleum and Natural
Resources), Abid Sher Ali (Water and Power), Annusha Rehman
(Information Technology), Usman Ibrahim (Capital Administration),
Pir Muhammad Aminul Hasnat Shah (Religious Affairs), Abdul
Hakeem Baloch (Railways).

In addition, there were three Advisors and Special Assistants. I was
appointed as Prime Minister's Advisor on Foreign Affairs and also
National Security Advisor.

Over the next four years, there were several changes and additions
in the Federal Cabinet. By the end July 2017, when Nawaz Sharif's
Cabinet was replaced by a new Cabinet under Shahid Khaqan Abbasi,
there were a total of thirty-two Ministers,fourteen Minister of States,
five Advisors and eight Special Assistants.

In his very first Cabinet meeting, on 11June 2013, Nawaz Sharif
recalled the basic message of PML(N) election manifesto that during
both its previous tenures, the PML(N) had fully demonstrated its ability
to focus on the economy as the centre piece of its priorities. Apart from
fundamental economic reforms in the 1990s, it had also achieved
notable success in resolving inter-provincial issues like the 1991 Indus
Basin Water Accord and 1991 National Finance Commission (NFC)
Award. But this time he said, PML(N) had inherited a very difficult
economic situation. It will therefore need to move on several fronts
simultaneously.

Nawaz Sharif then listed two important pre-requisites for the revival of the economy i.e. controlling militancy and terrorism and overcoming the energy crisis. The speed and determination with which Nawaz Sharif addressed these two issues over the next two years was outstanding.

The PML(N) Election Manifesto had already provided detailed guidelines, targets and policy options in these two areas which were based on solid research. As Chairman of the Manifesto Committee, I was able to draw on a considerable volume of this research, conducted by the Institute of Public Policy at my university Beaconhouse National University (BNU).

The Security Challenge

After a series of meetings between the Interior Minister, Chaudhry Nisar Ali Khan and the Army Chief, General Ashfaq Parvez Kayani, Prime Minister Nawaz Sharif decided to hold a special Cabinet meeting in Karachi on 3 and 4 September 2013, to address the serious problems of target killings, bomb blasts, suicide attacks and other acts of insurgency in and around Karachi. The formal Cabinet meeting was preceded by lengthy briefings on the ground situation by the Sindh Government and by D.G. Rangers, Major General Rizwan Akhtar.

In these briefings, it was reported that a total of 13,000 persons had been killed and 33,000 injured in 12,800 attacks since 2001. One third of these casualties were law enforcement personnel. Between 2008 and 2013, there were 350 drone attacks (with the highest number of 117 attacks in 2010). About 2500 persons were killed in these attacks including 570 foreigners.

It was also highlighted that between 2008 and 2013 a total of 2,500 persons had died in Karachi alone as a result of target killings.

It was obvious from this briefing that controlling these formidable security threats was beyond the capability of the Sindh Police Force. The need to entrust greater responsibility to the Rangers was therefore accepted but with the stipulation that Rangers would identify and apprehend terrorists and insurgents but the responsibility for investigation and judicial trials will remain with the Police.

The Cabinet, at its second meeting on 4 September 2013 approved a new law 'Protection of Pakistan Act, 2013' to give special policing powers to Sindh Rangers for a period of 2 years. These powers were extended by Sindh Government in September 2015 to enable the Rangers to act as the lead force.

Over the next four months, 13,900 suspected criminals were arrested and 48 criminals were killed in encounters. Large quantities of arms and ammunition were also recovered.

The next important initiative in dealing with the security challenge was the launch of Operation Zarb-e-Azb in North Waziristan, which had become a major sanctuary of many groups of local and foreign terrorists and militants. These included the Tehrik-i-Taliban Pakistan (TTP), the Haqqani Network, East Turkistan Islamic Movement (ETIM) and the Islamic Movement of Uzbekistan. Each group had built its own training centres for suicide attacks, IED factories, communication centres and underground medical facilities in different parts of North Waziristan.

The initial plan presented to the National Security Committee by General Raheel Sharif called for starting this operation in the first week of March 2015. But it was suggested that an attempt should be made to initiate a dialogue with the Tehrik-i-Taliban Pakistan (TTP) to persuade them to surrender their arms. Two different negotiating committees were set up amidst many speculations, but there was very little progress. The National Security Committee again met in the first week of June and decided to launch the operation from 15 of June. The Army had made elaborate arrangements to re-locate about half a million people to adjacent areas of Bannu and Dera Ismail Khan.

The operation, which lasted two years, was an outstanding success. At least 3,500 terrorists were killed and the writ of the state was established throughout North and South Waziristan. According to official reports about 7,500 ammunition factories and 990 hideouts were destroyed and 3,500 rockets and mortars, 253 tons of explosives were recovered.

The army suffered heavy casualties, with 500 deaths and twice as many injuries.

Another segment of the Operation Zarb-e-Azb was undertaken in Khyber Agency, and about 900 terrorists belonging to Lashkar-e-Islam and some other groups were eliminated.

On 16 December 2014, an unprecedented national tragedy descended on Pakistan like a major bolt from the blue. A group of terrorists from Afghanistan launched an attack on the Army Public School in Peshawar. Before the security forces arrived, the terrorists had killed 132 school children and 10 teachers in a matter of minutes, sending shock waves throughout the country.

Pakistan Air Force went into immediate action against the terrorists, hideouts and destroyed them. The Foreign Office also lodged a strong protest with the Afghan Government.

Within three days, Nawaz Sharif convened an All Parties Conference which was attended by leaders of all major political parties. The Conference decided to adopt a comprehensive National Action Plan to root out terrorism and extremism in all its manifestations. A drafting committee was set up and within a week the following twenty points National Action Plan was adopted.

National Action Plan – January 2015

1. Execution of convicted terrorists.
2. Establishment of special trial courts.
3. Ensure no armed militias are allowed to function in the country.
4. Strengthening and activation of National Counter Terrorism Authority (NACTA).
5. Countering hate speech and extremist material.
6. Choking financing for terrorists and terrorist organizations.
7. Ensuring against re-emergence of proscribed organizations.
8. Establishing and deploying a dedicated counter-terrorism force.
9. Taking effective steps against religious persecution.
10. Registration and regulation of madrassas.
11. Ban on glorification of terrorism and terrorist organizations.
12. FATA (Federally Administered Tribal Areas) Reforms.
13. Dismantling communication networks of terrorist organizations.
14. Measures against abuse of internet and social media for terrorism.
15. Zero tolerance for militancy in Punjab.
16. Taking the on-going operation in Karachi to its logical conclusion.
17. Reconciliation in Balochistan.
18. Dealing firmly with sectarian terrorists.

19. Policy to deal with the issue of Afghan refugees.
20. Revamping and reforming the criminal justice system.

Over the next four years, actions on some elements of the National Action Plan were reasonably successful and effective. These included 11 out of 20 points i.e. No.1, 2, 6, 8, 10, 12, 13, 14, 16, 17, and 19 listed above.

However, action on at least 5 points (No.5, 7, 9, 18 and 20) was by definition, a complex and a long term process which needed more time, patience and stronger public opinion.

On the remaining 4 points (3, 4, 11 and 15) some progress was registered but there were unexpected political and institutional difficulties in their implementation. More recently, because of the pressures generated by the Financial Action Task Force, some of these difficulties have been resolved, opening the prospects for speedier implementation of the National Action Plan as a whole.

In 2016, an elaborate plan was also prepared to fence the 2,600 kilometre border with Afghanistan. There would be several crossing points with adequate facilities to replace the previous system under which more than 50,000 persons crossed the border, both ways, every day, without any passports and visas. The new system was expected to ensure that the territory of both the countries was not used against either countries by insurgents, terrorists or smugglers.

In February 2017, a new Operation, code named Radd-ul-Fasaad was also launched by the new Chief of Army Staff, General Qamar Bajwa. This operation was aimed at rounding up scattered groups of terrorists and extremists who had escaped from the tribal belt and had taken shelter in surrounding areas of large cities and towns.

By May 2018, when the PML(N) government completed its tenure, the security situation in the country had seen a sea change and Pakistan had virtually turned the corner in its fight against terrorism and extremism.

National Security Committee (NSC)

In Chapter 11, I have explained at some length, the reasons for our continuing failure to evolve an effective national security system and also emphasized that as an inevitable consequence of the absence of such a system, there was a wide gap between the military establishment and the elected civilian set up on different aspects of national security policies. This gap was also partly responsible for recurrent political instability and for periodical tensions between the two.

In the second Cabinet of Nawaz Sharif, I had already served as Foreign Minister from August 1998 to October 1999. This time, in addition to Foreign Affairs, I was also appointed as National Security Advisor.

There was now, I recognized, an historic opportunity to create a National Security Committee with the right composition, comprehensive terms of reference and a well-equipped secretariat. The National Security Council, created by General Ziaul Haq in 1985 and that by General Musharraf in 2004 were actually meant to give the army an institutional role to supervise the political system. That is why these two Councils included the Chief Ministers of the Provinces but not the Ministers for Defence, Foreign Affairs or Interior. The first was deleted from the constitution within 9 months and the second never became functional.

A Defence Committee of the Cabinet has been in existence since 1956 but it met infrequently (held one meeting in 2008 and 2009, two in 2010 and four in 2011). It was utilized primarily for briefing the political leadership on security issues and not as a decision-making body on security issues. I suggested to the Prime Minister that a meeting of the Defence Committee of the Cabinet should be convened so that it can convert itself into a 'Cabinet Committee on Defence and National Security'. The option of calling it a 'National Security Council' was not considered because such a Council was created in the past under the President. A Cabinet Committee is always chaired by the Prime Minister.

The Defence Committee of the Cabinet met on 22 August 2013 and reconstituted itself as the 'Cabinet Committee on Defence and National Security'. In the second meeting held on 17 December 2013, the Prime Minister decided that the name of the Committee should be simplified to 'National Security Committee', as the principal decision making body on National Security. In addition to the Ministers of Defence, Finance, Foreign Affairs, Interior and Information, it would also include the Chairman, Joint Chiefs of Staff Committee (CJCSC), and

Chiefs of Army, Navy and Air Staff as members. This was a significant change because in the previous Defence Committee of the Cabinet, only four Ministers concerned were members and the Service Chief attended as non-members by special invitation.

An important component of the proposed national security system was the creation of two support institutions:

- A Planning Committee chaired by the National Security Advisor (NSA) with Secretaries of foreign affairs, defense, interior, heads of three intelligence agencies and the Chief of General Staff, to identify national security issues on which briefs and working papers would be prepared for consideration of the NSC and where necessary make arrangements for further research by public and private sector institutions.
- An Advisory Board, chaired by the NSA and consisting of heads of all the relevant think tanks including Institute of Strategic Studies, Islamabad (ISSI), Institute of Regional Studies (IRS), Institute for Strategic Studies, Research and Analysis, (ISSRA) and National Defence University (NDU) to conduct research on issues referred to them by the Planning Committee and also organize national and international seminars on national security issues.

At the second meeting, held in December 2013, the NSC approved in principle the creation of these two support bodies. In the third meeting held on 17 April 2014, the detailed TORs and composition of these bodies were submitted. However the approval was deferred since one member suggested they would like to give further thought to the composition of the Planning Committee. The item was again deferred at the fourth meeting held on 10 October 2014. Since no meeting of the NSC was held in 2015 and I was also replaced as NSA in October 2015, these two important bodies, so critical for the proper functioning of the National Security System, were never created.

Another important recommendation approved by the Prime Minister was to create a separate National Security Division to serve as the Secretariat of the National Security Committee. Mohammad Sadiq, a senior member of the Pakistan Foreign Service and at that time, Pakistan's Ambassador in Kabul was appointed as Secretary of the National Security Committee. However, since the National Security Division did not get the support of the proposed Planning Committee, and an Advisory Board, its capacity to undertake research or prepare substantive working papers was seriously handicapped.

My efforts to hold at least one meeting of the Committee every quarter did not succeed. After two meetings in 2013 (in August and December), the NSC met only twice in 2014 on 17 April and 10 October. No meeting was held throughout 2015 but two meetings were convened in 2016, 6 April and 22 July. Meanwhile, the previous practice of seeking Prime Minister's approval in restricted meetings with the Army Chief and his core team continued.

In October 2015, I was replaced as National Security Advisor by Lieutenant General (retd) Nasir Khan Janjua. I, however, continued as Advisor to Prime Minister on Foreign Affairs till July 2017.

Since its creation in August 2013, the National Security Committee has been useful on certain specific topics and initiatives like Operation Zarb-e-Azb, National Action Plan and FATA Reforms, but my long standing mission to create an effective National Security System with full powers to take decision on all matters of national security remained largely unfulfilled.

Foreign Policy Challenges

During the first half of PML(N) Government's five-year tenure (2013–2018), there were many positive developments on the foreign policy front:

- Strategic Dialogue with the US at Foreign Minister's level, which was suspended in 2011, was resumed, preparing the ground for an official visit by Nawaz Sharif to Washington DC in October 2013, followed by a second visit in October 2015.
- In May 2014, Prime Minister Narendra Modi invited Prime Minister Nawaz Sharif to attend his inauguration in New Delhi. The bilateral meeting on that occasion strengthened expectations that the composite dialogue with India could be resumed.
- In November 2014, President Ashraf Ghani of Afghanistan paid his first visit to Pakistan, after his election, sending strong signals of a new positive phase in Pak-Afghan relation.

- In April 2015, President Xi Jinping of China during his historic visit to Islamabad finalized a project portfolio of US$46 billion under the China-Pakistan Economic Corridor, creating a new threshold in the traditionally strong China-Pakistan relations.

At that time the US was planning to drastically reduce its military presence in Afghanistan from over 100,000 troops to only 10,000 by the end of 2014. It was therefore expecting Pakistan to facilitate this draw down by persuading the Taliban enter into peace talks.

President Ashraf Ghani's expectations were even higher. He felt that Pakistan had enough influence over the Taliban to persuade them to negotiate with his government.

With India, we never expected restoration of friendly relations anytime soon, but as a minimum we were seeking a resumption of dialogue, a quieter Line of Control in Kashmir and some confidence building measures.

Unfortunately, as explained in subsequent sections of this Chapter, many of these expectations did not materialize.

Relations with the US

Soon after I took over my new responsibilities at the Foreign Office, I received a message, through the US Embassy in Islamabad that Secretary of State, John Kerry would like to meet on 2 July 2013 on the side-lines of the Ministerial Session of Asian Regional Forum in Brunei Darussalam.

I conveyed to Secretary Kerry our appreciation for the President Obama's May statement, welcoming the new government in Pakistan, after a smooth democratic transition and expressed the hope that we will put behind us the past irritants and move forward our relations to a new strategic level. He quickly checked his diary and said the earliest he could visit Pakistan would be the last week of July 2013.

Secretary Kerry arrived in Islamabad on 31 July, as promised. We had a lengthy delegation-level meeting, preceded by a brief, one on one meeting and followed by an official lunch and a joint press briefing. Secretary Kerry also called on Prime Minister Nawaz Sharif. He also had a briefing session with the Army Chief, General Ashfaq Parvez Kayani.

My first detailed interaction with Secretary Kerry was very useful because both sides were able to spell out their respective concerns and expectations. The US agenda included (i) terrorism related issues (including safe havens of militants in Pakistan, cross border militancy, Haqqani network, and Al-Qaeda's links with certain Jihadi Organizations) (ii) Afghanistan reconciliation process, (iii), Pak-India relations and (iv) nuclear non-proliferation and development of tactical weapons.

The list of issues identified by Pakistan for discussions with the US apart from responding to issues raised by Secretary Kerry included (a) US drone strikes (b) revival of defence cooperation (c) greater market access (d) US investment in energy and other sectors (e) civil nuclear cooperation.

We had a very intense and frank exchange of views on all these topics. We agreed that we will continue these discussions in all our formal and informal interactions whenever and wherever we met.

An important outcome of this visit was an agreement in principle that Prime Minister Nawaz Sharif will pay an official visit to Washington DC in October 2013 in addition to an informal meeting between him and President Obama on the side-lines of the UN General Assembly in September, 2013.

Another important decision was to revive the Strategic Dialogue between US and Pakistan at Foreign Ministers level. This dialogue was initiated in 2010, supported by several Working Groups on energy, trade, economic cooperation, defence, law enforcement and counter terrorism and non-proliferation. But within a year the dialogue was suspended in 2011 after the Raymond Davis incident in Lahore and the Salala episode in Mohmand Agency. We agreed that the resumed dialogue will take place in Washington DC in January 2014, preceded by meetings of different Working Groups.

As already discussed, following the Salala episode, a 16-member Parliamentary Committee on National Security had been set up to evolve new guidelines for revised terms of engagements with the US/ Nato/ISAF. The Committee, chaired by Senator Raza Rabbani, held 10 meetings and submitted its report on 13 January 2012, containing 16 main recommendations and 24 sub-recommendations. Apart from closure of transit facilities to Afghanistan, the Report asked the US to review its footprints in Pakistan i.e. no drone strikes, no hot pursuit, no unauthorized activity by private security contractors. It also called for strategic parity with India, after the Indo-US nuclear deal.

These guidelines had virtually frozen US-Pakistan relations. That is why US was keen to revive this relationship through frequent high level interactions. That was the context in which Nawaz Sharif was invited on an official work visit to the US in October 2013 i.e. only a few weeks after he assumed office of the Prime Minister.

In his interactions with Nawaz Sharif, President Obama was gracious, respectful, and positive. He welcomed the smooth democratic transition from one elected government to another. He also expressed his appreciation for Nawaz Sharif's sincere efforts to improve relations with India. He said he would very much like to assist Pakistan in overcoming its economic difficulties and its energy crisis. We should, therefore deepen our bilateral economic cooperation. Various working groups under the Strategic Dialogue had already identified many specific areas for such cooperation.

During a separate meeting with my counterpart, National Security Advisor, Susan Rice openly expressed her frustration with President Karzai of Afghanistan. He was not ready to sign a Bilateral Security Agreement with the US or making much progress on reconciliation with the Taliban. She suggested that the US and Pakistan should evolve a 'Joint Strategy' for bringing peace to Afghanistan, so that US forces can withdraw without 'a stigma of defeat'.

In my remarks, in response to Susan Rice's comments on Afghanistan, I emphasized that we can bring durable peace to Afghanistan only through an inclusive process that is open to all Afghans, so that all have a stake in the peace process. Due to serious ethnic, tribal and cultural diversities, Afghanistan is polarized and fragile. Yet, we have to include all factions in the reconciliation process. If we exclude one important stakeholder which controls a sizeable portion of Afghanistan, namely the Taliban, by branding them as terrorists, we will not be able to achieve enduring peace.

She did not readily accept this approach for the way forward in Afghanistan at that time, but 5 years later, the Qatar process made progress only after US followed this important pre-requisite and accepted the need for an inclusive peace process.

The US had already announced that it will reduce the size of its troops in Afghanistan from over 100,000 to only 12,000 by December

2014. Their main concern now was the ability of the Afghan government to hold the ground against the Taliban. Secretary Kerry explained at some length their apprehensions that many groups of the Afghan Taliban like the Haqqani Network had sanctuaries in North Waziristan from where they provided logistic support to Taliban fighters and also launched attacks on selected targets.

At that time, I knew that a major anti-terror operation was being planned for North Waziristan by the Pakistan Army. Once that operation was successfully completed, all such sanctuaries of different groups will be wiped out. So I reassured him, in general terms, without indicating the timing of such an operation. Secretary Kerry responded very positively and said 'If that happens, US will offer Pakistan a major concession like preferential market access for its exports which Pakistan had been seeking for some time.

The Operation Zarb-e-Azb was launched on 15 June, 2014 and was successfully completed within 2 years to re-establish Pakistan's writ throughout the tribal belt. But the promise of preferential access for Pakistan's exports to the US was never fulfilled.

In January 2015, Secretary Kerry came to Islamabad for the next annual round of the Strategic Dialogue. Since this visit took place just a few days before President Obama's visit to India, I gave Secretary Kerry two 'non-papers' on Afghanistan and on strategic stability. My main emphasis in the second non-paper was that the US had every right to shape the scope and nature of its relations with India. However, in expanding its military and strategic cooperation, it should not ignore the impact of such cooperation on Pakistan's security concerns. He promised to convey these concerns to President Obama. However, as subsequent events clearly demonstrated, the strategic partnership between the US and India has been growing steadily with special emphasis on defence production and defence technologies. In complete contrast, the defence cooperation between the US and Pakistan had been shrinking. Even the sale of 8 F-16 fighter jets, for which funding had already been allocated, was blocked in 2015.

Prime Minister Nawaz Sharif's second official visit to the US between 20 and 23 October 2015 was more eventful than the first official visit in October 2013. A fortnight before the visit, Peter Lavoy a member of the White House staff came to Islamabad for finalizing the programme and the key issues for discussion. On his return, he sent to the Foreign Secretary, Aizaz Chaudhry a 'draft joint statement' which could be issued after incorporating any changes arising from the actual discussions. As we analysed the draft statement in the Foreign office, we found that it was attempting to cross several 'red lines' on many important issues. We accordingly made a presentation to the Prime Minister. He silently absorbed the presentation and then suddenly said 'If that is the outcome they expect from the visit, then let us cancel the visit'. He then asked me to call Susan Rice, the National Security Advisor in the White House and tell her that we are cancelling the visit.

When I called National Security Advisor, Susan Rice later that evening, she was taken by surprise, She called me back an hour later, and said 'the visit was only 6 days away and its sudden cancellation will lead to unnecessary speculations. The draft joint statement can be modified through mutual consultations'. I, then suggested that Foreign Secretary Aizaz Chaudhry will arrive two days in advance with a fresh draft of the joint statement and finalize it in consultation with your team. She agreed. That exercise was successful, even though it took 16 hours over two days to reach agreement on all, except two points. The brackets on these two points were removed later during my discussion with Advisor Rice and after the Prime Minister's meeting with President Obama.

The Prime Minister's meeting with President Obama was as cordial as in October 2013. But he was worried about the lack of progress in Afghanistan and about visible deterioration in Pakistan's relations with India and with Afghanistan. He said that he was now entering the final year of his 8 year Presidency and would like to leave behind a long term and enduring partnership between Pakistan and the US. Unfortunately, our expectation that after such a heavy mandate in the 2013 elections, one will be able to put the civil-military relations on an even keel, was not fully realized.

We had several in-depth review meetings after the Prime Minister's second visit to the US, to analyse the sense of frustration in the outgoing US Administration that most of US concerns about the Haqqani network, Shakil Afridi and particularly on the nuclear issues had not been addressed. We concluded that the US had overlooked the enormous progress that Pakistan had made in tackling the issue of terrorism, especially in the Tribal belt through Operation Zarb-e-Azb. Furthermore, the US was fully aware of the steps we had taken on nuclear safety. But on tactical nuclear weapons and the missile programme, the US should in fact recognize our growing concerns about India's nuclear programme. India had been deepening conventional asymmetry with Pakistan and was also developing a second strike nuclear capability. Having moved from defensive to offensive deterrence, it was also adopting a 'compliance posture'. Pakistan, had therefore, every right to safeguard its security as a de-jure and not de facto nuclear power because it had not signed the Non-Proliferation Treaty (NPT) but the US has not been fully sensitive to Pakistan's security concerns.

In January 2017, Donald Trump became as President and in the first few weeks, made unfriendly remarks about Pakistan in a series of Tweets 'US has given billions of dollars in aid to Pakistan, but Pakistan has done little for US', and 'It is sheltering those who are killing our soldiers in Afghanistan'.

Then on 20 August 2017, President Trump unveiled an expansive new Afghanistan South Asia Strategy in which he said:

Today, 20 US designated foreign terrorist organizations are active in Afghanistan and Pakistan, the highest concentration in any region, anywhere in the world. For its part, Pakistan often gives safe havens to agents of chaos, violence and terror. Pakistan is a major concern. It must stop providing safe havens for terrorists to rest and refit for actions in Afghanistan and elsewhere. Pakistan has much to gain from partnering with our efforts in Afghanistan and much to lose by continuing to harbour criminals and terrorists.

In comparison, the Trump, administration further intensified its conventional weapons cooperation with India, through joint manufacturing and transfer of advanced technologies. At the same time, it intensified pressure on Pakistan to counter terrorism. It endorsed India's stand on the issue in different fora by naming different groups like Jamaat-ud-Dawa and Jaish-e-Mohammed and taking a strong position in Financial Action Task Force (FATF) to move Pakistan once again to the 'Grey List'.

But within a few months of these tweets, the US started exploring options to open talks with the Taliban. As explained in the next section, the US policy on Afghanistan during the Obama Administration from January 2009 to December 2016, did not advance any of the goals for which the US and its allies had invaded Afghanistan in October 2001, causing a large number of casualties and inflicting prolonged suffering on the people of Afghanistan. So, it was time to revisit that policy.

The Unending Turmoil in Afghanistan

In Chapter 11, I have analysed the historical background of the multi-dimensional crisis in Afghanistan and pointed out how the US and its allies, after setting up, with Pakistan's support, hundreds of madrasahs in Afghanistan and Pakistan to train thousands of volunteers to fight and eventually defeat a super power, had walked away from Afghanistan, pushing it into a prolonged civil war. After 1994, these volunteers called the Taliban, gradually extended their writ and established their government in Kabul by 1998. They had eradicated poppy cultivation, disarmed different groups and warlords and were providing minimum necessary services in areas under their control. The 9/11 attack on the World Trade Centre marked the end of the Taliban regime in Afghanistan. None of those identified as responsible for the 9/11 attacks were Afghans, but by blaming Osama Bin Laden for 'inspiring' the attack, the US launched in October 2001, a brutal attack on the poorest country in the World. All independent observers are agreed on at least one point that none of the objectives, cited as justification for the 2001 attack on Afghanistan, namely bringing peace to Afghanistan, eliminating threat of terrorism, promoting democratic governance and initiating sustainable development, have been achieved. Nonetheless, the people of Afghanistan have continued to suffer death and destruction for over four decades.

In the light of this grim historical background, in June 2013, when I re-joined the Foreign Office, I was overwhelmed by the baffling array of additional blunders and miscalculations that had shaped the US policy in the preceding few years.

Soon after taking over in January 2009, President Obama had called for a strategic overview of the Afghan policy and also accepted Secretary of State, Hillary Clinton's recommendation to create a special Afghanistan-Pakistan (Afpak) Cell in the State Department under Richard Holbrooke, one the best US diplomats. The review went on for several months, with President Obama himself chairing at least 10 meetings of the National Security team, but there was no consensus on the way forward. The US State Department, under Hillary Clinton and Richard Holbrooke argued for diplomacy and political reconciliation with the Taliban but the Pentagon, the CIA and the White House were all opposed to this option.

Eventually, President Obama accepted the recommendation of General Stanley McChrystal, the new US Commander in Afghanistan to allow a surge of 30,000 additional troops in Afghanistan for 'finishing off' the Taliban insurgency.

During his election campaign, President Obama had promised to move away from Bush's 'militarized foreign policy', but in Afghanistan, he followed the Iraq's model of a counter insurgency strategy (code named COIN), although conditions in Afghanistan were radically different. He further diluted the impact of the strategy by announcing a deadline of July 2011 for the withdrawal of the bulk of the US troops from Afghanistan.

Subsequently, in June 2011, President Obama agreed to extend the deadline for troop withdrawal and also agreed to launch diplomatic efforts for reconciliation but the sequence and timing of these announcements were counterproductive. The Taliban had indicated as early as 2009 their willingness to talk to the US. If these negotiations had started then, along with the 'surge' and maximum number of troops on the ground, the US would have exerted much greater leverage. However, starting negotiations in 2011, when the 'surge' had not gained much on the ground and then to announce a new withdrawal schedule, was hardly a practical strategy. In such a situation, as subsequent events have proved, the Taliban would negotiate only for the total withdrawal of US troops without promising a ceasefire or serious negotiations with the Afghan Government.

In my assessment, President Obama was one of the best Presidents in US history and his resolve to improve relations with the Muslim world was also genuine. But on Afghanistan, the complexity of the crisis was so deep and the likely outcomes of different options so uncertain that he decided to follow the politically safer option of listening to his generals rather than the diplomats.

As many independent observers have pointed out, the US failure in Afghanistan was largely due to the mismatch between the goals, interests, and resources. The US stated goals were ambitious although its actual interests were more limited. The resources it deployed were not even adequate for the limited goals.

I and my colleagues in the Foreign Office devoted considerable time to the Afghan problem in a serious effort to facilitate a dialogue between the Taliban and the Afghan Government with the full involvement of the US. As a first step, we decided to invite President Karzai who was now in the final year of his second-five year term as President. After necessary consultations, I visited Kabul in July 2013 to personally deliver Prime Minister Nawaz Sharif's invitation for his visit to Islamabad. We had a detailed and in depth exchange of views before and after *Iftar* (breaking of fast) and President Karzai agreed to visit Islamabad in August 2013.

The following day after my return from Kabul, President Karzai issued a statement outlining some preconditions for his visit to Pakistan. He said the agenda should include 'serious and effective struggle against terrorism and for the peace process'. At that time, President Karzai had suspended the security talks with the US because the Taliban had styled their Doha office as an embassy of a government in waiting and by flying the Afghan Flag.

Despite these statements, President Karzai came to Islamabad as scheduled and had long interactions with the Prime Minister and the Army Chief. He had been President of Afghanistan for 12 years, including 3 years as interim leader before the 2003 elections. He was perceived as the most fashionable politician in Western capitals in the first few years but soon became the most disliked Afghan leader. Karzai, with his strong Durrani Tribal background and his key role in the success of the Bonn Conference of December 2001, hit back at his critics. He said, Afghanistan had become a side show after the war in Iraq and the US had no clear strategy for peace in Afghanistan. He reached out to some Taliban leaders for a dialogue and criticized US strikes that killed innocent civilians. He also brought back King Amanullah to the country from his exile with respect and dignity.

In July 2013, after my long conversation with President Karazi in Kabul, I knew that he wanted to remain popular in Afghanistan even after his retirement. So he openly criticized US policies and refused to become a scapegoat for NATO's failures. He was also lucky that unlike his two predecessors, Najibullah and Ustad Rabbani, he survived several assassination attempts.

As subsequent events have proved, not only has the US come back after wasting valuable years, to accept Karzai's strategy of talks with the Taliban but Karzai's role in peace talks with the Taliban in 2018–19 gradually moved ahead of President Ashraf Ghani's efforts.

My last interaction with President Karzai was in Dushanbe, Tajikistan in March 2014 at the Shanghai Cooperation Organization (SCO) Summit of heads of States. Since Pakistan was only an observer, Nawaz Sharif had decided that he will attend SCO Summits only after Pakistan became a full member. Meanwhile, Pakistan will be represented at Foreign Minister's level. I, therefore, represented Pakistan at all the six summits of the SCO at the head of state and head of government level between 2013 and 2016, when Pakistan became a full member of SCO in Ufa, Russia.

President Karzai was having a conversation with President Rouhani of Iran, just before the opening reception. When I joined the conversation in Persian, President Rouhani was very pleased that I could speak Persian (in fact *Darri*) so fluently. Hamid Karzai added that when Sartaj Aziz came to Kabul last year, we conducted our negotiations in four languages: Persian, Pashto, Urdu and English. Later, he said, I discovered that he also speaks Punjabi and Italian. Then, President Karzai suddenly became serious and said,

> But Mr Aziz is not helping me to bring peace to Afghanistan. My direct and indirect talks and contacts with the Taliban are making good progress. If Pakistan would offer to play a more active role, I would postpone the elections scheduled for April 2014 because bringing peace to Afghanistan is more important.

In response, I only asked, 'Is USA willing to allow you to continue with these peace efforts?' President Rouhani then diverted the conversation to another topic, after a meaningful smile.

The Afghan elections held on 5 April 2014, did not yield a clear winner and a second round was held on 14 June. In the first round, Abdullah Abdullah polled more votes than Ashraf Ghani, but in the second ballot, Ashraf Ghani secured 56 per cent of the votes and Abdullah Abdullah 43 per cent. Abdullah Abdullah refused to accept the results and there was a lengthy stalemate. Finally, the US Secretary of State, John Kerry negotiated a compromise deal which was signed on 8 August 2014. According to this deal, Ashraf Ghani would be

President and Abdullah Abdullah would also be sworn in as Chief Executive, with powers of a de facto Prime Minister. These powers were to be defined through constitutional amendments to be worked out by the two sides in the coming months.

On 29 September 2014, Ashraf Ghani was sworn in as President and Abdullah Abdullah as Chief Executive. However, the new arrangements for defining the powers of the Chief Executive were never finalized.

I visited Kabul on 19 October 2014 to invite President Ashraf Ghani to visit Pakistan. He not only agreed to undertake this visit in mid-November but was also very forthcoming in his commitment to make a new beginning in Afghanistan's relations with Pakistan. He said he wanted this 'window of opportunity' to become a door, the door to become a corridor and the corridor to become a highway through cooperation on multiple dimensions of the bilateral relationship, specially economic, security, intelligence, culture and refugees.

President Ashraf Ghani also suggested that it would be useful if the Chief of Army Staff, General Raheel Sharif would visit Kabul in the first week of November 2014. Similarly, the Afghan Finance Minister, Omar Zakhilwal and the National Security Advisor, Hanif Atmar would visit Islamabad two days before General Raheel Sharif's visit, for detailed discussions on economic and security cooperation. These visits took place as scheduled and provided a very comprehensive roadmap for bilateral cooperation.

Ashraf Ghani arrived in Islamabad on 14 November 2014. Since Nawaz Sharif's arrival from a visit abroad, due on the morning of 14 November, was delayed by a few hours, I decided that Ashraf Ghani's visit to the GHQ can take place on 14 instead of 15 November. This visit was very useful as the Director General of Military Operations (DGMO), General Aamir Riaz made a very exhaustive presentation on the security situation in the Region. President Ashraf Ghani was visibly impressed and asked many pertinent questions.

Later, in the afternoon, President Ashraf Ghani was formally received by Prime Minister Nawaz Sharif. In this meeting, Nawaz Sharif explored discretely the real question that was on everyone's mind: the capacity of the Afghan National Security Forces (ANSF) to operate on their own against the Taliban, after the drastic reduction in International Security Assistance Force (ISAF) troops from 140,000 to less than 14,000. The annual desertion rate in ANSF was almost

25 per cent. In 2014, there were at least 60 insider attacks on NATO/ ISAF forces. They may get some air support from ISAF, but it would be difficult to check the gradual advance of the Taliban who already controlled the Southern provinces of Kunar and Nuristan and overall about 45 per cent of rural areas of Afghanistan. Such turmoil in post 2014 Afghanistan could also lead to a renewed flow of refugees into Pakistan.

In response, President Ashraf Ghani said that he had already set up a Afghanistan High Peace Council to explore ways and means of political reconciliation with the Taliban. Pakistan, he said could play an important role in facilitating this process. Pakistan could also assist by denying some of the Afghan Taliban groups like the Haqqani Network the use of their safe havens in Waziristan.

The Prime Minister pointed out that a major counter insurgency campaign called Operation Zarb-i-Azb had been launched in North Waziristan in June 2014 and he was hopeful that in the next 12 months, all the safe havens of all the militant groups will be totally eliminated. Pakistan will also encourage the Taliban leaders to initiate talks with the Afghan government, but as history has shown, negotiating positions at a conference table are always determined by the ground situation. Pakistan does not, in any case, control the Taliban. It has contacts with some Taliban leaders and will do its utmost to persuade them for reconciliation talks.

Overall, President Ashraf Ghani's visit sent a strong signal of improved relations between the two countries. The economic agenda was implemented promptly specially on transit trade and speeding up various development projects financed by Pakistan from the initial pledge of US$500 million dollars.

Pakistan actively followed up on its promise to facilitate reconciliation talks. In February 2015, after a preliminary meeting with a delegation of the Taliban at Urumchi in China, it was agreed that the first formal round of talks with a delegation of the Afghan government will be held in Pakistan in July 2015.

Meanwhile, as already agreed, Prime Minister Nawaz Sharif accompanied by a high level delegation which included the Chief of Army Staff, General Raheel Sharif, paid a return visit to Kabul on 12 May 2015. The Prime Minister made the following important statement at a joint press conference with President Ashraf Ghani:

- We agreed that our bilateral relationship will continue to be guided by the following three principles: -

  • We will strictly adhere to the policy of non-interference.
  • We will not allow our respective territories to be used against the other, and
  • Afghanistan's enemies will be treated as Pakistan's enemies and Pakistan enemies will be treated as Afghanistan's enemies.

This statement was widely welcomed in both countries. The reconciliations talks were held in Bhurban, Murree on 7 July 2015 as scheduled. The Taliban sent a 5-member delegation and the Afghan official delegation had 7 members. Observers from the US Embassy in Islamabad and from the United Nations also attended. The dialogue which was chaired by the Foreign Secretary, Aizaz Chaudhry was held in a cordial atmosphere.

The success of this first, face to face, interaction between the Taliban and the Afghan Government can be judged from the fact that they agreed to meet again in the same month i.e. on 31 July, at the same location with a broader agenda and with a higher level Taliban delegation. We made all the preparations for this second round and the Taliban delegation arrived in Islamabad on 29 July in order to proceed to Murree the next day.

However, on the evening of 29 July, there was a surprising 'leak' from Kabul that the Chief Amir of Taliban, Mullah Mohammad Omar, who had ruled the Islamic Emirate of Afghanistan from1996 to 2001, had died 2 years earlier, in a Karachi hospital. This news had a devastating effect since in the absence of Mullah Omar, under whose authority would the Taliban delegation hold negotiations. The talk's scheduled for next day had to be cancelled.

I have often wondered about the motives of those who leaked the news that was two years old. The Afghan Intelligence Agency which was quoted by several news agencies as the source, obviously wanted to sabotage the talks with the Taliban. We also knew that many non-*Pakhtun* elements in the Afghan Government were not too unwilling to share power with the Taliban, but subsequent events have fully exposed the short-sightedness of this mind-set. In 2018, when the Taliban finally agreed to talk with the US, they flatly refused to talk to any representative of the Afghan Government.

This news leak also created the impression that Mullah Omar had lived and died in Pakistan. On the other hand, a Dutch journalist, Bette Dam, after 5 years of research and interviews, revealed in her book, *Searching for an Enemy*, that Mullah Omar never lived in Pakistan. Instead he was in Qalat, the capital of Zabul Province till 2004, when the US troops began building a Forward Operating Base (FOB) in Lagman, just a few minutes' walk from his hideout. Omar then moved to Shinkay district. When the US started building an FOB at Volverine, just 5 kilometres away, Omar decided not to move again. According to Dam, the Taliban leader died there from an illness on 23 April 2013.

The Taliban *Shoora* (a consultative council) promptly appointed Mullah Akhtar Mansoor as the new leader of the Taliban. On 23 May 2016, within a few months of his being appointed as leader, he was killed by a US drone attack on a vehicle in which he was travelling in Balochistan near the Afghan border. That proved to be the second major setback for direct peace talks between the Taliban and the Afghan Government.

In January 2016, a Quadrilateral Coordination Group (QCG) comprising Pakistan, Afghanistan, China and the United States was set-up to explore different options for a political solution to the Afghan conflict. Five meetings were held between January and April to define the terms of reference and a road map for the way forward. Fifteen months after Mullah Mansoor's death, the QCG was reconvened on 16 October 2017 in Muscat, Oman, following a visit to Kabul by the Pakistan Army Chief, General Qamar Bajwa. However, virtually no progress could be made because by then, President Trump had announced his preference for a military victory in Afghanistan, and also because of the varying expectations of QCG countries.

Meanwhile, the Taliban had expanded the area under their control from 45 per cent to 60 per cent. Faced with this grim reality and its anxiety to leave Afghanistan as early as possible, the US accepted the Taliban offer to talk to them directly. In the first round with the US delegation, led by Trump's special representative Zalmay Khalilzad, they restricted the agenda to two items: early withdrawal of US troops and not allowing Afghanistan to become a hub for terrorism against other countries. The Taliban were reluctant to discuss two other items, proposed by the US, a ceasefire to bring peace to Afghanistan and direct talks with the Afghan government to facilitate future power sharing. Subsequently, they agreed to talk to other Afghan leaders but not to the Afghan Government. On one occasion they allowed some Afghan officials to attend in their personal capacity.

During the first week of September 2019, Khalilzad declared that after nine rounds of talks, an agreement with the Taliban had been completed 'in principle'. Rumours also started circulating that President Trump had invited the Taliban leaders and President Ashraf Ghani to Camp David for a formal signing ceremony of the Agreement. But in a surprise tweet on Friday 6 September, President Trump announced that he had not only cancelled the secret meeting with the Taliban in Camp David but also the peace talks. The reason, he said, was a suicide attack in Kabul by the Taliban in which 12 people including an American soldier were killed.

Subsequent reports revealed other obstacles. One was President Ashraf Ghani's refusal to release Taliban prisoners, which was a part of the deal. Ashraf Ghani said that since Afghan Government was kept out of the talks, he was under no obligation to release the prisoners. Secondly, the Taliban wanted to visit the US after the agreement was signed and not before and they were also reluctant to meet Ashraf Ghani. There was also opposition to the visit of the Taliban so close to the 9/11 anniversary, within the US Congress.

Both sides have left the door open for a resumption of talks, but it is difficult to predict when that would happen and whether or not the resumed talks would lead to any reduction in violence. After the Geneva Accord of 1990, Russia withdrew its forces, but intra-Afghan hostilities reached their climax in the next few years. Similarly, it is quite possible that after the resumed peace talks and departure of US troops, intra Afghan violence may increase rather than diminish.

Relations with India

In Chapter 11, a brief overview of Pakistan's search for durable peace with India and a just solution of the Kashmir dispute have been presented. The pinnacle of these efforts was accomplished in February 1999, when Prime Minister Vajpayee visited Pakistan and signed the Lahore Declaration on 21 February 1999, committing both countries to intensify their efforts to resolve all issues, including the issue of

Jammu and Kashmir. This historic opportunity was however, derailed by the Kargil mis-adventure and then the military takeover in October 1999.

Another serious attempt to explore a negotiated settlement, issue was made in 2005–6, on the basis of General Musharraf 4 point's formula: (Identification of regions, demilitarization, self-governance and a joint mechanism)[1].

During the 10-year rule of the Congress Party under Prime Minister Manmohan Singh from 2004 to 2014, there was no major breakthrough but the composite dialogue initiated in September 1997, continued with frequent interruptions. The Line of Control (LOC) was quieter after the 2003 Agreement in which several new confidence building measures were agreed. Following Prime Minister Narendra Modi led Bharatiya Janata Party (BJP) government's takeover in May 2014, Pakistan-India relations have progressively deteriorated.

During Prime Minister Nawaz Sharif's visit to New Delhi to attend Prime Minister Modi's inauguration in May 2014, it was agreed that the two Foreign Secretaries will meet in August 2014 to discuss the agenda for further talks. However, the scheduled meeting was cancelled on the pretext of Pakistan High Commissioners' meeting with Hurriyat leaders in New Delhi. Subsequently, the meeting between the two National Security Advisors, agreed to during a meeting between the two Prime Ministers at the Ufa Summit in July 2015 was also cancelled.

In November 2015, Prime Minister Modi, probably responding to international pressures for engagement with Pakistan, approached Prime Minister Nawaz Sharif on the side-lines of the Paris Climate Change Conference and said 'let us make a new start'. Nawaz Sharif agreed and said he would welcome the participation of Indian Foreign Minister, Sushma Swaraj in the Heart of Asia Conference on Afghanistan scheduled in Islamabad on 9 December. Prime Minister Modi said that should be possible provided the two National Security Advisors(NSAs) can meet before the conference. Nawaz Sharif agreed and the two NSAs met in Bangkok on 6 December and Sushma Swaraj attended the Heart of Asia Conference in Islamabad. In our bilateral meeting after intense discussions, we agreed to resume the comprehensive dialogue on all issues under eight segments.

The positive signals emanating from this visit were further reinforced, when 16 days later, Prime Minister Modi flying from Kabul to New

Delhi, made a brief surprise stop-over in Lahore on 25 December to congratulate Nawaz Sharif on his birthday. The impression that Nawaz Sharif had invited Narendra Modi for the Lahore stop-over is completely wrong because if that was the case, either I or Tariq Fatemi would have reached Lahore for the meeting. The 3 hour surprise notice was too short for this journey but the Foreign Secretary, Aizaz Chaudhry was already in Lahore and attended the meeting.

This optimism proved short-lived as on 2 January 2016 there was a terrorist attack at Pathankot, and India once again cancelled the Foreign Secretaries' meeting which was to work out a time schedule for a comprehensive dialogue.

Then on 8 July 2016, a Kashmiri freedom fighter Burhanuddin Wani was martyred by the security forces leading to a new and prolonged intifada or uprising in the Indian Occupied Kashmir. This and the Uri attack in January 2017 added new layers of hostility to the India-Pakistan relations.

As we analysed these developments and India's overall strategy towards Pakistan, we came to the conclusion that, notwithstanding occasional gestures to satisfy international opinion, India under Modi, had launched an insidious plan to isolate Pakistan diplomatically and damage its image abroad 'as a safe haven for terrorists'. It had also intensified its efforts to support destabilizing elements within Pakistan to promote violence and insurgency. Simultaneously, it had started out-spending Pakistan on defence to force Pakistan to divert more resources from development to defence.

During the late 1990s, in my previous tenure in the Foreign Office, I had realized that friendship with India was not a realistic goal. However, if we could have 'normal co-existence', in which we could expand trade and sporting links and keep Kashmir on the agenda, at least some issues like Siachen and Sir Creek could be resolved and the people of Kashmir, while waiting for their inherent right of self-determination, will not suffer greater repression. Meanwhile, we could also expand cooperation in other areas under the SAARC umbrella.

Presently, we are facing a 'new normal' with India virtually setting new benchmarks, by escalating tensions with Pakistan without resorting to old style military build-up. Apart from unprecedented violations of the LOC and threats of surgical strikes, India unilaterally withdrew the Most Favoured Nation (MFN) status from Pakistan and threatened to terminate the Indus Water Treaty. In other words, if Pakistan wanted normal relations with India, it will be on Indian terms i.e. no talks on Kashmir. In fact, on 15 August 2016 Prime Minister Modi gave a clear message in his Independence Day speech that if Pakistan continued to highlight Kashmir atrocities, India will create complications for Pakistan in Balochistan. In August 2016, India actively persuaded some other South Asian Association for Regional Cooperation (SAARC) members to decline attendance at the SAARC Summit scheduled in Islamabad in November 2016. The letter of regret from four other members was identical to that of India. This cancellation of the SAARC summit has been a serious blow to this important regional organization.

The first major element of the counter strategy that Pakistan evolved to respond to India's game plan was to expose India's human rights violations and brutalities in Indian occupied Kashmir (IOC). In August 2016, these brutalities had become even harsher after widespread protest rallies throughout IOC following the brutal murder of Burhanuddin Wani, and the use of pellet guns on protestors. We prepared many dossiers with documentary evidence and photographs which were presented to the UN Secretary General and all the members of the Security Council. This created a strong wave of sympathy for the Kashmiris and also encouraged the UN Council for Human Rights (UNHCR) to send a mission to investigate these reports. India refused to receive this delegation, but Pakistan gave them full access to Azad Jammu and Kashmir and arranged their meetings with Kashmiri leaders.

In June 2017, the UN Human Rights Council released its report and was the first major UN intervention on the Kashmir Issue in two decades. Several Parliaments in Europe passed resolutions based on the Human Rights Commission Report. This HRC Report was followed up by a second report in July 2019, which fully exposed Indian repression and gross violations of human rights in IOK.

On the political front, we intensified our efforts to solicit stronger support from 56 members of Organization of Islamic Countries (OIC). The Council of Foreign Ministers in each of its Annual Meetings and the OIC Summit in April 2017 unanimously condemned Indian atrocities in Kashmir and called for resolving the issue in accordance with the UN Resolutions. These resolutions also underlined the indigenous character of the Kashmiris struggle.

We also began to share our concerns about serious violations of the fundamental rights of Muslims and other minorities in India with the media and other members of the international community. As BJP pursued its Hindutva agenda, its activists killed many Muslims only on the suspicious that they had eaten or sold beef meat. Many Christian churches were also burnt down in different parts of India. It was clear from these examples that India was no longer a safe country for minorities.

The next plan of this strategy was a counter campaign to expose the inconsistency in Indian claims on Pakistan's involvement in terrorist activities by highlighting the enormous progress Pakistan had made in eliminating terrorism and insurgency from Pakistan's tribal areas and urban centres. We also highlighted the Indian sponsorship of terrorist activities in Pakistan, as dramatically illustrated by the arrest of Kulbhushan Yadav.

In March 2017, Pakistan also organized a summit of the ten member states of the Economic Cooperation Organization (ECO) in Islamabad. It was attended by eight heads of state or government and exposed Indian security concerns as unfounded, when it forced the cancellation of the SAARC summit, scheduled for November 2016. It also effectively contradicted the false Indian propaganda that Pakistan was facing 'diplomatic Isolation' Pakistan's growing relations with China and Russia and close cooperation with Saudi Arabia, Turkey, Malaysia and the ECO clearly demonstrated that the Indian design to isolate Pakistan diplomatically had miserably failed.

While pursuing this strategy, in consultation with friendly countries, Pakistan also persisted with its public commitment to engage with India in an effort to address all outstanding issues through dialogue. This clearly portrayed our resolve to pursue a policy of peaceful neighbourhood. We also emphasized that the enormous economic benefits of regional connectivity and regional trade can be reaped by both countries only through dialogue and cooperation.

China

The most important foreign policy achievement of Nawaz Sharif's third tenure as Prime Minister was the path breaking transformation in Pakistan strategic partnership with China.

China was the first country that the Prime Minister visited in July 2013. President Xi Jinping's grand vision of OBOR (One Belt, One road) was just taking shape. It was agreed during this visit that an important component of OBOR would be a China-Pakistan Economic Corridor (CPEC). A Joint Cooperation Committee (JCC) co-chaired by the Planning Ministers of the two countries was established with four joint working groups on long term planning, energy, transport and Gwadar Port.

In November 2013, Prime Minister Nawaz Sharif again visited China to discuss specific projects and programmes that will be taken up under CPEC. It was agreed during the visit that President Xi Jinping will visit Pakistan in the second half of 2014 to formally launch CPEC. Meanwhile, the JCC and its Working Groups would finalize the list of projects and their estimated costs with as many feasibility studies as possible.

President Xi's visit was scheduled for the first week of September 2014 but had to be cancelled because the Pakistan Tehreek-e-Insaf had launched a sit-in (*dharna*) in Islamabad's Parliament Square (D-Chowk) from mid-August. We suggested that the scheduled visit can take place in Lahore rather than Islamabad but the Chinese authorities felt a postponement would be a better option.

A week after the decision to postpone the visit, I went to Tajikistan to attend an SCO Summit on 10 September. I was invited for a one on one meeting with President Xi Jinping in which he asked me to convey his sincere apologies to the Prime Minister for the cancellation of the visit. He said, he will reschedule it as early as possible.

President Xi Jinping's landmark visit finally took place on 9 and 10 April 2015. Prime Minister Nawaz Sharif himself supervised all the preparations for the visit, ranging from the airport ceremonies to the on-line inauguration of all the projects to be included. In all, fifty-one MOUs and agreements were signed, involving total investments and loans of US$46 billion. The joint communique announced the following guiding principles of CPEC: Consensus, Scientific Research, Sound Planning, Step by Step Approach, Mutual Win-Win and Market Principles.

In my long career, I have never seen a summit level visit that was so well organized, was so warm and spontaneous and generated so much goodwill among people in both the countries. President Xi Jinping was so impressed by the visit that two days later when we met in Jakarta, at the inauguration of Asia-Pacific Economic Cooperation (APEC) Summit, he came up to me and said 'Mr Aziz, I have come to Indonesia but my heart is still in Pakistan. Please convey my gratitude to Prime Minister Nawaz Sharif'.

Approximately two third of the initial CPEC portfolio of US$46 billion was allocated to 19 Energy projects in the form of investments by Chinese companies to generate about 11,000 Megawatts of electricity and improve the transmission system. These investments would not add to Pakistan's debt burden, since Pakistan will only pay for the electricity consumed, as compared to other Independent Power Producers (IPPs).

Other components of CPEC were road and rail infrastructure, development of Gwadar Port and several special industrial zones. Simultaneously, a long term plan was prepared by Chinese experts for Phase II of CPEC, to extend its scope to agriculture, tourism and science and technology with a potential investment of US$150 billion up to 2030.

Meanwhile, the first phase of CPEC expanded from US$46 to US$60 billion during 2016–18 after the provincial governments identified additional projects for inclusion and financing, to accelerate the growth of the economy, expand exports and provide much needed employment. By the end of 2018, 11 projects had been completed and 12 projects were under implementation. The total investment in these 23 projects is expected to be about US$20 billion. Another 20 projects are in the pipeline.

In May 2017, I accompanied Prime Minister Nawaz Sharif to the first OBOR Forum convened by President Xi Jinping to explain the scope and purpose of OBOR. It was attended by representatives of 80 countries, including 30 at the head of state or government level. After the formal opening speeches on the first day, a day long round table was held on 15 May 2017 by President Xi Jinping with all the Presidents and Prime Ministers accompanied only by their Foreign Ministers.

Over seven hours, President Xi Jinping responded to comments and questions from all his colleagues and emphasized the following key points: -

- Connectivity will break all bottlenecks.
- We have to go beyond physical connectivity to soft connectivity because we require connectivity among people, connectivity of minds and policy and connectivity of think tanks.
- In terms of mechanisms we should pay special attention to custom cooperation systems, and trade and investment facilitation.
- CPECs rapid progress has demonstrated that OBOR is a win-win initiative for all.
- Support for OBOR projects will be available not just from China but also several new financing institutions like Asian Infrastructure Investment Bank, Asian Silk Road Bank and New Development Bank formerly BRICS Development Bank.

In the initial presentation at the Forum, it was highlighted that OBOR was based on six different corridors: -

- New Eurasian Land Bridge, from China to Russia, connecting the Atlantic Ocean with the Pacific Ocean.
- The China-Mongolia Corridor connecting Russia with China through Mongolia.
- The China-Central Asia Economic Corridor connecting China with Turkey through the Central Asian countries.
- The China-Pakistan Economic Corridor to connect Western China with Pakistan and the port of Gwadar.
- The China-Indonesia Peninsula Economic Corridor connecting southern China to Singapore through Vietnam, Laos, Cambodia, Thailand, Myanmar and Malaysia via India and Bangladesh.
- Maritime-Silk Road connecting coastal China with Indian Ocean and the Arabian Sea terminating at Gwadar via Singapore and Malaysia.

For Pakistan, CPEC provides a golden opportunity to convert this major initiative into an economic and strategic game changer. China has already become the second largest economy of the World. It has made many impressive advances in education, science and technology. In artificial intelligence, which will have a far reaching impact on the global economy, China is ahead of the United States. Chinese foreign policy is not based on military alliances but on trade and investment with the outside World. Through OBOR, it is developing a network of corridors to expand connectivity and trade in an open and inclusive approach.

CPEC is a flagship of Belt and Road Initiative (BRI) and in terms of implementation is ahead of other corridors. It has great potential to:

- accelerate the rate of investment and growth in Pakistan in the coming years by at least 2 per cent of GDP;
- overcome the chronic energy crisis in Pakistan at affordable prices;
- help revive the industrial sector and especially the export industries, through special industrial zones in different parts of the country;
- open up, through the western route, growth and employment opportunities in Balochistan, Khyber Pakhtunkhwa (KP), and the Federally Administered Tribal Areas (FATA) now merged with Khyber Pakhtunkhwa, especially projects and employment for the youth in these less developed areas;
- Convert Gwadar into a major port for industrial development, petroleum refining and as a transit hub for connecting western China with the rest of the World;
- Upgrade technology and productivity in different sub-sectors through cooperation between public institutions and private enterprises in both countries;
- Attract investments from many other countries in the special industrial zones and other projects;
- Explore new areas of cooperation like agriculture, environment, tourism, and research under Phase II of CPEC. A long term plan for CPEC was signed at the Seventh Joint Cooperation Committee of CPEC on 21 November 2017.

But these vital objectives can only be fully achieved, if we keep CPEC away from controversies and unnecessary criticism. Initial concerns about western route were addressed through an All Parties Conference in 2016 and greater participation of Provincial Chief Ministers in the CPEC consultative processes.

In view of the strategic importance of CPEC, the Pakistan Army has extended full support to this initiative by creating a Special Security Division to provide full security to all the Chinese engineers and workers engaged in CPEC projects.

Unfortunately, after a change of Government in July 2018, some unnecessary controversies started surfacing. In October, the PTI government decided at Cabinet level, that the projects under CPEC should be reopened and reviewed. Then a government minister suggested that work on the CPEC projects might be stopped for one year. Another statement seeking 'strategic partnership' with Saudi Arabia in building an oil refinery at Gwadar under CPEC also caused some confusion. Since then, some attempts have been made to repair the damage but in view of the paramount importance of CPEC for Pakistan, such controversies should be carefully avoided in the future.

The Middle East

My four year stay in the Foreign Office coincided with a turbulent period in the history of the Middle East.

The phenomena of 'Arab Spring' erupted from a small incident in Tunisia on 18 December 2010. A young Tunisian graduate, who could not get a job, without a strong political recommendation, decided to set up his own stall on the roadside. When the police dismantled his unauthorized stall, he was so disgusted that he committed suicide by setting himself on fire. The public reacted strongly and small protests mushroomed into a major agitation against the autocratic regime of President Zain ul Abedeen. Shortly afterwards he escaped to Saudi Arabia and Tunisia began its much awaited journey towards democracy.

The example of Tunisia travelled quickly to next door Libya where people were already fed up with Muammar Gaddafi's 30-year dictatorship. The first anti-government demonstration took place in Benghazi. Gaddafi ordered a major crackdown on these 'rats' and thousands were killed in massive air raids. This led to a strong international reaction, US declared Libya a no-fly zone and NATO declared strong support for the protestors. Gaddafi had no option but to abandon office. He took shelter in a concrete pipe but the protestors found and killed him. Unfortunately, unlike Tunisia, Libya did not see either peace or democratic rule as it slid into a prolonged civil war between different factions, with strong foreign involvement in support of one side or the other.

The third important theatre of the 'Arab Spring' was the uprising in Egypt, where Hosni Mubarak had ruled for almost 30 years. Led by the Muslim Brotherhood, the strength of the revolutionaries kept growing as they occupied the famous Tahrir Square in January 2011. Finally, Hosni Mubarak gave up. He was arrested and tried. Egypt then went through its first democratic election in 2012 which was won by the only organized political force in the country, the Muslim Brotherhood.

Mohammad Morsi was elected President, but within a year the armed forces, under General Abdel Fattah el-Sisi led a coup against Morsi, deposed him and General el-Sisi took over on 3 July 2013. He was elected President in May 2014 and re-elected to a second term in March 2018. Thousands of Muslim Brotherhood activists were tried and hanged. Former President Morsi was also on trial but died while on trial in Court on 17 June 2019 at the age of 67 years. Human Rights groups have criticized the conditions in which he was kept for 6 long years. Thus, as a result of the Arab Spring, Egypt found renewed stability only under another military leader, but not genuine democracy for which Egyptian youth had protested in Tahrir Square for many weeks.

The advent of 'Arab Spring' in Syria was even more tragic. The majority Sunni population, launched its revolution against President Bashar Hafez al-Asad, who has been ruling Syria since 2000, after his father Hafez al-Asad, who was Syrian President for almost 30 years, died. Initially, it appeared that he would also look for an escape route. But apparently Iran came to his rescue, with tacit support from Russia, to safeguard the future of Alawite population which was only fifteen per cent of the total population. As a reaction, Daesh also known as Islamic State of Iraq and the Levant (ISIL) which had just established its foothold in Iraq and elements of Al-Qaeda jumped into the conflict to start a brutal civil war that led to one of worst humanitarian disasters in history. Initially, the US and other western powers, who wanted to replace Asad were indirectly supporting forces whom they were fighting elsewhere as hard-core terrorists. Turkey, which did not want Syrian Kurds to gain an upper hand, also joined anti-Asad forces. A result of this unending tragedy, triggered by the 'Arab Spring', many beautiful Syrian cities like Allepo and Mosul have been destroyed along with their historic heritage. At least 8 million Syrians or almost 40 per cent of its total population have become refugees in Jordan, Turkey and some countries in Europe. Gradually, Asad's forces supported by the Russian Air Force have gained control of most of Syria, but peace is still a distant dream for most Syrians.

Another victim of the 'Arab Spring', ravaged by unending warfare and a major humanitarian disaster, was Yemen. The uprising in 2011 uprooted Ali Abdullah Saleh, who had ruled Yemen for twenty-two years after North and South Yemen were merged into a single country in 1990. Under an agreement, negotiated by Gulf Cooperation Council (GCC), Abdrabbuh Mansur Hadi, his Vice President, became President in February 2012 on the understanding that Ali Abdullah Saleh's concerns and interests will be protected. This did not happen and within three years, many elements of the Yemen forces which were still loyal to Saleh, joined hands with Houthi forces, launched an operation and took control of the capital Sana'a in February 2015.

Saudi Arabia alleged that Iran was supplying weapons and missiles to the Houthis to target Saudi Arabia, but they will not tolerate such hostile elements in their backyard. On 25 March 2015, Saudi Arabia started air strikes against Houthi targets and announced that a ten member Islamic military Alliance had been formed 'to fight terrorism'. The list shared with the media included not only Arab countries (Saudi Arabia, UAE, Kuwait, Jordan, Qatar, Egypt and Morocco) but also three other Islamic countries, namely Turkey, Malaysia and Pakistan.

Prime Minister Nawaz Sharif received a call from the Deputy Crown Prince Mohammad Bin Salman bin Abdulaziz Al Saud on 27 March, seeking support in the form of troops and military aircraft to counter the terrorist threat from Yemen. The Prime Minister said he will send his Defence Minister and Foreign Minister as soon as possible for detailed discussions, after which a decision can be taken.

Khawaja Asif and I accordingly arrived at Riyadh Air Base on 31 March and were received by the Deputy Crown Prince Mohammad Bin Salman and given two-hour briefing by the Commander In-charge of the Yemen Operation, concluding with a working dinner.

During our dinner conversation, I told the Crown Prince that a guerrilla force like the Houthis will be difficult to defeat only through air power. Even ground troops require a different approach because the enemy is scattered and not easily distinguishable from ordinary citizens. I mentioned Pakistan's own counter insurgency experience and said, we had employed 200,000 specially trained troops in our tribal belt since 2009 and we have not yet fully established our writ in all in seven Tribal Agencies, whose population was much smaller than Yemen.

On our return, we submitted our report to the Prime Minister, advising against the option of sending troops to Yemen. It was a civil war with strong sectarian dimensions, the terrain was extremely difficult and it would not be easy for Saudi backed forces loyal to Mansur Hadi, to re-capture the capital Sana'a in the near future. The aerial bombardment will, however, destroy the already depleted infrastructure of Yemen, compounding the poverty and suffering of the population.

After receiving our report, the Prime Minister accepted the advice of some of his ministers, to consult the Parliament on the subject. The matter was taken up in Parliament on 7 April. After intense debate, the Parliament decided unanimously that Pakistan would stand firmly with Saudi Arabia for the defence of Harmain Al-Sharifain and for protecting the sovereignty and territorial integrity of the Kingdom of Saudi Arabia. Pakistan would support all efforts to counter international terrorism but the nature and extent of its participation will be decided in the light of the circumstances in each case. The actual resolution adopted by Parliament on 10 April 2015 is reproduced below:-

The *Majlis-e-Shoora* (Parliament) of Pakistan after its Joint Sitting held from 6 to 10 April, 2015, adopted the following Resolution:

Having considered the grave situation in Yemen and its implications for regional and international peace and security; and having noted that the war in Yemen is not sectarian in nature but has the potential of turning into a sectarian conflict, which will have a critical fallout in the region, including Pakistan:

1. Appreciates the decision of the Government to call the Joint Sitting of Parliament to consider Pakistan's response to the crisis in Yemen;

2. Expresses serious concern on the deteriorating security and humanitarian situation in Yemen and its implications for peace and stability of the region and supports all humanitarian initiatives aimed at bringing relief to the people caught in the conflict;

3. Calls upon the warring factions in Yemen to resolve their differences peacefully through dialogue;

4. Appreciates the arrangements made by the Government for the safe and swift evacuation of Pakistanis and nationals of many other countries from Yemen and expresses its gratitude to the People's Republic of China for its contribution in this regard;

5. Apprehends that the crisis in Yemen could plunge the region into turmoil;

6. Supports regional and international efforts for restoration of peace and stability in Yemen;

7. Underscores the need for continued efforts by the Government of Pakistan to find a peaceful resolution of the crisis, while promoting the unity of Muslim Ummah, in cooperation with the leaders of other Muslim countries;

8. Desires that Pakistan should maintain neutrality in the Yemen conflict so as to be able to play a proactive diplomatic role to end the crisis;

9. Urges the Muslim Ummah and the international community to intensify their efforts to promote peace in Yemen;

10. Express unequivocal support for the Kingdom of Saudi Arabia and affirms that in case of any violation of its territorial integrity or any threat to Harmain Al-Sharifain, Pakistan will stand shoulder to shoulder with Saudi Arabia and its people;

11. Expresses deep concern at the increasing threats posed by different terrorist groups and non-state actors to the security and stability of the region and advises the Government of Pakistan to enhance its friendship and cooperation with the Gulf Cooperation Council (GCC) and all other regional countries in combating extremism and terrorism; and

12. Desires that the Government of Pakistan initiate steps to move the UN Security Council and the Organization of Islamic Countries (OIC) to bring about an immediate cease-fire in Yemen.

Pakistan's position on the Yemen crisis, as reflected in this Resolution was not received positively by the media in the Gulf. 'Pakistan is not standing by us when we needed its support'. However, subsequent events, as the Yemen war dragged on for years, vindicated the sensible position Pakistan had adopted.

In December 2015, the Kingdom of Saudi Arabia had announced the formation of 34 Nation Islamic Military Alliance to combat terrorism and protect Muslim countries from all terrorist groups and extremist organizations irrespective of their sect, ideology, or name.

A fortnight later, Saudi Foreign Minister, Adel bin Ahmed Al-Jubeir visited Pakistan to explain the objectives and modalities of the Alliance. He said during our delegation level meeting that this was not a military Alliance. It is a coalition of 34 countries (41 by 2017) which will themselves decide which activities they would like to participate in.

On 2 February 2017, Saudi Arabia formally requested that General Raheel Sharif may be permitted to lead the 41-member Islamic Military Alliance. General Sharif had already retired as Chief of Army Staff in November 2016. After the Ministry of Defence issued the required No Objection Certificate, he joined his new assignment in Riyadh on 22 April 2017.

In April 2017, Director General, Inter-Services Public Relations (ISPR), Major General Asif Ghafoor clarified that 'Saudi Arabia had not so far formally requested for additional troop deployment. Pakistan currently has 1180 troops in Saudi Arabia under the 1982 bilateral agreement. If any additional troops are sent, they will not operate outside KSA'.

Many independent observers have been analysing the strategy underlying the formation of the Islamic Military Alliance. The 6 GCC countries despite enormous wealth had total troop strength of less than 350,000. Two other Arab Countries, namely Egypt and Jordan have sizeable forces (500,000 and 150,000 respectively), but these are not readily available to GCC countries. By forming a broader military alliance, the GCC countries, they concluded, would be in a stronger position to safeguard their security.

To sum up, the Arab Spring had become the Arab Autumn for all practical purposes, since all the countries, which saw the spontaneous uprising of youth, seeking better life and greater freedom ended up in turmoil especially in Libya, Egypt, Syria and Yemen. Iraq was already in shambles. External powers and forces had encouraged the 'Arab Spring Movement' in the name of democracy and human rights, without recognizing that if the old order, managed by dictators like Saddam Hussain, Gaddafi or Hosni Mubarak, were brought down, an alternative democratic order cannot replace it overnight since elements and institutions necessary for democracy take a long time to develop. Different political and social forces, trying to fill the resultant political vacuum started fighting each other and the result was chaos, civil wars, large scale displacement and millions of refugees moving in all directions in these divided countries. According to one estimate at least 40 million children have been traumatized by this turmoil and many would never fully recover and may even become terrorists in the future.

The transition in Tunisia was more successful because no outside power was involved. In Egypt, as the democratic experiment failed, another dictator took over to save the country from collapsing.

A very serious long term consequence of the turbulence in the Middle East is the emergence of ISIS or Daesh. Even after its defeat in Iraq and Syria, it will re-emerge under different labels in other parts of the world, unless the underlying causes of injustice are addressed. Whenever outside powers attempt regime changes in other countries or support efforts to de-stabilize a regime, the end is tragic. This is the key lesson the world should learn from this unfortunate phase of history.

PML(N) Government's Economic Record

The PTI Government, after assuming office in July 2018 under Imran Khan, has been shouting from the rooftop in Pakistan and abroad, that they had inherited a destroyed economy on the verge of collapse. All the institutions had been destroyed by corruption and inefficiency. The previous two governments had borrowed heavily, taking the total public sector debt of the country from Rs 6,000 billion in 2008 to Rs 30,000 billion in 2018. The new government has therefore no option but to cut down expenditure, slow down imports to stabilize the economy and also to secure loans from friendly countries to pay back past loans.

This politically motivated narrative is far from reality and so full of inaccuracies that it is imperative to place on record an objective and accurate assessment of the economic performance of the PML(N) government from June 2013 to May 2018:

PML(N) inherited an economy which in 2013 was plagued by serious problems and weakness. The average GDP Growth in 2008–13, at 2.8 per cent per annum, was the lowest in our history; inflation at an average of 12 per cent had remained in double digit throughout the 5 year period; Tax-GDP ratio had stagnated at 9.6 per cent; fiscal deficit was 8.2 per cent of GDP in 2012–13 and foreign exchange reserves had declined from US$10.8 billion to US$6 billion which were enough for only one of half month's imports.

Ishaq Dar, the Finance Minister designate, had done his homework well before the elections, since the PML(N) 2013 Election Manifesto had articulated a very comprehensive agenda and roadmap for economic revival, policies, and programmes for macro-economic stability, industrial growth, infrastructure, employment, and housing.

Nawaz Sharif in his very first Cabinet meeting had also emphasized that the two most important pre-requisites for economic revival were improvement in the security situation and overcoming the shortage of electricity and gas. So, while he himself launched determined efforts to address these two pre-requisites, Ishaq Dar successfully implemented most of the strategies and policies spelled out in the Manifesto: -

- He signed, an Extended Fund Facility (EFF) of US$ 6.2 billion with the International Monetary Fund (IMF) by the first week of July 2013, i.e. less than a month after the new government took over. The 3-year programme was successfully completed and most benchmarks were achieved.

- As a result of tight fiscal discipline, the rate of inflation was brought down to 4.5 per cent in 2014–15. Facilitated by a decline in oil prices, it remained below 4 per cent in the next 3 years. Correspondingly the State Bank policy rate was reduced to 6 per cent.

- The total tax revenues were doubled from Rs 2,200 billion in 2012–13 to Rs 4,000 billion in 2017–18, raising the tax GDP ratio from 10 to 12.9 per cent.

- With the speedy implementation of projects under CPEC, the public sector development programme was increased from Rs 350 billion in 2012–13 to Rs 850 billion in 2017–18.

- Most important of all, GDP growth increased to 5.8 per cent in 2017–18, the highest in 13 years.

Economic Indicators during PML(N) Government (2013–18)

Sectors	2013–14	2014–15	2015–16	2016–17	2017–18	Average 2014–18	2018–19 (P)
GDP Growth (%)	4.1	4.1	4.6	5.2	5.8	4.7	3.3
GDP (FC) Rs million	10,217,056	10,631,649	11,116,802	11,696,934	12,343,500	11,201,188.2	12,750,126
Agriculture (%)	2.5	2.1	0.2	2.2	3.9	2.2	0.9
Manufacturing (%)	5.7	3.9	3.7	5.8	5.4	4.9	-0.3
Services (%)	4.5	4.4	5.7	6.5	6.3	5.5	4.7
Inflation (%)	8.6	4.5	2.9	4.2	3.9	4.8	7.0
Current A/C Balance (US$ million)	-3,130.0	-2,795.0	-4,867.0	-12,621.0	-19,897.0	-86,623.0	-13,508.0
Export (US$ million)	25,078	24,090.0	21,972	22,003	24,768	23,582.2	24,224
Import (US$ million)	41,668	41,357	41,255	48,683	56,592	45,911.0	52,390
Total Revenues (Rs million)	3,637,297	3,931,042	4,446,979	4,936,723	5,228,014	4,436,011	4,900,724
Tax Revenue (Rs Million)	2,564,509	3,017,596	3,660,418	3,969,248	4,467,160	3,535,786	4,473,422
Non-Tax Revenue (Rs million)	1,072,788	913,446	786,561	967,475	760,854	900,224	427,302
Tax to GDP Ratio (% of GDP)	10.2	11.0	12.6	12.4	12.9	11.8	10.3
Budget Deficit (as % of GDP)	5.5	5.3	4.6	5.8	6.5	5.5	11.6
PSX 100 Index	29,652.5	34,398.9	37,783.5	46,565	41,911	38,062.2	8.9
Aggregate Market Capitalization	7,022.7	7,421.0	7,588.5	9,522.4	8,665.0	8,043.9	–

Source: Pakistan Economic Survey various years.

The only sector in which progress was less than expected, was exports which remained stagnant at US$ 23–24 billion. With a sharp increase in the import of machinery and petroleum products, the current account deficit in 2017–18 reached a record high level of US$19.8 billion. The average annual Current Account deficit for the 5 year period was however, US$8.6 billion.

The total public domestic and external debt which had increased from Rs 6,500 billion to Rs 14,200 billion during the 5 years tenure of the PPP government, increased to Rs 24.952 billion by June (and not to Rs 30,000 billion, as repeatedly claimed by the PTI government). As a percentage of GDP it went up from 62.4 to 75.2 per cent. As the experience of many other countries has shown, acceleration of growth is invariably accompanied by a proportionate increase in public debt. But it is important to contract such debt on reasonable terms, so that the burden of debt servicing remains manageable.

It should be clear from the foregoing that the narrative about a 'collapsed economy' and 'destroyed institution' is far from reality. In fact, almost all the positive indicators of PML(N) government became negative during the first year of the PTI government as shown in the preceding table.

The Panama Case

In April 2016, an International Consortium of Investigative journalists, leaked millions of documents of a law firm in Panama, called Mossack Fonseca, with detailed information of over 200,000 offshore companies. Among several prominent world leaders (like the Prime Minister of Finland, father of UK Prime Minister, David Cameron and President Putin of Russia) the properties owned by Nawaz Sharif's children in London were also listed in the Panama Papers.

The National Accountability Bureau (NAB) of Pakistan started, on the directives of the Supreme Court, an investigation in these reports and identified the following properties:

Four flats at Avenfield House, London purchased by two offshore companies, Nielson Holdings Limited and Nescol Limited in June 1993 and July 1996. These are being used by Nawaz Sharif and his family. Nawaz Sharif should provide a money trail to prove the source of funds for their purchase.

After many hearings and arguments in April 2017, the Supreme Court ruled by a 3:2 decision that since there was insufficient evidence, a Joint Investigation Team (JIT) should be constituted to further investigate the matter.

In June 2017, the JIT submitted its report to the Supreme Court. On 28 July, a 3 member bench of the Supreme Court consisting of Justice Ejaz Afzal, Justice Azmat Saeed and Justice Ijaz ul Ahsan disqualified Nawaz Sharif for life under Article 62(i)(f) of the Constitution and Section 99(i) (f) of Representation of People's Act for not declaring his 'receivable' salary of 10,000 dirhams from Capital FZE in his nomination papers for the 2013 elections. His plea that this was his son's company and a notional salary was indicated to facilitate his visas to UAE during his 8 years exile in Saudi Arabia and that he never actually received any salary, was ignored.

The Supreme Court also instructed NAB to file corruption and money laundering references against Nawaz Sharif and nominated Justice Ijaz ul Ahsan as the monitoring judge. Four references were filed against the Sharif family: London Avenfield properties, Flagship Investment Limited in UK. Azizia Steel Mills and Hill Metal Establishment in Jeddah. Maryam Nawaz and her husband Captain Safdar were named in the first reference and his sons, Hussain Nawaz and Hassan Nawaz in the other three.

In July 2018, Judge Muhammad Bashir of the Accountability Court convicted Nawaz Sharif in the Avenfield Apartment case, although the court did not find that Nawaz Sharif was either the owner of the apartments or he transferred funds to purchase them. The judgment stated:

Interviews of Hassan Nawaz and Hussain Nawaz, accused, are showing that they lived in these apartments during 1993 to 1996 which is when these apartments were purchased through offshore companies. The ages of the three children in 1993 were 20, 18 and 16 years respectively. They were dependent financially and could not purchase Avenfield apartments without anyone else's help. Generally, children remain dependant on their parents, during their tender ages, therefore accused No 1 cannot say that he has not provided any money to them to purchase the apartments.

Apparently, the court did not verify the dates of possession of different apartments or explain why it disregards the submission that the children's grandfather supported them. Nawaz Sharif was sentenced by Judge Bashir to a jail term of 10 years and his daughter Maryam Nawaz to 7 years because the Calibri Font used in the Trust Deed submitted by her was not commercially available before January 2007, so the deed was considered as fake and she was found guilty of abetting the crime of her father.

In two other cases, tried by Judge Arshad Malik of the Accountability Court, Nawaz Sharif was convicted in December 2018 to 10 years in one case (Azizia Steel Mills reference) but acquitted in the second case (Hill Metal Establishment). In July 2019, a major video scandal rocked the political landscape and the judicial system. A secretly recorded video showing Judge Arshad Malik confessing that he sentenced Nawaz Sharif under pressure, went viral. He is seen with representatives of PML(N) and also calling on Nawaz Sharif at his residence. In response to these accusations, Judge Arshad Malik claimed that he was actually pressurized and offered bribes to give inputs for Nawaz Sharif's appeal against the Azizia conviction.

While this controversy is being investigated under a directive of the Supreme Court, it has raised many questions about the conviction and disqualification of Nawaz Sharif. Surprisingly, despite this media hype and political slogan against corruption, not a single concrete charge of corruption has been levied against Nawaz Sharif so far.

As a result of the Supreme Court Judgment of 28 July 2017, Nawaz Sharif relinquished the office of the Prime Minister on that day. The media speculated that the Party will split over the issue of succession, but in a smooth transition, the Parliamentary Party of PML(N) elected Shahid Khaqan Abbasi as its leader and he took over as Prime Minister within a week on 4 August 2017.

Shahid Khaqan Abbasi as Prime Minister

Soon after Shahid Khaqan Abbasi was sworn in as Prime Minister, a new Cabinet was announced with several changes. Khawaja Asif was moved from the Ministries of Defence and Water & Power as Foreign Minister and in his place Khurram Dastgir was appointed as Defence Minister and Awais Leghari as Minister of Power. Ahsan Iqbal was given the additional charge of Minister of Interior and Miftah Ismail was appointed as Advisor for Finance to become Finance Minister later.

I was pleased when, in this reshuffle, I was appointed Deputy Chairman, Planning Commission. Having spent the ten best years of my career in the Planning Commission from 1961 to 1971, the opportunity to serve in that nerve centre of policy making on development issues was exciting.

Recognizing the importance of economic management, Prime Minister Abbasi assumed the chairmanship of the Economic Committee of the Cabinet (ECC), the Executive Committee of the National Economic Council (ECNEC) and the Cabinet Committees on Energy and Privatization. In September 2017, a new Cabinet Committee on CPEC chaired by the Prime Minister was set up to supervise the implementation of all CPEC projects. In October, another Committee chaired by the Prime Minister was set up for 'Digital Transformation and Implementation of E-government programme'. Prime Minister Abbasi also decided that the Federal Cabinet will meet every week. As a part of austerity measure, he announced that he would continue to reside in his own house and will not re-locate to the Prime Minister's House. But he never publicized this decision. His modesty was reflected in his protocol since his 'motorcade' consisted of only two cars.

In August 2016, the Supreme Court had decided that the term 'Government' means the cabinet and not the Prime Minister. This decision caused a mini upheaval in the central secretariat because in the past several decades, a large number of appointments equivalent to BPS 21 and 22 were recommended by the Ministries after processing by various selection committees and were then approved by the Prime Minister. Now all these cases started appearing on the Cabinet agenda. Prime Minister Abbasi's decision that the Cabinet will meet every week, made the Cabinet agenda more manageable.

Many development projects which the PML(N) government had initiated in the first three years of its tenure, had either been completed or were nearing completion. Shahid Khaqan Abbasi made a list of such projects and throughout his 10 months' tenure, he inaugurated one or two projects every week.

In my view, Prime Minister Abbasi's most outstanding contribution during his earlier tenure as the Minister for Petroleum was the setting up the first floating terminal in less than a year, to gasify imported LNG. A second terminal was added in 2017, ending a serious gas crisis for industrial, commercial and domestic consumers at competitive prices.

Another historic change in which Prime Minister Abbasi played a significant role was the merger of FATA in Khyber Pakhtunkhwa Province. The Nawaz Sharif Cabinet had approved the recommendations of the FATA Reforms Committee on 2 March 2017, for FATA's merger and the required legal and administrative actions that were reached during the transition period. It had also approved the recommendations that the FATA Reforms Committee, which I chaired, should be converted into an Implementation Committee. I suggested to the Prime Minister that it would be more useful if this Implementation Committee was chaired by the Prime Minister himself and also include the Chief of Army Staff. This recommendation was accepted. Prime Minister Abbasi in his 10 months' tenure convened four meetings of this high level National Implementation Committee to speed up all the required actions and complete them before the term of the PML (N) Government ended on 31 May 2018. As detailed in the next chapter, this objective was achieved and the Constitutional Amendments to merge FATA with Khyber Pakhtunkhwa, were adopted on 25 May 2018.

Prime Minister Abbasi also deserves the credit for finalizing the first ever National Water Policy during his tenure. This policy had been under preparation in the Water Division since 2006, but in the absence of inter-provincial consensus on many issues, the policy could not be finalized. The Seventh draft of the policy came up for consideration in a meeting of the Council of Common Interest (CCI) in November 2017 but there was again a deadlock. Prime Minister decided to set up a new high level Inter-provincial Committee chaired by me, with Minister of Water, Minister for Power, their Secretaries and the Chief Secretaries of the four provinces as members, to present an agreed and improved draft policy. The Committee held two meetings in January and February 2018 to discuss the new draft prepared by me. After addressing the concerns of the Chief Ministers expressed in the March meeting of the CCI, the National Water Policy was approved by CCI on 24 April 2018. This historic and comprehensive National Water Policy was signed by the Prime Minister and the four Chief Ministers in an impressive ceremony on that day.

Overall, Prime Minister Abbasi provided continuity and stability after a major political upheaval in which not only the Prime Minister but the leader of the ruling party was disqualified. The growth momentum of the previous four years was in fact accelerated by achieving a GDP growth of 5.8 per cent in 2017–18 and an inflation rate of less than 4 per cent. In meeting these difficult challenges, Prime Minister Abbasi followed an institutional approach to facilitate collective decision making.

In the light of this outstanding performance and an unblemished reputation, the arrest of Shahid Khaqan Abbasi in July 2019, on flimsy allegations will go down in our history as the worst example of political engineering in the name of accountability. That is why Chief Justice Asif Saeed Khosa, in a statement on 11 September 2019, said

> We, as a relevant organ of state, also feel that growing perception that the process of accountability being pursued in the country at present is lop-sided and is a part of political engineering, is a dangerous perception and some remedial steps need to be taken urgently so that the process does not lose credibility.

Nawaz Sharif's Score Card

Hardly any other politician has dominated the political landscape of Pakistan for such a long time, spreading over three decades. It is therefore, important to present an objective assessment of the remarkable factors behind his political career and also those that led to premature termination of each of his three terms as Prime Minister.

Entry into Politics

Mian Mohammad Sharif, the father of Nawaz Sharif migrated to Pakistan after Partition and set up an engineering workshop, the Ittefaq Foundry on Brandreth Road in Lahore. With his rich pre-Partition experience in steelmaking, his business expanded rapidly. In the early 1960s, when farmers in Punjab initiated a tube well revolution, Ittefaq water pumps emerged as one of the three most popular brands. Mian Sharif then set up the Ittefaq Complex with a large steel plant in Model Town. The complex included the Iffefaq Hospital and residences for all the family members. Mian Sharif's lifelong commitment to philanthropy continued when a few years later, he built the Sharif Medical City and Educational complex in Jati Umra on Raiwind Road where the Sharif family re-located to from Model Town, Lahore.

Nawaz Sharif had hardly finished his education, when the family had to migrate to Abu Dhabi because the PPP government of Zulfikar Ali Bhutto had nationalized 10 basic industries including the Ittefaq Steel Mills of Mian Mohammad Sharif. They returned to Pakistan after the military government of Gen Ziaul Haq denationalized their factories.

Nawaz Sharif started helping with his father's business and soon became an active member of Lahore society. He was also involved in many social and philanthropic projects that his father had initiated. In 1981, General (retd) Ghulam Jilani Khan, the Governor of Punjab invited Nawaz Sharif to join his Punjab Advisory Council on the recommendation of Corps Commander of Lahore, General Mohammad Iqbal. Two years later, in 1983, he elevated him as the provincial Finance Minister. That is when Nawaz Sharif's political journey began.

Within the next two years, Nawaz Sharif gained considerable recognition because he privatized many government owned enterprises in Punjab and presented two development-oriented budgets. In 1985, he became the Provincial President of Pakistan Muslim League (PML), with Ghulam Hyder Wyne as General Secretary. After that Nawaz Sharif's rise was meteoric. By 1985, he had done enough networking in Punjabi politics that after the non-party elections of that year, he was elected as Chief Minister of Punjab.

In 1988, the national elections were won by the Pakistan Peoples Party (PPP) under Benazir Bhutto but Nawaz Sharif's defiant policy as Chief Minister of Punjab further elevated his profile and he emerged as a counterweight to Benazir and PPP. PML won a majority in the Provincial Assembly and Nawaz Sharif continued as Chief Minister. He successfully defeated several moves to de-seat the PML government through floor crossing. He also set up the Bank of Punjab because the nationalized commercial banks had been directed by the Federal Government to stop financing businesses owned by the Ittefaq Group and other PML leaders.

Two years later, in November 1990, Nawaz Sharif became Prime Minister, when the 8-Party alliance of Islami Jamhoori Ittehad (IJI), won 106 out of 200 seats in the National Assembly. During the 1997 elections, Nawaz Sharif, now head of Pakistan Muslim League (Nawaz) (PML(N)) won by even a bigger margin (139 out of 200 seats). In 2013, he became Prime Minister for a record third time, by winning 180 seats in a house of 342. Thus for all his 3 tenures, he won an absolute majority and was able to form the government without needing any coalition partners.

Milestones

In Chapters 8 and 10, a chronology of Nawaz Sharif's two tenures has been presented in considerable detail. From these, it is not only easy to discern the main milestones in his remarkable political journey but also identify his strength and leadership qualities which elevated him to the highest political office in the country only 8 years after he entered politics. These milestones are summarized below:

1985: When the first non-party elections were held in 1985, after a gap of 8 years, Nawaz Sharif saw his opportunity. PPP and other MRD parties had boycotted these elections. Nawaz Sharif identified and cultivated many new candidates, especially those who had been elected in the local bodies' elections of 1983. Nawaz Sharif's supporters won a majority of seats in Punjab and he was elected Chief Minister of Punjab when he was just 35 years old.

1988: Based on his growing popularity and his performance as a development oriented Chief Minister, he quickly aspired for a rapid transition from provincial to national leadership. In fact, on 20 August, soon after the burial of General Ziaul Haq, he shared this dream with me and the Late Majid Nizami in these words:

> Benazir will be riding the populist wave created by her father 18 years ago, in the forthcoming elections, the first party based elections after 11 years. I do not think, Muslim League under Mohammad Khan Junejo, can take her on. I am the only leader in the Pakistan Muslim League, who can counter her populist platform and present an even stronger political alternative.

Because of a split in PML, between the Junejo and Nawaz Sharif factions, PML did not win the national elections in 1988, but in Punjab, Nawaz Sharif again won an absolute majority in the Provincial Assembly and continued as Chief Minister.

1990–93 Nawaz Sharif was able to realize his dream only two years later when he was sworn in as the Prime Minister of Pakistan on 6 November 1990. He was the first Punjabi Prime Minister, after Feroz Khan Noon in 1957, with a broader base of political support than almost any of his predecessors.

Nawaz Sharif's first 3 year tenure as Prime Minister will go down in the economic history of Pakistan as a period of major transformation, with basic structural reforms to deregulate the economy by doing away with import and exchange controls, undertaking a large scale privatization programme and opening up the banking, insurance, and telecommunication sectors to the private sector.

Nawaz Sharif also demonstrated real leadership when he secured agreement of the four Chief Ministers, for the historic Water Accord on sharing of the Indus Waters in March 1991.

On 17 April 1993, Nawaz Sharif graduated from being a traditional politician to become a bold radical leader when he addressed the nation in a strongly worded speech and said: 'I would not accept dictation from the Presidency. I would uphold the principles of democracy and the constitution'. Next day, the President dissolved the national Assembly and sacked his Government.

Nawaz Sharif continued with his defiant journey and the very next day on 19 April, despite serious efforts by the Punjab Government to cause disruption, he convened an emergency meeting of the PML Council. Nawaz Sharif was elected as President of PML in place of Mohammad Khan Junejo who had died a month earlier. This was an important political development because in October 1993 and the next 5 elections, the Party participated as PML(N) on the symbol of tiger. In his opening speech after his election, he emphasized the importance of political parties and said 'political parties are the main pillars of a democratic system. They not only mobilize voters but also give them a sense of direction'.

1993–1997: Benazir Bhutto's second term as Prime Minister lasted only 3 years from 1993 to 1996 and was marked by intense political confrontation between the PPP and PML(N). This confrontation was reflected in the ouster of the PML(N) government in NWFP, arrest of Nawaz Sharif's father and some other prominent PML(N) leaders and large scale extra judicial killings of MQM workers in Karachi. Nawaz Sharif launched a successful *Tehrik Nijat* in September 1994, and also concentrated on re-organizing the PML(N) as a major political party with strong grassroots support for the next elections. As a result, PML(N) under Nawaz Sharif won 138 or 69 per cent of the seats in the National Assembly, and 90 per cent of seats in Punjab Assembly. Chief Ministers in the coalition governments of Sindh and NWFP were also from PML(N). Its strength in the Senate also increased to 57 in a house of 87. During the next two and half years, Nawaz Sharif, with two third majority in both houses and PML governments in all the four provinces was at the pinnacle of his political journey.

1998: The 28 day of May 1998, will be recorded in the country's history as a major turning point, when Pakistan carried out 5 nuclear tests in response to India's tests of 11 May and became the seventh nuclear armed nation of the world. Nawaz Sharif successfully resisted serious pressures including 5 telephone calls from President Clinton and many offers of financial support and military hardware and restored Pakistan's strategic balance with India.

1999: Another foreign policy success for Nawaz Sharif during this tenure was the visit of the Indian Prime Minister Atal Bihari Vajpayee to Lahore on 20–21 February 1999. The historic Lahore Declaration was signed, recording the commitment of both countries to intensify their efforts to resolve all issues, including the issue of Jammu and Kashmir. As a follow up, I had negotiations with the Indian Foreign Minister, Jaswant Singh on the occasion of a SAARC Foreign Minister's meeting in Sri Lanka in March. But this important Lahore process was derailed by the Kargil misadventure of General Musharraf and then by his Martial Law in October 1999. The Kargil episode also seriously damaged Pakistan's standing as a responsible nuclear state.

The incalculable damage to the Kashmir cause by Pervez Musharraf scuttling the prospects of a negotiated settlement, became even starker on 5 August 2019 when Narendra Modi unilaterally annexed Indian Occupied Kashmir by illegally rescinding Articles 370 and 35-A of the Indian Constitution.

2006: After his exile from Pakistan in December 2000, Nawaz Sharif had realized the importance of bi-partisan working of the Parliament and the role of a vibrant opposition for a sustainable democratic system. On 14 July 2006, he signed a Charter of Democracy with Benazir Bhutto. It provided the basis for many important constitutional and legal reforms in the next few years, including the Eighteenth Amendment and the independence of judiciary. Both leaders had graduated from party leaders to national leaders.

2007: Nawaz Sharif returned to Pakistan after 8 years of forced exile on 25 November, only one day before the last day for filing nomination papers. His return changed the political landscape of the country. PML(N) won 91 seats in the National Assembly, compared to only 18 in 2002, when Nawaz Sharif was in exile. In these Elections, PML(N) emerged as the second largest party, after PPP, which received a very large sympathy vote as a result of the tragic death of Benazir Bhutto on 27 December 2007.

2009: On the second anniversary of 9 March 2007, when President Musharraf had dismissed Chief Justice Iftikhar Chaudhry, the lawyers announced a long march towards the federal capital, followed by a prolonged sit-in right in front of the Parliament on 16 March, till all the deposed judges had been restored. When PML(N) and three other political parties announced their support for the long march, the PPP government dismissed the PML(N) government in Punjab, imposed governor's rule and launched a major crackdown on the media. Yet, the long march started from Lahore on 15 March, Nawaz Sharif defied the ban and came out of his Model Town residence with his enthusiastic supporters. As the March started on GT Road, thousands joined the flood of humanity in vehicles and on foot. The barricades just melted away and many police officials refused to obstruct the long march. After several hours, the procession led by Nawaz Sharif had reached only Gujranwala when Prime Minister Yusaf Raza Gillani was forced to announce post-midnight that all the deposed judges will be restored. Thus, the threat of massive public uprising forced the government to cave in to this legitimate demand.

2010–12: The popularity of the PPP Government was declining sharply because of low growth and high inflation. Its difficulties were further compounded by a worsening energy crisis and gross mismanagement after the 2010 floods. Nawaz Sharif was under tremendous pressure from party hawks to launch an agitation campaign against the government but resisted. He said 'under the

2006 Charter of Democracy, even an inefficient democracy is better than no democracy. An agitation which brings down the government often sucks in undemocratic forces. Let us concentrate on organizing our party and prepare for the next elections in 2013'. His stance was vindicated in 2013, when there was a smooth transition from one elected government to another elected government for the first time in the history of the country.

2013–15: Nawaz Sharif entered the May 2013 Elections, with great confidence. He had given considerable personal attention to the Party Manifesto and to the selection of party candidates for the national and provincial elections. He also predicted that the entry of third major political party, the PTI, will not affect PML(N)'s vote bank. Disgruntled elements in PPP and PML(Q) could, however join PTI in large numbers. His political judgement proved right, as PML(N) won 126 out of 272 contested seats against PPP's 34 and PTI's 25. For the third time, PML(N) had won an outright majority and formed the Government, under Nawaz Sharif, without requiring coalition partners.

Nawaz Sharif's political instincts were very sharp but equally strong was his commitment to certain basic political principles. When the 120 day *dharna* (sit-in) of Tehreek-i-Insaf started in August 2014, within a year of the new government, he said to some of his closest colleague: 'I told you that as soon as you initiate any proceedings against General Musharraf for treason under Article 6, something will also start against you'. Then as the heat of the *dharna* grew and the Army Officers posted to protect the Parliament, did not act promptly enough and the agitators entered the premises after breaking the boundary wall and the fence, Nawaz Sharif again said 'It is far more important to stand up and survive with dignity rather than crumble under such pressure'.

2015: The much-awaited visit of President Xi-Jinping of China postponed from September 2014 to April 2015 because of the *dharna*, was another historic landmark in Nawaz Sharif's political career. In all, 51 MOUs and agreements were signed, involving total loans and investments of US$46 billion to formally launch the China-Pakistan Economic Corridor (CPEC) a flagship of President Xi's 'One Belt-One Road' initiative and a game changer for Pakistan.

Strengths and Qualities

I have presented the achievements and milestones of Nawaz Sharif's thirty-four years' political journey. The strength and qualities that made this rise possible can now be highlighted in order of their importance:

The most important quality of Nawaz Sharif, in my opinion, is his political charisma. That means a strong emotional connection with the supporters and workers, who not only support the party's policies and programmes, but also identify themselves as loyal devotees of their leader because they perceive an innate sincerity in him. Maryam Nawaz Sharif, who in all probability will inherit his mantle, has kept up and improved on that tradition. I personally saw a dramatic increase in the size of these devotees, very much like the PPP *Jiyala's* enthusiasm for Zulfikar Ali Bhutto. That is why one can categorize Nawaz Sharif, as the most charismatic leader after Zulfikar Ali Bhutto. One day, as I landed at the Lahore airport and started moving towards the lounge, a young man started walking with me and said 'Sartaj Sahib, I want to kiss your eyes because with these eyes, you see my leader every day'.

Nawaz Sharif's second major quality is his strong sense of patriotism. Like all political leaders, he guards his personal political interests very zealously but his commitment to the broader national interests is over-riding. He did not, for example, sack General Musharraf immediately after the Kargil fiasco, because at that time, in July 1999, India had published full page ads in the British media calling the Pakistan Army a 'rogue army'. When he went to Washington on 4 July 1999, to resolve the Kargil issue, he knew full well that he would be made a scapegoat. Similarly, Nawaz Sharif's determination to go ahead with the nuclear tests in May 1998 was based on his belief that Pakistan's strategic balance with India would be seriously jeopardized if these tests were not carried out immediately. He therefore went ahead, ignoring the advice that it would cost him dearly.

Nawaz Sharif pursued a policy of rapprochement with India because of his firm belief that a strong economy was the first pre-requisite for strategic balance. For that, a peaceful co-existence with India for a few years was necessary. He persisted with these policies despite the resistance of powerful forces, something which ultimately led to his downfall.

In addition to these qualities, Nawaz Sharif was steeped in certain basic values and traditions like respect for elders, helping others without any disclosure or announcement and unity of the family. Over the long period of my association with him, I never saw him using disrespectful language for anyone.

Nawaz Sharif's electoral success was largely due to his strong commitment to development as the first priority of his Government. In his first tenure, he launched far reaching reforms to open up the economy. In the early 1990s, Pakistan was ahead of India in ease of doing business and the Pakistani rupee was stronger than the Indian rupee. In 1997, despite the Asian Economic Crisis, he introduced further reforms in the banking sector and converted the Corporate Law Authority into the Securities and Exchange Commission. He also drastically reduced tariffs to make the industrial sector more competitive. In his third tenure, from 2013 to 2017, he succeeded in reversing the key indicators from 'low growth-high inflation' into 'high growth and low inflation'. His strong belief in the importance of infrastructure for development, specially energy and communications, was clearly visible in all his three terms, with the M2 Motorway and deregulating the telecom sector in his first tenure, M1 and Lahore Airport in his second term and China-Pakistan Economic Corridor (CPEC) in his third tenure.

Nawaz Sharif also recognized the paramount importance of channelling the fruits of growth to lower income groups and of creating new employment opportunities. His social initiatives included the Social Action Programmes of 1991, the National Rural Support Programme in 1992 and the Pakistan Poverty Alleviation Fund in 1997. He also launched several youth-employment programmes and allotted state land to landless rural families.

Causes of Instability

The counter point to Nawaz Sharif's brilliant political career, in which he was elected Prime Minister three times, is the stark reality that he was unable to complete his full 5-year tenure in any one of them. The reasons for each ouster were different and bring out his weaknesses and errors.

His first tenure which lasted for 33 months was cut short, because of serious differences with President Ghulam Ishaq Khan. There was a basic divergence on economic policies and economic management between the two: Nawaz Sharif hated lengthy procedures and cumbersome rules and Ishaq Khan was rule driven. Nawaz Sharif loved mega projects and dramatic announcements, which Ishaq Khan did not approve of. Nawaz Sharif had great belief in the role of the private sector in economic development, but Ishaq Khan was always complaining about the private sector's rent seeking activities and its unwillingness to pay taxes. Despite these differences, Ishaq Khan, having made it possible for Nawaz Sharif to become Prime Minister by dismissing the PPP Government in August 1990 after only 20 months, expected to be treated with respect and due deference. The cracks in the relationship started in January 1993, when Nawaz Sharif advised his colleagues in the Cabinet not to make any statement on the Presidential elections due in November 1993. That gave a clear indication to Ghulam Ishaq Khan that Nawaz Sharif had no intention to give him a second term.

Nawaz Sharif's second mistake was his premature announcement in the Senate on 28 February1993 that the process to delete clause 58-2(b) i.e. the power of the President to dissolve the National Assembly, had already started. That is when the President made up his mind to use these powers and he did so on 18 April 1993, despite last minute efforts to close the rift. The President's decision was held unconstitutional and the Assembly was restored on 26 May 1993 but Nawaz Sharif made his third mistake of imposing Governor's rule in Punjab, where the Provincial government of Mian Manzoor Wattoo was becoming increasingly hostile to the Federal Government. The Provincial government refused to honour the resolution of the Joint Session of the National Assembly and the Army also declined to intervene. The resultant constitutional deadlock was resolved by the Army Chief, General Waheed Kakar, through a formula under which both the President and the Prime Minister agreed to quit their respective offices.

In my opinion, Nawaz Sharif could have handled his relations with President Ghulam Ishaq Khan with greater tact and patience, by waiting for a few months and indicating his plans for Presidential elections only shortly before they were due. Nawaz Sharif could then have completed his tenure and probably also won the next elections, because of the remarkable turnaround in the economy.

Nawaz Sharif's second 32-month tenure ended abruptly on 12 October 1999. The Army Chief, General Pervez Musharraf had exceeded his authority when he launched his Kargil misadventure, without the express approval of the Government. He, therefore deserved to be, not only removed from his appointment but also tried under the relevant law. Nawaz Sharif's reluctance to sack him immediately after the fiasco is understandable and honourable but he should not have ordered his removal when he was on a flight back from Sri Lanka. The matter could have been given over to the Defence Standing Committee of both houses to look into and make recommendations. As it was, some of Musharraf's loyal colleagues reacted promptly to thwart the Prime Minister's action and provide an opportunity for Musharraf to take over, arrest Nawaz Sharif and then send him into exile for many years.

Nawaz Sharif's third tenure, 2013–2017, lasting 4 years ended when a 3-member bench of the Supreme Court, not only removed him from office but disqualified him from contesting elections for life. The decision was based on non-declaration of the salary receivable from his son's company in his nomination papers for the 2013 Elections!

It should be clear from these examples that he was a strong and decisive leader, which was his best quality in terms of governance. But the same quality became a drawback in adverse circumstances, which required tact, realism, and patience. Dramatic and impulsive moves, driven by his aggressive instincts, proved highly counterproductive for his political career. Seen from Nawaz Sharif's point of view, he found himself unable to compromise on the issues of sovereignty and civilian supremacy.

These repeated crises, prematurely ending all his tenures, also affected his psychology. He started giving greater importance to loyalty rather than competence and sincerity. As a result, in the last tenure, his inner circle was confined to his relatives or very loyal colleagues. That naturally affected not only the quality of governance but also his political decisions.

Relations with the Military

A major fatal fault line of Nawaz Sharif, in my assessment, was his inability to handle his relations with the military establishment. In the first phase, from 1985 to 1990, he was a 'selected' political leader of the military, as a potential candidate in opposition to counter PPP. But like all populist leaders, he gradually drifted away as he realized that his longer-term political future would be determined by his commitment to real democracy.

As a strong and decisive leader, Nawaz Sharif detested any undue interference in what he regarded as his domain or mandate. In fact, his first important comment on this subject which I heard in 1990, was well before he became the Prime Minister. Islami Jamhoori Ittehad (IJI) had won 106 out of 200 seats, including 92 from Punjab. Nawaz Sharif naturally expected that he would be asked to form the Government. However, President Ghulam Ishaq Khan took about 10 days to convene the National Assembly and rumours began to circulate that Ghualam Mustafa Jatoi was the establishment's first choice for prime minister. Nawaz Sharif came to my house and asked me to convey the following message to the President: 'we have to gradually reduce the role of these invisible forces in the political life of the country. Let the Assembly choose its leader according to democratic principles and the Constitution'.

For his second tenure from February 1997 to October 1999, he had won a two thirds majority and felt he could now fully assert the supremacy of the elected government. The Assembly passed the Thirteenth Amendment to delete the power of the President to dissolve the National Assembly and the Fourteenth Amendment to prevent floor crossing. But he soon developed differences with the third pillar of state, i.e. the judiciary because of his decision to set up special courts for speedy justice in terrorism cases. In the resulting judicial crisis, a 3-member bench under Chief Justice Sajjad Ali Shah, struck down the Thirteenth Amendment, restoring the power of the President to dissolve the Assembly. President Farooq Leghari was ready to use these powers but did not get a nod from the Army Chief, General Jehangir Karamat. As a result, President Farooq Leghari had to resign.

In this unfortunate phase of our history, Nawaz Sharif probably ignored the fact that Farooq Leghari, had made it possible for

Nawaz Sharif to return to power two years earlier, by dismissing the government of his own party and he, therefore expected better cooperation from the Prime Minister. Similarly, a few months later, when Nawaz Sharif asked General Jehangir Karamat to resign, he overlooked the fact that he had also played a major role in his survival in November 1998 by not supporting President Leghari's intended move to dissolve the Assembly.

In my assessment, the greatest blunder of Nawaz Sharif's political career was his decision to ask for General Jehangir Karamat's resignation only because he had mentioned the need for a National Security Council in his address at the Naval Staff College in Lahore. The history of Pakistan would have been different if he had not committed this blunder. General Jehangir Karamat would have in any case, retired 3 months later. In his place, probably General Ali Kuli Khan who was next in seniority and not General Musharraf would have become the Army Chief. There would have been no Kargil misadventure and no coup in October 1999. The democratic process would have continued and Nawaz Sharif would have completed his 5 year tenure rather than go into forced exile for 8 long years.

Musharraf's Martial Law came with the declared aim of excluding both the main parties, PML(N) and PPP from national politics. He failed in this task largely due to the Charter of Democracy (COD) signed in London in July 2006. I believe that the military establishment still maintained their aim of removing both the major political parties from national politics. Thus, it was convenient that after their return to Pakistan, the leadership of both the parties abandoned the spirit of COD and became unwitting accomplices of the plan to marginalize both the main parties. PML(N) became a party to the Memogate case, possibly on the behest of the establishment. The detention of Dr Asim Hussain, done to drive a wedge between PML(N) and PPP, was not recognized as such by Nawaz Sharif. Another questionable decision of Nawaz Sharif was his cancellation of a prearranged meeting with Asif Ali Zardari after he had used some strong words against the military establishment. This isolated Asif Ali Zardari who thought it propitious to leave the country and spend a period of time abroad in self-imposed exile. During this period, he was worked on to pay Nawaz Sharif in kind, something he managed with ruthless efficiency. The PPP adopted an active anti-Nawaz stand on the Panama case, played a pivotal role in dislodging the PML(N) government in Balochistan in 2018, and paved the way for the election of pro-establishment senators. In so doing, the PPP saved itself from the political machinations adopted against the PML(N) in Punjab and managed to form a government in Sindh. This is a classic case of game theory, where one of the prisoners acts against the other to save himself, only to find himself in equal trouble later on. In any case, the Charter of Democracy was mortally wounded.

Nawaz Sharif came to power for the third time, after the 2013 elections, against the wishes of the Establishment and without the support of other political parties that had endorsed the COD. This made it very difficult for him to function as an effective Prime Minister. There was a subtle campaign in the media to downplay the achievements of the government and to highlight negative attacks from the opposition. A strong anti-corruption drive also erupted during that period to further damage the image of politicians. As expected, Nawaz Sharif's third tenure ended prematurely on 25 July 2017, through judicial action.

Nawaz Sharif's transition away from the military Establishment grew incrementally when his core political interests or stakes were threatened by the absence of real democracy. Sadly, his belief in civilian supremacy was not accompanied by a deeper understanding of political realities. If he had such a grasp of the theoretical foundations of real democracy, he could have adopted a stronger institutional approach to civil-military relations. He could have convened weekly meetings of the National Security Committee, as in the UK, and presented all issues for discussion and collective decision making. That may not have solved all the problems but would have made the relationship more sustainable and negated the impression that he was the sole enemy of the de facto forces, inviting their wrath to his person.

Fundamentally, Nawaz Sharif did not fully comprehend the depth and strength of de facto forces and also ignored the importance of a broader coalition of political forces for establishing the supremacy of democratic institutions.

NOTE

1. See Khurshid Mahmud Kasuri, *Neither a Hawk nor a Dove: An Insiders' Account of Pakistan's Foreign Relations Including Details of the Kashmir Framework*, (OUP: Karachi, 2015), p. 223–4.

CHAPTER 16

The Merger of Federally Administered Tribal Areas with Khyber Pakhtunkhwa Province

Covering an area of 27,200 square kilometres, the Federally Administered Tribal Areas (FATA) comprise seven agencies and six tribal areas adjoining Peshawar, Kohat, Bannu, Lakki Marwat, Tank and Dera Ismail Khan districts, known as 'Frontier Regions' or FRs. According to the 2017 census, the total population of FATA and FRs was five million with the following breakdown and area of each Agency:

Agency	Area Sq. Km	Population**	Main Tribes
Bajaur	1,290	1,093,684	Utmankhel and Tarkhani
Mohmand	2,296	472,357	Mohmand, Safi and Utmankhel
Khyber	2,576	986,973	Afridi, Shelmani, Shinwari and Mulagori
Kurram	3,380	619,553	Sunnis: (Maqbal, Bangash, Ali Sherzai, Zadran), Shias: (Turi, Bangash, Badakhel, Hazara)
Orakzai	1,538	254,356	Sunnis (Utmankhel, Sheikhan, Bizoti), Shias (Manikhel Sepha)
South Waziristan	4,707	674,065	Wazir, Dawar, Utmanzai, Kharasin, Gurbaz
North Waziristan	6,620	543,254	Mehsud, Wazir, Ahmadzai
Frontier Regions	4,813	357,687	
Total:	**27,214**	**5,001,929**	

**Note: Representatives of FATA have been claiming that the total population of FATA was much larger than 5 million. The female population was not fully counted in every census because of social reasons and a sizable population of FATA citizens were working outside FATA in different parts of the country.

Historical Background

The tribal areas have been a gateway to the Indo-Pak sub-continent for centuries. The Mughals crossed the region in the early sixteenth century to capture Delhi and waged relentless military campaigns in the northwest to safeguard the security of their kingdom.

At the turn of the eighteenth century, Russia began to expand eastwards towards Central Asia. In order to ensure that Afghanistan does not fall under Russian influence, Britain fought two wars with Kabul in 1834 and 1878, to bring Afghanistan under British suzerainty. The boundary between Afghanistan and India was finalized between 1893 and 1895. In 1895, the Afghan boundary with Russia was demarcated.

Britain had realized that between the North West Frontier Province of India and Afghanistan, fiercely independent tribesmen could launch raids into adjoining districts for kidnapping and dacoity. To control these tribes, the British created the Khyber Agency in 1878, Kurram in 1892 and Malakand, Tochi and Wana in 1896.

After Lord Curzon became Viceroy of India, he introduced major changes in the tribal policy. In 1905, a new province called North West Frontier Province (NWFP) was created. The Chief Commissioner of NWFP became the Agent to the Governor General for the day to day management of the tribal areas through political agents. The 1876 version of the Frontier Crimes Regulations (FCR) was revised in 1901, which provided for the collective punishment of tribes if any infringement originated from their areas. New militias were created for different tribal areas like Khyber Rifles, Kurram Militia, and South Waziristan Militia, These militias known as 'Frontier Corps' were officered by the British Army Officers and one third of their strength was recruited from local tribes. Subsequently, a new force called 'Frontier Constabulary' was created to guard the border between the tribal areas and settled districts. It was officered by British police officers.

For the next half century, the tribal areas were ruled under this system as semi-governed no-man lands, without many roads or other infrastructure. In the absence of normal laws, the tribesmen were free to keep weapons and defend the border, in return for some rewards and titles, under the Malik System. The Malik was the head of a local group of tribal elders who were given special status and financial benefits to ensure, inter-alia, the safety of the roads, especially in 'protected' areas which fell under the direct control of the Political Agent. These protected areas were, initially, only 5 per cent of total tribal areas, but gradually expanded to 25 per cent.

Post–1947

After Independence in 1947, this tribal system was retained, partly because the new state of Pakistan did not have adequate resources or troops to fully patrol the border with Afghanistan and partly because the tribal Maliks requested the Quaid-i-Azam Mohammad Ali Jinnah, during his visit to Peshawar in 1948, not to make any changes in the administrative system without the tribesmen's consent. This commitment was subsequently enshrined in Article 247 of the 1973 Constitution:

247(3). No act of *Majlis Shoora* (Parliament) shall apply to any Federally Administered Tribal Area unless the President so directs.

(6) the President may at any time, by Order, direct that the whole or any part of a tribal area shall cease to be tribal Area and such Order may contain such incidental or consequential provisions as appear to the President to be necessary and proper.

Provided that before making any under this clause, the President shall ascertain, in such manner as he considers appropriate, the views of the people of the Tribal Area concerned as represented in tribal Jirga.

(7) Neither, the Supreme Court nor a High Court shall exercise any jurisdiction under the Constitution in relation to a Tribal Area unless *Majlis Shoora* by law otherwise provides.

As a result of this policy, FATA, over several decades, did not receive its due share in the financial allocations for development and non-development expenditures, compared to other provinces. This shortfall has been estimated at 30 to 40 per cent but more recently almost 50 per cent. Due to its difficult terrain, FATA would have received a higher per capita allocation, if it had become part of a Province.

On all major economic and social indicators like per capita income literacy and access to health facilities and drinking water, FATA has figured much lower than the national average or indicators for the adjoining Province.

The suffering and misery of the people of FATA, as a result of this chronic under development, was greatly compounded by the turmoil that started in Afghanistan in 1979 and especially after the catastrophic event of 9/11. Thousands of Taliban and other groups, which were trained in Pakistan with full support of the US, escaped to the Tribal belt and soon acquired control of many areas by killing tribal Maliks and imposing their own writ and taxes. The military operations that were undertaken from 2009 onwards uprooted thousands of tribal families from their homes and became Internally Displaced Persons (IDPs) for long periods.

During this turbulent period, FATA also became a major transit hub for a large number of smugglers, drug and arms traffickers and terrorists from Afghanistan. With an open border, more than 50,000 persons crossed the frontier every day without any passport or visa. The resultant insurgency in FATA inevitably spread to Pakistan in the form of bomb blasts and suicide attacks and became a serious threat to Pakistan's security.

Meanwhile, the tribal society had also changed with the emergence of new moneyed classes, with many links to Gulf workers and a growing army of disenchanted youth who had borne the brunt of dislocation and violence. They were openly agitating for security, education, and jobs.

FATA Reforms Committee

Having observed, with great anguish, these tragic circumstances and developments over two decades, I was desperately exploring practical options to fill the serious security vacuum in FATA and to improve the lives of the people.

In 2021, an opportunity presented itself, when I was appointed Chairman of PML(N)'s 2013 Manifesto Committee. The Manifesto as adopted contains the following recommendations in the chapter on 'Militancy and Terrorism':

Neither militancy nor terrorism can be countered by mere use of force. This is a problem that has penetrated deep into the vitals of society and therefore, needs a well-thought out, comprehensive and sustainable plan of action that should include economic, social, administrative, and political initiatives and measures to root out this menace. Some of the steps envisaged by PML(N) are:

- Integration of the Federally and Provincially Administered Tribal Areas into the country's political mainstream, by extending to its people the political rights enjoyed by the citizens of Pakistan.
- Establishment of schools and technical centres to create a pool of skilled manpower, not only for local enterprises, but for manpower export to friendly countries.
- Extending free health benefits to the disadvantaged classes, by providing mobile health units in these areas.
- A crash program to establish small and medium size industrial enterprises in the Tribal Areas that could provide gainful employment to the youth, making them stake-holders in peace and security of these areas.
- Extending special facilities for technical education to the female population of the area, so as to empower them economically and socially.
- Undertaking massive public education campaigns to create an alternate narrative to sustain efforts against terrorism and bring home the message that Islam is a religion of peace and that there is no moral or religious sanction for violence or extremism.
- Undertaking education reforms that will aim at eliminating different systems of education in the country, while ensuring that the Madrassahs too, follow the same syllabi as the government schools.

In order to achieve these important objectives, the Prime Minister's Secretariat notified on 8 November 2015, a Committee on FATA Reforms requesting me to be the Chairman, Governor Khyber Pakhtunkhwa, Sardar Mehtab Ahmed, Minister for States and Frontier Regions (SAFRON), Lt. General (rtd) Abdul Qadir Baloch, Minister for Law, Zahid Hamid and National Security Adviser, Lt. General (rtd) Nasir Khan Janjua, as members and the Secretary SAFRON, Muhammad Shehzad Arbab as Secretary.

The Committee was required to start working immediately and after consulting all stakeholders, propose concrete steps for the political mainstreaming of FATA areas.

It soon became clear to the Committee that political mainstreaming of FATA would be a very complex process because it would also involve legal, administrative, and security mainstreaming. Equally important would be the sequencing of these reforms and their complementarity in terms of timing and scale. Different attempts for reforms over the past forty years, though useful, did not bring about a fundamental mainstreaming of FATA because these elements were missing. The Committee, therefore decided to carry out an in-depth study of all previous FATA Reforms to determine why successive governments had failed in the past six decades in order to introduce meaningful reforms or undertake substantial development efforts.

The first serious attempt was made when Prime Minister Zulfikar Ali Bhutto formed a Committee under General (retd.) Naseerullah Babar, which included Hafeez Pirzada, Rafi Raza, and Dr Mubashar Hassan. The aim of the committee was to create a framework so that FATA could become a part of NWFP for the general elections to be held in March 1977. Later, it was decided to take up the issue after the elections. This did not happen because of the military coup in July 1977.

The second attempt came twenty years later when, in 1996, the government extended the adult franchise system to FATA, so that representatives from FATA could be elected to the National Assembly by the people directly and not through selected tribal maliks. This important step did not, however, increase self-governance, partly because of Article 247 of the Constitution and partly because FATA was not a province or part of another province and could not, therefore, elect its representatives to a provincial assembly, which actually elects ministers to govern the province.

Efforts to introduce the system of local bodies in FATA had totally failed. In 2002, the Government extended Local Government Regulation to FATA and in 2004, in some Agencies councillors were nominated by the Political Agents. However, the system did not take off because the general public had no confidence in the nominated office bearers who had no powers. In 2012, FATA Local Government Regulation 2012 was prepared to establish local bodies in FATA. However, the Regulation was never promulgated.

Another serious attempt at FATA Reforms was made in 2006, through a special committee, chaired by Sahibzada Imtiaz Ahmad.

The focus of this report was on administrative reforms and resulted in the increased independence autonomy of FATA Secretariat under a separate Additional Chief Secretary and a substantial increase in development funding for FATA. But in the absence of major legal reforms and concentration of all powers in the hands of political agents, there was no visible improvement in governance or development indicators. The security situation in FATA was also very fragile at that time and the resultant destruction of infrastructure and related facilities could not be restored by a few development projects undertaken by the government during that period.

In 2005, a Committee on legal reforms, chaired by Justice (R) Mian Muhammad Ajmal, had been constituted to recommend modifications in Frontier Crimes Regulations (FCR) following public consultation across FATA. The Committee recommended many important amendments in the FCR. Many of these were accepted and implemented in 2011. The amended FCR removed some of its shortcomings but more fundamental changes were needed to bring the judicial system in line with the rest of Pakistan and extend the jurisdiction of Superior Court to restore the fundamental rights of the people of FATA, as equal citizens of Pakistan.

In 2011, following the introduction of Adult Franchise Act, 1996, the Political Parties Order, 2002 was also extended to FATA, to allow political parties to campaign freely in FATA. This was an important step, but in the absence of provincial elections, its impact was limited. This step did, however, generate greater political awareness in FATA and also intensified the demand for fundamental reforms.

In addition to these partially successful attempts at FATA Reforms, there were many other studies, conferences, and seminars on different aspects of FATA Reforms during the past 10 years, which provided useful inputs for the Committee's work. A team of experts nominated by the United Nations Development Programme (UNDP) under the leadership of Khalid Aziz, former Chief Secretary of NWFP, to assist the Ministry of States and Frontier Regions on FATA Reforms, also played a valuable supporting role for the Committee.

The next important component of the Committee's work was the consultation process. Under Article 247(6) of the Constitution, the President was required before making any order, which the whole or any part of the Tribal Area shall cease to be Tribal Area, was to ascertain the views of the people of the Tribal Area concerned, as represented in tribal *jirgas*.

The Committee decided at its very first meeting held on 21 November 2015, that apart from visiting every Agency for holding *jirgas* with tribal maliks as required under Article 247(6), it should undertake a much wider process of consultation with (a) FATA members in the Parliament, (b) Representatives of political Parties in FATA and other members of the civil society including traders, lawyers, media and youth (c) Retired civil servants and professionals who had served in FATA.

The Committee held four meetings, at different stages of its work with 12 MNAs and 8 Senators from FATA. These members submitted a written and signed memorandum to the Committee calling for 'ending Article 247 and mainstreaming FATA through merger with Khyber Pakhtunkhwa, separate FATA Province or an elected Executive Council for FATA. Earlier on 7 September 2015, before the FATA Committee was set-up, 19 FATA Parliamentarians had submitted the draft of the Twenty-second Constitutional Amendment to the National Assembly to integrate FATA with Khyber Pakhtunkhwa.

The Committee visited all the 7 agencies on the date as indicated below and also a joint meeting of maliks from all the six Frontier Regions at Peshawar on 2 May 2016:

S.No.	Name of Agency	Date of Visit
1.	Bajaur Agency	31 December 2015
2.	Mohmand Agency	1 January 2016
3.	Khyber Agency	4 February 2016
4.	Orakzai Agency	28 March 2016
5.	Kurram Agency	28 March 2016
6.	North Waziristan Agency	4 April 2016
7.	South Waziristan Agency	25 April 2016
8.	Frontier Regions at Peshawar	2 May 2016

In each Agency, the Committee members attended a large *jirga* with about 450 to 500 tribal maliks over a three hour period. The *jirgas* were also attended by elected members of Parliament from that Agency. The combined *jirga* from all the Frontier Regions held at the Governor's House in Peshawar drew a large gathering of tribal maliks. Thus overall, the Committee was able to consult about 3000 Tribal maliks during these visits. Since the total number of tribal elders under the Malik system had been reduced from 39,000 to 6,000, the Committee was able to meet more than half the tribal maliks.

The afternoon sessions with representatives of political parties traders, lawyers, media and youth associations were also well attended and very lively. The most common slogan that was heard in all the Agencies, was 'Go-FCR-Go'.

The Committee had three meeting with the President. In December 2015, during the first meeting, the President's guidance was sought on the consultation process. In the second meeting, held on 30 August 2016, a presentation was made on the draft recommendations of the Committee. On 6 January 2017, a formal presentation on the final recommendations of the Committee was given to the President.

On 7 September 2016, the Committee had a day long meeting with the Chief Minister, Khyber Pakhtunkhwa, Parvez Khattak along with his colleagues in Peshawar. Following this meeting the Chief Minister sent detailed comments on the recommendations of the Committee. The Committee Secretariat kept a full record of the views expressed in each of the *jirga's* and other meetings. A summary of these views was then discussed in each meeting of the Committee on 16 February, 31 March, 9 May and 8 August 2016.

In these consultations, the stakeholders were asked to give their views on the following four options:

- Maintain the status quo with regard to the main elements of the present system in FATA, but introduce judicial reforms and increase focus on development activities.
- Grant special status to FATA with an elected FATA Council on the pattern of Gilgit-Baltistan Council.
- Create a separate Province of FATA comprising of seven Tribal Agencies.
- Integrate FATA with Khyber Pakhtunkhwa Province, each Agency becoming a separate district.

The key findings which emerged from these consultations, as incorporated in the Committee's Report, are summarized below: -

- There was little support for the status quo option or the option of a FATA Council. In fact, many *maliks* were aware that people of

Gilgit-Baltistan were not satisfied with their Council and wanted the de facto status of a Province.

- There were some *maliks* and representatives of certain political parties, who spoke about a separate Province for FATA. But they had no answer when it was pointed out that there was limited connectivity among different tribal Agencies, but each Agency was fully connected with the adjoining districts not only for trade and livelihoods but also in terms of tribal and cultural links. In addition, FATA did not have either the financial or the administrative capacity to sustain itself as a separate province.

- That effectively left only one option for the political mainstreaming of FATA namely merger with the Khyber Pakhtunkhwa Province. That is why in all the *jirgas* and other meetings there was a wide support for this option.

Despite this widespread support for the merger of FATA with KP, the 'special cultural, traditional features of FATA' and the *Rewaj* system were emphasized. It was also pointed out that the *thana-katchery* system of Pakistan was expensive, time consuming and corrupt. In comparison, the *jirga* system for dispute resolution was quicker and more in line with the traditional way of tribal life.

In some Agencies, especially North Waziristan and in Orakzai, there was much greater emphasis on the rehabilitation of IDPs and reconstruction work before the Reforms were undertaken.

There was strong support in every Agency, on accelerating development activities to expand educational and health facilities and providing employment. The main purpose of FATA Reforms, they said, should be improvement in the lives of the tribal people and specially the youth.

The Reform Committee's Recommendations

By the end of consultative process, the Reform Committee had concluded that the objective of political mainstreaming FATA can be achieved only through its merger with the Khyber Pakhtunkhwa Province. Earlier it had been pointed out, that political mainstreaming would also require complementary steps for the legal, administrative, and security mainstreaming of FATA. The timing, sequencing, and complementarity of these different dimensions of reform were, therefore the real challenge for the Committee. It proved much more difficult to reach a consensus on these aspects in the Committee work than I had initially anticipated.

One member in fact opposed the merger option because it could alter the sensitive demographic balance between Pakhtuns and non-Pakhtuns in KP. This could further intensify the demand for a separate Hazara Province. If as a result, Hazara separated from Khyber Pakhtunkhwa, a Pakhtun homogenous province bordering Afghanistan would emerge, with far reaching implications. Without revenues from Tarbela Dam and other hydro projects in Hazara, the financial viability of the new Khyber Pakhtunkhwa province, would become questionable. In fact, during the course of these discussions, a delegation of MNAs and MPAs from Hazara Division also sought a meeting with the Committee to reinforce these points. Other Committee members, however pointed out that many of the issues raised, including the demand for a separate Hazara Province were beyond the Terms of Reference of the FATA Reforms Committee.

Another member of the Committee argued strongly for a transition period of at least 10 years, as apart from the urgency of repatriation and rehabilitation of IDPs, it will take considerable time to build the administrative and judicial infrastructure that will be required before the actual merger. The counter-argument for a speedier process of merger was that the required infrastructure can be created only by the Khyber Pakhtunkhwa provincial government but it would not have the mandate or the jurisdiction to initiate this task until FATA is merged with Khyber Pakhtunkhwa. Eventually, a compromise was reached on a transition period of 5 years, although I felt, even 3 years would be adequate for the merger option i.e. by 2019. In addition, it was agreed that local bodies election could be held in FATA in 2017 and a special constitutional amendment could be made to enable the people of FATA to elect their representatives for the Provincial Assembly in the 2018 elections.

Another issue which the Committee considered at great length was how to retain, in accordance with the wishes of the people, some feature of the *Rewaj* system while extending the jurisdiction of the Superior Courts and repealing the Frontier Crimes Regulation. The Committee, therefore recommended a hybrid system, under which judicial processes based on *Rewaj* can be formulated and codified to become an integral part of the judicial system. It would also be ensured that the new codified *Rewaj* system is not in conflict with the fundamental rights as enshrined in the Constitution of Pakistan.

After this recommendation was approved, a *Rewaj Regulation* was drafted and submitted to the relevant Standing Committee of the National Assembly. However, it was not possible to achieve a consensus in the Standing Committee. It was then decided to give up the option of exploring a hybrid dispute resolution mechanism, in favour of the system that is the norm in the rest of the country.

Several important recommendations were finalized by the Committee for the Socio-economic development of FATA. These included (a) formulation of a 10-year Development Plan for FATA (b) a special annual allocation of 3 per cent of the divisible pool by the National Finance Commission for a period of 10 years for the implementation of the 10 year Development Plan (c) 30 per cent of this allocation to be channelled through the local bodies.

Discussions in Parliament

On 23 August 2016, the Committee presented its report to the Prime Minister and to the National Security Committee on 24 August. The Prime Minister, while appreciating the work of the Committee, decided that the Report should be presented to the Parliament for discussion and members of the public should also be invited to send their comments on the Report.

Accordingly, I tabled the Report of the Committee in the National Assembly on 9 September and in the Senate on 27 September 2016.

In the National Assembly, three full days were devoted to a discussion on the Report. A large majority of members who spoke at length supported the two main recommendations of the Report namely, FATA's merger with Khyber Pakhtunkhwa and repeal of Frontier Crimes Regulation. However, some members, notably from JUI(F) called for a referendum to decide if the tribal people wanted a separate province or merger with KP. Representative of Pashtunkhwa Milli Awami Party (PKMAP) also supported this proposal and suggested prior consultation with the Government of Afghanistan on

With President of China, Xi Jinping in Dushamber Tajikistan, September 2014

Photo Courtesy: Author's personal collection

With Ban Ki-moon, Secretary General of the United Nations, Islamabad, August 2013
Photo Courtesy: Author's personal collection

With the President of Iran, Hassan Rouhani in Tehran, April 2014
Photo Courtesy: Author's personal collection

With US Secretary of State John Kerry, in Islamabad, January 2015
Photo Courtesy: Author's personal collection

With Wang Yi, Chinese Foreign Minister in Islamabad, September 2015
Photo Courtesy: Press Information Department (PID), Islamabad

With Boris Johnson, then British Foreign Secretary in Islamabad November 2016
Photo Courtesy: Press Information Department (PID), Islamabad

With President Ashraf Ghani of Afghanistan, December 2016
Photo Courtesy: Press Information Department (PID), Islamabad

FATA Reforms. Other members of the National Assembly however, countered these arguments from the floor by saying that the option of a separate province for FATA was not a viable option so how can a referendum be held on an option that is not viable. There is effectively only one option, namely a merger with Khyber Pakhtunkhwa. Similarly, the reaction from the floor on the need for consultation with Afghanistan was very strong since it was entirely an internal policy matter for Pakistan to decide.

In the Senate, the Chairman set up a Committee of the Whole to discuss the Report of the FATA Reforms Committee on 6 December 2016. There was broad support for the recommendation to merge FATA with Khyber Pakhtunkhwa. However, some Senate members from FATA raised many questions about the adequacy of the consultation process and argued for retaining the tribal tradition, the *Rewaj* system and a gradual approach to FATA Reforms. Some other members responded to these comments and said, some members from FATA may be apprehensive that after FATA's merger, it would not have eight reserved Seats in the Senate. I assured the members that Senators who have already been elected would be allowed to complete their respective terms, even after FATA's merger with Khyber Pakhtunkhwa.

Cabinet Decisions

After the recommendations of the FATA Reform Committee received the support of all major political parties in Parliament, from the Khyber Pakhtunkhwa provincial government and also from the general public, the Report was submitted to the Cabinet for consideration and approval on 15 December 2016. The Cabinet decided that the Committee should make another effort to develop a consensus on the subject and submit a report to the next meeting of the Cabinet.

In the light of this directive, I had several meetings with Maulana Fazalur Rehman and in his absence with Akram Khan Durrani. They finally agreed with the merger option but insisted that it should take place after five years and not within five years. I promised to present this modification to the Cabinet for consideration. The Cabinet, however did not approve this change.

Finally on 2 March 2017, the dawn of a historic day, the Cabinet accorded its final approval to all the major proposals of the FATA Reforms Committee and approved in principle, the recommendations of the Committee to mainstream FATA in five years in consultation with different stakeholders of FATA. It also called for constitutional amendments to enable the people of FATA to elect their representatives to Khyber Pakhtunkhwa Assembly in the 2018 general elections and to hold party based local bodies election soon after.

Another important decision was the repeal of Frontier Crimes Regulations and extension of the jurisdiction of the Supreme Court and Peshawar High Court to FATA.

The Cabinet requested the inter-provincial National Finance Commission to consider making an allocation of 3 per cent of the divisible pool annually, for the implementation of the 10 year FATA Development Plan, in addition to the existing Public Sector Development Programme (PSDP) allocation of Rs 21 billion. The Cabinet also approved a number of other recommendations to accelerate the pace of development activities in FATA.

The complete 26 decisions on FATA Reforms approved by the Cabinet on 2 March 2017 is given in Box 16.1 at the end of this chapter.

Implementation

In order to ensure speedy and effective implementation of FATA Reforms in the right sequence, the Cabinet had approved the conversion of FATA Reforms Committee into a Cabinet Level Implementation Committee with the additions of Chief Minister and Chief Secretary Khyber Pakhtunkhwa, and Commander XI Corps, with the mandate to advise government on the timing and modalities of mainstreaming FATA.

Following the in-house change of Government in July 2017, I suggested to Prime Minister Shahid Khaqan Abbasi, that in view of the importance and complexity of the issues involved, it would be highly desirable, if the Cabinet Committee is chaired by the Prime Minister with the addition of the Chief Minister and Chief Secretary, Khyber Pakhtunkhwa, Commander XI Corps, as already approved by the

Cabinet, it should also include the Chief of Army Staff. The proposal was approved by the Prime Minister and subsequently by the Cabinet.

The new high level Committee, now called 'National Implementation Committee on FATA Reforms' held its first meeting on 8 September 2017 and took some important decisions: -

- The Ministry of States & Frontier Regions should identify, in consultation with Governor Khyber Pakhtunkhwa (KP) and Khyber Pakhtunkhwa Provincial Government, the administrative infrastructure that will be required for its political mainstreaming i.e. the merger of FATA with KP.
- Election Commission to make preparations for holding provincial elections in FATA in 2018.
- Legislative and administrative actions required for the repeal of Frontier Crimes Regulation should be fast tracked.
- Asked the Finance Minister to take up the proposal to allocate annually 3 per cent of the divisible pool at the next meeting of the National Finance Commission as a priority item.

The Committee also noted that the security situation had seen remarkable improvement in the past two years. This improvement will however, need further consolidation in the coming months by (i) expanding the strength and capacity of Frontier Constabulary and the Levies to convert them into an effective police force for the tribal districts (ii) setting up proper district headquarters and police stations in all the agencies (iii) expediting the fencing of the border with Afghanistan to regulate all movements through proper documents and procedures. The aim should be to extend the writ of the state right up to the border so that no security vacuum exists in the tribal districts.

The second meeting of the National Implementation Committee held on 17 October 2017, took note of the growing support for FATA's merger with Khyber Pakhtunkhwa, from almost all major political parties including PPP, PTI, ANP and JI. The option was also welcomed by other stakeholders like FATA Political Alliance. The FATA Youth Forum organized a number of events to call for early merger and also to counter the proposal for a referendum to decide if FATA should be merged with Khyber Pakhtunkhwa or made into a separate province. In the light of such widespread support and clear indications of a two third majority in Parliament for the required constitutional amendments, the Committee felt that the length of the transition period may have to be reconsidered.

The Committee also asked the Ministry of Law to expedite the passage of the bill to extend the jurisdiction of the Supreme Court and Peshawar High Court, which had already been endorsed by the Standing Committee on Law on 16 October 2017 and also requested the Peshawar High Court to set up Agency Courts in all the Seven Agencies as early as possible.

The Committee requested the Governor Khyber Pakhtunkhwa to fast track the preparation of the 10 year FATA Development Plan in consultation with the Provincial Government.

The Committee approved an allocation of Rs 250 million for 2017–18 to replace the expenditure previously financed from the Agency Development Fund collected through issue of permits and *rahdaris* (transit taxes) for exports from and imports into FATA. The Cabinet had already decided to abolish this system to bring down prices of essential items in FATA and to save traders in FATA from serious inconvenience caused by the system.

In the third meeting of the National Implementation Committee held on 18 December 2017, the Committee, apart from reviewing the progress on political, legal, economic, and administrative reforms, focussed on security mainstreaming. It called for urgent steps to screen all the personnel working in Frontier Constabulary, Levies or *Khasadars* in order to adjust those who qualify, against the requirements of 'agency police' that will take over policing duties in FATA, after the merger. Arrangements for the recruitment and training of additional levies already sanctioned by the Cabinet should also be expedited.

The first few months of 2018 saw very frantic activity for the implementation of legal reforms and financing of the 10 year FATA Development Plan. The bill to extend the jurisdiction of the Supreme Court and Peshawar High Court was passed on 14 May 2018 and preliminary work was initiated for repealing the FCR.

Meanwhile, the Special Committee under Governor Khyber Pakhtunkhwa had already submitted in January 2018, a preliminary document entitled 'Objectives and Sectoral Priorities of the 10 year

FATA Development Plan'. After earmarking 30 per cent for the local bodies, it had proposed sectoral allocations of Rs 700 billion. The largest allocation of Rs 160 billion was proposed for dams, small scale irrigation, agriculture, livestock and forestry. This was followed by urban centres' development (Rs 100 billion) connectivity (Rs 90 billion), governance (Rs 80 billion), energy (Rs 60 billion), industrial development (Rs 50 billion), and Rs 40 billion each for mineral development, education, health and special initiatives.

The special committee has also recommended that a 10-year plan should be formulated and implemented in three phases of 3, 3 and 4 years so that each phase can learn from the experience of the earlier phase.

This interim report of the Special Committee was presented to the National Economic Council on 24 April 2018 with the recommendation that financial requirements for the first three years should be fixed at 20 per cent or Rs 200 billion since it will take some time before larger projects are prepared and approved. Under the NFC formula, Rs 85 billion out of the proposed 3-year allocation of Rs 200 billion would be provided by the Federal Government and the remaining Rs 115 billion by the four provinces. The Federal Government and the KP government have already agreed to provide their respective shares over the next three years. In other words, half the funds required for the first three years of the 10 years Development Plan were already available. Work on the actual preparation and approval of the projects should therefore be taken in hand, without any delay. Meanwhile, the issue can be discussed in the next meeting of the Council of Common Interests so that the other three provinces can make their respective contributions. The National Economic Council endorsed these recommendations.

It was also emphasized that FATA's development would not be ensured only by allocating the required financial resources. Even the modest amount of Rs 20 to 25 billion allocated each year under the PSDP had never been fully utilized and the physical outcomes were even lower. A special fully staffed Planning Unit under a BPS-22 grade officer should be set up in the Provincial Planning Development as early as possible, exclusively for FATA.

The Final Phase

An important final meeting of the National Implementation Committee was held on 2 May 2018. The Committee recognized that the time was opportune for the political mainstreaming of FATA, through merger with Khyber Pakhtunkhwa, and this long standing issue can now be resolved. The Committee then set up a five member Committee under Barrister Zafarullah Khan to urgently draft a regulation for the repeal of FCR and for interim measures for the transition period, pending setting up of proper judicial infrastructure in FATA.

Similarly, the Prime Minister indicated that he was planning to meet leaders of Parliamentary Parties to discuss FATA Reforms and specifically the proposed Constitutional Amendment Bill to enable people of FATA to elect their representatives to the Khyber Pakhtunkhwa Assembly. This meeting was held on 7 May 2018 and was attended by Syed Khursheed Ahmad Shah and Naveed Qamar from PPP, Shah Mahmood Qureshi from PTI, Haji Ghulam Ahmed Bilour from ANP, Mohammad Khan Achakzai from PKMAP, Akram Khan Durrani from JUI(F), Aftab Sherpao from JWP, Farooq Sattar from MQM, Saibzada Tariqullah from JI, and Nasir Khan MNA from FATA. The National Assembly Speaker, Sardar Ayaz Sadiq, Ghalib Khan Wazir Minister of State, Barrister Zafarullah and I assisted the Prime Minister. Some additional members from these parties joined the subsequent meetings of this Group on 10 and 11 May.

While the representatives of JUI(F) and PKMAP persisted with their opposition to the merger option, representative of all other political parties expressed strong support for FATA's merger with KP. The Prime Minister informed the participants that a draft Constitutional Amendment Bill was almost ready and would be presented to them for consideration in the next two days. Some participants wanted to ensure that provincial elections in FATA should be held in July 2018 along with the general elections in the rest of the country. It was clarified that the Election Commission has to update the voters' lists and demarcate the constituencies. These tasks cannot be completed within the time available. However, the proposed legislation will indicate clearly that these provincial elections in FATA would be held within one year of the general elections.

On 8 May, the draft Constitutional Amendment was presented to the Cabinet and was approved in principle along with other consequential legal and administration measures.

The draft Constitutional Amendment Bill and draft Presidential Regulation to repeal the FCR were then discussed by the Prime Minister with the Parliamentary leaders in two marathon meetings held on 10 and 11 May 2018.

Two issues that came up for discussion in these meetings were about the number of seats ex-FATA MNAs will have in future in the National Assembly and the KP Assembly. In the past two decades, 12 National Assembly Seats were allocated to FATA, which was proportionately higher than its population, since FATA did not have any seats in the Provincial Assembly. In the proposed Bill, the number of National Assembly Seats had been reduced from 12 to 6. It was, however clarified by the Prime Minister that under a proviso in Section 3, the allocation of 12 seats for the 2018 Elections will remain and new allocations will apply to the next elections.

For the Provincial Assembly, FATA was allocated 21 seats (16 General, 4 Women and one non-Muslim). Parliamentary members from FATA pointed out that the population of FATA was under estimated in the 2017 census. It should, therefore be given additional seats. The Prime Minister explained that in view of limited time, no change is possible at this stage. However, the matter can be taken up at a later stage in Parliament.

It was also clarified that after merger of FATA, there will be no Separate seats for FATA in the Senate, in addition to 23 Senate seats allocated to KP. However, existing members of the Senate from FATA shall continue till the expiry of their respective terms.

Another important issue raised was that of taxation. It was pointed out that under Article 247(3) of the Constitution, four major tax laws namely Income Tax Ordinance 2001, Sales Tax Act 1990, Federal Excise Act 2005 and Customs Act 1969 were not applicable to FATA. After the merger, these would become operational immediately and adversely affect the efforts to accelerate the pace of development of these deprived areas. After lengthy discussions, the Prime Minister agreed that the pre-merged position of taxation would be continued in FATA for a period of five years.

After these clarifications and assurances, the meeting of Parliamentary leaders endorsed the draft Constitutional Amendment Bill for presentation to Parliament to merge Tribal Agencies and Tribal areas adjoining districts, in the KP province by amending Article 1, 51, 59, 62, 106 and 246 of the Constitution and the deletion of Article 247. The jurisdiction of the Peshawar High Court and the Supreme Court had already been extended to Tribal districts through a bill passed by Parliament on 14 May 2018.

The second important draft considered in these meetings was the FATA Interim Governance Regulation, to be issued by the President to repeal the FCR, convert all Agencies of FATA into Tribal Districts and re-designate the political agents as Deputy Commissioners. It also provided for an interim system of administration of justice, till the normal judicial infrastructure with required personnel had been established.

The Twenty–Fifth Constitutional Amendment Bill

On 24 May 2018, the Twenty–Fifth Constitutional Amendment Bill was passed by the National Assembly, by the Senate on 25 May 2018 and by the Provincial Assembly, as required on 27 May 2018. The President's Assent to the bill was accorded on 30 May 2018. The FATA Interim Governance Regulation 2018 was issued by the President the same day. All the members of the FATA Reforms Committee attended the memorable signing ceremony in the Presidency. Thus, these important requirements for the mainstreaming of FATA were completed only one day before the term of the PML(N) Government expired on 31 May 2018.

The jubilation in FATA, following its merger was enthusiastically renewed a year later, when elections were held in all tribal districts to elect 23 members to the Provincial Assembly of KP in June 2018. This completed the process of political mainstreaming of FATA.

Cabinet Decisions of 2 March 2017

The Cabinet considered the Summary dated, 27 January 2017 submitted by States and Frontier Regions Division on the **Report of the Committee on FATA Reforms 2016,** and decided as under: -

i) Approval in principle to the recommendation of the Committee to mainstream FATA in 5 years, in consultation with different stakeholders of FATA.

ii) Make provision, through a constitutional amendment, to enable the people of FATA to elect their representatives to the Khyber Pakhtunkhwa Assembly in the 2018 elections along with other consequential amendments.

iii) Frontier Crimes Regulations (FCR) will be repealed and replaced by a new *Rewaj* Regulation for Tribal Areas, in accordance with Constitutional provisions. In the new law provisions relating to collective/vicarious responsibility will be omitted, thereby making an individual responsible for his own acts.

iv) The target date for repatriation of all TDPs should be 30 April, 2017 and most activities under the reconstruction phase should be completed before the end of 2018.

v) A Special Committee of high level experts and officials should be formed under the Governor Khyber Pakhtunkhwa, to prioritize preparation of a 10-year Socio-Economic Development Plan for FATA by 30 April 2017.

vi) The NFC should be requested to consider making an allocation of 3 per cent of the gross federal divisible pool on annual basis for the implementation of FATA Development Plan. This will be in addition to the existing annual PSDP allocation of Rs 21 billion.

vii) 30 per cent of the allocation in the FATA Development Plan should be channelled through the local bodies.

viii) FATA Development Authority (FDA) may be reorganized under a Chief Operating Officer (COO) in BS-22 to supervise and coordinate the reconstruction phase and implementation of the 10-year Socio-Economic Development Plan for FATA.

ix) A Governor's Advisory Council consisting of all FATA Senators and MNAs may be set up to assist the Governor in carrying out development and administrative functions.

x) The approving powers of FATA Development Committee may be enhanced through due process from the present Rs 400 million to Rs 2 billion and that of FDWP from Rs 200 million to Rs 1 billion.

xi) Party based local bodies elections should be held in FATA soon after the 2018 general elections.

xii) Permit/*Rahdari* system for exports from and imports into FATA should be abolished to eliminate large scale corruption and to bring down prices of essential items in FATA. Correspondingly, necessary funds should be provided in the budget for operational expenditure of the political administration.

xiii) Auditor General of Pakistan should ensure that development funds and all other expenditure of local bodies in FATA are properly audited to ensure efficient utilization.

xiv) Jurisdiction of the Supreme Court of Pakistan and the Peshawar High Court should be extended to FATA through an Act of Parliament so that the inhabitants of FATA can enjoy equal rights.

xv) Additional posts in the Levies force may be sanctioned for performing agency/police functions in consultation with Finance Division. Destroyed/ damaged Levies posts should be reconstructed and provision of additional infrastructure for Levies to ensure round-the-clock security should be undertaken. Decision to create new wings in the civil armed forces will be reviewed.

xvi) Capacity building of FC should be undertaken and additional new wings of FC may be created for improved border management.

xvii) All posts in FATA should be upgraded and brought at par with Khyber Pakhtunkhwa. Salaries for the project personnel in FATA should be 20 per cent higher than that admissible under the project policy of Khyber Pakhtunkhwa.

xviii) Connectivity of FATA with CPEC should be ensured at suitable locations.

xix) State Bank of Pakistan (SBP) should encourage establishment of more branches of banks in FATA.

xx) The President Order No. 13 of 1972 regarding deputation of civil servants in FATA may be suitably revised to empower the Governor to attract competent officers from multiple sources for the transition period.

xxi) Land settlement should be planned and undertaken in consultation with the stake holders by using modern technology to create GIS based computerized individual record of rights.

xxii) Proper coverage of BISP, Bait-ul-Maal and microfinance schemes in FATA should be ensured.

xxiii) Quota of FATA students in education and health institutions in other provinces should be doubled and retained for 10 years after integration with Khyber Pakhtunkhwa.

xxiv) Set up a Directorate of Transition and Reform for coordinating and monitoring the reforms as recommended in Chapter 5 of the Report.

xxv) Approval for the conversion of FATA Reforms Committee 2016 into a Cabinet Level Implementation Committee with the addition of Chief Minister Khyber Pakhtunkhwa, Commander XI Corps, and Chief Secretary, Khyber Pakhtunkhwa with the mandate to also advise the government on the timing and modalities of mainstreaming FATA.

xxvi) Approval to the following three statutes annexed with the Summary:

a) The Constitutional Amendment Bill amending Article 106 of the Constitution.

b) The Supreme Court and High Court (Extension of Jurisdiction to Federally Administered Tribal Areas) Act, 2017.

c) The Tribal Areas *Rewaj* Regulations, 2017.

******

CHAPTER 17

Imran Khan as Prime Minister

Twenty two years after he launched a new political party, called Pakistan Tehreek-e-Insaf (PTI), Imran Khan was sworn in as the twenty-second Prime Minister of Pakistan.

Imran Khan was born into a respectable and well-to-do family from Mianwali in Punjab. He studied at Aitchison College, Lahore and then went to Oxford University. He soon became a star cricketer in a country that yearns for heroes. In March 1992, his sporting fame reached its pinnacle when Pakistan won the Cricket World Cup in Australia.

Soon after that, he decided to set-up the Shaukat Khanum Cancer Hospital in Lahore, in memory of his mother and launched a very successful fund raising campaign. During this fund raising campaign, Imran Khan focussed on educational institutions, with students donating small amounts from their pocket money. Instinctively and unknowingly, Imran Khan was cultivating his potential political supporters.

In 1996, Imran launched his political party PTI and jumped into the political arena by filing his nomination papers from 8 constituencies in the 1997 elections but could not win any of them because of PML(N)'s landslide victory in that election.

Five years later, after he lent his support to President Pervez Musharraf in the 2001 referendum, he expected to become Prime Minister by winning 80 to 100 seats in the 2002 elections. But Musharraf's kings party was PML(Q), so he offered him only 10 or maximum 20 seats, which he declined. In this election, Imran Khan's Party secured only one seat, from his home town constituency of Mianwali, which for some strange reason, he had not contested in 1997.

To gain popularity, Imran Khan soon become 'anti-Musharraf', and boycotted the 2008 elections.

In October 2011, Imran Khan's political future suddenly lit up, when PTI organized a public meeting in Lahore. The response was much bigger than anyone expected and the crowd had a large number of enthusiastic youth participation. Suddenly, Imran Khan had emerged as a national leader with an agenda for change, 'Naya (new) Pakistan' as he began to call it.

Imran Khan's rise coincided with PPP's decline in Punjab and Khyber Pakhtunkhwa provinces. Many PPP supporters, especially in Punjab found a welcome alternative in PTI. Similarly, PML(Q) which was created by Pervez Musharraf in 2000, to provide a civilian façade to his rule, was in disarray. Many of its members and supporters, who could not return to PML(N), also opted for PTI.

Despite this upsurge in PTI's popularity, PTI managed to win only 25 seats in the 2013 elections out of 272 contested seats. Immediately, Imran Khan started his campaign to brand the 2013 elections as rigged. He said his mandate was 'stolen'. Many independent observers pointed out that the margin of victory of PML(N) was very large (127 seats against PTI's 25), and even if rigging was alleged in some constituencies, it would not change the overall result. In August 2014, Imran Khan, raised the tempo of his protest movement and organized a *dharna* (sit-in) in D Square in front of the Parliament House in Islamabad. Many observers claimed that this sit-in could not have lasted 124 days without the active participation of Dr Tahir ul Qadri's semi-religious organization, the Pakistan Awami Tehreek of Minhaj-ul-Quran. The sit-in caused great disruption in the economic life of the country and led to many incidents of violence, including attacks on the Parliament building, the President House and the Pakistan Television Station.

The purpose of this *dharna*, it seems, was not to dislodge the government but to keep Nawaz Sharif under pressure. That objective was largely achieved. In addition, cumulative coverage of almost 20,000 hours on many TV channels, raised the political image and profile of Imran Khan. On the other hand, the *dharna* also brought PML(N) and PPP closer on the issue of 'saving democracy'. The PPP leaders called for a joint session of Parliament. The session went on for 12 days of heated debates and was greatly instrumental in ending the sit-in. In December 2014, the attack on the Army Public School in Peshawar in which 135 school children lost their precious lives was another factor.

In January 2015, the *dharna* was called off. It resulted in adding a new and dangerous dimension to Pakistani politics—'the container culture'. Any political leader could now stand on a container anywhere and hurl any manner of allegations and foul adjectives at his opponents. The long term consequences of this 'container culture' are yet to be assessed but it has already laid the foundations of a highly polarised political system, marked by intense hostility and uncompromising attitudes.

The 2018 Elections

Several months before the 2018 Elections, there were some unexpected political developments in Balochistan. In the first week of January 2018, 14 members of the Provincial Assembly filed a motion of no-confidence against the Chief Minister, Nawab Sanaullah Zehri of PML(N). The media described this move as 'a well thought out power manoeuvre to undertake, with one eye on the upcoming Senate elections, which will have a far reaching impact on national level politics'. At the same time three Ministers of the Zehri Cabinet, Mir Sarfraz Bugti, Sardar Sarfraz Dhomki and Prince Ahmed Ali tendered their resignations. With 21 seats out of 65 in the Baluchistan Assembly. PML(N) would have secured at least 4 out of 11 Senate seats in March 2018. With the imminent split in the party, Sanaullah Zehri was left with no option but to resign. In this phase, to the surprise of many, Mir Abdul Quddus Bizenjo of PML(Q) was elected as Chief Minister.

In March 2018, under this game plan a new political party Balochistan Awami Party (BAP) came into existence. It also managed to elect Sardar Sadiq Sanjrani as Chairman Senate, with support from PPP Senators. The Party which consisted mostly of dissidents from PML(N) and PML(Q) won 15 seats in the 65 members Provincial Assembly in the 2018 elections. Jam Kamal Ahmed Alyani of BAP was elected Chief Minister on 19 August, 2019, with support from PTI members.

Another unexpected development on the eve of 2018 elections was the creation of a South Punjab dissident group in PML(N) when 8 members of the National Assembly resigned from the Party and announced their support for PTI on the understanding that PTI will support their demand for a new South Punjab Province.

It was alleged from these developments that the Military Establishment had decided to facilitate the success of PTI in the 2018 elections. In 2018, a report prepared for the US Senate by the Congressional Research Service expressed the possible apprehension 'that Pakistan's security establishment covertly manipulated politics before and during the general elections of 2018, with the motive of removing Nawaz Sharif and his PML(N) from power'.

Under the shadow of these factors, it was not difficult to predict the outcome of the 2018 elections. It was, however expected that PML(N) may be able to retain its majority in the Punjab Assembly. It did win more seats (108) than the PTI (103), but then with a marathon and not so transparent effort to win over the majority of independent MPAs, PTI was able to form the Government of Punjab.

The results of 2018 National and Provincial Elections on contested seats are shown in the following table:

Pakistan General Elections 2018					
Party	NA	Punjab	Sindh	KP*	Balochistan
Pakistan Tehreek-e-Insaf	115	123	23	65	4
Pakistan Muslim League (N))	67	129	0	5	1
Pakistan Peoples Party Parliamentarians	43	6	75	4	0
Independent	14	28	0	5	5
Muttahida Majlis-e-Amal Pakistan	13	0	1	10	9
Mutatahida Qaumi Movement Pakistan	6	0	16	0	0
Pakistan Muslim League (Quaid-e-Azam)	4	7	0	0	0
Balochistan Awami Party	3	1	0	0	15
Balochistan National Party	3	0	0	0	6
Grand Democratic Alliance	2	0	11	0	0
Awami National Party	1	0	0	6	3
Awami Muslim League Pakistan	1	0	0	0	0
Total:	272	294	126	95	43

*Khyber Pakhtunkhwa

PTI's tally of 156 seats after adding women and minority seats, was short of the required majority of 172 seats in a house of 342, but with the support of PML(Q), MQM and Balochistan Awami Party, PTI was able to form the Federal Government and the Provincial Government in Punjab. In Khyber Pakhtunkhwa (KP), PTI increased its strength well above the 2013 level to 85 out of 125 seats. Surprisingly the four seats which Imran Khan wanted to open for recount in the 2013 elections, were again won by PML(N) in the 2018 elections.

In May 2018, in the run up to the 2018 Elections, PTI announced a '100 Days Agenda' promising sweeping reforms in all areas of governance. More specifically it promised:

- 10 million new jobs in first 100 days.
- A new Province in South Punjab.
- Fast tracking FATA's merger with Khyber Pakhtunkhwa.
- Improving law and order in Karachi.
- Better relations with Baloch political leaders.

Imran Khan addressed the nation soon after his swearing in. Apart from repeating the main points of the 100 days' agenda, he also announced 50 million new houses for low income groups and many austerity measures. He also promised to build and run Pakistan on the principles of the Islamic State of Medina. Most independent observers worried that the goals and targets Imran Khan had presented to the nation as benchmarks for a '*Naya* (New) Pakistan' had raised the expectation level of the common citizens and everyone expected a quick bonanza. However, in the first year of Imran Khan's government, the economy literally was in the ICU. Instead of relief, as explained in the next section of this chapter, the common man was overwhelmed by the sharp rise in prices and unemployment, largely due to the PTI government's unexpected failure to manage the economy.

Imran Khan's Economic Management

A few weeks before the elections, Imran Khan had indicated that if PTI won the elections, Asad Umar would be the Finance Minister. Everyone naturally expected that Asad Umar and some of his colleagues would have completed all the required home-work for managing the economy. But this expectation proved false.

Imran Khan had said, Pakistan would not go to the International Monetary Fund (IMF) because businessmen will pay taxes to an 'honest government' and, overseas Pakistanis will send huge amounts of foreign exchange to solve Pakistan's balance of payment problems. But in early September, Asad Umar told the media that he was going to Washington to negotiate a loan with the IMF 'in the larger national interest'. Obviously the discussions in Washington were difficult, so the Government decided to seek loans from friendly countries to avoid the option of seeking an IMF Programme. Imran Khan visited China, Saudi Arabia and UAE in quick succession. It was soon announced that a package of US$9 billion had been arranged. This will cover the current account deficit for this year and there will be no need to go to the IMF.

Apparently, the economic mangers had not calculated that the gap was much higher than US$9 billion. Soon after, Asad Umar returned from Washington and had briefed the media about his success in negotiating better terms with the IMF, there was a shock announcement that he had been removed from the post of Finance Minister and Hafeez Shaikh had been appointed as Advisor to PM on Finance. Simultaneously, the Governor State Bank (SBP), Tariq Bajwa was asked to resign and was replaced by Baqar Raza, the IMF Country representative in Egypt, as Governor SBP. The media readily speculated that Asad Umar was not perhaps ready to accept some of the tough IMF conditions. He was, therefore removed unceremoniously to make way for a team 'acceptable' to the IMF. Following this change, an IMF Extended Fund Facility of US$ 6 billion was finalized at the staff level within a few days and finally approved by the IMF Board on 3 July 2019. As explained later in the section, the impact of these IMF conditions on the business community and the common man were extremely negative.

Besides the dillydallying approach to the IMF issue, another factor which destroyed public confidence and the investment climate were Imran Khan's repeated statements, at home and abroad, that the country was on the verge of bankruptcy, its institutions were destroyed by the previous two regimes and rampant corruption and money laundering had emerged as the key issues for the new government. Government Ministers repeated these statements mentioning money laundering figures of US$ 10 billion every year. As a result, over US$500 million were pulled out of the stock market by foreign investors in the last quarter of 2018 and the stock market declined to its lowest in four years of 30,277 points as against 42,873 in the last week of August 2018. This decline of 12,596 points dropped the market capitalization by more than a trillion Rupees in the first year of PTI's rule.

The third important factor was the vagueness of Imran Khan's 'Agenda for Change'. Even after a year in office, the PTI spokespersons could not provide a list of Imran Khan's key priorities. The long list of objectives, plans and targets projected regularly on the media is similar to the past manifestos of other political parties. Realistic targets, supported by financial allocations and required policies or laws, will speak for themselves, when implemented and achieved. Good intentions and pronouncements are no substitute for actions.

As mentioned in the preceding chapter, the PML(N) government which took over in June 2013 succeeded in accelerating the annual rate of economic growth from 3 per cent to 5.8 per cent and bringing down the rate of inflation from 12 per cent to 4 per cent. This strategy, focussed on a higher rate of economic growth, and also helped in achieving other vital social targets, such as poverty reduction and employment.

The GDP growth of 5.8 per cent in 2017–18, the highest in 13 years, was made possible by a healthy growth of 3.5 per cent in agriculture, 6 per cent in large scale manufacturing, 9 per cent in the construction sector and 6.4 per cent in the services sector. This did lead to a sharp increase in imports, specially machinery and petroleum products, and therefore a higher current account deficit. Exports did not increase in the first three years mainly because of the energy crisis, but once the energy situation improved, exports also increased by 13 per cent in 2017–18.

Instead of evolving a balanced approach under which a selective stabilization programme could be combined with a strategy to sustain the growth momentum in the economy, the PTI government adopted the classical IMF approach to stabilization. In two mini budgets during 2018–19 and in the budget for 2019–20, it introduced the following measures; without understanding the full implications:

- Sharp increase in the prices of gas and electricity.

- Policy rate of the State Bank was raised from 6.25 per cent to 12.25 per cent and then 13.25 per cent.
- The exchange rate was allowed to depreciate by 38 per cent from Rs 115 to Rs 160 per dollar.
- Announced a revenue collection target of Rs 5,500 billion in 2018–19, implying a 40 per cent increase over actual collection of Rs 3,850 billion in 2018–19 (target was Rs 4,150 billion).
- To achieve this ambitious target, new taxes of Rs 516 billion were imposed in the budget, in addition to withdrawing exemptions worth Rs 300 billion.
- Public Sector Development Programme was drastically reduced. After taking into account the rate of inflation, the development expenditure in 2019–20 will be lower, in real terms, than in 2018–19.

As a result of these policies, it was no surprise that PTI government's economic performance in its first year was dismal. Almost every major indicator showed a negative trend:

- GDP growth slowed down from 5.8 per cent in 2017–18 to 3.2 per cent in 2018–19. The industrial growth was (-) 2 per cent and agricultural growth virtually stagnant.
- Rate of inflation went up from 4 per cent to 10.34 per cent with a serious drop in the purchasing power of low-income groups at a time when unemployment was also increasing.
- Total tax revenues which had doubled in the last 5 years (2013–18) from Rs 2,000 billion to 4,000 billion, declined to Rs 3,842 billion, for the first time in Pakistan's history. The budget deficit at 8.9 per cent was also higher than 6.8 per cent in 2017–18.
- Exports in 2018–19 actually declined to US$22.97 billion from previous years' US$ 23.4 billion, despite continuing depreciation in the exchange rate. Imports were however compressed from US$60.8 billion to US$ 54.8 million due to a slowdown in the economy and decline in machinery imports.
- The stock market index declined to 34,000 points on 30 June 2019, compared to 41,900 in June 2018.
- Forecast GDP growth for 2019–20 is less than 3 per cent.

Following, the implementation of the IMF Programme, some of these indicators may deteriorate further. The IMF predicted in its report that the rate of GDP growth in 2019–20 is not likely to exceed 2.4 per cent but the rate of inflation will be higher at 13 per cent against 10 per cent in June 2019.

The big hike in the prices of gas and electricity, the increase in general price level due to currency depreciation and the impact of additional taxes in the budget suddenly became a lethal combination against which threats of strikes and public protests have seen an increase. After sporadic strikes in some cities, the trader's associations, called for a nationwide strike against such heavy taxes on a stagnant economy.

Business leaders are also apprehensive that government will not be able to meet the targets agreed with the IMF and that may lead to further taxation and other stabilization measures. As a result of the hike in State Bank's policy rate and the large devaluation of the rupee, a large part of the additional tax revenues of Rs 1,500 billion 'expected' in 2019–20 will be absorbed by additional debt servicing, caused not by excessive borrowings of the previous two regimes, but the policy actions of the PTI government. This will make it impossible to achieve the unprecedented fiscal adjustment of 2.3 per cent in a single year.

Similarly, the IMF Programme requires the government to give up the use of many administrative measures, such a cash margins or regulatory duties to curtail imports. So the only option left for 'correcting' the balance of payments will be the exchange rate. Will the government be able to allow further large and continuing depreciation of the rupee with its harmful side-effects on the rate of inflation and on debt servicing?

As in previous IMF reports, it has again listed many structural weaknesses of the Pakistan economy i.e. chronically weak tax administration, difficult business environment, inefficient loss making state owned enterprises and a large informal economy. However, recognizing the political obstacles in addressing these weaknesses, the IMF has now focussed on monetary and fiscal 'structural weaknesses'; some of which have already been implemented as prior actions; namely:

- Adoption of a 'free floating exchange rate' without any intervention from government or the State Bank.
- Raising the policy rate by 350 bps from 9.75 to 13.25 per cent.

- Restrictions on the government not to borrow from the SBP to cover its fiscal deficit, initially as a policy commitment but through legislation before the end of 2019.
- A comprehensive plan by September 2019, to eliminate the circular debt on electricity and gas through automatic 10 per cent adjustment in rates every quarter.

These reforms are well meaning and badly needed but the time frame in which these are to be implemented is completely unrealistic. Also, at a time when the economy is slowing down, it will be prudent to implement only those structural reforms that would not further depress the economy and the growth rate. The rest can be taken up when the economy has recovered. This is the essence of the required balance between growth and stability.

IMF has also introduced for the first time, conditionalities related to Financial Action Task Force (FATF). Since FATF has already become a politically biased process, the risk to the IMF programme from any adverse decision, will be disastrous.

To explain away this multi-dimensional crisis afflicting the economy, Imran Khan and his Ministers have been harping on a single narrative throughout their first year in office:

The previous two governments in the past 10 years have been borrowing recklessly and have increased the country's debt burden, from Rs 6,000 billion to Rs 30,000 billion. Now we have to borrow money from friendly countries and IMF only to pay back these loans. There was widespread corruption and the rulers transferred these borrowed funds to their personal accounts abroad. Even if half of this looted wealth is brought back, the country's balance of payments problem will be solved.

In my entire career I have never heard such an oversimplified and misleading narrative on such vital aspects of a country's economy and that also on the basis of inaccurate facts:

The PTI government in projecting the figure of Rs 30,000 billion has deliberately ignored the definition of public debt under the Fiscal Responsibility Law of 2005 and included many other liabilities like provincial borrowings for commodity operations or loans contracted by the private sector. According to figures released by the State Bank in September 2019, the correct figures of public debt at the end of 2017–18 was Rs 23,051 billion and not Rs 30,000 billion.

According to these figures, the PPP government in its 5 year tenure, added Rs 7,807 billion to the public debt and PML(N) Rs 9,594 billion during its 5 year tenure. But the PTI government has added Rs 10,000 billion to the stock of public debt in a single year!

The State Bank and Economic Affairs Division have complete records of these loans and the international financial institutions have elaborate accounting and auditing procedures to monitor their respective loans.

In the light of these facts to create a false impression for political point scoring, that previous rulers have eaten away loans totalling Rs 24,000 billion is at the least unfortunate. If Imran Khan has been making these allegations without verifying the facts, then serious questions will arise about his sense of responsibility. Furthermore, if he repeated these allegations, with the knowledge of actual facts, then his claim for total integrity will flounder. According to many scholars, intellectual and moral integrity is as important as financial integrity.

The need for a 'Charter of the Economy' has been widely discussed but how can a consensus-based Charter be evolved in a politically charged atmosphere when the PTI government insists that all the policies introduced by the previous two governments destroyed the economy. Every government, in order to survive and retain its vote bank, initiates policies and reforms to solve the problems of the people. Some are more successful than others. But it is an on-going process since new reforms are built on the edifice of reforms built by the previous governments. In some cases, old initiatives are re-branded and presented by the new government as 'first time ventures'.

Pakistan's economy has huge potential for economic and social progress but that requires stable political environment and economic stability. The Fitch Solution Report of 4 January 2019 states, 'Political confrontation in Pakistan is brewing and runs the risk of bogging down the wheels of policy making in a political stalemate. The Ruling Party is over extended in ruinous confrontation, which is further depressing the economy'.

Foreign Policy under Imran Khan

Imran Khan's domestic agenda especially on the economic front began to flounder in the very first year of the PTI government. There was a natural urge to play up any success on the foreign policy front. Unfortunately, each one of these 'success stories' either proved short-lived or backfired.

There were three visits to Saudi Arabia and two to UAE followed by announcements that a package of US$ 9 billion had been arranged to resolve the current account problem facing the economy. Soon after the visits, it was disclosed by the media that a part of the package will be delivered over three years, and most of it will be in the form of short term interest bearing deposits in our Central Bank.

The impression projected that these visits were turning points in our, relations with these countries, was nullified in August, 2019 when after Modi's annexation of Indian occupied Kashmir, the UAE, Ambassador in India called it an internal matter and UAE, along with Bahrain, conferred their highest civilian honour on Narendra Modi, totally ignoring the plight of eight million Kashmiri Muslims. After their visit to Pakistan in September, the Foreign Ministers of Saudi Arabia and UAE did not address a joint press conference with Pakistan's Foreign Minister nor issued any statement condemning gross violations of human rights in Kashmir.

The manner in which Imran Khan took another U-turn by going back on his commitment to attend the Kuala Lumpur Summit convened by Prime Minister Mahathir Mohamad on 18–20 December 2019, due to unusual pressure exerted by Saudi Arabia, was termed by the media as another example of amateurish diplomacy.

Imran Khan also visited China to seek financial assistance, in a U-turn on his declared policy of not seeking such assistance, at a time when the PTI government had started throwing cold water on many projects under CPEC. The Chinese were however, gracious enough to offer US$ 3 billion but the damage caused to this most vital bilateral relationship between Pakistan and China has not been fully repaired.

In July 2019, the hype about foreign policy achievements reached a new crescendo after Imran Khan's well-publicised meeting with President Trump and his address to the UN General Assembly in September 2019.

As already mentioned in Chapter 15, President Trump had issued many tweets, after taking over as President in January 2017, to criticize Pakistan while praising India's role in Afghanistan as a 'key component of any strategy in the Region'. Although the victory of Imran Khan in the 2018 elections went unnoticed, in comparison, President Obama had invited Nawaz Sharif for his first visit to Washington within 3 months but Imran Khan had to wait for a whole year before he was invited by the White House for his first visit.

This change of policy towards Pakistan occurred because President Trump was now preparing for the 2020 Presidential election and extricating the US from Afghanistan had become one of his key priorities. Senator Lindsay Graham, who had been coming to Pakistan regularly with his close friend the late Senator John McCain, again visited Pakistan and was told that if the US would accept the proposal to talk directly to the Taliban, it may get a face saving formula, with or without peace, to leave Afghanistan. President Trump accepted the advice and appointed Zalmay Khalizad as his special representative for talks with the Taliban. Since, several rounds of these talks were held in Doha and made good progress, President Trump decided that Imran Khan should be invited to visit Washington. Initially, the State Department professed ignorance about the visit but after the White House clarified, they withdrew their denial. However, the Secretary of State, Mike Pompeo did not attend President Trump's meeting with Imran Khan. He called on him separately.

During his meeting with Imran Khan, President Trump praised him and also publically acknowledged Pakistan's key role in facilitating the Afghan 'Peace Process'. He also urged Pakistan to persuade the Taliban to accept the other two agenda points, namely a ceasefire and direct talks with the Afghan Government. However, the Taliban had already announced that they would not talk to the Afghan government but would have an intra-Afghan dialogue after the schedule for the withdrawal of US troops had been agreed upon. Some representatives of the Afghan government may attend this dialogue in their personal capacity. As mentioned in the previous Chapter, President Trump through a tweet on 6 September 2019, not only cancelled his secret meeting with the Taliban in Camp David but also the peace talks. This cancellation could also renew pressures on Pakistan 'to do more' to persuade the Taliban for 'real peace'.

To everyone surprise, President Trump also offered to mediate on Kashmir. India, as expected, readily rejected any such possibility. But in Pakistan, Trump's reference to Kashmir and his offer to mediate was played up as a big diplomatic coup. Only three weeks later, the reality of this mediation offer was totally exposed when India unilaterally ended, on 5 August, Indian Occupied Kashmir's special status and brought it under the direct control of New Delhi. Any remnants of this dubious mediation offer were further shredded in Paris on 25 August. At President Trump's meeting with Narendra Modi in France at the G7 Summit, Modi brazenly said, 'all issues between India and Pakistan are bilateral'. President Trump readily agreed and said I hope they will resolve the issue bilaterally but I am available if needed!

In September 2019, Imran Khan had another meeting with President Trump on the side-lines of the UN General Assembly. President Trump again praised Imran Khan for his leadership and renewed his offer to mediate if both India and Pakistan invited him to assist in resolving the long standing issue. But these pleasantries were not adequate to balance the impact of Modi's 'Howdy Modi mega event in Houston Texas' in which President Trump along with several high ranking Americans also participated. On 27 September, Imran Khan delivered an impressive and eloquent speech in the UN General Assembly to warn the world about the explosive situation created by Modi in Indian Occupied Kashmir (IOK).

As a result of a strong media campaign and diplomatic offensive, a section of the western media criticized Modi's actions of 5 August, his disregard of international agreements and gross violations of human rights but there was no clear indication of UN action or any international initiative to reverse these actions and force India to seek the wishes of the Kashmiri people. However, everyone in Pakistan is confident that whenever the prolonged curfew and lockdown is lifted there will be an unprecedented backlash from the people of IOK to reaffirm their inherent rights of self-determination. This will fully expose the hollowness of Indian efforts to annex Kashmir by force.

In July 2019, after his return from Washington, the Foreign Minister, Shah Mehmood Qureshi also said that Imran Khan's visit to the US had finally ended Pakistan's 'diplomatic isolation'. Since it is common practice in PTI, this statement was repeated and exaggerated by many other PTI Ministers and spokespersons for political point scoring. As highlighted in the previous chapter, diplomatically isolating Pakistan has been one of main planks of India's anti-Pakistan strategy, but it did not succeed. During PML (N) government's 5 years, Pakistan deepened its relations with China, Russia, Turkey and Central Asian States. In July 2016, there was the full membership of SCO and in March 2017, the ECO Summit in Islamabad, were visible landmarks in Pakistan's diplomatic journey.

The Annexation of Indian Occupied Kashmir

The biggest foreign policy challenge for Imran Khan was the bombshell dropped by Narendra Modi on 5 August 2019, when he unlawfully changed the status of the Indian Occupied Kashmir (IOK).

At the time of Partition of India in 1947, the 560 princely states were given the choice, under the Indian Independence Act of 1947, to remain independent or accede to the two new states of India or Pakistan. However, the accession by a Ruler, who belonged to different religion than the majority population of the state, would not be acceptable until the wishes of the people were ascertained through a referendum. There were three states which came under this clause: Hyderabad, Junagarh and Kashmir. The Nizam of Hyderabad wanted independence but India dispatched its army to occupy the state because the majority population was non-Muslims. The Nawab of Junagarh acceded to Pakistan but India nullified this accession by occupying the state by force and allowed the Nawab to escape to Pakistan. In the third case, India did not follow the same logic. Maharaja Hari Singh, the ruler of Muslim majority Jammu and Kashmir declared that Kashmir will stay independent but signed a standstill agreement with Pakistan to provide certain services like post, telegraph and railway to Kashmir. No such agreement was signed with India. When Pakistan saw India occupying Hyderabad and Junagarh by force, it decided to follow the same course in Kashmir. Pakistan's military units were still moving from India to Pakistan, so Pakistan organized some tribal *lashkars* to join the limited troops to enter Kashmir. They reached Srinagar but failed to capture the airport. The Indian forces started arriving and a war broke out. Meanwhile, the Maharaja of Kashmir, was trying, with the help of RSS Volunteers, to force Kashmiri Muslims to migrate to

Pakistan or face extermination, as in East Punjab. When the tribal *lashkars* reached Srinagar, he escaped to Jammu, appealed to India for military assistance and also signed a dubious instrument of accession with India, on 26 October 1947. Since this accession was in conflict with the Indian Independence Act, the Governor General of India, Lord Mountbatten accepted the accession on the condition that 'as soon as law and order was restored in Kashmir and her soil cleared of the invader, the question of accession should be settled by a reference to the people'.

On 1 January 1948, India took the question of Kashmir to the United Nations. The Security Council passed several resolutions. In the second resolution passed on 20 January, 1948, it set up a 5-member Commission to arrange a plebiscite, after both sides have withdrawn or reduced their troops. A third resolution was adopted on 21 April 1948. This plebiscite was never held, despite continuing demand by the people of Kashmir, to this day.

In 1950, when the Indian Constitution was being adopted, it was recognized that, pending the promised plebiscite, Kashmir required special treatment. Article 370 was accordingly included as an interim system to give constitutional cover to the Instrument of accession by exempting Jammu & Kashmir (J&K), from the provision of the Indian Constitution and restricting the Indian Parliament's legislative power to three subjects, namely defence, foreign affairs and communications. In 1951, India also convened a Constituent Assembly to formulate a Constitution for J&K which was rejected by major political parties of Kashmir. This Assembly was dissolved in 1957 after it adopted a new "constitution" declaring that the whole of the state was an integral part of India. The Security Council, however passed another resolution No.122 of 1957 to reaffirm that the action taken by the Constituent Assembly would not satisfy its earlier resolution calling for a plebiscite.

Another constitutional Amendment, 35-A, protected the local population of Kashmir by preventing people from the rest of India to buy properties, acquire permanent residence of Kashmir or avail local government jobs.

On 5 August 2019, India repealed both Articles 370 and 35-A of the Indian Constitution through the Jammu and Kashmir Reorganisation Act of 2019 and the Presidential Order C.O. 272. The Reorganisation Act abolished the State of Jammu & Kashmir and divided it into two union territories of Ladakh and Jammu & Kashmir, to be ruled directly from New Delhi: 'Under CO 272; all references to the Government of J&K would henceforth be construed as reference to the Governor of J&K'.

These unilateral actions to unlawfully annex a disputed territory involved serious violations of international law and also the Indian Constitution as shown below: -

- The 1947 Instrument of Accession by Maharaja Hari Singh, which says 'the terms of this instrument shall not be varied by any amendment of the Act or of the Indian Independence Act, unless such amendment is accepted by me through a supplementary instrument;
- Resolutions of the UN Security Council which clearly call for ascertaining the will of the people, before its formal status is determined';
- The Simla Agreement of 1972, which clearly says in Para-ii 'Pending the final settlement of any of the problems between the two countries, neither side shall unilaterally alter the situation and both shall prevent the organization, assistance or encouragement of any act detrimental to the maintenance of peaceful and harmonious relations';
- The Indian Constitution has been clearly violated since these measures were promulgated without consulting the Legislative Assembly of Jammu & Kashmir, which had been dissolved in November 2018.

Human Rights Violations in Indian Occupied Kashmir

Human rights violations in the Indian Occupied Kashmir are a more serious dimension of the crisis than the legal or constitutional violations. India is fully aware that a large majority of the people had not accepted the Indian occupation under a dubious instrument of accession. All major political parties had boycotted successive elections held in the Indian Occupied Kashmir, under the Indian Constitution.

After 1989, with continuing increase in repression by Indian Security forces and massive rigging in the 1987 elections, the agitation by Kashmiris turned into violent freedom struggle. Over the next 30 years more than 100,000 Kashmiri freedom fighters have been martyred and many more have disappeared. India has been referring to them as "terrorists" but the whole world was aware that it was an indigenous uprising for their right of self-determination promised to them by the United Nations.

After the tragic death of Burhanuddin Wani in July 2016, the temperature of agitation or intifada reached its peak in the next 3 years. It is astounding that the BJP government under Narendra Modi should totally ignore this 70 year old history and impose a drastic 'solution' in violation of its own international commitments and the international humanitarian laws.

Anticipating violent reaction to these changes and the plans to bring about a demographic change by relocating a large number of Hindus to IOK, India converted it into a vast prison, a few days before the black day of 5 August. All tourists and pilgrims were asked to leave. All communications including telephone lines and internet were blocked and a curfew was imposed 'until further orders'. Another 100,000 troops were moved to IOK to take the total to over 900,000 and making IOK the most densely militarized territory in the world.

As expected, Pakistan reacted to this deepening tragedy with full determination to stand with the people of Kashmir. On 30 August this solidarity was displayed in all parts of Pakistan when representatives of all political parties and common people from every city, town, and village came out in rallies with flags of Azad Jammu and Kashmir. As already mentioned Pakistan also launched a strong diplomatic campaign to inform the international community about the grave implications of this confrontation between two nuclear powers. Pakistan downgraded its diplomatic representation, and suspended all trade with India. The UN Security Council met in an informal session on 16 August to discuss the Kashmir crisis and many parliaments around the world have scheduled a discussion on the Kashmir Issue.

It is difficult to predict if all the members of Security Council will show adequate foresight and political will to call upon India to undo their actions of 5 August in view of their rejection by a large majority of the affected population. But the ultimate outcome will depend on the sacrifices of the Kashmiri people. History has repeatedly shown that freedom movements cannot be suppressed by force.

Accountability

Rooting out corruption was listed as one of the most important objectives in the Pakistan Tehreek-e-Insaf (PTI) Election Manifesto. This topic, therefore occupied centre stage in almost every public statement that Imran Khan made at home or abroad.

In July 2017, Nawaz Sharif had been disqualified from holding public office and convicted in the Avenfield Apartment case in July 2018 i.e. a month before Imran Khan took over as Prime Minister. But during the next 14 months a large number of PML(N) leaders were arrested on different charges. These leaders included Shahbaz Sharif, Hamza Shahbaz, Maryam Nawaz, Shahid Khaqan Abbasi, Saad Rafiq and his brother Salman Rafiq, Miftah Ismail, and Rana Sanaullah. In most of these cases, no references had been filed or specific charges framed, even several months after these arrests. This bizarre legal situation developed due to a very unusual provision in the 2002 National Accountability Bureau (NAB) Ordinance which gave this power to the NAB Chairman to arrest a person, on the basis of a preliminary complaint, even if specific charges have yet to be framed. Even more draconian was another provision under which the Accountability Court had no power to grant bail to an arrested person under this law. Only the High Court concerned could grant bail.

These arrests were not confined to PML(N). Many leaders of PPP including the former President Asif Ali Zardari, his sister Faryal Talpur, Syed Khurshid Shah and Agha Siraj Durrani were arrested before filing any reference or charges against them.

From the outset the Opposition launched a vigorous attack in Parliament and outside it against this one sided process of accountability and cited many cases of PTI leaders which were being investigated but they had not been arrested. On 11 September 2019, Chief Justice Asif Saeed Khosa in a statement said,

We, as a relevant organ of state, also feel that growing perception that the process of accountability being pursued in the country at present is lopsided and is a part of political engineering, is a dangerous perception and some remedial steps need to be taken urgently so that the process does not lose credibility.'

On 19 November, Chairman NAB, Justice Javed Iqbal also indirectly confirmed a degree of bias when he said, 'So far we have focussed on old outstanding cases of previous regimes. But now we are also taking up cases against ministers or leaders of the present government. The direction of wind is changing'.

The months of October-November, however witnessed a very unpleasant episode arising from Nawaz Sharif's illness. He was already serving his sentence in Kot Lakhpat jail in Lahore for many months. But in the first week of October NAB 're-arrested' him in another case and moved him to NAB's Headquarters in Lahore on physical remand. A week later, Dr Adnan, personal physician to Nawaz Sharif noticed a sudden deterioration in his health and wrote to NAB authorities for urgent action. Government Minsters and spokespersons however downplayed these reports and Nawaz Sharif remained jailed in NAB Headquarters. On 21 October a simple blood test revealed that Nawaz Sharif's platelet count had gone down to 16000, well below the minimum normal level of 150,000. The NAB authorities then realized their folly of moving him from the Jail hospital and requested the Punjab government to admit him to a hospital immediately. He was admitted to the Services Hospital the same day, while government Ministers in Islamabad were still mocking reports about his medical condition. But this ill-advised controversy suddenly turned into panic the next day, when fresh tests showed that Nawaz Sharif's platelets had plummeted to only 2000. The Punjab Health Minister Dr Yasmin Rashid rushed to the hospital and took personal charge of supervising his treatment and also keeping Islamabad informed. Specialists were flown in from Karachi and the Prime Minister himself conveyed his best wishes to Nawaz Sharif through Dr Yasmin Rashid.

On the following Monday, Shahbaz Sharif filed an application on behalf of Nawaz Sharif in Lahore High Court on grounds of health. The High Court called for medical reports and testimony of two Medical Boards which the government had set up to examine Nawaz Sharif. These reports revealed that Nawaz Sharif's prognosis was very serious because of his past history of three coronary bypasses, kidney ailment and his diabetic condition. The medical reports also confirmed that certain tests needed to diagnose the actual causes of the platelet problem were not available in Pakistan. Based on these reports, the NAB authorities did not object to the grant of bail. The Lahore High Court granted the bail so that Nawaz Sharif could seek the required medical facilities 'in Pakistan or abroad'.

The next requirement was removal of Nawaz Sharif's name from the Exit Control List (ECL). After the High Court granted bail several spokespersons of the government indicated that Prime Minister Imran Khan had agreed to remove Nawaz Sharif"s name from the ECL and a formal decision would be taken at the next Cabinet meeting on 12 November. The Prime Minister was obviously worried about political backlash if anything happened to Nawaz Sharif, but he could not forget his 'no deal' mantra. So, when the issue came up before the Cabinet, it 'graciously' granted a one- time waiver from ECL for a period of one month, provided Nawaz Sharif provided an indemnity bond of Rs 7 billion, which would be confiscated if he did not return after 1 month.

The PML(N) leadership rejected this 'offer' straight away and said that PTI was playing politics with Nawaz Sharif's health and wanted to demonstrate to its voters that it had let Nawaz Sharif go after extracting the alleged ill gotten money from him. In other words, PML(N) would by implication accept the PTI allegation of corruption. One PML(N) spokesperson said 'Nawaz Sharif might prefer his physical death to this political suicide.'

The next day, PML(N) filed a petition against this order in the Lahore High Court on the plea that the ECL Ordinance had no provision for indemnity bonds. The High Court heard the case on Friday 15 November and decided to continue the hearing on Saturday 16 November in view of the urgency of Nawaz Sharif's treatment abroad. After three sittings, the High Court accepted the plea of PML(N) that the condition of indemnity bond of Rs 7 billion could not be imposed under the law. However, both Nawaz Sharif and Shahbaz Sharif would file a written personal affidavit on a stamp paper of Rs 50 'that Nawaz Sharif will return to Pakistan within four weeks or as and when certified by doctors that he has regained his health and is fit to return to Pakistan.'

Following these rulings of the Lahore High Court, Nawaz Sharif flew to London on the morning of 19 November but that did not end this unpleasant saga.

A day after Nawaz Sharif's departure, Imran Khan while inaugurating the Hazara Motorway raised a fresh controversy by asking Chief Justice Asif Saeed Khosa and his successor, Justice Gulzar Ahmad to come forward and restore public trust by ending the impression that there is a different legal system for the powerful.

The Chief Justice responded to this loaded statement the next day. Addressing an inaugural event in Islamabad on 20 November, he departed from his written English statement and spoke in Urdu for several minutes. He said,

> Please do not taunt us for favouring the powerful. The courts had convicted a Prime Minister and disqualified another. A decision about a former army chief was also expected soon. Last year, 3,100 judges in the judiciary had decided 3.6 million cases and apart from a few powerful individuals, all the litigants belonged to the weak and down trodden classes. Please reconsider your statement about the imbalance in dispensing justice. A silent revolution has already taken place. Don't compare us with the pre-2009 judiciary. Times have changed. Now, we are deciding matters strictly in accordance with the law. In fact, the decision on the ECL Issue was taken by the government and not by the Court. The Court only addressed the resultant modalities.

The Prime Minister asked his Ministers not to comment on the statement of Chief Justice but could not take his mind away from Nawaz Sharif. The following day, while addressing an event in Mianwali he said, "As I watched on TV how Nawaz Sharif climbed the stairs into the aircraft and then his arrival in London, I again looked at his medical reports which had suggested that he was critically ill and could die any day. Are these reports credible?"

The media was quick to point out that Nawaz Sharif had used a forklift to enter the aircraft. It also recalled the flash back of all the U-turns and conflicting positions which Imran Khan and his government had adopted at different stages of this episode. But, the Ministers now turned their criticism towards the media for overplaying and dramatizing the illness of Nawaz Sharif. To the relief of many, this saga suddenly disappeared from the TV screens when three important cases descended like a thunderstorm on the political horizon of the country: the extension granted to General Qamar Javed Bajwa, the trial of former President, Pervez Musharraf, under Article 6, and the investigation into the foreign funding case against the PTI by the Election Commission.

General Bajwa's Extension

On 26 November 2019, the Supreme Court cancelled the following notification, issued on 19th August 2019 under the signature of Prime Minister Imran Khan:

> General Qumar Javaid Bajwa is appointed Chief of Army Staff for another term of three years from the date of the completion of current tenure. The decision has been taken in view of the regional security environment.

A day earlier, a petitioner, Riaz Hanif Rahi had pleaded before the Court under Article 184(3) to set aside the August 19 notification for being unconstitutional. When the Supreme Court began hearing this petition, it was informed that the Court had received an unsigned hand written application from the petitioner seeking to withdraw his petition. The three member bench of the Supreme Court, (Chief Justice Asif Saeed Khosa, Justice Mazhar Alam, and Justice Syed Mansoor Ali Shah) rejected this application and said, 'this matter involves a question of public importance and the individual capacity of the petitioner pales into insignificance'.

The Attorney General, Anwar Mansoor Khan, thereupon presented photocopies of the relevant orders passed by the President for the extension/re-appointment of General Bajwa. After examining the documents, the Court passed the following short order:

> The stated purpose for the proposed reappointment/extension in the term of office of the incumbent Chief of the Army Staff is "regional security environment". The said words are quite vague and if at all there is any regional security threat then it is the gallant armed forces of the country as an institution which are to meet the said threat and an individual's role in that regard may be minimal. If the said reason is held to be correct and valid then every person serving in the armed forces would claim re-appointment/extension in his service on the basis of the said reason.
>
> The points noted above call for a detailed examination of the matter of extension/re-appointment of General Qamar Javed Bajwa, Chief of the Army Staff and, therefore, he is hereby made a respondent to this petition and the office is directed to carry out the necessary addition in the memorandum of this petition. Let notice of this petition be issued to all the respondents for tomorrow, i.e. 27.11.2019, as requested by the learned Attorney General for Pakistan. In the meanwhile the operation of the

impugned order/Notification in respect of extension/re-appointment of General Qamar Javed Bajwa, Chief of the Army Staff for another term in the said office shall remain suspended.

Source: Supreme Court Order of 26th November 2019 in Constitution Petition Number 39 of 2019. https://www.supremecourt.gov.pk/

Recognizing the gravity of this epic legal battle, an emergency meeting of the cabinet was convened the same afternoon. The cabinet cancelled the previous three year extension order of the COAS signed by the Prime Minister on 19th August and issued a fresh extension order. It also amended Section 255 of the Army Regulations, by incorporating the words 'extension in tenure'. The fresh extension order was approved by the President. Three ministers then addressed a press conference to emphasize that no irregularity or negligence had been committed and the procedural lacuna had now been addressed. It was also announced that the Law Minister had resigned in order to represent General Bajwa in the Supreme Court.

When the Court resumed hearing of the case on 27 November, it took strong exception to the government coming up with different versions while moving a fresh summary notifying extension in service of General Bajwa.

Two meetings were held and we hoped that big minds assembled would present some good, but we have been thoroughly disappointed. Nobody even bothered to go through the summary before issuing it', the CJP remarked and said, 'there are three issues to be considered: one, whether the matter has any legal backing, second, if the procedure and process was adopted as per law and thirdly reasons for appointment. For us only the first two are very important.

The following day, the Attorney General submitted, on behalf of the government, a new summary on the re-appointment of General Bajwa. The Chief Justice took exception to a reference to the Court's proceedings in the summary and said 'don't bracket us with your actions'. He also pointed out that the summary mentions a fresh tenure of three years, although Article 243 of the Constitution does not mention any tenure.

The Court asked the Attorney General to submit an amended notification in the light of these remarks by 1 p.m. the same day, along with an affidavit to undertake that the earlier practice of granting extensions to the Army Chief would be codified under the law by legislation through parliament within a period of six months.

After receiving the revised notification and the affidavit, the Court passed the following short order:

> We have examined Article 243(4)(b) of the Constitution, Pakistan Army Act, 1952, Pakistan Army Act Rules, 1954 and Army Regulations (Rules), 1998 and in spite of the assistance rendered by the learned Attorney General, we could not find any provision relating to the tenure of COAS or of a General and whether the COAS can be reappointed or his term can be extended or his retirement can be limited or suspended under the Constitution or the law. The learned Attorney General has taken pains to explain that the answers to these questions are based on practice being followed in the Pakistan Army but the said practice has not been codified under the law.
>
> The learned Attorney General has categorically assured the Court that this practice being followed is to be codified under the law and undertakes that the Federal Government shall initiate the process to carry out the necessary legislation in this regard and seeks a period of six months for getting the needful done. Considering that the COAS is responsible for the command, discipline, training, administration, organization and preparedness for war of the Army and is the Chief Executive in General Headquarters, we, while exercising judicial restraint, find it appropriate to leave the matter to the Parliament and the Federal Government to clearly specify the terms and conditions of service of the COAS through an Act of Parliament and to clarify the scope of Article 243 of the Constitution in this regard. Therefore, the current appointment of General Qamar Javed Bajwa as COAS shall be subject to the said legislation and shall continue for a period of six months from today, where after the new legislation shall determine his tenure and other terms and conditions of service. This petition is disposed of in the above terms.

(Detailed judgment at https://www.supremecourt.gov.pk/)

With this order a major crisis was averted, and the nation heaved a sigh of relief after three days of extreme uncertainty. Most experts and observers welcomed the restraint shown by the Supreme Court and acknowledged that in true spirit of democracy the Parliament has been asked to make clear provisions through legislation for the tenure and other terms and conditions of the Army Chief.

On 16 December, the Supreme Court issued its detailed judgment in this case. The main point of this 42 page judgment, authored by Justice Mansoor Ali Shah, can be summarized as follows:

- There is no provision in law for the extending the service of the Army Chief for second term, nor was there any consistent and continuous institutional practice of granting such extension which could be enforced in the absence of the law on the subject.
- The crucial matter of the tenure of COAS and its extension which has a somewhat checkered history is before the parliament to fix for all times to come and it is now for the people of Pakistan and their chosen representatives in the Parliament to come up with a law that will provide certainty and predictability to the post of COAS remembering that in strengthening institutions nations prosper.
- If the Federal Government remains unable to regulate the tenure and terms of the service of the General and as a consequence of COAS, through an appropriate legislation by parliament within a period of six months, the tenure of the constitutional post of COAS could not be left totally unregulated and to continue forever. In case of such failure, the institutional practice of the retirement of a General on completion of the tenure of three years, as pleaded by the Attorney General and borne out from the record, shall stand enforced to regulate the tenure of General Bajwa.
- The President should on the advice of the Prime Minister appoint a serving General Officer as the new COAS.

Chief Justice Asif Saeed Khosa while agreeing with the detailed judgment wrote an additional note and observed that,

For an Army Chief who held a powerful position any unbridled power or position, like unstructured discretion was dangerous. It was a shocking revelation that the terms and conditions of service and the extension and tenure of his office or his reappointment to that office had remained unregulated by any law so far. In the backdrop of the last 3 scores and 12 years of our history, I may observe with hope and optimism, that framing of a law by the Parliament, regulating the terms and conditions of the office of COAS may go a long way in rectifying multiple historical wrongs and in asserting sovereign authority of the chosen representatives of the people, besides making exercise of judicial power of the courts all pervasive.

(Detailed judgment at https://www.supremecourt.gov.pk/)

In compliance with this judgment, the Parliament initiated the required amendments in the Pakistan Army Act, 1952, with the support of the Opposition Parties, during the first week of January 2020.

The Opposition's 'Azadi March'

On 27 October 2019, the 'Azadi March' organized by Maulana Fazlur Rehman, left Karachi for Islamabad. It was welcomed by representatives of other opposition parties as it moved north. By 31 October when it reached the 9H Grounds in Islamabad, it was the largest crowd the citizens of Islamabad had ever seen.

This march of protesters, which was estimated to be over 50,000 and possibly 100,000 at its peak, then became a *dharna* or sit-in, for the next two weeks, despite the rains and logistical difficulties.

Several days earlier, Maulana Fazlur Rehman had been discussing his planned Azadi March with other political parties, notably PML(N) and PPP. These parties supported the march in principle but urged him to delay it for a few months to give them time to mobilize their workers. However, Maulana Fazlur Rehman was adamant that they had been preparing for this march for many months. It would, therefore start on 27 October. Eventually both the parties agreed to this schedule but emphasized that they would join the march but not the *dharna*. PML(N) stated that it had criticized the PTI *dharna* in 2014 as unlawful so they could not join a JUI(F) *dharna*. PPP also said they could not support any agitation that could lead to violence and as a result derail the democratic system. The differences within PML(N) were resolved when Nawaz Sharif wrote a letter to Shahbaz Sharif, the President of PML(N), to extend full support to JUI(F)'s chief.

An All Parties Conference of opposition parties had set up a *Rahbar* (steering) committee to coordinate and supervise the Azadi March. The *Rahbar* Committee, chaired by Akram Durrani of JUI(F) agreed to put forward the following four demands:

- Immediate resignation of Prime Minister Imran Khan.
- Snap mid-term elections in the country.
- No role for the army in the electoral process.
- Supremacy of the Constitution, with assurances to safeguard all the Islamic provisions in the 1973 Constitution.

By the time the Azadi March reached Islamabad, six other opposition parties had announced their support for the march. These included the Awami National Party (ANP), Pashtunkhwa Milli Awami Party (PKMAP), National Party (NP), Qaumi Watan Party (QWP), and National People's Party (NPP). The heads of these parties including Shahbaz Sharif, Bilawal Bhutto, Asfandyar Wali, Mahmood Khan Achakzai, Hasil Bizenjo, Aftab Sherpao and Sajid Mir joined the opening session of the Azadi March on 1 November and addressed the large and enthusiastic crowd. Many workers of PML(N), PPP and ANP also joined the *dharna* for the first two days.

Maulana Fazlur Rehman and other opposition leaders, in their speeches strongly criticized the PTI Government's performance during its past 15 month tenure and highlighted the following points:

- The PTI had mismanaged the economy, causing great misery to the people of Pakistan. Due to unprecedented increase in the prices of electricity and gas, the sudden jump in the policy rate of the State Bank to 13 per cent and 35 per cent devaluation of the Pakistan Rupee, the rate of inflation had increased from 4 per cent in 2017–2018 to over 11 per cent in 2018–2019. As a result, the common man could no longer provide two square meals for his family or pay for his children's school fees.
- The PTI Government made tall promises before and after the elections, but had not fulfilled any of them. It promised, for example to provide 10 million new jobs in the first 100 days but due to the serious slowdown in the economy, millions had lost their jobs at a time of high inflation.
- Clear evidence was claimed of serious irregularities in the 2018 general elections, casting serious doubts on the credibility of the elections as a whole. In response to the opposition's demand, a Parliamentary Committee had been set up more than a year ago to look into these allegations, but it had not met even once.

- Imran Khan's political agenda was based on the vilification of all other political parties and political leaders. As a result of this polarizing attitude, important institutions like the Parliament and the Election Commission had become dysfunctional.
- In the field of external relations, the PTI had failed to mobilize international support to challenge and undo the unconstitutional acts of the Modi Government to annex Indian Occupied Kashmir by repealing article 370 and 35 of the Indian Constitution.

Initially, the reaction of PTI ministers to the Azadi March was dismissive, but the arrival of such a large crowd of disciplined and charged workers of JUI(F) had a sobering effect. The government nominated a high level negotiating committee to hold discussions with Maulana Fazlur Rehman and the Rahbar Committee. The Committee chaired by Pervez Khatak, Defence Minister, included Sadiq Sanjrani, Chairman of the Senate; Asad Qaiser, speaker of the National Assembly; Parvez Ilahi, Speaker of the Punjab Assembly; Shafqat Mahmood, Education Minister; and Noor-ul-Haq Qadri, Minister of Religious Affairs.

Several negotiating sessions were held between the two Committees in the first week of November, but the deadlock over the main demand for the resignation of the Prime Minister persisted.

Meanwhile, Chaudhry Shujaat Hussain and Chaudhry Pervez Ilahi also had several meetings with Maulana Fazlur Rehman to explore some middle ground to resolve the deadlock. On 13 November, Maulana Fazlur Rehman called off the 14 day *dharna* and announced that, under Plan B, the programme of agitation against the Government would continue. JUI(F) workers would peacefully block several major arteries all over the country, but the movement of humanitarian workers, ambulances and fire fighting vehicles would not be obstructed.

On 19 November, after a meeting of the Rahbar Committee, it was announced that plan B of the Azadi March would also be terminated, but under Plan C, joint protest meetings of opposition parties would now be held at the district level. The opposition will also visit the Election Commission to demand day to day hearing of the 'foreign funding case' against the PTI.

In response to this demand, the Election Commission announced that it would conduct daily hearing of this case from 26 November. The media suddenly grasped the serious implications of this renewed spotlight on a case that had been pending for five years due to delaying legal tactics adopted by the PTI.

In this context, the opposition also registered its concern about the serious situation that would arise in December 2019 when the Chief Election Commissioner retired. That would make the Election Commission dysfunctional because the government had failed to fill the two vacant posts of members of the Election Commission in accordance with the Constitution. Now, when the Chief Election Commissioner retires, the five member commission will no longer have the minimum strength required for its functioning as a Commission.

It is too early to assess the full impact of the Azadi March. Realistically, even Maulana Fazlur Rehman could not have expected that his demand will be accepted and the Prime Minister will resign. But, due to the size, discipline and enthusiasm of the crowd, the success of the March probably exceeded his own expectations.

Just as PTI's 2014 *dharna* did not overthrow the government, but prepared the ground for PTI's success in the 2018 elections, this *dharna* could also lead to a similar impact because of its negative impact on the vote bank of the PTI in the next elections whenever these are held. Correspondingly, PML(N) may improve its vote bank since its comparative performance in managing the economy was highlighted in the Azadi March. Similarly, JUI(F)'s show of street power will enhance its political influence and standing.

An important question which the *dharna* has not yet answered is whether or not Imran Khan will review his attitude towards the opposition and recognize its role in promoting political stability, which is an essential prerequisite for economic stability. Even in highly polarized societies, democratically elected governments treat members of the opposition with respect and dignity. It is equally important to recall that in the 2018 elections, the opposition parties collectively received twice as many votes as the ruling party; that the role of the opposition is laid down in the Constitution and that the Parliament and many other institutions of state cannot function properly without the active participation of the opposition.

Epilogue 1
Dreams Never Die

Excessive emotions and concealed prejudices that dominated the writing of history in Pakistan in its initial years have somehow created a culture of what might be called 'subjective history'. Under this culture, events are seen through coloured glasses, conclusions are rooted in pre-conceived notions and heroes and villains are identified within this biased framework. That is why we have very few authentic and objective books on the history of Pakistan. This is sad, not only from an academic standpoint, but also in terms of practical politics because many important lessons of our history are not available to our leaders and policy makers in an objective manner.

Pakistan came into existence under exceptionally difficult circumstances with very poor infrastructure and hardly any industry. Its own ethnic and social heterogeneity was accentuated by large-scale migration when millions of Muslim refugees flooded into Pakistan with nothing but their worn out clothes. The social turmoil created by partition was also compounded by the scramble for evacuee properties and a few jobs that became available. In this chaotic and unsettled state, the nation had to fight a war with India over Kashmir that erupted in October 1947. As if these difficulties were not enormous enough, the founding father of the new state, Quaid-i-Azam Mohammad Ali Jinnah, died on 11 September 1948—only thirteen months after the creation of Pakistan. Three years later, Prime Minister Liaquat Ali Khan was assassinated on 16 October 1951.

That Pakistan was able to overcome these enormous difficulties and survive as a viable and progressive state is a testimony to its will, determination and resilience as a nation. I have no doubt that these inherent qualities will steer Pakistan in the future also, provided all the stakeholders in society learn the right lessons from all the turning points of its turbulent history.

Many writers and observers, both inside and outside the country have questioned the very 'idea of Pakistan'. Most of them have argued

481

that the concept of nationhood in a multi-ethnic and diverse population should be based on common geography and common history rather than culture or religion.

Stephen Cohen of the Brookings Institution in Washington and a well known scholar on South Asia, published in 2005, a book entitled *The Idea of Pakistan*. In this book he analyses the factors that led to the success of the Pakistan Movement and the difficulties that threaten its existence. He then identifies five kinds of failure in his diagnosis of Pakistan as a 'failed state':

- '*The failure to live up to past expectations, one's own and those of others*. Nations seldom fulfil their high ideals and early promise. Pakistan, created as a haven for Indian Muslims, was to be a stable and prosperous Islamic state. The discrepancy between its early aspirations and contemporary reality is one of the country's more notable features.
- *Failure of vision*. Pakistan's founders expected the idea of Pakistan to shape the state of Pakistan; instead, a military bureaucracy governs the state and imposes its own vision of a Pakistani nation.
- *Economic failure*. With the loss of the very poor East Wing in 1971, Pakistan expected to gain middle-income status. But the economy did not fire up, and its per capita income today is below that of India.
- *Failure of leadership*. Pakistan has a distinct political and governing class: the 'Establishment', a moderate oligarchy that has presided over many political, economic, and strategic disasters, and whose most promising leaders, notably Benazir Bhutto, have by and large disappointed their ardent supporters, creating further disillusionment with the political process.
- *Catastrophic failure*. Failing states, at one time absorbed by imperial powers or neighbours or placed under international trusteeship, today pose a highly visible and serious problem for the world, complicated by refugees and migrants, televised holocausts, and the internationalization of ethnic conflict. An additional concern in Pakistan's case is the possible spread of nuclear weapons, missiles, and Islamic radicalism: a catastrophically failed Pakistan would become a matter of grave concern to many states.'[1]

In the summer of 2003 Stephen Cohen, while attending a seminar in Islamabad, had distributed some portions of the manuscript of this book. In response to his request for reactions, I sent him the following comments in my letter of 25 September 2003:

Dear Steve,

I was in Washington D.C. last week to attend a meeting hosted jointly by the World Economic Forum and Brookings. I was planning to call you to explore the possibility of a meeting, but unfortunately Brookings was closed on Thursday and Friday due to Hurricane Isabel. I am, therefore, writing this letter to offer some comments on your paper 'The Nation and the State of Pakistan', which I was hoping to share with you if we had met:

- In the historical context, your starting point that Pakistan was to be a 'homeland for Indian Muslims and an ideological and political leader of the Islamic world' is not quite accurate. Jinnah's concept of Pakistan was based on a more limited premise: that Muslims should rule in areas where they are in a majority. 'A homeland for Indian Muslims' would have meant a tacit commitment to accommodate all the Muslims living in post-1947 India, which was not practicable. Similarly, Jinnah never promoted pan-Islamism. The Pakistan he conceived was a Muslim state and not an Islamic state. Pakistan did support Islamic causes in the UN and elsewhere but without claiming to be the 'leader' of the Islamic world. Some groups started promoting pan-Islamism at a later stage but it was long after Jinnah's death.
- To say that Pakistan presents an 'existential' challenge to its neighbours is not, in my view, a fair assessment. In fact, Pakistan has been under threat from a much larger and stronger neighbour, which has territorial or ethnic disputes and problems with all its other neighbours also. With the exception of India, Pakistan has good relations with all its SAARC neighbours. Afghanistan is a different subject and was complicated further by the Russian invasion in 1979.
- The militarization of Pakistan society and the growth of extremist organizations can be traced directly to the US strategy to defeat the Russians in Afghanistan in the 1980s in cooperation with Pakistan. After the war, USA and other western countries walked away from Afghanistan, leaving Pakistan to handle the consequences by itself, in terms of weapons, drugs and 3.5 million refugees. If the promised financial assistance for the reconstruction of Afghanistan had been provided in the early 1990s, many mujahideen would have found jobs

and the circumstances which led to emergence of the Taliban in 1994, would have been mitigated to a large extent.

- The statement on page 114 that Islamic parties in Pakistan want to wage a Jihad in India to liberate 140 million Muslims goes too far. There have been protests against the destruction of Babri mosque and large-scale killings of Muslims in Gujarat, but there has never been any serious threat that will justify such a statement. In fact in 2002, Pakistan was under constant threat from India, which had brought a million troops to the Pakistan border.

Your overall analysis of the difficulties Pakistan is facing is on the whole correct as is your prediction that Pakistan will continue to live on the border of democracy. In this context, the following sentence succinctly sums up the dilemma facing Pakistan: 'Pakistan is in the ambivalent position of having an army that can neither govern nor allow civilians to rule.' However, more than half the developing countries are in a similar situation and do not have a functioning democracy. But for various reasons, that I have never fully understood, Pakistan's failings and difficulties are always over-projected.

There is one other aspect, which has not received full attention. Absence of democracy in Islamic countries does not create the problems that caste ridden societies face. India, for example, needs democracy to override the social inequality inherent in its caste system. Muslim societies on the other hand, have an inherent egalitarian culture reflected not just in praying and eating together but also equalizing wealth through Zakat and other institutions. That is why a large number of Islamic countries, with monarchies do not experience any mass movements to seek a democratic system. In fact, they find democratic rulers elsewhere too weak to control such volatile societies.

I am not arguing against democracy. Every society should strive to evolve strong democratic institutions adjusted to its own circumstances. But we should bear in mind that in the transition period, Islamic societies have some inherited assets, which can and do smooth the transition.

I do not agree that 'The Idea of Pakistan' is failing. You have effectively redefined the 'idea' and then argued that it is failing. But the actual idea was more modest—to enable the Muslims living in Muslim majority areas to manage their own affairs. Today, Muslims in India are decidedly worse off than the average Indians and the average Pakistani is still better off than the average Indian, despite recent progress there. This is not only in terms of living standards but to have a 'homeland' in which to live freely according to one's own culture and beliefs. In India, only those Muslims can go forward who do not show their identity as Muslims. In that sense, the idea of Pakistan remains valid.'

During a visit to Pakistan, Steve Cohen thanked me for these comments and said he had to revise several portions of his book after receiving my comments.

Lessons of History

My main purpose in writing this book was to convey to the coming generations, with all the emphasis at my command, four important lessons from our history:

1. That Pakistan can survive as a dynamic and viable political entity only through a genuine democratic framework, since democracy ensures a sense of identity and a sense of participation to all the federating units and sub-units, while being a part of a coherent political framework.
2. That a self sustaining democratic framework can only be built on strong institutions and the rule of law, under civilian supremacy. Military rule with a civilian façade can never become a substitute for genuine democracy.
3. A democratic system and especially a parliamentary federal system can survive only if the three pillars of state: namely the parliament, the judiciary and the executive function within the parameters laid down by the constitution. If the executive becomes too powerful, as has happened under frequent military takeovers in Pakistan, then the other two pillars become much weaker and cannot perform their primary function of protecting fundamental rights and provincial rights as laid down in the constitution. That can shake the very foundations of state structure.
4. The vitality of a nation does not come only from its economic progress and the size of its military, but also from its shared values, cultural heritage and social energy. In this context the classical definition of a 'nation' with a common language and a common culture, has been replaced with the modern concept of the nation state with a diverse range of cultures, languages and ethnic groups.

This diversity, if properly harnessed and harmonized through democratic principles and forces can increase the inherent vitality of the nation.

The causes of the failure of democracy in Pakistan are many but unless we identify and remedy the principal causes, it will be difficult to build the edifice of genuine democracy on solid foundations. The first important step in this task is to list the initial violations of democratic principles which in turn generated serious fault lines in the country's political structure.

In the very first decade of Pakistan's existence, a basic democratic principle was violated when East Pakistan was denied its due share in the political power structure in proportion to its population, which was larger than that of the four provinces of West Pakistan. To resolve the deadlock over constitution making, an artificial 'parity' was created between East and West Pakistan by merging in 1955, the four West Pakistan provinces into a single 'Unit' and giving equal seats to the two provinces. In a genuine democratic framework, imbalances in population are often accommodated by having an upper house or Senate, with equal representation from all provinces.

This injustice was further compounded by General Ayub Khan when he promulgated his 1962 constitution. He had taken over in October 1958 after abrogating the 1956 constitution, only a few months before the first general elections under this constitution could be held in February 1959. The new constitution concentrated all powers in the hands of a president, who was indirectly elected through 80,000 'basic democrats'. He also retained his military position by assuming the lifelong rank of a Field Marshal. Under this constitution, Ayub Khan drastically reduced the quantum of provincial autonomy by exercising all effective powers through nominated governors rather than giving them to elected assemblies, thus creating serious political fault lines which ultimately led to the Bangladesh movement and the break-up of the country in December 1971.

The second major cause of the failure of democracy has been the dominant role of the military in the country's power structure. The first war between India and Pakistan over Kashmir broke out within a year of Pakistan's birth. The foundations of a 'security state' were thus laid from the very outset. The next two India–Pakistan wars in 1965 and 1971 were fought when Pakistan was under army rule and further reinforced the paramount supremacy of defence and national security in the national agenda. That is why even the short periods of civilian rule that were allowed by the Establishment, were largely overshadowed by the military's influence on key policies.

Civil–Military Relations

Throughout Pakistan's history, there has been a serious debate about whether the ultimate responsibility for the failure of democracy lies with the military for taking over so frequently on one pretext or another or with political parties which did not follow democratic principles or traditions whenever they got a chance to rule, nor provided good governance.

The pro-military school argues that developing countries like Pakistan are not yet ripe for western style democracy. They need a 'managed system' of democracy under military's supervision especially in view of the difficult geo-political conditions surrounding Pakistan.

The pro-democracy school however rightly argues that democracy has never been given a chance in Pakistan. It takes time and collective efforts of all the stakeholders to nurture the plant of democracy. If it is uprooted every 8 or 10 years, it cannot develop roots, nor allow genuine grass-root political leadership to emerge. In fact, almost all the leaders that assumed power during brief civilian interludes were the 'products' of the military managed political dispensations.

The pro-military school has often argued that military was 'invited' by opposition politicians to takeover, or there was serious infighting among politicians that effectively 'sucked in' the army. This line of argument is not supported by the history of army takeovers.

Ayub Khan's 1958 coup was no doubt caused by an image of political instability especially on the issue of provincial autonomy, but once agreement was reached on the 1956 constitution, it was very important to hold the first general elections under that constitution, scheduled for February 1959 to give an opportunity to elected representatives to resolve the remaining differences. Ayub Khan, by taking over, in fact, further complicated the issue of provincial autonomy, leading to the break-up of the country. Nor did he evolve a stable political process during his 11-year rule. In March 1969 he had to hand over power to General Yahya Khan whose rule lasted two and a half years. Thus after thirteen years of military rule, half the country was lost and 90,000 soldiers languished as Indian Prisoners of War (POWs) for two years.

Ziaul Haq's coup in July 1977 was also without any justification because Zulfikar Ali Bhutto had reached a compromise with the opposition over re-elections in several constituencies. Bhutto had no doubt alienated several segments of society including the business community and the bureaucracy, and his rule was marked by many contradictions inherent in his strong personality, especially because he had greater trust in his own ability than the strength of the institutions on which democracy is built. But the ultimate accountability must rest with the electorate. In this case, Ziaul Haq took advantage of Bhutto's unpopularity in many powerful circles, including the United States, and fulfilled his inherent ambition to assume power. But by the end of Ziaul Haq's 11-year rule, there were three million AK-47s in circulation in the country, over a million Pakistanis were heroin addicts, and we had three and half million Afghan refugees. We were also deeply involved in Afghanistan, the consequences of which are still threatening our national existence.

Pervez Musharraf's takeover of October 1999 was essentially a 'countercoup' in that he wanted to cancel his removal as army chief. The prime minister had the authority to sack the army chief, but the army chief did not have the power to dismiss an elected government with two-thirds majority. No one can claim that after nine years of Musharraf's rule Pakistan is more secure and more prosperous than it was in 1999. Throughout 2007, more people have died in suicide blasts in Pakistan than Iraq and Afghanistan combined. The Pakistan army has killed more people in Balochistan and the tribal areas, than the US and her allies have in Afghanistan. The Pakistan army has suffered more casualties in the tribal areas than the US and Allied troops in Afghanistan.

It should be clear from these examples that there is no firm evidence of 'invitation' from opposition politicians. In any case, the army as an institution should never take such an important extra constitutional step simply because some disgruntled politicians are urging them to do so. In fact under-development and fragmentation of politics in Pakistan is entirely attributable to long periods of military rule in Pakistan.

Irrespective of the initial reasons for any army takeover, the net impact of such takeovers has been highly negative for the strength and unity of the federation and for the growth of a sustainable political process. Military rule invariably over-centralizes power in the executive to deliver 'quick results' and then seeks legitimacy by forcing the Judiciary to sanctify the takeover on grounds of state necessity. It further weakens the democratic process by weakening the role of the parliament and by manipulating certain political parties to obtain 'positive results' which means victory for parties that provide a civilian façade for continuing military rule. How many military dictators who have held sway over the politics of this country would volunteer to go through an accountability process that top PML or PPP leadership has undergone, or even face a genuine accountability process for that matter?

The military no doubt has the power, the experience and a strong desire to dominate the core political institutions to protect and promote what it regards as vital national interests, but it has not yet recognized that this responsibility to define and protect national interests should essentially rest with the country's political leadership. In each of its tenures the military has failed to create a durable political structure. If anything it has weakened the political structure, by manipulating and dividing various political parties, managing elections and giving a bad name to politics and politicians.

The system, which brought Musharraf to power and sustained him there, cannot escape total responsibility for where this country finds itself today. It is also incumbent on that power structure to take the lead in remedial measures.

The bewildered people of this country, subject to daily suicide bombings in the major cities and full-scale military actions in other parts of the country, want someone to take responsibility for what has gone wrong. The officers and *jawans* of the Pakistan army also need to know why they cannot walk proudly in the bazaars and streets of their own country wearing their uniforms. What happened to this nation's love and respect for them, which did not wane even after the humiliating defeat of 1971, they wonder.

The current military leadership owes to the people of this country, and no less to the Pakistan army's rank and file, a moment of retrospection. They must consider the possibility that the undoing of this nation has come about, at least partially, not despite but actually because of the repeated direct and indirect involvement of the armed forces in politics.

The Silver Lining

At the end of each period of military rule, the army as an institution has an underlying desire to withdraw from politics and concentrate on its core function of protecting the country's frontiers. The directions issued by the new army chief, General Ashfaq Parvez Kayani to withdraw army officers from civilian posts and to ask army officers and institutions not to interfere in political matters clearly reflect this desire. This provides a very positive juncture to replant the roots of genuine democracy and put the system back on the rails.

The recent civil society movement led by the lawyers, and the media, and supported by all major opposition parties is another historic turning point. This movement is seeking not only to restore the judiciary to the position it occupied on 2 November 2007, but also to establish the *supremacy of the rule of law* in the country. As experience in many other parts of the world has shown, genuine democracy cannot flourish without the active involvement of the civil society. Whenever the dominant segments of any society decide that henceforth they want to live under the rule of law and not the tyranny of a gun, no power can stop them from their goal.

The concept of rule of law and justice is all encompassing and includes the integration and reconciliation of conflicting claims and passions. This superb quality of justice to promote togetherness as the most important motivation of a nation has been manifest in all the stable democracies of the world. The importance of justice as a unifying ideology for a nation underlines the historic nature of the lawyers' movement for an independent judiciary and the rule of law.[2]

The third silver lining is the resolve of all the main political parties to work together for reconciliation and national consensus and for initiating a genuine democratic process, based on the rule of law and independence of judiciary, without any interference from the army. Even though the PPP–PML(N) coalition could not continue beyond August 2008, due to differences over the issue of the restoration of deposed judges, PML(N)'s conduct in Parliament, as an opposition party is very different from that witnessed in the 1990s. New pressures are also emerging in the face of a worsening economic crisis and the spate of suicide bombings in different parts of the country, that at this critical juncture, the country needs a government of national unity in which all political parties represented in parliament should participate, and demonstrate convincingly that democracy can work in Pakistan.

In the final analysis a multi-party democratic system based on strong institutions and a free media has a much better chance to create a new vitality to fight extremism and evolve a more tolerant society that accommodates different cultures, languages and ethnic groups.

Pakistan may be a new political entity on the map of the world but the history of its people goes back thousands of years to the Harappa and Mohenjo-Daro civilizations on the banks of the river Indus. They have a rich and diverse heritage of culture. In the eighth century, the advent of Islam in the Indian subcontinent brought a new dynamism and many saints. The saints spread their spiritual and moral message among millions of low caste inhabitants who embraced Islam to gain identity and equality in society. The Mughal rulers who came to India in the sixteenth century not only generated wealth and prosperity on a significant scale, but also brought about a cultural revival in the field of poetry, music, art and literature. These were the historical foundations on which the movement for an independent homeland for the Muslims of the Indian subcontinent was conceived and successfully accomplished by Quaid-i-Azam Mohammad Ali Jinnah and his colleagues. We will have to regain that momentum to revive the cultural values and social vitality of our nation-state.

Pakistan is located at a geo-strategic crossroad in Asia, linking Western Asia and Central Asia with South Asia. It can build a strong and prosperous economy on these geo-strategic foundations if it can put its own house in order by strengthening its constitutional, political and moral foundations. This is a gigantic task that will require the collective will and efforts of all the stakeholders including the armed forces. Once the foundations of democracy are well established, the focus of the entire nation should shift to development and good governance.

The dream of Pakistan should never be allowed to die.

NOTES

1. Stephen Phillip Cohen, *The Idea of Pakistan*, Vanguard Books (Pvt.) Ltd., Lahore and Brookings Institution Press, Washington D.C., 2005, pp. 3–4.
2. In the Second World War, as German forces overran Europe and defeated the British troops at Dunkirk, there was imminent danger of an invasion of Great Britain. In the middle of that crisis, Prime Minister Churchill wrote a letter to the Lord Chancellor (chief justice) asking him if 'the British Courts were functioning well'. He got an affirmative answer but sometime later, the Chancellor asked Churchill, 'Prime Minister, in the midst of your heroic preoccupations, what made you think of the functioning of the courts?' Churchill replied, 'I knew that if the common man in England knew that the justice he enjoyed would be denied if the island was occupied by the Nazis, people would offer resistance on the beaches. People will fight neither for you, nor for me, but for justice.'

Epilogue 2
A New Charter of Democracy

Some reviews of the first edition of this book, while appreciating the lessons of history that were presented, pointed out that I had failed to identify some basic flaws and fault lines in the society that had not allowed Pakistan to realize the Quaid-i-Azam's vision of a progressive, tolerant and inclusive nation and realize its full development potential.

In Chapter 2 of this book, I have in fact listed two important factors which led to the failure of democracy in Pakistan. Firstly, the death of Quaid-i-Azam Mohammad Ali Jinnah only one year after Pakistan came into existence and the assassination of Prime Minister Liaquat Ali Khan three years later. This made it difficult to resolve political differences on basic issues and erect the Constitutional edifice on which a democratic and workable political system could be built. Some of the top leadership of Muslim League in Pakistan had migrated from India, leaving their native constituencies behind. This dislocation deprived them of territorial base in any elections, thus avoiding renewal of popular mandate. This problem could easily have been addressed with some political ingenuity such as proportionate representation or provincial list systems.

Secondly, a new Constitution was adopted in 1956, but before elections under that Constitution could be held, General Ayub Khan took over in 1958, declared Martial Law and abrogated the Constitution. He introduced a new system of indirect elections under the 1962 Constitution. This Constitution, which was flawed ab initio ('I Field Marshal Ayub Khan... give you this constitution...', instead of 'We, the People'), led to serious agitation in East Pakistan and did not survive a day after Ayub Khan's departure. In 1969, a new Legal Framework Order (LFO) was issued by General Yahya Khan. In 1970, the first general elections were held under this LFO i.e. a full twenty-three years after Pakistan was created.

Thirdly, an important factor highlighted in Chapter 2 and in Epilogue I-*Dreams Never Die*, was the dominant role of the military in the country's power structure. Thirty years of direct military rule and many more years of indirect rule, stultified the political process which could have produced outstanding political leaders. Almost all the political leaders after 1958 have been the product of a military managed political system which they created to provide a civilian facade to indirect military rule.

Some other factors responsible for recurrent political instability in Pakistan, such as the polarization of the society along religious, ethnic, sectarian and tribal lines and the growth of violent extremism after 9/11, have been discussed in different chapters. But the lethal mixture of all these factors, compounded by many geopolitical fault lines, had a much more devastating effect on the political system, the economy and society as a whole.

Before discussing these grave structural issues, let me summarize some of the milestones and turning points of our history to clarify the context.

On 14 August 1947, when I witnessed the raising of the Pakistan flag for the first time in Abbottabad, it was a sight to behold. We had a nation to be proud of, our own country, to have and to live in, and our own Quaid-i-Azam to lead us, and for us to follow him and to die for. A dream that became true in all the colours of a rainbow. That is the dream I have held on to all my life.

The death of the Quaid in 1948 devastated us but we were back on our feet within weeks. The Quaid was no more but two of his loyal lieutenants were there; Liaquat Ali Khan and Khawaja Nazimuddin. Nothing could go wrong, or so we thought. Liaquat Ali Khan's assassination, three years later and the political musical chairs that followed, began to ruin our dream.

In 1958, Ayub Khan's Martial Law was welcomed by many because everyone was yearning for stability. By 1964, Pakistan was a vibrant economy with sustained growth and rapid industrial progress. But economic development without social and political development is like a sand castle, which is washed away by the first high tide of political turmoil. This high tide did come in 1971 and not only washed away the decade of development but also half the country. East Pakistan becoming Bangladesh was a catastrophic blow to the country and our dreams.

Our hopes were revived when Zulfikar Ali Bhutto came to power. His charisma pulled the prostrate nation up. He gave us a new Constitution which has stood the test of time. He brought back our prisoners of war from India. He started the nuclear programme and established a respectable place for the country in the Muslim World. He rekindled hope and the Pakistan dream began to shine once more. But Bhutto also had his failings: a socialist mind imprisoned in a feudal body, a democrat at heart but an autocrat in actions. These contradictions allowed the forces that had retreated after the December 1971 catastrophe to reassert themselves with a vengeance. In 1979, Bhutto was hanged after a military coup by General Ziaul Haq, through a court decision which is now universally recognized as judicial murder.

Under Ziaul Haq, the Pakistan dream, based on Quaid-i-Azam's vision of a democratic, progressive welfare state, was replaced by an elaborate security state, which operated through selected agencies and non-state entities. He joined the Afghan Jihad and trained, with US support, thousands of armed and indoctrinated cadres of *Jihadis* (Islamic militant) from Pakistan and abroad. This brought to the country, religious intolerance, sectarian strife and gun culture, with far reaching consequences. Foreign Policy was reduced to a series of transactional arrangements and the resultant access to loans and grants created a model of development that was over dependent on foreign assistance rather than on our own human and material resources.

Under Ziaul Haq, the Pakistan Army, apart from its basic responsibility for defending the country's geographical borders, also became responsible for defending its 'ideological frontiers'. Accordingly, he elevated the Army Chief to the proverbial 'Defender of Faith' status. In the process, many Islamic political parties and groups began to advocate a state under strict Islamic Law, effectively negating the political logic for the creation of Pakistan and also the vision of Allama Iqbal and Quaid-i-Azam for an inclusive democratic state.

Since ideology is an all-pervasive concept, reflected in a society's culture, political system and educational policies, the Pakistan Army gradually extended its mandate to control virtually all the streams of national life. The pliant elected set-up was thus left with only the mundane. When Prime Minister Junejo tried to extend the

Parliament's writ through the Eighth Amendment, he was sent home and the Assembly was dissolved.

Benazir Bhutto won the 1988 general elections, following Ziaul Haq's death in an air crash. She was kept waiting for several days until she agreed to all the conditions that had been set out and signed on the dotted line. Only then was the National Assembly convened to elect her. As her compliance was less than expected, a campaign to destabilize her government was started fairly soon and her government was sacked after only 20 months, on charges of 'corruption'.

Nawaz Sharif, who followed her into the Prime Minister's House, found the same straight jacket of de facto forces unbearable. In April 1993, he came on National TV to declare, 'I will not take dictation from the Presidency'. He was sacked the following day on similar charges which the Supreme Court set aside six weeks later.

Benazir Bhutto's second term was largely pliant, yet she faced turmoil and conspiracies, like the murder of her brother Murtaza Bhutto, for which her husband, Asif Zardari was blamed. This tragedy weakened her moral authority and popularity, making it easier for her own handpicked President, Farooq Leghari, to dismiss her government in August 1996.

In his second tenure, with two third majority in Parliament, Nawaz Sharif tried to wrench back some of the lost territory for the civilian set up, by repealing Article 58-2(b), carrying out nuclear tests and inviting Vajpayee to Lahore. But his decision to sack Musharraf for the Kargil misadventure, which even the Chiefs of the Air Force and the Navy had openly questioned, led to his removal from office. For posterity, it must be said that the decision was correct, but the timing was three months too late, giving Musharraf the time to recover and to take appropriate measures to pre-empt what must have seemed inevitable to him. The Parliament was dissolved, and Musharraf ruled for the next 8 years.

In each of these episodes, as mentioned elsewhere, there were several other contributing factors, but under the surface there was a persistent campaign to defame politics and politicians. Under Musharraf's successor, army personnel were withdrawn from various civilian positions but the long-term goal of marginalizing both major political parties remained in place.

By the time General Kayani left, a new assertive phase of military involvement was fully operational. The Zarb-e-Azb Operation and improvement of law and order in Karachi gave legitimacy to this phase and by 2016 the encirclement of the political system was well advanced. The 'REJECTED' tweet was a proclamation of a new paradigm. The WhatsApp JIT and the Iqama decision, were all milestones of this new paradigm shift. The Faizabad *Dharna* of November 2017, and the resultant unconditional surrender of the civilian government was the crowning moment in the triumph of de-facto forces over the de jure civilian setup.

In 2018, these de facto forces not only facilitated the victory of PTI in the elections but stitched together the required parliamentary coalition. It also became an active participant in managing the economy and the administrative structure, with full control of the media and strategic communications. On 11 September 2019, Chief Justice Asif Saeed Khosa observed that, 'Receding political space in governance does not augur well for the country and growing censorship is a serious threat to democracy'.

Corruption and abuse of authority has been another consistent weapon against politicians, starting from Elected Bodies Disqualification Order (EBDO) to the present anti-narcotic imprisonment of political opponents. Every misdemeanour by politicians was brought under the microscope, who were proven guilty as charged under the force of propaganda, and if need be, judicial process. Fatima Jinnah, H. S. Suhrawardy, Zulfikar Ali Bhutto, Mohammad Khan Junejo, Benazir Bhutto, Asif Zardari, Nawaz Sharif, Shahid Khaqan Abbasi were all unworthy politicians. 'Corruption' and 'abuse of authority' was billed as a unique Pakistani phenomenon, making a military rule or, at any rate, a military guided political dispensation as the only viable option. A cursory look at the world's contemporary political scene negates this narrative. Many former Presidents and Prime Ministers have faced corruption charges in the courts. But in none of these countries did the defense forces jump in to save the country from 'corrupt politicians'. Every head of state or government has to make a large number of decisions. It is very easy for their political rivals to single out some of these decisions for investigation. But few of them are eventually proved in a court of law.

Surprisingly, this overwhelming ingress of the military in all facets of national life has been met with acquiescence rather than rejection, except from some opposition leaders and certain civil society organizations. This was achieved by a long term, two pronged, consistent and coordinated strategy. To legitimize the illegitimate, the legitimate must be stigmatized first. On the one hand, not only politicians but the very institution of politics had to be undermined; on the other, the people were to be convinced that the armed forces of Pakistan were all that stood between them and cataclysm. The success of this strategy was also enhanced by certain ground realities:

1. Throughout the past seven decades, 1971 notwithstanding, the armed forces of Pakistan have successfully defended the territorial integrity and sovereignty of the country against an adversary that is 7 times larger in terms of population and 10 times larger in terms of GDP. People, therefore talk proudly about the quality and bravery of the armed forces.

2. The armed forces have rendered huge sacrifices in meeting the internal security challenges from militant extremism and terrorism, which had become an existential threat, not just in FATA but also in many other parts of the country.

3. Several geopolitical factors and the geostrategic location of Pakistan have attracted the interest of great powers. The containment of the Soviet Union in the 1960s and 1970s, the US Sponsored Afghan Jihad and war on terror after 9/11, provided the Pakistan Army with financial assistance, military aid and diplomatic support, thus enhancing its standing vis-a-vis the civilian rulers during that period.

4. All stakeholders who strongly believe in civilian supremacy, acknowledge that the democratic governance, which Pakistan has seen for brief periods, has not been as competent, fair, and accountable as required by our circumstances, ignoring in the process the circumstances and the limitations under which civilian governments had to perform.

5. Everyone agrees that, for these reasons, we cannot weaken the military in order to strengthen democratic governance. But will a strong and overbearing military then allow space and opportunity to civilians to upgrade their capacity to govern. Once prolonged military rule, with a pliant civilian façade, becomes the

'norm', the tree of real democracy cannot grow under its shadow. That is the real dilemma facing Pakistan today.

It is absolutely vital to resolve this dilemma. The hybrid plus model of governance that Pakistan has glided into, is neither viable nor sustainable. In fact, it has already reached a dead-end, and is certainly not capable of dealing with the multidimensional crisis Pakistan is facing at present:

- A serious economic crisis, with declining business confidence, and shortfalls in tax revenues, exports, industrial production and the stock market, leading to low growth combined with high inflation and rising unemployment.
- Dangerously polarized politics, with increasing tensions between the government and the opposition seriously affecting the working of the Parliamentary System. This polarization is becoming more serious because the Establishment is openly and aggressively supporting the ruling party, violating the sanctity of institutional neutrality and blurring the distinction between Government and State.
- Basic principles of constitutional rule and a federal structure are being violated through disregard of the separation of powers and undermining the rights of the federating units.
- Erosion of independence of judiciary and the rule of law, through overwhelming pressures from the deep state, is dismantling the platform on which a modern state can be built.
- Unprecedented restrictions and curbs on the electronic and print media and on civil society organizations is alienating large and vital segments of society.
- Serious security challenges on all our three borders especially after Indian unilateral actions of 5 August 2019, the breakdown of the Afghan peace negotiations, and more recently the escalating tensions between Saudi Arabia and Iran.

These far reaching and inter-related problems cannot be resolved overnight by any political party or any general. The most fundamental prerequisite, before we begin to address these problems, is a constitutional and democratic framework in which the voters and not the military establishment decide which party will rule Pakistan for the next 5 years. This will automatically lead to participatory decision making, an independent parliament, empowered provincial assemblies and self-governing local bodies, all committed to safeguarding national security, reviving the economy and ensuring the well-being of the people of Pakistan. Perhaps the Parliament can initiate a Grand National Dialogue among all stake holders to evolve a new Charter of Democratic Governance.

International experience has clearly shown that prolonged military rule, whether direct or indirect, causes much greater damage to the economic and political system, than civilian misrule. It also affects the military's ability to perform its core function i.e. to safeguard the country's security in case of war.

Between 1950 and 1990, a large number of countries in Asia and Africa were ruled by the military because of geo-political factors arising from the cold war between the US and USSR. In the past three decades this number has declined sharply and most countries like Argentina, Brazil, Indonesia, and Turkey have made better economic and social progress than they did under military rule. The time has come for Pakistan to draw lessons from history.

In this book's Epilogue 1, *Dreams Never Die*, one of the most important lessons of our history was presented in the following words:

> The vitality of a nation does not come only from its economic progress or the size of its military but also from its shared values, cultural heritage and social energy. In this context, the classical definition of a 'nation' with a common language and a common culture has been replaced with the modern concept of the nation state with a diverse range of cultures, languages and ethnic groups. This diversity, if properly harnessed and harmonized, through democratic principles and forces can increase the inherent vitality of a nation.

The national interest of a thriving state is in fact the sum total of its national cohesion, internal and external security, health of its economy, a credible and just judicial system, depth and quality of its education system; a rational and coherent foreign policy, and above all, singularity of the locus of state authority.

These important ingredients can be harnessed over time only through a broader and inclusive democratic system. That is the only way to ensure that 'the dream of Pakistan is never allowed to die'.

APPENDICES

List of Appendices

Appendix I: Economic Contingency Plan
(See page 196)

In the Cabinet meeting held on 14 May 1998, it was decided that an Economic Contingency Plan should be formulated in case Pakistan decides to go ahead with the nuclear explosion and has to face economic sanctions. This paper has been prepared in response to this directive.

2. If and when Pakistan decides to go for the nuclear option, there will be a strong reaction from the market, even before the actual sanctions are announced. To deal with this reaction and to safeguard against a sudden flight of capital, the following measures would have to be adopted immediately.

   i. An ordinance will have to be issued to suspend the operation of the protection of Economic Reforms Act of 1991.
   ii. The Foreign Currency Accounts (FCAs) of resident Pakistanis will be converted into rupees at the official exchange rate (about $7 billion). The banks will be directed to offer attractive rates on these rupee accounts.
   iii. Foreign Currency Accounts of non-residents ($4 billion) will not be converted, but will be temporarily brought under SBP restrictions, so that there is no sudden withdrawal. However SBP may allow some withdrawals on a case to case basis, to avoid hardship.
   iv. In line with the decision in (ii) above, holding of FCAs by residents will be discontinued, along with the suspension of licenses held by money-changers.
   v. A bank holiday will be declared on Day 1, to facilitate the implementation of these measures.

3. While these measures are intended to safeguard the balance of payments, some measures should also be announced to safeguard the budgetary situation. These would include:

   (i) 10–15 per cent cut in non-development budget
   (ii) New ordinance to speed up the recovery of stuck up loans
   (iii) A major austerity drive

4. It will take a few days after the tests, before we know about the nature, scope and severity of the sanctions that may be imposed on Pakistan. But keeping in view the sanctions imposed on India, we could lose foreign assistance of about $2 billion, (over and above the projected BOP gap of $2 billion forecast for the year 1998–99), as detailed below:

		$billion
(i)	Loss of Programme Loans from WB ADB & Japan	1.00
(ii)	Loss of about 25 per cent of the expected project assistance (Total for 1998-99 estimated at $1.7 billion)	0.40
(iii)	Loss of credits lined up for wheat imports of 1.5 million tons	0.26
(iv)	Loss of 3rd & 4th installments of IMF loans under ESAF/EEF	0.50
	Total:	2.16

5.   This amount is about 1/6th of the projected imports of about $12 billion in 1998–99. Our first priority will be to compress our imports by this amount or arrange alternative sources of credit to finance some of these imports, as detailed below:

Petroleum Products	$1.90 billion
Wheat	$0.26 billion
Fertilizer (DAP)	$0.17 billion
Edible oils	$0.75 billion
Total	$3.08 billion

6.   It will be necessary to send special representatives, without any loss of time, to various Islamic and friendly countries to arrange credits (hopefully for 3–5 years) for these imports. (Saudi Arabia, UAE, Kuwait, Malaysia). IDB may also finance wheat imports or fertilizer imports from Islamic countries. Some of them may provide financial aid or special deposits.

7.   Simultaneously we should launch a crash agricultural programme to achieve self sufficiency in wheat and edible oil, and to expand our exportable commodities like cotton and rice.

8.   Out of the total estimated loss of $2.16 billion in foreign assistance, a loss of $1.5 billion (Rs65 billion) will also affect the budget. For this purpose:

   a.   Non-development and non essential expenditures will have to be curtailed; Provinces will be asked to do the same.

   b.   No new projects to be undertaken in the PSDP, but aided on-going projects to be protected to utilize more aid from the pipeline and thus assist the balance of payments.

   c.   New tax measures may have to be introduced to cover increased defence expenditures that may arise in view of tensions with India.

   d.   Quasi-fiscal deficit of public sector agencies, i.e. WAPDA, KSE, Railways will have to be recouped through reduction in cross subsidies and adjustment in tariffs.

9.   In the short run, Pakistan's vulnerability is much greater than India's, which has exchange reserves of $25 billion (6 months imports) and its reliance on foreign aid as a proportion of its imports are much smaller (about 10 per cent). By

comparison, foreign assistance finances about 25 per cent of Pakistan's imports and its foreign exchange reserves are only $1.4 billion (6 weeks' imports), with short term liabilities of $12 billion ($11 billion in Foreign Currency Accounts and $1 billion in short term loans).

10. If sanctions are imposed, Pakistan will not be able to raise any new short term loans in the Bond markets, while it needs to roll over the loans obtained in earlier years. Confidence in the stock market will also be shaken and some of the foreign portfolio investors will withdraw their funds. This would mean a further decline in the stock market. (It is already touching a two year low of 1374 on 18 May). Our Privatization Programme will also receive a set back because those buying assets in Pakistan will not be able to get financial backing from Banks in USA and other countries imposing sanctions.

11. An important issue in this context will be our Debt Repayment Policy which will have to be formulated in the light of the sanctions and their scope. The estimates in para 4 above assume that aid in the pipeline will continue (except perhaps from Japan) but new credits may not be forthcoming.

12. One option would be to stop loan repayment and interest payment to countries that impose sanctions (namely USA, Japan) and save about $1 billion. But that may involve further sanctions (including those that may affect our exports) that apply to loan defaulters in the 'Paris Club'.

13. Similarly, outflow of direct foreign investment or portfolio investment may have to be allowed, so that our ability to borrow from foreign commercial banks is not affected very seriously, although we will have to pay higher rates.

14. There may be some difficulty in imports, if our LCs are not honoured by foreign banks, but special steps may have to be taken to seek the support of foreign banks in Pakistan to counter-guarantee LCs issued by our Banks.

15. Another issue that will have to be taken up will be the need for import restrictions. Depending on the emerging situation and if our efforts to mobilize compensatory resources do not succeed according to our expectations, we may have to impose restrictions on certain imports. This will be a very serious step because it would lead to inflation and affect the cost of living of the common man. So this extreme step should be taken only as a last resort.

16. To coordinate and implement this Contingency Plan, it will be necessary to setup a small Committee, preferably as a Sub-Committee of the ECC, to watch the situation on a day-to-day basis and take decisions in a timely manner. (Finance Minister; Commerce Minister; Petroleum Minister; Deputy Chairman, Planning Commission; Chairman, Board of Investment; and Governor State Bank of Pakistan).

Sartaj Aziz
Finance Minister
19.05.1998

Appendix II: Joint Statement on Prime Minister Vajpayee's Visit to Lahore on 20–21 February 1999

(See page 224)

In response to an invitation by the Prime Minister of Pakistan, Mohammad Nawaz Sharif, the Prime Minister of India, Shri Atal Bihari Vajpayee visited Pakistan from 20–21 February 1999, on the inaugural run of the Delhi–Lahore bus service.

2. The Prime Minister of Pakistan received the Indian Prime Minister at the Wagah border on 20 February 1999. A banquet in honour of the Indian Prime Minister and his delegation was hosted by the Prime Minister at Lahore Fort, on the same evening. Prime Minister Atal Bihari Vajpayee visited Minar-e-Pakistan, Mausoleum of Allama Iqbal, Gurdawara Dera Sahib and Samadhi of Maharaja Ranjeet Singh. On 21 February, a civic reception was held in honour of the visiting Prime Minister at the Governor's House.

3. The two leaders held discussions on the entire range of bilateral relations, regional cooperation within SAARC, and issues of international concern. They decided that:

    a. The two Foreign Ministers will meet periodically to discuss all issues of mutual concern, including nuclear related issues.

    b. The two sides shall undertake consultations on WTO related issues with a view to coordinating their respective positions.

    c. The two sides shall determine areas of cooperation in Information Technology, in particular for tackling the problems of Y2K.

    d. The two sides will hold consultations with a view to further liberalizing the visa and travel regime.

    e. The two sides shall appoint a 2-member committee at ministerial level to examine humanitarian issues relating to Civilian detainees and missing POWs.

4. They expressed satisfaction on the commencement of a Bus Service between Lahore and New Delhi, the release of fishermen and civilian detainees and renewal of contacts in the field of sports.

5. Pursuant to the directive given by the two Prime Ministers, the Foreign Secretaries of Pakistan and India signed a Memorandum of Understanding on 21 February 1999, identifying measures aimed at promoting an environment of peace and security between the two countries.

6. The two Prime Ministers signed the Lahore Declaration embodying their shared vision of peace and stability between their countries and of progress and prosperity for their people.
7. Prime Minister Atal Bihari Vajpayee extended an invitation to Prime Minister Mohammad Nawaz Sharif to visit India on mutually convenient dates.
8. Prime Minister Atal Bihari Vajpayee thanked Prime Minister Mohammad Nawaz Sharif for the warm welcome and gracious hospitality extended to him and members of his delegation and for the excellent arrangements made for his visit.

Lahore
21 February 1999

Lahore Declaration

The Prime Ministers of the Islamic Republic of Pakistan, and the Republic of India:

Sharing a vision of peace and stability between their countries, and of progress and prosperity for their peoples;
Convinced that durable peace and development of harmonious relations and friendly cooperation will serve the vital interests of the peoples of the two countries, enabling them to devote their energies for a better future;
Recognizing that the nuclear dimension of the security environment of the two countries adds to their responsibility for avoidance of conflict between the two countries;
Committed to the principles and purposes of the Charter of the United Nations, and the universally accepted principles of peaceful co-existence;
Reiterating the determination of both countries to implementing the Simla Agreement in letter and spirit;
Committed to the objective of universal nuclear disarmament and non-proliferation;
Convinced of the importance of mutually agreed confidence building measures for improving the security environment;
Recalling their agreement of 23 September 1998, that an environment of peace and security is in the supreme national interest of both sides and that the resolution of all outstanding issues, including Jammu and Kashmir, is essential for this purpose;

Have agreed that their respective governments:

- shall intensify their efforts to resolve all issues, including the issue of Jammu and Kashmir.
- shall refrain from intervention and interference in each other's internal affairs.
- shall intensify their composite and integrated dialogue process for an early and positive outcome of the agreed bilateral agenda.
- shall take immediate steps for reducing the risk of accidental or unauthorized use of nuclear weapons and discuss concepts and doctrines with a view to elaborating

measures for confidence building in the nuclear and conventional fields, aimed at prevention of conflict.

- reaffirm their commitment to the goals and objectives of SAARC and to concert their efforts towards the realization of the SAARC vision for the year 2000 and beyond with a view to promoting the welfare of the peoples of South Asia and to improve their quality of life through accelerated economic growth, social progress and cultural development.
- reaffirm their condemnation of terrorism in all its forms and manifestations and their determination to combat this menace.
- shall promote and protect all human rights and fundamental freedoms.

Signed at Lahore on the 21st day of February 1999.

Memorandum of Understanding

The Foreign Secretaries of Pakistan and India:

Reaffirming the continued commitment of their respective governments to the principles and purposes of the UN Charter;

Reiterating the determination of both countries to implementing the Simla Agreement in letter and spirit;

Guided by the agreement between their Prime Ministers of 23 September 1998 that an environment of peace and security is in the supreme national interest of both sides and that resolution of all outstanding issues, including Jammu and Kashmir, is essential for this purpose;

Pursuant to the directive given by their respective Prime Ministers in Lahore, to adopt measures for promoting a stable environment of peace, and security between the two countries;

Have on this day, agreed to the following:

1. The two sides shall engage in bilateral consultations on security concepts, and nuclear doctrines, with a view to developing measures for confidence building in the nuclear and conventional fields, aimed at avoidance of conflict.
2. The two sides undertake to provide each other with advance notification in respect of ballistic missile flight tests, and shall conclude a bilateral agreement in this regard.
3. The two sides are fully committed to undertaking national measures to reducing the risks of accidental or unauthorized use of nuclear weapons under their respective control. The two sides further undertake to notify each other immediately in the event of any accidental, unauthorized or unexplained incident that could create the risk of a fallout with adverse consequences for both sides, or an outbreak of a nuclear war between the two countries, as well as to adopt measures aimed at diminishing the possibility of such actions, or such incidents

being misinterpreted by the other. The two sides shall identify/establish the appropriate communication mechanism for this purpose.

4. The two sides shall continue to abide by their respective unilateral moratorium on conducting further nuclear test explosions unless either side, in exercise of its national sovereignty decides that extraordinary events have jeopardized its supreme interest.

5. The two sides shall conclude an agreement on prevention of incidents at sea in order to ensure safety of navigation by naval vessels, and aircraft belonging to the two sides.

6. The two sides shall periodically review the implementation of existing Confidence Building Measures (CBMs) and where necessary, setup appropriate consultative mechanisms to monitor and ensure effective implementation of these CBMs.

7. The two sides shall undertake a review of the existing communication links (e.g. between the respective Directors General, Military Operations) with a view to upgrading and improving these links, and to provide for fail-safe and secure communications.

8. The two sides shall engage in bilateral consultations on security, disarmament and non-proliferation issues within the context of negotiations on these issues in multilateral fora.

Where required, the technical details of the above measures will be worked out by experts of the two sides in meetings to be held on mutually agreed dates, before mid 1999, with a view to reaching bilateral agreements.

Done at Lahore on 21 February 1999 in the presence of Prime Minister of India Atal Bihari Vajpayee and Prime Minister of Pakistan Mohammad Nawaz Sharif.

(Shamshad Ahmad)   (K. Raghunath)
Foreign Secretary of the   Foreign Secretary of the
Islamic Republic of Pakistan.   Republic of India.

Appendix III: Musharraf–Aziz Conversations (May 1999)

(See pages 261 and 269)

Transcripts of two telephone conversations between Lt.-Gen. Mohammad Aziz Khan, Chief of General Staff and General Pervez Musharraf, Chief of Army Staff, then on a visit to China on 26 and 29 May 1999, and intercepted by Indian Intelligence Agency (RAW)

P: Pakistan: Lieutenant General Mohammad Aziz Khan

C: China: General Pervez Musharraf

First recording (26 May 1999)

P: How is the visit going?

C: Yes, very well, Okay. And, what else is the news on that side?

P: *Ham-dul-ullah*. There is no change on the ground situation. They have started rocketing and strafing. That has been upgraded a little. It has happened yesterday also and today. Today high altitude bombing has been done.

C: On their side, in those positions?

P: In those positions, but in today's bombing about three bombs landed on our side of the Line of Control. No damage, Sir.

C: Is it quite a lot?

P: Sir, about 12–13 bombs were dropped, from which three fell on our side, which does not appear to be a result of inaccuracy. In my interpretation, it is a sort of giving of a message that if need be, we can do it on the other side as well. It is quite a distance apart. Where the bombs have been dropped, they have tried to drop from a good position where they are in difficulty, from behind the LoC but they have fallen on our side of the LoC. So I have spoken to the Foreign Secretary and I have told him that he should make the appropriate noises about this in the Press.

C: They (Indians) should also be told.

P: That we have told, Foreign Secretary will also say and Rashid will also say. He will not, generally speaking, make any such mistake about those other bombs falling on the other side, our stand should be that all these bombs are falling on our side. We will not come into that situation. The guideline that they have given, we have stressed that we should say that this build-up and employment of air strike which has been done under the garb of....us (?), actually they are targeting our position on the LoC and our logistic build-up, these possibly they are taking under the garb having intention for operation the craft (?) Line of Control, and this need to be taken note of and we would retaliate in kind....is what happened? So, to the entire build-up we want to give this colour.

C: Absolutely okay. Yes, this is better. After that, has there been any talk with them? Any meetings etc?

P: Yesterday, again, in the evening.

C: Who all were there?

P: Actually, we insisted that a meeting should be held, because otherwise that friend of ours, the incumbent of my old chair, we thought lest he give some interpretation of his own, we should do something ourselves by going there.

C: Was he a little disturbed? I heard that there was some trouble in Sialkot.

P: Yes, There was one in Daska. On this issue there was trouble. Yes, he was a little disturbed about that but I told him that such small things keep happening and we can reply to such things in a better way.

C: Absolutely.

P: There is no such thing to worry.

C: So that briefing to Mian Sahib that we did, was the forum the same as where we had done previously? There, at Jamshed's place?

P: No. In Mian Sahib's office.

C: Oh I see. There. What was he saying?

P: From here we had gone—Choudhary Zafar Sahib, Mahmud, myself and Tauqir. Because before going, Tauqir had spoken with his counterpart. We carried that tape with us.

C: So, what was he (Indian counterpart) saying?

P: That is very interesting. When you come, I will play it for you. Its focus was that these infiltrators, who are sitting here, they have your help and artillery support, without which they could not have come to J and K. This is not a very friendly act and it is against the spirit of the Lahore Declaration. Then Tauqir told him that if your boys tried to physically attack the Line of Control and go beyond it....and that the bombs were planted on the Turtok bridge and the dead body received in the process was returned with military honours and I said, I thought that there was good enough indication you would not enter into this type of misadventure, and all this build-up that you are doing—one or more brigade strength and 50–60 aircraft are being collected. These are excuses for undertaking some operations against the various spaces, so I had put him on the defensive. Then he said the same old story. He would put three points again and again that they (militants) should not be supported, and without your support they could not be there, they have sophisticated weapons and we will flush them out, we will not let them stay there. But this is not a friendly act.

C: So, did they talk of coming out and meeting somewhere?

P: No, no, they did not.

C: Was there some other talk of putting pressure on us?

P: No. He only said that they (militants) will be given suitable reception. This term he used. He said they will be flushed out, and every time Tauqir said that please tell us some detail, detail about how many have gone into your area, what is happening there? Then I will ask the concerned people and then we will get back to you. So whenever he asked these details, he would say, we will talk about this when we meet, then I will give details. This means, they are possibly looking forward to the next round of talks, in which the two sides could meet. This could be the next round of talks between the two PMs which they are expecting it....Sir, very good thing, no problem...

C: So, many times we had discussed, taken your (PM's?...) blessings and yesterday also I told him that the door of discussion, dialogue must be kept open and rest, no change in ground situation.

P: So, no one was in a particularly disturbed, frame of mind.

C: Even your seat man?

P: Yes, he was disturbed. Also, Malik Sahib was disturbed, as they had been even earlier. Those two's views were that the status quo and the present position of Gen Hassan (?) no change should be recommended in that. But he was also saying that any escalation after that should be regulated as there may be the danger of war. On this logic, we gave the suggestion that there was no such fear as the scruff (*tooti*) of their (militants) neck is in our hands, whenever you want, we could regulate it. Choudhary Zafar Sahib coped very well. He gave a very good presentation of our viewpoint. He said we had briefed the PM earlier and given an assessment. After this, we played the tape of Tauqir. Then he said that what we are seeing, that was our assessment, and those very stages of the military situation were being seen, which it would not be a problem for us to handle. Rest, it was for your guidance how to deal with the political and diplomatic aspects. We told him there is no reason of alarm and panic. <u>Then he said that when I came to know seven days back, when Corps Commanders were told</u>. The entire reason of the success of this operation was this total secrecy. Our experience was that our earlier efforts failed because of lack of secrecy. So the top priority is to accord confidentiality, to ensure our success. We should respect this and the advantage we have from this would give us a handle. (*underlining added*).

C: Rest (*baqi*), is Mian Sahib okay?

P: Ok. He was confident just like that but for the other two. Shamshad as usual was supporting. Today, for the last two hours the BBC has been continuously reporting on the air strikes by India. Keep using this—let them keep dropping bombs. As far as internationalization is concerned, this is the fastest this has happened. You may have seen in the press about UN Secretary General Kofi Annan's appeal that both countries should sit and talk.

Second recording (29 May 1999)

P: This Is Pakistan. Give me Room No. 83315 (same room number). Hello.

C: Hello Aziz.

P: The situation on ground is okay, no change. This area but it is not brought down by attack. One of their MI-17 arms (?) was brought down. Further, the position is, we had approached to our position, it was brought down. Rest is okay. Nothing else except, there is a development. Have you listened to yesterday's news regarding Mian Sahib speaking to his counterpart. He told him that the spirit of Lahore Declaration and escalation has been done by your people. Specially wanted to speak to me thereafter. He told Indian PM that they should have waited instead of upping the ante by using Air Force and all other means. He (Nawaz) told him (Indian PM) that he suggested Sartaj Aziz could go to New Delhi to explore the possibility of defusing the tension.

C: Okay.

P: Which is likely to take place, most probably tomorrow.

C: Okay.

P: Our other friend (Lt.-Gen. Ziauddin, DG ISI…?… or could be United States) might have also put pressure on. For that, today they will have a discussion at Foreign Office about 9.30 and Zafar Sahib (Lt.-Gen. Saeed-uz-Zaman Zafar, GOC 11 Corps and Acting Chief) is supposed to attend.

C: Okay.

P: Aziz Sahib (Sartaj Aziz, Foreign, Minister) has discussed with me and my recommendation is that dialogue option is always open. But in their first meeting, they must give no understanding or no commitment on ground situation.

C: Very correct. You or Mahmud (GOC X Corps, Rawalpindi) must have to go with Zafar. Because, they don't know about the ground situation.

P: This week, we are getting together at 8'o clock because meeting will be at 9.30, so Zafar Sahib will deliberate it. We want to suggest to Zafar that they have to maintain that they will not be talking about ground situation. All that you say. So far as the ground situation is concerned. Subsequently, DGMOs can discuss with each other and work out the modus operandi.

C: Idea on LoC.

P: Yes. Hint is that, given that the LoC has many areas where the interpretation of either side is not what the other side believes. So, comprehensive deliberation is required. So, that can be worked out by DGMOs.

C: If they are assured that we are here from a long period. We have been sitting here for long. Like in the beginning, the matter is the same—no post was attacked and no post was captured. The situation is that we are along our defensive Line of Control. If it is not in his (Sartaj Aziz's) knowledge, then discuss it altogether. Emphasise that for years, we are here only.

C: Yes, this point should be raised. We are sitting on the same LoC since a long period.

P: This is their weakness. They are not agreed on the demarcation under UN's verification, whereas we are agreed. We want to exploit it.

C: This is in Simla Agreement that we cannot go for UN intervention.

P: Our neighbour does not accept their presence or UNMOGIP arrangement for survey for the area. So, we can start from the top, from 9842 (NJ 9842). On this line, we can give them logic but in short, the recommendation for Sartaj Aziz Sahib is that he should make no commitment in the first meeting on military situation. And he should not even accept ceasefire, because if there is ceasefire, then vehicles will be moving (on Dras-Kargil highway). In this regard, they have to use their own argument that whatever is interfering with you. That we don't know but there is no justification about tension on LoC. No justification. We want to give them this type of brief so that he does not get into any specifics.

C: Alright.

P: In this connection, we want your approval and what is your programme.

C: I will come tomorrow. We are just leaving within an hour. We are going to Shenzhen. From there, by evening, we will be in Hong Kong. There will be a flight tomorrow from Hong Kong. So, we will be there at Lahore in the evening, via Bangkok flight.

P: Sunday evening, you will be at Lahore. We will also indicate that, if there is more critical situation, then it (Sartaj visit) should be deferred for another day or two. We can discuss on Monday and then do.

C: Has this MI-17 not fallen in our area?

P: No sir. This has fallen in their area. We have not claimed it. We have got it claimed through the mujahideen.

C: Well done.

P: But top wise side, crashing straight before our eyes.

C: Very good. Now are they facing any greater difficulty in flying them? Are they scared or not? This also you should note. Are they coming any less nearer?

P: Yes. There is a lot of pressure on them. They were talking about greater air defence than they had anticipated. They can't afford to lose any more aircraft. There has been less intensity of air flying after that.

C: Very good. First class. Is there any build up on the ground?

P: Just like that but the movement is pretty sluggish and slow. One or two are coming near no. 6. Till now only one call sign in which one has not reached the valley so far. Now the air people and the ground people will stay back and then the situation will be okay.

C: See you in the evening.

Appendix IV: Review Petition in the Supreme Court (May 2000)

(See page 295)

In the Supreme Court of Pakistan Review Petition under Article 188 of the Constitution of Pakistan on The Judgement dated 29 May 2000 on Const. Petition No. 63 of 1999

1. Wasim Sajjad
    Son of (Late) Sajjad Ahmed Jan
    (Chairman Senate)
    R/o H.No. 28, St. 5,
    Sector E-7, Islamabad.

2. Illahi Bux Soomro
    Son of Haji Allah Bux Soomro
    (Speaker National Assembly)
    R/o 232 Somerset Street
    P.I. Lines, Karachi.

3. Raja Zafar ul Haq
    Son of Raja Fazal dad Khan
    (Leader of the House in the Senate)
    R/o H.No. 36, St. 39,
    Sector G-7/4, Islamabad.

4. Ch. Pervez Elahi
    Son of Ch. Manzoor Elahi
    (Speaker Punjab Provincial Assembly)
    R/o 33-C, Gulberg, Lahore

....Petitioners

VS

1. Federation of Pakistan,
    Through Secretary Cabinet Division

2. General Pervez Musharraf
    Chief Executive

516

3.   National Security Council
      Islamabad.

RESPONDENTS

Invocation of the Law of Necessity

The judgement of this Hon'ble Court has far reaching implications for democracy and the Constitutional dispensation in Pakistan. This Hon'ble Court has justified suspension of the Constitution and the removal of democratically elected governments by the armed forces on the ground of state necessity. This Court has also held that the Constitution of Pakistan remains the Supreme Law of the land and the Superior Courts continue to function there-under. There is thus an error apparent on the face of the record because these propositions being contradictory in nature cannot both be correct. Either the Constitution can be supreme or the law of necessity is supreme. By holding that the constitution can be validly suspended on grounds of state necessity, this Hon'ble Court has in fact relegated the Constitution to a position inferior to the law of necessity. In substance it means that the constitution which embodies the will and aspirations of the 140 million people of Pakistan can be nullified by the act of an individual or a group of individuals on grounds of state necessity.

It is a matter of public knowledge that on 12-10-99, when the army intervention took place, all the institutions created under the Constitution were functioning. Sessions of the National Assembly and the Senate had been called and they were to meet within days. The civil administration was performing its duties in the normal manner. Business and industrial activities were proceeding normally. The courts were also performing their duties in accordance with the Constitution and the Law. There was thus no break-down or collapse of the Constitutional machinery....

The petitioners had submitted before this Hon'ble Court that the Law of Necessity was a dead doctrine and was wrongly invoked in the Nusrat Bhutto Case. Since the judgement was delivered in 1977, this Hon'ble Court has itself observed in the Liaquat Hussain Case that the Law of Necessity can not be invoked if its effect is to violate any provision of the Constitution. Nevertheless, even these factors were not present on 12-10-99 to re-invoke the Law of Necessity. There is thus, an error apparent on the face of the record in the extension of the Nusrat Bhutto Case to the situation as it existed on 12 October 1999 because as a consequence, military intervention can take place any time, to remove any constitutionally elected government reducing the Constitution to a meaningless piece of paper. Allegations of corruption against the Government and its functionaries (which have been denied and will be dealt with later) misgovernance, tapping of telephones etc. are allegations which have consistently been made in the past and will continue to be made in the future. As a result Constitutional governance—which is the only way in which civilized countries are ruled—will for ever remain an elusive dream in Pakistan.

That it is a matter of faith with the people of Pakistan that Supreme Sovereign is Almighty Allah and the Constitution and other laws are made by the representatives of the people under this delegated Authority. In such an ideological state, the concept of necessity has no place whatsoever and in any case is contrary to Article 2A of the

Constitution of Pakistan, which incorporates the preamble to the Constitution as a substantive part thereof. In the respectful submission of the Petitioners, Article 2A can never be suspended nor is there a finding by this Hon'ble Court to the contrary. There is thus an error on the face of the record in as much as Article 2A has not been considered at all in the context of the over all judgement of the Court.

In invoking the doctrine of necessity this Hon'ble Court has observed that the constitution had been rendered un-workable and provided no solution to the situation that had arisen. The immediate cause for the military take-over on 12-10-99 was the removal by the Prime Minister of the Chief of Army Staff and Chairman Joint Chiefs of Staff Committee and his replacement by Lt.-Gen. Ziauddin. The Chief of Army Staff is on record having stated that what happened on 12-10-99 was not a coup but a counter coup. That being so the question arises whether the Constitution provided a remedy for this situation and if so what is the nature of that remedy. An obvious answer is that if the Chief of Army Staff felt aggrieved by the action taken he had a remedy by way of petition before this Hon'ble Court as well as the High Court. He could have urged—as has been suggested by this Hon'ble Court, that the action was taken without a show cause notice. It may be pointed out that there is a precedent when a Prime Minister wrongly removed from office was re-instated under orders of the Supreme Court. Reference may be made to PLD 1993 SC 473 by which judgement Nawaz Sharif was restored to the office of Prime Minister after the court held that his removal by the President was against the Constitution. Thus there was a solution within the Constitution for the situation which led to military action.

In any event while holding that removal of the Chief of Army Staff was invalid for the reason that he had not been served with a show cause notice, this Hon'ble Court failed to notice that holders of several Constitutional Posts like the Chairman Senate and Speaker National Assembly and speaker of Provincial Assemblies were also removed/suspended without a show cause notice. On a parity of reasoning all those holders of Constitutional positions were similarly entitled to reinstatement and to a declaration that their removal/suspension was illegal.

None of the alleged grievances against the government—including the charges of corruption and lack of good governance were such which could not have been redressed within the four corners of the Constitution. Laws and machinery to redress such grievances were already in existence and further, if as alleged, the government of the day did not take appropriate steps it was open to this Hon'ble Court to direct the taking of specific steps in exercise of powers under Article 184(3) of the Constitution read with Article 187 thereof. Therefore the observation of this Hon'ble Court that Law of Necessity could validly be invoked to suspend the Supreme Law of the country namely the Constitution as it had no answer to the situation that had arisen needs to be reviewed....

Collapse of the Economy

In paragraphs 237 and 238 of the judgement, this Hon'ble Court has dealt with the argument that the economy had collapsed thus justifying military take-over. The court has observed 'that the combined effect of the overall policies and methodology adopted by the former government was the total collapse of the country's economy in as much as GDP growth during the past 3 years had hardly kept pace with the growth of population and Pakistan has a debt burden which equals the country's entire national income. The Court also took judicial notice of the fact that the trade imbalance was persistent and due to defective economic policies and lack of economic discipline by the previous regime, the industrial sector had suffered a great set-back.

The concern of this Hon'ble Court regarding the state of Pakistan's economy is understandable; however it would be an over-simplification to place the entire responsibility for the bad state of the economy on the performance of the Government during the last 30 months prior to military take-over. The economy of the country is a very complex phenomena and there are many chronic factors which are responsible for the state of affairs in which the country finds itself today. Dr Hafiz Pasha, the former Deputy Chairman Planning Commission and currently a member of Economic Advisory Committee of the present government, presented on 27 October 1999, a statement to the five member Commonwealth Ministerial Delegation led by Lloyd Axworthy, Foreign Minister of Canada. The main purpose of this statement was to answer the fundamental questions 'whether the economy was beginning to show some signs of recovery or was in a state of collapse at the time of military take-over'.

After a succinct and objective analysis of all the relevant factors and figures, the statement presented the following main conclusions to the Commonwealth delegation:

a)   The main indicators of an economic collapse, in the light of recent East Asian crisis, include (i) steep currency depreciation along with a severe haemorrhaging of the foreign exchange reserves; (ii) banking system comes under severe strain and share prices tumble precipitously; (iii) there is a run on deposits and some banks may even fail; (iv) interest rates shoot up and the process of financial dis-intermediation becomes clearly visible; (v) prices of essential commodities rise exponentially, with shortages and import bottlenecks.

b)   None of these manifestations of a financial crisis was evident on 12 October 1999. The exchange rate was stable with a depreciation of only 1 per cent in 4½ months and foreign exchange reserves of $1.5 billion were the highest in three years. The share market index having declined to 750 in December 1998 as a result of the sanctions imposed in June 1998 had recovered to 1257 on 12 October 1999. The banking system was not under any exceptional strain, the fiscal deficit had declined and the inflation rate had fallen to a record low of 3.3 per cent in July–September 1999.

c)   The real economy was also showing signs of recovery; industrial production had been showing a steady growth of 5 per cent since February 1999 and with a bumper cotton crop, agricultural growth was recovering.

d)   Overall, it would be fair to say that the economy was not in a state of collapse on 12 October 1999. If anything, there were visible signs of recovery both in financial and real sectors of the economy.

The London 'Economist' of October 23-29, 1999, in its comments on the military take-over echoed similar views in the following words:

'The economy the General inherited from Nawaz Sharif was reviving. Growth for the fiscal year, which ends on 30 June, was expected, before the coup to be 3.9–4.4 per cent. Inflation is at its lowest level in 12 years. After a <u>de facto</u> default last year, Pakistan has built up an adequate level of foreign exchange. Before the coup, the government was close to an agreement with the IMF that would have released a vital $280 million loan instalment'....

In the light of the comparison of certain key economic indicators before and after 12 October 1999, the performance of the economy is not and cannot be valid factor for the removal of an elected government or for invoking the Law of Necessity.

Duration of Military Rule

This Hon'ble Court has allowed a period of 3 years to the Chief Executive for return to democratic constitutional government with effect from 12 October 1999. In fixing the period of 3 years, this Hon'ble Court has been influenced by the following factors:

a)   That according to the Attorney General, the Chief Election Commissioner had reported that the preparation of Electoral Rolls will take two years. Thereafter, some time will be required for delimitation of constituencies and disposal of objections, etc.

b)   Judicial notice has been taken of the fact that ex-Senator Sartaj Aziz moved Constitutional Petition No. 15 of 1996 seeking a mandamus to the concerned authorities for preparation of fresh electoral rolls as according to him, the position to the contrary was tantamount to perpetuate dis-enfranchisement of millions of people of Pakistan in violation of Articles 17 and 19 of the Constitution. Similar petition bearing No. 53 of 1996 had also been filed by the MQM.

Section 17 of the Electoral Rolls act, 1974 places a responsibility on the Chief Election Commissioner to revise the rolls annually. This is also the practice in countries which have a Parliamentary System of government because in such systems, elections may be called at any time. In view of statuary provisions, there cannot be any justification for requiring 2 years to prepare fresh electoral rolls.

According to a report published in the 'Daily News' Lahore of June 2000, the Chief Election Commissioner has asked the National Database and Registration Authority to prepare computerized electoral rolls by September 2000 for the local council elections. According to this schedule, even the fresh draft electoral rolls will be ready by September 2000 and the final rolls by November 2000. The basis on which this Hon'ble Court has provided a 3 years time frame for holding elections would not therefore appear to be justified.

In addition this Honourable Court has committed a fundamental error, which is apparent from the face of the record, in holding (in paragraph 15 of the Short Order) that Sartaj Aziz had filed C.P. No. 15 of 1996 seeking a direction to the concerned authorities for preparation of fresh electoral rolls. The factual position is not merely different but, in fact, is the exact opposite. C.P. No. 15 of 1996 was filed seeking not a direction for preparation of fresh electoral rolls but a direction preventing the preparation of fresh electoral rolls since the argument was that the law contemplated an annual process of revising and updating electoral rolls and not a preparation of fresh electoral rolls. This is an error apparent on the face of the record which can be confirmed by a perusal of the said petition. It is respectfully submitted that, in the light of the above, it is clear that this Honourable Court has committed two errors, one of which pertains to procedure and the other which relates to substance.

On the procedural plane it has to be pointed out that C.P. No. 15 of 1996 was neither referred to in the arguments advanced on behalf of the Petitioner and nor in those put forward o behalf of the Respondents. This Honourable Court referred to the said petition on its own and without seeking the benefit of arguments from either side. If this Honourable Court had sought a clarification form the counsel appearing in the case in relation to the facts of the above mentioned petition this error would not have occurred.

Secondly, as far as the substantive aspect of the matter is concerned, now that the correct facts have been brought to the notice of this Honourable Court, it will be manifest that the decision to grant time for preparation of fresh electoral rolls was taken on the basis of a fundamental misconception and thus needs to be reconsidered. It is prayed that the period of 3 years be curtailed and the Chief Executive be directed to hold elections forthwith.

It is therefore prayed that the short order dated 12 May 2000 and the detailed judgement dated 29 May 2000 be reviewed and the Army takeover of the country on 12 October 1999 the Provisional Constitution Order No. 1 dated 14 October 1999, the proclamation of emergency of the same date and all orders, enactments and instruments issued thereunder be declared to be violative of the constitution and of no legal effect. It also prayed that the judgement aforesaid be reviewed and:

a) The power of amendment of the constitution granted to the Chief Executive be withdrawn being against all notions of democracy and the basic principles of the constitution as also of Article 2A thereof.

b) The period of 3 years granted to the Chief Executive for return to constitutional and democratic governance be curtailed as it is based on a serious misconception and fundamental error and the Chief Executive be directed to hold elections forthwith to the Provincial Assemblies, the National Assembly and the Senate.

c) Any other relief to which the petitioners may be entitled from the facts and circumstances stated in this petition may also be granted.

Appendix V: The Charter of Democracy (July 2006)

(See page 311)

The Charter of Democracy signed between Nawaz Sharif and Benazir Bhutto in London on 14 July 2006

We the elected leaders of Pakistan have deliberated on the political crisis in our beloved homeland, the threats to its survival, the erosion of the federation's unity, the military's subordination of all state institutions, the marginalization of civil society, the mockery of the Constitution and representative institutions, growing poverty, unemployment and inequality, brutalization of society, breakdown of rule of law and, the unprecedented hardships facing our people under a military dictatorship, which has pushed our beloved country to the brink of a total disaster.

Noting the most devastating and traumatic experiences that our nation experienced under military dictatorships that played havoc with the nation's destiny and created conditions disallowing the progress of our people and the flowering of democracy. Even after removal from office they undermined the people's mandate and the sovereign will of the people.

Drawing history's lesson that the military dictatorship and the nation cannot co-exist—as military involvement adversely affect the economy and the democratic institutions as well as the defence capabilities, and the integrity of the country—the nation needs a new direction different from a militaristic and regimental approach of the Bonapartist regimes, as the current one.

Taking serious exception to the vilification campaign against the representatives of the people, in particular, and the civilians, in general, the victimization of political leaders/workers and their media trials under a Draconian law in the name of accountability, in order to divide and eliminate the representative political parties, to Gerrymander a king's party and concoct legitimacy to prolong the military rule.

Noting our responsibility to our people to set an alternative direction for the country saving it from its present predicaments on an economically sustainable, socially progressive, politically democratic and pluralist, federally cooperative, ideologically tolerant, internationally respectable and regionally peaceful basis in the larger interests of the peoples of Pakistan to decide once for all that only the people and no one else has the sovereign right to govern through their elected representatives, as conceived by the democrat par excellence, Father of the Nation Quaid-i-Azam Mohammad Ali Jinnah.

Reaffirming our commitment to undiluted democracy and universally recognized fundamental rights, the rights of a vibrant opposition, internal party democracy, ideological/political tolerance, bipartisan working of the parliament through powerful committee system, a cooperative federation with no discrimination against federating units, the decentralization and devolution of power, maximum provincial autonomy, the empowerment of the people at the grassroots level, the emancipation of our people from poverty, ignorance, want and disease, the uplift of women and minorities, the elimination of Kalashnikov culture, a free and independent media, an independent judiciary, a neutral civil service, rule of law and merit, the settlement of disputes with the neighbours through peaceful means, honouring international contracts, laws/covenants and sovereign guarantees, so as to achieve a responsible and civilized status in the comity of nations through a foreign policy that suits our national interests.

Calling upon the people of Pakistan to join hands to save our motherland from the clutches of military dictatorship and to defend their fundamental, social, political and economic rights and for a democratic, federal, modern and progressive Pakistan as dreamt by the Founder of the nation; have adopted the following, 'Charter of Democracy':

Text of the Charter of Democracy

A. CONSTITUTIONAL AMENDMENTS

1. The 1973 Constitution as on 12 October 1999 before the military coup shall be restored with the provisions of joint electorates, minorities, and women reserved seats on closed party list in the Parliament, the lowering of the voting age, and the increase in seats in parliament and the Legal Framework Order, 2000 and the Seventeenth Constitutional Amendment shall be repealed accordingly.

2. The appointment of the governors, three services chiefs and the CJCSC shall be made by the chief executive who is the prime minister, as per the 1973 Constitution.

3. (a) The recommendations for appointment of judges to superior judiciary shall be formulated through a commission, which shall comprise of the following: (i) The chairman shall be a chief justice, who has never previously taken oath under the PCO. (ii) The members of the commission shall be the chief justices of the provincial high courts who have not taken oath under the PCO, failing which the senior most judge of that high court who has not taken oath shall be the member. (iii) Vice-Chairmen of Pakistan and Vice-Chairmen of Provincial Bar Association with respect to the appointment of judges to their concerned province. (iv) President of Supreme Court Bar Association. (v) Presidents of High Court Bar Associations of Karachi, Lahore, Peshawar, and Quetta with respect to the appointment of judges to their concerned province. (vi) Federal Minister for Law and Justice. (vii) Attorney General of Pakistan. (a-i) The commission shall forward a panel of three names for each vacancy to the prime minister, who shall forward one name for confirmation to joint parliamentary committee for confirmation of the nomination through a transparent public hearing process. (a-ii) The joint parliamentary committee shall comprise of 50 per cent members from the treasury benches and the remaining 50 per cent from opposition parties based on their strength in the parliament nominated by respective parliamentary leaders.

(b) No judge shall take oath under any Provisional Constitutional Order or any other oath that is contradictory to the exact language of the original oath prescribed in the Constitution of 1973.

(c) Administrative mechanism will be instituted for the prevention of misconduct, implementation of code of ethics, and removal of judges on such charges brought to its attention by any citizen through the proposed commission for appointment of Judges. (d) All special courts including anti-terrorism and accountability courts shall be abolished and such cases be tried in ordinary courts. Further to create a set of rules and procedures whereby, the arbitrary powers of the chief justices over the assignment of cases to various judges and the transfer of judges to various benches such powers shall be exercised by the Chief Justice and two senior most judges sitting together.

4. A Federal Constitutional Court will be setup to resolve constitutional issues, giving equal representation to each of the federating units, whose members may be judges or persons qualified to be judges of the Supreme Court, constituted for a six-year period. The Supreme and High Courts will hear regular civil and criminal cases. The appointment of judges shall be made in the same manner as for judges of higher judiciary.

5. The Concurrent List in the Constitution will be abolished. A new NFC award will be announced.

6. The reserved seats for women in the national and provincial assemblies will be allocated to the parties on the basis of the number of votes polled in the general elections by each party.

7. The strength of the Senate of Pakistan shall be increased to give representation to minorities in the Senate.

8. FATA shall be included in the NWFP province in consultation with them.

9. Northern Areas shall be developed by giving it a special status and further empowering the Northern Areas Legislative Council to provide people of Northern Areas access to justice and human rights.

10. Local bodies election will be held on party basis through provincial election commissions in respective provinces and constitutional protection will be given to the local bodies to make them autonomous and answerable to their respective assemblies as well as to the people through regular courts of law.

B. CODE OF CONDUCT

11. National Security Council will be abolished. Defence Cabinet Committee will be headed by prime minister and will have a permanent secretariat. The prime minister may appoint a federal security adviser to process intelligence reports for the prime minister. The efficacy of the higher defence and security structure, created two decades ago, will be reviewed. The Joint Services Command structure will be strengthened and made more effective and headed in rotation among the three services by law.

12. The ban on a 'prime minister not being eligible for a third term of office' will be abolished.

13. (a) Truth and Reconciliation Commission be established to acknowledge victims of torture, imprisonment, state-sponsored persecution, targeted legislation, and

politically motivated accountability. The commission will also examine and report its findings on military coups and civil removals of governments from 1996. (b) A commission shall also examine and identify the causes of and fix responsibility and make recommendations in the light thereof for incidences such as Kargil. (c) Accountability of NAB and other Ehtesab operators to identify and hold accountable abuse of office by NAB operators through purgery and perversion of justice and violation of human rights since its establishment. (d) To replace politically motivated NAB with an independent accountability commission, whose chairman shall be nominated by the prime minister in consultation with the leader of opposition and confirmed by a joint parliamentary committee with 50 per cent members from treasury benches and remaining 50 per cent from opposition parties in same manner as appointment of judges through transparent public hearing. The confirmed nominee shall meet the standard of political impartiality, judicial propriety, moderate views expressed through his judgements and would have not dealt.

14. The press and electronic media will be allowed its independence. Access to information will become law after parliamentary debate and public scrutiny.

15. The chairmen of public accounts committee in the national and provincial assemblies will be appointed by the leaders of opposition in the concerned assemblies.

16. An effective Nuclear Command and Control system under the Defence Cabinet Committee will be put in place to avoid any possibility of leakage or proliferation.

17. Peaceful relations with India and Afghanistan will be pursued without prejudice to outstanding disputes.

18. Kashmir dispute should be settled in accordance with the UN Resolutions and the aspirations of the people of Jammu and Kashmir.

19. Governance will be improved to help the common citizen, by giving access to quality social services like education, health, job generation, curbing price hike, combating illegal redundancies, and curbing lavish spendings in civil and military establishments as ostentious causes great resentment amongst the teeming millions. We pledge to promote and practice simplicity, at all levels.

20. Women, minorities, and the under privileged will be provided equal opportunities in all walks of life.

21. We will respect the electoral mandate of representative governments that accepts the due role of the opposition and declare neither shall undermine each other through extra constitutional ways.

22. We shall not join a military regime or any military sponsored government. No party shall solicit the support of military to come into power or to dislodge a democratic government.

23. To prevent corruption and floor crossing all votes for the Senate and indirect seats will be by open identifiable ballot. Those violating the party discipline in the poll shall stand disqualified by a letter from the parliamentary party leader to the concerned Speaker or the Chairman Senate with a copy to the Election Commission for notification purposes within 14 days of receipt of letter failing which it will be deemed to have been notified on the expiry of that period.

24. All military and judicial officers will be required to file annual assets and income declarations like Parliamentarians to make them accountable to the public.
25. National Democracy Commission shall be established to promote and develop a democratic culture in the country and provide assistance to political parties for capacity building on the basis of their seats in parliament in a transparent manner.
26. Terrorism and militancy are by-products of military dictatorship, negation of democracy, are strongly condemned, and will be vigorously confronted.

C. FREE AND FAIR ELECTIONS

27. There shall be an independent, autonomous, and impartial election commission. The prime minister shall in consultation with leader of opposition forward up to three names for each position of chief election commissioner, members of election commission and secretary, to joint parliamentary committee, constituted on the same pattern as for appointment of judges in superior judiciary, through transparent public hearing process. In case of no consensus, both prime minister and leader of opposition shall forward separate lists to the joint parliamentary committee for consideration. Provincial election commissioner shall be appointed on the same pattern by committees of respective provincial assemblies.
28. All contesting political parties will be ensured a level playing field in the elections by the release of all political prisoners and the unconditional return of all political exiles. Elections shall be open to all political parties and political personalities. The graduation requirement of eligibility which has led to corruption and fake degrees will be repealed.
29. Local bodies elections will be held within three months of the holding of general elections.
30. The concerned election authority shall suspend and appoint neutral administrators for all local bodies from the date of formation of a caretaker government for holding of general elections till the elections are held.
31. There shall be a neutral caretaker government to hold free, fair, and transparent elections. The members of the said government and their immediate relatives shall not contest elections.

D. CIVIL–MILITARY RELATIONS

32. The ISI, MI and other security agencies shall be accountable to the elected government through Prime Minister Sectt, Ministry of Defence, and Cabinet Division respectively. Their budgets will be approved by DCC after recommendations are prepared by the respective ministry. The political wings of all intelligence agencies will be disbanded. A committee will be formed to cut waste and bloat in the armed forces and security agencies in the interest of the defence and security of the country. All senior postings in these agencies shall be made with the approval of the government through respective ministry.
33. All indemnities and savings introduced by military regimes in the constitution shall be reviewed.
34. Defence budget shall be placed before the parliament for debate and approval.

35. Military land allotment and cantonment jurisdictions will come under the purview of defence ministry. A commission shall be setup to review, scrutinize, and examine the legitimacy of all such land allotment rules, regulations, and policies, along with all cases of state land allotment including those of military urban and agricultural land allotments since 12 October, 1999 to hold those accountable who have indulged in malpractices, profiteering, and favouritism.
36. Rules of business of the federal and provincial governments shall be reviewed to bring them in conformity with parliamentary form of government.

(Mohtarma Benazir Bhutto)   **(Mr Nawaz Sharif)**
Chairperson   **Quaid**
Pakistan Peoples Party   **Pakistan Muslim League (N)**

Dated: 14th May, 2006

Appendix VI: APC Declaration of 8 July 2007

(See page 312)

The Declaration adopted by the Conference of 28 Political Parties convened by Mr Nawaz Sharif in London on 8 July 2007, under the title of APC Declaration

We the political parties assembled here together declare that: military dictatorship has brought Pakistan to the edge of a precipice, leading to strife, chaos and the threat of disintegration. The Musharraf regime uses brute state force against its peoples to perpetuate its illegitimate rule and suppress dissent. Innocent citizens are kidnapped by the state as militancy and sectarianism thrive. Provincial autonomy has been denied, leading to further strains in the federation. From Khyber to Karachi, the regime is unable to maintain the writ of the state, and as a consequence there is a total breakdown of law and order.

Parliament has been marginalized and stripped of all its powers. It has no access to information, nor can it legislate or hold the regime accountable. Both houses have been reduced to a rubber stamp for the Chief of Army Staff who unconstitutionally occupies the office of the President. The Cabinet too is subject to the whims of an individual.

Instead of resolving the crisis, the regime muzzled the media to black out ground realities and block live coverage of the turbulence on the streets. Working journalists have been murdered, kidnapped, tortured, detained and harassed. Today, Pakistan has been declared the third most dangerous country for journalists. Having failed to suppress the truth, the regime on 5 June 2007, promulgated an Ordinance while the Senate was in session and the National Assembly was to meet the next day.

On 12 May 2007, at Karachi, an engineered massacre of Opposition workers was orchestrated, unarmed political workers were at the mercy of gun-toting Muttahida Qaumi Movement (MQM) workers while the police and rangers watched. The High Court was laid siege and judges had to run to save themselves. The district courts were surrounded by MQM activists and lawyers including women were beaten. While the federal and provincial regimes watched, 48 innocent people lost their lives and over 200 were injured; yet General Musharraf says there is no need for an inquiry.

Today Balochistan bleeds under the heels of an Army operation, where gunship helicopters are used for silencing dissenting political voices. The murder of Sardar Akbar Bugti on instructions of General Musharraf is most condemnable.

The Musharraf regime is responsible for the highest unemployment in the country. Low grade employees have been axed, trade unions banned, and anti-labour laws have been promulgated and enacted. This, coupled with the cartelization of the economy has allowed big businesses to reap huge profits at the cost of the common man. It has resulted in unprecedented price hike. Today wealth is concentrated in a few big business houses and the market manipulators are in control of political offices.

The regime continues to spend billions of rupees on a political witch-hunt against the Opposition. It continues to institute concocted cases under laws that fail the test of international norms of justice or judicial review. No institution is safe. The due process of law is subverted with impunity and the violation of fundamental rights is the norm. The assault on the judiciary reflects the regime's contempt for law, justice and institutional autonomy. The summoning of the Chief Justice of Pakistan [Iftikhar Muhammad Chaudhry] to the Army House, meeting him in uniform along with heads of intelligence agencies and using coercive measures for his resignation amounts to a total desecration of the office of the Chief Justice of Pakistan. This is General Musharraf's attempt at creating a pliant court in a year when his quest for the presidency is going to be riddled with inherent constitutional disqualifications. The resistance by the bar is unprecedented, it has involved members of the bench, political parties and civil society.

The Musharraf regime is in the process of rewriting the civil military equation, to the advantage of the latter. There is a deliberate attempt at militarization of civil society which is evident from the large scale induction at all levels of serving or retired Army personnel in the civil bureaucracy, police, autonomous and semi-autonomous corporations and bodies.

The national wealth has been plundered through the use of ministerial offices, cartels, stock exchanges, misuse of official information and non-transparent privatization. The mega scams to mention only a few are: the Pakistan Steel Mills, oil pricing, sugar prices, cement prices, Habib Bank, Karachi Electric Supply Corporation, Pakistan Telecommunication Limited, railway engines and locomotives, sale of islands in Sindh, railway golf course, black cabs, purchase of defence lands and the Defence Housing Authority, loan write offs from the banks and not to mention the scandals that have been exposed by the Public Accounts Committee of the National Assembly.

The APC [All Parties Conference] notes that the Charter of Democracy [COD] initiative ratified by the Alliance for the Restoration of Democracy [ARD] is a positive step toward the restoration of the supremacy of civil society and democratic governance.

Since the unconstitutional takeover on 12 October 1999, the state and its institutions have been used to perpetuate General Musharraf's rule. After creating laws that were aimed only to serve one man, the regime now seeks to elect General Musharraf in uniform as the President of Pakistan through the existing assemblies. This act is unconstitutional, morally unjustifiable and smacks of political bankruptcy. Assemblies whose terms are to expire in one month have no moral justification to elect a person for a term of five years. This will constitute 'the mother' of all pre-poll rigging.

It is clear that the Musharraf regime is incapable of holding free, fair and honest elections. The strings of bye-elections held by the regime have exposed its nefarious motives. The Election Commission has been reduced to a hand-maiden of the executive, the electoral rolls prepared by them are seriously flawed, wherein; the number of voters in various districts has been reduced from the rolls of 2002. The orders of the Chief Election Commissioner are flouted and ignored by the federal and provincial functionaries. Polling stations are changed, ballot boxes stuffed, law enforcement agencies used to prevent Opposition voters from coming to the poll stations, polling staff impersonated, false ID cards used, in short the Opposition is contesting the election against the state apparatus. The recent bye-elections in Sindh clearly demonstrated the intent of the regime.

Robbing the people of their democratic right to bring about a peaceful change of government is fraught with dangerous consequences not only for the region, but the federation itself.

Therefore, we the parties assembled here together pledge, in order to make Pakistan a truly democratic state, express our utmost joint commitment towards establishing supremacy of Constitution & rule of law, independence of judiciary, ensuring fair and free election, protecting freedom of media, and depoliticizing military:

(1) To carry on the struggle within and outside Parliament for the restoration of the 1973 Constitution as on 12 October 1999, before the military coup with the provisions of joint electorate, minorities and women reserved seats on closed party list in Parliament, the lowering of the voting age, and the increase in seats in Parliament. The Legal Framework Order [LFO] 2000 and the Seventeenth Constitution Amendment shall be repealed.

(2) The APC demands the immediate resignation of General Musharraf to pave way for holding of fair and free elections under a neutral caretaker government in the country. The APC is of the view that no fair and free election is possible under General Musharraf. If an attempt is made to hold rigged election, as is likely, it further resolves that it shall prevent the rigging of the electoral process at all costs through a coordinated democratic popular movement.

(3) To strongly resist the election by the incumbent assemblies of General Musharraf for the office of the President of Pakistan through all means including the option of resignations from Parliament and the provincial assemblies.

(4) **To jointly struggle for:**

1. The formation of a caretaker government of national consensus, in consultation with the Opposition parties to hold free, fair and honest elections. Its members will not contest the elections.

2. The appointment of a neutral Chief Election Commissioner and members of the Election Commission in consultation with the opposition parties.

3. The dissolution of the local governments three months prior to the holding of the general elections.

4. The caretaker government of national consensus shall appoint officers with no political affiliation in the Election Commission, federal, provincial and district governments.

5. Repeal of all discriminatory election laws, to ensure even playing fields and the implementation of fair election proposals.

6. Implementation of the jointly agreed criteria for holding of fair and free elections as in the annexure.

7. To keep under review the steps being taken to ensure free, fair and honest elections, and to collectively through consensus take any decision, which

may include a boycott of elections in the extreme case at the appropriate time.

8. To firmly resist collectively the machinations of the regime to postpone the general elections by imposing emergency or under any other pretext.

(5) To struggle collectively for the removal of dictatorship from Pakistan and confine the role of the armed forces to that prescribed in the Constitution of 1973. It demands immediate withdrawal of military personnel from all civilian departments and posts. It demands closure of the political cells of all the military, security and intelligence agencies.

(6) **The APC demands in Balochistan the following:**

1. That the Army operation against innocent people of Balochistan is stopped immediately. That all political workers and leaders be released immediately. The construction of cantonments and the deployment of police instead of the levies are stopped. The practice of enforced abductions should be stopped immediately.

2. The APC further resolves that the Army operation against innocent people of tribal areas is stopped immediately. Tribal areas should be cleared of all outside elements, pressures and influences.

(7) To review the current quantum of provincial autonomy and to develop a national consensus on the basis of federal principle to remove grievances of smaller provinces through a consensus.

(8) To ensure the return of Benazir Bhutto and Muhammad Nawaz Sharif, and will resist any attempt on the part of the regime to prevent or take into custody the popular leadership on their return.

(9) We demand that the state stop with immediate effect the kidnapping of its citizens and release immediately all those kidnapped by or through the state. In case of any substantive offence to charge them before a competent court of jurisdiction, allowing defence counsel of their choice and access to family members. It should release all political prisoners including Javed Hashmi, Akhtar Mengal, Afaq Ahmad, Amir Khan, Allama Shabbir Hashmi, Mian Aslam and others.

(10) We reject the construction of new GHQ in Islamabad because a country mired with poverty, unemployment and illiteracy can't afford such mega housing and real estate project costing over $4 billion in market value.

(11) We demand the immediate withdrawal of the Reference and the reinstatement of the Chief Justice of Pakistan. We further pledge to carry on the movement for the independence of the judiciary while wholeheartedly supporting the legal fraternity and civil society in its struggle for rule of law.

(12) We reject the PEMRA Ordinance dated 4 June 2007, while assuring all forms of the media in Pakistan of our fullest support in their struggle for freedom of media and reaffirm our commitment to the freedom of expression.

(13) The APC holds General Musharraf, the Sindh Governor and the provincial government, and the MQM responsible for the carnage carried out in Karachi on 12 May 2007, and demands an independent judicial enquiry by a judge of the Supreme Court to ascertain and identify the persons involved.

(14) The APC condemns recent acts of terrorism in the UK. It further resolves to write a joint memorandum to the UK Government for initiating necessary legal proceedings against Mr Altaf Hussain for his alleged role in incidents of terrorism in Pakistan.

(15) The APC resolves that independent and sovereign foreign policy based on national interests should be pursued. The solution of Kashmir dispute should be found according to wishes and aspirations of the people of Jammu and Kashmir.

Appendix VII

PRESENT:
Mr. Justice Asif Saeed Khan Khosa, CJ
Mr. Justice Mazhar Alam Khan Miankhel
Mr. Justice Syed Mansoor Ali Shah

Constitution Petition No. 39 of 2019
(Against Extension of Tenure of Chief of Army Staff)

The Jurists Foundation through its Chairman

...*Petitioner*

versus

Federal Government through Secretary Ministry of Defence, etc.

...*Respondents*

For the petitioner:	Nemo.
For the respondents:	Mr. Anwar Mansoor Khan, Attorney-General for Pakistan Mian Asghar Ali, Deputy Attorney-General for Pakistan
Date of hearing:	26.11.2019

ORDER

Asif Saeed Khan Khosa, CJ.: The Court-Associate has produced before us a handwritten application statedly submitted by the petitioner seeking permission to withdraw this petition. The petitioner has failed to appear in person nor anybody else has appeared on his behalf. The application received does not carry any date and the same is not accompanied by any affidavit. There is nothing before us to accept or to presume that the said application has actually been submitted by the petitioner himself or that he has submitted the same voluntarily. Be that as it may the petition in hand invokes Article 184(3) of the Constitution and the subject matter of the petition involves a question of public importance with reference to enforcement of fundamental rights and, thus, the individual capacity of the petitioner pales into insignificance even if he decides not to pursue the present petition. The application attributed to the petitioner is, therefore, not entertained.

2.   The learned Attorney-General for Pakistan is in attendance on his own and he has presented before us photocopies of many documents leading to an order passed by the President approving the summary sent to him by the Prime Minister along with his advice for extension/re-appointment of General Qamar Javed Bajwa, Chief of the Army Staff for a fresh term of three years in that office after expiry of his first term in that office. With the assistance of the learned Attorney-General for Pakistan we have gone through the said documents and have *ex facie* noticed the following things:

i)   A summary had initially been moved by the Ministry of Defence for extension of the term of office of the Chief of the Army Staff and subsequently he was appointed as Chief of the Army Staff for a second term of three years after completion of his first term in that office but the learned Attorney-General for Pakistan has not been able to refer to any provision in any legal instrument regarding extension in service of a Chief of the Army Staff upon completion of his first term in that office or for his re-appointment to that office after completion of his first term.

ii)   In the case in hand the Prime Minister had himself passed an order appointing the current Chief of the Army Staff for a second term in that office on 19.08.2019 whereas under Article 243 of the Constitution it is the President who is the appointing authority for that office. Apparently that mistake came to notice straightaway and on the same day, i.e. 19.08.2019 a summary was moved from the Prime Minister's office to the President for extension/re-appointment of the incumbent Chief of the Army Staff and on that very day, i.e. 19.08.2019 the President was pleased to approve the summary in that regard and, hence, the advice of the Prime Minister was apparently accepted and acted upon. It appears that even that process was found to be flawed and on that very day it was realized that the Prime Minister or the President could not take the above mentioned actions without the approval of the Cabinet and, thus, on the next day, i.e. 20.08.2019 a summary was moved in the relevant regard for approval of the Cabinet and on 21.08.2019 the Cabinet was said to have approved the said proposal through circulation. The opinion of the Cabinet recorded in this regard, photocopies whereof have been produced before us, shows that there are 25 members of the Cabinet and out of those 25 members only 11 had agreed to the proposal which shows that the majority of the Cabinet had not approved the said proposal. Yet another peculiar aspect is that after the purported or so-called approval of the Cabinet regarding extension/re-appointment of the incumbent Chief of the Army Staff the matter was never sent to the Prime Minister or the President again for the purposes of a fresh advice or a fresh order of the Prime Minister and the President respectively.

iii)   After our repeated queries the learned Attorney-General for Pakistan has referred to Regulation No. 255 of the Army Regulations (Rules) according to which a retirement of an Army officer can temporarily be suspended or limited. By placing reliance upon the said Regulation the learned Attorney-General for Pakistan has maintained that the Federal Government has the requisite authority to re-appoint or extend the services of an incumbent Chief of the Army Staff prior to his retirement if the exigencies of the service so require or the public interest so demands. A bare perusal of Regulation No. 255, however, *prima facie* shows that the said provision can be invoked after an officer has already retired from service and that is why the said Regulation speaks of suspension of retirement or limiting of retirement. Suspending a retirement or limiting a retirement before the retirement has actually taken effect may amount to putting the cart before the horse. The learned Attorney-General for Pakistan has, however, very candidly submitted before us that in the entire body of laws pertaining to the Pakistan Army there is no express provision available regarding re-appointment or extension in the service of a Chief of the Army Staff.

iv)   The stated purpose for the proposed re-appointment/extension in the term of office of the incumbent Chief of the Army Staff is "regional security environment". The said words are quite vague and if at all there is any regional security threat then it is the gallant armed forces of the country as an institution which are to meet the said threat and an individual's role in that regard may be minimal. If the said reason is held to be correct and valid then every person serving in the armed forces would claim re-appointment/extension in his service on the basis of the said reason.

3.   The points noted above call for a detailed examination of the matter of extension/re-appointment of General Qamar Javed Bajwa, Chief of the Army Staff and, therefore, he is hereby made a respondent to this petition and the office is directed to carry out the necessary addition in the memorandum of this petition. Let notice of this petition be issued to all the respondents for tomorrow, i.e. **27.11.2019**, as requested by the learned Attorney-General for Pakistan. In the meanwhile the operation of the impugned order/Notification in respect of extension/re-appointment of General Qamar Javed Bajwa, Chief of the Army Staff for another term in the said office shall remain suspended.

Chief Justice

Judge

Judge

Islamabad
26.11.2019

Source: https://www.supremecourt.gov.pk/)

Appendix VIII

IN THE SUPREME COURT OF PAKISTAN
(Original Jurisdiction)

PRESENT:
Mr. Justice Asif Saeed Khan Khosa, CJ
Mr. Justice Mazhar Alam Khan Miankhel
Mr. Justice Syed Mansoor Ali Shah

Constitution Petition No. 39 of 2019
(Against Extension of Tenure of Chief of the Army Staff)

The Jurists Foundation through its Chairman

...*Petitioner*

versus

Federal Government through Secretary Ministry of Defence, etc.

...*Respondents*

Petitioner:	In person.
For the respondents:	Mr. Anwar Mansoor Khan, Attorney-General for Pakistan with
	Mr. Sajid Ilyas Bhatti, Addl. Attorney-General
	Mr. Amir-ur-Rehman, Addl. Attorney General
	Ch. Ishtiaq Ahmed, Addl. Attorney General.
	Mr. Sohail Mehmood, Dy. Attorney General.
	Mian Asghar Ali, Dy. Attorney General.
	Assisted by Ms. Faryal Shah Afridi, Advocate.
	Syed Iqbal Hussain, ASC.

Brig. Falak Naz, Director (Law), M/o Defence.
Flt. Lt. Khalid Abbas, Asst. Director (Law), M/o Defence.
Brig. Muhammad Khalid Khan, JAG Department, GHQ.
Lt. Col Rai Tanveer Ahmed Kharral, OIC, JAG Department, GHQ.
Dr. Farogh Nasim, ASC for respondent No.4, alongwith
Mr. Abid S. Zuberi, ASC.
assisted by M/s Ayan Memon, Mr. Shahid Naseem Gondal & Barriser Neelum Bukhari.

Date of hearing: 28.11.2019

ORDER

For detailed reasons to be recorded later we pass the following short order:-

2.   The extension/reappointment of General Qamar Javed Bajwa, Chief of the Army Staff (**"COAS"**) has been challenged before us. In the proceedings before us during the last three days the Federal Government has moved from one position to another referring to it as reappointment, limiting of retirement or extension of tenure and has also interchangeably placed reliance on Article 243(4)(b) of the Constitution of the Islamic Republic of Pakistan, 1973 (**"Constitution"**) and Regulation 255 of the Army Regulations (Rules), 1998. However, finally today the Federal Government through the learned Attorney General for Pakistan has presented this Court with a recent summary approved by the President on the advice of the Prime Minister alongwith Notification dated 28.11.2019 which shows that General Qamar Javed Bajwa

has been appointed as COAS under Article 243(4)(b) of the Constitution with effect from 28.11.2019.

3.   We have examined Article 243(4)(b) of the Constitution, Pakistan Army Act, 1952, Pakistan Army Act Rules, 1954 and Army Regulations (Rules), 1998 and inspite of the assistance rendered by the learned Attorney-General, we could not find any provision relating to the tenure of COAS or of a General and whether the COAS can be reappointed or his term can be extended or his retirement can be limited or suspended under the Constitution or the law. The learned Attorney-General has taken pains to explain that the answers to these questions are based on practice being followed in the Pakistan Army but the said practice has not been codified under the law.

4.   Article 243 of the Constitution clearly mandates that the Federal Government shall have control and command of the Armed Forces and the supreme command of the Armed Forces shall vest in the President. It further provides that the President shall, subject to law, have power to raise and maintain the military, etc. and it is the President who on the advice of the Prime Minister shall appoint, inter alia, COAS. Article 243 of the Constitution, therefore, clearly shows that the President shall, subject to law, raise and maintain the military, however, the laws referred to above do not specify the tenure, retirement, re-appointment and extension of the COAS or of a General of the Pakistan Army.

5.   The learned Attorney-General has categorically assured the Court that this practice being followed is to be codified under the law and undertakes that the Federal Government shall initiate the process to carry out the necessary legislation in this

initiate the process to carry out the necessary legislation in this regard and seeks a period of six months for getting the needful done. Considering that the COAS is responsible for the command, discipline, training, administration, organization and preparedness for war of the Army and is the Chief Executive in General Headquarters, we, while exercising judicial restraint, find it appropriate to leave the matter to the Parliament and the Federal Government to clearly specify the terms and conditions of service of the COAS through an Act of Parliament and to clarify the scope of Article 243 of the Constitution in this regard. Therefore, the current appointment of General Qamar Javed Bajwa as COAS shall be subject to the said legislation and shall continue for a period of six months from today, whereafter the new legislation shall determine his tenure and other terms and conditions of service.

6.   This petition is disposed of in the above terms.

Chief Justice

Judge

Judge

Islamabad,
28th November, 2019

Source: https://www.supremecourt.gov.pk/)

Index